THE AMERICAN PRESIDENCY

Clinton Rossiter is John L. Senior Professor of American Institutions at Cornell University, and has also been Pitt Professor of American History at Cambridge University. His books include *The Supreme Court and the Commander in Chief, Constitutional Dictatorship, The American Presidency, Parties and Politics in America, Marxism: The View from America, Conservatism in America,* and *Seedtime of the Republic,* for which he received the Bancroft Prize, the Woodrow Wilson Foundation Award, and the prize of the Institute of Early American History and Culture.

Mr. Rossiter has been a consultant to the Ford and Rockefeller Foundations, is general editor of the series of books on "Communism in American Life" sponsored by the Fund for the Republic, and was a contributor to *Goals for Americans,* the Report of the President's Commission on National Goals (1960).

THE
AMERICAN
PRESIDENCY

by Clinton Rossiter

A Harvest Book

Harcourt, Brace

& World, Inc.

New York

To My Students, Past and Present, in
        The American Presidency (Government 216)
        Cornell University

"Methought I heard a voice cry, 'Sleep no more!' "
                    —*Macbeth*, II, i, 36

Preface to the First Edition

This book is a revised version of six lectures given on the Charles R. Walgreen Foundation at the University of Chicago, April 23–May 3, 1956. I am grateful to the officers of the Foundation for giving me this opportunity to rethink the thoughts of fifteen years on the Presidency. I am also grateful to James M. Burns, Edward S. Corwin, Arch Dotson, Richard P. Longaker, Alexander J. Morin, Richard E. Neustadt, J. Francis Paschal, John P. Roche, and, most of all, Mary Crane Rossiter, for their help and advice.

CLINTON ROSSITER

Ithaca, New York
March, 1956

Preface to the Second Edition

This book is a revised version of the revised lectures of 1956. In addition to strewing second thoughts all through these pages, I have tried to bring fresh materials, drawn largely from the conduct of the Presidency in the past four years, into chapters 1, 2, 4, and 8. I have added new passages on such topics as the process of impeachment and the President's responsibility in the broad field of science, and two new chapters on the currently agitated questions of election and succession to the Presidency. Least important to my own purposes but probably most interesting to readers and reviewers of this book, I have made a second attempt (based on seven years of observation rather than just three) to assess the performance of Dwight D. Eisenhower and to predict his place in the history of the Presidency. In all this I have been helped by the comments—some friendly, some critical, and some explosive—of hundreds of persons who took the trouble to write me about the first edition. To them, to Gladys Kessler, and once again to Mary Crane Rossiter I am genuinely grateful.

CLINTON ROSSITER

Ithaca, New York
December, 1959

CONTENTS

PREFACE TO THE FIRST EDITION 7

PREFACE TO THE SECOND EDITION 9

1. THE POWERS OF THE PRESIDENCY 15

2. THE LIMITS OF THE PRESIDENCY 44

3. THE PRESIDENCY IN HISTORY 74

4. THE MODERN PRESIDENCY 109

5. THE MODERN PRESIDENTS 142

6. THE HIRING OF PRESIDENTS 182

7. THE FIRING, RETIRING, AND EXPIRING OF PRESIDENTS 207

8. THE FUTURE OF THE PRESIDENCY 237

APPENDIX I: THE PRESIDENTS OF THE UNITED STATES 263

APPENDIX II: THE PRESIDENCY IN THE CONSTITUTION 264

APPENDIX III: A BIBLIOGRAPHY OF THE PRESIDENCY 272

INDEX 277

THE AMERICAN PRESIDENCY

CHAPTER 1

THE POWERS OF THE PRESIDENCY

Sometimes the stranger outside the gates has a clearer vision of an American institution than we who have lived with it all our lives. John Bright, best friend in all England of the embattled Union, paid this tribute to the Presidency in 1861:

> I think the whole world offers no finer spectacle than this; it offers no higher dignity; and there is no greater object of ambition on the political stage on which men are permitted to move. You may point, if you will, to hereditary rulers, to crowns coming down through successive generations of the same family, to thrones based on prescription or on conquest, to sceptres wielded over veteran legions and subject realms,—but to my mind there is nothing more worthy of reverence and obedience, and nothing more sacred, than the authority of the freely chosen magistrate of a great and free people; and if there be on earth and amongst men any right divine to govern, surely it rests with a ruler so chosen and so appointed.

My purpose is to confirm Bright's splendid judgment by presenting the American Presidency as what I honestly believe it to be: one of the few truly successful institutions created by men in their endless quest for the blessings of free government. This great office, like even the greatest men who have filled it, displays its fair share of warts, and I shall try to paint them as large as life. Yet I would be less than candid were I not to make clear at the outset my own feeling of veneration, if not

15

exactly reverence, for the authority and dignity of the Presidency.

This book is very far from a detailed or definitive portrait of this astounding institution. It is at best an impressionistic rendering of the main dimensions, and I beg early forgiveness for all the things I cannot possibly find room to say about it. My hope is simply that those who read these chapters may come to a sharper understanding of the position the Presidency occupies in the annals of our past and the hopes of our future.

This presentation must begin with a careful accounting of those tasks we call upon the President to perform, for if there is any one thing about him that strikes the eye immediately, it is the staggering burden he bears for all of us. Those who cherish Gilbert and Sullivan will remember Pooh-Bah, the "particularly haughty and exclusive person" in *The Mikado* who filled the offices of "First Lord of the Treasury, Lord Chief Justice, Commander-in-Chief, Lord High Admiral, Master of the Buckhounds, Groom of the Back Stairs, Archbishop of Titipu, and Lord Mayor, both acting and elect." We chuckle at the fictitious Pooh-Bah; we can only wonder at the real one that history has made of the American President. He has at least three jobs for every one of Pooh-Bah's, and they are not performed with the flick of a lacquered fan. At the risk of being perhaps too analytical, let me review the functions of the modern President. These, as I interpret them, are the major roles he plays in the sprawling drama of American government.

First, the President is Chief of State. He remains today, as he has always been, the ceremonial head of the government of the United States, and he must take part with real or apparent enthusiasm in a range of activities that would keep him running and posing from sunrise to bedtime if he were not protected by a cold-blooded staff. Some of these activities are solemn or even priestly in nature; others, through no fault of his own, are flirtations with vulgarity. The long catalogue of public duties that the Queen discharges in England, the President of the Republic in France, and the Governor-General in Canada is the President's responsibility in this country, and the catalogue is even longer because he is not a king, or even the agent of one, and is therefore expected to go through some rather undignified paces by a people who think of him as a combination of scoutmaster, Delphic oracle, hero of the silver screen, and father of the multitudes.

As figurehead rather than working head of our government, he greets distinguished visitors from all parts of the world, lays wreaths on the tomb of the Unknown Soldier and before the statue of Lincoln, makes proclamations of thanksgiving and commemoration, bestows medals on flustered pilots, holds state dinners for the diplomatic corps and the Supreme Court, lights the nation's Christmas tree, buys the first poppy from the Veterans of Foreign Wars, gives the first crisp banknote to the Red Cross, throws out the first ball for the Senators (the harmless ones out at Griffith Stadium), rolls the first egg for the Easter Bunny, and in the course of any month greets a fantastic procession of firemen, athletes, veterans, Boy Scouts, Campfire Girls, boosters, hog callers, exchange students, and heroic school children. The annual United Fund Drive could not possibly get under way without a five-minute telecast from the White House; Sunday is not Sunday if the President and his lady skip church; a public-works project is not public until the President presses a silver key in Washington and explodes a charge of dynamite in Fort Peck or Hanford or the Tennessee Valley.

The President is not permitted to confine this sort of activity to the White House and the city around it. The people expect him to come to them from time to time, and the presidential grand tour, a precedent set conspicuously by George Washington, is an important aspect of the ceremonial function. Nor is this function, for obvious political and cultural reasons, untainted with commercialism. If it isn't one "Week" for him to proclaim or salute, it's another, and what President, espe-

cially in an election year, would turn away the Maid of Cotton
or the Railroad Man of the Year or, to keep everybody happy,
the Truck Driver of the Year from the White House door?

The President, in short, is the one-man distillation of the
American people just as surely as the Queen is of the British
people; he is, in President Taft's words, "the personal embodiment and representative of their dignity and majesty." (Mr.
Taft, it will be remembered, was uniquely shaped by nature's
lavish hand to be a personal embodiment of dignity and majesty.) Or as Attorney General Stanberry argued before the
Supreme Court in 1867 in the case of *Mississippi* v. *Johnson:*

> Undoubtedly so far as the mere individual man is concerned there
> is a great difference between the President and a king; but so far as
> the office is concerned—so far as the great executive office of this
> government is concerned—I deny that there is a particle less dignity
> belonging to the office of President than to the office of King of
> Great Britain or of any other potentate on the face of the earth. He
> represents the majesty of the law and of the people as fully and as
> essentially, and with the same dignity, as does any absolute monarch
> or the head of any independent government in the world.

The role of Chief of State may often seem trivial, yet it cannot be neglected by a President who proposes to stay in favor
and, more to the point, in touch with the people, the ultimate
source of all his power. It is a conspicuous thief of his precious
time, yet more than one President, most notably Harry S Truman, has played it in such a way as to gain genuine release
from the routine tasks and hard decisions that filled the rest of
his day. And whether or not he enjoys this role, no President
can fail to realize that all his powers are invigorated, indeed are
given a new dimension of authority, because he is the symbol
of our sovereignty, continuity, and grandeur. When he asks a
Senator to lunch in order to enlist his support for a pet project,
when he thumps his desk and reminds the antagonists in a
labor dispute of the larger interests of the American people,
when he orders a general to cease caviling or else be removed

from his command, the Senator and the disputants and the general are well aware—especially if the scene is laid in the White House—that they are dealing with no ordinary head of government. The framers of the Constitution took a momentous step when they fused the dignity of a king and the power of a prime minister in one elective office. And, if they did nothing else, they gave us a "father image" that should satisfy even the most demanding political Freudians.

The second of the President's roles is that of Chief Executive. He reigns, but he also rules; he symbolizes the people, but he also runs their government. "The true test of a good government is its aptitude and tendency to produce a good administration," Hamilton wrote in *The Federalist*, at the same time making clear that it would be the first duty of the proposed President to produce this "good administration." For reasons that I shall touch upon later, the President (and I mean any President, no matter how happily he may wallow in the details of administration) has more trouble playing this role successfully than he does any of the others. It is, in fact, the one major area of presidential activity in which his powers are simply not equal to his responsibilities. Yet the role is an important one, and we cannot savor the fullness of the President's duties unless we recall that he is held primarily and often exclusively accountable for the ethics, loyalty, efficiency, frugality, and responsiveness to the public's wishes of the two and a third million Americans in the national administration.

Both the Constitution and Congress have recognized his authority to supervise the day-to-day activities of the executive branch, strained and restrained though this supervision may often be in practice. From the Constitution, explicitly or implicitly, he receives the twin powers of appointment and removal, as well as the primary duty, which no law or plan or circumstance can ever take away from him, to "take care that the laws be faithfully executed." He alone may appoint, passage from the *United States Code* makes clear that Congress itself expects much of him:

The President is authorized to prescribe such regulations for the admission of persons into the civil service of the United States as may best promote the efficiency thereof, and ascertain the fitness of each candidate in respect to age, health, character, knowledge, and ability for the branch of service into which he seeks to enter; and for this purpose he may employ suitable persons to conduct such inquiries, and may prescribe their duties, and establish regulations for the conduct of persons who may receive appointment in the civil service.

It might be useful to hear the opinion of the acknowledged experts in this field. I take these paragraphs from the report of the sixth American Assembly, which met at Arden House in October 1954 to consider the "character, prestige, and problems" of the public service:

The President has the responsibility for leadership of the Executive Branch of the Federal Government service. Constitutional principles, the necessities of our national life and the example of successful corporate enterprise all underscore the indispensability of executive responsibility for the personnel policies and the personnel management of the Federal Government.

This leadership must be acknowledged and supported by the heads and employees of executive departments, by the party leaders and by the members of the Congress. This leadership must be accepted and exercised by the President, if the business of the National Government is to be efficiently performed.

Whether it is his letters or his taxes the ordinary citizen wants more efficiently collected, he looks first of all to the President as business manager of the administration. There was a time when Presidents could and did pay strict attention to matters such as these, and about a hundred million people still do not seem to realize that the time has long since passed.

The President's third major function is one he could not escape if he wished, and several Presidents have wished it mightily.

The Constitution designates him specifically as "Commander-in-Chief of the Army and Navy of the United States, and of the militia of the several States when called into the actual service of the United States." In peace and war he is the supreme commander of the armed forces, the living guarantee of the American belief in "the supremacy of the civil over military authority."

In time of peace he raises, trains, supervises, and deploys the forces that Congress is willing to maintain, and he has a great deal to say about the size and make-up of these forces. With the aid of the Secretary of Defense, the Secretaries of the three services, the Joint Chiefs of Staff, and the members of the National Security Council—every one of these men his personal choice—he looks constantly to the state of the nation's defenses. He is never for one day allowed to forget that he will be held accountable by people, Congress, and history for the nation's readiness to meet an enemy assault. There is no more striking indication of the present latitude of the President's military power than these matter-of-fact words in the Atomic Energy Act of 1946:

Sec. 6(a) Authority. The *Commission* is authorized to—
 (1) conduct experiments and do research and development work in the military application of atomic energy; and
 (2) engage in the production of atomic bombs, atomic bomb parts, or other military weapons utilizing fissionable materials; except that such activities shall be carried on only to the extent that the express consent and direction of the President of the United States has been obtained, which consent and direction shall be obtained at least once each year.

The President from time to time may direct the Commission (1) to deliver such quantities of fissionable materials or weapons to the armed forces for such use as he deems necessary in the interest of the national defense or (2) to authorize the armed forces to manufacture, produce, or acquire any equipment or device utilizing fissionable material or atomic energy as a military weapon.

It should be added that, despite the wounded protests of Senator Bricker, most citizens agreed with Mr. Truman's brisk assertion in 1950 that it was for the President to decide whether the H-bomb should be built. Congress might have refused to grant funds for such an undertaking, but this would not have stopped the President from pushing ahead as best he could with the other resources at his command. And, as the same doughty man demonstrated in 1945, it is for the President to decide in time of war when and where and how the H-bomb or A-bomb or any other bomb should be dropped.

In such time, "when the blast of war blows in our ears," the President's power to command the forces swells out of all proportion to his other powers. All major decisions of strategy, and many of his tactics as well, are his alone to make or to approve. Lincoln and Franklin Roosevelt, each in his own way and time, showed how far the power of military command can be driven by a President anxious to have his generals and admirals get on with the war. No small part of his time, as we know from Lincoln's experience, can be spent searching for the right generals and admirals.

But this, the power of command, is only a fraction of the vast responsibility the modern President draws from the Commander in Chief clause. The framers of the Constitution, to be sure, took a narrow view of the authority they had granted. "It would amount," Hamilton wrote offhandedly in *The Federalist,* "to nothing more than the supreme command and direction of the military and naval forces, as first General and Admiral of the Confederacy." This view of presidential power as something purely military foundered on the hard facts of the first of our modern wars. Faced by an overriding necessity for harsh, even dictatorial action, Lincoln used the Commander in Chief clause, at first gingerly, in the end boldly, to justify an unprecedented series of measures that cut deeply into the accepted liberties of the people and the routine pattern of government. Wilson added another cubit to the stature of the wartime Presidency by demanding that Congress give him those powers over the economy about which there was any constitutional doubt, and Franklin Roosevelt, who had read about Lincoln and lived with Wilson, carried the wartime Presidency to breath-taking heights of authority over the American economy and social order. The creation and staffing of a whole array of emergency boards and offices, the seizure and operation of more than sixty strike-bound or strike-threatened plants and industries, and the forced evacuation of 70,000 American citizens of Japanese descent from the West Coast are three startling and prophetic examples of what a President can do as Commander in Chief to stiffen the home front in support of the fighting forces. It is important to recall that Congress came to Roosevelt's aid in each of these series of actions by passing laws empowering him to do what he had done already or by fixing penalties for violating the orders of his subordinates. Congress, too, likes to win wars, and Congressmen are more likely to needle the President for inactivity and timidity than to accuse him of acting too swiftly and arbitrarily.

Now that total war, which ignores the old line between battlefield and home front, has been compounded by the absolute weapon, which mocks every rule we have ever tried to honor, we may expect the President to be nothing short of a "constitutional dictator" in the event of war. The next wartime President, who may well be our last, will have the right, of which Lincoln spoke with feeling, to take "any measure which may best subdue the enemy," and he alone will be the judge of what is "best" for the survival of the republic. We have placed a shocking amount of military power in the President's keeping, but where else, we may ask, could it possibly have been placed?

Next, the President is Chief Diplomat. Although authority in the field of foreign relations is shared constitutionally among three organs—President, Congress, and, for two special purposes, the Senate—his position is paramount, if not indeed dominant. In 1799 John Marshall, no particular friend of executive power, spoke of the President as "the sole organ of the nation in its external relations, and its sole representative with foreign nations." In 1936 Justice Sutherland, no particular friend of executive power and even less of Franklin D. Roosevelt, put the Court's stamp of approval on "the very delicate, plenary and exclusive power of the President as the sole organ of the government in the field of international relations."

The primacy of the executive comes under vigorous attack from time to time, chiefly from those who object to a specific policy even more strongly than to a President's pursuit of it, and it is true that he acts more arbitrarily and independently than the framers of the Constitution ever intended him to act. Yet the growth of presidential authority in this area seems to have been almost inevitable, and hardly the outcome of a shameful conspiracy by the three Democratic Presidents of the twentieth century. Constitution, laws, custom, the practice of other nations, and the logic of history have combined to place the President in a dominant position. Secrecy, dispatch, unity, continuity, and access to information—the ingredients of successful diplomacy—are properties of his office, and Congress, I need hardly add, possesses none of them. It is a body with immense power of its own in the field of foreign relations—a fact perfectly symbolized by the unprecedented conference between Prime Minister Macmillan and the leaders of Congress in March 1959—but the power is essentially negative in character and application. And as if all this were not enough to insure the President's dominance, he is also, as we have just noted, Commander in Chief, the man who controls and directs the armed might of the United States in a world in which force, real or threatened, is the essence of diplomacy.

The field of foreign relations can be conveniently if somewhat inexactly divided into two sectors: the formulation of policy and the conduct of affairs. The first of these is a joint undertaking in which the President proposes, Congress disposes, and the wishes of the people prevail in the end. The President's leadership is usually vindicated. Our most ancient and honored policy is significantly known as the *Monroe* Doctrine; our leading policies of recent years have been the *Truman* Doctrine and the *Eisenhower* Doctrine. From Washington's Proclamation of Neutrality in 1793 to Eisenhower's decision to stand fast in Berlin in 1959, the President has repeatedly committed the nation to decisive attitudes and actions abroad, more than once to war itself. Occasionally Congress has compelled him to abandon a policy already put forward, as it did in the case of Grant's plans for Santo Domingo, or has forced distasteful policies upon him, as it did upon Madison in 1812 and McKinley in 1898. Nevertheless, a stubborn President is hard to budge, a crusading President hard to thwart. The diplomatic lives of the two Roosevelts are proof enough of these assertions. Mr. Truman was not exaggerating much when he told an informal gathering of the Jewish War Veterans in 1948: "I make American foreign policy."

The transaction of business with foreign nations is, as Jefferson once wrote, "executive altogether," and Congress finds it difficult to exercise effective control or to deliver constructive criticism, not that Congress can be accused of lack of trying. The State Department carries on its many activities in the name of the President, and he is or ought to be in command of every procedure through which our foreign relations are carried on from one day to the next: negotiation of treaties and executive agreements, recognition of new governments and nations, selection and supervision of diplomatic personnel, adjustment of tariff barriers within statutory limits, direction of our delegation to the United Nations, and communications with foreign powers. As Commander in Chief he deploys our armed forces abroad and occasionally supports our policies with what is known as "presidential warmaking." The conduct of foreign relations as a short-range proposition is a presidential prerogative, and short-range actions—the recognition of a revolutionary regime in Cuba, the reception of a Burmese prime minister, the raising of the duty on Swiss watches—can have long-range consequences.

In recent years, the role of Chief Diplomat has become the most important and exacting of all those we call upon the President to play. Indeed, when one thinks of the hours of "prayerful consideration" President Eisenhower devoted each week to briefing sessions with the Dulles brothers, conferences with the National Security Council, lunches with Senators Fulbright and Wiley, chats with Nehru or Macmillan or Diefenbaker or whoever else might be in town, explanatory and inspirational speeches to the nation, and lonely wrestling bouts with appointments and reports and messages to Congress—not to mention his correspondence with Khrushchev, Zhukov, and Bulganin—it is a wonder that he had a moment's time for any of his other duties.

The President's duties are not all purely executive in nature. He is also intimately associated, by Constitution and custom, with the legislative process, and we may therefore consider him to be the Chief Legislator. Congress has a wealth of strong and talented men, but the complexity of the problems they are asked to solve by a people who assume that all problems are solvable has made *external* leadership a requisite of effective operation. The President alone is in a political, constitutional, and practical position to provide such leadership, and he is therefore expected, within the limits of constitutional and political propriety, to guide Congress in much of its lawmaking activity. Indeed, since Congress is no longer organized to guide itself, not even under such tough-minded leaders as Senator Johnson and Speaker Rayburn, the refusal or inability of the President to point out the way results in weak or, at best, stalemated government.

Success in the delicate area of executive-legislative relations depends on several variables: the political complexion of President and Congress, the state of the Union and of the world around us, the vigor and tact of the President's leadership, and the mood of Congress, which is generally friendly near the beginning of a President's term and rebellious near the end. Yet even the President whose announced policy is to "restore our hallowed system of the separation of powers" and leave Congress strictly alone (Coolidge is a capital example, one not likely to be repeated) must exercise his constitutional option to veto or not to veto about a thousand times each session, must discourse once a year on the state of the Union and occasionally recommend "such measures as he shall judge necessary and expedient," must present the annual budget, and must make some effort to realize at least the less controversial promises in his party's platform. "After all," Mr. Eisenhower told a press conference in 1959, "the Constitution puts the President right square into the legislative business." In the hands of a Wilson or a Roosevelt, even at times in the hands of an Eisenhower, the Presidency becomes a sort of prime ministership or "third House of Congress," and the chief concern of the President is to push for the enactment of his own or his party's legislative desires.

Upon many of our most celebrated laws the presidential imprint is clearly stamped. Each of these was drafted in the President's offices, introduced and supported by his friends, defended in committee by his aides, voted through by a party over which every form of discipline and persuasion was exerted, and then made law by his signature. The signature, of course, was affixed with several dozen fountain pens, which were then passed out among the beaming friends and aides. Among the "ploys and gambits" the President may have used in the process were the White House breakfast with his chief lieutenants, or perhaps with his chief obstructionists; the fireside chat with his constituents, some of whom were also constituents of the obstructionists; the press conference, in which he proclaimed his astonishment at the way Congress was dragging its feet; the dangled patronage or favor, which brought a wavering or even hostile Senator to his side; and the threat of a veto, which he brandished like the Gorgon's head to frighten the mavericks into removing objectionable amendments to the bill he had first sent over.

Even the President who lacks a congressional majority must go through the motions of leadership. The Republicans in the Eightieth Congress always waited politely for Mr. Truman's proposals on labor, taxes, inflation, civil rights, and education, however scant the regard they intended to pay them. The Democrats, if we may believe the protests of Speaker Rayburn and Senator Johnson, were impatient to hear President Eisenhower's proposals and to feel the lash of his leadership. In any case, the chief responsibility for bridging the constitutional gulf between executive and legislature now rests irrevocably with the President. His tasks as leader of Congress are difficult and delicate, yet he must bend to them steadily or be judged a failure. The President who will not give his best thoughts to guiding Congress, more so the President who is temperamentally or politically unfitted to "get along with Congress," is now rightly considered a national liability.

Chief of State, Chief Executive, Commander in Chief, Chief Diplomat, Chief Legislator—these functions make up the strictly constitutional burden of the President. As Mr. Truman himself allowed in several of his folksy sermons on the Presidency, they form an aggregate of power that would have made Caesar or Genghis Khan or Napoleon bite his nails with envy. Yet even these are not the whole weight of presidential responsibility. I count at least five additional functions that have been piled on top of the original load.

The first of these is the President's role as Chief of Party, one that he has played by popular demand and to a mixed reception ever since the administration of Thomas Jefferson. However sincere Washington's abhorrence of "factions" may have been, his own administration and policies spawned our first two parties, and their arrival upon the scene altered the character of the Presidency radically. No matter how fondly or how often we may long for a President who is above the heat of political strife, we must acknowledge resolutely his right and duty to be the leader of his party. He is at once the least political and most political of all heads of government.

The value of this function has been attested by all our first-rate Presidents. Jackson, Lincoln, Wilson, and the two Roosevelts were especially skillful party leaders. By playing the politician with unashamed zest the first of these gave his epic administration a unique sense of cohesion, the second rallied doubting Republican leaders and their followings to the cause of the Union, and the other three achieved genuine triumphs as catalysts of congressional action. That elegant amateur, Dwight D. Eisenhower, played the role with devotion if not exactly zest. It would have astonished George Washington, but it cannot even ruffle us, to learn that the President devoted breakfast and most of the morning of June 20, 1955—a day otherwise given over to solemn celebration of the tenth birthday of the United Nations—to mending a few fences with Republican leaders of California. He was demonstrating only what close observers of the Presidency know well: that its incumbent must devote an hour or two of every working day to the profession of Chief Democrat or Chief Republican. The President dictates the selection of the national chairman and other top party officials, reminds his partisans in Congress that the legislative record must be bright if victory is to crown their joint efforts, delivers "fight talks" to the endless procession of professionals who call upon him, and, through the careful distribution of the loaves and fishes of federal patronage, keeps the party a going concern. The loaves and fishes are not so plentiful as they were in the days of Jackson and Lincoln, but the President is still a wholesale distributor of "jobs for the boys."

It troubles many good people, not entirely without reason, to watch their Chief of State dabbling in politics, smiling on party hacks, and endorsing candidates he knows to be unfit for anything but immediate delivery to the county jail. Yet if he is to persuade Congress, if he is to achieve a loyal and cohesive administration, if he is to be elected in the first place (and re-elected in the second), he must put his hand firmly to the plow of politics. The working head of government in a constitutional democracy must be the nation's number-one boss, and most Presidents have had no trouble swallowing this truth.

Yet he is, at the same time if not in the same breath, the Voice of the People, the leading formulator and expounder of public opinion in the United States. While he acts as political leader of some, he serves as moral spokesman for all. Well before Woodrow Wilson had come to the Presidency, but not before he had begun to dream of it, he expressed the essence of this role:

His is the only national voice in affairs. Let him once win the admiration and confidence of the country, and no other single force can withstand him, no combination of forces will easily overpower him. His position takes the imagination of the country. He is the representative of no constituency, but of the whole people. When he speaks in his true character, he speaks for no special interest. If he rightly interpret the national thought and boldly insist upon it, he is irresistible; and the country never feels the zest for action so much as when its President is of such insight and calibre.

Throughout our history there have been moments of triumph or dedication or frustration or even shame when the will of the people—would it be wrong to call it the General Will?—demanded to be heard clearly and unmistakably. It took the line of Presidents some time to grasp the meaning of this function, but since the day when Andrew Jackson thundered against the Nullifiers of South Carolina no effective President has doubted his prerogative to speak the people's mind on the great issues of his time, to act, again in Wilson's words, as "the spokesman for the real sentiment and purpose of the country."

The coming of the radio, and now of television, has added immeasurably to the range and power of the President's voice, offering the man who occupies this "bully pulpit" (as Theodore Roosevelt described it) an opportunity to preach the gospel of America in every home and, indeed, in almost every land. Neither Steve Allen nor Ed Sullivan, neither Bishop Sheen nor Edward R. Murrow—not even, I would insist, the men of the mythical West who fill every channel with the sound of their guns—can gain access to so many millions of American homes. Indeed, the President must be especially on his guard not to pervert these mighty media that are his to command. It is one thing for a huckster to appeal to the people to buy a mouth-wash; it would be quite another for a President to appeal to them to stampede the Senate. I like to think that our sales resistance would be as dogged in the second case as in the first, but there is no denying that, even in defeat, a President could do a great deal of damage to our scheme of representative government.

Sometimes, of course, it is no easy thing, even for the most sensitive and large-minded of Presidents, to know the real sentiment of the people or to be bold enough to state it in defiance of loudly voiced contrary opinion. There are definite limits to presidential free speech, as Mr. Eisenhower learned in 1959 when he was egged into a few plaintive comments on the size and shape of American automobiles. Yet the President who senses the popular mood and spots new tides even before they start to run, who practices shrewd economy in his appearances as spokesman for the nation, who is conscious of his unique power to compel discussion on his own terms, and who talks the language of Christian morality and the American tradition, can shout down any other voice or chorus of voices in the land. There have been times, to be sure, when we seemed as willing to listen to an antagonist as to the President—to Senator Taft in 1950, General MacArthur in 1951, Clarence Randall of Inland Steel in June 1952—but in the end, we knew, and the antagonist knew, too, that the battle was no Armageddon, that it was a frustrating skirmish fought between grossly ill-matched forces. And if we learned anything from Senator Johnson's speech of January 6, 1958, to his Democratic colleagues, it was that two addresses on the state of the Union are one too many.

The President is the American people's one authentic trumpet, and he has no higher duty than to give a clear and certain sound. "Words at great moments of history are deeds," Clement Attlee said of Winston Churchill on the day the latter stepped down in 1945. The strong and imaginative President can make with his own words the kind of history that Churchill made in 1940 and 1941. When the events of 1933 are all but forgotten, we shall still recall Roosevelt's words, "The only thing we have to fear is fear itself."

In the memorable case of *In re Neagle* (1890), which still makes good reading for those who like a touch of horse opera in their constitutional law, Justice Samuel Miller spoke with feeling of the "peace of the United States"—a happy condition, it would appear, of domestic tranquillity and national prosperity that is often broken by violent men and forces and just as often restored by the President. Perhaps the least known of his functions is the mandate he holds from the Constitution and the laws, but even more positively from the people of the United States, to act as Protector of the Peace. The emergencies that can disturb the peace of the United States seem to grow thicker and more vexing every year, and hardly a week now goes by that the President is not called upon to take forceful steps in behalf of a section or city or group or enterprise that has been hit hard and suddenly by disaster. Generally, it is for state and local authorities to deal with social and natural calamities, but in the face of a riot in Detroit or floods in New England or a tornado in Missouri or a railroad strike in Chicago or a panic in Wall Street, the people turn almost instinctively to the White House and its occupant for aid and comfort.

And he, certainly, is the person to give it. No man or combination of men in the United States can muster so quickly and authoritatively the troops, experts, food, money, loans, equipment, medical supplies, and moral support that may be needed in a disaster. Are thousands of homes flooded in the Missouri and Ohio Valleys?—then the President will order Coast Guardsmen and their boats to be flown to the scene for rescue and patrol work, and he will go himself to bring cheer to the homeless. Are cattle starving on the snow-bound western plains? —then the President will order the Air Force to engage in Operation Haylift. Are the farmers of Rhode Island and Massachusetts facing ruin in the wake of a September hurricane?— then the President will designate these states as disaster areas and order the Secretary of Agriculture to release surplus foods and make emergency loans on easy terms. Is Maine scourged by forest fires? Is Texas parched with drought? Is Kansas invaded by grasshoppers? Is Little Rock soiled with the blood of men and tears of children?—then in every instance the President must take the lead to restore the normal pattern of existence.

Or are we having a March 1933 all over again, and are we caught up in the first dreadful moments of a financial panic?— then the President will issue the necessary orders on the authority of two laws that have been waiting quietly on the books since the first years of the New Deal:

Section 4 of the Emergency Banking Act of 1933:

In order to provide for the safer and more effective operation of the National Banking System . . . during such emergency period as the President of the United States by proclamation may prescribe, no member bank of the Federal Reserve System shall transact any

banking business except to such extent and subject to such regulations, limitations and restrictions as may be prescribed by the Secretary of the Treasury, with the approval of the President.

Section 19 (a) of the Securities Exchange Act of 1934:

The Commission is authorized . . . if in its opinion the public interest so requires, summarily to suspend trading in any registered security on any national securities exchange for a period not
exceeding ten days, or with the approval of the President, summarily
to suspend all trading on any national securities exchange for a
period not exceeding ninety days.

If I may reduce the meaning of these two laws to simple
terms, they empower the President to meet the challenge of
any future panic like that of March 1933 by declaring a state
of financial martial law. At the same time, he remains constitutionally, we might even say extraconstitutionally, empowered
to respond to an atomic attack by declaring straight-out martial
law through all the land. This, be it noted for future reference,
is exactly what President Eisenhower pretended to do in the
simulated hydrogen-bomb attack of June 1955. One of the remarkable events of that three-day test of our readiness for
atomic war was the startled discovery by Mr. Eisenhower and
his staff that "the inherent powers of the Presidency," something about which Republicans usually maintain uneasy silence,
would be the nation's chief crutch in the aftermath of the
ultimate disaster. This fact, and thus his status as Protector of
the Peace, had already been recognized by a group of Senators
who called on Mr. Eisenhower to "assume personal responsibility" for creating an adequate program of civil defense,
something he shortly proceeded to do within the limits of his
budget and our expectations.

There is at least one area of American life, the economy, in
which the people of this country are no longer content to let
disaster fall upon them unopposed. They now expect their
government, under the direct leadership of the President, to
prevent a depression or panic and not simply to wait until one

has developed before putting it to rout. Thus the President has a new function, which is still taking shape, that of Manager of Prosperity.

The origin of this function can be fixed with unusual exactness. The Employment Act of 1946 was the first clear acknowledgement by the federal government of a general responsibility for maintaining a stable and prosperous economy:

Sec. 2. The Congress hereby declares that it is the continuing policy and responsibility of the Federal Government to use all practicable means consistent with its needs and obligations and other essential considerations of national policy, with the assistance and cooperation of industry, agriculture, labor, and State and local governments to coordinate and utilize all its plans, functions, and resources for the purpose of creating and maintaining, in a manner calculated to foster and promote free competitive enterprise and the general welfare, conditions under which there will be afforded useful employment opportunities, including self-employment, for those able, willing, and seeking to work, and to promote maximum employment, production, and purchasing power.

The significant feature of this law from our point of view is the deliberate manner in which, in section after section, the President is singled out as the official who is "to foster and promote free competitive enterprise, to avoid economic fluctuations or to diminish the effects thereof, and to maintain employment, production, and purchasing power." He is granted the handsome gift of the Council of Economic Advisers; he is requested to make the annual Economic Report and such supplementary reports as may be advisable; he is expected to propose "a program for carrying out the policy declared in section 2, together with such recommendations for legislation as he may deem necessary or desirable." There is apparently no doubt in Congress's collective mind that one of the President's prime duties is to watch like a mother hen over all the eggs in all our baskets. As for the American people, it is a notorious fact that we give our President small credit for prosperity and full blame for hard times.

Yet even if the Employment Act had never been passed, he would have this duty and most of the powers that go with it. We have built some remarkable stabilizing devices into our political economy since 1929, and the men who control them —in the Federal Reserve System, the Securities and Exchange Commission, the Federal Security Agency, the countless credit organizations, the Federal Deposit Insurance Corporation— are wide open to suggestions, even directions from the President. There are limits, both strategic and physical, to what can be done in the White House, but certainly the alert President stands always ready to invite the managers of a sick industry or the leading citizens of a city plagued by chronic unemployment to come together and take counsel under his leadership. Of course, it is not his counsel but a well-placed government contract or a hike in the tariff or a dramatic recommendation to Congress for which they have come. Fortunately for the President, his position as overseer of the entire economy is obvious to even the most embittered spokesmen for special interests, and he can take refuge from their pleas for relief by insisting that he must consider the whole picture before deciding on action in their behalf.

The very notion of the President as Manager of Prosperity strikes many people as an economic and political heresy, especially those who still swear allegiance to the tattered doctrine of the self-healing economy. Most of us, however, now accept the idea of a federal government openly engaged in preventing runaway booms and plunging busts. We need only think of Mr. Eisenhower's creditable performance in the slack days of 1954—or, for that matter, of his uninspired performance in the harder days of 1958-1959—to recognize the central position of the Presidency in this new kind of government. Lest there be any doubt how the President himself felt about the new dimension of government responsibility, let me quote from his message to Congress accompanying the Economic Report for 1953:

The demands of modern life and the unsettled status of the world require a more important role for government than it played in earlier and quieter times. . . .

Government must use its vast power to help maintain employment and purchasing power as well as to maintain reasonably stable prices.

Government must be alert and sensitive to economic developments, including its own myriad activities. It must be prepared to take preventive as well as remedial action; and it must be ready to cope with new situations that may arise. This is not a start-and-stop responsibility, but a continuous one.

The arsenal of weapons at the disposal of Government for maintaining economic stability is formidable. It includes credit controls administered by the Federal Reserve System; the debt-management policies of the Treasury; authority of the President to vary the terms of mortgages carrying Federal insurance; flexibility in administration of the budget; agricultural supports; modification of the tax structure; and public works. We shall not hesitate to use any or all of these weapons as the situation may require.

And this from a Republican President dedicated to the glories of free enterprise! Thus far have we and the Presidency moved in a generation of welfare and warfare.

In order to grasp the full import of the last of the President's roles, we must take him as Chief Diplomat, Commander in Chief, and Chief of State, then thrust him onto a far wider stage, there to perform before a much more numerous and more critical audience. For the modern President is, whether we or our friends abroad like it or not, marked out for duty as a World Leader. The President has a much larger constituency than the American electorate: his words and deeds in behalf of our own survival as a free nation have a direct bearing upon the freedom and stability of at least several score other countries.

The reasons why he, rather than the British Prime Minister or French President or an outstanding figure from one of the smaller countries, should be singled out for supranational

leadership are too clear to require extended mention. Not
only are we the richest and most powerful member of any
coalition we may enter, not only are we the chief target of
the enemy and thus the most truculent of the powers arrayed
against him, but the Presidency, for the very reasons I have
dwelled upon in this chapter, unites power, drama, and prestige
as does no other office in the world. Its incumbent sits,
wherever he sits, at the head of the table. Winston Churchill,
an A-plus student of our system of government, recognized
this great truth with unerring eye when he insisted that not
he, the elder statesman, but Mr. Eisenhower, the American
President, take the chair in the middle at the Big Three conference in Bermuda in 1953. No British Prime Minister would
ever be likely to forget that the President with whom he must
deal every week of the year is a head of state as well as a
head of government, a king and a prime minister rolled into
one.

This role is not much more than a decade old, although there
was a short rehearsal of it in late 1918 and the first few months
of 1919. Whether it will continue to grow in the years of tension
ahead depends, of course, on just how high the tension remains.
It does seem probable that the President will have no choice
but to act consciously for and speak openly to the nations
with whom we are associated in defense of freedom—to act
as Truman did in the North Korean aggression of June 1950,
to speak as Eisenhower did in his proposal for an international
atomic-energy pool delivered to the Assembly of the United
Nations in December 1953, to act and speak together as Eisenhower did in the Berlin crisis of 1959. If the British Prime
Minister often seemed to be the most influential figure in the
Atlantic coalition during the first part of that nerve-racking
year, this could be ascribed to the reluctance of the President
rather than to any decline in the stature of the Presidency. Whoever the incumbent of our first office may be, its stature in the
world grows mightier with every passing year. For some time to

come the President of the United States will also be the "President of the West."

Having engaged in this piecemeal analysis of the Presidency, I hasten to fit the pieces back together into a seamless unity. For that, after all, is what the Presidency is, and I hope this exercise in political taxonomy has not obscured the paramount fact that it is a single office filled by a single man. I feel something like a professor of nutritional science who has just ticked off the ingredients of a wonderful stew. The members of the audience may be clear in their minds about the items in the pot, but they have not the slightest notion of what the final product looks like or tastes like or will feel like in their stomachs. The Presidency, too, is a wonderful stew whose unique flavor cannot be accounted for simply by making a list of its ingredients. It is a whole greater than and different from the sum of its parts, an office whose power and prestige are something more than the arithmetical total of all its functions. The President is not one kind of official during one part of the day, another kind during another part—administrator in the morning, legislator at lunch, king in the afternoon, commander before dinner, and politician at odd moments that come his weary way. He is all these things all the time, and any one of his functions feeds upon and into all the others. He is a more exalted Chief of State because he is also Voice of the People, a more forceful Chief Diplomat because he commands the armed forces personally, a more effective Chief Legislator because the political system forces him to be Chief of Party, a more artful Manager of Prosperity because he is Chief Executive.

At the same time, several of these functions are plainly in competition, even in conflict, with one another, and not just in terms of their demands on the President's time and energy. The roles of Voice of the People and Chief of Party cannot both be played with equal fervor, as Mr. Truman proved on several occasions that had best be forgotten, while to act as Chief Diplomat but to think as Chief of Party, as he was apparently persuaded to do in the Palestine crisis of 1948, can throw our foreign relations into indelicate confusion. Mr. Eisenhower certainly had his periods in which, despite perfect health, he reigned too much and thus ruled too little, and one can think of several competent Presidents—Cleveland and Taft and Hoover, to name three out of the last hundred years—who tried much too hard to be faithful Chief Executives.

There is no easy formula for solving this problem inherent in the nature of the office. If the Presidency is a chamber orchestra of ten pieces, all played by the leader, he must learn for himself by hard practice how to blend them together, remembering always that perfect harmony is unattainable, remembering, too, with Whitman, to "resist anything better than my own diversity." The only thing he can know for certain before he begins to make presidential music is that there are several parts, notably those of Chief of Party and Chief Executive, that he must not play too long and loud lest he drown out the others.

The burden of these ten functions is monstrous, and the President carries it as well as he does only because a remarkable array of administrative machinery has been invented to help him in his daily tasks, because

> Thousands at his bidding speed,
> And post o'er land and ocean without rest.

Yet the activities of this train of experts, the Executive Office and the Cabinet and all their offshoots and auxiliaries, must not draw our final attention away from the man all alone at the head. The Presidency, as I shall try to show in Chapter 4, has been converted into an institution during the past quarter-century, and we can never again talk about it sensibly without accounting for "the men around the President." Yet if it has become a thousand-man job in the budget and in the minds of students of public administration, it remains a one-man job in the Constitution and in the minds of the people—a truth of which we were dramatically reminded when the President fell ill in September 1955. Since it is a one-man job, the one man who holds it can never escape making the final decisions in each of the many areas in which the American people and their Constitution hold him responsible.

Mr. Truman, so it is said, used to keep a sign on his desk that read: "The buck stops here." That, in the end, is the essence of the Presidency. It is the one office in all the land whose occupant is forbidden to pass the buck.

CHAPTER 2

THE LIMITS OF THE PRESIDENCY

The American Presidency is not universally admired. Most of us may think of it as a choice instrument of constitutional government, but there are loud dissenters in this country, especially in deep right field, and sharp dissenters abroad, especially in those happy lands where the parliamentary system is counted a success. If the opinions of the former are generally too mixed up with politics to demand serious attention, the opinions of the latter deserve a hearing and rebuttal. The particulars of their bill of indictment against the Presidency read as follows:

1) The President and Congress, thanks chiefly to the independence that each enjoys under the Constitution, are set perennially at odds with one another. Antagonism is built into the system, and the President is forced willy-nilly to choose between meek withdrawal, which leaves the government leaderless, or bold aggression, which throws it into turmoil.

2) The President, thanks chiefly to his fixed term and his exemption from the final penalty of a vote of no confidence by the legislature, is held neither continuously responsible for his general conduct of office nor ever responsible for specific acts and policies. He feels not at all the kind of day-to-day, act-to-act accountability that compels the working head of

government in a parliamentary system to mind every important step.

3) The Presidency, thanks to the whole of Article II of the Constitution, combines power and independence to a dangerous degree. It is, indeed, a "matrix for dictatorship," as the Swiss took pains to point out while writing their Constitution of 1848. The sad history of the Presidency south of Florida and Texas is a warning to Americans that they had better think of reducing either the power or independence of the original model at home.

The American rebuttal to the case against the Presidency makes three general points: that all these criticisms add up to a caricature of the real office, that they ignore the broad pattern of constitutional morality into which this office fits, and that their contempt for history is so flagrant as to raise laughs rather than doubts in the minds of all reasonable men. More specifically, we reject the first particular by answering that the founding fathers "planned it that way," preferring imperfect safety to perfect efficiency, and that we their descendants are coming more and more to suspect that they wrought more shrewdly than they knew in separating the executive and legislative powers. Would this giant democracy of ours—spread over an entire continent, undisciplined by the sanctions of a clear-cut class structure, assaulted daily by the massed voices of vulgarity and unreason—make as safe and sane a success of parliamentary government as it seems to be making of our divided system? This is a question to which even the most perceptive of our resident and visiting critics have yet to address themselves at all persuasively.

We reject the second particular not quite so confidently, for it would have been rather healthy, I think, to have held Roosevelt accountable for the "Court-packing" scheme, Truman for his proposed draft of the railroad strikers in 1946, and Eisenhower for the debacle over the Salk polio vaccine. But we cannot have the best of both great systems, and this, the too easy manner in which Presidents escape paying any real penalty for their blunders, is part of the minimum price we must meet in return for the benefits of the independent Presidency. And, after all, how do we know which kind of executive we would get if we were to adopt the parliamentary system in order to secure the blessings of continuous, piecemeal responsibility: the British Prime Minister, who operates just about as freely as an executive should, or the French Premier under the Fourth Republic, who was harassed at every step?

To the last criticism, that the Presidency blends too much power with too much independence, we can only make answer by inviting its critics to look back over the whole sweep of American political and constitutional history. Whatever grotesque shapes the Presidency may have assumed in Latin America, it has not been a matrix for dictatorship here in the United States; and I hardly think it an act of bravery, even an act of faith, to predict that it will not become one for a very long time, if ever. The Presidency, like every other instrument of power we have created for our use, operates within a grand and durable pattern of private liberty and public morality, which means that it operates successfully only when the President honors the pattern by selecting ends and means that are "characteristically American." I may well be accused of begging the question of dictatorship by saying that the American system simply would not permit it, but I know of no better way to underline the impossibility of our spawning and then succumbing to a Perón or a Batista than to point to the history and people and climate of opinion of the United States and let it go at that.

The Presidency, be it noted, presents a most convincing argument in its own behalf and in that of the American people: 170-odd years and thirty-three Presidents—and still no despot or profligate or scoundrel has made the grade. In my opinion, no despot or profligate, and no scoundrel except Aaron Burr, ever made a good race, and perhaps the Presidency would have sobered even that "damaged soul." It was then and it is now the most thoroughly American of institutions, and I trust I will be excused from any further laboring of the plain historical and sociological truth that it is not a standing invitation to counterrevolution.

Yet, if we should not lose sleep over the possibility of a presidential *coup d'état,* we do have a right to worry about occasional abuses of power. The President is in a position to do serious damage, if not irreparable injury, to the ideals and methods of American democracy. Power that can be used decisively can also be abused grossly. No man can hold such a concentration of authority without feeling the urge, even though the urge be honest and patriotic, to push it beyond its usual bounds. We must therefore consider carefully the various safeguards that are counted upon to keep the President's feet in paths of constitutional righteousness. I have already discussed the powers of the President, as most writers on the subject delight to do, and now I think it proper to discuss the limits on him, as most do not. Blended together in judicious amounts, powers and limits make up a constitution, and the Presidency is nothing if not a constitutional office. Its powers are huge, but they are of no real effect unless exercised through constitutional forms and within constitutional limits.

The search for limitations begins with the written and unwritten law, and thus with the Constitution. Like the good constitution it is, it grants spacious authority in a few frugal words (for which we must be ever grateful to the one-legged man who polished them so brightly) and then clamps on limitations with equal economy of detail. Restrictions on the President are sprinkled all through the Constitution. One has only to think of the rigid four-year term of office, the qualifications on the power of veto, and, to prove that we are not yet entirely content with the bounds fixed by the framers, the

flat ban on a third term established in the Twenty-second
Amendment. Perhaps even more important than these specific
restrictions are the powers the Constitution withholds silently
from the President or bestows bountifully on other organs
over which he has no control. The prime constitutional limit
on the Presidency is the existence of Articles I and III.

The laws of Congress are full of implicit or explicit limitations. For one example, they rarely extend the President substantial authority today without requesting him to report to
Congress annually or semiannually on his use thereof, or at
even briefer intervals. For another, appropriations are more
often than not made in such painful detail that he and his
lieutenants are left with scant discretion to spend them with
any flexibility. For a third, he is limited sharply in his power
of appointment by the many qualifications—as to citizenship,
loyalty, political affiliations, professional attainments, residence,
and the like—that the laws fix in varying degrees on "offices
under the United States." The laws, like the Constitution, are
full of indirect checks on the President, especially those statutes
which set up agencies and commissions independent of his
direction.

Like Congress and the Justices themselves, the President can
show eye-opening ingenuity in bypassing decisions of the
Supreme Court. Yet no President can fail to recognize the
restrictions set upon the free play of his executive will in such
famous cases as *Humphrey's Executor* v. *U.S.* (1935), which
upheld the power of Congress to protect certain administrative
officials against arbitrary removal from office, and *Youngstown
Sheet and Tube Co.* v. *Sawyer* (1952), which denied Mr.
Truman authority to seize and operate the steel industry.
Custom, too, can be ignored in unimportant matters and for
short periods, but it has a way of asserting itself against the
most strong-willed President. The ancient custom of senatorial
courtesy, which appears to have burst full-grown from the
heads of the Senators from Georgia in the first year of Wash-

ington's administration, puts narrow limits on the President's power of appointment to hundreds of offices.

Most of these restrictions are fine and welcome, and they should be studied more thoughtfully by students of American government. Yet they exist on paper, and paper limitations, even those in the Constitution, need the support of living people and going institutions if they are to be of any force. We must therefore look further, into the political and social system all about us, if we are to learn what really puts the brakes on the President who has a mind to wander too far afield. "Brakes" is perhaps not the happiest word to use in this instance, because I am concerned with persons and institutions and centers of power that not only block the President's way, convincing him that a course of action is more trouble than it is worth or even frustrating him flatly, but often force him to take a course of action that he does not want to take at all. What are some of these, and how do they operate to restrain or persuade him?

The first and most vigorous is the Congress of the United States —a concourse of self-willed persons, a venerable institution, a fiercely independent center of power. Some of the weapons with which it may check or persuade the President are bright with use; others have not been hauled out and brandished for many years. Yet all must be reckoned with by the President who sets out upon an extraordinary line of conduct, or even, for that matter, by the President who simply tends quietly to his legitimate business. Let me list them briefly and add one or two comments.

The power of legislation is one that I have already touched upon sufficiently by indicating some of the ways in which the President is limited by statute. I would add only the observation that this power is a great deal easier for Congress to wield over future Presidents than over the President of the moment. Yet the Humphrey-Stennis joint resolution of July 1955, which set up the Wright Commission to investigate and report on the loyalty and security program, shows that pressure can sometimes be applied by law to an incumbent President. This shrewdly designed statute persuaded Mr. Eisenhower much against his stated will to join in re-examining a program for which he was primarily responsible. The Senate and the House, acting separately or concurrently, can also exert strong pressure on the President through the agency of a resolution, even though such a resolution is nothing more than an expression of opinion. No President is likely to help Communist China take a seat in the United Nations so long as Congress keeps on resolving unanimously that "such admission would gravely injure the United Nations and impair its effective functioning." It may be argued that such resolutions have only moral force, but ours is a system of government in which moral force is often the only kind that really counts.

Another check, whose potentialities (and constitutionality) have yet to be fully explored, is the provision occasionally inserted in broad delegations of emergency power that permits the power to be recaptured by concurrent resolution, that is, without the President's consent. A variation on this check is the provision in the Reciprocal Trade Act of 1958 that permits Congress, by a two-thirds vote in both houses, to overrule presidential objections to decisions of the Tariff Commission. Many grants of power, of course, are made for limited periods; some of the most important wartime statutes named specific terminal dates. And there is always the "rider" placed artfully in a bill the President cannot afford to veto. Rutherford B. Hayes, I am told by residents of Fremont, Ohio, still shakes in his grave every time a President is forced to protest against this practice. No President was ever more beset by "riders," nor ever flung them back more boldly at the gamesmen in Congress.

The power of investigation, which includes the power to ask questions if not always to get answers from the President's chief lieutenants, calls for even less comment. The excellent uses and disgraceful abuses of this power over the past generation are etched sharply in our memories, and it is scarcely necessary to point out that in many of the leading investigations of this period (those, for example, conducted by Senator McCarthy in 1953 and Senator Kefauver in 1955) the real target was the President himself. While these men were engaged in high theater, other Congressmen, less ambitious and more merciful, were plodding quietly ahead with the routine inquiries into administrative purposes, methods, and shortcomings that do much to keep the Chief Executive and his helpers in touch with democratic realities. Hardly less effective as a limit upon the strong-minded President is the vast web of informal contacts and friendships and understandings between the old hands in Congress and the old hands in the civil service. Many of these relationships, which are rarely publicized, are maintained in blithesome disregard of the stated policies of the President—but he, after all, is only passing through.

The power of the purse was once upon a time considered the most formidable of Congress's weapons, and there are those who persist in talking about it as did Madison in *The Federalist:*

This power over the purse may, in fact, be regarded as the most complete and effectual weapon with which any constitution can arm the immediate representatives of the people, for obtaining a redress of every grievance, and for carrying into effect every just and salutary measure.

I am afraid we must enter a dissent to this much too mechanical evaluation of a power more vaunted than viable. Instances in which Congress slapped a President, and hurt him, by withholding funds from schemes in which he had an intense personal interest do not come to mind in bunches. Perhaps the most notable use of this weapon in recent years was the senseless murder of the National Resources Planning Board in 1943 by the Seventy-eighth Congress. In the same year, however, Mr. Roosevelt sent in a budget of $100,000,000,000, and Congress fell all over itself trying to give the Commander in Chief every-

thing he needed to win the war—everything, that is, but the
National Resources Planning Board. In the warfare-welfare
state, which Madison could hardly have foreseen, the power of
the purse exists more in rhetoric than in fact. Indeed, the evidence is rather convincing that in time of emergency, when
controls on expenditures are most needed, Congress itself takes
the lead in loosening them. In this permanent emergency
through which we seem to be living, the annual defense budget
makes a cruel mockery of all claims for the power of the purse.

The power of impeachment is the "extreme medicine" of the
Constitution, so extreme—and so brutally administered in the
one instance in which it was prescribed for a President—that
most observers now agree with Jefferson that it is a "mere scare-
crow" and with Henry Jones Ford that it is a "rusted blunderbuss, that will probably never be taken in hand again." The one
instance, of course, was the audacious attempt of the Radical
Republicans in Congress to have done once and for all with
Andrew Johnson. Johnson was impeached by the House of
Representatives in March 1868 on eleven counts. The key
charge was his alleged violation of the Tenure of Office Act of
1867 in insisting on his right to remove the faithless Edwin M.
Stanton from his position as Secretary of War, but in point of
fact the whole attack was vengefully political in motivation and
purpose. In the trial before the Senate—with Chief Justice Chase
presiding in keeping with the Constitution and with the President absenting himself in keeping with the dignity of his office
—he was thrice saved from removal by a margin of one vote.
The votes of thirty-six Senators were necessary to convict under
the two-thirds rule laid down in the Constitution, and on three
counts the vote to convict was 35 to 19. This fact, coupled with
the arguments of Johnson's counsel and the wording of the
charges, made clear for all time that impeachment is not an
"inquest of office," a political process for turning out a President whom a majority of the House and two-thirds of the Senate simply cannot abide. It is certainly not, nor was it ever

intended to be, an extraordinary device for registering a vote of no confidence. Yet, rusted though the blunderbuss may be, it still endures, stacked away defiantly in the Constitution, and it could yet be used to bring down a President who engages openly in "treason, bribery, or other high crimes and misdemeanors." If it is not, as Professor Edward S. Corwin has written, "an effective weapon in the arsenal of liberty," this must be largely due "to the fact that Presidents have in the past kept pretty clear of courses which might make people think seriously of so extreme a discipline." I predict confidently that the next President to be impeached will have asked for the firing squad by committing a low personal rather than a high political crime—by shooting a Senator, for example. Lest someone take the phrase "firing squad" seriously, I invite my readers to turn to Appendix II and read for themselves in the Constitution what penalties can be inflicted upon a wrongdoing President by an outraged Senate.

Congress, or either house, also retains the power of "soft impeachment," although this, too, has been used on a President only about once a century. The Senate's censure of Andrew Jackson in 1834 for "the late executive proceedings in relation to the public revenue" was the most drastic exercise of this extraordinary power. It cannot be said to have had much influence on Jackson's subsequent conduct; rather, it proved to be one of the most deadly boomerangs in American political history. An interesting variation on the power of censure was the resolution of the Republican conferences in the House and Senate in December 1950 demanding the removal of Secretary of State Acheson. This unprecedented "vote of no confidence" by the minority party may have hurt Mr. Acheson's prestige at the Brussels parley, but it, too, proved a boomerang. One suspects that nothing short of a gun at his head, and perhaps not even that, could thereafter have persuaded Mr. Truman to throw his Secretary of State from the sleigh to the Republican wolves.

Finally, I need hardly do more than point with awe to the

three great negative powers of the Senate, two of which it draws
from the Constitution, the third of which it has bestowed upon
its own grateful self: 1) the power of a majority to withhold
consent from the President's nominations; 2) the power of one-
third (plus one) "of the Senators present" to withhold consent
from the treaties he submits to it; and 3) the power of a "little
group of willful men, representing no opinion but their own,"
to hamstring the desire of a majority of both houses to give the
President a grant of authority or money for which he may have
desperate need. Some of the most celebrated filibusters in the
Senate's history have been directed against the policies and even
the person of a President.

The real power of Congress to check or persuade a President
lies in none of the positive weapons I have just reviewed, for
the real power of Congress over him is essentially negative in
character. Two points are worth remembering in this connection: first, that no great policy, domestic or foreign, can be
maintained effectively by a President without the approval of
Congress in the form of laws and money; and second, that there
is no way under our Constitution for a President to force Congress to pass a law or spend money against its will. In the
course of this book I have several times pointed with pride and
awe to the unique independence of our executive, but I could
also have pointed, with no less pride and perhaps more awe, to
the unique independence of our legislature. If the members of
Congress cannot force the President to resign by a vote of no
confidence, neither can he dissolve Congress. If his term is
rigidly fixed, so, too, is theirs. Ours is just about the only legislature in the world over whose decisions the executive has no
final power of persuasion, either in political fact or constitutional theory. He has *influence,* and the influence may be great,
as Franklin Roosevelt proved in March 1933, but he has no
power. Nor is the indissolubility of Congress the only bulwark
of its independence. It, too, draws its authority directly from

the Constitution; it, too, arises out of a constituency essentially its own.

Let me illustrate this point with the aid of a passage from Beard's *Republic*. The Glaucon of the piece, Dr. Smyth, has just made a sweeping assertion of presidential power in foreign affairs—something like the one I made in the first chapter—and Socrates, Professor Beard, is not the man to let him get away with it:

Now let me put some yes or no questions to you, the kind you like to put to me. Can the President alone regulate intercourse with other countries at his pleasure—that is, tariffs, tonnage duties, financial exchanges, and travel?

No. Congress has that power.

Can the President at his pleasure regulate immigration and emigration?

No. Congress passes immigration acts.

Can the President determine the conditions of naturalization and the rights of aliens in the United States?

No.

Can the President fix the size and nature of our army, navy, and other armed forces?

No.

Can the President alone set up ministries and consulates in other countries and pick his own ministers and consuls?

No. Since Congress must provide the money for them, it could control this branch of foreign business, if it wanted to do so. Besides, the Senate must approve the persons named by the President as ministers or ambassadors.

Can the President make treaties with other countries?

No. A treaty must have the approval of two-thirds of the Senate. But the President can make minor agreements without asking the consent of the Senate.

Can the President declare war?

No. That power is supposed to be in the hands of Congress.

Can the President make peace?

If it takes a treaty, the Senate must approve.

Can the President declare the foreign policy of the United States and impose it on the country by his own will?

There are two questions. Certainly the President can declare the foreign policy of the United States. But he cannot impose it upon the country by mere declaration.

There is more of this kind of talk, but the passage will suffice to remind us of the President's reliance on Congress for support of even his most splendid prerogatives.

I could proceed indefinitely discussing this most crucial relationship in our system of government, yet I trust I have made my point with sufficient vigor: the most reliable single limitation on the American Presidency is the independent existence of a proud, jealous, watchful co-ordinate branch. No President ever lived who would not have agreed, reverently or ruefully, with this statement.

The restricting powers of the third independent branch are a delusive shadow compared with the sweep of authority just reviewed. For most practical purposes, the President may act as if the Supreme Court did not exist. It takes a raw action by an imprudent President to invite judicial condemnation, and most exertions of executive power, however raw, are directed to questions over which no court would presume to exercise the slightest measure of supervision or even judgment.

This is especially true of the President's activities in time of war, as one may read for himself in the *United States Reports* published during and after our three great conflicts. At the very moment when the President, whether Lincoln or Wilson or Roosevelt, was drawing most audaciously on the Commander in Chief clause for authority to regulate the lives and property of the people, the Court was drawing most sheepishly on its bag of tricks to avoid a showdown with him and his military subordinates. The reason for excessive judicial self-restraint in time of war is, of course, obvious and compelling. A challenge in court to an evacuation order or a plant seizure or a suspension of the writ of habeas corpus raises a question so politically explosive, perhaps so vital to national survival, that the very notion of "government by lawsuit" becomes unthinkable. Whatever we allow this process to settle in time of peace, we cannot submit to its vagaries in time of war—a truth that the Court itself has been the first to acknowledge by avoiding unfavorable judgments on the President's orders as Commander in Chief. Like Congress's power of the purse, the Court's power of judicial review is least useful when most needed.

Yet the Court does own a few spectacular victories over the President. Several of these, like *Humphrey's Executor* v. *U.S.* (1935), came too late to be of much use or warning to anyone involved. The most famous and confidently quoted of all limiting decisions, *Ex parte Milligan* (1866), was announced a full year after the assassination of the President who was being censured, in this instance for authorizing the trial of civilians by military commission in an area far removed from the theater of war. Cases like *Schecter Bros.* v. *U.S.* (1934) and *Youngstown Sheet and Tube Co.* v. *Sawyer* (1952), however, shot down high-flying Presidents at the top of their trajectories. Whatever else may be said of the Schecter case, which cut the legal ground from under the National Recovery Administration, it was a healthy exhibition of constitutional government in action, and it was the President, not the Court, who took the crucial step by ordering the N.R.A. to fold its tents without delay. The Steel Seizure case was an equally dramatic vindication of constitutional practice, and again it was the President who bowed deeply, if hardly reverently, to constituted authority by ordering the Secretary of Commerce to relinquish possession of the steel mills. To bring the story up to date, President Eisenhower was handed two irritating rebuffs by the Supreme Court in 1958: *Kent* v. *Dulles,* in which the Secretary of State's practice of using his own power to deny passports as an instrument of foreign policy was limited if hardly eliminated, and *Cole* v. *Young,* in which the Court chopped down the area to which the

President's statutory power of removal had been extended "in the interest of the national security of the United States"—or, in other words, put a crimp in his loyalty program.

In none of these cases was the President himself before the Court. Jefferson's rejection of Marshall's *subpoena duces tecum* in the Burr trial and Chase's opinion in *Mississippi* v. *Johnson* (1867), which spared Andrew Johnson the necessity of answering a writ of injunction, make clear that the judiciary has no power to enjoin or mandamus or even question the President. His subordinates, however, do not share his immunity from the judicial process. Whenever a claim or justification is based on the authority of a presidential order, the order itself may come under challenge in the form of a suit against those seeking to enforce it. The interesting old case of *Little* v. *Barreme* (1804) presents one clear-cut instance in which the Court held a presidential order to be without legal warrant; *Panama Refining Co.* v. *Ryan* (1934) presents another.

I do not wish to sound too harsh or hopeless in my final estimate of the Court as a restraint on presidential activity. No one can doubt the high moral standing of a case like *Humphrey's Executor* v. *U.S.*, least of all some future President who decides to stir up the hornets by removing a commissioner from one of the independent agencies. Even as he chooses a course of action that permits him to ignore Justice Sutherland's opinion in that case, he will have to explain carefully to Congress and people, and in time to the Court, just what distinguishes this removal from that effected by Franklin Roosevelt in 1934. Yet as the Humphrey case demonstrated and *Wiener* v. *U.S.* (1958) confirmed, the President can remove just about any official if he wants to badly enough, and the Court will not be able to give the removed man anything more than sympathy and some back salary. We delude ourselves cruelly if we count on the Court at all hopefully to save us from the consequences of most abuses of presidential power. The fact is that the Court has done more over the years to expand than to contract the authority of the

Presidency—as witness the *Prize Cases* (1863), in which it supported Lincoln's blockade of the South; *In re Debs* (1895), in which it approved Cleveland's strong line of action in the Pullman strike; *Myers* v. *U.S.* (1926), in which a President-turned-Chief Justice cut through every restriction ever thrown about the removal power; *United States* v. *Curtiss-Wright Export Corp.* (1936), in which the Court spoke glowingly of the President's power in foreign relations; and the long series of cases in which it purified and strengthened the powers to pardon offenses and veto bills. In the nature of things judicial and political, the Court can be expected to go on rationalizing most pretensions of most Presidents. It is clearly one of the least reliable restraints on presidential activity.

A more reliable restraint is to be found in the federal administration: in the persons and politics and prejudices of, let us say, the top 20,000 civil and military officials of the government of the United States. Were the Presidents of the last fifty years to be polled on this question, all but one or two, I am sure, would agree that the "natural obstinacy" of the average bureau chief or commissioner or colonel was second only to the "ingrained suspicions" of the average Congressman as a check on the President's ability to do either good or evil. Several would doubtless go further to insist that the President's hardest job is, not to persuade Congress to support a policy dear to his political heart, but to persuade the pertinent bureau or agency or mission, even when headed by men of his own choosing, to follow his direction faithfully and transform the shadow of the policy into the substance of a program. No President, they would tell us sadly, can accomplish anything lasting in influence without the energetic assistance of a whole train of civil servants, most of whom were on the job long before he arrived and will be there long after he has departed, and without the loyal support of a motley array of political executives, most of whom he had never heard of until the day he sent in their names to the Senate. In seeking to win this kind of assistance, in trying to "get on top and stay on top" of his administration or even a part of it, a President can easily dissipate all his time, energy, and capacity for leadership.

This is not to say that the federal administration is led and staffed by men whose one purpose in life is to ignore, emasculate, or otherwise frustrate the legitimate wishes of the President. Quite the contrary, our public servants are no less anxious than he to get on with the business of good and democratic government. But his idea and their idea of what is "good" or "democratic" must often be at stiff odds with one another, especially when he is pushing some untried and unconventional policy, even more especially when they have the support of strong men and groups in Congress. It is too much to expect, short of the kind of drastic therapy or surgery that may well leave an agency in no condition to act at all, that such a policy can be the same in execution as it was in conception. I think, in this instance, of all the written and spoken directives of our last three Presidents aimed at eliminating racial discrimination in the civil service and the armed forces, and I wonder how many thousands of times some stubborn or fainthearted official has made a mockery of the President's good intentions. I think, too, of the trials undergone by Truman and Eisenhower in persuading certain chiefs of staff, whose official lives depend entirely on the President's pleasure, to shape their acts and speeches to the policies of the administration. And I top off these thoughts with a memorable observation by a man who knew firsthand about the severe limits on the President's power to influence administrators, Franklin D. Roosevelt:

The Treasury is so large and far-flung and ingrained in its practices that I find it is almost impossible to get the action and results I want—even with Henry [Morgenthau] there. But the Treasury is not to be compared with the State Department. You should go through the experience of trying to get any changes in the thinking, policy and action of the career diplomats and then you'd know what a real problem was. But the Treasury and the State Department put together are nothing compared with the Na-a-vy. The admirals are really something to cope with—and I should know. To change anything in the Na-a-vy is like punching a feather bed. You punch it with your right and you punch it with your left until you are finally exhausted, and then you find the damn bed just as it was before you started punching.

I shall have more to say about the President's difficulties as an administrator in later chapters. Here I need only call attention to certain broad features of the administrative branch that can be counted on to hobble a crusading President, even when the crusade is obviously launched against the forces of darkness. The first of these is the mere size of the federal administration, which now makes it impossible for a President to know or see or influence personally more than a handful of those men whose day-to-day activities will determine whether some cherished policy is to succeed or fail. What Burke said of the old British Empire, we may say of the new American government: "In large bodies, the circulation of power must be less vigorous at the extremities. Nature has said it." At many extremities of the federal administration the circulation of presidential power cannot be felt at all.

The second feature is pluralism in law, and a close corollary is pluralism in fact. Many agencies are rendered independent of the President's immediate supervision by statute; many more are exempt from his influence because of political and personal circumstances. The most unusual circumstance, one that can frustrate any President, is that of an upright agency headed by a case-hardened chief who numbers more real friends among the leaders of Congress than any President who ever lived, not even excluding William McKinley. The Federal Bureau of Investigation under J. Edgar Hoover, the Passport Office under Mrs. Ruth Shipley and Miss Frances Knight, and the Corps of Engineers under almost anyone are examples of what I mean by "pluralism in fact." Although a President may count on these agencies to execute the laws faithfully according to their own lights, he would invite disaster, both administrative and political, if he tried to alter the course that each has been following for these many years. Mr. Hoover has a kind of tenure that even the most carefully sheltered administrator should have reason to envy; his time-tested ability to outlast the President of the moment must always give that President pause. I cannot help wondering how often President Truman thought of relieving Mr. Hoover—and then thought a second time, sighed, and went about his business.

Finally, I need only mention such qualities of any administration as tradition, pride, inertia, and professional knowledge to show that the President, be his intentions good or bad, is checked sharply by the mere existence of all those thousands of top-grade public servants over whom he simply cannot expect to have the control in fact that he does in law, and of those hundreds over whom he has no effective control at all. Nor does it afford him much comfort to know that he hires and fires the men on top of the executive departments, for few of these are his unquestioning supporters and all must suffer the existence of bureau and division heads who make their own deals with congressional committees for power, funds, and prestige. There are more programs under way in the federal administration than any one President has ever dreamed of initiating, terminating, or bending to his will.

Another series of restraints upon the President arises out of our political system, by which I mean the two major parties. We all know well the many ways in which the leaders of the opposition party can make hash of his plans and a misery of his existence. They can badger his assistants, investigate his methods, vote down his requests, question his motives, keep a record of the times he plays golf, and, as in the congressional elections of 1918 and 1946 and perhaps even in 1958, beat him in the process of beating his party at the polls. If the President is the grand sachem of his own party and thus the symbol of its hopes and instrument of its principles, the party that fought him tooth and nail at his election must continue to fight him, with perhaps a little more restraint now that he is President, all through his four years in office. His record is essentially the record of his party, and the party in opposition, which wants desperately to put its own man in the White House, cannot be expected to let him have his own way except in matters that touch upon our survival as a nation. Even as he struggles with these matters he will be harassed by the enemy's irregulars. Not the least effective check in our system of checks and balances is one the framers themselves tried to save us from with all their skill: the party in opposition, which now means the party that lost the Presidency in the last election. No party can think of itself as the governing party in this country unless it can claim the authority and prestige of the White House. Indeed, ours is just about the only country in the world in which a party can dominate the national legislature for years on end and still be described correctly as "the party out of power"—a commentary on the unique character and authority of the American Presidency that must be worth at least ten thousand words.

If the opposing party is a roadblock in the path of the President, his own party is at best a drag. He draws great power from his position as Chief of Party, but with it comes the obligation to work and live with the men who elected him to office —an obligation of which Representative Simpson of Pennsylvania reminded Mr. Eisenhower with a fervor just short of anger in January 1959. Not only must he be careful not to plunge too far ahead or lag too far to the rear of his allies in Congress; he must pay homage to the traditions of his party, select his chief lieutenants from its ranks, act as "honest broker" among its squabbling wings, and endure silently attacks upon his integrity by men who roam the outer reaches of party loyalty. In doing all these things for the sake of harmony, and for the sake of victory in the next election, he cannot help losing some of his zest for bold experiment. In most instances that matter he must work with the party or not at all. The party, as we well know from the history of a dozen administrations, is more likely to tame him than he is to reshape it. Franklin Roosevelt, supposedly the most dominant of political leaders, felt the drag of his own party through most of his years in office. The Democrats on the House Rules Committee and Senate Judiciary Committee, not the Republicans huddled together in the Cave of Adullam, were the impenetrable barrier between him and some of his most ardently sought goals. Dwight D. Eisenhower, a man with little taste for adventure, was certainly hampered rather than invigorated by his leadership of the Republican party. The party that makes him also brakes him: this is the lot, not entirely unhappy, of the modern President.

When we look beyond the national government and the parties that are its lifeblood, we note at least three other centers or dispersions of power that stand in the President's way and often force him to take troublesome detours. The first of these is the federal system—an involved network of fifty separate and independent governments and their countless subdivisions, all of which possess powers whose use or disuse can seriously embarrass the President and his policies. Although the states no longer have the restraining influence of the days when they defied Jefferson, ignored Madison, and heckled Lincoln, they remain an obstacle to the determined President, especially to one who is eager to push ahead boldly with experiments in education and racial justice. In conducting foreign relations, too, the President may discover that the states and even the cities still hold some power to irritate if not to persuade him. Theodore Roosevelt's Japanese policy nearly foundered on the anti-Oriental obstinacy of the San Francisco Board of Education; the Board gave way to the President only after he had promised to see what he could do to reduce the flow of Japanese immigrants into California. The Republican-dominated legislature of California made even more trouble for President Wilson by passing an

alien land law aimed primarily at the Japanese, despite the
earnest pleas of the President, which Secretary of State Bryan
delivered personally in Sacramento, that the nation be spared
the consequences of this insult to proud Japan. Our policy in
the Middle East, which has never been celebrated for its clarity
of purpose, was thrown into even more of a state of frustrated
confusion in 1957 by Mayor Wagner's childish behavior on the
occasion of King Ibn Saud's visit to New York City. While I
am on the subject of the Middle East, an area in which oil is
the beginning and end of our foreign policy, I might call attention to the existence of the Texas Railroad Commission. One of
these days we may need to export unusual quantities of oil to
Western Europe—as we did for a short time in the Suez crisis
of 1957—and just how much persuasion will our President be
able to visit upon this powerful agency which, as few Americans
seem to realize, has effective authority over the rate of production in most of the oil fields in the United States? I suppose we
can always count on Texas to remind us that the states still exist.

Far stronger than the states as a check on the Presidency is
the American system of free enterprise—that fabulous galaxy
of corporations, small businesses, partnerships, individual enterprises, trade associations, co-operatives, unions, consumer
groups, and foundations through which the power of economic
decision is splintered and diffused in the interest of freedom and
progress. The President must enlist a great deal of private support among both management and labor if he is to make his
authority as Manager of Prosperity felt in the face of impending economic disaster. His bid for support may often be spurned
by some group of men in the economy who just do not want to
be managed into prosperity, at least prosperity as the President
defines it.

And he can be spurned—no doubt of that. There have been
several occasions in recent years when free enterprise, or even
a single free enterpriser, has defied a President with impunity
and even brought him to terms. John L. Lewis, the last of the

robber barons, has driven at least three Presidents to consider either homicide or suicide, and Clarence Randall, a man who has served this country well, may be remembered most vividly for his televised attack on President Truman's order to seize the steel industry in April 1952. Mr. Randall's opening and closing words on that occasion are well worth recording, for they give a candid picture of an American mind wrestling with the prickly truth that the politician in the White House is also a king, and vice versa:

I have a deep sense of responsibility as I face this vast audience of the air. I am here to make answer on behalf of the steel industry to charges flung over these microphones last night by the man who then stood where I stand now. I am a plain citizen. He was the President of the United States.

Happily we still live in a country where a private citizen may look the President in the eye and tell him that he was wrong, but actually it is not the President of the United States to whom I make answer.

It is Harry S. Truman, the man, who last night so far transgressed his oath of office, so far abused the power which is temporarily his, that he must now stand and take it.

I shall not let my deep respect for the office which he holds stop me from denouncing his shocking distortions of fact. Nor shall I permit the honor of his title to blind the American people from the enormity of what he has done.

He has seized the steel plants of the nation, the private property of one million people, most of whom now hear the sound of my voice. This he has done without the slightest shadow of legal right. . . .

For whom has he done this? Let no American be misled. This evil deed, without precedent in American history, discharges a political debt to the C.I.O. Phil Murray now gives Harry S. Truman a receipt marked "paid in full." I present this forthright reply to the President only because I believe deeply in the truth of what I have said. I should feel derelict in my own duty as a citizen if I did not tonight call upon Americans everywhere to take up the challenge the President threw down last night.

Whereupon Mr. Randall and his associates took up the challenge themselves and, eight weeks later, drove the President and Secretary of Commerce Sawyer headlong from their mills. Their troubles were far from over, but they had defeated a President in a battle of his choosing.

I have already referred to the President's obligations to his colleagues and constituents overseas. No obligation that goes with this new dimension of leadership is more certain and pressing than his duty to listen carefully, and to pay heed when he can, to the suggestions of our friends, real or simply wished for, throughout the world; for on these terms alone can we maintain the alliances upon which we depend for survival as a self-governing people. This means, of course, that in shaping a military or foreign policy the President must give careful thought to how persons outside as well as inside the country will respond. He must henceforth sense a reduction in his freedom to conduct the delicate business of diplomacy and the nasty business of war because of pressures flowing from London and Paris and Tokyo, as well as from New Delhi and the United Nations building in New York. Dozens of times since World War II our Presidents have acted as they have because Sir Winston Churchill or Sir Anthony Eden or General de Gaulle or, let us not forget, Syngman Rhee has persuaded them to act that way. Would Mr. Eisenhower have gone to the Summit in 1955 if he had not been entreated by Eden and Premier Faure? And would Sir Anthony have entreated quite so persuasively had he not been faced with a general election, one that Mr. Eisenhower had a strong desire to see him win? Would not the way to the Summit in 1959-1960 have been a great deal easier if it had not been littered with the suspicions of Adenauer and de Gaulle? And would they have been so suspicious had they not been persuaded of the reluctance of millions of Germans and Frenchmen to face the Russians at the bargaining table? It would seem that the people as well as the political leaders of other nations can occasionally speed a President up or slow him down.

This brings me to the last and, over the long run, most effective check upon the President: the opinions of the people of the United States, which our pressure groups can be counted on to express with zeal. Lincoln is supposed to have said that he could do anything with "public sentiment" but nothing without it or against it; and if he did not say it, we can say it for him. The President draws immense authority from the support of the American people, but only if he uses it in ways they understand and approve, which generally means ways that are fair, digni- fied, traditional, and familiar. He can lead public opinion, but only so far as public opinion is willing to go, and it is splendidly inert on dozens of great issues. Indeed, there are times when it will not rouse to any appeal, when it wearies, as Franklin Roose- velt once confessed to a friend, of being "attuned . . . to a constant repetition of the highest note in the scale," which is another way of saying that the President must be careful not to become a bore.

The President can steer public opinion a bit, too, and occa- sionally redirect its course, but he cannot make it take a direc- tion that goes against what I have called our "grand and durable pattern of private liberty and public morality." For if he flouts either the considered judgments or ill-considered prejudices of any vocal segment of the people, if he chances to roam too far outside the accepted limits of presidential behavior, he will find himself exposed to all those enemies who multiply like mos- quitoes in a Jersey August whenever a President plays the game too hard. No President, certainly no peacetime President, ever wielded more power with less need to worry about the political consequences than did Franklin Roosevelt in 1933, yet even then the assumption was abroad that there were some steps he could not take, some measures he could not recommend to Con- gress, in his effort to rescue "a stricken Nation in the midst of a stricken world." Let me drive this point home with a few words from a devoted admirer of the President, Professor Harold Laski, who wanted a new deck more than a New Deal:

Vast innovations for which the public is unprepared are almost bound to fail, because they are almost certain to shock. There can be experiment in the tactics of policy; there can hardly, without great danger, be experiment in fundamental ideas. Those observers who say that Mr. Roosevelt missed a great opportunity in 1933 when he did not nationalize the banking system seem to me wholly to misconceive the nature of the presidential office. While it was possible that, at that grave moment, the president might have carried through such a scheme, it was so widely outside the range of common expectation that it would have destroyed his authority for the rest of his term in office. Nothing in previous discussion had prepared the public for such a measure. Nothing in the electoral conception of Mr. Roosevelt had prepared the public to associate him with such a strategy. He might have won the battle; he would have lost the campaign.

Thinking of Mr. Roosevelt's defeat in his fight to enlarge the Supreme Court in 1937, I would go a step beyond Laski and assert that he would not even have won the battle. Public opinion in this country in 1933, or at least the opinion of a large and dogged segment of it, would never have made peace with the idea of nationalizing the banking system, and it would surely have found a dozen ways to harry the President into surrender. These ways still exist and have, if anything, grown stronger in the past several decades. And by "ways" I do not mean simply such outlets for American opinion as radio, television, Gallup and Roper polls, letters to the White House, or even elections, useful as all these may be as storm warnings to a President. The real force of public opinion as a limit on the Presidency is felt through the other restraints I have described in this chapter. Public opinion, that is to say, works most effectively on a President when it encourages Congress to override a veto, persuades an investigating committee to put a White House intimate on the grill, stiffens the resolve of a band of

Senators to talk until Christmas, convinces an ousted commissioner that his ouster is worth fighting in the courts, and puts backbone in a Supreme Court asked to nullify a presidential order. The various institutions and centers of power that check the President are inept and often useless without public opinion —and with it wondrously armed.

All this is especially true of Congress, which never feels that life is so worth living as when it condemns the President or refuses to grant his request for power because it senses that for once it, not he, has "rightly interpreted the national thought." If he tries to persuade Congress improperly or pushes ahead in defiance of all the rules, he invites the one disaster from which Presidents rarely recover: the loss of genuine popular support.

In the end, of course, the checks that hold the President in line are internal rather than external. His conscience and training, his sense of history and desire to be judged well by it, his awareness of the need to pace himself lest he collapse under the burden—all join to halt him far short of the kind of deed that destroys a President's "fame and power." He, like the rest of us, has been raised in the American tradition; he, perhaps better than the rest of us, senses what the tradition permits and what it forbids in the conduct of high office. If he knows anything of history or politics or administration, he knows that he can do great things only within "the common range of expectation," that is to say, in ways that honor or at least do not outrage the accepted dictates of constitutionalism, democracy, personal liberty, and Christian morality.

And so we return to the point from which we set forth on this journey around the perimeter of presidential power, and again I beg the question of dictatorship by saying that the American system would not permit it. This republic has had its share of "God's angry men," and some of them have climbed up to high places and set off damaging explosions. But none has even got a good start on the climb to the highest place of all. Our political rules demand categorically that a candidate for the Presidency be, first, a politician able to unite a party in whose house there are a hundred mansions and, second, a statesman able to bid confidently for the votes of a majority of the American constituency. It has unfailing ways of singling out and rejecting the man who cannot do these things because he is too angry or anxious or unprincipled. Men like Thaddeus Stevens and Huey Long and Senator McCarthy may wield vast powers of provocation and intimidation in their time, but no party with the faintest hope of winning the big election will ever nominate such a man to lead it. I think a good test of a man's understanding of the American system was his recognition, even in 1952 and 1953, that Senator McCarthy might help to make or break a President but could never be one himself. At least one of Hamilton's confident observations in *The Federalist* still rings true:

The process of election affords a moral certainty, that the office of President will never fall to the lot of any man who is not in an eminent degree endowed with the requisite qualifications. Talents for low intrigue, and the little arts of popularity, may alone suffice to elevate a man to the first honors in a single state; but it will require other talents, and a different kind of merit, to establish him in the esteem and confidence of the whole Union, or of so considerable a portion of it as would be necessary to make him a successful candidate for the distinguished office of President of the United States. It will not be too strong to say, that there will be a constant probability of seeing the station filled by characters preeminent for ability and virtue.

Or at least by characters with enough ability to lead an American-style party and enough virtue to appeal to a majority of one of the world's most enlightened electorates.

Let me refix attention upon the President who is already in office, upon the one, indeed, in office at the moment of writing. Like all our Presidents, he is quite unlikely to hazard a dictatorship; but, again like all of them, he is quite likely to indulge in occasional misuses of power. My concern has been to describe the network of restraints that keeps him from indulging

too often and too perniciously in such misuses, and I think it
essential to round off this description with two observations.
First, no one of these mighty centers of power—Congress,
Court, administration, parties, states, economy, people—operates alone in restraining him. They form, as I have said, a network, and the strength of the network arises from the interlocking of all its parts. One fortifies the other and is in turn
fortified by it. A genuinely indecent performance by the President will arouse fierce opposition in every part of our system,
and even a questionable course of action, such as Eisenhower's
series of blunders in the Dixon-Yates affair, will move Congressmen, administrators, lobbyists, and politicians to unite in opposition. Several observers were moved to remark in the midst of
that controversy that the President seemed never to have heard
of John C. Calhoun's doctrine of the "concurrent majority," or
surely he would have realized that no important program can
be brought off in this country without the concurrence of a clear
majority of the social and economic interests with a stake in the
outcome. One always had the feeling that Eisenhower would
lose in the end—if not the battle, certainly the campaign. And
when he did lose the battle, he lost not only to the city of
Memphis but to a whole host of other interests that had fought
him implacably on a dozen fronts. There are those, to be sure,
who think of the Dixon-Yates contract as a proper agreement
properly made, which is as useful a thought as any to illustrate
the truth that the system can prevent a President from doing
good as well as evil. In the end, however, we must hold fast to
the faith, which is surely borne out by history, that the network
of restraints on the President works about as well as we have
a right to expect our institutions to work. Much, after all, is left
to chance among free men. As we cannot expect power to be
used only to do good, so we cannot expect limitations to be
used only to block evil.

My second point is that the President is not a Gulliver immo-
bilized by ten thousand tiny cords, nor even a Prometheus

chained to a rock of frustration. He is, rather, a kind of magnificent lion who can roam widely and do great deeds so long as he does not try to break loose from his broad reservation. Our pluralistic system of restraints is designed to keep him from going out of bounds, not to paralyze him in the field that has been reserved for his use. He will feel few checks upon his power if he uses that power as he should. This may well be the final definition of the strong and successful President: the one who knows just how far he can go in the direction he wants to go. If he cannot judge the limits of his power, he cannot call upon its strength. If he cannot sense the possible, he will exhaust himself attempting the impossible. The power of the Presidency moves as a mighty host only *with* the grain of liberty and morality.

CHAPTER **3**

THE PRESIDENCY IN HISTORY

The roots of the American Presidency run deep into history. In a world in which model constitutions with their model executives have come and gone in profusion over the past 150 years, this office stands forth as a truly venerable institution. We cannot take its full measure unless we know something of its history, and its history, in any case, is worth studying for its own exciting sake. With no further ado I plunge headlong into it.

The point of origin to which I would first direct attention is the Constitutional Convention of 1787, although like all such points it had origins of its own, in this instance far back in English constitutional history. To understand the kind of executive created in Article II of the Constitution, we must know something of the men who wrote it, the purposes they had in mind, the materials with which they worked, and the experience that was their "final guide."

The men most influential in shaping the Presidency were James Wilson, who campaigned tirelessly for an executive that could operate with "energy, dispatch, and responsibility"; James Madison, who swung around slowly, but in the end decisively, to Wilson's advanced yet sensible views; and Gouverneur Morris (the one-legged man of page 47), who led the battle for an energetic executive on the floor of the Convention and then sealed the victory by writing the final draft of the Constitution.

Hamilton and Washington, too, each in his own way, deserve some credit for the original Presidency.

The purposes of all these men were the purposes of the whole Convention: to rescue the new republic from the turbulent aftermath of revolution by establishing a government with sufficient energy to insure domestic tranquillity, secure the blessings of ordered liberty, protect private property, create conditions favorable to commercial prosperity, gain respect for itself and fair treatment for its citizens abroad, unite the states in pursuit of common ends, and return the reins of power to the "enlightened gentry." Men like Wilson and Morris understood more clearly than men like Roger Sherman and Edmund Randolph that a strong and independent executive was an essential element of any such government.

The materials with which they worked were the colonial governorships and thus, more remotely, the British monarchy, the various solutions to the problem of executive power in the first state constitutions, the administrative departments that had developed under the Articles of Confederation, and the writings of such exponents of balanced government as Locke and Montesquieu. The experience, both happy and unhappy, of the leaders of the Convention finally dictated the choice of the New York Constitution of 1777 and the Massachusetts Constitution of 1780 as the chief materials. The contrast between these two states, where independent executives served the cause of stability and order, and states like North Carolina and Rhode Island, where unchecked legislatures engaged in all sorts of unseemly activities, did not escape the attention of the delegates at Philadelphia. They had had their fill of governments, both state and national, in which "everything has been drawn within the legislative vortex." Between 1776 and 1787 there had been a noticeable shift in the constitutional theory of the moderate Whigs, from whose ranks came the framers of the Constitution —a shift away from innate confidence in popular assemblies and toward the suspicion that, as Jefferson wrote in his *Notes on Virginia,* "173 despots would surely be as oppressive as one." The sharp decline in the prestige of Congress and the state assemblies among conservatives throughout the new republic was a major factor in the decision to adopt a form of government in which the legislature would be balanced by a strong executive, not mismatched with a "mere Cipher." Even George Mason went on record as opposing "decidedly the making the executive the mere creature of the legislature as a violation of the fundamental principle of good government."

The progress of the Convention toward this decision was labored and uncertain, however, and it often seemed that the hard lessons of the previous decade would be wasted on a majority of the delegates. Persistent voices were raised against almost every arrangement that eventually appeared in Article II, and Wilson and his colleagues were able to score their final success only after a series of debates, decisions, reconsiderations, references to committees, and private maneuvers that still leave the historian befuddled. I have followed the tortuous progress of the incipient Presidency through Madison's *Notes* several times, and I am still not sure how the champions of the strong executive won their smashing victory. It can be said for certain, however, that at least eight decisions on the structure and powers of the executive were taken at different stages of the proceedings, and that out of these arose the Presidency. Every one of these decisions, with one partial exception that history was shortly to remedy, was taken in favor of a strong executive. The consequences for the Presidency, indeed for our whole system of government, would have been enormous had any one of them been taken differently—as it could easily have been. Let me list these decisions briefly, first giving notice that this list lends a deceptive appearance of order to a highly disordered train of events:

1) An executive would be established separate from the legislature. Although this was surely the easiest of all eight deci-

sions to adopt, there were those like Sherman who continued to wonder aloud if it would not be wiser to leave the legislature free to create and appoint such executives "as experience might dictate." To most delegates it was clear from the outset that the executive should be created in the Constitution itself. This had not been done in the first American constitution, and most hardheaded patriots considered this one of the serious defects in the Articles of Confederation.

2) The executive would consist of one man, a President of the United States. This fateful decision was taken only after considerable debate, and only after Wilson had used his position as chairman of the Committee on Detail to spike the plans of those like Randolph who feared the one-man executive as a "foetus of monarchy." Had Randolph and his friends had their way, the Presidency, or whatever it might have been called, would probably have been shared among three men.

3) The President would have a source of election outside the legislature. To no problem of the executive did the framers devote more time, talk, and votes. Most of the delegates originally shared Sherman's view that the executive "ought to be appointed by and accountable to the legislature only, which was the depository of the supreme will of the Society." Both the Virginia and the New Jersey plans provided for election of the executive by the legislature, and five times in the course of the Convention the delegates voted for this method. Not until the very end were enough of them swayed by the eloquence and diplomacy of Morris to adopt the electoral system outlined in Article II, Section 1, which was borrowed from the method for electing state senators in the Maryland Constitution of 1776. Morris and Wilson, an ill-assorted pair of prophets, were the only delegates to raise their voices clearly for election by the people. Another forty to fifty years would pass before the onward sweep of American democracy would carry the election of the President the rest of the way to the people, but the key

decision in behalf of his independence was taken at Philadelphia: the removal of the regular machinery for choosing him to a location outside the legislature and beyond its control.

4) The President would have a fixed term of office, which could be terminated only by the extraordinary method of conviction on impeachment for a high crime or misdemeanor. Hamilton devoted an entire number of *The Federalist* to arguing the vast merits of this decision, which, he insisted, would guarantee the "personal firmness" of the President and the "stability" of his administration. Yet neither he nor any of his associates recognized the real implication of the fixed term: that it would render impossible the rise of a parliamentary form of government. They can hardly be blamed for not recognizing it, since the sharpest minds in England had not yet noticed how far their constitution had moved in the direction of responsible cabinet government.

5) The President would be eligible for re-election to an indefinite number of terms. Had this decision been taken differently, had no President been permitted even to seek a second term, the office would surely be a less splendid and powerful one than it is today. The second terms of Washington, Jackson, Wilson, the two Roosevelts, and Truman, landmarks in the evolution of the Presidency, would never have taken place at all; and their first terms, no mean landmarks themselves, would have been severely hampered had not friend and foe alike expected them to go for a second. And as Hamilton wrote in *The Federalist:*

Would it promote the peace of the community, or the stability of the government to have half a dozen men who had had credit enough to be raised to the seat of the supreme magistracy, wandering among the people like discontented ghosts, and sighing for a place which they were destined never more to possess?

6) The President would be granted his own powers by the Constitution. It is a matter of great moment that he has prerogatives of his own, that all his authority does not come to him in

the form of grants from Congress. What would he be without the constitutional right to command, nominate, pardon, negotiate treaties, supervise the execution of the laws, convene Congress, and, above all, defend himself with the qualified veto? How could Hamilton, writing as *Pacificus,* have vindicated Washington's proclamation of neutrality in 1793, how could the first Roosevelt have spun out his "Stewardship Theory," how could Chief Justice Taft have written the breath-taking opinion in *Myers* v. *U.S.*—if the opening words of Article II were not so inclusive in their simplicity? "The executive power shall be vested in a President of the United States of America": could an apologist for the strong Presidency ask for anything more?

7) The President would not be encumbered with a council to which he would have to go for approval of his nominations or vetoes or other acts. In every state government of the time the executive was restrained in the use of one or more of his powers by a "council of revision," and the disappointed advocates of a plural executive insisted strenuously that the unity of the Presidency be qualified at least to this extent. "The Grand Signor himself," Mason grumbled, "had his Divan," but he grumbled in vain. The last of a persistent series of efforts to saddle the President with a council was beaten off at the end of the Convention. The unity of the executive had been preserved against all assaults.

8) A clause was inserted in Article I that would forbid any "person holding any office under the United States" to be a "member of either house during his continuance in office." The concern of the delegates over "corruption and the low arts of intrigue" was responsible for this copy of the ill-fated Place Bill of 1692; its real significance, which naturally escaped their notice, lay in the roadblock it still throws up against the evolution of any system of cabinet responsibility to Congress. A motion to strike this clause from the Constitution in preparation was frustrated by a tie vote. There is no telling what a President like

James Monroe or Franklin Pierce, or even Thomas Jefferson, might have made of the absence of this prohibition against a backstairs union of executive and legislature.

It is not hard to think of decisions the Convention might have taken to strengthen the Presidency even further. It could have fixed a longer term, granted the President an item veto over appropriations, named four or five departments and made them clearly responsible to him, and required only a majority of the Senate to confirm treaties. But we can well be satisfied with Article II. When we realize that just two weeks from the end of the Convention the proposed Senate held exclusive authority to make treaties and appoint ambassadors and justices, we must marvel at the way in which the story came to a happy ending for Wilson and Morris.

The framers were fully aware, as they read over their finished work, that the Presidency would come under severe attack from those who had opposed the whole idea of the Convention from the beginning and were now about to learn that some of their worst fears had been realized. The case against the Presidency was well summed up in Patrick Henry's warning that this new executive office was an "awful squint toward monarchy." Hamilton, to be sure, proved equal to the task of refuting the charge. One can almost hear him sigh under the burden as he begins the eleven numbers of *The Federalist* devoted to the Presidency with the remark:

There is hardly any part of the system which could have been attended with greater difficulty in the arrangement of it than this; and there is, perhaps, none which has been inveighed against with less candor or criticized with less judgment.

The big if silent gun in the arsenal of those who insisted upon the essential republicanism of the proposed Presidency was the universal assumption that George Washington, the Cincinnatus of the West, would be chosen as first occupant of the office, and chosen and chosen again until claimed by the grave. This assumption surely had something to do with the fact that all arguments over the executive at Philadelphia were resolved in favor of power and independence. As Pierce Butler wrote to a relative in England about the powers of the executive, "Entre nous, I do [not] believe they would have been so great, had not many of the members cast their eyes toward General Washington as President; and shaped their ideas of the Powers to be given a President, by their opinions of his Virtue." And it made things a good deal easier for those who carried the brunt of the debate in 1788.

Let me now review briefly the outlines of the Presidency as it left the hands of the framers. Considering the temper of the times, it was an office of remarkable vigor and independence. Hamilton pointed out in *The Federalist* that it combined energy, unity, duration, competent powers, and "an adequate provision for its support" with "a due dependence on the people" and "a due responsibility." The President had a source of election divorced from the legislature, a fixed term, indefinite re-eligibility, immunity from conciliar advice that he had not sought, and broad constitutional powers of his own. It was his first task to run the government: to be its administrative chief, to appoint and supervise the bureaucrats, and to "take care that the laws be faithfully executed." He was to be ceremonial head of the nation, a republican king with the prerogative of mercy, and he was to lead the government in its foreign relations, whether peaceful or hostile. Despite the principle of the separation of powers, he was not to be completely isolated from the houses of Congress. To them he could tender occasional advice, and over their labors he held a qualified but effective veto. The President was to be a strong, dignified, nonpolitical chief of state and government. In two words, he was to be George Washington.

The Presidency today has much the same general outlines as it had in 1789, but the whole picture is a hundred times magnified. The President is all the things he was intended to be, and he is

several other things as well. If we compare the Presidency under
Washington with the Presidency under Eisenhower, we can see
several remarkable changes in its character.

First, it is distinctly more powerful. It cuts deeply into the
powers of Congress; in fact, it has quite reversed the expectations of the framers by becoming itself a vortex into which these
powers have been drawn in massive amounts. It cuts deeply into
the lives of the people; in fact, it commands authority over their
comings and goings that Hamilton himself might tremble to
behold.

Next, the President is more heavily involved in making national policy. It was, to be sure, the nineteenth-century Whigs
who insisted most arrogantly that his sole task was to carry out
the policies determined by an all-wise Congress, but even Washington cannot be said to have taken much of a hand in making
policy except in the fields of foreign and military relations.
Although Hamilton, his Secretary of the Treasury, exercised
imaginative leadership and independent judgment in the areas
he occupied by right or had invaded by stealth, his was considered a virtuoso performance that would probably not be
repeated. Yet it has been repeated and much improved upon by
every President worth his salt. Whether as legislator, opinion-
maker, commander, or administrator, the President molds lasting policy in every sector of American life.

To a large extent this is true because he is now so highly
political a figure, and over this development the framers would
have shaken their heads in wonder and sorrow. The plunge of
the Presidency into party politics, which Jefferson took for himself and all his successors, may seem to have been unavoidable. The framers, however, would not have seen it that way.
They believed sincerely in the idea of a patriot President, one
who would rise coolly above the "heats of faction"; they would
have considered it a mockery of all their pains to create a republican king if the king, like George III, were to turn his
energies to party intrigue.

Another development would probably have shocked the framers, although one or two of them seem to have suspected that it was in the offing: the conversion of the Presidency into a democratic office. The extent to which he has become the "tribune of the people" is never so apparent as in an election year. When we contrast the decentralized, nonpolitical, dignified election of Washington with the "heats and ferments" of the presidential canvass as it has existed at least since 1840, we begin to sense how far the American people have gone to make the Presidency their peculiar possession.

Finally, the office has a kind of prestige that it did not know under Washington and lacked as late as the turn of this century. Washington, after all, lent his prestige to the Presidency, but today quite the reverse process takes place when a man becomes President. He becomes the great figure in our system because the office is the great institution. We forget too easily that Congress—with sometimes the House on top and at other times the Senate—was the focus of the people's interest in their government through most of the first century under the Constitution. The Presidency carried with it very little of the magic that is now so notable an element in its strength.

All this evidence leads me to assert that the outstanding feature of American constitutional development has been the growth of the power and prestige of the Presidency. This growth has not been steady, but subject to sharp ebbs as well as massive flows. Strong Presidents have been followed by weak ones; in the aftermath of every "dictator," Congress has exulted in the "restoration of the balance wisely ordained by the fathers." Yet the ebbs have been more apparent than real, and each new strong President has picked up where the last strong one left off. Lincoln took off from Jackson and Polk, not from Pierce and Buchanan. Franklin Roosevelt looked back to Wilson over the barely visible heads of the three Presidents who came between them. As to the fate of the Presidency under the assaults of Thaddeus Stevens, Ben Wade, Schuyler Colfax, and their friends and heirs, I call Henry Jones Ford to witness: "Although once executive power, in the hands of an accidental President, was bent and held down by the weight of a huge congressional majority, its springs were unbroken, and it sprang up unhurt when the abnormal pressure was removed." In the face of history, it seems hard to deny the inevitability of the upward course of the Presidency—discontinuous, to be sure, but also irreversible.

Why should the Presidency have proved so resilient and resolute? Why has it outstripped both Congress and Court in the long race for power and prestige? The answer lies in the whole history of the United States. Let me dwell for a few pages on the major forces in our history that have hastened the ascent of the Presidency.

The first of these is the rise of the "positive state," the big government that regulates, stimulates, and operates in every part of the American economy and society and, further, strikes "a respectable posture of defense" in a shrinking world. The growth of our industrial civilization has brought in its train a thousand problems of huge concern to the American people, and the people have turned again and again to beg their national government for help in solving them. Congress has responded, too eagerly for some Americans and too timidly for others, by passing laws that reach deeply into our lives and even more deeply into our pockets. To execute these laws, Congress has created more than two million federal jobs. The positive state, that is to say, is the administrative state, and although much of the administration operates by design or default outside the President's range of supervision, much operates in his name and under his final direction. Moreover, as I have noted before, no law of Congress, no tricky technique aimed at insuring independence for some new arm of the positive state, can ever rob him of the exclusive constitutional power to "take care that the laws be faithfully executed." The historic shift in the nature of our Constitution away from a catalogue of limitations and toward a grant of powers has singled out the President as its chief beneficiary. Our progress as an industrial people has elevated him to a position of administrative authority without precedent in all history. Indeed, his authority is so vast that he cannot begin to exert it.

No book on an American subject is thought complete these days without a few insightful words from Alexis de Tocqueville, so I call upon that prince of cultural anthropologists to point out the second development that has raised the Presidency so high. Seeking for those "accidental causes which may increase the influence of executive government," Tocqueville commented:

It is chiefly in its foreign relations that the executive power of a nation finds occasion to exert its skill and its strength. If the existence of the Union were perpetually threatened, if its chief interests were in daily connection with those of other powerful nations, the executive government would assume an increased importance in proportion to the measures expected of it and to those which it would execute.

So long as America held relatively aloof from the world, Congress could pose as the dominant branch of our government. Our self-elevation to the status of a major power, however, upset the old balance of the nineteenth century completely and finally. Woodrow Wilson wrote in Theodore Roosevelt's last year in office:

The President can never again be the mere domestic figure he has been throughout so large a part of our history. The nation has risen to the first rank in power and resources. The other nations of the world look askance upon her, half in envy, half in fear, and wonder with a deep anxiety what she will do with her vast strength. . . . Our President must always, henceforth, be one of the great powers of the world, whether he act greatly or wisely or not. . . . We can never hide our President again as a mere domestic officer. We can never again see him the mere executive he was in the thirties and forties. He must stand always at the front of our affairs, and the office will be as big and as influential as the man who occupies it.

Even more influential and bigger, one may say with assurance, for even a Harding or Pierce or a succession of Fillmores could not remove America from the top of the world and turn the Presidency back into a cipher, and even an army of Radical Republicans in Congress led by a healthy Thad Stevens would not be equal to the tasks of negotiation and force. Congress continues to take a major part in shaping foreign policy and overseeing foreign affairs, but it can no longer seriously challenge the leadership of the President. We may take it as an axiom of political science that the more deeply a nation becomes involved in the affairs of other nations, the more powerful becomes its executive branch. The authority of the President has been permanently inflated by our entrance into world politics and our decision to be armed against threats of aggression, and as the world grows smaller, he will grow bigger.

An associated cause of the growth of the Presidency is the shattering series of emergencies, both foreign and domestic, that have been our lot during the past century—especially the emergency of all-out war. Another axiom of political science would seem to be this: great emergencies in the life of a constitutional state bring an increase in executive power and prestige, always at least temporarily, more often than not permanently. As proof of this point, we need only think of the sudden expansion in power that the Presidency experienced under Lincoln as he faced the rebellion, under Wilson as he led us into a world war, or under Franklin Roosevelt as he called upon Congress to extend him "broad Executive power to wage a war" against depression. Each of these men left the Presidency a visibly stronger instrument than it had been before the crisis. Nor should we forget lesser Presidents in lesser crises, for these men, too, left their mark on the office. When Hayes dispatched troops to restore peace in the railroad strike of 1877, when McKinley sent 5,000 soldiers and marines to China during the Boxer uprising, and when Harry Truman acted on a dozen occasions to save entire states from the ravages of storm or fire or flood, the

Presidency moved to a higher level of authority and prestige, principally because the people had now been taught to expect more of it.

The long decline of Congress has contributed greatly to the rise of the Presidency. The framers, as I have explained, expected Congress to be the focus of our system of government. The President was granted several of his powers not so much for the sake of efficiency as to keep him from being drawn out of his orbit into that of the legislature, there to tag along weakly in the wake of this sovereign force. What the framers did not reckon with was the astounding growth of the republic, which has turned Congress into a cumbersome pair of assemblies that speak in a confusion of tongues. Congress is a mighty instrument of constitutional democracy, one of which Americans may well be proud. Yet it is an instrument that cannot, by reason of its structure, constituency, and mission, do some things very well and other things at all. It cannot operate in the grand style without external leadership, which the President alone is in a position to offer. When Congress finally gave up primary responsibility for preparing the budget in 1921, it had no choice but to call on the President to come to the rescue. By abdicating an ancient function it could no longer perform, it gave a tremendous boost to the power of the President, not only to control his administration, but to influence the legislative process.

The knife of reality cuts even deeper: Congress generally cannot exercise its own authority without, in turn, increasing that of the President. There are obvious limits to what it can accomplish effectively by setting up independent commissions to execute new laws, and he must therefore be the chief beneficiary of most expeditions into unexplored territory. A delicious example of the way in which Congress is forced to expand his power while expanding its own is Title II of the Taft-Hartley Act of 1947. Few Congresses have ever distrusted presidential power more earnestly than that led by Joseph W. Martin and Robert A. Taft. Yet in enacting the long-awaited law "to bring the unions into line," it had to grant the President new statutory authority to act in major strikes. To make the whole episode even more delicious, it will be recalled that Mr. Truman spurned the gift, had it forced upon him by two-thirds of each house, and then used it spectacularly on ten separate occasions. Whether because of its exertions or insufficiencies, Congress has done its part to make the President what he is today.

Henry Jones Ford, in his perceptive *Rise and Growth of American Politics* (1898), was the first to call attention pointedly to the one giant force that has done most to elevate the Presidency to power and glory: the rise of American democracy. Most men who feared the proposed Presidency in 1787 were prisoners of the inherited Whig assumption that legislative power was essentially popular and executive power essentially monarchial in nature. The notion that a democratic President might be pitted against an oligarchical legislature occurred to few at the time, most notably to Gouverneur Morris, who spoke of the executive, with his tongue somewhere in his cheek, as "the guardian of the people" against the tyranny of the "great and wealthy who in the course of things will necessarily compose the legislative body." As a matter of history, it took only about forty years to make Morris's masked prophecy come true. Since the days of Andrew Jackson the Presidency has been generally recognized as a highly democratic office. It depends directly on the people for much of its power and prestige; it shrinks to a rather mean thing when it loses their support. It is not, I feel sure, an accident of history that the upsurge of democracy and Jackson's resurrection of the Presidency went hand in hand, nor that he gave his name to the mighty movement that swept him into office and bade him act boldly in the name of the people. Our Presidents could never have challenged Congress so often and successfully were they, too, not popularly elected and popularly sustained. American democracy finds in the President its single most useful instrument. Small wonder, then, that he stands as high as he does in the mythology and expectations of the American people. There is virtually no limit to what the President can do if he does it for democratic ends and by democratic means.

It is all very well to write about the forces that have made the Presidency what it is today, but I think it high time that I also wrote about men. None of these mighty events—the upbuilding of the positive state, our plunge into the world, the crises of war and depression, the hard times of Congress, or the triumph of democracy—would have had such influence on the Presidency if strong, alert, capable men had not come to this high office and shaped the event to their ends. The President acts every day, consciously or unconsciously, in the image of the Presidents who have gone before him. There are a hundred things he could not do, certainly not without raising a deafening outcry, if his predecessors had not done them already. The Presidents, too, helped build the Presidency, and I would therefore think it proper to devote the rest of this chapter to a review of the major contributions of the major Presidents. Just who those Presidents were—I count eight—will shortly become clear. At the same time, I shall not neglect entirely those other Presidents—I count six—who also gave strength to the Presidency, if only by defending it valiantly in a period of congressional ascendancy. Let it be clear that I am judging these men as Presidents and weighing their contributions to the Presidency. Herbert Hoover is a much abler man than he was a President; James Madison's total impact on history should not be judged by his bumbling activities between 1809 and 1817.

George Washington enjoyed a long head start toward being a great President simply because he was the first man to fill the office. This, however, is far from the whole story of George Washington. The most meaningful judgment one can make of his eight years is that he fulfilled the hopes of the friends of

the Constitution and spiked the fears of its critics, and that in
turning both these tricks with vigor and dignity he proved himself the best of all possible first Presidents.

The hopes of its friends were that the creation of an energetic
executive, independent of the legislature yet integrated into the
constitutional structure, would introduce the one factor most
sorrowfully missing from the equation of government under the
Articles of Confederation: authority to execute the laws of the
United States with force and dispatch. The government of the
new republic was in desperate need of power—power to make
policy and power to carry it through. Article I of the Constitution as interpreted by Madison, Ellsworth, and the other
gentlemen of Congress proved to be the answer to the first
half of this need. Article II as interpreted by Washington
proved to be the answer to the second half.

He was certainly not a President in the image of the Roosevelts or Harry S Truman. When faced with a situation that
called for decisive action, he took a painfully long time to
make up his mind. For example, he sought the advice of both
Hamilton and Jefferson even when he knew that they would
only confuse and delay him with their antithetical counsels.
He recognized that his decisions would quite possibly set
precedents for men who would still be unborn when he was two
centuries in his grave, and this recognition gave an extra measure of gravity to his conduct of office. When Washington was
ready to act, however, he acted with confidence and courage.
The remarkable thing is how consistently he chose to act
strongly rather than to abstain huffily, to advance rather than to
retreat in his skirmishes with Congress over the uncharted territory left between them by the Constitution. In the field of
foreign relations alone he set a dozen precedents that no later
period of congressional ascendancy could ever erase—for example, the recognition of republican France, the proclamation
of neutrality, the reception and dismissal of the French Minister
Genêt, the negotiation of Jay's Treaty, the use of executive

agents, and the refusal to lay diplomatic correspondence before the House. Thanks to Hamilton he was an influential leader of legislation, thanks to his experience he was an excellent administrator, and thanks to himself he was a head of state who made every king alive seem like a silly goose.

The fears of the critics of the Constitution were that the executive outlined in Article II would prove too rich a blend of strength and independence, and that the government of the United States would go the way of most other popular governments in history: straight into tyranny. That it did not go this way was the result of many factors: the political maturity of the people, the widespread spirit of liberty, the vigilance of the opposition, the excellence of the Constitution, and, not least important, the single-minded devotion of Washington to the principles of republican government. It was no easy trick to be the first occupant of a mistrusted office under a dubious Constitution. Two or three missteps might have touched off a popular demand for an amendment designed to cut the Presidency down to size—the size, for example, of the governorship of North Carolina. But Washington, who had a nice feeling for the delicacy of his task, never did commit a serious misstep. His conduct was always eminently constitutional, and he repeatedly proved the point that Hamilton had labored in *The Federalist:* that executive power was wholly "consistent with the genius of republican government" and even essential to the steady conduct of such government. "For he was no monarchist from preference of his judgment," Jefferson wrote some years after Washington's death. "The soundness of that gave him correct views of the rights of man, and his severe justice devoted him to them." Washington's Presidency was nothing if not painfully constitutional.

It is not easy or indeed pleasant to imagine the fate of this great gamble in constitutional government if Washington had refused to accept his election to the Presidency. If he had stayed at Mount Vernon, as he wanted desperately to do, another man—probably John Adams or John Rutledge or John Jay or George Clinton—would have been the first President of the United States, and that could easily have meant the undoing of the Constitution. We can go right down the list of all those who ever held high office in the United States and not discover a man so perfectly suited for the delicate task of finding the right balance of authority and restraint in the executive branch. Washington did the new republic a mighty service by proving that power can ennoble as well as corrupt and by fitting the Presidency carefully into the emerging pattern of American constitutionalism.

He did a great deal more than this, of course, for he lent his vast prestige to the new Constitution and thus rendered it acceptable to the American people. Men like Senator Maclay of Pennsylvania poked fun at the pomp and circumstance of "the Washington court," but they did not understand as clearly as he that magic may be reduced but never eliminated entirely from the processes by which free men are governed. John Adams did, however, and he explained it all to Benjamin Rush many years after Washington's death:

Washington understood this Art very well, and we may say of him, if he was not the greatest President he was the best Actor of the Presidency we have ever had. His address to The States when he left the Army: His solemn Leave taken of Congress when he resigned his Commission: his Farewell Address to the People when he resigned his Presidency. These were all in a strain of Shakespearean and Garrickal excellence in Dramatic Exhibitions.

Even the Republicans could not deny that Washington's grand tours through the states—for example, through New England in 1789 and the South in 1791—strengthened the people's trust in the Constitution and excited their interest in the Presidency. On the first of these trips he fought a polite but dogged battle with Governor John Hancock of Massachusetts over one of the most ancient questions of applied political science: who should call first on whom? The battle was fierce, and consumed most of his first two days in Boston; but a stubborn Washington, who insisted icily that Hancock make the first call, finally won a victory of profound symbolic importance for the authority of the new national government and, more to the point, for the prestige of its Chief of State. The humbling of vain John Hancock in 1789 and the enforcement of the laws in the Whiskey Rebellion of 1793 are two precedents that stood Dwight D. Eisenhower in good stead in the Little Rock crisis of 1957.

Washington's great gifts to the Presidency and to the republic were dignity, authority, and constitutionalism, and the greatest of these, surely, was constitutionalism. It has been said of him that he could have been a king but chose to be something more exalted: the first elected head of the first truly free government. In his inaugural address he made clear the solemnity of his mandate:

The preservation of the sacred fire of liberty and the destiny of the republican model of government are justly considered, perhaps, as *deeply,* as *finally,* staked on the experiment entrusted to the hands of the American people.

It was Washington's glory as President that he never broke faith with this solemn vision of the American Mission. Well could Jefferson write in gratitude that he had conducted the councils of the new nation "through the birth of a government, new in its form and principles, until it had settled down into a quiet and orderly train," chiefly by "scrupulously obeying the laws through the whole of his career, civil and military, of which the history of the world furnishes no other example." And lest we forget that Washington was also a human being, I end with this passage from Senator William Maclay's delightful *Journal,* which describes a scene in which members of Congress waited upon the President:

The President took his reply out of his coat pocket. He had his spectacles in his jacket pocket, having his hat in his left hand and his paper in his right. He had too many objects for his hands. He shifted his hat between his forearm and the left side of his breast. But taking his spectacles from the case embarrassed him. He got rid of this small distress by laying the spectacle case on the chimney piece. . . . Having adjusted his spectacles, which was not very easy considering the engagements of his hands, he read the reply with tolerable exactness and without much emotion.

The Presidency of Thomas Jefferson presents a slippery problem to the judgment of history. That he was a great man there can be no doubt, but that he was a great President there is considerable doubt. To his lasting credit are the injection of large doses of republicanism into an office that was coming to look just a shade too kingly, the breath-taking assertion of power (which took even his own breath away) in the purchase of Louisiana, and the flat declaration of presidential independence in his rejection of Marshall's subpoena in the Burr trial.

His most important contributions, of course, were his conversion of the Presidency to a political office and his leadership of Congress, and it is exactly at these two points that we run into trouble with Jefferson's reputation as a strong President. His successes in molding and leading a party and then in using it to influence Congress leave us no choice but to judge him an effective leader. As Professor Binkley has written: "No president has ever exceeded Jefferson's feat of putting the extraordinarily drastic Embargo Act through Congress in one day, December 22, 1807." Yet the very methods through which he brought strength to his own Presidency were calculated to weaken the office grievously once he had turned it over to lesser men, to men who were not and could never be the kind of party chieftain and ideological arbiter that he had proved to be. John Marshall made a remarkable prediction about Jefferson's methods and influence in a letter written to Hamilton while the election of 1800 hung in the balance.

Mr. Jefferson appears to me to be a man, who will embody himself with the House of Representatives. By weakening the office of President he will increase his personal power. He will diminish his responsibility, sap the fundamental principles of the government, and become the leader of that party which is about to constitute the majority of the legislature.

We need not subscribe to the full bitterness of this statement to recognize that Marshall was a shrewd observer and an even shrewder prophet. Jefferson did embody himself in the House of Representatives, thereby increasing his power ten times over. The power, however, was personal and not presidential; it flowed from him and not from his office. The leaders of Congress were his trusty lieutenants, the party caucus was his instrument to use pretty much as he pleased—so long as he did not wander from Republican principles. (And who, after all, had first defined these principles?) Timothy Pickering, another bitter foe, wrote that Jefferson tried to "screen himself from all responsibility by calling on Congress for advice and direction. . . . Yet with affected modesty and deference he secretly dictates every measure which is seriously proposed." This, I think, was the essence of Jefferson's Presidency, and this is why our final judgment of his influence must always be ambiguous. If we concentrate our gaze on his eight years, then shift it swiftly down to the middle of either the nineteenth or twentieth centuries, we can say that it was a strong and great Presidency. If we let our gaze halt at any year between 1809 and 1829, we must conclude that Jefferson damaged the office severely by compromising its independence. Since we are dealing with one of the greatest Americans, perhaps we should take the long-range view and hail him as a President whom it would be unthinkable to exclude from the inner circle of greatness.

Andrew Jackson plucked Jefferson's chestnuts from the fire by putting on a show of authority that still commands our fascinated respect. Coming as it did after twenty years of con-

gressional supremacy and government by committee, his resolute Presidency was, in Professor Corwin's words, "no mere
revival of the office—it was a remaking of it."

Jackson regained control over his own house by putting
each department head in his place and cutting the Cabinet
down to size, distributed the spoils of victory in such a way as
to build a team almost fanatical in its loyalty to him, revived
the veto and purified it of the niceties that had grown up
around it, acted simultaneously as an imposing Chief of State
and a hard-driving Chief of Party, and made clear to South
Carolina that his power to execute the laws would be fully
equal to the task of preserving the Union. He never missed
an opportunity, by word or deed, to reassert the independence
of an office that had become much more dependent on Congress
than the framers could possibly have intended. His veto of
the Bank Bill, his proclamation against the Nullifiers, and his
"solemn protest" against the Senate's resolution of censure are
assertions of presidential independence and authority that make
exciting reading even today.

Small wonder that Jackson's enemies, who remembered the
deferential years of Madison and Monroe, should judge his
performance to be subversive of the republic. "I look upon
Jackson," Chancellor Kent wrote to Justice Story, "as a de-
testable, ignorant, reckless, vain and malignant tyrant." "The
President carries on the government," Webster cried in the
Senate; "all the rest are subcontractors." And Clay spoke for
all the Whigs:

> We are in the midst of a revolution, hitherto bloodless, but tend-
> ing rapidly toward a total change of the pure republican character
> of the Government, and to the concentration of all power in the
> hands of one man.

Clay was right: he and his friends were caught up in a
revolution, but he was incapable of noting its origin or character. The revolution was abroad among the people, shifting the

basis of our government from aristocracy to democracy without destroying its essential republicanism. Jackson was more a beneficiary than a leader of this revolution. He rode into office on a wave of protest that he never directed and whose character he barely understood himself. Yet he was exactly the kind of President—truculent, charismatic, and more than a little bit demagogic—the revolution needed to bring it full circle. The Presidency would surely have become a democratic office had Jackson never held it, but he was the one who presided imperiously over the radical reversal in the roles of President and Congress as instruments of popular power and targets of popular feeling. And it is here, of course, that Clay and his friends went astray, for they could not rid their minds of the assumption, the very marrow of Whiggery, that executive power is inherently antipopular. Jackson's insistence that he, too, represented the people, at least as well as the House and better than the Senate, seemed to them the babbling of a fool or the bluster of a tyrant. No small part of his success may be traced directly to the fact that he was the first President of the United States elected by the people, and to the added fact that he knew it:

The President is the direct representative of the American people; he possesses original executive powers, and absorbs in himself all executive functions and responsibilities; and it is his especial duty to protect the liberties and rights of the people and the integrity of the Constitution against the Senate, or the House of Representatives, or both together.

Jackson's mistakes were many, his legacies not all bright; more than one such President a century would be hard to take. Yet he was a giant in his influence on our system of government, and the influence, on balance, seems to have been wholesome. Well might he write in defense of his conduct: "I shall anticipate with pleasure the place to be assigned me in the history of my country." I would place him fifth in the list of

Presidents in terms of performance and impact on history, and second only to Washington in terms of influence on the Presidency.

The reaction to Jackson's Presidency was pronounced and prolonged; it was still in progress when Lincoln entered the White House. Yet the reaction, even though aided immeasurably by the depressing influence of the slavery issue on the Presidency, could never undo the work the old hero had done. The Jacksonian theory of the office prevailed, and Lincoln, untutored as an administrator but richly experienced in the arts of purposeful politics, drew upon it resolutely in his hour of need.

Lincoln came to the Presidency with very few advance thoughts about the authority it embodied. He had never put himself publicly in either the Whig or Jacksonian camps (I am speaking, of course, of theories of the Presidency and not of party politics), and many of his critics were certain that his administration would prove too feeble for the awesome task at hand. Lincoln soon proved them grossly wrong in their judgments of his character and in their fears for the Presidency. He had sworn "an oath registered in Heaven" to defend the Constitution, and in his inaugural address he promised his fellow citizens to save the Union without which the Constitution would be nothing but a scrap of paper. In sharp contrast to the vacillating Buchanan, who had denied his own authority to coerce a state to remain in the Union, he turned to military force as the final answer to secession. He was never greatly concerned about the forms his actions might take. It was enough for him to act—as commander in chief, as supervisor of the faithful execution of the laws, as sole legatee of the shapeless grant of power we can read for ourselves in the opening words of Article II of the Constitution.

It became necessary for me to choose whether, using only the existing means, agencies, and processes which Congress had provided, I should let the Government fall at once into ruin or whether, availing myself of the broader powers conferred by the Constitution in cases of insurrection, I would make an effort to save it, with all its blessings, for the present age and for posterity.

In his effort to save the government and the Union, Lincoln pushed the powers of the Presidency to a new plateau high above any conception of executive authority hitherto imagined in this country. During the course of his famed eleven-week "dictatorship" he called out the militia, clamped a blockade on the South, enlarged the regular army and navy beyond their statutory limits, advanced public moneys to persons unauthorized to receive them, pledged the credit of the United States for a sizable loan, closed the mails to "treasonable correspondence," authorized the arrest of potential traitors, and, in defiance of all precedent, suspended the writ of habeas corpus along the line of communication between Washington and New York. In a message to Congress of July 4, 1861, the date he had selected for convening the houses in special session, he described most of the actions he had taken, rationalized the more doubtful of these by referring to "the war power of the government" (his phrase and evidently his idea), and invited congressional ratification. Lincoln himself apparently entertained no doubts about the legality of his calling out the militia and establishing the blockade, nor did he find it necessary to explain why he had chosen to postpone the emergency meeting of Congress to July 4. For his actions of a more legislative and therefore constitutionally more doubtful character, he advanced a different justification:

These measures, whether strictly legal or not, were ventured upon under what appeared to be a popular demand and a public necessity, trusting then, as now, that Congress would readily ratify them. It is believed that nothing has been done beyond the constitutional competency of Congress.

He asserted that the power to suspend the writ of habeas corpus could belong to him as well as to Congress, but he tactfully left the subsequent disposal of this matter to the legislators. The whole tenor of his message implied that the government of the United States, like all governments, possessed a final power of self-preservation, a power to be wielded primarily by the President of the United States. And this power extended even to the breaking of fundamental laws of the nation —if such a step were unavoidable.

Are all the laws but *one* to go unexecuted, and the Government itself go to pieces lest that one be violated? Even in such a case, would not the official oath be broken if the Government should be overthrown when it was believed that disregarding the single law would tend to preserve it?

In other words, in an instance of urgent necessity, an official of a constitutional state may act more faithfully to his oath of office if he breaks one law in order that the rest may endure. This was a powerful and unique plea for the doctrine of paramount necessity. It established no definite rule for the use of emergency power in this country, but it does stand as a fateful example of how a true democrat in power is likely to act if there is no other way for him to preserve the constitutional system he has sworn to defend.

Once Congress had reassembled in answer to the President's call, it did what it could to cut him down from an Andrew Jackson to, at the very most, a James K. Polk. Lincoln, however, although always respectful of Congress, went forward resolutely on his power-directed course, taking one extraordinary action after another on the basis of the "war power." In all this activity he had the help, if never the full respect, of what many historians consider the most effective Cabinet ever assembled. Having brought the office of the Presidency to new heights of prestige, he kept it there to the end. His interpretation of his powers was stabilized at an exalted level, and it appears that he considered himself constitutionally empowered to do just about anything that the military situation demanded. "As

Commander-in-Chief in time of war," he told some visitors from Chicago, "I suppose I have a right to take any measure which may best subdue the enemy." We need not look beyond the Emancipation Proclamation and the declaration of martial law in Indiana to learn what he meant by "any measure."

There is a good deal more than this to tell about Lincoln's Presidency: the shabby performance as administrator, the creditable performance as diplomat, and the astounding performance as politician and leader of public opinion, not to mention the refusal of Congress to acquiesce in either the sweep or exclusiveness of his assertion of the war power. Enough has been said, I trust, to make this point clear: through the boldness of his initiative, through an unprecedented plea of necessity, and through a unique interpretation of executive power, Lincoln raised the Presidency to a position of constitutional and moral ascendancy that left no doubt where the burden of crisis government in this country would thereafter rest. When Eisenhower's lieutenants spoke in 1955 of the "inherent powers of the Presidency" as our chief crutch in the wake of atomic disaster, they were reaching out to the mighty figure of Abraham Lincoln. And as they did, I trust that they pondered the truth that Lincoln was a democrat as well as a "dictator," that he went to the well of power in behalf of humanity and rededicated the Presidency to the cause of liberty.

Lincoln, like Jefferson, left the Presidency temporarily enfeebled. The reaction was savage, and poor Andrew Johnson, a far braver President than Madison, was left to reap the wild wind that Lincoln had sowed unconcernedly when he permitted the War Department and Congress's Committee on the Conduct of the War to strike up an intimate relationship. There were times in the next thirty years—especially under Grant and Harrison—when the Presidency seemed to have declined permanently in relation to Congress. But our rise to industrial might and our grand entrance upon the stage of world politics turned the course of the Presidency once more upward, and Colonel Roosevelt galloped into the White House as our first modern President.

It is hard to come to grips with Theodore Roosevelt, just as it is with any boy of six. There are times when he has the look of a genuinely great man, and times when he has the look, as Mark Hanna said, of a "damned cowboy." He was, beyond a doubt, a strong President, and no small part of his strength lay in the fact that he always was a kind of cowboy. Roosevelt gave the Presidency the absorbing drama of a Western movie, and he never left the audience in doubt that he was the "good guy" and the other fellows—Democrats, Senators, monopolists, Socialists, diplomats, "nature fakers," muckrakers—the "bad guys." With the help of an attractive and active family, he put the Presidency on the front page of every newspaper in America, and there it has remained ever since with huge consequences for its status and authority. Teddy lived the dreams of every red-blooded American boy of his time: he punched cattle, led a cavalry charge, became President, argued with the Pope, and, when it was all over, went off to shoot lions and elephants in Africa.

Roosevelt himself described a significant milestone in the evolution of the Presidency:

When the dinner was announced, the mayor led me in—or to speak more accurately, tucked me under one arm and lifted me partially off the ground, so that I felt as if I looked like one of those limp dolls with dangling legs carried around by small children. . . . As soon as we got in the banquet hall and sat at the head of the table the mayor hammered lustily with the handle of his knife and announced, "Waiter, bring on the feed!" Then, in a spirit of pure kindliness he added, "Waiter, pull up the curtains and let the people see the President eat."

T. R. contributed a great deal more to the office than a cheerful willingness to let the people see him eat. He was a brilliant molder and interpreter of public opinion, who confessed happily that the White House was a "bully pulpit." He scored several genuine triumphs as leader of Congress and thus gave substance to his theory that "a good executive under present conditions of American life must take a very active interest in getting the right kind of legislation." He conducted our diplomacy with unusual vigor, although his stick was not so big nor his voice so soft as he liked to boast. Still, the Panama Canal and the Treaty of Portsmouth were rather substantial achievements for those days, and who can say that he did not act grandly when he started the fleet off around the world and left it up to Congress to buy enough coal to bring it back?

Unfortunately for the Colonel, but probably fortunately for the country, there was no real crisis in all his seven years that would permit him to prove conclusively that he was, as he insisted, a "Jackson-Lincoln" as opposed to a "Buchanan" President. The nearest thing to such a crisis was the anthracite coal strike of 1902, which he managed to settle before being pushed into executing his plans, first revealed fully in his *Autobiography* (1913), to have the army seize and operate the mines. This event, his land withdrawals, and several other minor exertions of authority led him to state the famed "Stewardship Theory," which is still the most adroit literary justification of the strenuous Presidency:

The most important factor in getting the right spirit in my Administration, next to the insistence upon courage, honesty, and a genuine democracy of desire to serve the plain people, was my insistence upon the theory that the executive power was limited only by specific restrictions and prohibitions appearing in the Constitution or imposed by the Congress under its Constitutional powers. My view was that every executive officer, and above all every executive officer in high position, was a steward of the people bound actively and affirmatively to do all he could for the people, and not to content himself with the negative merit of keeping his talents undamaged in a napkin. I declined to adopt the view that what was imperatively necessary for the Nation could not be done by the President unless he could find some specific authorization to do it. My belief was that it was not only his right but his duty to do anything that the needs of the Nation demanded unless such action was forbidden by the Constitution or the laws.

William Howard Taft, speaking also as a former President, derided the notion that the "executive . . . is to play the part of a universal providence and set all things right," and the strict theory of the Constitution is certainly on his side. Whatever the theory, the facts have always been with Roosevelt in moments of extreme national emergency.

Woodrow Wilson was the best prepared President, intellectually and morally, ever to come to the White House. I have quoted several times from the chapter on the Presidency in his *Constitutional Government* (1908), and I think it fair to sum up the first four years of his Presidency by saying that he went as far as any man could go in converting those elegant, somewhat exaggerated words into reality. He was an able administrator, a shrewd leader of his party, a sensitive "spokesman for the real purpose and sentiment of the country," an impressive head of state, and, thanks to his academic theory of the President as a prime minister in relation to Congress, a genuinely effective leader of legislation. A devoted traditionalist, he was nevertheless unafraid of innovation. I would give a considerable sum to have seen Theodore Roosevelt's face when he picked up his evening paper April 8, 1913, and read that Wilson, honoring tradition and working innovation in the same act, had brought off successfully the first personal appearance of a President before Congress since the days of John Adams. Many historians think that the American Presidency, and with it our whole system of government, reached its highest peak of democracy, efficiency, and morality in the first four years of Woodrow Wilson.

In his second term, to be sure, he came to grief in more ways than one, although his record as a wartime President is every bit as admirable as the records of both Lincoln and the second Roosevelt. The most striking feature of this record is the way in which he acquired his vast authority over the American economy. Most of his emergency powers were delegated to him by laws of Congress. Confronted by the problem of raising and equipping an army to fight overseas rather than by a sudden threat to the Republic, Wilson chose to demand express legislative authority for almost every unusual step. Lincoln had shown what the office was equal to in crises calling for solitary executive action. Now Wilson showed what it could do by working with the legislature. The source of Lincoln's power was the Constitution, and he operated in spite of Congress. The source of Wilson's power, except in the area of command and a few related matters, was a batch of statutes, and he cooperated with Congress.

In the end, sad to relate, he lost his hold on Congress, the country, and even himself. His haughty appeal for a Democratic Congress in 1918 was a serious blunder; his whole course of action in behalf of the League of Nations foundered on his own obstinacy. Yet his journey to Europe in December 1918 was a herald of things to come, a rehearsal of the grand role the President would fill in the aftermath of World War II. Wilson carried the Presidency to new moral and political heights, and the strength of his days can be measured in the weakness of those that followed.

My seventh and eighth candidates for presidential greatness are Franklin D. Roosevelt and Harry S Truman, but I am going to put off the pleasure of dealing with them until Chapter 5. In the meantime, what of those men who, if not worthy to be ranked with Washington and Lincoln at the top, with Wilson and Jackson at the next level down, or with T. R. and Jefferson just below them, were none the less Presidents who turned in

creditable or at least unusual performances? Let me call off
these six names in order, several of which, I am aware, are
not on every historian's roll of notable Presidents:

Grover Cleveland, whose persistent display of integrity and
independence (symbolized by the 414 vetoes of his first term)
brought him very close to greatness in the Presidency.

James K. Polk, the one bright spot in the dull void between
Jackson and Lincoln, of whom the historian George Bancroft
could write a half-century later:

> His administration, viewed from the standpoint of results, was
> perhaps the greatest in our history, certainly one of the greatest.
> He succeeded because he insisted on being its center and in over-
> ruling and guiding all his secretaries to act so as to produce unity
> and harmony.

Dwight D. Eisenhower, of whom more hereafter.

Rutherford B. Hayes, a vastly underrated President, whose
successful struggle to name his own Cabinet, dogged devotion
to civil-service reform, seven stout vetoes of legislative riders,
and dispatch of troops in the railroad strike of 1877 were all
long steps forward from the Waste Land of Grant.

John Adams, who had the misfortune to follow Washington,
but whose grand theory of the President as a "patriot king"
was applied with rare stoutness of heart in the move for peace
with France in 1799.

Andrew Johnson, a man of few talents but much courage,
whose protests against the ravages of the Radicals in Congress
were a high rather than a low point in the progress of the
Presidency.

This is not, be it noted, a list based exclusively on intelligence
or even competence. There have been at least seven men—John
Quincy Adams, Van Buren, Tyler, Arthur, McKinley, Taft,
and Hoover—who were far better Presidents than Johnson
from a technical point of view. None of them, however, was
so important to the history of the Presidency as the despised
man from Tennessee.

To round out the presidential list, an irresponsible sort of exercise when done so abruptly, let me place Madison, Monroe, Fillmore, Benjamin Harrison, and Coolidge in the next slot down; W. H. Harrison, Taylor, and Garfield in a category that reads "insufficient data for ranking"; and Pierce, Buchanan, Grant, and Harding at the bottom. Buchanan was a man of rich experience, Grant a genuinely great general, and Harding a gentle man, but each in his own way was a near disaster for the Presidency. As for Pierce, let us nod to Nathaniel Hawthorne's reaction to the news of his election—"Frank, I pity you—indeed I do, from the bottom of my heart"—and then let the gentle poet from New Hampshire have the last word:

> She had one President (pronounce him Purse,
> And make the most of it for better or worse.
> He's your one chance to score against the state).

It would be a near disaster for me to end this chapter on so low a note, and I therefore call attention once again to the six—I am still avoiding Roosevelt and Truman—who contributed most handsomely to the Presidency as it stands today. These men were more than eminent characters and strong Presidents. They were and are luminous symbols in our history. We, too, the enlightened Americans, feel the need of myth and mystery in national life—of magic parchments like the Declaration of Independence, of shrines like Plymouth and the Alamo, of slogans like "Fifty-Four Forty or Fight!," of hymns like "America," of heroics like Pickett's charge, of heroes like John Paul Jones. No one can have lived through Davy Crockett and deny the force of the American myth; no one can stand at Gettysburg and deny its meaning. And who fashioned the myth? Who are the most satisfying of our folk heroes? With whom is associated a wonderful web of slogans and shrines and heroics? The answer, plainly, is the six Presidents I have pointed to most proudly. Each is an authentic folk hero, each a symbol of some virtue or dream especially dear to Americans.

Together they make up almost half of the company of American giants, for who except Christopher Columbus, Benjamin Franklin, Daniel Boone, Robert E. Lee, and Thomas A. Edison in real life, Deerslayer and Ragged Dick in fiction, and Paul Bunyan and the Lonesome Cowboy in myth can challenge them for immortality? Washington the spotless patriot, Jefferson the democrat, Jackson the man of the frontier, Lincoln the emancipator and preserver of the Union, Theodore Roosevelt the All-American Boy, Wilson the peacemaker—these men are symbols of huge interest and value to the American people.

Lincoln is the supreme myth, the richest symbol in the American experience. He is, as someone has remarked neither irreverently nor sacrilegiously, the martyred Christ of democracy's passion play. And who, then, can measure the strength that is given to the President because he holds Lincoln's office, lives in Lincoln's house, and walks in Lincoln's way? The final greatness of the Presidency lies in the truth that it is not just an office of incredible power but a breeding ground of indestructible myth.

CHAPTER **4**

THE MODERN PRESIDENCY

The Presidency to which Dwight D. Eisenhower came on January 20, 1953, was a visibly different office from the Presidency that Herbert Hoover had surrendered on March 4, 1933. In the course of these twenty years it had been laden with all kinds of new duties by a people unwilling to submit patiently to the disorders of an industrial civilization or to withdraw sullenly from the turmoils of a mad world. It had taken on all kinds of new help, both personal and institutional, to save it from collapse under the mounting burdens of war and peace. And it had moved even higher, if that were possible, in the esteem of the American people, most of whom counted it a mighty weapon in the struggle for liberty at home and security abroad. The Presidency had been modernized, conspicuously if not completely.

My purpose in this chapter is to examine the new dimensions added to the office by Presidents Roosevelt and Truman. Lest it be thought that this is a partisan review, I hasten to point out that Dwight D. Eisenhower moved ahead, steadily if not quite so theatrically, with the work of modernization begun by the Democrats who preceded him. If he was not as strong a President as Roosevelt or Truman, he occupied an equally strong Presidency. He was, in any case, the first beneficiary of two decades of unusual executive activity. The Presidency, like any vital institution, is always in transition, but this has been

109

an especially propitious period for experiment and growth, and we must now take account of the significant changes in the authority and structure of the Presidency during the past quarter-century.

The first change is in the working relations of President and Congress. I have already made some comments on the President's part in the lawmaking process, the sum of which was that he has now become a sort of prime minister or "third House of Congress." He is no longer restricted in his legislative activities to the points of input and output on the congressional transmission belt, that is, to recommending measures in general terms at one end and then, after sitting quietly for a decent or indecent interval, to stamping the mangled results "OK" or "Reject." Rather, he is now expected to make detailed recommendations in the form of messages and proposed bills, to watch them closely in their tortuous progress on the floor and in committee in each house, and to use every honorable means within his power to persuade the gentlemen of Congress to give him what he wanted in the first place. One of the chief concerns of the modern President is to push politely but relentlessly for enactment of his own or his party's legislative program. If he lacks a program of the most detailed nature, he is considered a sluggard; if he cannot persuade Congress to enact at least a few of the details, he is considered a failure. In judging the performance of the modern President, we rely heavily on the "box score" of his hits and outs and errors in the game of persuasion he is always playing with Congress.

It was not always thus. The role of the President as active participant in every stage of the legislative process is almost wholly the creation of three twentieth-century incumbents: Theodore Roosevelt, Woodrow Wilson, and Franklin D. Roosevelt. Each of these men came to the Presidency from a successful tenure as governor of a progressive state, and the extent of his success had been measured in terms of his leadership of the legislature. Each came at a time when the state of the Union demanded that new laws be placed on the books; none was strangled by wearing the "old school tie" of either house of Congress. The meeting of their forceful personalities with the crises of the age produced a revolution in the relations of the President to Congress and in the standards with which the American people rate his total performance.

This revolution, it should be noted, was still unfinished in the last days of Franklin Roosevelt, for Congress, the party of the second part, remained unconvinced of the President's right to interest himself so strenuously in its independent activities. The members of Congress could hardly be blamed for believing that the times were out of joint, that Roosevelt had exerted a kind of leadership that would not outlast his incumbency or the end of the emergency, and that there would be a retreat to Hoover (if never again to Harding) under the next President. But the next President, despite the perky pride with which he himself wore the old school tie, refused to play dead. Mr. Truman kept the pressure turned on throughout his eight years, even when his hopes of accomplishing anything constructive must have been entirely empty, and by the end of his second term even the Republicans in Congress professed an eagerness to have his thoughts on such red-hot issues as labor, taxes, inflation, and education. What is still more revealing of the change of climate, they considered it a wholly natural thing to be invited to the White House to hear from the President directly what he had in mind. Things had moved a long way from the days when Senator George F. Hoar had testified:

The most eminent senators would have received as a personal affront a private message from the White House expressing a desire that they should adopt any course in the discharge of their legislative duties that they did not approve. If they visited the White House, it was to give, not to receive, advice. Any little company or coterie who had undertaken to arrange public policies with the president and to report to their associates what the president thought would have rapidly come to grief. . . . Each of these stars kept his own orbit and shone in his sphere, within which he tolerated no intrusion from the president or from anybody else.

This development has been carried the rest of the way (beyond the point of no return, I would judge) by President Eisenhower. That point was reached and passed in a press conference on January 13, 1954. During the first session of the Eighty-third Congress Mr. Eisenhower had submitted few proposals to Congress and had exerted little continuous pressure in their behalf. Observers were wondering aloud whether he was aware of the change that had come over the Presidency or of Congress's need for prudent guidance. But as the second session approached, the President began to gather steam, and within a few days of the opening of Congress in 1954 he was sending over detailed messages outlining his wishes on farm policy, social security, foreign policy, labor, and finance. And now at the press conference this exchange took place:

Q. Mr. President, could you say what percentage of your recommended proposals you would expect to be passed at this session?

A. The President said, Look, he wanted to make this clear. He was not making recommendations to pass the time away or to look good. . . . He was going to work for their enactment. Make no mistake about that. That was exactly what he was in the White House for and what he intended to do.

Fifty years ago this remark, especially as and to whom delivered, would have brought most members of Congress spluttering to their feet and set the President's few remaining friends to shaking their disbelieving heads. Even as late as twenty years ago it would have been considered a gratuitous insult by the die-hards and a show of bad taste by the moderates in Congress. In 1954 it passed unchallenged and even unnoticed except by those whose reaction was "Well, it's about time."

From that moment of awakening on, President Eisenhower did his best, within the obvious limits of his tastes and politics, to make good his pledge. He used arts of persuasion that were once controversial but are now considered altogether regular, and that is the essence of this first ingredient of the modern Presidency: the irregular has become the regular, the unexpected the expected, in the area of executive-legislative relations. The President has no weapons that were not available to Harding or, for that matter, to McKinley. The appeal to the people is more easily brought off in the age of electronics; on the other hand, the dangled patronage has lost much of its influence, thanks to the success of civil-service reform. The White House conference, the appeal to party loyalty, the threat of a veto—these weapons, too, are no keener than they were a half-century ago. The President's own machinery for drafting legislative proposals and for maintaining good relations with Congressmen is vastly enlarged and improved; Congress itself calls ever more insistently upon the President for reports and recommendations. Yet the two houses, despite the pleas of Senators Kefauver and Monroney, have made no important institutional changes in recognition of his increased responsibility for providing them with leadership. And the Constitution, needless to say, reads exactly as it did in 1789 in those passages that govern the relations of executive and legislature. The remarkable change in these relations has been neither institutional nor constitutional but, rather, meteorological, a change in the climate of politics and custom. The country now expects the President to have a program and to work hard for its enactment. He is more likely to be criticized in today's press for timidity and inertia than for resolution and activity. What the country expects, Congress also expects. Henceforth it will react with mild irritation rather than wild indignation to presidential attempts to goad it into action.

The President's right, even duty, to propose detailed legislation to Congress touching every problem of American society, and then to speed its passage down the legislative transmission belt, is now an accepted usage of our constitutional system. So far has this revolution gone that the thought occurs: we need new standards with which to judge the "strength" of a President. We need new techniques of executive-legislative co-operation, too, and I shall return to this persistent problem in my final chapter.

The emergence of the President as active leader of Congress has been accompanied by a second change: the opening of new channels of communication through which he can mold and measure public opinion. Who can say how much power and drama have flowed toward the President and away from the houses of Congress because he can chat with the nation easily over radio and television and they cannot? Programs like "Capitol Cloakroom" and "Face the Nation" have never been in the same class as a fifteen-minute broadcast and telecast from the White House. Nor can the "spectaculars" staged by Senators McCarthy and Kefauver for the housewives of America be said to have raised our interest in or respect for Congress as an institution. Let us acknowledge that the President has been the chief gainer from the miracles of electronics, and let us pray that Congress never succumbs to the urge to compete with him by putting its regular proceedings on the air. What Stephen Potter would call the "natural one-upness" of the President is a hard fact of life with which Congress must learn to live, just as he has had to learn to live with the hard fact that, thanks to his uniquely exposed position, privacy is a right to which he has practically no claim at all so long as he is President.

The most influential channel of public opinion to and from the President that has been opened up in recent years is the press conference. The President's regular meeting with the press is now a completely accepted institution, and it therefore comes as a surprise to recall that its unbroken existence in present form dates only from the first year of Franklin Roosevelt. The Presidents have been in close touch with the press from the beginning, but not until the administration of Woodrow Wilson was the regularly scheduled conference, open to newspaper-men as a matter of right and not of personal privilege, established on a fixed footing. When America entered World War I, Wilson abandoned the conference to avoid embarrassment to his administration, and the three Republican Presidents who followed him were unable or unwilling to match his able performance between 1913 and 1917. Harding made such a mess of several hot grounders hit in his direction that he changed the rules and required questions to be written out and submitted in advance; Coolidge continued this practice and generally kept the press at arm's length; and Hoover, who also insisted on written questions, held fewer and fewer conferences until finally, as the darkness of impending defeat gathered over his head, he abandoned them altogether.

Franklin Roosevelt, who would have been lost without the press, revived the conference and brought it to new heights of influence and public interest. Any journalist certified by the correspondents' own association was admitted to the conference, and questions were asked and answered "from horseback." Roosevelt maintained the wise rule first laid down by Wilson that he was not to be quoted directly without specific permission, but otherwise the conference became a wonderful game of give-and-take—with the President, a genius at sarcasm, doing most of the giving. Mr. Truman, despite some occasional lapses in his first term, carried forward the precedents set by President Roosevelt. He gets the credit and blame, which have been dished out in roughly equal amounts, for shifting the conference from the President's office to the "treaty room" in the old State building, an auditorium with seats for several hundred persons, and thus for establishing it on a much more formal basis.

Mr. Eisenhower, too, did his manful best to meet the press once a week when he happened to be in Washington, and he went on record repeatedly and "emphatically" in praise of the press conference as "a very fine latter-day American institution." On January 19, 1955, a day to remember, he presided over the first press conference ever to be filmed by television and newsreel camera; millions of Americans sat at home that evening and watched their President go through his paces. He went through them, let it be recorded, with an air of dignity, sincerity, and competence, and even the most hardened observers fell all over themselves praising this "marvelous example of democracy at work." There were some complaints, largely political in inspiration, over the decision of the White House to review the footage before releasing it to the telecasters and movie companies, but this was a perfectly proper extension of the well-understood prohibition against quoting the President directly without permission. The experiment having succeeded, the televised press conference has become a regular weekly feature. As might be expected, it is losing its appeal to many people, and the networks now present only the juiciest excerpts from the conferences. The moral is an old one, familiar to all the able Presidents: when you find a bright new tool, don't dull it with too much use. So long as the televised press conference is not overdone, it bids well to remain an important, not to say informative and entertaining, technique of American democracy. More than that, the taped films of the press conference will provide a kind of documentation for future historians that should make the writing of presidential biographies a happier if less creative experience.

Televised or not, the presidential press conference is now a fixed custom in our system of government. It is conceivable that a President with no taste for this kind of half-circus, half-inquisition could cut the growth of custom short, but the next President would be certain—in fact, he would pledge himself bravely while still a candidate—to start it up again. In part this is true because the people have come to expect it and dislike being disappointed in their expectations, in part because it is, on balance, so useful a platform for the man who stands on it. No President can afford to be without it, certainly no sociable, outgoing President of the kind we are likely to elect from now on.

There has been considerable talk in the press and in text-books about the kinship of the President's press conference and the question-and-answer period in the British House of Commons. The press conference does serve us in some ways as a method for interrogating the government of the day, but several sharp differences are to be noted. The President controls the questions (if only by retreating into the shell of "no comment") as the Prime Minister does not. The questioners are in no sense his peers, even though they like to think of themselves as representatives of the American people, a fourth estate with a grave responsibility. To the best of my knowledge, no gentleman of the press has ever risen to scold the President for an unsatisfactory answer and to push him for a better one. Indeed, the first gentleman to do it will probably be the last. And the questions must generally be of a kind that, far from nailing the President to the wall on a specific point, permit him to take off on a free flight in any direction he chooses. The fact is that the President could not ask for a tool of leadership more perfectly designed to his ends, for a pulpit more artfully constructed from which to preach sermons to us and to the world, for a listening device more finely tuned to hear the opinions and fears and complaints of the American people. As Mr. Eisenhower himself testified:

> As a matter of fact, I think this is a wonderful institution. I have seen all kinds of statements that Presidents have considered it a bore and a chore, but it does a lot of things for me personally.
>
> Moreover, I rather like to get the questions because frequently I think they represent the kind of thinking that is going on.

The press conference is not a restraining but an enabling device, as our last three Presidents have demonstrated repeatedly; and that, I would guess, is why it will never again be abandoned outright nor even reduced to the cold, gray event it was under Herbert Hoover. An unbriefed, irritable,

shoot-from-the-hip sort of President may do himself serious
damage in the give-and-take of the press conference, but so
may he in reaching out along any of his channels to the people.
I conclude with a comment from Louis Brownlow, certainly
the wisest head among those who watched the press conference
grow to its present stature.

It would be almost impossible, in my opinion, for any President
now to change this pattern or to interfere in any material way with
this institution, set up without authority of the law, required by no
Constitutional mandate, embodying no rights enforceable in a court
of law, but nevertheless an institution of prime importance in the
political life of the American people.

It would be almost impossible and altogether imbecile. No
President in his right mind would surrender gladly the power
he draws from this unique institution, which puts him, in a
light that he selects for himself, on the front page of every
newspaper in the land and, as often as not, in the world.

The role of the President that has undergone perhaps the most
rapid growth in the past quarter-century is that of Protector of
the Peace. Thanks to the eagerness with which Roosevelt and
Truman responded to calls for help from the people, we now
look upon the President as a one-man riot squad ready to rush
anywhere in the country to restore peace and order. While state
and local authorities usually deal with fire, drought, flood,
pestilence, or violence, disasters that spread over several states
or touch upon federal interests or are simply too hot for a
locality to handle can be sure of attention and action from the
White House.

This is especially true of labor disputes that disturb the
peace of the United States. The sudden expansion of government interest in labor-management relations under the New
and Fair Deals has worked visible influence upon the office and
powers of the President. He has little to do with the normal
processes of government participation in such relations, but

in labor disputes that are national emergencies he has now become, even when he refuses to act, a dominant third party. The Taft-Hartley Act of 1947 speaks wistfully of "sound and stable industrial peace." The prime responsibility of the President to preserve and protect the peace is now universally assumed. His powers in this area fall under three headings:

1) The power literally to "keep the peace of the United States" by instituting military action in strikes attended by violence and public disorder.

In most cases the policing of disorderly strikes is the duty of state and local authorities. The President will intervene in industrial warfare in two situations only: when he has been requested to act by the proper authorities, who thereby acknowledge their own inability to preserve order; or when federal laws and rights are being openly flouted and the national interest in a restoration of order is clear. The President may refuse to intervene when asked; he may also, as Cleveland proved in the Pullman strike of 1894, intervene unbidden and even unwanted. In recent years this power has rested on the shelf. We seem to have less violence in our labor disputes, and local officials seem better qualified to handle them in the severe yet neutral fashion the public interest demands. Yet the power remains in the President's possession, stretching all the way from the mere threat of force to outright martial law, and I suspect we will live to see it used again.

2) The power to remove obstructions to the flow of industrial production in time of war, or just before or after war.

The President must display unusual interest in wartime labor disputes. As Commander in Chief he is concerned before all others that production and delivery of weapons and supplies continue without interruption. Under conditions of total war he becomes the dominant figure in industrial relations. His power is exerted along two related lines. First, he makes it his immediate business to see that peaceful relations are maintained between labor and management. To this end he institutes special agencies to aid them in resolving their differences. Second, he enforces the rulings and orders of these agencies by applying "indirect sanctions"—for example, by focusing publicity on a recalcitrant union or employer, by threatening to reclassify workers in the draft, or by cutting off a plant's supply of scarce raw materials—and he prevents critical work stoppages by the final sanction of presidential seizure. Presidents Roosevelt and Truman both wielded this vast authority with vigor and considerable success. Between them they ordered more than sixty seizures in the years 1941-1946. The most notable of these was the "Battle of Montgomery Ward" in 1944, in which the enemy was finally defeated by the simple maneuver of having its commander, Mr. Sewell Avery, carried from his office by two bewildered enlisted men of the United States Army whose mothers had certainly not raised them to be this kind of soldier. This power received a salutary if hardly crippling check in the Steel Seizure case of June 1952.

3) The power to intervene in disputes that constitute economic national emergencies.

Quite apart from the open threat to our national well-being presented by large-scale violence or a halt in war production is the continuing problem of strikes in the basic industries and transportation system. The American people know from experience how injurious a widespread stoppage of work in the telephone system or steel mills can be, and long before Judge T. Alan Goldsborough began his famous lecture course for John L. Lewis (which the student failed miserably), we were aware that a strike of long duration in the railroads or coal mines might cause "society itself" to "disintegrate." It is therefore not surprising that the wave of strikes in 1946 and 1947 should have persuaded the authors of the Taft-Hartley Act to insert broad provisions authorizing the President to act in disputes "imperilling the national health and safety." He already had some power in this area: his prestige as President, which allowed him to intervene informally in the manner of Theodore

Roosevelt in the anthracite coal strike of 1902, and a grant of limited authority, which had been enfeebled by overwork, in the Railway Labor Act of 1926. Now Congress was prepared to go further and empower the President to seek an injunction in the federal courts that would delay a crippling strike for eighty days. Although Mr. Truman, in vetoing the Taft-Hartley Act, expressed particular disapproval of its emergency provisions, he made use of them on seven occasions in 1948 and on three in his second term, for the most part with circumspection and at least modest success. Mr. Eisenhower, who presided in less turbulent times and was more reluctant than Mr. Truman to brandish this kind of power, nevertheless used this power himself seven times in his first seven years. The dock and steel strikes of 1959 revealed all too painfully the limited reach of Title II of the Taft-Hartley Act, and a stronger set of emergency provisions would seem to be on the agenda of the future.

Whatever techniques we may create to prevent the crippling of the nation by widespread strikes, it should be plain to see that from this time forward the most important single factor in labor disputes of this character will be the heart, mind, and politics of the President of the United States. His position in such disputes is, to be sure, extremely delicate. As the final guardian of the public interest he must stand clear of partisanship and wield his weapons with discretion. In particular, he must avoid using them in such a manner that one of the parties to a dispute will go out of its way to invite intervention. He must recognize that his powers in this field are emergency powers only, that the regular processes of collective bargaining and of government mediation and conciliation are not to be disturbed. He must draw upon his matchless capacity to mobilize and express public opinion with shrewd frugality. He must resist the temptation to interpose his prestige in disputes that are being threshed out, however slowly, by regular statutory and administrative machinery, or he may pull down the whole structure of government intervention about his ears. "Equality for both and vigilance for the public welfare" must be the President's high resolve.

Limited though his powers are, we are better off with them than without them. It is reassuring to know that in an economic system that invites and rewards the struggle for self-interest there is a boundary beyond which the contestants will push at some peril, and that we have a high sheriff to patrol it.

It might be well to close this discussion by recalling my comments in Chapter 1 on a role that is still very much in its infancy, that of Manager of Prosperity. The President is now expected to act before and not just after an economic crisis develops, and he is steadily amassing powers with which to do it. It is still too early to measure the full dimensions of this role, but not too early to recognize that they are genuinely impressive. When we come face to face with the next grave threat of depression, the President, whoever he may be, will be a "spectacle unto the world."

If there is any one point I have hammered on in this book, it is that the Presidency is an essentially democratic office. The people have done much to make it what it is today; the man who holds it reaches out to them for support and repays them with guidance and protection. There is no more impressive evidence of this truth than a fourth development in the modern Presidency: the elevation of this office to a commanding position in the ongoing struggle for civil liberties and civil rights. We have become increasingly conscious of our shortcomings and wrongdoings in these related fields in recent years. Even as we sin against one another in the area of freedom of expression, even as we drag our feet in the march toward justice for our minorities, we feel the gaze of the whole world upon our necks and are uncomfortable. And as we have become more conscious, the President, who has a sizable part of this world for a constituency, seems to have grown in stature as a friend of liberty.

Here as everywhere he operates under severe limitations. A

wing of his party may have a stake in discrimination; public opinion may be riding a wave of intolerance; Congress may refuse him even the most watered-down authority to protect minorities against intimidation. Yet there are many things he can do if he is resolute and perceptive, if he steers a middle course between serene abstention and demagogic meddling in events and areas critical for American liberty. Here are some of his powers, all but one or two of them the creations of our last three Presidents:

He can recommend legislation to Congress—in the grand style of Harry S Truman's message of February 2, 1948, which made ten controversial proposals ranging from the establishment of a fair employment practices commission to home rule for the District of Columbia, or in the more modest manner of Dwight D. Eisenhower's request for legislation to permit federal prosecution of private persons, as well as state and local officials, for intimidating voters in presidential or congressional elections. And he can summon all his authority as Chief Legislator to push his proposals past the recalcitrants in Congress.

He can veto illiberal legislation, as Presidents Cleveland, Taft, and Wilson all vetoed bills that set up a literacy test for immigrants. (For the record, such a bill was finally passed into law over Wilson's veto in 1917.) So long as the Supreme Court stays "on the hot spot" in the continuing struggles over freedom of expression and desegregation, it will need all the protection it can get against an irate Congress; and I can think of no protection quite so comforting as the President's power to veto genuinely ill-willed and ill-considered attempts to limit the Court's jurisdiction.

He can make broad use of his authority as Commander in Chief. Like Roosevelt he can establish an F.E.P.C. by executive order as a means of speeding up production in time of war, like Truman he can establish a President's Committee on Equality of Treatment and Opportunity in the Armed Forces, and like Eisenhower he can push ahead with the work begun by his two predecessors aimed at putting an end to segregated units in all branches of the service. Few Americans seem to realize how far we have gone, thanks largely to the President's authority as Commander in Chief, toward eliminating segregation as a way of life on military bases throughout the United States.

He can issue similar orders and push for similar practices in his capacity as Chief Executive. Examples of this use of presidential authority are Truman's regulations of 1948 prohibiting discrimination in personnel practices "throughout the federal establishment" and Eisenhower's Committee on Government Contracts, which was set up to secure compliance with fair employment practices by companies with government contracts.

He can use his power of appointment to strengthen the Supreme Court as a bulwark of freedom, or to bring acknowledged friends of civil liberty and representatives of minority groups into the top levels of the administration; he can use his power of removal, if he doesn't mind the storm he will surely raise, to dismiss officials who insist on ignoring or even sabotaging his antidiscrimination orders.

He can prod his chief assistant for law enforcement, the Attorney General, to push steadily for relief and assistance to minority groups in the federal courts. Like Eisenhower, he can order him to file a brief as "friend of the court" in private suits against segregation in education; like Truman, he can order him to institute actions under Title 18, chapter 13, sections 241-242 of the *United States Code*. These provisions, which date from 1870, make it a federal offense to engage in various activities that "injure, oppress, threaten, or intimidate any citizen in the free exercise or enjoyment of any right or privilege secured to him by the Constitution or laws of the United States." They are not easy to use, but an occasional conviction has been obtained under them. The President can also prod the Federal Bureau of Investigation to be on the alert for offenses in this category. Another string was added to the President's bow in the Civil Rights Act of 1957, which authorizes the Department of Justice to seek injunctions in the federal courts against state or local officials who discriminate against Negro voters.

He can establish commissions of distinguished citizens to survey and report on the state of freedom in this country, or co-operate wholeheartedly with one established by Congress. The leading example of such a commission was Mr. Truman's own Committee on Civil Rights, whose memorable report of 1947 pointed out the way for many of our advances in recent years.

He can use a number of his ancient and honorable powers to advance the cause of justice and humanity: for example, the pardoning power to correct a sentence made heavier because of the criminal's race, the treaty-making power to pledge his own faith (if not the Senate's) to wiping genocide from the face of the earth, and his power as chieftain of his party to bring leaders of minorities into its high councils.

He can take special pains to eliminate the disgraceful vestiges of discrimination in the District of Columbia. Although Truman was doubtless correct in denying that he had the power to end racial segregation outright in the District by executive order, there is much the President can do with a quiet order here and a good example there. For example, Attorney General Brownell's vigorous intervention in a case in 1953 resulted in the Supreme Court's upholding legislation prohibiting discrimination in Washington restaurants, after which a commissioner of the District government appointed by the President gave restaurant owners forty-eight hours to comply with the law.

I doubt that any one in the world who has heard the words "Little Rock" needs to be reminded of the existence of still another of the President's powers in this controversial area, but let me at least set down the fateful truth that his broad authority to keep the peace of the United States with armed might extends forcefully to situations like that faced by Mr. Eisenhower in September 1957. Whether the President mixed force and prudence to the proper degree in that great constitutional and social crisis is a question we will be arguing for years to come, but the argument over his power to use the United States Army to enforce the desegregation orders of a federal court came to an end the very day it began. If he cannot use bayonets to pave the road to a more just and decent America, he can certainly use them to hold the road open.

Finally, and most important, he can draw upon his authority as spokesman for the nation in such a way as to inspire those who are working for a more democratic America and to rebuff those who would drag us backward into the swamps of primitivism and oppression—or, better still, to educate all of us in the ways of brotherhood. The moral force of this great office is never so apparent as when he lashes out at the vigilantes who spoil the vines of the First Amendment, its prestige never so imposing as when he sets out quietly to persuade the leaders of Southern opinion that a new day has dawned. One thing is certain about our attempt to solve the crisis of desegregation in the schools: a key factor in the equation of success will be a succession of Presidents determined to use all the resources of this great office.

I am aware that I have given only one side of the picture in this review. The President also has it in his power to dampen the struggle for civil rights by his indifference and to invade the field of civil liberties in force. Franklin Roosevelt's order authorizing the evacuation of all persons of Japanese ancestry from the Pacific Coast in early 1942 and the combined Truman-Eisenhower record in the area of loyalty and security are proof that even the most conscientious President may blunder or be pressured into dubious acts. I am aware, too, as I noted at the outset of this discussion, that he must use his powers shrewdly and with an eye out for the limits of possibility. He cannot, for example, comment critically on every patent violation of liberty and justice throughout the land, especially when the violence is done by judges and juries; he cannot declare rhetorical war on an entire section or interest or school of opinion in this country, not if he expects to get on with his other tasks. Yet he is now in a position to be one of the most potent forces behind our progress in civil rights and our defense of civil liberties. From this time forward the President will have no choice but to serve as the conscience and strong right arm of American democracy.

The most notable development in the Presidency in recent years is a change in structure rather than a growth in power, although the latter is certainly the first cause of the change. As the burdens of the President have mounted steadily, he has taken on auxiliary machinery to help him bear them. Inseparable from the modern Presidency, indeed essential to its effective operation, is a whole train of officers and offices that serve him as eyes, ears, arms, mouth, and brain. The encompassing title of this machinery is the Executive Office of the President, and it numbers roughly a thousand persons whose sole purpose in public life is to aid the President in the execution of his own duties. The Executive Office exists for him, and he could not exist without it.

The Executive Office was established in 1939 through the associated, if not entirely harmonious, endeavors of Franklin D. Roosevelt and the Seventy-sixth Congress. The immediate impulse for organizing it was Roosevelt's own candid recognition that an otherwise professional performance during his first term in the Presidency had been hampered by the lack of a staff to help him stay on top of his ever-growing duties. He was not the first person to make this discovery. Long before the New Deal began to pile new burdens on the Presidency, students of the national government, the most vocal of them the Presidents themselves, had been calling the attention of Congress and the nation to the hapless plight of the "final object of the public wishes."

Mr. Roosevelt's solution was thoroughly in character. Never one to let an important problem lie around unstudied by a special commission, he set the wheels turning in early 1936 with the appointment of the President's Committee on Administrative Management. Under the adroit guidance of Louis Brownlow (Chairman), Charles E. Merriam, and Luther Gulick, a corps of noted scholars probed every part of the federal administration. Particular attention was devoted to the heart of the system, the Presidency itself. The Committee reported to Mr. Roosevelt in January 1937, and in the shortest scholarly sentence on record told him what he had known ever since his first day in the White House: "The President needs help." In forwarding the Committee's reports to Congress, Mr. Roosevelt summed up the parlous state of the Presidency in these words:

The Committee has not spared me; they say, what has been common knowledge for twenty years, that the President cannot adequately handle his responsibilities; that he is overworked; that it is humanly impossible, under the system which we have, for him fully to carry out his constitutional duty as Chief Executive, because he is overwhelmed with minor details and needless contacts arising directly from the bad organization and equipment of the Government. I can testify to this. With my predecessors who have said the same thing over and over again, I plead guilty.

The controversial recommendations of the President's Committee ranged the whole field of executive management. Central to its purposes, however, was the immediate problem of the presidential burden, which it proposed to lighten by creating a team of six executive assistants and an administrative staff of experts who would handle the President's managerial functions in budgeting, planning, and personnel management. These proposals ran afoul of the epic battle over the "Court-packing" scheme and the efforts of numerous members of the Seventy-fifth Congress to pin the label of "dictator" on the President. Not until two years later did Congress grudgingly bestow on Mr. Roosevelt a limited power of executive reorganization. The sweeping proposal of the Committee on Administrative Management that "the whole Executive Branch of the Government should be overhauled and the present 100 agencies reorganized under a few large departments in which every executive authority would find its place" was frustrated by those sections of the Reorganization Act that forbade the President to lay profane hands upon a full nineteen agencies, including the Civil Service Commission. With the latter exception, however, he was able to deal pretty much as he saw fit with his own problems.

This he did in Executive Order 8248, dated September 8, 1939, and described correctly by Mr. Gulick as a "nearly unnoticed but none the less epoch-making event in the history of American institutions." The effect of the order was to create the Executive Office, designate six components within it, and authorize the President to appoint the personal assistants for whom the Committee on Administrative Management had called. The logic of this order can be most clearly grasped by quoting a passage from Professor Leonard D. White, in which he succeeded admirably in expressing the "basic objectives" underlying the "proper organization of any large-scale executive office in government." These, it would seem, were the purposes for which the Executive Office was created:

1. To insure that the chief executive is adequately and currently informed.
2. To assist him in foreseeing problems and planning future programs.
3. To ensure that matters for his decision reach his desk promptly, in condition to be settled intelligently and without delay; and to protect him against hasty and ill-considered judgments.
4. To exclude every matter that can be settled elsewhere in the system.
5. To protect his time.
6. To secure means of ensuring compliance by subordinates with established policy and executive direction.

There was a more profound purpose, too, for this was a President, not just a department head, who was to be rescued from overwork—but more of that presently.

Through all the years of crisis since 1939 the Executive Office has functioned at a high level of proficiency and morale. By no means a faultless instrument of public administration, it has nevertheless served President and nation with distinction and has given an entirely new cast to the question of executive management in the national government, as well as to the Presidency itself. For some years now, it has been popular, even among his friends, to write off Mr. Roosevelt as a "second-rate administrator." In the light of Executive Order 8248, an accomplishment in public administration superior to that of any other President, this familiar judgment seems a trifle musty.

Rather than wander wearily through the many changes in the Executive Office under each of the last three Presidents, let me describe the major components that exist today. This is the President's "general staff":

The White House Office, which serves him directly and intimately, numbers about two dozen top-flight personal aides, two dozen aides to these aides, and roughly 350 clerks, stenographers, messengers, and secretaries who are needed to handle the documents and correspondence and appeals for help that descend upon the White House in torrents. Although each President can be expected to divide his personal load in whatever way seems to suit him best, some positions in the White House have already taken on an air of permanence, notably those of the Assistant to the President, Press Secretary, Staff Secretary, Special Counsel, Secretary to the Cabinet, secretary for appointments, liaison man with Congress, and chief speech writer. Associated with these men are a whole crew of Assistants, some labeled "Special" and others "Administrative," who cover a wide range of presidential responsibilities—economic problems, science, minority relations, government personnel, liaison with the states, foreign affairs, patronage, and any other problem, such as disarmament or farm surpluses or air safety, that calls loudly for the attention the President wishes he could give it himself. The President may often designate officials with jobs of their own to serve him personally, as Mr. Eisenhower designated Chairman Lewis L. Strauss of the Atomic Energy Commission and Chairman Philip Young of the Civil Service Commission, and he may quietly borrow officials with special skills from any part of the administration for just about any length of time. Finally, he has one aide for each of the armed services.

The National Security Council was established in 1947 "to advise the President with respect to the integration of domestic, foreign, and military policies relating to the national security." The current membership of the Council includes the President, the Vice-President, the Secretaries of State and Defense, and the Director of the Office of Civil and Defense Mobilization. The core of this interdepartmental committee is a permanent staff headed by an executive secretary. Suspended from the National Security Council, although not an integral part of the Executive Office, is the Central Intelligence Agency. The Council, which usually invites other officials like the Joint Chiefs of Staff and the Secretary of the Treasury to sit with it, is actually a specialized cabinet to advise the President in the whole field of foreign and military affairs. In 1957 the Operations Coordinating Board was placed within its structure as a kind of expediting agency for the Council's policies—that is to say, the President's policies—in this critical area. The total personnel of N.S.C. and O.C.B. is about sixty.

The Council of Economic Advisers, a team of three economists aided by thirty staff and clerical aides, joined the presidential camp under the terms of the Employment Act of 1946, which directed it to assist and advise the President in the preparation of an annual economic report on the state of the Union; "gather timely and authoritative information concerning economic developments and economic trends" and submit studies based on this information to the President; "develop and recommend to the President national economic policies" designed to "promote maximum employment, production, and purchasing power"; and "make and furnish such studies, reports thereon, and recommendations with respect to matters of federal economic policy and legislation as the President may request." The breadth of this mandate affords the Council full opportunity to serve the President as a formalized "brain trust" in all matters that touch upon the economic state of the Union. Without it he could hardly be expected to be our Manager of Prosperity.

The Office of Civil and Defense Mobilization is the result of a merger in 1958 of the Federal Civil Defense Administration and the Office of Defense Mobilization. It is charged "with the responsibility of directing, planning, and coordinating the mobilization and non-military defense functions of the nation," and as such it very obviously helps the President to discharge several of his major duties as Commander in Chief. Despite this fact, and despite the technical location of O.C.D.M. in the Executive Office, it hardly seems sensible to class this 1,600-man agency as an integral part of the presidential machinery. Perhaps we can compromise with the cold logic of the *Government Organization Manual* by agreeing that the top three or four officials in O.C.D.M. are servants primarily of the President, but why not then go on to include the Civil Service Commission in the Executive Office?

Last but far from least in importance is what Richard Neustadt salutes as "the oldest, toughest organism in the presidential orbit," the Bureau of the Budget, which serves the President as an "administrative general staff." The Bureau is one of the two original components of the Executive Office, having been transferred in 1939 from the Treasury Department, and is sure to be functioning in much the same way when most other components have passed into history. Without it the President could not begin to do his job as Chief Executive or Chief Legislator. In addition to taking the burden of the budget almost completely off his back, it engages in a broad range of activities designed to achieve "more efficient and economical conduct of the Government service," assists in preparing the President's executive orders and proclamations, and acts as his clearinghouse for proposed legislation and enrolled bills. To cite only one instance of the importance of the Bureau in the pattern of presidential responsibility, its Office of Legislative Reference shoulders every part of the burden of the veto power except the final decision to say "yes" or "no." The Bureau counts 420 employees, and no one in his right mind has ever suggested that it could get along with any fewer.

In and around the four key agencies, especially the White House Office, swirls a whole galaxy of persons—Secretaries, Under Secretaries, study groups, presidential commissions—. who give some, most, or all of their time and best thoughts directly to the President. One of the features of the White House Office is its unusual plasticity. The President is, as he should be, entirely free to parcel out his immediate burden among his assistants, to establish or disestablish interdepartmental committees or secretariats, to call on persons anywhere in the executive branch to perform special tasks, and, like all who preceded him, to take counsel with private citizens. If Mr. Eisenhower chose to use Sherman Adams as a chief of staff or to put special trust in his Vice-President or to revive the Cabinet as a co-ordinating agency, if he chose to take his television cues from Robert Montgomery or to ask Willie Mays about juvenile delinquency or to hold a White House Conference on Education, that was entirely his business. He ran his team in one way, each of the men he succeeded ran his in another, the men who succeed him will run theirs in ways yet unimagined.

At the same time, we must understand that the hard core of this machinery, especially the Bureau of the Budget, is now a permanent fixture in the national government. Many persons in it can look forward confidently to a long life of service for a long line of Presidents. Although those immediately around him are his personal choices, most of the men and women who serve them have tenure in their jobs. Although his personal touch is necessary to give the whole Executive Office its sense of direction, it could run for some time entirely on its own. The fact is that the Presidency has become "institutionalized," and if it is a fact to cause us concern—as I shall point out in my final chapter—it is also one that is here to stay. The President is still one man, but he is also, like any man with a thousand helpers, an institution. Most of the wheels go around steadily whether he watches them or not, as we learned so well during Eisenhower's illnesses. Many orders and suggestions and leaks emerge from "the White House" about which the President knows nothing. One must be especially careful today in reading newspapers to distinguish among what he says for himself, what his aides say for him, and what his aides say for themselves. If the distinction is not easy to make (and Washington is full of people who wish they could make it unerringly), that should remind us of the unity into which President, White House, and Executive Office finally merge.

I have already pointed out, with the help of Professor White, the momentous administrative significance of this development in the modern Presidency. Its constitutional significance, it seems to me, is even more momentous. It converts the Presidency into an instrument of twentieth-century government; it gives the incumbent a sporting chance to stand the strain and fulfill his constitutional mandate as a one-man branch of our three-part government; it deflates even the most forceful arguments, which are still raised occasionally, for a plural executive; it assures us that the Presidency will survive the advent of the positive state. Executive Order 8248 may yet be judged to have saved the Presidency from paralysis and the Constitution from radical amendment. At $8,000,000 (the annual appropriation for the four key agencies), the Executive Office of the President is almost the best bargain we get in the federal budget.

I trust it will be thought proper in a book of nearly three hundred pages on the Presidency to devote seven to the Vice-Presidency, although even this ratio of forty to one is no measure of the vast gap between them in power and prestige. The Presidency is the greatest constitutional office the world has known, a splendid chieftainship sought eagerly by just about every first-rate political figure in the nation, not to mention a horde of second-raters. The Vice-Presidency is a hollow shell of an office, an uncomfortable heir apparency sought by practically no one we should like to see as President. It has perked up noticeably in the years since 1948, but fundamentally it remains a disappointment in the American constitutional system.

The Vice-Presidency is one of our oldest problems. Some of the more astute members of the Convention of 1787 doubted that there was any need for a Vice-President, and Hamilton was forced to refute numerous criticisms of the office in *The Federalist*. There were apparently three reasons for creating the Vice-Presidency: to establish a constitutional heir for the President, to facilitate the selection of "continental characters" under the original electoral system (of which more hereafter), and to provide a presiding officer for the Senate not immediately devoted to the interests of any particular state. The framers also recognized the advantage of a moderator for this body with a deciding vote in the event of a tie. In general, they expected the office to be filled by the nation's number-two political figure, the man who had polled the second highest number of votes in the presidential election.

However cogent the reasons of the framers, and however high their expectations, the Vice-Presidency was a failure, and was recognized as such, almost from the outset. John Adams, the first to hold it, lamented that "my country has in its wisdom contrived for me the most insignificant office that ever the invention of man contrived or his imagination conceived." Thomas Jefferson, his successor, said something more meaningful than he realized when he described the "second office of government" as "honorable and easy," "the first" as "but a splendid misery." And several early statesmen referred to the Vice-President as "His Superfluous Excellency." The rise of the Federalist and Re-

publican parties, the near disaster of the Jefferson-Burr election
of 1800-1801, the consequent adoption of the Twelfth Amendment, and the establishment of the "Virginia Succession" (under which the Secretaryship of State became the "bullpen" of
the Presidency) all contributed to the decline of the office. The
first two Vice-Presidents may have been Adams and Jefferson,
but the fifth and sixth were Elbridge Gerry and Daniel D.
Tompkins; the seventh, John C. Calhoun, resigned to enter the
Senate. And somewhere along the line there was a Vice-President named Throttlebottom—and a good one, too. Public men
then, like public men today, apparently preferred misery with
power to ease without it.

For the record, let me set down the powers of the Vice-
President as they exist today. He draws two clear duties from
the Constitution—to preside over the Senate and exercise a tie-
breaking vote—and, as I count them, six from the laws: 1) to
appoint five midshipmen to the Naval Academy; 2) to appoint
four Senators to its Board of Visitors; 3) to recommend two
candidates to the President for appointment to the Military
Academy; 4) to sign enrolled bills and joint resolutions before
they are sent to the President; 5) to be a member of the Smithsonian Institution and its Board of Regents; and 6), the one
grant of any consequence, to sit as a statutory member of the
National Security Council. Occasionally he is designated to appoint several members to a special commission. He also draws
his pay: $35,000 a year plus $10,000 for expenses.

These, plainly, are dimensions of impotence, and impotence
is the mark of a second-class office. Suspended in a constitutional limbo between executive and legislature, and in a political
limbo between obscurity and glory, the Vice-Presidency has lost
most of its significance as an instrument of government. Woodrow Wilson summed up the problem of the Vice-Presidency
neatly when he wrote in exasperation: "The chief embarrassment in discussing his office is, that in explaining how little
there is to be said about it one has evidently said all there is

to say." I would sum it up myself by taking note of the fact
that there have been fifteen occasions in the history of the republic, a total of more than thirty-six years, when we had no
Vice-President and never knew the difference.

The fact that the Vice-President has little to do is not in
itself a danger spot in our constitutional system. In considering
what he is, however, we must remember what he may be:
President of the United States. John Adams, discerning as ever,
remarked in the very first days: "I am possessed of two separate powers, the one *in esse* and the other *in posse*. I am Vice
President. In this I am nothing, but I may be everything." The
reality of vice-presidential impotence has generally loomed far
more prominently in the nation's political consciousness than
the possibility of a succession to the Presidency; the *esse* of the
office has too often blotted out the *posse*. The real danger of
the powerless Vice-Presidency is therefore this: that it is rarely
occupied by a man for whom a majority of the people would
have voted as a candidate for the Presidency. The potential importance of the Vice-President as heir apparent to the President,
pointed up by seven successions in 170-odd years, has not been
sufficient to attract leading political figures to seek it as a matter
of course. Most men of ability and ambition would still rather
be a leading Senator or Secretary of State than Vice-President,
even after all the good and exciting times enjoyed by Richard
Nixon. While the office is not quite the political county farm
that some of its critics have portrayed, few men of presidential
stature have occupied it since Adams and Jefferson, and they
usually had to be dragooned into accepting their party's nomination. We have had distinguished Vice-Presidents, but who since
Van Buren has been second only to the President as a political
figure, even of his own party? Mr. Dooley's creator echoed our
opinion of most Vice-Presidents when, alarmed at the prospect
of Charles W. Fairbanks as President, he pleaded with Theodore
Roosevelt not to go down in a submarine, and ended on the
note, "Well, you really shouldn't do it—unless you take the

Vice-President with you." Roosevelt had already added his bit to the lore of the Vice-Presidency by stating, "I would a great deal rather be anybody, say a professor of history, than Vice-President." The man who served under Wilson and longed for a good five-cent cigar, Thomas R. Marshall, went Roosevelt one better by describing himself as "a man in a cataleptic fit," who "is conscious of all that goes on but has no part in it," and then topped that by noting the propriety of his membership in the Smithsonian Institution, where he had "opportunity to compare his fossilized life with the fossils of all ages."

Like the Vice-Presidency itself, the danger of a second-rater as Vice-President is everything *in posse* and little *in esse*. Many a party hack has served his four years presiding over the Senate and passed into oblivion. On the other hand, several party hacks have succeeded to the Presidency with rather painful results. Only one of the original reasons for this office is valid today—the necessity of a constitutional heir for the President—and it is exactly here that the Vice-Presidency has failed most conspicuously. The only ways to erase the danger spot are to eliminate the office or to make it a highly attractive place of honor and power. If the history of the Vice-Presidency means anything, the former course is inconceivable and the latter unlikely.

To the credit of both Presidents Truman and Eisenhower, the Vice-Presidency has experienced something of a renaissance in recent years. Alben Barkley was probably the most distinguished man nominated for the office since John C. Calhoun, and he proved extremely useful to Mr. Truman as a link to Congress. Richard Nixon, however—and I do not mean this disrespectfully—was hauled up to the second rung from far down the ladder for reasons that had nothing to do with his qualifications for the Presidency. Mr. Nixon, thanks to the President's mind and the President's heart, was easily the busiest and most useful Vice-President within memory. Yet he was still inferior to Secretary of State Dulles or Speaker Rayburn or a dozen Senators in influence and prestige, and the Vice-Presidency is still very far from being in fact the "second office of the land." One of the few lessons we should have learned clearly from the anxious weeks following Mr. Eisenhower's heart attack was that the Vice-President, even when favored openly by the President, is unsuited to serve in emergencies as an "acting President"—unless, of course, the President's disability is clearly established. Sherman Adams, George Humphrey, John Foster Dulles, James Hagerty—all these men were more important and influential than Mr. Nixon in the conduct of the Presidency during those troubled weeks. The weaknesses of the Vice-Presidency were never more dramatically exposed than at the moment when a bewildered nation turned to it for strength and guidance. Neither in law, custom, nor political circumstance was it prepared to assume the burden that many well-meaning citizens tried to thrust upon it, and tried again after each of the next two illnesses.

Mr. Nixon, to be sure, made as much of a success of this frustrating office as any man could be expected to make. He sat by invitation in the Cabinet and presided over it in the President's absence, sat by right in the National Security Council and took part in decisions of great moment, made important statements of policy that might have been impolitic for the President to make, relieved the President of any number of trips to the airport to greet distinguished visitors, served as chairman of both the Committee on Government Contracts and the Cabinet Committee on Price Stability for Economic Growth, visited several dozen countries (not all of them exactly friendly) as special envoy of the President, served as chief campaigner in 1958, and acted as both trouble-shooter and pacifier in executive-legislative relations. Most important of all, on two occasions he stood for a few days—and stood with reserve and dignity—on the brink of the Presidency; and he was surely the first Vice-President in history to state publicly that he had stopped off at the White House on the way home from work "to see if there are any loose ends I can take care of." Yet even on the brink he was a thousand times bigger *in posse* than he was *in esse*.

Within the inherent limitations of the office, which have never been more apparent, the Vice-Presidency is generally what the President chooses to make it. President Eisenhower chose to make it something much more than it usually is, and Vice-President Nixon, unlike many of his predecessors, was delighted to go along. It must be recognized, however, that no permanent solution to the problem has been worked out, and I doubt very much that it can be. From time to time it is suggested that the Vice-President be converted into the President's top executive assistant—I once made such a proposal myself, which I hereby recant—but the road to this revolution would, I feel sure, prove rocky and dangerous. If an officer not subject to the power of removal should be authorized to execute the laws in the President's name, it would violate one of the soundest principles of our system of government. The Vice-Presidency would be a dagger aimed constantly at the precious unity of the executive power, and that would be a condition we could not tolerate. The leading men in the State Department seem to have had some such thought in their minds when they successfully thwarted Nixon's appointment to the chairmanship of the Operations Coordinating Board, and we can hardly blame them for their concern lest a barrier of unpredictable obduracy be placed between them and the President.

The most we can now hope for, I think, is that Congress will increase the Vice-President's emoluments, establish an official residency, and give him an even larger staff of his own; that a series of Presidents will follow Mr. Eisenhower's lead and fix some of these recent departures in constitutional custom; and that the parties will seek consciously to nominate men who are qualified by experience, character, and prestige to succeed to the Presidency. It would be reassuring to know that from this time forward neither party would nominate a man to the second office who had not been considered seriously for the first. There is evidence that the people think a great deal more of it than do the politicians, and the latter should face up to the blunt fact that every time they select a candidate for the Vice-Presidency they are selecting one for the Presidency. It might be of interest to hear Eisenhower's testimony on this subject, delivered at a press conference in 1955:

Q. (by Mr. Reston of the New York *Times*) Mr. President . . . what I was trying to get at was what is your philosophy about the role of the nominee in the selection of the Vice-President? Is it your view that the convention is sovereign, it can pick anybody it likes, or should it, in your judgment, follow the recommendation of the Presidential nominee?

A. Well, I would say this, Mr. Reston: It seems obvious to me that unless the man were acceptable to the Presidential nominee, the Presidential nominee should immediately step aside. . . . If there isn't some kind of general closeness of feeling between these two, it is an impossible situation, at least the way I believe it should be run.

I personally believe the Vice-President of the United States should never be a nonentity. I believe he should be used. I believe he should have a very useful job.

Plainly, then, it is up to each future President—first as nominee, then as incumbent—to make whatever can be made of this disappointing office.

To return in conclusion to the Presidency, I have tried to indicate some of the major developments that lead many observers to believe that the office is in a period of pronounced transition. There were other developments to which I might have called attention—for example, the blending of the President's roles as Chief Diplomat and Commander in Chief (to the advantage of each) and the addition of new statutory emergency powers to his already large stock—but the five discussed in detail are evidence enough of this transition. His strong posture of legislative leadership, his new channels of opinion, his increased concern for domestic peace and prosperity, his emergence as a leader in the struggle for personal liberty and racial equality, and above all his conversion into an institution—these are the fresh ingredients of the Presidency. If I may mix the metaphor, the foundations of the office remain as firm as ever, but there are some interesting changes going on in the superstructure.

CHAPTER **5**

THE MODERN PRESIDENTS

It has not been easy to suppress the giddy urge to liven up this portrait of the Presidency with comments about the men who have been in and around it during the past quarter-century, and now I am about to give way all at once. I do not give way merely to gratify a weakness for gossip about "the man in the White House." We cannot come to close grips with the modern Presidency as an institution or as a force in history unless we talk in highly personal terms about the men who have held it. Woodrow Wilson once remarked that "governments are what politicians make them, and it is easier to write of the President than of the Presidency." With his blessing I turn to the delicate but delightful task of judging the performances of Franklin D. Roosevelt, who created the modern Presidency, of Harry S Truman, who defended it, and of Dwight D. Eisenhower, who inherited it and made it acceptable to the American people. Let us place ourselves, if we can, on the throne of posterity, and from that serene point of vantage let us look back objectively, as we expect our great-grandchildren to look back, at the achievements of each of these men.

"Ranking the Presidents" has always been a Favorite Indoor Sport of history-minded Americans, and I see no reason why we should not play it with Roosevelt, Truman, and Eisenhower as happily as we play it with Jackson, Cleveland, and Harding.

I am especially concerned to anticipate the opinions of our descendants about the "greatness" of our last three Presidents. Will Roosevelt be ranked with Lincoln or Wilson? Will Truman be compared with Johnson or Theodore Roosevelt? Will the old soldier named Eisenhower be placed just below the old soldier named Washington or just above the old soldier named Grant? The answers to these questions lie in still other questions which historians like to ask about Presidents long dead. I have made a rough content analysis of more than one hundred serious presidential biographies, and I have found the same standards applied again and again. These are the questions, the accepted standards of presidential achievement, against which I propose to measure Roosevelt, Truman, and Eisenhower and thus attempt to predict the judgments of our posterity on the Presidents of our time:

In what sort of times did he live? A man cannot possibly be judged a great President unless he holds office in great times. Washington's eminence arose from the founding of the republic, Jackson's from the upsurge of democracy, Lincoln's from the Civil War, and Wilson's from World War I. We have no right even to consider a man for membership in this exclusive club unless he, too, presides over the nation in challenging years. This standard may work unfairly on Presidents who live under sunny skies, but that is the way that history is written.

If the times were great, how bravely and imaginatively did he bear the burden of extraordinary responsibility? A successful President must do a great deal more than stand quiet watch over the lottery of history: he must be a forceful leader—of Congress, the administration, and the American people; he must make the hard decisions that have to be made, and make most of them correctly; he must work hard at being President and see that these decisions are carried out.

What was his philosophy of presidential power? To be a great President a man must think like a great President; he must follow Theodore Roosevelt and choose to be a "Jackson-Lincoln," a man of strength and independence, rather than a "Buchanan," a deferential Whig. Indeed, if he is not widely and persistently accused in his own time of "subverting the Constitution," he may as well forget about being judged a truly eminent man by future generations.

What sort of technician was he? How efficiently did he organize his energies, direct his lieutenants, and thus exercise his powers? Lincoln could be an indifferent administrator and yet a great President, but the rise of the modern state has made it impossible for an inefficient President to discharge even a fraction of his duties with much hope of success.

What men did he call on for help? Did he, like Washington, have his Jefferson and Hamilton? Did he, like Lincoln, have his Seward and Chase? Did he have his great lieutenants, and his efficient sergeants, too? If the modern Presidency, as I have insisted, is irrevocably institutionalized, the modern President must do even better than Washington and Lincoln on this score, for he can no longer expect to accomplish much of anything unless he surrounds himself with able technicians as well as wise statesmen and shrewd politicians.

What manner of man was he beneath the trappings of office? We remember a President as much for his quirks and quips as for his deeds and decisions. If he is not the sort of man around whose person legends will arise in profusion, he will surely not meet the final test of presidential greatness: to be enshrined as a folk hero in the American consciousness.

What was his influence on the Presidency? We are not likely to rate a President highly if he weakens the office through cowardice or neglect. A place at the top of the ladder is reserved only for those Presidents who have added to the office by setting precedents for other Presidents to follow.

Finally, what was his influence on history? In particular, did he inspire or represent, and find words to explain, some earth-shaking readjustment in the pattern of American society? More than one President has been granted a high place in history because he sensed the direction of American democracy in his times and bent or hastened its onward course—or even, as in the case of Theodore Roosevelt, confined himself largely to pointing out the way that his successors would have to travel.

Before I hazard this informed guess about the future status of Roosevelt, Truman, and Eisenhower, let me remind my readers of one cardinal fact: American history is written, if not always made, by men of moderate views, broad interests, and merciful judgments. Time works for, rather than against, most Presidents. The men who write texts for our great-grandchildren, like the men who wrote them for us, will be concerned with broad accomplishments and failures, not with petty tales of corruption, ill temper, and intrigue, and I would hope that some of their spirit would rub off on this effort to anticipate them.

Franklin D. Roosevelt's times may well be judged to have been the most exciting and demanding in the history of the republic, as uncertain as the first fluid years under Washington, as hazardous as the first dark years under Lincoln. We bestow the accolade of greatness on a President like Wilson for having led the nation safely through one major crisis. Franklin Roosevelt, who led us through two, must therefore enjoy a long head start toward the eminence he surely wished for in his heart. It would have been sufficient unto posterity for him to have weathered the Hundred Days and launched the New Deal. What can posterity do but think grandly of a President who also led us into, through, and very nearly out of the greatest war in history, and in the midst of this travail launched the United Nations? The willingness of the American people to give Roosevelt a third term and then a fourth is the most eloquent of all witnesses to the glory of his times.

The essence of Roosevelt's Presidency was his airy eagerness to meet the age head on. Thanks to his flair for drama, he acted as if never in all history had there been times like our own. Thanks to his sense of history, he exulted in the vast responsibilities that were thrust upon him even as he sought them. In the first Hundred Days he gave Congress a kind of leadership it had not known before and still does not care to have repeated. In the golden days of the New Deal he initiated a dozen programs designed to save a society from the defects of its virtues. In the hard days before Pearl Harbor he led us step by step to a war we always knew we would have to fight, and in the harder but somehow happier days thereafter he was a Commander in Chief no less awesome than Lincoln himself.

His blunders and trimmings are all on record: the casual manipulation of the dollar in 1933, the ill-conceived assault upon the Court in 1937, the ill-starred interference in the primaries in 1938, the shabby hesitation in the Spanish Civil War, the offhand acquiescence in the evacuation of the Japanese-Americans from the Pacific Coast in 1942, the misplaced confidence in his own ability to "handle Stalin," the shocking unconcern over the education of his Vice-President in 1945, and above all the failure of the New Deal to achieve genuine economic recovery. Yet I have an idea that most of these black marks will be expunged from the memories of our posterity by his undoubted successes in launching the Tennessee Valley Authority and social security, swinging the Lend-Lease Program and the "Destroyer Deal," setting the grand strategy of the war, initiating the atom-bomb project, and converting America into a bountiful arsenal for fifty countries in addition to his own. Nor are these memorable events the whole story of his capacity for decision and leadership. When many of his acts as Commander in Chief are long forgotten, grateful men will remember that he was as devoted a conservationist as Theodore Roosevelt, as warm a friend of culture as Jefferson, and as ardent a free trader as any President who ever lived. We may never hear the end of arguments over the direction in which he led us, but few are left to argue that he preferred drifting to leading. "He demonstrated the ultimate capacity to dominate and control a supreme emergency," Sumner Welles has written, "which is the rarest and most valuable characteristic of any statesman."

No sane observer has ever placed Franklin Roosevelt in the Buchanan line of Presidents. He was, to be sure, a constitutionalist, but his Constitution was that of Jackson, Theodore Roosevelt, Lincoln, and Wilson. Like the first of these he considered the independence of the office to be its most precious asset, like the second he thought of himself as a steward of the people, like the third he made himself a "constitutional dictator" in time of severe national emergency. The gamy flavor of his theory of presidential power may be tasted in some remarkable words delivered to Congress on September 7, 1942. In demanding the repeal of an inflationary provision in the Price Control Act of 1942 he stated flatly:

I ask the Congress to take this action by the first of October. Inaction on your part by that date will leave me with an inescapable responsibility to the people of this country to see to it that the war effort is no longer imperiled by threat of economic chaos.

In the event that the Congress should fail to act, and act adequately, I shall assume the responsibility and I will act. . . .

The President has the power, under the Constitution and Congressional acts, to take measures necessary to avert a disaster which would interfere with the winning of the war. . . .

The American people can be sure that I will use my powers with a full sense of my responsibility to the Constitution and to my country. The American people can also be sure that I shall not hesitate to use every power vested in me to accomplish the defeat of our enemies in any part of the world where our own safety demands such defeat.

When the war is won, the powers under which I act automatically revert to the people—to whom they belong.

Finally, like Wilson he considered himself a lay preacher to the American people. Just a few days after his first election he remarked:

The Presidency is not merely an administrative office. That is the least of it. It is pre-eminently a place of moral leadership.

All of our great Presidents were leaders of thought at times when certain historic ideas in the life of the nation had to be clarified. Washington personified the idea of Federal Union. Jefferson practically originated the party system as we know it by opposing the democratic theory to the republicanism of Hamilton. This theory was reaffirmed by Jackson.

Two great principles of our government were forever put beyond question by Lincoln. Cleveland, coming into office following an era of great political corruption, typified rugged honesty. Theodore Roosevelt and Wilson were both moral leaders, each in his own way and for his own time, who used the Presidency as a pulpit.

That is what the office is—a superb opportunity for reapplying, applying to new conditions, the simple rules of human conduct to which we always go back. Without leadership alert and sensitive to change, we are bogged up or lose our way.

Not more than two or three Presidents, it seems safe to say, ever took so broad a view of their constitutional and moral authority as did Franklin D. Roosevelt.

Even his stoutest friends admit that Roosevelt was not much of an administrator. His working habits were casual, personal, and opportunistic; he permitted the inevitable feuds of an active administration to flare too hotly and run too long; he was unbelievably reluctant to discipline the feckless and fire the useless; he was an improviser who lacked the improviser's most essential quality—the candid courage to admit a failure and begin all over again. Yet it is possible that his friends give away too much to his enemies on this particular count. Governments bent on social reform are bound to be wasteful of time and money; Presidents who lead such governments have bigger things to think about than petty details of administration. Roosevelt was aware of his own shortcomings and took a bold step to correct the most glaring of them in Executive Order 8248, which I described in Chapter 4. Beyond that he did not care to go, for he chose to save his energies for his larger responsibilities as leader of the American people. A successful President is something more than a skilled administrator; it almost seems as if Roosevelt set out consciously to reverse the record of Hoover by being a second-rate administrator and a first-rate President. In the end, his deficiencies as an administrator were nearly swallowed up in his genius for bringing politics to the support of policy. A master politician, he rarely lost sight of a truth that most politicians have yet to perceive: that politics is only a game, and a shabby game at that, if it is not directed to larger and nobler ends. His generally masterful leadership of Congress was the most significant application of this principle.

In the course of two major crises and twelve strenuous years, Roosevelt called on hundreds of able men to help him in his tasks. He called on some odd and disreputable characters, too, four or five of whom had no business being within fifty miles of the White House, but for the most part he displayed a remarkable talent for putting the right man in the right job. Harold Ickes as Secretary of the Interior, James A. Farley as chairman of the Democratic National Committee, David Lilienthal as head of T.V.A., Robert H. Jackson as Attorney General, Harold D. Smith as Director of the Budget, Sumner Welles as Under Secretary of State, Robert E. Sherwood and Samuel Rosenman as speech writers, and Stephen Early as Press Secretary are a few examples of what I mean by "the right man in the right job."

In time of war, when it was no longer necessary for the President to confine his search for help to men of his own political stripe, this talent broadened into genius. It is easy to forget that Leahy, Marshall, King, Arnold, Eisenhower, Stimson, Vinson, Patterson, Land, McCloy, Knudsen, Forrestal, Winant, Nelson, Byrnes, Harriman, Donovan, and all the others were, in almost every instance, his personal choices to fill their critical positions. It is just as easy to forget that several of his appointments to the Supreme Court were extremely distinguished or that his elevation of Harlan Fiske Stone to the Chief Justiceship was, in the context of the times, an act of statesmanship. In the end, what impresses me most vividly about the men around Roosevelt is the number of flinty "no-sayers" who served him, loyally but not obsequiously, and the way in which he always remained "the boss." I think, in this regard, of Nathaniel Hawthorne's musing on Andrew Jackson, a President who was also thought to be inferior in intellect to the clever men surrounding him:

Surely he was a great man, and his native strength, as well of intellect as of character, compelled every man to be his tool that came within his reach; and the more cunning the individual might be, it served only to make him the sharper tool.

Roosevelt is already well on his way to enshrinement as folk hero, although, to be sure, he will have to double as folk devil for at least another generation. Those millions who still hate him lavishly may as well face the hard fact bravely that *Sunrise at Campobello* will be in the repertory of every amateur company, and that their great-grandchildren's children will read with affectionate interest of the bird walks on the Hudson, the manly training under Dr. Peabody, and the dogged triumph over crippling pain. Roosevelt's virtues and faults are either too well known or too bitterly contested for me to review in this short space, but I would like to point to several qualities that made him a man for posterity to remember: his buoyancy, which made it possible for him to love the job as no other President except the first Roosevelt had loved it; his breadth of vision, which in time of war gave him a clearer grasp of America's productive potential than the leaders of industry seemed to have themselves; his delight in danger, which made him a natural leader for a generation whose lot was, as a critic remarked, "one damned crisis after another—and with F.D.R. the damnedest crisis of all"; his sense of history, which invited him even before his inauguration to join the company of Presidents to whom monuments are raised long after their death; and his personal conservatism, which provided a solid base for his political liberalism and kept it from running beyond the aspirations of the American people. (To those who doubt the existence or influence of this last quality, I recommend a trip through the old house at Hyde Park.) Roosevelt will never, I am sure, be ranked with Washington and Lincoln, for there were touches of softness and mummery about him that will keep him from sainthood. If he was as busy as Rabbit and as bouncy as Tigger, he was too often, I fear, as big a bluffer as Owl.

Roosevelt's influence on the Presidency was tremendous. Only Washington, who made the office, and Jackson, who remade it, did more than he to raise it to its present condition of strength, dignity, and independence. I often wonder if Mr. Eisenhower ever paused during his period of apprenticeship to think how many of the powers and privileges he commanded, and how much of the respect and assistance he enjoyed, were a direct gift from Franklin Roosevelt. The press conference, the Executive Office, the right to reorganize the administration, and the powers to protect industrial and financial peace are all parts of Roosevelt's legacy to the modern President. Generals obey the President, Congress defers to him, and leaders of other nations honor him far more readily than they would if Roosevelt had not been so forceful a President. Like every such President, he left his successor in boiling water, and in at least one instance—the passage of the Twenty-second Amendment—the reaction to his high-riding incumbency was sufficiently angry to weaken the office permanently. Yet the verdict of history will surely be that he left the Presidency a more splendid instrument of democracy than he found it.

His influence on history is something for our descendants to assess. They will know firsthand, as we can only guess from afar, whether the two great "revolutions" he set in motion turned out to be blessings or curses for the American people. The first of these was the New Deal, which was essentially a decision to preserve American capitalism by invoking the positive power of the national government to support and stabilize the economy. Roosevelt, the master of public opinion, found the words to rationalize this vast readjustment in our ways of thinking and doing. He will long be remembered, fondly by some, contemptuously by others, for having read the word "security" into the American definition of "liberty."

The second great change took form in the coalition of warring powers and the plans for the United Nations, both of which involved a series of decisions aimed at plunging America permanently, for America's own sake, into world affairs. Roosevelt's skill with words was again equal to the high occasion, and men in every land will quote them for centuries to come. We must not forget that this record in war and diplomacy made him a giant figure in world as well as in American history. If we fail to honor him, other men will do it for us, as Winston Churchill honored him in the House of Commons:

> Of Roosevelt, however, it must be said that had he not acted when he did, in the way he did, had he not felt the generous surge of freedom in his heart, had he not resolved to give aid to Britain, and to Europe in the supreme crisis through which we have passed, a hideous fate might well have overwhelmed mankind and made its whole future for centuries sink into shame and ruin. It may well be that the man whom we honor today not only anticipated history, but altered its course, and altered it in a manner which has saved the freedom and earned the gratitude of the human race.

This has been much too simple a review of a complicated man and his turbulent times, but it would be capricious of me not to end by registering my opinion, to which I did not come easily, that Franklin Roosevelt is fixed firmly in the hierarchy of great Presidents a small step above Jackson and Wilson, a sizable step, which may grow smaller over the years, below Washington and Lincoln. He had his own rendezvous with history, and history will be kind to him.

Harry S Truman presents a much tougher case for objective evaluation than does Franklin D. Roosevelt. At times he had the look of greatness, at times he gave off the sound of meanness. But lest we prejudge him too easily and emotionally, let us subject him to our eight tests of presidential greatness. In so doing, I would recall my warning, which is especially pertinent to his amazing Presidency, that history is written, if not always made, by men of moderate views.

His times were not so laden with drama and hazard as those of Franklin Roosevelt, but they were at least as decisive for the American future as those of Jefferson and Wilson. He, too, has a head start for glory, a point that his most savage detractors must concede in his favor. In his two terms we passed through a whole series of nagging crises. We had decadence and destruction prophesied for us again and again. Yet on January 20, 1953, we stood before the world a free, prosperous, liberty-loving people with no more wounds and neuroses than we probably deserved. History may record that it was no mean achievement simply to have gone through the motions of being President in these eight years. This fact alone will surely elevate Mr. Truman above the Adamses and McKinley and quite probably above Polk and Cleveland.

The larger fact is that Harry Truman, once he had got the bearings that Roosevelt neglected to give him, did a great deal more than go through the motions of forwarding messages to Congress, greeting kings and Eagle Scouts, paying political debts, and saying "no comment" to the press. He studied, read, conferred, and dictated as long and hard as any President who ever lived, and he faced up to at least a dozen decisions that gave the world a hard shake. He, too, has a record of sins of commission and omission, especially in domestic affairs. In the former category, I would list his proposal to draft the railroad strikers in 1946 and his seizure of the steel industry in 1952, in the latter his offhand manner toward painful evidence of subversion, corruption, and shoddiness in high places. Yet these must certainly fade into obscurity before the dropping of the first atom bomb (and the second), the pursuit of nuclear research and production on a massive scale, the Truman Doctrine and the Berlin airlift, the Marshall Plan and the North Atlantic

Treaty Organization, and the decision to resist in Korea. Not one of his grave steps in foreign and military affairs, not even the fateful and controversial decision to use the atom bomb on live targets, has yet been proved wrong, stupid, or contrary to the best judgment and interests of the American people. He took all of them as the people expect their President to take such fateful steps: resolutely, solemnly, and hopefully. Truman rarely if ever had Roosevelt's sure touch of leadership, perhaps because he often appeared dizzy from the speed of his ride to the top, but there is small disposition among either his admirers or detractors to hold anyone but him responsible for his actions.

Truman came in time to an even more exalted view of the Presidency than did Roosevelt. His spacious understanding of its powers and obligations will surely impress posterity more than his disturbing lapses from decorum. Certainly no President ever spoke so grandly and yet humbly of his authority. Certainly no President ever gave a more imaginative and accurate description of his job:

> And people talk about the powers of a President, all the powers that a Chief Executive has, and what he can do. Let me tell you something—from experience!
>
> The President may have a great many powers given to him in the Constitution and may have certain powers under certain laws which are given to him by the Congress of the United States; but the principal power that the President has is to bring people in and try to persuade them to do what they ought to do without persuasion. That's what I spend most of my time doing. That's what the powers of the President amount to.

An entirely new theory of the Presidency can be spun out of that folksy statement, which Truman repeated with amusing variations on at least a dozen occasions.

If he did not always show himself sufficiently aware of the limitations of his office, it must be remembered that less impetuous men than he—Lincoln, Wilson, and Franklin D. Roosevelt—might also have considered themselves empowered to seize the steel mills in 1952. In any case, for all his alleged lack of learning and of disposition for pondering great truths, Mr. Truman demonstrated a more clear-cut philosophy of presidential power than any predecessor except Woodrow Wilson. The heaviest black mark against his reading of the Presidency, in my opinion, was his cavalier disregard of the sensibilities and prerogatives of Congress in the harsh debate of 1951 over the power to station troops in Europe. His failure to associate Congress more quickly and positively in the decision to fight the Korean war and his partisan seizure of the steel mills were hardly less censurable.

As a technician Truman had few equals in the long history of the Presidency. Most experienced students of public administration agree that he organized his time, which meant a seventy-hour week, and distributed his energies, which were legendary, with the sure touch of the professional. Yet he was not a professional at all, which is another way of saying that he learned his job on the job with astounding success. On several counts he is open to severe criticism: his methods of dealing with Congress were inexcusably irritating; he permitted raw politics to hold sway in areas to which it should have been rigidly denied entry; the moral tone of his administration unsettled even some of his most devoted admirers. Yet in the White House itself things were remarkably serene and efficient. The conjunction of cold war, which threw a hundred new burdens on an already overburdened office, and Mr. Truman, who learned to delegate his own authority as well as any President in this century, speeded and made secure the institutionalization of the American Presidency. To those around him he was the very model of a modern executive.

One final point might illustrate both his technical competence and his awareness of his responsibilities. At the very moment when his stature seemed at its lowest, when he seemed to many Americans to have surrendered all sense of dignity or authority, Mr. Truman did something that not a single President in history had cared to do: with efficient grace he transferred power and information to an incoming administration of the opposite political party. From this time forward, outgoing Presidents will be expected to assist incoming Presidents in the image of his high-minded co-operation with Dwight D. Eisenhower.

The roll call of those whom Truman enlisted in his staff and ranks runs the whole scale of virtue and talent from selfless greatness to dishonest incompetence. It has been suggested by some observers, and I am inclined to agree, that he made a more or less conscious deal with himself to insist upon non-partisan excellence in military and diplomatic affairs and to tolerate partisan mediocrity in domestic affairs. The names of Marshall, Lovett, Forrestal, Acheson, Bedell Smith, Hoffman, Bohlen, Symington, Foster, Bradley, Clay, Lewis Douglas, Kennan, Draper, Jessup, Harriman, Finletter, Patterson, McCloy—and of Eisenhower and Dulles—are proof enough that Truman mobilized even more talent than Roosevelt in the areas that touch upon survival. The names of McGrath, McGranery, Snyder, Caudle, and Sawyer should be enough to remind us that the rest of the nation's business was carried on with little distinction and much bumbling. To complete a group portrait that has General Marshall sitting on one side of the President and General Vaughan on the other, I think we may say with sorrowful conviction that Truman's appointments to the Supreme Court were about the least distinguished in history.

Harry S Truman is a man whom history will delight to remember. Those very lapses from dignity that made him an object of scorn to millions of Republicans—the angry letters, testy press conferences, whistle stops, impossible sport shirts, and early-morning seminars on the streets of dozens of American cities—open his door to immortality. It is a rare American, even a rare Republican, who can be scornful about a man one hundred years dead, and our descendants will be chuckling over his Missouri wit and wisdom long after the "five-per-centers" have been buried and forgotten. They will read with admiration of the upset he brought off in 1948, with awe of the firing of General MacArthur, and with a sense of kinship of the way he remained more genuinely "plain folks" than any other President. They will be moved by the simple dignity of his confession: "There are probably a million people in this country who could do the presidential job better than I, but I've got the job and I'm doing the very best I can." He was fascinating to watch, even when the sight hurt, and he will be fascinating to read about. The historians can be expected to do their share to fix him securely in history, for he provides a classic case study of one of their favorite themes: the President who grows in office.

Truman's influence on the Presidency can be summed up in the simple judgment that he was a highly successful Andrew Johnson. The Presidency had grown enough in Franklin Roosevelt's time to satisfy most Americans for at least another generation; it was his successor's high duty to see that the new tools of democratic leadership were not blunted or stolen by the forces of reaction. This duty Mr. Truman discharged with enthusiasm and success. He defended the integrity of the Presidency stoutly against the grand challenge of MacArthur and the sabotage of McCarthy, and even after his departure he defended it against the vulgar showmanship of Representative Velde, whose subpoena to appear before the House Committee on Un-American Activities in 1953 Truman thrust aside magisterially. Whatever damage he did to the office by intruding too one-sidedly into labor disputes or by insulting Congress gratuitously or by losing control of some of his subordinates was altogether temporary in effect. The office he handed over to Eisenhower was no less magnificent than the office he inherited from Roosevelt. Looked at in the light of what took place during the term of every other man who succeeded a great President

—John Adams, Madison, Van Buren, Johnson, Taft, and Harding—this may well appear as Truman's most remarkable achievement.

There appear to have been two great events in Truman's eight years for which he may be remembered as Madison or Grant or Taft or Hoover will never be remembered. One was domestic in character: the first real beginnings of a many-sided program toward eliminating discrimination and second-class citizenship in American life. The other was international: the irrevocable commitment of the American people to active co-operation with other nations in search of world peace and prosperity. Over neither of these vast beginnings did Mr. Truman exercise much control, yet to each he gave the full support of the Presidency. He will surely be remembered, and may yet be supremely honored, for the President's Committee on Civil Rights and the resulting message to Congress of February 2, 1948. He will as surely be remembered, and as possibly supremely honored, for his action in support of collective security against Communist aggression. It was a grand accomplishment in the total sweep of American history to take this nation into its first peacetime military alliance (NATO), to commit us for the first time to defend an area in which we had no obvious national interest (the Greek-Turkish program), to meet Communist force with force of our own making (Korea, 1950), and to call for a long-range constructive program that could open the gate to world peace (Point Four). The Marshall Plan is also credited to his account.

Mr. Truman often remarked that equal opportunity for all Americans and lasting peace for all men were the two consuming goals of his administration. The achievement of these goals (if we are blessed enough to achieve them) must inevitably add luster to his name. His uncompromising opponents are certain that both courses, civil rights and internationalism, will lead us to disaster. As Truman himself often reminded us, we must all wait for history to judge between him and Governor

Byrnes in the struggle for equal opportunity, and between him and Senator Bricker in the search for peace with freedom. My feeling is that he may wait with confidence.

On the basis of this evidence I am ready to hazard an opinion, to which I came, I confess manfully, with dragging feet, that Harry S Truman will eventually win a place as President alongside Jefferson and Theodore Roosevelt. There will be at least a half-dozen Presidents strung out below him who were more able and large-minded, but he had the good fortune to preside in stirring times and will reap large credit for having survived them. I cannot, in good conscience, predict the greatness of Washington, Lincoln, Franklin Roosevelt, Wilson, and Jackson for his name. Certain deficiencies of intellect and perception must always bar him from the seats of the mighty. We must remember that his consuming hobby has always been political and military history. He knew that there was a game called "Ranking the Presidents"; he confessed repeatedly, and with a candor that embarrassed his listeners, that he was an accident of history who did not belong on the ladder at all. Despite or because of this harsh self-appraisal, he made a determined effort to climb the ladder by imitating the well-remembered Presidents of the past and by acting beyond his gifts. As he himself put it, "I may not have been one of the great Presidents, but I had a good time trying to be."

Harry S Truman will be a well-remembered President because he proved that an ordinary man could fill the world's most extraordinary office with devotion and high purpose. He may serve as a lasting symbol of the noble truth that gives strength and meaning to the American experiment: plain men *can* govern themselves; democracy *does* work. And his epitaph will read: He was distressingly petty in petty things; he was gallantly big in big things.

I feel bound to preface my prediction of Dwight D. Eisenhower's standing among all the Presidents by confessing to a downward shift of opinion between the first and second editions of this book.* I now foresee, not the least bit happily, a somewhat lower ranking for the third of our modern Presidents than I had anticipated in 1956. At that time I wrote in conclusion to my assessment: "Eisenhower already stands above Polk and Cleveland, and he has a reasonable chance to move up to Jefferson and Theodore Roosevelt. To label this President another Grant is merely absurd. We shall all say a lot of silly things for or against Eisenhower before this campaign is over, but we really should let General Grant rest in peace."

General Grant, I think, may continue to rest in peace; General Eisenhower will surely be placed well above him by our descendants. Just how far above him is a guess I will hazard only at the end of these remarks, limiting myself to the preliminary observation that he fumbled away that "reasonable chance" early in his second term, and that I now expect him to be left outside the magic circle of presidential greatness. It is, of course, an act of temerity if not folly to attempt the long view of a man with whom we have all lived, so to speak, in daily intimacy. Still, this is a game that is fun to play even on a muddy field and a murky day, and so let us ask our eight questions about Dwight D. Eisenhower—the President, not the General.

His times were certainly less exacting than those of Roosevelt and Truman. They were difficult, to be sure, but they were not perilous, and it is out of peril that men have risen to glory in the American Presidency during the twentieth century. I think it important to make a distinction, which I will make at several points in this survey, between the first and

* Although this assessment was written at the end of Eisenhower's seventh year, it is pitched in a style and tense more appropriate to a final reckoning. I have done this for the sake of art, objectivity, and convenience—and in full recognition of the fact that I have taken something of a gamble on the President's performance in his eighth year. I have followed the same practice throughout the book, most noticeably in my discussion of Vice-President Nixon on pages 137-140.

second terms of Eisenhower's Presidency. The first was, almost by definition, a time in which a President could win gratitude but not immortality. For all his bold talk as a candidate in 1952 about a "crusade," we knew (and if we did not know it in 1952, we knew it by 1953) that his mission was to bring us peace at home and abroad, even at the price of a future reckoning. We were weary of reform in the one area and of adventure in the other, and we elected a President who would give us a breathing spell from both without taking us back over the ground we had already covered. We got that spell, and we can be thankful that we did. Mr. Eisenhower would be the last man to complain of the price he paid in the coin of a diminished reputation in the annals of history. Not only was he elected in a time of conservatism; he elected to be a conservative President, and I doubt that he knew or cared that history finds it hard to rise in wild acclaim of such a President in such a time.

In his second term events began to move a little faster, but the crisis of our age is still more impending than real. Things at home and abroad are going to get a lot worse before they get a lot better, but it would be hard to convince most Americans, including President Eisenhower, that this is the true nature of our present discontents. We are still basking in the luxury of catching our breath. The most strong-minded and adventurous of Presidents would have had trouble stirring us to actions that do more than hold the line, and Mr. Eisenhower was certainly never that kind of President. In short, he was not cut off completely from greatness by the nature of his times and mission, but he, like Theodore Roosevelt, was asked to travel farther and faster in search of it. As a gradualist in a time of gradualism, an earth-smoother rather than an earth-shaker, he never really put his heart in the attempt. He had very little sense of history to begin with; and even if he had had it to the full measure of Harry S Truman, he was too modest to do an imitation of Jackson and Lincoln. I think it both cruel and crude to describe the Eisenhower years as a time in which "the bland led the bland," but I also think it absurd to acclaim them as a time in which a crusader led a crusade.

President Eisenhower's manner of meeting his responsibilities at home and abroad was that of the moderate conservative he repeatedly professed to be. To his credit are the measures against recession in 1954, the improved administration of the defense budget, the initiation of a major program of highway construction, the modest efforts in behalf of civil rights, and such sporadic displays of executive independence as the angry veto of the natural-gas bill in 1956 and the rejection of congressional attempts to remake his Cabinet. To his debit are the blunder of Dixon-Yates, the injustices and inanities of the loyalty-security program (more apparent in his first term than in his second), the miscalculation of the public interest in the broad fields of conservation and regulation, the untidy handling of the government's obligations in the polio vaccine fiasco, the unprecedented refusal to support his own budget in 1957, and all the starts and stops and wrong turns in pursuit of his promise to get the farm problem into manageable shape. In the unceasing campaign against corruption in high places, Eisenhower was largely content to govern by setting a tone for others to match as best they could, and by cutting a man loose when he had made too unpleasant a mess, something he rarely did with either grace or candor. The departures into limbo of Edmund F. Mansure, Harold E. Talbott, and above all Sherman Adams did nothing to enhance the President's reputation for either political finesse or administrative command. I must leave it to each reader to decide for himself whether Eisenhower handled the challenge of Senator McCarthy in a manner consistent with his position as President. I limit myself to the double-barreled observation that the Senator was a badly beaten man long before his death in 1957, and that Eisenhower may well have done all that he could do (within the limits of dignity he had imposed upon himself) to help administer the beating.

All these pluses and minuses are likely to fade into insignificance, however, in the harsh light of Mr. Eisenhower's two most apparent failures to focus his unique prestige upon domestic problems: his abdication of both moral and political leadership in the crisis of integration in the South, and his refusal to push steadily for solutions to the crisis of education throughout the Union. In each of these situations, which deteriorated visibly during his years in office, his pattern of action was one of long periods of drift punctuated by sharp bursts of anger, a pattern hardly calculated to persuade the recalcitrants in Little Rock or in the House of Representatives to take even the first step into a future that must surely come. The temper of the times, the folkways of the people, and the hostility of some of the nation's most vested interests were all ranged against him in his appeals for peaceful schools in the South and adequate schools everywhere, yet he fought back, when he fought at all, with only a fraction of his powers. Worse than that, he too often talked more boldly than he was prepared to act. As James Reston put it, "Both in golf and in politics, his backswing has always been better than his follow-through." Other Presidents have failed in such matters as these and been pardoned by history, but this President, I fear, may be dealt with much more harshly by a posterity that, God willing, will have made a reality of our present hopes. It was not so much that he failed to catch the right vision of the future, but that he was unwilling to draw steadily on his overflowing reservoir of popularity to get us moving in the direction of the vision. Historians will be reluctant to accord the judgment of greatness to a President who kept so much of his immense influence in reserve. To put the matter another way, no President in history was ever more powerfully armed to persuade the minds of men to face up to the inevitable—and then failed more poignantly to use his power.

In foreign affairs Mr. Eisenhower was, on his own terms, a successful President, thanks largely, we can agree, to a Secretary of State with no superior in history for courage and devotion to duty. For a man who had been around as long as he had in the hot spots of diplomacy, Eisenhower got off the mark like a lead-footed amateur. But he rallied quickly, especially after the armistice in Korea, and no one can deny that we have all come a long way back from the degrading days when Cohn and Schine roamed Europe and the image of a free America was tarnished in the eyes of even our most steadfast and forgiving friends. The President gave us as satisfactory a peace as we could possibly have expected in Korea; he kept us from being bogged down in the morass of French colonialism; and he took the lead—not a bold lead, but at least a prudent one—in bringing the atom to the service of all mankind. We went once to the Summit at Geneva and heard our President speak for peace with honor as only he could do; we went twice to the wall at Quemoy and roused to his refusal to give way meekly to the blackmail of force. Few will deny that he acted with prudent resolution in his successful effort to save the legitimate government of Lebanon from subversion in 1958. He had his failures, in Cairo and Caracas and Congress, but even the most alert and purposeful President will have his fair share of failures from now on. Success in diplomacy must be judged in the perspective of the long years, and it is altogether possible that Eisenhower —and the battle-scarred Secretary of State who gave him the best six years of his own life—may eventually be given credit for a successful performance. (I doubt, however, that any sizable part of his success will be attributed to the Grand Tours of 1959. Grand Tours of our Presidents are exciting to follow, to be sure; but, as Woodrow Wilson proved a full forty years ago, they are no substitute for tough diplomacy.)

Yet he was a success, I repeat, on his own terms, and they were never the terms of creative greatness. If he is remembered by history for his feats of diplomacy, it will be as the President who "kept the shop," faithfully but unimaginatively, which was set up before him by Harry S Truman in pursuit of the general directions of Franklin D. Roosevelt. I cannot think of a single

major departure in the course of Eisenhower's stewardship from
the new line of diplomacy that was first laid out in the Truman
Doctrine, the Marshall Plan, the Reciprocal Trade Acts, the
Point Four program, and our simultaneous commitment to
NATO and the United Nations; and I take wry comfort in the
knowledge that neither the Chicago *Tribune* nor the *Nation* can
think of one either. If history finally decides that this was the
line to take, the President will be remembered for having carried it forward dutifully. If history decides that it was a mistake
from the beginning, he may suffer even more than the men who
launched us upon it. By 1958 we knew far better than we did
in 1948 the price we might have to pay for collective security
against Soviet designs.

Taken all in all, Mr. Eisenhower's performance in the Presidency was not the kind that will bring posterity to its feet in
waves of applause. Indeed, if we put his performance to the
three tests of leadership I mentioned on page 143, we are bound
to say that he never did measure up to the lofty expectations
of the American people—expectations, alas for him, that no
President could have satisfied. We called upon him to lead
Congress, but he simply could not bring himself to dish out
steadily those plums to the good boys and spanks to the bad
that do more than a thousand speeches to influence the legislative process. The kind of decisive influence he exerted in behalf of labor-reform legislation in 1959 was only rarely brought
to bear in the course of his presidential career. It may be said
in his defense that he had to face a Democratic majority in
Congress for fully three-fourths of his tenure, but this defense
collapses before the notorious fact that his prerogatives as
President were more carefully respected by Senators Johnson,
Russell, George, and Green than they were by Senators Knowland, Taft, Bricker, and McCarthy, and before the related fact
that most points in his programs were at least as appealing to
the opposition as to his own party.

He was not much more determined a leader of the administration. If moral exhortation (at which Mr. Eisenhower was admittedly a genius) is not enough to goad Congress into action, it is even less effective as an ingredient of presidential leadership of the makers and executors of policy in the federal administration, and in this area, too, he was a disappointment to those who thought of him as another Jackson. No President could have had a more eager and devoted team (with a few glaring exceptions like Scott McLeod), and no team could have been more consistently befuddled about the coach's plans to move the ball. Mr. Dulles knew the President was all for peace, but he could never be sure what price the President was willing to pay for peace at each of the major trouble spots around the world. Mr. Rogers knew the President was all for brotherhood, but he never got the kind of support he had a right to expect in Little Rock and Atlanta and Montgomery. Mr. Brundage handed the President a "modern Republican" budget to lay before Congress in 1957, but he found out to his surprise (or was he surprised?) that Mr. Humphrey had another kind of budget in mind. The plain truth is that Mr. Eisenhower was not especially interested in either the purposes or mechanics of most parts of the federal administration, and the first requisite of a successful administrator at the top of the pyramid is, surely, an unforced interest in what goes on below.

Finally, history will very likely judge Mr. Eisenhower's leadership of the American people to have been most disappointing of all. No man ever got a more astounding show of support in the one popularity poll that counts—a margin of 6.5 million in 1952 and of 9.5 million in 1956—and no man since Harding (another big winner) had less success in exchanging this popularity for the hard currency of influence. By running more than seven million votes ahead of his party in 1956 he scored a personal triumph without parallel in American history, but this feat could also be looked at as a shocking default of political leadership. It was the first time in more than a hundred years that a President had gained re-election and his party had failed to capture control of Congress. Future historians may have trouble understanding how a President could persuade so many Americans to vote for him but not for his party. They are sure to have a field day accounting for his failure to live up to the popular image of an iron-willed leader, but they are all likely to agree on the first and greatest reason: that he could not lead because he would not lead.

A dozen factors militated against a steady display of Jacksonian leadership in these years, but the most important factor of all, we must acknowledge regretfully, was Mr. Eisenhower's inability or unwillingness (they are really the same thing) to "work hard at being President." I could drag up a score of examples of his refusal to apply himself eagerly and consistently to the job at hand, but one should suffice to make the point: his general inaccessibility to individual members of Congress. It is astounding to note that those Congressmen who seem to have had the hardest time getting in to see him were his most zealous supporters. If any Senator can beat Clifford Case's record for cooling his heels at the White House door, I have not heard of him. Not all Congressmen are as loyal and forgiving as Senator Case, and a good part of the blame for Mr. Eisenhower's indifferent leadership of Congress can be laid to his refusal to cultivate the garden personally. There are limits to the practice of personal leadership in this and the other areas in which the President must set men into creative motion, but Mr. Eisenhower, it now seems plain, never even approached these limits for more than a few short periods in his years in the Presidency, notably the opening months of 1954 and 1959. The eagerness with which most Washington correspondents and Republican politicians seized upon and paraded each scrap of evidence of a "new Ike" (or, more exactly, of the "old Ike") is evidence itself that the President rarely operated under a full head of steam. By 1959 he was getting extravagant praise for sporadic displays of the sort of leadership that Wilson and the Roosevelts offered throughout their careers.

One clearly established reason for this refusal to play the strong leader day in and day out was Eisenhower's modest conception of the authority of the Presidency. He came to the office with practically no thoughts of his own about its powers and purposes. He came, moreover, as a Republican, and therefore committed to the Whig theory of a partnership between President and Congress in which the latter sets the nation's goals without much help from the former. He had swallowed a good deal of the propaganda directed at Roosevelt and Truman, and the result was a first year in office during which his view of his powers was not much different from that announced long ago by William Howard Taft. In the late fall of 1953 he began to broaden this view considerably. His matured theory of the Presidency should not be confused with that of Taft or even Hoover, for he proved himself on several occasions to be a staunch defender of the independence of the executive. But it also should not be confused with that of Lincoln or even Washington, the two Presidents he is said to have considered his favorites, for he never really saw himself, neither in his proudest moments nor in his most humble, as the steady focus of the American system of government. Nothing is more revealing of this modest philosophy than his request early in 1955 for authority to defend Formosa and the Pescadores, a request repeated in 1957 for similar authority in the Middle East. It is obvious that Eisenhower, quite unlike Truman, considered the President to be under stern moral obligation to ask approval of Congress—certainly when there is time to ask it—for the use of powers in the twilight zone between them. Stern morality, needless to say, may also be good politics in situations like these. Speaker Rayburn, it should be noted, took the lead among those who wondered aloud if these two requests would not cripple the striking power of the Presidency in a sudden crisis, but the point seemed to trouble Mr. Eisenhower not at all. In any case, he was much less impressed with the authority of the Presidency than were his Democratic predecessors, and if this, too, was a brake on his progress toward the stature of a great President, he did not appear to be overly worried. He may well have thought that posterity was for once ready to salute a President who saw no threat to his own position in being polite to Congress.

Eisenhower's competence as a technician is a subject of hot dispute. His supporters insist that he moved beyond Roosevelt and Truman in distributing the routine burdens of the Presidency efficiently among an industrious and loyal team. His critics reply that he learned the lesson of his army days much too thoroughly, for he delegated not only the use but the control of some of his highest prerogatives and lost his freedom of maneuver to an outsized, self-directing staff. From the very beginning, they say, he reigned too much and ruled too little; indeed, the "Eisenhower regency" began to function long before September 24, 1955.

The truth, I think, rests just about in the middle of the extreme claims of his friends and his foes. The Presidency was at least as efficiently organized as it was in the best days of Harry Truman, and by delegating responsibility on a broad and imaginative scale the President himself gained more hours for his own use than either of his predecessors enjoyed. Far more important in the light of history, his plans and methods—and a touch of Eisenhower luck—made it possible on three occasions for the Presidency to run for weeks almost without a President and almost without a hitch. At the same time, it can hardly be denied that Mr. Eisenhower came much closer than did either of the other two modern Presidents to becoming a prisoner in his own overorganized house—a house in which his press secretary often said "we" when he meant "the President," in which Sherman Adams ruled for several years as an autocrat who seemed to know the workings of the Presidency far better than the President himself, and in which "the White House" took on the dimensions of an independent center of power, most notably in the dumping of Joseph W.

Martin from his position as minority leader in the House in 1959.
I shall have something to say in my last chapter of the dangers to
the Presidency that lurk in the growing pattern of institutionalization, but I must say now that I had President Eisenhower specifically in mind when I wrote the words of caution that appear on
pages 243-244. There are many levelheaded students of the Presidency who think of him as a man who was spared, who allowed himself to be spared, a little too much of the suffering
and glory of democratic leadership. I myself would still think
that the main fire of his critics should be directed against the
use he made of all those extra hours which Governor Adams
and General Persons gave him, although some might also
be directed against his too ready reliance on his own team for
information and advice. He should have tried a little harder
to keep the back door open to callers of his own choosing,
and he should have devoted a few more of those pleasant
evening hours to reading the newspapers, especially the ones
that criticized him. Be all that as it may, he did himself and
the Presidency a great service by carrying the process of institutionalization at least a step and a half farther than Truman.
If he went too far in surrendering control of some of his powers,
the next President should have no trouble recovering it.

The men around Eisenhower, like the men around Roosevelt and Truman, presented a composite picture of all the
virtues and most of the faults (if not the sins) of public life.
In these years of gradualism there was a clear reduction in
vision and daring and humor among the men who ran the
country, but there was also a clear expansion in probity and
frugality and attention to the business at hand. In the still of
the night and with the eye of his mind Mr. Eisenhower must
have often looked back sheepishly to his campaign promise of
1952 to mobilize "the best brains of America," for it is one
promise he did not even come close to keeping, even on his
own terms. Yet how could he, a career soldier, have known
that his freedom of choice would be narrowed so drastically

by Republican politics and American folkways? Not only was
he pledged in ways he could barely understand to concentrate
on "jobs for the boys" rather than "boys for the jobs"; his, after
all, was a businessman's government, and businessmen are
understandably more reluctant than, let us say, professors to
drop everything and rush to their President's call. It seems
plain that Eisenhower will not be especially remembered for
the talents he assembled about him. He was clearly more successful in finding the right men for his immediate staff than
for the great offices of state. James C. Hagerty, Arthur Burns,
Gabriel Hauge, Gerald D. Morgan, Robert E. Merriam, Bernard M. Shanley, General Goodpaster, General Persons, Roger
Jones, Robert Cutler, and, yes, the unlamented Sherman Adams
were a far better team in their league than the department
heads were in theirs. Of the nineteen men and one woman who
headed the executive departments, a good deal less than one-
third, notably John Foster Dulles, Marion Folsom, James P.
Mitchell, and William P. Rogers, turned in first-class performances, and a roughly equal number, notably Charles E.
Wilson and Mrs. Hobby, were unrelieved disasters. In the
offices that really count—the Secretaryships of State, Defense,
and Treasury, the positions on the Joint Chiefs of Staff, the
chairmanship of the Atomic Energy Commission, and the key
embassies—Mr. Eisenhower was content, indeed seemed well
content, with a team that will never, I am certain, be mentioned
in the same breath with that wonderful band of stalwarts who
helped see Lincoln through to glory: Seward, Chase, Stanton,
Welles, Charles Francis Adams, Sherman, and Grant. Only
Secretary Dulles may have been in their class, but that is a
judgment I prefer to leave to the future. For only the future
can tell whether his obdurate but not fanatical anti-Communism
was the correct policy for our times, and whether his fame
will therefore prosper. If it does, it will very possibly be at
the expense of the fame of that President for whom Dulles
ran the diplomatic show as no Secretary of State had run it for

generations, certainly not for any President with a claim to distinction. The amazing relationship between Eisenhower and Dulles brought far more credit to the servant than it did to the master, and in this relationship future historians may very well find conclusive evidence of Eisenhower's refusal to make his own rendezvous with history. An important bit of the evidence in this matter will be the apparent shift in our policy toward the U.S.S.R. that followed the death of Mr. Dulles. One is bound to ask whether the Khrushchev visit would have taken place if Dulles had been alive and healthy—and bound to answer that it is not very likely. Who, then, we must go on to ask, was the effective molder of our foreign policy between 1953 and 1959?

One final point can be made emphatically in Eisenhower's favor: his appointments to the Supreme Court were vastly superior to Truman's. Indeed, I think it altogether possible that the future may salute him as the unwitting and perhaps unwanting molder of one of the great Courts in American history. Mr. Eisenhower did his work; the rest is up to Chief Justice Warren and his colleagues.

About the man himself there is nothing to say that has not been said a thousand times, except that despite his unique hold on the people of this country, or perhaps because of it, he is less likely than Roosevelt to project his personality forcefully on the consciousness of history. A President who is adored by a little more than half the people and despised by the rest is a more probable candidate for immortality than a President who is liked by all those in the center, which means most Americans, and disliked only by those on the fringes. The very qualities of decency and affability that made him exactly the man the American people wanted at a restful stage in their pilgrimage may be woven by time into a curtain of indifference that will hang darkly between our posterity and our most popular President. He aroused his fair share of enthusiasm but not of anger, and I can think of no memorable President after Washington who did not arouse both to a pronounced degree. (Washington aroused pure awe, but that is a feeling in which, for better or worse, modern men do not indulge.)

President Eisenhower's public character was not above criticism. He was a dogged anti-intellectual in an age when intellect alone stands between us and annihilation, a man of hot temper who boiled over at the wrong times and for the wrong reasons, a rather poor judge of the qualities of mind and heart that are needed in high places. Even his admirers were troubled by the gap that often yawned between what the President said and what he did about reducing tariffs or protecting our natural heritage or playing fair with those accused of disloyalty or educating the white South in the ways of tolerance. Yet it cannot be doubted that his character, like his life, was an amazingly accurate projection of much of what is best in the American dream. He had been a small-town boy with a job in the local dairy, a West Point halfback with a trick knee, a soldier who stood close to Marshall and MacArthur, a commander with a genius for molding diverse spirits into a fighting force, a grandfather with a small but active crew of appealing descendants, a man known to swear because he missed a two-foot putt. He was manly, brave, charming, honest, capable, friendly, fair-minded, and incredibly lucky—and who, except for the Muse who keeps the rolls of true greatness, could have asked for anything more?

Eisenhower's influence on the Presidency passed through three fairly distinct stages. During his first year it often seemed that his incumbency would prove a disaster for the office. It was not so much his unwillingness to exercise his legitimate prerogatives that troubled students of the Presidency, but rather his indifference to an unruly Congress celebrating the end of twenty years of "executive encroachment" with some encroachments of its own. Sometime in 1953 Eisenhower came to a clearer understanding of the modern Presidency, and for the next two years he was, if not a "strong" President, certainly a firm one. The manner of his tenure throughout those most vigorous of his years was, in point of historical fact, a huge blessing for the office, for in his own quiet way he introduced many of the precedents of Roosevelt and Truman, about which the touch of crisis or partisanship still lingered, into the normal pattern of the Presidency. To put the matter another way, the Presidency called loudly for a Republican in 1952, for not until the Republicans had learned by experience that Whiggery was obsolete could the modernization of the Presidency be considered complete. Eisenhower proved himself a strong enough President to hold the line that his predecessors had staked out, but not too strong to lose touch with the Whigs in his party and thus miss a wonderful chance to educate them. We may go beyond this general observation to give him credit for these specific actions: his decisive opposition to the Bricker Amendment, his efforts to save the Cabinet from further decline, his reinvigoration of the National Security Council, his further refinement of the press conference, his personal solution to the problem of disability (of which more in Chapter 7), and his gallant attempt to do something with the Vice-President if not with the Vice-Presidency. All in all, it was a long journey uphill from 1953 and his needless surrenders to "the courtesy of the Senate" to 1955 and his bold announcement that he would ignore a provision of an act he had just signed—because he, the President, thought the provision unconstitutional.

The three successive illnesses of 1955 and 1956 ushered in the third stage of Mr. Eisenhower's influence on the Presidency. He never forgot the painful lessons of 1953, and he kept the power and prestige of the office intact against the forces in Congress and country that wanted to "cut the President down to size." If he reduced the effectiveness of the Presidency itself, it was only because he let his staff bear more than its proper share of his political burden. The "White House," I repeat, took over a little too much of "the Presidency" in Mr.

Eisenhower's second term. But that, I insist, is an imbalance that his successors should be able to correct with no difficulty. Mr. Eisenhower once told his Cabinet, according to Robert Donovan, that he did not want to "become known as a President who had practically crippled the Presidency," and certainly he need have no fears on this score. His new show of vigor in 1959, which was not entirely a figment of the wishful imaginations of Henry Luce and Arthur Krock, was a genuine boon to the Presidency. Indeed, historians may record, although I remain somewhat doubtful, that Eisenhower's last two years—the years without Humphrey, Dulles, and Adams—were a fourth and generally more successful stage in his presidential career.

To speak of Eisenhower's influence on history is to soar on wings of brass into the realms of fantasy. History plays malicious tricks, especially on historians with a penchant for prophecy, and I am well aware that before I am gathered to my fathers I may have to eat all these words without benefit of spice or sauce. But having come this far I cannot turn back, and so I make bold to predict that Mr. Eisenhower will finally be judged to have been a faithful if not farsighted son of his own time; and the time, as I said before, was the kind in which a President could win gratitude but not immortality.

His total performance in the Presidency will be assessed, I think, at two levels, which even now seem to match up fairly closely with his two terms. At the first level, that is to say, in his first term, he gave us just about the most satisfactory dose of conservatism we have taken since the administration of Rutherford B. Hayes—or would it be John Quincy Adams? He not only kept the shop but put it back in order; he not only offered us a rest but made us take it. He "widened the vital center" so steadily that the American people enjoyed a climate of unity that they had not known for thirty years or more. Mr. Eisenhower did all this largely through his leadership of that difficult but essential minority, the Republican party. He did not succeed as much as he might have liked in remolding it in his own image of moderate conservatism, but he did persuade most of its leaders to follow him into the twentieth century. By a route that often seemed much too circuitous but had a final logic of its own, he brought the Republican party, and with it the business community, very near to accepting once and for all the ground rules of the New Economy and the burdens of the New Internationalism. He did a job the American people wanted to have done—not an exciting job, to be sure, but one for which history, too, had been calling— and history ought to make a special effort to remember him for it. I cannot emphasize too strongly that it usually prefers to ignore the President who promises peace rather than prog- ress. Yet Eisenhower's conservatism was obviously of a newer and higher order than that of McKinley or Taft or Coolidge, and it is possible that he may be richly honored for it. It is possible, too, that the credentials of presidential greatness may be revised in the next generation to permit an occasional earth-smoother to sit in glory with the earth-shakers. Knowing what I do of history and historians and, for that matter, of the American people, I doubt it strongly, but for a man like Mr. Eisenhower the knowledge of a job well done is a reward more precious than any premonition of immortality.

By 1957, I would think, we had had our fill of moderate conservatism. Even as most of us went on catching our own breaths, we began to feel the breaths of countless others upon us—of Soviet scientists and Chinese steelmakers, of angry Latins and even angrier Virginians, of American men unable to find work in a booming economy. The times had begun to run ahead of our will and imagination, and they called for a leader who would rouse us from the lethargy of "fat-dripping prosperity" and point out the hard road we would have to travel into a demanding future. Mr. Eisenhower, I repeat, was not that kind of leader. The temper of the times was against him, and so were many circumstances—the nature of his

mandate, the division in the ranks of his party, the new constitutional provision that rendered him a "lame duck" at the very
moment of his smashing re-election, the three illnesses in a
row, the general loss of vigor. But most serious of all as a
factor in a performance that failed to shake history was his
whole approach to life—his character, his methods, his cast of
mind. His character was that of the peacemaker, the man who
wants to like everyone and wants everyone to like him. "Eisenhower's personal inclination," James Reston has written, "always has been to try to talk and conciliate. It was the talker
and the conciliator in him that brought him to the pinnacle of
American public life in the first place." It would have been
a far different Eisenhower who could have acted consistently
on the memorable advice of Herbert Bayard Swope: "I don't
have a formula for success, but I know the sure formula for
failure; try to please everybody." His methods were those of
a man with a distaste for aggressive politics and a horror of
administrative detail. "He has never been willing," Walter
Lippmann has written, "to break the eggs that are needed for
the omelet." His cast of mind was of the genuine conservative. He seems to have been made aware of the magnitude
of the impending crisis, but he acted, however bravely he
may have talked from time to time, like a man who preferred to let problems solve themselves. Unfortunately for
his future reputation, he was President in the age in which it
finally came home to most Americans that the problems of
the modern world are of a different order of nastiness and
urgency. It would have been enough for him to have pointed
them out with a harsh finger, as did Theodore Roosevelt in his
last two years, or to have chalked up a gallant failure in a
premature effort to solve one of them, as did Woodrow Wilson.
But the best he could do in the years in which we first reached
into space—and found the Russians there to greet us—was to
talk like a Coolidge of a balanced budget and a reduction in
taxes. If we find a new road to peace, if we make a mockery of

Khrushchev's promise to "bury" us, if we win new opportunity and respect for the Negro, if we get control of the population explosion, if we win something more than cheap glory in our explorations in space, it will not, alas, be thanks to him. He will be remembered, I fear, as the unadventurous President who held on one term too long in the new age of adventure. Like Washington, he was already a legend when he entered the White House, and it helped to make him the best Chief of State since our very first President. Unlike him, he gained no added luster from his service as President. I make bold to predict that the historians of a century hence, and the people who learn from them, will rank him outside the first eight, even outside the first ten of the Presidents who went before him. He was a good President, but far from a great one. If our descendants judge him finally to have been a truly great man, it will be the General rather than the President who has taken their fancy.

It may appear to some of my readers that I have been too hard on Eisenhower and too easy on Truman. To this indictment I return two pleas: First, I have tended to be more negative in the case of Eisenhower and more positive in the case of Truman because popular opinion appears to hold exactly the reverse of my predictions. And second, I have tried to anticipate the judgments of posterity with all the objectivity I can command. In so doing I have surprised even myself, and I trust that my readers will give me credit for having risen at least a few feet above my own political prejudices. I must come back in the end to take refuge in the simple truth that popularity in one age does not guarantee fame in another. The examples of Truman and Eisenhower may conspire to prove that the combative, unpopular President is the fellow with the head start to glory. I am left with the prickly suspicion that history, after all, is wiser than the people.

It would seem useful to conclude by drawing a few impersonal lessons from this exercise in personality. I propose, therefore,

with only the barest comment, to list certain qualities that a
man must have or cultivate if he is to be an effective modern
President. In this instance I am more concerned with success
than with greatness, with the needs of our contemporaries than
with the judgments of our descendants. This is not a catalogue
of every habit and talent we should hope for in our President.
Like most Americans, I should be delighted if he would practice, faithfully but not self-righteously, all those virtues celebrated in the New Testament, *The Compleat Gentlemen, The
Way to Wealth,* and the handbook of the Boy Scouts of
America. It can go without my saying that we like our President to be brave, clean, kind, industrious, frugal, and honest.
My list of stocks is short, but each item on it pays rich divi-
dends:

Bounce: Not only must the President be healthy, in the sense
of freedom from ailments; he must have that extra elasticity,
given to few men, which makes it possible for him to thrive
on the toughest diet of work and responsibility in the world.
This quality, I would suppose, is to be found in full measure
only in those Presidents who really enjoy themselves in the
White House, who welcome the challenges of the office as
delightedly as they do the privileges. Franklin Roosevelt learned
at first hand about the importance of being bouncy. As a small
boy he had stood before Grover Cleveland, who hoped out loud
that he would never be so unfortunate as to grow up and become President. As a young man he had heard someone ask
his cousin Theodore what kind of time he was having in the
White House, whereupon the Colonel replied with a roar,
"Ripping, simply ripping!" I leave it to my readers to decide
what sound moral the second Roosevelt drew from this experience.

Affability: The President's heart must be not only stout but
warm. He must care deeply about people in the flesh, show
an unfeigned interest in everything from dogs to the Dodgers,
be willing to live his private life publicly, and have the sure

instincts of the democrat. The Presidency is a people's office, and there is no room in it now for a man with ice in his veins.

Political skill: We used to hear a lot of wailing about men who were "too high-minded ever to be nominated and elected" but who none the less "would make excellent Presidents." If this was ever true, it is true no longer. The man who lacks the little arts to be elected President lacks the little arts to be President. How can he persuade people to do "what they ought to do without persuasion" if he cannot persuade them first of all to give him the job?

Cunning: We do not openly admire this quality, and too much of it can destroy the most dedicated man. Yet a President cannot get the best out of the dozens of able figures around him or keep them under his command unless he is a master in the delicate art of manipulating men.

A sense of history: This cast of mind raises him above all those around him, sobering yet exalting him with the thought that he sits in Lincoln's seat. No man or combination of men can match his power to influence history, and his grasp of this stark truth can save him from going astray into the fields of petty strife. It can save him, too, when he must act arbitrarily, from the backlash of opinion. There is practically nothing a President may decide to do in a moment of crisis that Washington or Jackson or Lincoln, or often Harding and Coolidge, did not already do in a similar spot.

The newspaper habit: The modern President must be on guard lest he be cut off from harsh reality. He needs badly to know what people are thinking about events and about his handling of them. If he values his independence, he must have clear channels to the outside, and there is no substitute —certainly not a one-page digest of news and opinion prepared by his own secretaries—for a front page of the New York *Times* or the Chicago *Tribune,* an editorial in the St. Louis *Post-Dispatch* or the New York *Daily News,* a cartoon by Herblock or Fitzpatrick, a column by Alsop or Pearson, or a magisterial lecture on the Constitution by Lippmann or Krock. An occasional half-hour in the appendix of the *Congressional Record* is another experience no President should miss.

A sense of humor: If he reads the *Record* and the *Tribune* at all faithfully, he will need a thick skin and a light heart. At least two recent Presidents have testified convincingly that they could not have survived in office if they had been unable to laugh at the world and themselves. It is remarkable how many of our admitted failures in the Presidency were men who could not chuckle at an unfriendly cartoon, much less frame the original for hanging in the President's study—a happy practice engaged in by several of our admitted successes.

Any one of these habits or talents can be a snare to a President who turns to it too often and confidently, but so, too, can almost every virtue in the American catalogue. The most we can hope for is a man who blends self-confidence and self-restraint in the balanced attitude that all our successful Presidents have struck. In the end, perhaps, it is essential (if far from enough) for him simply to look the part. Woodrow Wilson took hold of a momentous truth when he remarked in awe: "The office is so much greater than any man could honestly imagine himself to be that the most he can do is look grave enough and self-possessed enough to seem to fill it."

CHAPTER **6**

THE HIRING OF PRESIDENTS

The air of satisfaction with which most Americans gaze upon the Presidency turns suddenly chilly when they shift their attentions to the patched-up machinery for nominating and electing a man to fill it, even chillier when they look around and fail to find any machinery at all with which to replace a President who has lost the physical or mental capacity to govern. The problem of choosing an able President is one about which we have been disturbed almost without rest since the election of 1796; the problem of removing or sequestering a disabled President is one about which we have got heated up only occasionally, that is, on every occasion a President has appeared to be disabled. Popular unrest with the whole question of the selection and tenure of Presidents has reached a new peak in the years since World War II; almost every week of every session of Congress some member (as often as not a would-be President) rises to propose an amendment to the Constitution that would spare us the real or imagined horrors of a minority President or a sick President or no President at all.

In the next two chapters I intend to take serious note of this unrest, in particular to judge whether it is justified by the realities and probabilities of American politics. My opinion is that most of it is not, but I would not want to state such an opinion with conviction until I had reviewed the evidence. Let me therefore turn to consider four specific issues of selection and tenure that have been widely discussed, and in two instances acted upon, during the past fifteen years: in this chapter, nomination and election; in the next, disability, succession, and re-eligibility.

The framers of the Constitution, who were obsessed with the notion that all men are real or potential fools, devoted an unusual amount of thought to devising a foolproof system of filling the office of President with a man whose authority to govern would be recognized as legitimate. "The subject has greatly divided this House," James Wilson observed on the floor of the Convention. "It is in truth the most difficult of all on which we have to decide." Not until the framers had slogged their way through more than thirty votes did the Committee of Eleven come up with the general method finally laid out in Article II, Section 1, clauses 2-4 of the Constitution.

I would ask my readers to turn to Appendix II and study these clauses. They should pay particular attention to the federal character of the electoral process (for example, the unrestricted power of the state legislatures to determine the manner of choosing electors); to the total exclusion of national legislators and officeholders from participation in the activity of the electoral college; to the contingent role of the House of Representatives; and to the ingenious provision through which each elector was to vote for *two* men as President, "of whom one at least shall not be an inhabitant of the same State" as himself.

One reason for this double vote was to guarantee the presence of a first-class man in a second-class office, the Vice-Presidency; but far more important a consideration was the certainty that the electors would be forced to look beyond the boundaries of their own states to search for men with national reputations. The framers of the Constitution were genuinely concerned with the persistence of provincialism in the politics of the new republic. They assumed that the electors in each state, with or without the directions of the people, would almost always vote for a native son for President. The double vote, they thought, would be the one sure way in which to raise "continental characters" above the dull herd of native sons. I would ask my readers to bear this fact in mind as they study the original electoral system, and I would ask them to read into these clauses four other expectations shared by the most perceptive of the framers: that the electors, in Hamilton's straightforward words, would be "chosen by the people"; that, once assembled "in their respective States," they would exercise discretion but not independence in casting their double vote for President; that the whole process would operate in a decentralized and largely unorganized way; and that, as the chief result, many elections would be settled finally in the House of Representatives. In general, then, they meant to remove the entire process of electing the President, or at least a key stage, to a point outside the legislature, and to mingle in this process both the will of the people and the judgment of the gentry. And once they had made their intentions known, they began to think rather highly of them. Hamilton spoke for most of the framers in *The Federalist* when he "hesitate [d] not to affirm that if the manner" of electing the President "be not perfect, it is at least excellent."

So long as Washington was available for the Presidency, the original system operated well enough to justify Hamilton's confidence. But the retirement of the one truly continental character, the rise of the Federalist and Republican parties, and the establishment of the congressional caucus to nominate candidates for the Presidency all conspired to bring this system to an early demise. Perhaps the most serious blow to the sanguine hopes of the framers was the natural insistence of the electors on discriminating in their minds (as they could not in their ballots) between the man they really wanted to make President and the man they intended to be Vice-President. The result of all these new departures was the election of 1800, and the result of that fiasco (and of some shameless Federalist "politicking") was the

Twelfth Amendment, which I also invite my readers to study with care. I trust they will note the one major change it worked in the original plan of election: henceforth each elector would cast one vote for one man as President and a distinct vote for a second man as Vice-President.

More than 150 years have passed since the adoption of the Twelfth Amendment, and still it continues to govern our manner of choosing the President. But it operates within a context of national custom and state law that has converted the election into a process of decision-making far more centralized, direct, protracted, hot-blooded, and popular, one might even say *plebiscitary,* than the framers could have imagined in their most restless nightmares. Almost every major feature of this context of law and custom was in full operation in the fabled election of 1840 between Harrison and Van Buren. The question ignored by the framers—how to nominate candidates for consideration by the people and the electors—had been answered once and for all by the collapse of the congressional caucus and the emergence of the nominating conventions. The first such convention met in Baltimore in September 1831 to nominate William Wirt for President on the Anti-Masonic ticket, and the two major parties, who have never scrupled to steal our third parties blind, held their first nominating conventions before the passage of another year. The question answered gingerly by Hamilton—how to "appoint" the electors in each state—had been answered resoundingly by the rise of American democracy. Only South Carolina still held out against white manhood suffrage in the choice of electors in the election of 1840. The people had been moving toward the last step to a truly popular system of electing the President—the conversion of the electors into "mere agents" for registering the wishes of the voters— almost from the beginning, and the abandonment of the double vote in 1804 wiped out any lingering hope (or worry) that the electors would be anything more elevated than "mere agents" or "mouthpieces" or "puppets on a string." In 1796 an elector in Pennsylvania had ignored a pledge to vote for Adams and had voted instead for Jefferson. The complaint of a Federalist voter still rings through our political consciousness: "Do I choose Samuel Miles to determine for me whether John Adams or Thomas Jefferson is the fittest man for President of the United States? No, I choose him to act, not to think."

To these three extraconstitutional changes in the method of electing a President yet a fourth was added in these years of the upsurge of democracy: by 1840 every state except South Carolina had adopted the so-called "general-ticket" system of choosing electors or, more exactly, of casting the state's electoral vote. Under this arrangement the total electoral vote in each state went to the candidate with the highest popular vote. Once some of the states had adopted it, all of them had to, and since 1892 it has prevailed throughout the Union. The people and politicians even of Nevada and Alaska are apparently convinced that their influence in a presidential election is a good deal larger because they give all their electoral votes in one lump to one lucky candidate. As to New York and California, their larger-than-life importance in the calculation of those who nominate candidates and conduct their campaigns depends almost entirely on the maintenance of the general-ticket system. Finally, most of the paraphernalia of the nationwide popular election were on full display throughout the Union in the battle between "Old Tippecanoe" and "Van, Van, the used-up Man," and in some regions well before then. The appeal of each candidate for the Presidency was henceforth and forever to be directed to the people, and it was to be an appeal to their fears and fancies as much as to their powers of rational decision.

Our machinery for electing a President, which has been functioning virtually without change for a century and a quarter, operates today in five successive stages:

1) In the period from March to June of each presidential election year, delegates are chosen to the nominating conven-

tions of the two major parties. In roughly one-third of the states the voters of each party have a voice in this process, in two-thirds the delegates are chosen by party machinery.

2) In the period between mid-June and late July (or even as late as August if one of the parties is running a popular President for re-election) the nominating conventions meet to choose their candidates for President and Vice-President. So familiar is the sight and sound of these quadrennial extravaganzas to all Americans who own TV sets (perilously close to *all* Americans) that I hardly think it necessary to describe the events that take place. I will confine myself to the observation that they fill a yawning void in the electoral system designed for us by the framers and their immediate successors.

3) On the first Tuesday after the first Monday in November, a day fixed uniformly by law of Congress (November 8 in 1960, November 3 in 1964), the people of the United States go to the polls to vote—in fact and fancy for President and Vice-President, in law and Constitution for electors for these two offices. By midnight in San Francisco, if not hours before, they almost always know the results of their part in the election, which they correctly consider the only part that really counts.

4) On the first Monday after the second Wednesday in December, a day also fixed by law (December 19 in 1960, December 14 in 1964), the electors of the successful candidates in each state meet and cast their solemn and meaningless votes for the men to whom they have been pledged. For those who care about such details, I should point out that in some states the electors are chosen by party conventions, in others by party primaries, in still others by party organizations, and in hard-headed Pennsylvania by the party's candidate for President. In more than half the states the names of the electors never even appear on the ballot; in only two (California and Oregon) are they commanded directly by law to follow the custom of the country and honor their pledges to the people who chose them.

5) On January 6 of the following year, just two weeks before inauguration day, the Senate and House sit as one body to count the electoral votes of the states. A certification of the validity of each state's votes by its "executive" is declared by law to be "conclusive." Except in unusual circumstances, which need not concern us in a survey as general as this, Congress acts simply as a recording machine. When the count has been completed, the President of the Senate rises to announce the results, and then proclaims the winner "President-elect of the United States." A President of the Senate named John Adams was once put in the embarrassing position of proclaiming himself President-elect; being an Adams, he performed this task with courage if not with relish.

Twice in our history there has been one further stage to pass through before we could be certain of the identity of our rightful President. The ironic and almost tragic tie in 1800 between Jefferson and Burr and the failure in 1824 of either Jackson or John Quincy Adams to secure a majority of the electoral vote both set the contingent machinery of the Constitution into operation; and the House of Representatives was called upon to make the final choice. To bring the continued possibility of this contingency closer to home, many of my readers will remember the morning hours of November 3, 1948, when it appeared that neither Truman nor Dewey, thanks to Thurmond and Wallace, would achieve the necessary constitutional majority. If such had been the outcome of the popular election in November, the House of Representatives would have moved immediately after the inconclusive count of January 6, 1949, to ballot for President. In keeping with the straightforward command of the Constitution, the members of the House would have been restricted in their choice to the three leaders— Truman, Dewey, and Thurmond—and the vote of each state delegation would have been counted as one. Twenty-five would have been the magic number for election in 1949; it is, of course, twenty-six today.

This machinery operates within the climate of opinion and expectation known as the American way of life. At least three features of this climate, three notable characteristics of the American people, pervade and shape the whole process of electing a President.

First, we are a political people, and it is therefore a highly political process, one in which all our units of public decision—from the biggest party to the smallest interest group, from the broadest ethnic minority to the most exclusive clique in "the power elite"—play a lively part. The importance of the Presidency for the character and very existence of our parties is even greater than the importance of the parties for the support and control of the Presidency. Arthur Macmahon comes close to the truth of the matter when he remarks that the two great parties "may be described as loose alliances to win the stakes of power embodied in the Presidency." The one persistent purpose of their existence on a national scale is to elect a President.

Second, we are a rich people, and the bill for all the fun and frolic and hard labor of seating a President in the White House now runs into tens of millions of dollars. No man for whom other men are unwilling to spend vast sums of money has much right to think about nomination as candidate for President in the affluent society. If he is the kind of man who can and should be nominated, he will have little trouble gathering it together. In any case, at least one sizable stretch of the path to the White House is paved with greenbacks.

Third, we are a modern, industrialized people, citizens of a mass society, and we rely heavily on the instruments with which we communicate with one another—newspapers, periodicals, books, the mails, opinion polls, advertising media, radio, and above all television—to keep the machinery of election in purposeful motion. The election of the President is truly a mass experience; it is the one great national ritual in which all Americans, whether they vote or not, have no choice but to join with shouts of glee or despair. The media of communication have helped mightily to make it such a ritual—like all public rituals (like all men, for that matter) a fantastic blend of the solemn and the silly. Yet, to tell the truth, the election has been a mass experience since as far back as 1840, perhaps even 1828. The paving of Madison Avenue and the triumph of television added a new quality but not a new dimension to the workings of the Twelfth Amendment.

Let me conclude this brief survey as dramatically as I can: no power of the Presidency is more fateful and symbolic than its power to force all thinking Americans to speculate constantly about the identity of the next man to occupy it. I go most of the way with Professor Binkley, who wonders "how else the electorate as a whole could be made so acutely aware of the very existence of our national state," and all the way with Walt Whitman, who wrote in *Democratic Vistas,* "I know nothing grander, better exercise, better digestion, more positive proof of the past, the triumphant result of faith in human kind, than a well-contested American national election." The American people are rightly convinced that they have no more solemn task to perform and gripping melodrama to enjoy than to elect a President every four years. Hamilton engaged in one of his keenest displays of prophecy when he foretold a time "when every vital question of state will be merged in the question, 'Who will be the next President?' " That time has come, and it is a time that has no stop. The next election for President now begins the day the last election ends.

In the light of the significance, both rational and emotional, we attach to placing the best of all Americans in the presidential office, it is hardly surprising that we should feel so uneasy about the machinery with which we are asked to do it. It is complicated and costly, a weird design of bits and pieces put together by countless hands, and no one starting out to construct a new method of election would dream of copying it.

Many years have passed since anyone has commented upon the electoral system with the smugness of Hamilton. Committee after committee, text after text, editorial after editorial have paraded before us the dangers and injustices of the system, especially those of the nominating conventions and the electoral college, and most Americans now assume that there is something terribly wrong with it.

The case against the nominating convention is almost too familiar to bear repeating. I doubt that I need rehearse the cultural sins of which it is accused by sensitive observers. It should be enough to remind ourselves that this windy, vulgar circus is met to nominate a candidate for the most powerful office on earth, and to wonder if there could be any gathering of men that seems less in character with its high purpose, that seems more unhappily to express what Henry James called "the triumph of the superficial and the apotheosis of the raw." The convention is certainly a gross distortion of that picture of intelligent men reasoning together which we carry in our heads as the image of free government. It was the sight of an American convention that led a famous European scholar (Ostrogorski) to observe, first, that "fifteen thousand people all attacked at once with Saint Vitus' dance" was not his idea of democracy; and, second, that God in His infinite wisdom watches benevolently over drunkards, little children, and the United States of America.

And yet the case against the convention as a cultural abomination is itself a distortion. It is, indeed, a barrage directed through clouded sights at the wrong target. For the plain truth is that most criticisms of this noisy, plebeian, commercial institution are really criticisms of the noisy, plebeian, commercial civilization within which it operates. We see our follies as a people in the follies of the convention, and unless we reform ourselves, which I know we will not and suspect we dare not do, the convention will continue to disturb the reasonable, shock the fastidious, and fascinate all of us. In any case, it is yet to be proved that men who act like deacons can make a better choice of candidates for the Presidency than men who act like clowns, and that—the kind of choice the convention makes—is the meaningful test of its value as an institution of American life.

The more technical charges against the nominating convention are that it is undemocratic, since it cuts the rank and file of the party out of the process of selecting a candidate; unreliable, since it ignores or distorts the real sentiment of the party in making the selection; and corrupt, since it puts a premium on the kind of horse trading in which men cannot expect to succeed unless they unlearn every rule of public and private morality. The convention, we are told, offers us a man we neither want nor deserve, and it offers him on a platter of corruption and cynicism. Those who make these charges usually go on to advocate some sort of nationwide presidential primary. The convention would become a pep rally to shout approval of the people's choice or, quite possibly, would be abolished altogether.

These charges, it seems to me, are a caricature of reality. The first and third might just as easily be leveled at Congress as at the nominating convention, while the second, which is most often and earnestly advanced, simply cannot stand up under the scrutiny of history. When in the twentieth century, except perhaps in the Republican convention of 1912, has a majority of the voters of either great party been handed a candidate it did not want? When, except in the nomination of Harding in 1920, did a convention pass over several first-rate men to choose an acknowledged second-rater? Quite to the contrary of accepted legend, the convention has done a remarkable job over the years in giving the voters of each party the man whom they, too, would have selected had they been faced with the necessity of making a responsible choice. The convention is anxious to satisfy, not frustrate, the hopes of the members of the party; if the latter give an unmistakable sound, the former will echo it gladly and faithfully. If they speak in a babble of voices, if they cannot agree on a clear choice, the convention will choose their man for them, even if it take a hundred ballots, and the choice, moreover, will be made finally with near or complete unanimity. One of the undeniable merits of the convention, as opposed to the primary, is that it heals most of the wounds that are inevitably laid open in the rough process of making so momentous a political decision.

There is something to be said, I suppose, for the efforts of Senator Douglas and his friends to encourage the growth of presidential-preference primaries. In more than one-third of the states of the Union the voters of each party are now given some chance to elect or instruct their delegation to the convention, and no one would argue that professional politicians should be protected against such expressions of the public mood or choice. Yet it would be a mistake to make these exercises in public opinion much more uniform in pattern or binding in effect than they are at present. Reformers should be careful not to upset the nice balance that history has struck between the hard responsibilities of the professionals at the convention and the vague wishes of the voters at home. The real question about our presidential primaries, it seems to me, is not whether they should take over completely the key role of the convention, which is an academic question at best, but whether they are worth all the fuss they cause in the minds of the public and all the strain they put upon even the most hard-shelled candidates. The active campaign for the Presidency becomes much too long drawn out a process; money becomes much too decisive a factor in the hopes and plans of any one candidate; some of the best candidates are torn between the responsibility of the important positions they already fill and the lure of the one after which they hunger and thirst. Under the system as it now operates, even the most popular candidates are hostages to whim and accident, especially to the whim of the "favorite sons" who sprout quadrenially and to the accident of the timetable of the primaries. The Democrats of New Hampshire, where the first primary is usually held, are all fine people, I am sure, but neither so fine nor so wise that they should be able to make or break a presidential aspirant all by themselves. I am inclined to agree with Adlai Stevenson, who speaks to the point with matchless authority, that the presidential primaries are a "very, very questionable method of selecting presidential candidates." Rather than have a handful of primaries spread carelessly over the months between February and July, it might be the wiser and even more democratic thing to have none at all. I for one would be happy to see our strongest candidates take the advice of the publisher of the *Adirondack Daily Enterprise,* James Loeb, Jr., and join in boycotting the present system entirely. It is, by almost any standard, one of the failures of our political system.

The convention, to the contrary, is a clear if not brilliant success. It meets the one test to which we like to put all our institutions: it does the job it is asked to do, and does it remarkably well. Indeed, one can be more positive than this in defense of the convention, for it performs several tasks that no other institution or arrangement can perform at all. Not only does it serve as the major unifying influence in political parties that are decentralized to the point of anarchy; it is, as Professor V. O. Key has written, "part and parcel of the magic by which men rule." And Americans, I again insist, are far from that enlightened condition in which political magic has lost its usefulness. The nominating convention fills a constitutional void; it unites and inspires each of the parties; it arouses interest in the grand plebiscite through which we choose our President. We will have to hear more convincing charges than have hitherto been pressed against the convention before we tamper with this venerable instrument of American democracy.

The case against the electoral system is much more impressive, so impressive indeed that it led two-thirds of the Senate in 1950 to propose an amendment to the Constitution, the Lodge-

Gossett amendment, abolishing the electoral college, retaining the electoral vote, and dividing it within each state in exact proportion to the percentages of the popular vote cast for candidates for the Presidency. Not satisfied with this compromise between the old federal republic and the new continental democracy, former Senator Lehman and friends would like to institute a national plebiscite, that is, to sweep away the whole machinery of the electoral college in favor of direct election by all eligible voters without regard to state boundaries. Former Representative Coudert, on the other hand, has stated the case for the district system, which was much used in the early years of the republic. Under this system each state would be divided into as many electoral districts as it has representatives in the House. The voters in each district would choose one elector; the voters in all the districts together would choose the two additional electors to which they are entitled by reason of their representation in the Senate.

All these men, whatever their particular panacea, unite in condemning the present system, concentrating most of their fire on those injustices and inconsistencies that arise out of the tyranny of the general ticket. And these are the criticisms in which they join most insistently:

1) The electoral vote distorts, often radically, the real sentiment of the country; a close election can have the appearance of a landslide.

2) Millions of votes go practically uncounted, and many Americans, at least in Vermont and Georgia, are doomed indefinitely to cast their presidential ballots in vain. As a result, many voters do not even bother to turn out.

3) The system, in the words of Lucius Wilmerding, one of its most effective critics, "puts a premium on accident." It is entirely possible for us to elect (indeed we have several times elected) a "minority President," a man who has not received even a plurality of the popular vote.

4) The parties are forced to concentrate much too heavily

and corruptly on the large and unsure states, and the system becomes an invitation to fraud. Moreover, minorities in these states swing political power out of all proportion to their size and importance.

5) The small states, even though overrepresented in the electoral count, are ignored as sources of presidential and even vice-presidential talent.

Harsh criticisms have also been aimed at other parts of the system. Some feel it potentially dangerous for the electors to retain, constitutionally and legally, their freedom of choice. Others argue that the House of Representatives, with each state delegation casting one vote, is about the last place in which a President should be chosen in the event that no one candidate secures an electoral majority. And we can all imagine the crisis that might develop if a President-elect were to die between the election in November and the casting of the electoral vote in December. There is no provision whatever, in Constitution or in law or in custom, for such a situation.

Distortion, injustice, apathy, accident, fraud, sectionalism— these are powerful arguments against our system of choosing the President, and yet the system, having survived the challenge of 1950, bids well to endure in unreconstructed glory for years to come. The case against either the Lodge-Gossett or Coudert proposals, which like the proposals themselves is now largely political in inspiration, has been stated with refreshing frankness on the floors of both houses. The decisive obstruction to reform is the general expectation that various minorities outside the South (in particular, labor unions and ethnic groups) would lose much of their present hold over both parties, especially over the Democrats, if the presidential vote were to be divided in proportion to the popular vote of each state. This explains why the chief sentiment for rewriting the Twelfth Amendment is now centered in the conservative South, the chief sentiment for holding fast in the progressive North. There can be no doubt that the one-party South, where the electoral margin for the victorious candidate would be not much less than it has been in most elections in the past, would gain in political power at the expense of the two-party North, where the margin in the large states would often be shaved as thin as a wafer. Men who already decry the disproportionate power of the South in Congress can hardly be expected to welcome such a shift in the power base of the Presidency. Many continue to advocate direct election of the President by the whole nation, but they couple their advocacy, as well they should, with a condition that has no hope of realization in the face of old history and new politics: that qualifications for the presidential suffrage be fixed by national law.

There is innate wisdom, if not always reasoned delicacy, in the stand of those who oppose drastic revision of the present system. One may take this stand for either or both of two solid reasons. The first is essentially conservative in mood and essence, for it is the argument of those who, recognizing that constitutional perfection is a cruel will-o'-the-wisp, would simply leave well enough alone. Such men, if I understand them rightly, are not unmindful of the defects of our electoral system. Yet they are sincerely convinced that a reformed system, from which all present dangers and injustices had been eliminated, would soon enough develop dangers and injustices of its own; some of these might be far nastier than any we are asked to suffer at present. They argue, further, that many of the dangers in the present system are hypothetical, many of the injustices not unjust at all. There is, for example, no indication that our political life has been hurt by distortions such as those registered in 1860 and 1936, and the American people should be given credit for ability to recognize an obvious distortion when they see one. There has been no convincing instance, certainly not in 1824 and 1876 and probably not even in 1888, in which a candidate was cheated out of the Presidency in spite of a clear plurality in the popular vote. A single elector might exercise his alleged freedom of choice, as James Russell Lowell was

vainly implored to do in 1876, but the chances that it could
make any difference are one in ten thousand. Only twice in more
than 150 years has an elector clearly voted for someone other
than the candidate to whom he was pledged—William Plumer
of New Hampshire for John Quincy Adams instead of James
Monroe in 1820, W. F. Turner of Alabama for Judge Walter
B. Jones instead of Adlai Stevenson in 1956—and each instance was a show of harmless eccentricity. As to the point
pressed vigorously by Senator Lodge—the way in which men
from the small states are passed over abruptly as candidates
for the Presidency—I doubt seriously that his scheme would
change our political folkways. We turn to the large states for a
dozen reasons, not least because they are far more likely than
the small states to produce the kind of large-calibered men we
need in the American Presidency.

And so it goes with the whole attack on the present system:
men who are understandably unsettled by the fantasy of our
machinery for electing a President are determined to replace
it with one that is simple and rational, no matter what new
and unsuspected problems they may raise in the process. Such
men, say defenders of the present system, are digging into the
foundations of the state—always a dangerous thing to do, but
especially in a time of watchful waiting.

The second reason for opposing change is directed, at least
in terms of current party politics, to liberal ends. The men who
make it are frank to concede that the present electoral system
is gerrymandered in favor of the urban vote, but this distortion,
they assert, is a necessary counterbalance to the overrepresentation of rural interests in the House and Senate. The various
proposals to eliminate the general ticket of electors in each
state would upset the balance of representation in our total
political system, and it would be even more difficult than at
present for the forces of reform to come to grips with the
problems of our industrial society. The Presidency, like Congress, would fall into the hands of the standpatters rather than

the progressives in each party. Indeed, the character of the Presidency as a great democratic office might well be jeopardized were its constituency thus altered. These men are not so much concerned about the system of electing the President as about the kind of President it produces. An urban civilization, they argue forcefully, deserves at least one urban-oriented institution in the complex of effective power at the national level.

Each of these arguments has much to be said for it, and for the present at least we should be content to rest upon them and contemplate the electoral system with wry tolerance. I would certainly favor abolishing the electoral college. If the electors are puppets, they are useless; if they are free agents, as several Southern states have tried to make them, they are 175 years out of date. I see no reason why we should not take steps to plug the gap between November 8 and December 19. It is absurd for us to rely on the party of the successful candidate to choose a man in his place, even his running mate, if he were to die in these six weeks. This would put a strain on the "old pros" in the party, not to mention the semipros in the electoral college, that neither we nor they could be at all happy about. There is even less reason to go on ignoring the problems that might arise between December 19 and January 6. The Twentieth Amendment lists several rude possibilities in Sections 3 and 4, but Congress has thus far refused to accept its flat invitation to "provide" against them "by law." And the only reason I have ever heard raised against having the House and Senate meet jointly (with each member casting one vote) to decide inconclusive elections is that the small states would never permit it, which is not a reason at all but a sigh of despair.

There are several reasons, all of them convincing, why we should hesitate a long time before replacing a humpty-dumpty system that works with a neat one that may blow up in our faces. All the arguments for the system are practical; most of those against it are theoretical. Until we are sure that the Presidency itself will not suffer from a radical change in the

method of election, we had best stand fast on tradition and prescription.

So much for the machinery, but what about the products?
What kind of men does it give us to be President of the United
States? The answer, as I tried to show in Chapters 3 and 5,
is all manner of men—men of the twentieth century, for example, so different in belief and style and competence as
Theodore Roosevelt and Calvin Coolidge, Herbert Hoover and
Harry S Truman, Woodrow Wilson and Warren G. Harding,
Franklin D. Roosevelt and Dwight D. Eisenhower. At the same
time, we should not make too much of these differences, for
these men also had important qualities in common. They all had
to meet certain tests to which the American people like to subject candidates for the Presidency. Not all of these tests are
polite or even reasonable; they are none the less a formidable part
of our electoral system. The question they raise in my mind, and
which I pose in conclusion to this chapter on nomination and
election, is this: What kind of man is most likely to be nominated as a candidate for President of the United States? What
kind of man can never hope to be nominated? To put the question another way, how large is the pool of men who are really
eligible for the Presidency? I have already mentioned some of
the qualities a man must have or cultivate if he is to be an
effective modern President. Now I am concerned with the
attributes he must have, many of which are impossible to cultivate, before he has a right to think of being President at all. I
am no less concerned with those attributes—physical, political,
ethnic, religious, cultural, social—that disqualify a man no
matter how noble and talented he may be.

Let me put the answer to this question of who can and who
cannot hope for the lightning to strike in the form of a list
that may not seem very scientific but is loaded with hard fact.
If my reading of American history and understanding of Ameri-

can mores is at all correct, then we may say of a man who
aspires to the Presidency:

He must be, according to the Constitution:
　　at least 35 years old,
　　a "natural born" citizen,
　　"fourteen years a resident within the United States," what-
　　　　ever that means.
He must be, according to unwritten law:
　　a man,
　　white,
　　a Christian.
He almost certainly must be:
　　a Northerner or Westerner,
　　less than sixty-five years old,
　　of Northern European stock,
　　experienced in politics and public service,
　　healthy.
He ought to be:
　　from a state larger than Kentucky,
　　more than forty-five years old,
　　a family man,
　　of British stock,
　　a veteran,
　　a Protestant,
　　a lawyer,
　　a state governor,
　　a Mason, Legionnaire, or Rotarian—preferably all three,
　　a small-town boy,
　　a self-made man, especially if a Republican,
　　experienced in international affairs,
　　a cultural middle-brow who likes baseball, detective stories,
　　　　fishing, pop concerts, picnics, and seascapes.
It really makes no difference whether he is:

a college graduate,

a small businessman,

a member of Congress,

a member of the Cabinet,

a defeated candidate for the Presidency, providing that he emerged from his defeat the very image of the happy warrior.

He ought not to be:

from a state smaller than Kentucky,

divorced,

a bachelor,

a Catholic,

a former Catholic,

a corporation president,

a twice-defeated candidate for the Presidency,

an intellectual, even if blooded in the political wars,

a professional soldier,

a professional politician,

conspicuously rich.

He almost certainly cannot be:

a Southerner (for more reasons than one, I am at a loss to know whether Texas is in the South or West),

of Polish, Italian, or Slavic stock,

a union official,

an ordained minister.

He cannot be, according to unwritten law:

a Negro,

a Jew,

an Oriental,

a woman,

an atheist,

a freak.

He cannot be, according to the Constitution:

a former President with more than a term and one half of service,

less than thirty-five years old,
a naturalized citizen,
an expatriate.

Several things should be noted about this list. First, I have purposely left out a number of intangibles—achievement, friendliness, moral repute, presence, eloquence, intelligence, moderation in views and tastes, rapport with the current mood of the country, willingness to serve faithfully (and, before that, to run hard), the look of a winner—that are obviously factors of decisive importance in transforming men who are merely "available" into serious contenders for nomination. What I have tried to list here are those self-evident qualifications and disqualifications which act almost automatically to dry up the pool of available men to probably not more than seventy-five to one hundred Americans, less than one out of every million adults.

Second, any rule in the fourth and sixth categories, if not exactly made to be broken, can certainly be broken with relative impunity by a man who scores high on the other self-evident tests of availability, especially if his intangibles are all in working order. Wendell Willkie was a corporation president, Adlai Stevenson was divorced, William Jennings Bryan was a twice-defeated candidate, Al Smith was a Catholic, and yet they were nominated by hardheaded men who hoped they would win. None of them did win, be it noted, and we are left with the almost certain feeling that each of them lost a sizable number of votes by reason of his particular disqualification. I need hardly point out that the pluses and minuses on this list apply even more forcefully to the two candidates for election than to the many candidates for nomination.

They do not apply quite so forcefully, however, to aspirants for the Vice-Presidency. No man born and living in the South has been nominated for the Presidency on a major party ticket since the Whigs came up with Zachary Taylor in 1848, but the nomination of John Sparkman of Alabama in 1952 is proof enough that the Democrats will give second place on their ticket to a man ineligible for first. So, too, will the Republicans, who could not have dared nominate a man as young as Richard Nixon for President in 1952, but who gave freshness to their ticket by putting him up for Vice-President.

I hasten to proclaim that I cannot guarantee the applicability of every item on this list, especially those in the middle categories, any longer than the next quarter-century. Although many of our common tastes and expectations (and, alas, our prejudices) are constant to the point of obduracy, many, too, are likely to change, as they have changed in the past, under the pressures of social progress and readjustment. If men of Italian or Polish descent are not eligible today, they may very well be in the year 2000. Catholics were certainly not eligible in 1900, but they have become more eligible with every new census of religious affiliation in the United States. Indeed, we may very well have reached the point at which a party, especially the Democratic party, would hurt itself more by refusing nomination to a Catholic otherwise fully available and qualified than by defying an ancient taboo that is slowly losing its force. Assuming that their qualifications are otherwise identical, however, a Protestant is still more likely than a Catholic to be nominated and elected President.

In conclusion, I would call attention to the special problem of each of our two great parties. It is an established fact, the kind of fact that tough-minded men take fully into account, that the Democrats are now the majority party and the Republicans the minority party in the American political system. What the Republican party enjoyed from 1896 to 1934 the Democratic party enjoys today: the allegiance at the polls, where allegiance pays off, of a clear majority of the voters of this country. Other things being equal, which they are perhaps more often than not, the Democrats should win every presidential election they contest. Their special problem, therefore, is to nominate a candidate who can bring the party's own voters to the polls. It is important to find a man who can appeal to the floaters in the center and to the deviants in the Republican party, but it is even more important to find one who can hold together the squabbling legions of this astounding coalition, who can please both the United Automobile Workers and the United Daughters of the Confederacy, the Irish of Boston and the Jews of Brooklyn, the professors and the professionals, the farmers and the factory-workers, the white supremacists of Georgia and the Negroes of Harlem. An unwritten law governs the proceedings of the Democratic national convention, commanding the delegates to nominate a candidate for President who is 1) a loyal son of the party, a warrior with scars, 2) not too closely identified with any of the major elements in the coalition, and 3) not openly hostile to any one of them. If anyone doubts the force of this law, let him try to account in any other way for the nomination of so reluctant a man as Adlai Stevenson in 1952. If Stevenson had been from Missouri, and had not been divorced, he would have been the almost perfect candidate of the modern Democratic party.

The trouble was, of course, that he ran head-on into the absolutely perfect candidate of the Republican party—and in a year, when, thanks to "Communism, Corruption, and Korea," all other things were far from equal. The special problem of the Republicans, needless to say, is to nominate a candidate who can bring the party's voters to the polls and, further, attract several million persons who normally vote Democratic or not at all. A man like Eisenhower was designed in heaven for just such a purpose, and I have always thought that there was something a little unreal about the savagery of the struggle between Eisenhower and Taft at the Chicago convention in 1952. Senator Taft, I am certain, would know what I mean when I say that if he had been as good a Democrat as he was a Republican, he would have been the candidate of "that other party" at least twice in his life. Unfortunately for him, he went down more than twice to what now seems a preordained defeat because his party was driven by the logic of its minority position to seek a candidate with more appeal for that bogey of all good Republicans, the "independent vote." So long as the tides of politics run as they are running today, the Republicans, like the Democrats from Buchanan to Roosevelt, choose suicide if they choose a party stalwart with no visible appeal beyond the ranks of the faithful. A man who aspires seriously to the Republican nomination for the Presidency must be (or appear to be) a "modern Republican."

These, if not the laws, are at least the axioms of presidential politics in the United States, and I do not expect to see them ignored with impunity for some years to come.

CHAPTER 7

THE FIRING, RETIRING, AND EXPIRING

OF PRESIDENTS

Once settled in office, a President can look forward confidently to four years of power and service. If he chooses, and we choose, too, his course can run eight years. We may refuse him re-election, but his party is rarely in a position to refuse him renomination. (Taft in 1912, Hoover in 1932, and Truman in 1948 all demonstrated the power of even the most whipsawed President to insist on a second shot at the grand prize.) Beyond eight years not even the most popular and dominant President can now go—but of that I shall have more to say in a few pages.

The prospect of a full term should fill a President with confidence, but not with serenity. Nothing in life is that certain, and every incumbent knows perfectly well that there are at least four ways in which his tenure can be cut short. All of them are openly contemplated in the Constitution.

The first is conviction by a vote of two-thirds of the Senators "present" on impeachment by the House on charges of "treason, bribery, or other high crimes and misdemeanors." I have already said most of what needs to be said about "the extreme medicine of the Constitution." I would call fresh attention only to the point that impeachment is not a *political* process, an inquest of office by the House and Senate acting as legislative bodies, but a *judicial* process, a trial of the President for crimes known to law in which the House acts as prosecutor, the Senate as jury, and the Chief Justice as presiding judge. Despite what I said in jest on page 53 about "the next President to be impeached," I do not think we are likely ever again to witness such a trial.

The second is death, which comes to Presidents perhaps more easily than it does to other men of their years. Many of our political calculations—for example, our choices of candidates for Vice-President—would be differently made if we were to face the fact that seven of the twenty-nine elected Presidents, just about one in four, have died in office. For those who care about such details, this little table should prove interesting.

President who died	Date of death	Cause of death	Unexpired portion of term
William H. Harrison	April 4, 1841	pneumonia	3 years, 11 months
Zachary Taylor	July 9, 1850	cholera morbus (acute indigestion)	2 years, 7 months, 23 days
Abraham Lincoln	April 15, 1865	assassination (lingered 9 hours)	3 years, 10 months, 17 days
James A. Garfield	Sept. 19, 1881	assassination (lingered 80 days)	3 years, 5 months, 13 days
William McKinley	Sept. 14, 1901	assassination (lingered 8 days)	3 years, 5 months, 18 days
Warren G. Harding	Aug. 2, 1923	embolism (on top of broncho-pneumonia, on top of a gastrointestinal attack)	1 year, 7 months, 2 days
Franklin D. Roosevelt	April 12, 1945	cerebral hemorrhage	3 years, 9 months, 8 days

Those who think that our Constitution is all written provision and no unwritten precedent should take a good look at what happened upon the occasion of each of these deaths, for what happened on the first occasion and has been happening ever since is in clear if sensible disregard of the wording of Article II, Section 1, clause 6 of the Constitution (which was not, to be sure, its most precise admonition) and of the intentions of the framers (which are not, to be sure, binding upon us). Constitutional historians are in unanimous agreement that the framers intended the Vice-President to act as President but not to be President whenever the office should fall vacant. Yet, when the office did fall vacant for the first time, upon the death of Old Tippecanoe, his Vice-President, John Tyler, strengthened in resolution by the tough-minded support of Secretary of State Daniel Webster, took over the power, duties, emoluments, residence, status, *and* title of the President almost without opposition. Except for eight Senators, a handful of editors, and, as one might expect, crusty old John Quincy Adams, no one was disposed to challenge Tyler's description of the event as "my accession to the Presidency."

The next time the office fell vacant, upon the death of Zachary Taylor, this shaky precedent hardened into a rock against which no one has been disposed to butt his head from that day to this. The Cabinet dispatched official notice of Taylor's death to Vice-President Fillmore in a message addressed to "the President of the United States," and Fillmore took the oath of office as President the very next day before a joint session of Congress. Despite the introduction of a resolution in the House describing Andrew Johnson as "the officer now exercising the functions pertaining to the office of President of the United States," he was finally accorded the signal honor of being impeached as President.

The last four Vice-Presidents to succeed to the Presidency have done so without challenge or even question. One of these, Calvin Coolidge, took the oath of office as President of the

United States from his own father, a notary public in Plymouth, Vermont, and in his father's house. The story had every prop for which a sentimental nation could have asked, from an old man "standing like a ramrod" to an old kerosene lamp with "etched sides," but that did not stop Coolidge from quieting his own doubts about the legality of this ceremony by taking a second oath from a federal judge in Washington two weeks later. The judge was sworn to secrecy by the Attorney General, and the secret was kept until 1932, by which time the elder Coolidge was safely past all caring.

No President has ever chosen the third and only voluntary way out of office, resignation, although one, Woodrow Wilson, seems to have contemplated it seriously. (I assume that every President with a skin less than six inches thick contemplated it half-seriously at least once in his term of office.) Just before the election of 1916 Wilson wrote a letter to Secretary of State Lansing suggesting that, if he were to lose to Charles Evans Hughes, he would appoint Hughes to Lansing's position and then, along with Vice-President Marshall, whose advice in the matter had not been asked, resign abruptly. Under the succession law as then written, Hughes would have become acting President almost four months before his elected term was scheduled to begin, and thus, in Wilson's words, the country would be "relieved" of the "perils" of a President "without such moral backing from the nation as would be necessary to steady and control our relations with other governments." Unfortunately for this story if not for history, Wilson was re-elected, and we shall never know if he really meant it. Two days after the election of 1920 Williams Jennings Bryan called on Wilson publicly to appoint the victorious Harding as Secretary of State, and then do manfully what he had promised to do in 1916. Bryan's proposal was greeted with icy silence.

So, too, was Senator Fulbright's well-meaning but ill-considered call for Truman's resignation after the Republican victory in the congressional elections of 1946; so, too, were the calls, just as well-meaning and not much more carefully considered, for Eisenhower's resignation issued from time to time in his second term. I question the essential wisdom of all such appeals for a President's resignation, principally because they seem to ignore the solemn nature of the mandate he holds from the people. We elect our Presidents on the assumption that, barring death or disability, they will go the whole way. A President-by-election proceeding at three-quarters speed is still preferable to a President-by-succession going full blast. The Presidency is indeed a kind of "republican kingship" which a man would abdicate rather than resign if he were to throw it over. Be all that as it may, resignation is contemplated by the Constitution and provided for in a law of 1792. By "an instrument in writing" signed and then "delivered into the office of the Secretary of State," a President or Vice-President may consummate an intention to resign or, for that matter, may refuse to accept election. One Vice-President, John C. Calhoun, did resign with two months of his term still to run. The Senate called him back, and he answered eagerly.

The Constitution points to a fourth way out of the Presidency, whether for a short time or for good, in a passage that speaks cryptically of "inability to discharge the powers and duties of said office." The word "disability" is used later in the same clause and may be regarded as exactly interchangeable with this phrase. John Dickinson asked his colleagues on the floor of the Convention to tell him what was meant by "disability" and who should decide that it existed, but no one found it necessary or possible even to hazard a guess. We will never know what the framers had in mind. This is clearly an instance in which we must find our own way, something we have hitherto done with no success whatever.

There have been two occasions in the history of the United States on which a President was unquestionably in no condition for a considerable length of time "to discharge the powers and

duties of said office." From the day Garfield was shot until the
day he died, a period of more than eleven weeks, he was unable
to put his mind to a single issue of importance for the country;
his one official act was to sign an extradition paper. In the
last few weeks his mind seems to have deteriorated along with
his wounded body. From the day of Wilson's breakdown of
September 25, 1919 (followed by a paralyzing stroke a few
days later) until well into 1920, he, too, was at his best only
a fragment of a President. Acts of Congress became law because
of his failure to pass on them; he did not meet his Cabinet for
eight months, nor did he learn for four months that it was
meeting without him; requests for information by the Senate
Committee on Foreign Relations went unanswered. Wilson's
disability was, in an objective sense, more acute than Garfield's
because the times called more loudly for a show of presidential
leadership. His collapse took place during a nationwide tour
designed to win friends and influence Senators in the history-
making debate over the League of Nations.

There have been other occasions on which the Presidency
was, in effect, a fully paralyzed office (if not institution)—
the last few days of Harrison, Taylor, McKinley, and Harding,
the last few hours of Lincoln and Franklin Roosevelt, and the
first few hours or days after each of Eisenhower's three sudden
illnesses—but all were self-resolving crises of short duration
which, except perhaps for the instances in which Eisenhower
was the stricken protagonist, no one wanted to complicate
further by insisting upon a heavy-footed interpretation of the
Constitution. To these should be added two potential cases
of disability that tease the historian's imagination almost to
distraction: the chaotic situations that would have arisen if
either Madison or Lincoln, as was altogether possible, had been
captured by enemy forces. Quite needless to add, except that
we have a habit of ignoring it, is the plain truth that every
day of his life every President has faced, like everyone else
in the country, the chance that accident or disease would strike

him helpless or even unconscious without striking him dead.

The problem of disability is, then, a real problem, real in history and even more real in the threat of demoralized chaos it constantly poses. Perhaps the single most pressing requirement of good government in the United States today is an uninterrupted exercise of the full authority of the Presidency. We need a man in the Presidency at all times who is capable of exercising this authority; we need one, moreover, whose claim to authority is undoubted. No man should be expected or permitted to wield the power of the Presidency without the clearest of titles to it. Whatever arguments may exist for the grand doctrine that all power must be first of all legitimate apply twice as severely to the power that is lodged in the American Presidency. For this reason, if for no other, the problem of disability in the Presidency presses hard upon us, and we have a right to expect our men of decision, which in this instance means the men who lead Congress, to do their statesmanlike best to provide the most workable solution of which American ingenuity and common sense are capable. We have done a lot of talking about this problem in the years since September 24, 1955, just as we did in the first years after July 2, 1881 and September 25, 1919, but thus far the only acting has been done by Dwight D. Eisenhower. Our continued failure to come to grips with it is not, I am sure, a product of carelessness or petty politics. It is, rather, our left-handed way of acknowledging how slippery a problem it really is.

The road to a workable solution must be built out of reasonable answers to four questions raised directly or obliquely, and answered not at all, in the Constitution.

1) What is "disability" in the Presidency?

2) Who decides that disability exists?

3) In the event of a clear-cut case of disability, what does the Vice-President assume—"the powers and duties of the said office" or the office itself? Is he acting President or President pure and simple?

4) If he is only acting President, that is to say, if the Presidency is recoverable, who decides that disability, in the words of the Constitution, has been "removed"?

After all the hearings and editorials and learned commentaries of the past few years, there is nothing new to be said on any of these questions. Let me sum up the present consensus on each (or where no consensus exists, the most important points of disagreement) and see if we can make a good start down the road to that "workable solution."

1) Most persons who have done any sound thinking at all on the subject would now agree with Professor Ruth Silva, who has done more sound thinking on it than all the members of Congress put together, that the words of the Constitution contemplate "any *de facto* inability, whatever the cause or the duration, if it occurs at a time when the urgency of public business requires executive action." Since the state of the President and the state of the Union must both be considered in any judgment of disability, it would be the height of folly to define disability any more precisely than this. A detailed law imagining all possible cases of disability would prove, as Emerson said of all "foolish legislation," a "rope of sand" that would "perish in the twisting." It might be pointed out in passing that, thanks respectively to Andrew Johnson and Woodrow Wilson, neither impeachment nor voluntary absence from the country falls within the definition of disability.

2) No one has ever doubted the President's right to decide and proclaim his own disability; few have doubted the Vice-President's duty—in a situation so obvious that even the inner circle at the White House would be anxious to give way—to initiate a determination of disability in the absence or even defiance of the President's express wish. But what of situations in which some doubt exists? What, in particular, of a Vice-President as reluctant as Vice-Presidents Arthur, Marshall, and Nixon all proved to be? How could he be persuaded to assume the powers of the Presidency? And how could we be persuaded

that his assumption was constitutionally and morally legitimate? The answer that appeals to most persons who have thought about it at all is: a decision of disability by an organ so legitimate in its own right, so laden with power and prestige, that the nation would be disposed to accept its judgment without hesitation. Congressmen, editors, lawyers, and professors of political science have had a field day trying to imagine the identity or composition of such an organ in the last few years, and their imaginations have stretched as far as all these possibilities:

The Vice-President alone, who would act according to his conscience and take his chances with Congress, the Supreme Court, public opinion, and history.

The Cabinet, whether a) with or b) without the consent of the Vice-President, and with the concurrence of a) an ordinary or b) an extraordinary majority of its members.

The Secretary of State, with the advice and consent of the Cabinet.

Congress, which would act by concurrent resolution a) on its own initiative, b) on application of the Cabinet, c) on application of the Vice-President, or d) on application of both. The vote in Congress would be a) by a simple majority in each house, b) by a two-thirds majority, or c) by a three-fourths majority. (If my readers are beginning to see spots before their eyes, so did I in reading through the hearings and debates on this subject in the seven Congresses that have discussed it seriously.)

The Supreme Court, acting a) in its capacity as a court or b) as a special tribunal, and by margins ranging from a simple majority to unanimity.

The governors of all or some of the fifty states.

A panel of leading physicians.

A panel of eminent private citizens, including all former Presidents of the United States.

Any one of the several dozen combinations that can be

constructed out of the officers and institutions listed above.

A special tribunal composed of great officers of state—for example, the Chief Justice, two senior Associate Justices, the Speaker of the House, the President pro tem of the Senate, the minority leaders in both houses, and the Secretaries of State, Treasury, and Defense. Some of those who propose such a privy council would make its decision binding; others would limit its role to giving advice to Congress or the Cabinet or the Vice-President, as the case might be. At least one learned publicist would reserve a place on this tribunal for the President's wife.

I do not wish to render this problem even more confusing than it must now appear, but it should be pointed out that there is a serious division of opinion between those experts (and who is not one in this matter?) who think it can be settled by statute and those who insist upon an amendment to the Constitution.

3) We have already noted that the framers of the Constitution never intended the Vice-President to become President except by election in his own right. If John Tyler and his associates had paid heed to these intentions (or, to be fair to Tyler, if the intentions had been proclaimed in unmistakable language), this third question would never have arisen. And if it had never arisen, the question of disability would not have been half so difficult to answer. Neither Arthur nor Marshall could have been persuaded to take over from his ailing President because too many men whose co-operation was needed were certain that such a transfer was irrevocable. A President who moved or was pushed aside, they argued, was no longer President at all; indeed, it was constitutionally impossible to have two Presidents at the same time, one acting and one mending on the shelf. For every one person who was certain that this was the meaning of the Constitution as it had developed through precedent, there were another ten who were at least in doubt. Under these circumstances of doubt, neither Arthur nor Marshall could have been permitted to take over. These doubts have been largely but not entirely laid to rest in recent years, and so long as a man, even a cranky

man, in a position as central as that of Speaker of the House expresses them, they will continue to plague all honest efforts to solve the problem of disability.

4) Although almost every method proposed for determining that disability exists has also been proposed for determining that it has come to an end, once again the chief responsibility is pinned on the President himself. His announcement that he was ready to reassume his powers would, in the nature of things political and constitutional, be conclusive. I am assuming, of course, that a deranged President would not be permitted to announce anything to anyone who would dare or care to "leak" it to the press. I could be wrong.

What then should be our solution to the problem of disability? Before I try to answer this question, let me record the circumstances and details of the only arrangement for a transfer of power that has ever been given formal expression. I speak, of course, of the Eisenhower-Nixon agreement, which was revealed in outline by the President February 26, 1958, and in detail (by popular demand) five days later. For months Mr. Eisenhower had been asking Congress to bring some order out of the confusion raised in all our minds by his three illnesses, and, then, despairing of legislative action, he decided to do the best he could simply as President. This he did by coming to a "clear understanding" with his Vice-President, which was announced to the nation in these words:

The President and the Vice-President have agreed that the following procedures are in accord with the purposes and provisions of Article 2, Section 1, of the Constitution, dealing with Presidential inability. They believe that these procedures, which are intended to apply to themselves only, are in no sense outside or contrary to the Constitution but are consistent with its present provisions and implement its clear intent.

(1) In the event of inability the President would—if possible— so inform the Vice-President, and the Vice-President would serve as Acting President, exercising the powers and duties of the Office until the inability had ended.

(2) In the event of an inability which would prevent the President from communicating with the Vice-President, the Vice-President, after such consultation as seems to him appropriate under the circumstances, would decide upon the devolution of the powers and duties of the Office and would serve as Acting President until the inability had ended.

(3) The President, in either event, would determine when the inability had ended and at that time would resume the full exercise of the powers and duties of the Office.

Speaker Rayburn and Mr. Truman raised objections to this arrangement that can be described only as "talmudic," and that made sense only as one more way for them to express their well-known contempt for Vice-President Nixon. Otherwise there was nothing but praise, warm or cool according to the political allegiance of the man who spoke it, for this simple and sensible arrangement. It remains to be seen whether Mr. Eisenhower has set a precedent for future Presidents, but at least he did all that he could have done to solve the problem for the duration of his own Presidency.

In my own opinion, we need something more than this arrangement, however compelling a precedent it may be for future Presidents, and something less than one of the grandiose schemes presented for our consideration in the past few years. I say "something more" because there are simply too many people of influence who remain in doubt about this question, "something less" because it would be either feckless or reckless to lay out an elaborate plan to solve a problem that in one sense is not much of a problem at all and in another is quite insoluble.

I would agree with those Congressmen and scholars who think that most of what we can reasonably hope to do can be done by a simple concurrent resolution of Congress. Such a resolution could end debate on at least five doubtful issues; the rest could properly be left to the men of good will and good sense we expect to govern us in the years to come. And these are the points it could make with conviction, principally because they express what has always been the most thoughtful opinion on the matter:

1) The President of the United States has the right to declare his own disability and to bestow his powers and duties upon the Vice-President or, in the event there is no Vice-President, upon the next officer in line of succession.

2) If the President is unable to declare his own disability, the Vice-President is to make this decision on his own initiative and responsibility.

3) In the event of disability, the Vice-President shall only act as President; his original oath as Vice-President shall be sufficient to give full legitimacy to his orders, proclamations, and other official actions.

4) The President may recover his powers and duties simply by informing the Vice-President that his disability no longer exists.

5) Disability, to repeat Professor Silva's words, means "any *de facto* inability, whatever the cause or the duration, if it occurs at a time when the urgency of public business requires executive action."

I am not a lawyer, and I would expect that these points could be made with a good deal more precision than I have given them. They are, in any case, the common sense of the matter, conformable alike to the intentions of the framers, to the assumptions of those who initiated the Twentieth and Twenty-second Amendments (which teem with men "acting as President"), and to the foreseeable needs of the nation. They add exactly nothing, in my opinion, to the situation as it now exists, and as it was so honestly put by President Eisenhower; but if a resolution incorporating them would help clear the air of doubt, let us by all means have it. And for the benefit of those who would still have doubts, let us at the same time move to declare these principles in an amendment to the Constitution.

Let us be careful to do no more than that. Let us not write a law that tries to provide for all the eventualities that might arise, lest we trap our descendants in a snare of technicalities. Let us not go beyond the President and Vice-President in search of machinery to decide doubtful cases of disability, lest we construct a monstrosity that raises more doubts than those it is supposed to settle. I see almost nothing to give us confidence, rather a great deal to give us pause, in the dozens of schemes that would drag Congress or the Cabinet or the Supreme Court or former Presidents into the picture. A judgment of presidential disability would be, in both great senses of the word, a *political* decision—a determination of high policy, and thus a task for men who can be held accountable to the country; a demonstration of "the art of the possible," and thus a task for men (the same men, I would think) who are permitted to practice their art under the most favorable circumstances. The men who count politically, whether in Congress or in the Cabinet, will have their say in any case, and I think we should leave it to them to decide how best to have it. The men who do not, among whom I would include all governors, physicians, private citizens, former Presidents, presidential spouses, and Justices of the Supreme Court, should speak only when spoken to— and, in the case of the Justices, not even then. It is comforting to learn that all members of the present Court are said to agree with this argument. They want no part of any of the schemes that would incorporate them, whether as Court or as individuals, into the machinery of decision in this delicate area.

As to the proposal of a special tribunal, a Presidential Disability Commission, the notion that it could lay our doubts to rest seems quite unsubstantial. The last thing we should do is to provide a method that resembles a trial, complete with expert witnesses and cross-examination. In circumstances that called for action it would use up too much time; in a crisis that called for unity it would open up needless wounds. The next to last thing is to provide a method that would make it too easy for a President to surrender his powers temporarily. We have labored for generations to preserve the unity of the Presidency, and I for one would tremble to see us open the door even a little way to pluralism in this great office. All suggestions that an indisposed President can, like an indisposed corporation executive or union chief or general or even Secretary of State, hand over his powers formally to his first deputy betray a lack of understanding of the qualitative difference between this office and all others in or out of the government of the United States. They ignore, too, the harsh fact of history that the Vice-President is very seldom the President's "first deputy," that he is as likely as not to be someone who stands well outside the President's inner circle. This was certainly one of the difficulties of Arthur's position, for he was a "Stalwart" who had been placed on the ticket to heal the wounds opened by the nomination of a "Half-Breed" (we would call him a Modern Republican) like Garfield. Marshall, too, was an outsider whom the President had never taken into his confidence. Worse than that, he was Thomas R. Marshall and the President was Woodrow Wilson; the contrast between their relative standings in the eyes of Congress, the Cabinet, the American people, and the world was so sharp that the notion of the one acting for the other in any important way still seems ridiculous. Marshall might have signed a few laws and made a few appointments, but he could hardly have done anything to influence the debate over the League of Nations. The one thing we could not expect an acting President to do would be to commit his disabled chief to a policy or bargain which the chief would never have made himself.

I am led by all these considerations to repeat my observation that in one sense, probably the most important sense, the problem of disability is quite insoluble. We may yet solve it legally by framing an understanding in law and custom that leaves no doubt about the terms on which power is to be transferred from an ailing President to a healthy Vice-President; we can even do away with the practical difficulties we have already met in the Vice-President who is an outsider or the President who is a giant, not to mention the President who is mentally alert but physically confined. A period of clearly established presidential disability will always be a messy situation, one in which caution or even timidity must mark the posture of the acting President.

A period of doubt, a time in which a Roosevelt declines or an Eisenhower recovers, will be even messier, and it is really no help at all to ask why a Truman or a Nixon should not take over in such a situation. The answer is that he *cannot,* that the Presidency is an office governed by none of the ordinary rules, that a wise custom of the American people commands us at all reasonable costs to guard the unity of the Presidency and the dignity of any man who holds it. This, in any case, is what has troubled the people, the professors, and the politicians over the past few years: not the memory of Garfield or the phantom of another Wilson, but the disturbing sight of the partial paralysis that stole over the White House during the confused days after each of Eisenhower's three illnesses. We had a right to be troubled, and at least one ingredient of our discomfort was the realization that we were caught up in a situation that had no easy solution, perhaps no solution at all except patience, prayer, and improvisation. To expect any neater solution than we got on each of those occasions is to ask something of our political institutions that they cannot give. Putting aside the plain fact that Eisenhower was not disabled except for a few hours or days, that not a single piece of routine business failed to get done, we might ask just what it was that Nixon could have done any better or would have done any differently during the weeks in which, on each of these occasions, the President was recovering. And the answer is: exactly nothing. As acting President he would have done just what he and the other members of the Eisenhower team did so well in so painful a pause: he would have kept the shop. Let us be entirely clear on this point: the only thing a Vice-President can do, so long as there is the slightest chance that the President will recover, is to keep the shop. All the machinery in the world cannot alter that fact, which is inherent in the status and functions of all great offices of state, and most especially in the unique case of the American Presidency.

I conclude by expressing my own modest hope that Congress will move in good time to enact a law expressing "the common sense of this matter" as I tried to describe it a few pages back. Armed with such a declaration, with our compelling instruments of publicity, and with the knowledge that decency and patriotism and political maturity still pervade the upper reaches of our government, we can face this problem with as much confidence as we can ever expect to muster in the face of chance. I would call special attention to those "instruments of publicity," for they have already gone far, in my opinion, to correct the unpleasant situation that arose in the illnesses of Garfield and Wilson. We have long since reached and passed the point of no return in our journey toward what I would call "the public Presidency." The American people now assume that nothing of this nature is to be kept from them, and they would expect and surely get daily, if necessary hourly, reports on the condition of a stricken President. The palace guard now exists to feed information, not to withhold it.

For those who entertain doubts on this score, I would recommend thoughtful study of the sharp contrast between the way things were done in Cleveland's day and the way they have been done in Eisenhower's. Grover Cleveland underwent an operation for cancer of the jaw in 1893, and the first credible news the nation had of it was in 1917, nine years after his death, twenty-four after the fact. Dwight D. Eisenhower had a heart attack in 1955, and the news, which was both credible and full, started to gush forth within a couple of hours. In less than forty-eight hours, with an explanation that it would be "good for the morale of the people," Dr. Paul Dudley White and James Hagerty were telling us all about the President's bowel movements. I mention this with no relish, because I think it was a show of vulgarity rendered even more vulgar by White's remark that "the country is so bowel-minded anyway," but simply to clinch my argument that henceforth and forever we will be informed directly of every bit of information on a stricken President's condition necessary for us to make our own judgment about his ability to bear the burden of his office. If we cannot have confidence in our ability to make such a judgment as men of sense and decency, then what in heaven's name can we have confidence in at all?

The problem of succession is in some ways stickier than the problem of disability. The Presidency is an office that can never, so to speak, be left empty for a moment; the authority of the man who wields its mighty powers must be recognized as constitutionally and morally legitimate by Congress, the courts, the people, and history. It is therefore imperative, especially under conditions of modern existence, that a line of succession be marked out clearly, that the line be extended downward through a number of persons, and that these persons be men of standing in the national community.

The framers of the Constitution handled this problem in characteristic fashion. They designated the Vice-President, whom they expected to be a man of genuine standing, as heir apparent, and then invited Congress to guard against the calamitous event of a double vacancy (or a vacancy combined with a disability, or even a double disability) by enacting a law "declaring what officer shall then act as President." Congress has responded to this invitation on three occasions—1792, 1886, and 1947— each time with a law that has pleased just about no one who studied it with a lawyer's care or a historian's imagination. Fortunately, we have thus far been spared the necessity of doing anything more than study these three laws for imperfections. In the course of 170-odd years we have lost seven Presidents and eight Vice-Presidents during their terms of office, which comes to a total of fifteen occasions when the heir apparent to the authority if not the office of the Presidency was marked out by law. But never yet, thanks, I suppose, to the same luck of which Ostrogorski spoke, have we lost both men whom we had elected to serve us for four years. This is no guarantee for the future.

There are two obvious pools of talent and prestige upon which the nation can be expected to draw for an acting President: the heads of the executive departments and the leadership in Congress. Those notable pools that spawn generals, Justices, and state governors are all, for one sound reason or another, a little too muddy to be tapped with confidence, and Congress has refused to look beyond the Cabinet and its own leadership for men to entrust with the powers of the Presidency in the event of a double vacancy.

Congress came up with its first shaky solution to the problem of succession in 1792; the solution, be it noted by those who like to make bloodless gods of the founding fathers, was a product of political animosity rather than of creative statesmanship. Instead of designating the Secretary of State as first in line after the Vice-President (the sensible solution, except that the Secretary of State was Thomas Jefferson), the conservative leadership in Congress picked on the President pro tempore of the Senate and, after him, the Speaker of the House. Neither of these officers was to be President, but was only to act the part. Further, if the double vacancy were to occur during the first two years and seven months of any given presidential term, the Secretary of State was to proceed "forthwith" to call a special election.

Despite many doubts about both the constitutionality and practicality of this law, Congress did not make a real attempt to improve upon it until 1886. Then, for motives so mixed that I beg to be excused from deciphering them, the two houses turned abruptly to the other great pool of talent and prestige, the President's own Cabinet. Henceforth, in the event of a double vacancy, the succession was to run down the line from Secretary of State to Secretary of the Interior. Upon such

a child of fortune only the "powers and duties" of the Presidency were to devolve, but he was to hold them all the way
to the next regular election. The provision for a special election
in the law of 1792 was consigned to oblivion—and with it
another clear but never clearly stated expectation of the framers
of the Constitution.

Just before leaving for Potsdam in 1945, Harry S Truman
asked Congress to reconsider the succession established in 1886.
As an old legislative hand he had been strongly impressed by
the argument that it would be more "democratic" to have an
elected rather than an appointed official in line right after him.
When this argument was first put forward for Truman's consideration, Edward R. Stettinius was Secretary of State, and the
chance to replace him as crown prince with Sam Rayburn,
Speaker of the House, was enough to get the wheels of Congress
in motion. After James F. Byrnes had taken over from Stettinius, however, the wheels ground to a halt. The victory of the
Republicans in the congressional elections of 1946 provided Mr.
Truman with a matchless opportunity to act the statesman; this
he did by once again asking Congress to recast the succession in
favor of the Speaker, who had now been transformed by the
alchemy of politics from a man named Sam Rayburn to a man
named Joseph W. Martin. Congress responded with the law of
1947, which we are likely to carry on the books for some time
to come, praying all the while that we shall never have to use it.

The Presidential Succession Act of 1947 draws primarily on
the legislative pool, keeping the Cabinet in reserve for the most
contingent of contingencies. It is a complicated piece of legislation, and I will limit this exposition of it to those provisions
designed to produce an acting President in the event both the
Presidency and Vice-Presidency have fallen vacant. In such an
unhappy event, "the Speaker of the House of Representatives
shall, upon his resignation as Speaker and as Representative
in Congress, act as President." If there is no Speaker, or if
"the Speaker fails to qualify as Acting President, then the Presi-

dent pro tempore of the Senate shall, upon his resignation as President pro tempore and as Senator, act as President." If there is no Speaker or no President pro tempore, or if neither is qualified (for example, neither is a natural-born citizen), the line of succession then runs down through the Cabinet to the first of its members "not under disability to discharge the powers and duties of the office of President," which is to say that he must be "eligible to the office of President under the Constitution," must hold his office "with the advice and consent of the Senate," and must not be under impeachment. Such a man would be an acting President twice over, for he would serve only until a Speaker or President pro tempore had qualified to take over. As in the law of 1886, no provision at all is made for a special election.

A number of substantial objections have been raised against this latest arrangement for the succession to the Presidency. For one thing, it is a quite unsettled question whether either the Speaker of the House or the President pro tempore of the Senate is an "officer" within the meaning of the Constitution. For another, as Professor Silva points out, the Succession Act of 1947 perversely requires the man upon whom the powers and duties of the Presidency devolve to resign the very office— the one he is already holding—to which these powers and duties are attached by law. Congress, that is to say, has power to attach the authority of the Presidency to an office, but not to decide what officer shall become President, which is exactly what it has done in the Act of 1947. Even if these are technicalities that we could overcome with a show of common sense, would it not be more sensible to return to the Act of 1886 and designate the Secretary of State as statutory heir apparent and to line up the other members of the Cabinet behind him? At least three reasons can be mustered in support of the contention that the Act of 1886 is superior to the Acts of 1792 and 1947: first, that we have several times been without a Speaker or President pro tempore; second, that the Secretary of State (or Treasury or Defense) would be more likely to provide continuity in the executive branch; and third, to be as realistic as possible, that more men of presidential stature have presided over the Department of State than over the House of Representatives. If the Speaker of the House is a more "democratic" choice than the Secretary of State, it is not by a very substantial margin, certainly not while most Speakers rise to the top by way of the "safe district," seniority, and faction.

The problem of succession as it has existed up until now is, all things considered, one over which we cannot be expected to lose much sleep. It is pleasant to speculate about alternative solutions, and I think we should debate the possibility of a special election in the event of a double vacancy during the first year and a half of a regular term. But here, too, I think we can trust to common sense and patriotism to carry us through a crisis which could never, by means of any conceivable solution, be made a happy time for the nation.

What I am concerned about is the problem of succession as it will exist from now on. If we are only poorly prepared for a double vacancy, we are not prepared at all for a multiple vacancy; and it is this kind of vacancy, so I am told by colleagues who deal in the laws of probability, that we are most likely to be faced with during the next hundred years and beyond. One well-aimed bomb, or at the most three or four, could leave us with no one to exercise the authority of the Presidency and, perhaps worse, with several persons to claim it —and all this at a moment in history when, as in April 1861, our future would rest in the capacity of the Presidency to provide autocratic leadership. How are we to provide against this ghastly contingency? By placing still other executive offices in the line of succession? By insisting that several men at the top live and work in other parts of the country? By dragging in the Governor of New York or the Commanding General of the Sixth Army? Or by trusting in Providence or, as some would prefer, providence? I leave this question to a posterity which, I pray, will never have to answer it. If we can hold off the great cataclysm, we need worry no more than we have worried in the past. If we cannot, if we are bombed in full force by the Soviet Union or China (or in time by Egypt or Ghana or Andorra), we may be past all worrying. How thoroughly smashed can a nation be and still remain a salvageable political entity? This may not be the place to raise such a question, but I raise it none the less.

The other problem of selection and tenure that has been acted upon formally in recent years has to do with the number of terms for which any one man can be elected to the Presidency. The framers of the Constitution gave the most serious consideration to limiting each President's tenure to one term or at most to two consecutive terms. In the end, they decided to make him re-eligible for election to any number of terms. Hamilton laid out all the rational arguments for indefinite re-eligibility in *The Federalist,* but one suspects that the real reason for the absence of any restriction in the Constitution was the strong hope that George Washington would be willing to serve as first President and the even stronger expectation that the people would want to keep him in command until the day he died.

If Washington was only indirectly responsible for the absence of all restrictions on re-eligibility in the Constitution, he was directly responsible for initiating the wholesome custom that made it possible for the American people to live calmly for more than 150 years with this "open door to dictatorship" and to shrug off all attempts (and there have been hundreds) to close it with the aid of a constitutional amendment. I refer, of course, to the two-term tradition, which he and the three other Virginia Presidents of the early days made a compelling if not compulsive precedent of our political system. More than one man in the long line of two-term Presidents between Washington and Franklin D. Roosevelt was tempted by his vanity, his ambition, or his train of friends, or by all three in concert, to ask for a third helping of glory. More than one kept his hand firmly on the great lever of political power by refusing to back off from the possibility of a third term until the last possible moment. But there was never much doubt in the popular mind that this was an almost sacred tradition that could never be suspended except in the most unusual circumstances.

We would still be sailing along calmly under the terms of the casual arrangement in the Constitution had it not been for the circumstances of 1940, the most unusual of which was the emergence of the first President in history who was ready to brave the storms of a violated tradition and seek a third term in office. Franklin D. Roosevelt got his third term, and at least part of a fourth term, too, and we got the Twenty-second Amendment. History may yet judge it a fair bargain, and I mean both the history written by his friends and the history written by his foes.

Congress proposed the Twenty-second Amendment in 1947, with not a single dissenting vote in the Republican majority in either house, and it was ratified by the requisite number of state legislatures in 1951. There can be no mistaking the intention of its key passage:

No person shall be elected to the office of the President more than twice, and no person who has held the office of President, or acted as President, for more than two years of a term to which some other person was elected President shall be elected to the office of the President more than once.

This amendment is apparently designed, in contrast to comparable restrictions in state constitutions, to impose *permanent* ineligibility for re-election on any person who has been President of the United States for six years.

The case for the Twenty-second Amendment was stated with eloquence in both the House and Senate in 1947. Senator Revercomb of West Virginia went to "the real heart" of the matter by insisting, in effect, that the longer any one man held on to the Presidency, the closer this country drew to "autocracy," to "the destruction of the real freedom of the people." A clever and ambitious President, Senator Wiley agreed, was in an ideal position to increase and perpetuate his authority: by dispensing the many favors in his possession to men willing to do his bidding, whether in the administration, the armed forces, the judiciary, or even in Congress; by buying the extra votes necessary to secure his repeated re-election; and by posing at all times as "the indispensable man" whom the people should support and Congress never thwart. David Lawrence has recently echoed the key argument of these men by describing the proposal to repeal the Twenty-second Amendment as the "dictatorship amendment." If a "dictatorship" were ever "to arise in America," he writes, it would probably "come out of the tremendous powers derived by a President from the right to continuous office." This fear of presidential dictatorship was and still remains the surface logic of the Twenty-second Amendment.

The case against the amendment was stated by men like Representatives Sabath and Kefauver and Senators Kilgore, Pepper, and Lucas. Although they fought in a losing cause, their appeal to history was forceful, and their cause has been slowly attracting new converts over the intervening years. President Eisenhower several times described the flat ban on a third term as "not wholly wise," although he reversed himself obliquely in 1959 by permitting Attorney General Rogers to advise Congress to "defer any legislative action in regard to the amendment to permit further experience thereunder"—in other words, to wait and see how it works over a sizable period of time. Former President Truman, with whom Speaker Rayburn agrees, puts the Twenty-second Amendment in a class with the Eighteenth. And such doughty characters as Senator Neuberger and Representatives Celler and Udall have offered resolutions designed to do away with it. The arguments of all these men, and of the political scientists who support them, are summed up in this indictment of the Twenty-second Amendment:

1) It bespeaks a shocking lack of faith in the common sense and good judgment of the people of the United States, who apparently cannot be trusted to decide for themselves when an extraordinary situation demands an extraordinary break with the customary pattern of politics.

2) As a corollary to the first point, it should be noted that this amendment was not, like the Twenty-first, submitted to ratifying conventions elected by the people. Suspecting that the voters who elected Roosevelt for two extra terms would resent this oblique rebuke, the Republican leaders in Congress went back to the old method of seeking ratification from the state legislatures, which were then worked over one by one while most people were looking the other way.

3) It puts a new element of rigidity in a Constitution whose flexibility has been one of our most precious possessions, and thus subjects future generations of Americans needlessly to "government from the grave."

4) Although we may have to wait many years to see this critical weakness reveal itself fully, sooner or later we will find ourselves trapped in a severe national emergency and be anxious to keep the incumbent President in office. Against our own will, and in submission to the will of men who acted hastily and vindictively far back in 1947, we will have to put aside the man to whom we would otherwise choose overwhelmingly to recommit our destiny. Then we will be sorry that we did not pay heed to the advice of Washington, who, in writing to Lafayette about this very matter, professed to see no sense at all "in precluding ourselves from the services of any man who on some emergency shall be deemed universally most capable of serving the public."

5) We already have evidence before our eyes that the second term of even the most popular President will henceforth be an especially unhappy time for executive leadership. No second-

term President except Jackson, not even Jefferson or the two Roosevelts, finished his eighth year as strong a leader as he had been in his seventh or sixth year or especially in his fourth, and his decline began the day when he admitted, or his friends and foes could assume, that he was not a candidate for re-election. As William Plumer, of New Hampshire, put it in 1806:

It seems now to be agreed that Mr. Jefferson is not to be a candidate at the next Presidential election. The disclosure of this fact, thus early, is an unnecessary and imprudent letting down of his importance. Most men seek the rising rather than the setting sun.

Now that every President's sun starts to set forever the day he begins his second term—to be less poetic, now that he is a "lame duck" a full four years before his certain demise—we must expect to see a steady deterioration in his capacity to persuade people "to do what they ought to do without persuasion." This is not a serene prospect for the second half of the twentieth century, years in which we will be in no position to afford the old luxury of having Presidents who have lost their political grip. We have dealt the modern Presidency a grievous blow by depriving the second-term President of that notable political weapon, his "availability," with which men as different as Coolidge and Truman, not to mention Jackson and Grant, kept their troops in line by keeping them guessing.

6) Finally, the Twenty-second Amendment disfigured the Constitution with words that still express the sharp anger of a moment of reaction rather than the studied wisdom of a generation. It was, indeed, although the fact may no longer be relevant, an undisguised slap at the memory of Franklin D. Roosevelt. No one can ever question the inalienable right of Americans to be critical of dead Presidents as well as of the living, but the Constitution is not the place to engage in a display of rancor. A concurrent resolution of Congress redirecting our attention to the rectitude of the two-term tradition would have accomplished the purpose just as well.

The fourth and fifth particulars in this bill of indictment are the essence of the case against the Twenty-second Amendment, and I am bound to say that I find them convincing. To the fourth there is no rebuttal except that there may never be so desperate a crisis combined with so badly needed a man, to which I can only reply grimly: Just wait and see. To the fifth there are two rebuttals, which arise out of different theories of the Presidency and are rarely joined together. The first is the argument that the President who cannot hope for re-election is uniquely situated to rise above politics and to act, as no President since Washington has acted, the noble role of "leader of all the people." As one hopeful citizen, Mr. William B. Goodman, of Flushing, New York, framed this argument in a letter to the New York *Times* just after President Eisenhower's re-election:

> He has nothing to lose. He cannot be re-elected. He may reconsider foreign and domestic policies he could not politically afford to suggest were less than adequate during his first term. He no longer need consider what, for example, the Senatorial opposition in his own party can do to him. He can do more to them if he will organize Congressional support of his policies solely around agreement to them rather than to the membership in a party over which he has steadily decreasing control. His appeal to the people on issues need no longer carry the mark of party.
>
> Thus to free the President from mere partisanship, while not the intent of the Twenty-second Amendment, may well be its result. Freeing the President for truly national leadership as it does, the amendment also makes him a lonelier figure—but his freedom is worth such isolation for the freedom of action it confers. He can maneuver, wheel, and fight, as no President has ever been able to before.

I confess that my own spirit rouses to the note of antique patriotism in this message, but I do not see how we can escape the blunt lesson of history that a President "free" from "mere partisanship" is a *roi fainéant,* a man commanded to "maneuver, wheel, and fight" with a blunted sword in hand. Any second-term President who tried seriously to abdicate his role as leader of his party would be worse than a lame duck: he would be a dead one. And as if that were not a cruel enough fate, some men might also consider him an ingrate or even a renegade. The party that elected him twice to the Presidency would have every right to expect him to "go all out" for the party's candidate in the next election. While the vision of the nonpartisan President will always beckon us, it is fated to remain no more than a vision.

The second rebuttal is simply that, if the hard choice must be made, it is more important to guard against the pretensions of a third-term President than to strengthen the hand of a second-term President. In point of fact, most of those who support the Twenty-second Amendment do not consider this a hard choice at all. If this amendment has served to weaken the Presidency, they argue, so much the better for the health of our democracy. The real logic of the Twenty-second Amendment is, then, that it helps to shift the balance of power in our government away from the executive and back toward the legislature, thus reversing a trend that had appeared irreversible by any ordinary exertion of the will of Congress. Senator Revercomb came near to expressing this inarticulate major premise when he said:

It may be argued that the Congress, the membership of which is elected from term to term, might well be sufficient assurance of safety against individual power in the Executive. I submit that the Congress cannot stop the growth of Executive powers which may be gained by an individual through long tenure in so powerful an office as that of President of the United States. There are immense innate powers in that office. They can be mushroomed fast or gradually grown until the strength of thorough despotism may be in the hands of one man, or a group of individuals, for that matter, to rule the people by his will and not by laws. If such a situation should be brought about it would be, in summary, the very destruction of government by free and independent people and a move toward the creation of dictatorship in fact.

And I submit that it was not the possibility of dictatorship but the reality of the strong Presidency, not the shadow of a third-term President but the substance of any President, that gave force to the successful drive for the Twenty-second Amendment. When all the arguments and rebuttals and prophesies of doom have been mustered by each side, the fact remains that those who take pride and comfort in the amendment are Whigs, men who fear the Presidency and put their final trust in Congress, and that those who propose to repeal it are Jacksonians, men who respect Congress but look for leadership to the Presidency. Since this whole book is a salute to the modern Presidency, I doubt that I need to explain any further why the Twenty-second Amendment should be stricken from the Constitution. (I doubt that it will be, but that is no reason to think it should not be.) I would be sorry to see it stricken, however, without a dramatic reaffirmation, by Congress and the President then in office, of the essential wisdom of the two-term tradition. Let it thereafter be left to the American people to decide whether, in the event of another 1940, this tradition should be honored in the observance or in the breach.

CHAPTER 8

THE FUTURE OF THE PRESIDENCY

★

We need no special gift of prophecy to predict a long and exciting future for the American Presidency. There are those who dream of a President in the image of Calvin Coolidge; there are those who fear that the Presidency will be sapped by "the assaults of ignorance and envy." Neither the dream nor the fear is likely to find much substance in coming events. All the great political and social forces that brought the Presidency to its present state of power and glory will continue to work in the future. Our economy and society will grow more rather than less interdependent, and we will turn to the President, anxiously if not always confidently, for help in solving the problems that fall thickly upon us. Our government will become more rather than less involved in the affairs of "mankind, from China to Peru," and the peoples of the world will look to its head for bold and imaginative leadership. Emergencies will grow nastier; Congress will become more unwieldy; politics will take on more and more the spirit of a vast town meeting. And one of the few things we can say for certain about the next war is that it will convert our form of government overnight into a temporary dictatorship of the President of the United States.

Another thing we can say for certain is that we have not seen our last great man in the White House. The people of the United States are no longer interested in presidential aspirants

who promise only to be meek and mild. In the foreseeable
future, as in the recent past, they will expect and get a full
measure of presidential leadership. Even the Republicans, who
have always been distinctly less enamored of the strong Presidency than have the Democrats, are coming to realize that the
scales of power have tipped drastically and probably permanently toward the White House and away from Capitol Hill.
There is a Presidency in our future, and it is the Presidency
of Jackson and Lincoln rather than of Monroe and Buchanan,
of Roosevelt and Truman rather than of Harding and Coolidge.

If any of my readers doubts the validity of this prediction,
let him make a list of the gravest social problems we now face
in this country, and then let him ask himself whether a single
one of them is ever going to be solved to the satisfaction of
the American people without a persistent and vigorous display
of presidential leadership. My own list, for what it is worth,
would begin with four—the crisis in race relations, the intolerable incidence of crime and delinquency, the lag in education,
and the blight of our cities—and would end with the observation that the first step toward the solution of each of these and
of many other problems must be the determination of the President to bring all his power and prestige to bear upon them.
These problems call for state and local action, but such action
now seems doomed to failure in the absence of co-ordination,
stimulation, and even direction from the federal government.
They call for bold legislation by Congress, but for a complex
of historical, sectional, and political reasons Congress seems
powerless to move forcefully against them. As a result, we have
never been in more obvious need of presidential manipulation
of all the techniques that are available to him to mold opinion,
goad Congress, and inspire public officials at all levels.

Within the federal government itself the need for presidential
leadership is no less pressing. We have talked ourselves dizzy in
recent years about the steps we ought to take toward more
effective co-ordination and supervision of the government's

wide-ranging and costly activities in the rapidly expanding realm of science. I have no intention of aggravating this state of dizziness, but I would like to point out that a good deal of it would disappear quickly if all participants in this great conversation, especially the scientists themselves, were to recognize the paramount position the President must occupy in any reasonable solution. He is Commander in Chief, and fully eighty per cent of the four billions of dollars we now spend annually on scientific research and development is devoted to purposes of national security; he is Chief Executive, and science, like every other activity in the government, reduces in the end to questions of budgeting, reporting, and the choice and supervision of personnel; he is, above all, the President of the United States, and we have a national habit of sooner or later bringing our major problems to focus in the office of Washington, Lincoln, and Roosevelt. I do not know what the solution is to this complicated problem, or whether, indeed, there is any solution that can ever satisfy all the many constituencies that must be satisfied. I know only that the Presidency is the peg on which we will surely have to hang all co-ordination and supervision, not to mention inspiration and direction, of scientific endeavor under the auspices of the federal government. And I know, too, that Eisenhower's appointment of James A. Killian, Jr., in November 1957 to the post of Special Assistant to the President for Science and Technology was only a first timid step toward the kind of bold solution—perhaps a new unit in the Executive Office, perhaps a Department of Science, perhaps a tightly reined group of interdepartmental committees—to which we must surely come in time. My own preference would be for a combination of the first and third of these loudly voiced proposals, not least because it would acknowledge the President's central position and draw authority directly from his prestige. If we have to have a "czar of science" in Washington in the years ahead, the only candidate I can imagine our swallowing would be the President himself.

I trust that no one will interpret this last remark as a plea for central direction of our scientific effort from the White House. The President already has far too many other eggs to watch without asking him to take immediate command of the race into space or the search for new sources of energy or the attempt to control the weather; and, in any case, that is not the way we get great things accomplished in our society. But I would still insist that whatever hope we have for a more alert, rational, economical management of the human and financial resources our government contributes to research and technology depends to a large degree on the capacity of the Presidency to co-ordinate the kind of activity in which dozens of federal agencies must necessarily be involved. I am not nominating the President for the role of Chief Scientist; neither he nor science nor the American cause would profit from such a development. I am merely expressing what seems to be the common sense of the matter: that every President from now on must give considerable time and thought to the serious problem of how to make the government of the United States a benevolent force in our advance into the wonders of the future, and that he must serve consciously as the center of gravity around which the scientific endeavors of the federal government revolve in a multitude of orbits. Science demands a pattern of pluralism, inside as well as outside our government, but pluralism is anarchy without a common point of reference. For the National Science Foundation, the Atomic Energy Commission, the National Aeronautics and Space Administration, the Advanced Research Projects Agency, and all other major agencies and committees that we may in time create, this point of reference can only be the President of the United States.

Since the Presidency of the future will grow out of the Presidency of the present, it is imperative to go one step farther with this appraisal. The total picture of the office drawn in this book has been perhaps more cheerful than it should be. In attempting to point up sharply the elements of strength and reliability in the Presidency, I have passed too lightly over problems and weaknesses to which some of our most useful public servants and astute political scientists have addressed themselves with fervor and ingenuity. Let me now turn to examine the most pressing of these. This is not, be it noted, an appraisal of the American system of government, even less of American society. I must assume that we have the society we deserve; I do assume that it would be neither possible nor sensible to alter the main outlines of our government. I propose to concentrate on the Presidency as it is and might be constituted, and to call attention to those defects, real or alleged, about which men of good will and good sense are most earnestly agitated. I will also have something to say about the wisdom and feasibility of current proposals to eliminate these defects.

To the worst of these, the patched-up machinery for electing an able President and the missing machinery for relieving a disabled one, I have already devoted most of two full chapters. I have nothing to add except one fearless prediction: Barring a calamity that frightens us half out of our wits, nothing will be done about them for years to come, if ever.

A third major defect that men find in the Presidency is the intolerable burden laid upon him who holds it. I am not talking here about the great functions of state he discharges in our behalf, for I cannot imagine how a single one of these could be transferred safely and effectively to some other officer in the national government. It would be a constitutional disaster if the President were even to attempt to surrender his final responsibility in the areas of war, peace, politics, opinion, ceremony, and management. I am talking, rather, of the routine of these functions: of the mechanical tasks he is required to perform by law and custom; of the briefings, appointments, speeches, conferences, and appearances; of the letters he must answer and signatures he must affix. Much has been done in recent years to relieve him of his petty burdens without relieving him of his great responsibilities, and we can be grateful to Franklin Roosevelt and his successors for having taken the lead in improving their own lot. Yet much, too, remains to be done. We should expect future Presidents, Congresses, and Executive Offices to co-operate in guarding the Presidency against the paralysis of detail. Considerable authority is already in the President's hands. For example, in 1950 Congress enacted a brief provision permitting the President to delegate functions vested in him by statute, and it is comforting to learn that Mr. Eisenhower used this authority to rid himself of hundreds of petty duties we had no business laying upon the President in the first place. We may be sure that every President from this time forward will press the search for functions to delegate to his chief lieutenants.

In seeking to lighten the President's burden, we would do well to recall the warning of Woodrow Wilson: "Men of ordinary physique and discretion cannot be Presidents and live, if the strain be not somehow relieved. We shall be obliged always to be picking our chief magistrates from among wise and prudent athletes—a small class." At the same time, we should also recall that a long list of routine tasks, each of which appears "nonessential" when viewed by itself, may well add up to an inspired performance of a great function of state. The President cannot be a successful Chief of State if he turns all the little ceremonies and visits over to the Vice-President. He cannot lead Congress if he is unwilling to spend hours listening to Congressmen. And he cannot be a vigorous Commander in Chief unless he studies the defense budget item by item. For him as for all of us there is no final escape from hard and pedestrian labor. And as the gentlemen of Congress warned in the law of 1950 I have just mentioned: "Nothing contained herein shall relieve the President of his responsibility" for the acts of those "designated by him to perform [his] functions." As Mr. Truman would say, the President may pass the details but not the buck.

The Executive Office itself presents a number of problems, although it, too, is a huge improvement over the haphazard machinery on which our Presidents had to rely before 1939. For one thing, the President still lacks complete control over the organization of this machinery; he should be completely free to establish, regroup, or eliminate the components of the Executive Office on his own order, and to experiment with the internal structure of each component. For another, there has never been a satisfactory arrangement within the Executive Office to assist him in handling his numerous duties as chief personnel officer of the national government. And for a third, he still lacks adequate assistance, in the form of a single staff agency or perhaps of several agencies, in co-ordinating the many elements in his total program.

The real problem of the Executive Office is potential rather than actual: the danger that the President might be buried under his own machinery. The institutionalization of the Presidency could be carried so far that the man who occupies it would become a prisoner in his own house, a victim of too much and too rigid organization. I doubt very much that such a situation could last for long if it did develop. Andrew Jackson proved once and for all the capacity of a determined President to burst the bonds of restrictive custom and legislation and to beat a retreat to the plain words of Article II. Yet rather than make it necessary for another Jackson to blow across Washington like a "tropical tornado," we should be alert to steps that might weaken or smother the President's position of dominance over his own auxiliaries. Much depends, of course, on his intimate advisers. It is their unrelenting duty to protect the President against all but the most essential problems in their designated areas, to present these in such form that they can be readily mastered, and especially to preserve the President's freedom of choice among competing alternatives. Needless to say, the President himself must set the tone for the operations of the Executive Office. He must insist that he be spared routine but not thought and decision, for he is, after all, the responsible head of government. He must be careful not to rely too heavily on the briefings and opinions of his own staff, for he will soon find himself out of touch with harsh reality. Above all, he must leave channels open to the political and social pressures that excite imagination and breed sensitivity. Unfriendly visitors, hostile newspapers, and free-swinging press conferences are three such channels he must have the insight and bravery not to block off. The Presidency must not become so highly mechanized that the President himself is spared the "suffering and glory of democratic leadership."

The Executive Office never will or should take on a permanent pattern of organization. Each President must feel free to tinker with it; no part of it, not even the Bureau of the Budget, should be considered too sacred to touch. The President, like the Red Queen, must run as fast as he can to stay in the same place. He must make a half-dozen adjustments in the course of his incumbency simply to keep pace with the rising tempo of his duties. The need in this vital area is for change and experiment, for an Executive Office that is not so much a perfect design as a plastic mosaic of formal and informal arrangements. There is, however, an outer limit beyond which it would be unwise to expand the Executive Office. It must be big enough to make it possible for the President to supervise the administration, but not so big that he has trouble supervising it. It must have enough officers and agencies and committees to make it possible for him to make up his mind, but not so many that his mind is made up for him. In the White House itself, as in the administration that sprawls all around it, we have quite possibly reached the limit of "government by committee."

The Cabinet has been a problem for at least a generation—in George Graham's words, "a bleeding and anemic patient." Only tough custom and past glory have kept it from sliding noiselessly into oblivion. It is no longer a body upon which the President can rely for sage advice on great issues of state; it is not even, in its formal composition, a gathering of his most important and intimate associates. It is at best a relic of a simpler past when department heads were thought to be men of broad interests and held in their own hands the whole power of administration.

Mr. Eisenhower, to be sure, did his best to restore the Cabinet to full duty. He invited such key officials as the Director of the Budget and the Chairman of the Civil Service Commission to attend regularly. He went ahead to institute what other Presidents had only talked about vaguely: a formal Cabinet secretariat to organize its work, keep the necessary records, and follow through on decisions. In addition to setting up a subcabinet to support the Cabinet itself, he continued the practice of authorizing Cabinet-level committees to deal with special problems, which in his incumbency ranged all the way from the co-ordination of foreign-aid activities to a drive on narcotics. He even reminded us of the existence of the Cabinet by staging one of its sessions on television, although the chief result of this exercise in the "soft sell" was to dramatize the unimportance of a council whose proceedings could be tuned in (and tuned out) by an entire nation. Eisenhower followed Truman in the practice of using the National Security Council (which has *not* appeared on television) as a functional cabinet in matters of military and foreign policy, leaving the Cabinet to devote itself narrowly to domestic, administrative, and political affairs. A group that takes no real part in making and co-ordinating policy in the area of national survival can hardly be considered a great council of state in the image of the Cabinets of our past.

It remains to be seen whether any efforts to revive the Cabinet prove successful. Eisenhower bucked an ebb tide that has been running for a long time, and it is just possible that his successors could ride this tide to a happier solution. The President needs conciliar advice, in national as in international affairs; he needs agencies to co-ordinate executive policy, in the government at large as in the White House. Yet it is clear that the Cabinet cannot serve these two high purposes as well as other groups and agencies that exist already or could be set up without too much difficulty. What would probably serve the President best is a series of functional cabinets and Cabinet-level committees, each with a secretariat of its own and each recognizing him or his deputy as chairman. The Cabinet itself, which has been around too long to be allowed to disappear entirely, might well be doubled in size and raised to the status of a privy council. It would meet only at moments of solemn decision; it would be a dignified holding company for the several subcabinets to which pertinent members of the parent body would belong. Though I tread here in fields of fancy, I think it altogether possible that the Cabinet's future lies in this direction.

Perhaps the softest spot of all in the general health of the Presidency lies in the gap between responsibility and authority, between promise and performance, in the area of public administration. The President, as I pointed out in Chapter 1, is held primarily responsible for the ethics, loyalty, efficiency, frugality, and responsiveness to the public's wishes of the two million and more Americans in the national administration. He is the Chief Executive, the general manager of the business of government, the one officer designated by the Constitution to "take care that the laws be faithfully executed." Yet his authority over the administration is in no way equal to his responsibility for its performance. Many executive functions are placed by statute beyond his reach in the independent commissions; many are carried on by bureaus and offices upon which time, tenure, and politics have bestowed an autonomy he challenges at his peril. Committees of Congress, themselves practically independent of their parent bodies, maintain more intimate relations with many agencies than those enjoyed by the President and his department heads. His own subordinates are often vested by statute with direct authority to conduct important programs; at the same time, they are granted appropriations in such detailed form that neither they nor the President can administer them with the necessary freedom of maneuver. Almost everywhere the President turns to supervise and discipline, he is trapped in the toils of pluralism, tradition, politics, professionalism, and inertia.

Here, too, improvements have been wrought in recent years, although it is always a question whether these have kept pace with the careening growth of the administration. The most essential of these improvements, of course, was the incorporation of the Bureau of the Budget in the Executive Office, for without its help in both fiscal and administrative affairs the Presidency would long since have sunk without a trace. And here, too, much remains to be done, as the first Hoover Commission reminded the nation forcefully. Most of those who have lived with the problem and gone home to write about it agree that the President would benefit most as Chief Executive from these steps, no one of them easy to take:

The President should be granted full and permanent statutory power, subject to congressional disapproval within a specified time, to reorganize the internal structure of the executive branch, and then he should use this power to straighten out the lines of control throughout the administration.

Congress should help him to reduce the pockets of obstinate independence for whose existence there are not even convincing political reasons, and together they should work to cut down the number of officials whom the President is expected to supervise directly.

Congress should resist the urge to insert in the laws needlessly detailed instructions to those designated to execute them.

The President himself should experiment with groups and procedures designed to co-ordinate policy throughout the administration.

An entirely new study should be made of the independent regulatory commissions, and steps should then be taken to bring their strictly executive functions more clearly into the President's area of responsibility. To integrate the commissions completely in the executive branch would be, I think, to pile one gross mistake on top of another, but much can be done to give more purposeful direction to our celebrated "headless fourth branch of government."

The whole system of personnel administration in the national government should be overhauled. On one hand, a reformed Civil Service Commission should be located within the Executive Office; on the other, the actual selection and management of personnel should be largely decentralized to department and commission heads.

We must not be misled by counsels of perfection in this confused area; we must not expect too much of the man who is supposed to supervise it. Inertia and tradition are found in all human organizations, and as often as not they serve some good purpose. There will always be conflict of purpose between the administrator with his professional knowledge and the politician with his constituency. In the very nature of things political and administrative, many tasks of government have to be performed with little or no opportunity for the application of over-all management. The "perfect pyramid" of administration is more a delusion than a panacea; rivalry and friction have virtues of their own. As long as power is both divided and shared by Congress and President, the former must be expected to take an active role in overseeing administration, and the role, as we know, can be played usefully as well as actively. The most essential point of all is to remember that the President has responsibilities that range far beyond his formless duty "to produce a good administration," and that many of these are impossible to delegate and disastrous to ignore. He has other and more important roles to play, and if he works too hard, if he succeeds too auspiciously, as Chief Executive, this is a certain sign that he is neglecting his high duties as Chief Diplomat or Commander in Chief.

It may well be time to readjust our thinking about the President's responsibility and authority as Chief Executive. If we cannot level the latter up, perhaps we should level the former down. We should not hold him to such strict account, as we still do in the country at large, for every blunder and fraud throughout the administration. He can never surrender constitutionally, nor should he surrender effectively, the final duty to oversee the execution of the laws. But we should ask no more of him than that he set a high personal example of integrity and industry, choose able men to administer the nation's business, delegate his administrative powers broadly and support his deputies faithfully, give a clear political lead that can be transmitted downward through his chief lieutenants, and act magisterially to punish glaring breaches of decorum and democracy. Perhaps we should be more tolerant of our President, at least in his capacity as Chief Executive.

Since the opening day of Washington's administration the President's relations with Congress have been a target of criticism; the target is still being shot at with enthusiasm and at least passing accuracy. Much of this criticism is irrelevant, since it ignores the blunt truth that we long ago made our irrevocable choice of co-ordinate rather than unified government. Much is soft-headed, since it refuses to rise above the political and personal frictions that are the mark, but not the only mark, of such government. Yet much hits the target squarely, and I think we should take notice of two major areas in which the hope of improvement must never be abandoned.

In the first place, the President's leadership of Congress remains spotty and discontinuous. Although he is acknowledged widely to be the Leader of Legislation, his tools of persuasion, except his own machinery for drafting, clearing, and forwarding legislative proposals, are not one bit sharper than they were forty years ago. Here, too, as in the field of administration, there is a widening gap between what the people expect and what he can produce. He must have a program and push for its enactment, but he has no way to force a decision upon a reluctant Congress.

There have been a dozen or more proposals, some modest and others extravagant, to stabilize the President's leadership and increase his influence in Congress. Senator Kefauver has taken up Representative Pendleton's ancient plan for a question-and-answer period for department heads on the floor of either house. Professor Corwin predicts great gains for harmony if the President would choose part of his Cabinet from leading members of Congress. The La Follette–Monroney Committee of 1946 recommended a joint council of congressional leaders and Cabinet officers who would presumably work together in making and executing national policy. Some political scientists talk fondly of "responsible party government"; others put their trust in elaborate schemes for parallel organization of each major department or agency and its related committee in Congress. All these proposals are well-intentioned, and one, the establishment of an executive-legislative council by joint resolution, might be worth a try. Most, however, are not nearly so clever or feasible as they may seem at first glance, and several might have results far different from those predicted. In particular, it is not impossible that the President's leadership, which we have labored long to fix in custom, would suffer grave damage.

Is there nothing, then, that we can do to achieve a more stable relationship between the two great political branches? Nothing, I would answer, that ignores these facts, some of which I have already stated: First, superficial remedies will not cure, and may only quicken, the nervous tension between President and Congress that is endemic to our system. Second, stronger remedies, such as those proposals of a parliamentary system we have heard from Professor W. Y. Elliott and Thomas

K. Finletter and David Lawrence, are just not called for in the present situation, nor would the patients submit to them in any situation. Third, we cannot have the best of both possible worlds, the rugged safeguards of our own system and the sweet harmonies of the British. To mix the metaphor hopelessly, there is no such thing as a happy mongrel that combines the good points of both parents. And finally, the affliction of dissension and irresponsibility arises from much deeper causes in our system than the arrangements of the Constitution. Those who insist that the affliction is a disease, and also think they can cure it, must go beyond government to reform politics and beyond politics to reform society—which is another way of saying that they should take the sage's advice to "relax and enjoy the inevitable."

In the last reckoning, we will continue to make progress toward firmer and friendlier executive-legislative relations by traveling the familiar path hacked out by the successful Presidents of this century. By following this path, even when it wandered through the swamps of petty politics, we have moved to a point at which co-operation under the President's guidance is far more certain that it was before 1900. Term by term, crisis by crisis, men in and out of Congress have been educated to accept the necessity of presidential leadership, and the Presidents have gone through a cumulative learning process of their own. This process of education in statesmanship must be carried on indefinitely, for in prescriptive growth, not in clever "gimmicks," lies our best hope for the co-operation we have a right to expect.

Most political observers are now more concerned with the other side of the two-way street between President and Congress. While he is busy asserting leadership in making laws, Congress is busy asserting control over their execution, and there is evidence to support the charge that Congress has roamed farther out of bounds than the President in the past few years. It is, to be sure, an axiom of co-ordinate government that the independent legislature must exercise oversight of the administration. Congress, too, must be concerned with ethics, loyalty, efficiency, frugality, and responsiveness in the public service; it must judge for itself whether the laws are being faithfully executed. No one can argue that it has any less constitutional right than the President to stake its claim to the disputed territory between them. But it does not have the right, probably not constitutionally and certainly not morally, to take over effective control of any part of the executive branch. It may inquire, expose, encourage, and warn, but it may not direct; and this—straight-out direction of various agencies and officers—is what Congress has been doing too much of in recent years. The result has been disorder, dissension, indecision, and disruption of morale at key points in the public service. Needless to say, Congress as a whole is guilty only of nonfeasance. It is the members of Congress, operating as committees, subcommittees, or lone wolves, who have poked their inquiring noses beyond the limits of political decorum and constitutional practice.

Concern over improper congressional meddling in the business of the executive reached a peak of indignation in the heady days when Senator McCarthy was asserting with implausible gall his right of espionage in the executive branch. It did seem for a while as if he and his friends might do permanent damage to those vague but visible lines drawn by custom between President and Congress. The decline of the Senator, matched and hastened by the rise of the President, did much to restore the old condition of equilibrium in this delicate area. There are even those who feel that the lines were made more visible by Mr. Eisenhower's ordeal, or, rather, by the ordeal of those whom he seemed unwilling to protect; many members of Congress are now said to be more aware of the limits beyond which they cannot go in their search for misconduct in the administration. Surely we are all much clearer in our minds about the responsibility of the President and his chief lieutenants to keep Congress out of the executive sphere. It would be pleasant to think that each of the houses would have enough sense and bravery to hold its marauders in check, but while we await the Golden Age of congressional self-discipline, we must put our trust in the truth that power alone can check power. It is up to the President, exercising his rightful power, to hold the lines of constitutional sanity against those who would break through them in reckless quest of notoriety or sincere inquest of wrong-doing. He must defend his own authority while conceding that of Congress.

He has the best chance of doing this, it seems to me, by applying prudently this tested rule: The head of a department or agency, who has the power to give orders to his subordinates, must in turn stand ready to answer for the manner of their execution. The pertinent corollary is this: The head has the right and duty to interpose his authority, as best he can, between the investigator and the subordinate and give the necessary answers himself to congressional committees. In terms of recent experience, it was not a question of Senator McCarthy's right to ask "who promoted Major Peress," which we must concede with a grimace; it was a question of who should give the answer—the responsible head and his chief deputies, or a procession of bewildered and belabored subordinates. The responsible head, not a marauding Senator, must command the loyalty of the men for whose performance he is constitutionally and legally accountable. There are limits, of course, both political and practical, to the authority of a top administrator to control, defend, and speak for the public servants under his direction. Yet not until this wise old rule is established in our constitutional thinking will peace (as much peace as we can expect under our system) reign on this side of the street between President and Congress.

It may be thought irrelevant to call attention to the defects of Congress, but it is generally conceded that a strengthening of the national legislature in terms of its own internal structure would do much to improve working relations with the President. He has nothing to fear, to the contrary, he has much to gain, from the adoption of most proposals for reform that have been pressed on Congress by some of its best friends. Congress as a whole presents no improper threat to his legitimate control over the operations of the administration. Small groups and freewheeling individuals strike illicit bargains, plant co-operative friends, and ask indecent questions; small groups and freewheeling individuals hamstring the power of legislative decision and bring Congress into disrepute. Any step, therefore, that would lead to tighter organization, to a situation in which the houses could exercise some discipline over their outlaws and control over their obstructionists, would be a blessing alike to President and Congress. Any step toward efficiency, for example, a reduction in the number of committees, could not fail to give the President satisfaction. He has no stake in an inefficient and overburdened Congress. He has a sizable stake, as do all of us, in the reform of Congress.

There is one final defect in the relations of President and Congress of which we should take careful note, especially since its correction would strengthen the President's control over the administration as well as his influence in Congress. I refer to his lack of any power to veto separate items in the overstuffed appropriations bills presented for his approval. The President often feels compelled to sign bills that are full of dubious grants and subsidies rather than risk a breakdown in the work of whole departments. While it salves his conscience and cools his anger to announce publicly that he would veto these if he could, most Congressmen have learned to pay no attention to his protests. The champions of the "item veto," who point out that forty governors have a power denied to the President, insist that nothing but great good would come from giving it to him, whether through a constitutional amendment or, failing that, a self-denying ordinance of Congress. On one hand, his leadership of Congress would be strengthened, for he would hold an efficient new weapon, one that works out in the open, for reminding Congressmen that economy in the national interest is just as important as spending in the local interest. On the other, his work as Chief Executive would run more smoothly, since he would at last have full authority to match his responsibility for the executive budget. No agency of the government would be spending new money on a project of which he had the courage to disapprove sharply.

The loudest argument that has been raised against the item veto is that it might strengthen the President's hand just a little too much in his dealings with Congress. It would open the door to presidential pressure on individual Congressmen, and thus to bargains of the hardest kind. There is much to be said for this argument, and we might well pause before amending the Constitution to grant this new power to the President. But there is no reason why Congress itself should not experiment with an occasional appropriations bill that authorizes the President to eliminate or reduce specific items subject to congressional reversal by concurrent resolution within a specified number of days. We have the assurance of several prominent constitutionalists that such a device would violate neither the letter nor the spirit of the Constitution. If Congress could once give this power outright to the governors of several territories, it can certainly give it now under wraps to the President of the United States. If we learn through these experiments that the power is one he ought to have, and is unlikely to abuse, we could then catch up with the Confederate States of America by writing it into the Constitution. We should hesitate much longer to grant him power to veto items in ordinary bills. Although the practice of attaching "riders" may often set our teeth on edge, Congress, too, needs weapons for the perpetual struggle, and we have no right to expect it to surrender this ancient blunderbuss.

★

Many Americans, not all of them Miniver Cheevys, would insist that I have thus far passed over with intent or in ignorance the gravest defect in the Presidency: the high concentration of power that rests in the President's hands, the startling expansion of this power over the past generation, the frustrations that face Congress in the attempt to regain its share and thereby to "restore the balance of the Constitution." This was not my intent, nor am I ignorant of this charge and the supporting evidence. No one who pays even passing attention to American politics can fail to know the full particulars of the case against the strong Presidency and the proposed steps to restore the old balance. Senator Taft's challenge to Truman's initial action in Korea, Representative Coudert's attempt to limit Eisenhower's power to station troops in Europe by "rider," Senator Bricker's campaign to reduce any President's power to negotiate treaties and agreements with other nations, Judge Pine's restatement of the Whig or "errand-boy" theory of the Presidency in the District Court decision in the Steel Seizure case, Senator McCarthy's riotous assault on the first principles of the Constitution—all these are straws, or whole bales of hay, in a wind that beats relentlessly on the White House. Challenges arise in every Congress to the scope if not the existence of the President's power to adjust tariffs, issue ordinances, make appointments, and influence the passage of legislation. And in persuading the country to adopt the Twenty-second Amendment, the opponents of the strong Presidency struck a mighty blow for their cause.

Their cause, I am bound to say, is ill-considered and ill-starred. It is ill-considered because any major reduction now in the powers of the President would leave us naked to our enemies, to the invisible forces of boom and bust at home and to the visible forces of unrest and aggression abroad. In a country over which industrialism has swept in great waves, in a world where active diplomacy is the minimum price of survival, it is not alone power but a vacuum of power that men must fear.

It is ill-starred because the Whigs, who may win skirmishes

and even an occasional battle, cannot win a war against American history. The strong Presidency is the product of events that cannot be undone and of forces that continue to roll. We have made our decisions for the New Economy and the New Internationalism, and in making them we have made this kind of Presidency a requisite for the effective conduct of our constitutional system. No government can exercise the supervision that ours does over the economy at home or honor the bargains that ours has made abroad unless it has a strong, unified, energetic executive to lead it.

I do not mean to say—I have not meant to say throughout this book—that "strength" in the Presidency is to be equated with "goodness" and "greatness." A strong President is a bad President, a curse upon the land, unless his means are constitutional and his ends democratic, unless he acts in ways that are fair, dignified, and familiar, and pursues policies to which a "persistent and undoubted" majority of the people has given support. We honor the great Presidents of the past, not for their strength, but for the fact that they used it wisely to build a better America. And in honoring them we recognize that their kind of Presidency is one of our chief bulwarks against decline and chaos.

In point of fact, the struggle over the powers of the Presidency, fierce though it may seem, is only a secondary campaign in a political war, now pretty well decided, over the future of America. Few men get heated up over the Presidency alone. Their arguments over its powers are really arguments over the American way of life and the direction in which it is moving. The strong Presidency is an instrument and symbol of the 1960's; the weak Presidency is an instrument and symbol of the 1920's. Those who truly yearn to "go home again," like John T. Flynn and Clarence Manion and the Daughters of the American Revolution, are right in thinking that a reduction in the powers of the Presidency would be an excellent first step to the rear, although it would be only a first step. It should be clearly understood that an attack on the Presidency like the Bricker amendment is aimed beyond the Constitution at America's position in the world. The backers of this amendment may be greatly worried about the potential dangers of "presidential autocracy," but they are even more worried about the present consequences of the New Internationalism. Conversely, many voices that are raised for an even stronger Presidency are really raised for an even bigger government with even more control of society.

We should not look with equanimity on the Presidency and its huge arsenal of authority. We should be careful about giving the President additional powers, alert to abuses of those he already holds, cognizant that the present balance of the Constitution is not a cause for unlimited self-congratulation. But we can look on it with at least as much equanimity—each of us according to his own blend of blood, bile, phlegm, and melancholy—as we do upon the present state of the Union. For the strength of the Presidency is a measure of the strength of the America in which we now live. Those who reject this America and are alarmed by the course we are taking reject the strong Presidency angrily. Those who accept this America and do not fear the one that is coming accept the strong Presidency soberly.

As I look back through this book, I detect a deep note of satisfaction, although hardly of complacency, with the American Presidency as it stands today. A steady theme seems to have run all through this final review of its weaknesses and problems, a theme entitled (with apologies to the genius of Thurber) "Leave Your Presidency Alone!" This feeling of satisfaction springs, I am frank to admit, from a political outlook more concerned with the world as it is than as it is said to have been by reactionaries and is promised to be by radicals. Since this outlook is now shared by a staggering majority of Americans, I feel that I am expressing something more than a personal opinion. If we accept the facts of life in the 1960's, as we must, and if we shun the false counsels of perfection, as we do, then we are bound to conclude that we are richly blessed with a choice instrument of constitutional democracy. Judged in the light of memory and desire, the Presidency is in a state of sturdy health, and that is why we should not give way easily to despair over the defects men of too much zeal or too little courage claim to discover in it. Some of these are not defects at all; some are chronic in our system of government; some could be cured only by opening the way to others far more malign.

This does not mean that we should stand pat with the Presidency. Rather, we should confine ourselves to small readjustments—I have noted a dozen or more that might be worth a try—and leave the usual avenues open to prescriptive change. We should abolish the electoral college but leave the electoral system to pursue its illogical but hitherto effective way. We should plan carefully for mobilization in the event of war but take care that the inherent emergency power of the President—the power used by Lincoln to blockade the South, by Wilson to arm the merchantmen, and by Roosevelt to bring off the Destroyer Deal—be left intact and untrammeled. We should experiment with a joint executive-legislative council and the item veto but be on our guard against the urge to alter radically the pattern of competitive coexistence between Congress and President. We should give the President all the aides he can use but beware the deceptively simple solution of a second and even third Vice-President for executive purposes. And we should tinker modestly with the President's machinery but wake from the false dream of perfect harmony in high places, especially in the highest place of all. For if the Presidency could speak, it would say with Whitman:

> Do I contradict myself?
> Very well then I contradict myself.
> (I am large, I contain multitudes.)

"Leave Your Presidency Alone": that is the message of this chapter, and I trust I have made clear in all these chapters why I transmit it so confidently. To put the final case for the American Presidency as forcefully as possible, let me point once again to its essential qualities:

It strikes a felicitous balance between power and limitations. In a world in which power is the price of freedom, the Presidency, as Professor Merriam and his colleagues wrote in 1937, "stands across the path of those who mistakenly assert that democracy must fail because it can neither decide promptly nor act vigorously." In a world in which power has been abused on a tragic scale, it presents a heartening lesson in the uses of constitutionalism. To repeat the moral of Chapter 2, the power of the Presidency moves as a mighty host only *with* the grain of liberty and morality. The quest of constitutional government is for the right balance of authority and restraint, and Americans may take some pride in the balance they have built into the Presidency.

It provides a steady focus of leadership: of administration, Congress, and people. In a constitutional system compounded of diversity and antagonism, the Presidency looms up as the countervailing force of unity and harmony. In a society ridden by centrifugal forces, it is, as Sidney Hyman has written, the "common reference point for social effort." The relentless progress of this continental republic has made the Presidency our one truly national political institution. There are those who would reserve this role to Congress, but as the least aggressive of our Presidents, Calvin Coolidge, once testified, "It is because in their hours of timidity the Congress becomes subservient to the importunities of organized minorities that the President comes more and more to stand as the champion of the rights of the whole country." The more Congress becomes, in Burke's phrase, "a confused and scuffling bustle of local agency," the more the Presidency must become a clear beacon of national purpose.

It is a priceless symbol of our continuity and destiny as a people. Few nations have solved so simply and yet grandly the problem of finding and maintaining an office of state that embodies their majesty and reflects their character. Only the Constitution overshadows the Presidency as an object of popular reverence, and the Constitution does not walk about smiling and shaking hands. "The simple fact is," a distinguished, disgruntled Briton wrote at the end of the "Royal Soap Opera" of 1955, "that the United States Presidency today is a far more dignified institution than the British monarchy." In all honesty and tact we must quickly demur, but we can be well satisfied with our "republican king."

It has been tested sternly in the crucible of time. Our obsession with youth leads us to forget too easily how long our chief instruments of government have been operating in unbroken career. The Presidency is now the most venerable executive among all the large nations of the earth, and if one looks back beyond 1787 to "times of ancient glory and renown," he will find that the formula has worked before. "The truth is," Henry Jones Ford wrote with grace and insight,

that in the presidential office, as it has been constituted since Jackson's time, American democracy has revived the oldest political institution of the race, the elective kingship. It is all there: the precognition of the notables and the tumultuous choice of the freemen, only conformed to modern conditions. That the people have been able . . . to make good a principle which no other people have been able to reconcile with the safety of the state, indicates the highest degree of constitutional morality yet attained by any race.

It is, finally, an office of freedom. The Presidency is a standing reproach to those petty doctrinaires who insist that executive power is inherently undemocratic; for, to the exact contrary, it has been more responsive to the needs and dreams of giant democracy than any other office or institution in the whole mosaic of American life. It is no less a reproach to those easy generalizers who think that Lord Acton had the very last word on the corrupting effects of power; for, again to the contrary,

262   *The American Presidency*

his doctrine finds small confirmation in the history of the Presidency. The vast power of this office has not been "poison," as Henry Adams wrote in scorn; rather, it has elevated often and corrupted never, chiefly because those who held it recognized the true source of the power and were ennobled by the knowledge.

The American people, who are, after all, the best judges of the means by which their democracy is to be achieved, have made the Presidency their peculiar instrument. As they ready themselves for the pilgrimage ahead, they can take comfort and pride in the thought that it is also their peculiar treasure.

THE PRESIDENTS OF

THE UNITED STATES

	Date of Inauguration	Age at Inauguration	State of Residence	Politics	Date of Death
George Washington	1789	57	Va.	Fed.	1799
John Adams	1797	61	Mass.	Fed.	1826
Thomas Jefferson	1801	57	Va.	Dem.-Rep.	1826
James Madison	1809	57	Va.	Dem.-Rep.	1836
James Monroe	1817	58	Va.	Dem.-Rep.	1831
John Q. Adams	1825	57	Mass.	Dem.-Rep.	1848
Andrew Jackson	1829	61	Tenn.	Dem.	1845
Martin Van Buren	1837	54	N.Y.	Dem.	1862
William H. Harrison	1841	68	Ohio	Whig	1841
John Tyler	1841	51	Va.	Whig	1862
James K. Polk	1845	49	Tenn.	Dem.	1849
Zachary Taylor	1849	64	La.	Whig	1850
Millard Fillmore	1850	50	N.Y.	Whig	1874
Franklin Pierce	1853	48	N.H.	Dem.	1869
James Buchanan	1857	65	Pa.	Dem.	1868
Abraham Lincoln	1861	52	Ill.	Rep.	1865
Andrew Johnson	1865	56	Tenn.	Dem.(Union)	1875
Ulysses S. Grant	1869	46	Ill.	Rep.	1885
Rutherford B. Hayes	1877	54	Ohio	Rep.	1893
James A. Garfield	1881	49	Ohio	Rep.	1881
Chester A. Arthur	1881	50	N.Y.	Rep.	1886
Grover Cleveland	1885	47	N.Y.	Dem.	1908
Benjamin Harrison	1889	55	Ohio	Rep.	1901
Grover Cleveland	1893	55	N.Y.	Dem.	1908
William McKinley	1897	54	Ohio	Rep.	1901
Theodore Roosevelt	1901	42	N.Y.	Rep.	1919
William H. Taft	1909	51	Ohio	Rep.	1930
Woodrow Wilson	1913	56	N.J.	Dem.	1924
Warren G. Harding	1921	55	Ohio	Rep.	1923
Calvin Coolidge	1923	51	Mass.	Rep.	1933
Herbert Hoover	1929	54	Cal.	Rep.	—
Franklin D. Roosevelt	1933	51	N.Y.	Dem.	1945
Harry S Truman	1945	60	Mo.	Dem.	—
Dwight D. Eisenhower	1953	62	N.Y. (Pa.)	Rep.	—

THE PRESIDENCY IN THE

CONSTITUTION

Those passages in the Constitution that touch directly upon the Presidency run as follows:

Article I

Section 3:

6. The Senate shall have the sole power to try all impeachments. When sitting for that purpose, they shall be on oath or affirmation. When the President of the United States is tried, the Chief Justice shall preside; and no person shall be convicted without the concurrence of two-thirds of the members present.

7. Judgment in cases of impeachment shall not extend further than to removal from office, and disqualification to hold and enjoy any office of honor, trust, or profit under the United States; but the party convicted shall, nevertheless, be liable and subject to indictment, trial, judgment, and punishment, according to law.

Section 7:

2. Every bill which shall have passed the House of Representatives and the Senate shall, before it becomes a law, be presented to the President of the United States; if he approve he shall sign it, but if not he shall return it, with his objections, to that house in which it shall have originated, who shall enter the objections at large on their journal and

proceed to reconsider it. If after such reconsideration two-thirds of that house shall agree to pass the bill, it shall be sent, together with the objections, to the other house, by which it shall likewise be reconsidered, and if approved by two-thirds of that house it shall become a law. But in all such cases the votes of both houses shall be determined by yeas and nays, and the names of the persons voting for and against the bill shall be entered on the journal of each house respectively. If any bill shall not be returned by the President within ten days (Sundays excepted) after it shall have been presented to him, the same shall be a law, in like manner as if he had signed it unless the Congress by their adjournment prevent its return, in which case it shall not be a law.

3. Every order, resolution, or vote to which the concurrence of the Senate and House of Representatives may be necessary (except on a question of adjournment) shall be presented to the President of the United States; and before the same shall take effect, shall be approved by him, or being disapproved by him, shall be repassed by two-thirds of the Senate and House of Representatives, according to the rules and limitations prescribed in the case of a bill.

Article II

Section 1:

1. The executive power shall be vested in a President of the United States of America. He shall hold his office during the term of four years, and, together with the Vice-President, chosen for the same term, be elected as follows:

2. Each state shall appoint, in such manner as the legislature thereof may direct, a number of electors, equal to the whole number of Senators and Representatives to which the State may be entitled in the Congress; but no Senator or Representative, or person holding an office of trust or profit under the United States, shall be appointed an elector.

[3. The electors shall meet in their respective States and

vote by ballot for two persons, of whom one at least shall not be an inhabitant of the same State with themselves. And they shall make a list of all the persons voted for, and of the number of votes for each; which list they shall sign and certify, and transmit sealed to the seat of the government of the United States, directed to the President of the Senate. The President of the Senate shall, in the presence of the Senate and House of Representatives, open all the certificates, and the votes shall then be counted. The person having the greatest number of votes shall be the President, if such a number be a majority of the whole number of electors appointed; and if there be more than one who have such majority, and have an equal number of votes, then the House of Representatives shall immediately choose by ballot one of them for President; and if no person have a majority, then from the five highest on the list the said House shall in like manner choose the President. But in choosing the President the votes shall be taken by States, the representation from each State having one vote; a quorum for this purpose shall consist of a member or members from two-thirds of the States, and a majority of all the States shall be necessary to a choice. In every case, after the choice of the President, the person having the greatest number of votes of the electors shall be the Vice-President. But if there should remain two or more who have equal votes, the Senate shall choose from them by ballot the Vice-President.]

4. The Congress may determine the time of choosing the electors and the day on which they shall give their votes, which day shall be the same throughout the United States.

5. No person except a natural born citizen, or a citizen of the United States at the time of the adoption of this Constitution, shall be eligible to the office of President; neither shall any person be eligible to that office who shall not have attained to the age of thirty-five years, and been fourteen years a resident within the United States.

6. In case of the removal of the President from office, or of his death, resignation, or inability to discharge the powers and duties of the said office, the same shall devolve on the Vice-President, and the Congress may by law provide for the case of removal, death, resignation, or inability, both of the President and Vice-President, declaring what officer shall then act as President, and such officer shall act accordingly until the disability be removed or a President shall be elected.

7. The President shall, at stated times, receive for his services a compensation, which shall neither be increased nor diminished during the period for which he shall have been elected, and he shall not receive within that period any other emolument from the United States or any of them.

8. Before he enter on the execution of his office he shall take the following oath or affirmation:

"I do solemnly swear (or affirm) that I will faithfully execute the office of President of the United States, and will to the best of my ability preserve, protect, and defend the Constitution of the United States."

Section 2:

1. The President shall be Commander-in-Chief of the Army and Navy of the United States, and of the militia of the several States when called into the actual service of the United States; he may require the opinion, in writing, of the principal officer in each of the executive departments, upon any subject relating to the duties of their respective offices, and he shall have power to grant reprieves and pardons for offenses against the United States, except in cases of impeachment.

2. He shall have power, by and with the advice and consent of the Senate, to make treaties, provided two-thirds of the Senators present concur; and he shall nominate, and, by and with the advice and consent of the Senate, shall appoint ambassadors, other public ministers and consuls, judges of the Supreme Court, and all other officers of the United States,

whose appointments are not herein otherwise provided for, and which shall be established by law; but the Congress may by law vest the appointment of such inferior officers, as they think proper, in the President alone, in the courts of law, or in the heads of departments.

3. The President shall have power to fill up all vacancies that may happen during the recess of the Senate, by granting commissions which shall expire at the end of their next session.

Section 3:

He shall from time to time give to the Congress information of the state of the Union, and recommend to their consideration such measures as he shall judge necessary and expedient; he may, on extraordinary occasions, convene both houses, or either of them, and in case of disagreement between them with respect to the time of adjournment, he may adjourn them to such time as he shall think proper; he shall receive ambassadors and other public ministers; he shall take care that the laws be faithfully executed, and shall commission all the officers of the United States.

Section 4:

The President, Vice-President, and all civil officers of the United States shall be removed from office on impeachment for and conviction of treason, bribery, or other high crimes and misdemeanors.

Amendment XII

The electors shall meet in their respective States and vote by ballot for President and Vice-President, one of whom, at least, shall not be an inhabitant of the same State with themselves; they shall name in their ballots the person voted for as President, and in distinct ballots the person voted for as Vice-President, and they shall make distinct lists of all persons voted for as President and of all persons voted for as Vice-President, and of the number of votes for each; which lists they shall sign and certify, and transmit sealed to the seat of the government of the United States, directed to the President of the Senate. The President of the Senate shall, in the presence of the Senate and House of Representatives, open all the certificates and the votes shall then be counted. The person having the greatest number of votes for President shall be the President, if such number be a majority of the whole number of electors appointed; and if no person have such majority, then from the persons having the highest numbers not exceeding three on the list of those voted for as President, the House of Representatives shall choose immediately, by ballot, the President. But in choosing the President the votes shall be taken by States, the representation from each State having one vote; a quorum for this purpose shall consist of a member or members from two-thirds of the States, and a majority of all the States shall be necessary to a choice. And if the House of Representatives shall not choose a President whenever the right of choice shall devolve upon them, before the fourth day of March next following, then the Vice-President shall act as President, as in the case of the death or other constitutional disability of the President.

The person having the greatest number of votes as Vice-President shall be the Vice-President, if such number be a majority of the whole number of electors appointed; and if no person have a majority, then from the two highest numbers on the list the Senate shall choose the Vice-President; a quorum for the purpose shall consist of two-thirds of the whole number of Senators, and a majority of the whole number shall be necessary to a choice. But no person constitutionally ineligible to the office of President shall be eligible to that of Vice-President of the United States.

Amendment XX

Section 1:

The terms of the President and Vice-President shall end at

noon on the 20th day of January, and the terms of Senators and Representatives at noon on the 3d day of January, of the years in which such terms would have ended if this article had not been ratified; and the terms of their successors shall then begin.

Section 2:

The Congress shall assemble at least once in every year, and such meeting shall begin at noon on the 3d day of January, unless they shall by law appoint a different day.

Section 3:

If, at the time fixed for the beginning of the term of the President, the President elect shall have died, the Vice-President elect shall become President. If a President shall not have been chosen before the time fixed for the beginning of his term, or if the President elect shall have failed to qualify, then the Vice-President elect shall act as President until a President shall have qualified; and the Congress may by law provide for the case wherein neither a President elect nor a Vice-President elect shall have qualified, declaring who shall then act as President, or the manner in which one who is to act shall be selected, and such person shall act accordingly until a President or Vice-President shall have qualified.

Section 4:

The Congress may by law provide for the case of the death of any of the persons from whom the House of Representatives may choose a President whenever the right of choice shall have devolved upon them, and for the case of the death of any of the persons from whom the Senate may choose a Vice-President whenever the right of choice shall have devolved upon them.

Amendment XXII

No person shall be elected to the office of the President more than twice, and no person who has held the office of President, or acted as President, for more than two years of a term to which some other person was elected President shall be elected to the office of the President more than once. But this Article shall not apply to any person holding the office of President when this Article was proposed by the Congress, and shall not prevent any person who may be holding the office of President, or acting as President, during the term within which this Article becomes operative from holding the office of President or acting as President during the remainder of such term.

Appendix III

A BIBLIOGRAPHY OF THE

PRESIDENCY

The Presidency has been the subject of a vast amount of writing both good and bad. What I have tried to do in the following list is to separate the wheat of the fifty or so most rewarding books on the Presidency from the chaff of the hundreds that one would have to read to exhaust the subject. The ones I have starred are, if I may be pardoned the expression, the cream of the wheat. Some of the best writing on the Presidency, of course, is to be found in general histories of the United States, treatises on the national government, and the dispatches of such perceptive observers as James Reston and Walter Lippmann.

I. GENERAL WORKS

Wilfred E. Binkley, *The Man in the White House,* Baltimore, 1958
*Edward S. Corwin, *The President: Office and Powers,* 4th Edition, New York, 1957
Edward S. Corwin and Louis W. Koenig, *The Presidency Today,* New York, 1956
*Sidney Hyman, *The American President,* New York, 1954
Sidney Hyman (ed.), *The Office of the American Presidency,* in *The Annals of The American Academy of Political and Social Science,* Vol. 307, 1956
*Harold J. Laski, *The American Presidency,* New York, 1940, also issued in paperback
J. Francis Paschal (ed.), *The Presidential Office,* in *Law and Contemporary Problems,* Vol. 21. 1957

Robert S. Rankin (ed.), *The Presidency in Transition*, in *The Journal of Politics*, Vol. 11, 1949

II. SPECIAL STUDIES

*Lawrence H. Chamberlain, *The President, Congress and Legislation*, New York, 1946

Richard F. Fenno, Jr., *The President's Cabinet*, Cambridge, Mass., 1959

*Joseph P. Harris, *The Advice and Consent of the Senate*, Berkeley, Calif., 1953

Pendleton Herring, *Presidential Leadership*, New York, 1940

Edward H. Hobbs, *Behind the President*, Washington, 1954

W. H. Humbert, *The Pardoning Power of the President*, Washington, 1941

Harry S. Learned, *The President's Cabinet*, New Haven, Conn., 1912

Richard E. Neustadt, *Presidential Power*, New York, 1960

Bennett Milton Rich, *The Presidents and Civil Disorder*, Washington, 1941

Clinton Rossiter, *The Supreme Court and the Commander-in-Chief*, Ithaca, N. Y., 1951

Glendon A. Schubert, Jr., *The Presidency in the Courts*, Minneapolis, 1957

Norman J. Small, *Some Presidential Interpretations of the Presidency*, Baltimore, 1932

Ruth C. Silva, *Presidential Succession*, Ann Arbor, Mich., 1951

Irving G. Williams, *The Rise of the Vice-Presidency*, Washington, 1956

*Lucius Wilmerding, Jr., *The Electoral College*, New Brunswick, New Jersey, 1958

III. PRESIDENTIAL POLITICS

Paul T. David, Malcolm Moos, and Ralph M. Goldman, *Presidential Nominating Politics*, 5 vols., Baltimore, 1954

Malcolm Moos, *Politics, Presidents, and Coattails*, Baltimore, 1950

Eugene H. Roseboom, *A History of Presidential Elections*, New York, 1957

IV. HISTORIES

*Wilfred E. Binkley, *President and Congress*, New York, 1947

George Fort Milton, *The Use of Presidential Power*, Boston, 1944
Charles C. Thach, Jr., *The Creation of the Presidency, 1775-1789*,
Baltimore, 1922
*Leonard D. White, *A Study in Administrative History*, 4 vols.,
New York, 1947-1958. The titles of the volumes are *The Fed-
eralists, The Jeffersonians, The Jacksonians, The Republican
Era.*

V. AUTOBIOGRAPHIES, DIARIES, INSIDE GLIMPSES

Grover Cleveland, *Presidential Problems*, New York, 1904
Herbert Hoover, *Memoirs*, 3 vols., New York, 1951-1952
David F. Houston, *Eight Years with Wilson's Cabinet*, New York,
1926
*James K. Polk, *The Diary of a President*, Allan Nevins (ed.),
New York, 1929
W. C. Redfield, *With Congress and Cabinet*, New York, 1924
*Theodore Roosevelt, *Autobiography*, New York, 1913
*Robert E. Sherwood, *Roosevelt and Hopkins*, New York, 1948
William Howard Taft, *Our Chief Magistrate and His Powers*, New
York, 1916
William Howard Taft, *The Presidency*, New York, 1916
Harry S Truman, *Memoirs*, New York, 1955-1956
*Gideon Welles, *Diary of Gideon Welles*, Boston, 1909

VI. BIOGRAPHIES

Irving Brant, *Madison the President*, Vol. V, New York, 1957
*James M. Burns, *Roosevelt: The Lion and the Fox*, New York,
1956
Robert J. Donovan, *Eisenhower: The Inside Story*, New York, 1956
Douglas S. Freeman, *George Washington*, Vols. VI-VII, New York,
1954-1957
*Burton J. Hendrick, *Lincoln's War Cabinet*, Boston, 1946
*Herbert Hoover, *The Ordeal of Woodrow Wilson*, New York,
1958
*Marquis James, *Andrew Jackson: Portrait of a President*, New
York, 1937
*Margaret Leech, *In the Days of McKinley*, New York, 1959
Robert J. Morgan, *A Whig Embattled*, Lincoln, Neb., 1954
Allan Nevins, *Grover Cleveland: A Study in Courage*, New York,
1932

Roy F. Nichols, *Franklin Pierce: Young Hickory of the Granite Hills,* Philadelphia, 1931

*Henry F. Pringle, *Theodore Roosevelt,* New York, 1931, also issued in paperback

Henry F. Pringle, *The Life and Times of William Howard Taft,* New York, 1939

*J. G. Randall, *Lincoln the President,* 4 vols. (fourth volume by Randall and Richard N. Current), New York, 1945-1955

Arthur M. Schlesinger, Jr., *The Crisis of the Old Order,* Boston, 1957

Arthur M. Schlesinger, Jr., *The Coming of the New Deal,* Boston, 1959

INDEX

Acheson, Dean, 53
Adams, Henry, 262
Adams, John, 92, 104, 106, 135, 137, 158, 188
Adams, John Quincy, 106, 175, 188, 209
Adams, Sherman, 133, 162, 169, 170, 171, 175
administration, federal, 19-22, 50-51, 59-62, 84-85, 127-134, 148, 241-249
Arthur, Chester Alan, 106, 214, 216, 221
atomic energy, 23-24, 240

Barkley, Alben, 138
Beard, Charles A., 55-56
Binkley, W. E., 94, 190
Bricker, John, 24, 165, 256
Bricker amendment, 159, 256
Bright, John, 15
Brownlow, Louis, 118, 128
Brundage, Percival F., 166
Buchanan, James, 98, 107
Bureau of the Budget, 132-133, 244, 247
Burns, Arthur F., 171
Butler, Pierce, 81
Byrnes, James F., 158-159, 226

Cabinet, 96, 100, 215, 225-228, 244-246
Calhoun, John C., 72, 136, 211
Case, Clifford, 167
Celler, Emanuel, 231

Chase, Salmon P., 52, 58
Churchill, Sir Winston, 34, 40, 67, 152
Clay, Henry, 96, 97
Cleveland, Grover, 42, 106, 119, 123, 179, 223
Congress, 19-22, 26-27, 28-30, 44, 48, 49-56, 60, 70, 82, 84, 86, 87-88, 95, 96, 110-114, 173, 188, 199, 215, 225-228, 235, 238, 246-247, 252-255, 260
relations with President, 28-30, 44, 48, 49-56, 87-88, 104, 110-114, 146, 235, 242, 249-255
reform of, 253-255
Constitution, 19-20, 26, 44-45, 47-48, 74-81, 84-85, 113, 136, 183, 209, 233, 264-271
Constitutional Convention (1787), 74-81, 135, 183, 224
conventions, nominating, 140, 185, 186-187, 191-194
Coolidge, Calvin, 29, 107, 115, 176, 210-211, 233, 260
Corwin, Edward S., 53, 96, 250
Coudert, Frederic R., 195, 196, 256
Council of Economic Advisers, 37, 131-132
Cutler, Robert, 171

disability, presidential, 174, 211-224
Donovan, Robert, 175
Douglas, Paul, 193

Dulles, John Foster, 163-165, 171, 172, 175

Eisenhower, Dwight D., 21, 29, 31, 33, 36, 38-39, 40, 42, 45, 50, 57, 60, 63-64, 67, 72, 109, 112, 115-117, 121, 123-126, 133, 134, 138-141, 142-143, 156, 205, 211, 212, 217-218, 222, 223, 231, 242, 245, 252
  evaluated, 106, 160-178
elections, presidential, 77-78, 135, 182-200
  criticisms, 190-194, 195-200
  reforms, 196-200
Elliott, W. Y., 250
Executive Office, 127-134, 151, 243-244, 247

Farley, James A., 149
federalism, 64, 119
Federalist, The, 19, 24, 51-52, 71, 78-81, 91, 135, 184, 229
Fillmore, Millard, 107, 209
Finletter, Thomas K., 251
Folsom, Marion, 171
Ford, Henry Jones, 52, 84, 88, 261
Fulbright, J. William, 28, 210-211

Garfield, James A., 107, 208, 212, 221
George, Walter, 165
Goodman, William, 234
Goodpaster, A. J., 171
Graham, George, 244
Grant, Ulysses S., 27, 101, 107, 160, 233
Green, Theodore F., 165
Gulick, Luther, 128, 129

Hagerty, James, 171, 223
Hamilton, Alexander, 19, 24, 71, 74-81, 82, 90-91, 135, 184, 190, 229

Hancock, John, 92-93
Harding, Warren G., 107, 115, 158, 192, 208, 212
Harrison, Benjamin, 101, 107
Harrison, William Henry, 107, 185, 208, 212
Hauge, Gabriel, 171
Hayes, Rutherford B., 50, 86, 106, 175
Henry, Patrick, 80
Hoover, Herbert, 42, 89, 106, 115, 207
Hoover, J. Edgar, 61-62
Humphrey, George, 166, 175
Hyman, Sidney, 260

impeachment, 52-53, 207-208
item veto, 80, 255

Jackson, Andrew, 31, 32, 53, 88, 108, 143, 147, 150, 151, 188, 233, 243
  evaluated, 95-98, 105, 152
Jefferson, Thomas, 27, 30, 52, 58, 75-76, 80, 82, 90, 93, 108, 135, 188, 225, 233
  evaluated, 94-95, 105, 159
Johnson, Andrew, 52, 58, 101, 106, 158, 209, 214
Johnson, Lyndon, 28, 30, 34, 165
Jones, Roger, 171

Kahn, A. E. ("Fred"), 37, 131-132
Kefauver, Estes, 51, 113, 231, 250
Key, V. O., 194
Knowland, William F., 165
Krock, Arthur, 181

Laski, Harold, 69
Lawrence, David, 231, 251
Lehman, Herbert, 195
Lewis, John L., 65, 120
Lilienthal, David, 149

Lincoln, Abraham, 24, 25, 31, 59, 83, 86, 105, 108, 143, 144, 147, 168, 180, 208, 212, 259
evaluated, 98-101, 105, 151, 152
Lippmann, Walter, 177, 181, 272
Lodge, H. C., 194, 198
Loeb, James, Jr., 194

MacArthur, Douglas, 34, 157
Maclay, William, 92-94
Macmahon, Arthur, 189
Madison, James, 27, 51-52, 74-81, 89, 96, 107, 158, 212
Marshall, John, 26, 58, 94
Marshall, Thomas R., 210, 214, 216, 221
Martin, Joseph W., 169-170, 226
Mason, George, 76-80
McCarthy, Joseph, 51, 71, 157, 162, 165, 252-253, 256
McKinley, William, 27, 106, 176, 208, 212
Merriam, Charles E., 128, 260
Merriam, Robert E., 171
Mitchell, James P., 171
Monroe, James, 80, 96, 107
Monroney, Mike, 113, 250
Morgan, Gerald D., 171
Morris, Gouverneur, 74-81, 88

National Security Council, 23, 131, 136, 245
Neustadt, Bertha, 276
Neustadt, Richard E., 132
Nixon, Richard, 137-140, 204, 214, 217-218

Office of Civil and Defense Mobilization, 132
Operations Coordinating Board, 131, 140

parties, 30-32, 62-64, 82, 140, 204-205

Persons, Wilton B., 170, 171
Pierce, Franklin, 80, 107
Polk, James K., 106
Potter, Stephen, 114
Presidency:
    burden, 30, 41-43, 144, 241-246
    criticisms of, 44-47, 190-194
    dangers of, 44-47, 229-236, 256-258
    as democratic office, 77-78, 83, 88, 96-97, 102, 122-127, 179-180, 189-190, 261-262
    election to, 77-78, 135, 182-200
    growth, reasons for, 83-89, 134, 237-238, 256-257
    history, 74-108
    as institution, 41-43, 127-134, 169-170, 174-175, 222-223, 241-246
    limitations, 44-73, 126-127
    qualifications for, 71, 78, 178-181, 200-206
    qualities, 220-221, 256-257, 260-262
    recent changes, 109-141
    reform of, 193-194, 241-255
    relations with Congress, 28-30, 48, 49-56, 87-88, 104, 110-114, 146, 235, 242, 249-255
    staff, 41-43, 127-134, 222-223, 241-246
    succession to, 209-210, 224-229
    as symbol, 16-18, 39-41, 81, 83, 93, 102, 107-108, 144, 148, 150, 156-157, 172-173, 260-261
    theories of, 79, 88, 98, 103, 143-144, 147-148, 154-155, 168-169
President, powers of:
    general, 16-43, 78-79
    administrative, 19-22, 41, 59-62, 84-85, 87, 127-134, 144, 148, 155, 240, 241-249

ceremonial (Chief of State), 16-18, 39-41, 81, 83, 93, 260-261
diplomatic, 25-28, 39-41, 67, 85, 90-91, 103, 105, 131
economic, 36-39, 41, 122, 131-132
in emergencies, 34-39, 86-87, 98-101, 118-122, 147, 259
in field of civil liberties, 122-127
in labor disputes, 118-122
legislative, 41, 110-114, 132-133, 249-255
military (Commander in Chief), 22-25, 35, 39-41, 57, 86-87, 98-101, 105, 119, 123, 125-126, 131-132, 239-240
political, 30-34, 41, 62-64, 82, 94-95, 114-118, 125, 180, 189-190, 207, 235
removal, 20-21, 57-58
in science, 238-240
press conference, 114-118, 151
public opinion, 32-33, 41, 68-70, 103, 114-118, 223

Randall, Clarence, 34, 65-67
Randolph, Edmund, 75-80
Rayburn, Sam, 28, 30, 168, 218, 226, 231
Reston, James, 141, 163, 177, 272
Revercomb, Chapman, 230, 235
Rogers, William P., 166, 171, 231
Roosevelt, Franklin D., 21, 24, 25, 29, 31, 45, 51, 54, 57, 58, 60-61, 64, 68-69, 83, 86, 109, 110-111, 114-115, 118, 120, 126, 127-130, 142, 143, 154, 164, 174, 179, 208, 212, 230, 233, 259
    evaluated, 105, 145-152
Roosevelt, Theodore, 31, 33, 64, 79, 85, 104, 108, 110, 121, 143-144, 145, 147, 161, 177, 179, 233
    evaluated, 102-104, 105, 159
Russell, Richard B., 165

Senate, 54, 80, 135
Shanley, Bernard M., 171
Sherman, Roger, 75-80
Silva, Ruth, 214, 219, 228
Stanton, Edwin M., 52
Stevens, Thaddeus, 71, 83
Stevenson, Adlai, 194, 203, 205
Stone, Harlan Fiske, 149
Supreme Court, 48, 56-59, 69, 120, 123-124, 125, 172, 215, 220
    cases involving Presidency, 18, 34, 48, 56-59, 120, 256
Sutherland, George, 26, 58

Taft, Robert A., 33, 87, 165, 205, 256
Taft, William Howard, 18, 42, 59, 79, 104, 106, 123, 158, 168, 176, 207
Taft-Hartley Act, 87-88, 119-121
Taylor, Zachary, 107, 203, 208, 209, 212
Tennessee Valley Authority, 21
third-term tradition, 151, 229-236
Tocqueville, Alexis de, 85
Truman, Harry S, 18, 21, 24, 27, 30, 40, 41, 43, 45, 53, 60, 62, 66-67, 86, 88, 109, 111, 115, 118, 120, 121, 123-126, 142, 143, 161, 162, 164-165, 168-169, 172, 174, 178, 207, 210, 218, 226, 231, 256
    evaluated, 105, 152-159
Twenty-second Amendment, 151, 229-236, 256
Tyler, John, 106, 209, 216

Udall, Stewart L., 231

Van Buren, Martin, 106, 158, 185
Vice-Presidency, 131, 134-141, 174, 183, 208-211, 214-228, 259

Warren, Earl, 172
Washington, George, 17, 27, 30, 31, 75, 78, 80-81, 82, 98, 108, 143, 144, 168, 178, 184, 229, 232
  evaluated, 89-94, 105, 151, 152
Welles, Sumner, 147, 149
White, Leonard D., 129, 134

White House Office, 130-131, 133-134
Wiley, Alexander, 28, 231
Wilmerding, Lucius, 195
Wilson, James, 74-81, 183
Wilson, Woodrow, 24, 29, 31, 32, 64, 85, 86, 108, 110, 114, 123, 136, 142, 143, 147, 152, 155, 164, 177, 181, 210, 212, 214, 221, 242, 259
  evaluated, 104-105

World Map 2, © 1989 by Nina Katchadourian

Late Editions
Cultural Studies for the End of the Century

6

PARANOIA WITHIN REASON

A CASEBOOK ON CONSPIRACY AS EXPLANATION

George E. Marcus, EDITOR

The University of Chicago Press
Chicago and London

George E. Marcus is professor of anthropology at Rice University. He is coauthor of *Anthropology as Cultural Critique* (University of Chicago Press, 1986) and was the inaugural editor of the journal *Cultural Anthropology*.

The University of Chicago Press, Chicago 60637
The University of Chicago Press, Ltd., London
© 1999 by The University of Chicago
All rights reserved. Published 1999
Printed in the United States of America
08 07 06 05 04 03 02 01 00 99   1 2 3 4 5

ISBN: 0-226-50457-3 (cloth)
ISBN: 0-226-50458-1 (paper)

ISSN: 1070-8987 (for Late Editions)

CONTENTS

Preface: A Reintroduction to the Series ix

Introduction to the Volume: The Paranoid Style Now
GEORGE E. MARCUS 1

1 Conspiracy Theory's Worlds
KATHLEEN STEWART 13

2 Paranoid, Critical, Methodical: Dalí, Koolhaas, and . . .
JAMER HUNT 21

I. Paranoia within Reason
3 The Extraterritoriality of Imre Lakatos: A Conversation with
János Radványi
JOHN KADVANY 39

4 Entangled States: Quantum Teleportation and the "Willies"
MICHAEL FORTUN 65

5 The Detection and Attribution of Conspiracies: The Controversy
Over Chapter 8
MYANNA LAHSEN 111

6 The New Alienists: Healing Shattered Selves at Century's End
MICHAEL F. BROWN 137

7 Due Diligence and the Pursuit of Transparency: The Securities
and Exchange Commission, 1996
KIM AND MICHAEL FORTUN 157

II. Paranoid Histories
8 The Usual Suspects
ANDREA AURELI 197

9   A Toast to Fear: Ethnographic Flashes and Two Quasi-Aphorisms
        LUIZ E. SOARES   225

10 The Return of the Repressed: Conversations with Three Russian
        Entrepreneurs
        BRUCE GRANT   241

11 *Udbomafija* and the Rhetoric of Conspiracy
        TATIANA BAJUK   269

III. Paranoid Presents

12 The Judas Kiss of Giulio Andreotti: Italy in Purgatorio
        ROBIN WAGNER-PACIFICI   299

13 Tactical Thuggery: National Socialism in the East End of London
        DOUGLAS R. HOLMES   319

14 Lone Gunmen: Legacies of the Gulf War, Illness, and Unseen
        Enemies
        KIM FORTUN   343

15 Deus Absconditus: Waco, Conspiracy (Theory), Millennialism,
        and (the End of) the Twentieth Century
        JAMES D. FAUBION   375

16 An American Theme Park: Working and Riding Out Paranoia in
        the Late Twentieth Century
        SCOTT A. LUKAS   405

        Contributors   429

        Index   431

PREFACE:

A REINTRODUCTION TO THE SERIES

This is the sixth volume of an annual series that will be published until the year 2000. In this series we are as much interested in the widespread self-awareness of massive changes in society and culture globally, especially among those who write about the contemporary world, as we are in the facts and lived experiences of these changes themselves. Indeed, this self-awareness among both writers and their subjects *is* one of the major facts about this moment. This dual interest and a particular strategy for pursuing it in producing the series are what we believe make these volumes distinctive.

Perhaps the single most striking rhetorical characteristic of writing about the contemporary in this fin de siècle (and probably of others before it) is the hyperawareness that the velocity and immensity of changes are beyond the conceptual grasp of writers of various kinds to describe and interpret them. For some, this rhetoric of the insufficiency of the means of representation in the face of watershed changes constitutes a kind of discourse of marveling that ironically enhances conventional, distanced descriptions of events and processes. A rhetoric of a struggle to keep up with what is happening often frames and creates a special urgency—a newsworthiness—for the most mundane as well as the very best conventional print and electronic journalism. The aura of both the fear and wonder of the present emerging into the future is what "current events" best-sellers are made of and is also a key "visionary" component in arguing for government programs and policies. However, media commentaries, best-sellers, and policies are only cogent if they still speak compellingly in comfortable, taken-for-granted terms and story lines even though these might indeed be under erasure, so to speak.

For others who write about the present—and here I have in mind those large segments of the academic world who have been in a sense prepared for the fin de siècle by the deep influence on them of the 1980s critiques of longstanding languages, rhetorics, and practices of scholarship about culture and society—the self-awareness of the inadequacy of past means of representation has led to a vast outpouring of experimentation with modes of writing, theorizing, scholarly practice, and a questioning of the purposes of scholarship itself. One thing for sure is that the standard modes of realist narrative storytelling about the momentous present as it unfolds is not enough for historians, anthropologists, literary critics, film- and videomakers, philosophers, and other scholars of the present. The latter are characteristically expected to be more reflective than journalists or policymakers, and they are certainly not subject to the demands of communicating to a broad, imagined public. Typically, the call among academic cultural critics has been for new vocabularies for new social and cultural realities, but this is too sanguine a response to the sensibility operating among critical scholars who have been profoundly influenced by the challenge to conventional narrative practices in such intellectual movements as feminism, postcolonialism, and post-structuralism. Any new "language" to grasp the present unfolding will not be anything like past languages or models of discourse that become in some sense standardized and authoritative, even in a self-conscious critical mode. Rather, the new languages or vocabularies will remain for the foreseeable future embedded in and inextricable from the messy, contestatory discussions that predominate in the wake of the widely acknowledged crisis of representation. In this domain, marveling about the unspeakability of the present unfolding, associated with the rhetoric of insufficient language, is tinged with a skepticism that doubts whether straightforward, distanced stories about the present can be told in any compelling way without constant interruption and the negotiation of heterogeneous voices.

In this series we try to steer a course between these two tendencies of writing about the contemporary. While we recognize the ironic seduction of a posited inadequacy of language to keep doing the same old kind of "voiceover" description and narration about events and changes, we also understand that the deep and widespread urge to document and witness in a stark, straightforward way cannot be denied. We merely claim that distanced, expository discourse and representations—whether theoretical, descriptive, or media commonsensical—are inadequate without the collaboration and exposure of the discourse of situated persons, who become the subjects of the contributions on the various fin-de-siècle themes taken up by this series.

Our strategy to achieve this mix of distance and engagement is to impose some variation of an interview/dialogue/conversation format upon the mostly academic authors of this series. While in their research they indeed operate in a world of interviews and conversations, such authors in their writing are accustomed to the analytic, descriptive discourse of scholars. In a sense, each piece in this series is an experiment in suppressing the enunciatory mode of academic/journalistic writing, or at least in pursuing insights and arguments by other means, through the voices of situated others.

The situated conversation or interview is of course the mise-en-scène of research in anthropology, but the interview specifically as a form of writing creates a certain intimacy, an experiential yet distanced access to events and processes, known otherwise through day-to-day reporting and commentary in the media. The interview form in the hands of academic writers uncertainly employing it delivers both a strong reality effect and also an undermining of the effect by knowing readerships wise to the deceits of any kind of representation that appeals to a transparent real. Thus the interview as experimented with here can potentially occupy that difficult middle ground within a form that documents while constantly giving indications of its constructedness, of the ambivalences of its interlocutors, and of both occlusions and statements that seem just right in relation to encompassing events and processes. In other words, the use of the interview holds promise of just those mixed characteristics of discourse that can navigate the shoals of writing in the shadow of a crisis of representation.

The interview intruded on the habit of exposition is thus the main emblem of the series and its wager concerning what is effective discourse at the moment about contemporary change. Yet displayed in these volumes are not accomplished examples of the interview form, but various kinds of struggle with it. Indeed, some of the pieces evolve in other directions—as biographical profiles, as personal memoirs, as the juxtaposed representation of documents, as interesting accounts of failed conversations. A recurrent question voiced at our annual collective editorial meetings is about how much context (read, how much background necessary for the unititiated reader as well as enunciative prose from the schoarly specialist) is necessary and appropriate for various pieces, indexing a persistent relative discomfort among authors with yielding so much space to the exposure of encounters and staged conversations rather than direct authorial interpretations of them. The results are varied and mixed, with occasional rough edges, but we hope they are always interesting and imaginative.

The short-term time-space of this series is signaled by the loaded label, fin de siècle, in which it periodizes and limits itself, and cultivates a certain detachment, while understanding that this is not the old claim to value neutrality enabling the truth. Detachment arises from and is a way to cope with bewilderments and cynicisms that seem so much a part of the age. It seeks not to close down optimism or pander to pessimism but struggles for a documentation that, through the interview or some variation on it, is a kind of cultural activism. These volumes do not attempt authoritatively to review or survey fields, but rather are carefully constructed assemblages that seek to play on associations among diffuse pieces not only within particular volumes but across them as natural accumulations of producing the series.

In this series, then, rather than the marveling side of the rhetoric of writerly insufficiency, we tend to display its anxious side. Fin-de-siècle perspective for us communicates more anticipation and responses to "first signs" than a sense of the reality of changes. Most of the situations explored through personal accounts in this series were produced implicitly or explicitly in anticipation of these great changes. This posture of waiting through all the coping and envisioning at present is definitive of a fin-de-siècle mood. There is indeed a lot of futurism in current thinking, but it is much more anxiety filled than, for example, the earlier bout of futurist writing in the 1960s (books with titles like *Toward the Year 2000*). The future is actually experienced now through all sorts of new requirements and disruptions in the present without being clearly conceived or imagined. The notion of emergence—the future in the rapidly unfolding present—so salient in contemporary discourse, communicates this ambiguous posture of anticipatory waiting in relation to an unimaginable future.

Readers familiar with previous works in this series will be aware of the unusual combination of modesty and chutzpah by which this project is motivated. Its modesty is in our sense of the limitations of distanced commentaries on contemporary events and processes in conveying an understanding of them commensurate with their complexity and ambiguity. In no sense is this series meant to be a substitute for such conventional ethnography or social-science writing, but it is meant as a distinctive, valuable, and sometimes challenging supplement to them. The chutzpah of this project is in the alternative that we offer—in effect, a series of experiments with form—in which value is claimed for paying primary attention to the exposure of material that is usually masked and subordinated to more "finished" commentary, description, and argument. Because of the conceptual work and rethinking that is done in many settings by social actors, we believe that emphasizing the exposure of eliciting conversations and embedded discourses provides equivalents and even more complex understandings of social processes and institutions undergoing fin-de-siècle transformation than authoritative, expert discourse on society and culture. Consequently, the resulting pieces of these volumes might seem more raw and messier than conventional academic scholarly papers in the material they present, and they certainly require more in the way of indulgence and participation from the reader.

The volumes of this series are generated by a standard cycle of production. Two meetings are held annually and in conjunction with each other during the late spring at the Rice University anthropology department. One is a collective editorial meeting on the current year's project; the other is a separate stimulus meeting for the next volume, attended by the contributors to the current year's volume, to discuss possible themes and to suggest likely contributors. In succeeding months, I contact and invite prospective participants, who in the past have mostly been scholars at various stage of career development, typically from anthropology, history, sociology, literary studies, or interdisciplinary fields. They are asked to propose contributions that will take them back to sites of past interest or to already collected material, but will require them to operate in an unconventional genre, built on the interview format. In a sense, the pieces that are developed for the series represent negotiations between me as the editor and upholder of the rationale of the series and the contributors who have developed highly variant and always interesting accommodations to this rationale. Drafts of pieces are circulated prior to the collective editorial meeting held in late May, attended by as many contributors who are able. At this meeting there are discussions about revisions for final drafts to be submitted in the fall. Most interestingly, a general sense of a particular volume's ethos emerges through discussions that focus on details, unsuspected connections among pieces, and the variant forms that they take. The result always remains an assemblage that does not approximate, nor seeks to do so, the mostly elusive ideal of the neatly interlocking, comprehensive scholarly collection as treatise. Still, our assemblages have managed to evidence consistencies and striking points of coherence.

Before proceeding with our present survey of paranoia as a mode of contemporary social thought, we should perhaps summarize, as a reintroduction to the series, the major distinctive features of its pieces and volumes.

Ideally, in this series, the necessary framing or contextualization of pieces should be embedded in the interviews and conversations themselves. In practice, such embedded framing is rarely sufficient, so that authorial voice is often present and gravitates between making an argument and scene setting.

Because so much emphasis is placed on edited conversations and the exposure of subjects' discourses, there is always more in pieces than might be intended by authorial design. We consider the excess, or slippage, so to speak, in each piece to be more of a virtue than a flaw of the series since it often allows for connections and associations to be made by readers out of the control of the series' rationale. Indeed, a speculative questioning by readers of "signs" or "clues" of motivation, intent, and ambivalence in these pieces on the part of both interviewers and their interlocutors is the most valuable way that their broader contexts and implication can be developed.

The emphasis of these pieces is not so much on the specific telling of highly individual stories or on the singular case, as might be supposed from the use of the subject-focused interview genre. Rather, what is special about most of these pieces is that they provide *perspective,* speak the general, from a situated actor's point of view in which the latter's conditions, purposes, and idioms are highly visible, or at least the ambiguities of which are accessible to the reader. It is precisely this imputed heightened tendency at present of the social actor, self-conscious of great transformations and breaks with the past, to reassess and "size up" his or her milieu that fascinates and motivates this project, and suggests what it can offer that other more conventional "voiceover" modes of exposition cannot.

While working within common themes like science, political change, media, and corporations, for each of which there exists extensive literatures, the volumes of this series, taking shape as somewhat opportunistic assemblages, often compromise unusual juxtapositions and inclusions that stretch the common-sensical boundaries of a particular theme. For example, in the present volume, theme parks, scientific controversies, the practice of therapists, and the authoritarian tendencies of past and present governments are juxtaposed sites for the probing of paranoid thinking and conspiracy theories. Again, this is a kind of slippage characteristic of our project that we consider, on balance, more a virtue than a vice.

From its inception, this series has been supported annually by generous funds from Rice University administered through the dean of the School of Social Sciences and the Center for the Study of Cultures.

George E. Marcus

INTRODUCTION:
THE PARANOID STYLE NOW

In the United States, the classic statement of conspiracy theories as a mode of social thought is historian Richard Hofstadter's 1952 essay, "The Paranoid Style in American Politics." While he shows that this mode of thought has deep and continuous roots in American culture, and while he allows for its apearance equally on the Right and Left of the political spectrum, his particular treatment of it in the early, McCarthyite years of the cold war was conceived as a sharp critique of right-wing mentality in its perception of the pervasive infiltration of American government and institutions by communists. In this critique, Hofstadter brilliantly captured the general defining features of paranoid social thought:

> What distinguishes the paranoid style is not, then, the absence of verifiable facts (though it is occasionally true that in his extravagant passion for facts the paranoid occasionally manufactures them), but rather the curious leap in imagination that is always made at some critical point in the recital of events. (37)

> The typical procedures of the higher paranoid scholarship is to start with such defensible assumptions and with a careful accumulation of facts, or at least of what appear to be facts, and to marshall these facts toward an overwhelming 'proof' of the particular conspiracy that is to be established. It is nothing if not coherent—in fact the paranoid mentality is far more coherent than the real world since it leaves no room for mistakes, failures, or ambiguities. (36)

> A feeling of persecution is central to the paranoid style, but whereas the clinically paranoid person perceives a world hostile and conspiratorial against him or herself, the spokesperson for the paranoid style finds it directed against a nation, a culture, a way of life whose fate affects not himself alone but millions of others. . . . His sense that his political passions are unselfish and patriotic, in fact, goes far to intensify his feeling of righteousness and his moral indignation. (4)

There is indeed a distinct appreciation in Hofstadter's writing of the very
ambiguous relationship of the paranoid mode of social thought, at least as a
matter of form, to rationality and logic—the sense in which the former might
be seductively mistaken for or identified with the latter. Yet given his pursuit of
a pointed critique and exposure of the excesses of a certain trend of politics in
the United States, he has no feel or sympathy for the "reasonableness" of
thinking in terms of conspiracy theories under particular conditions, or of a
substantial paranoid potential in the most rational or commonsensical frames
of thought that readily emerges at certain moments.

Nowadays, Hofstadter's precise take on the paranoid style would serve well
as a means of understanding all of the recent reporting on the seemingly pervasive visions of conspiracy, perpetrated by big government, as an expression
of popular resentments in U.S. society, and located in groups organized by
fundamentalism, extremisms, and cult religions of various kinds. While there
are at least two pieces in this assemblage that address contexts of this sort
(those by Holmes on English Nazis, and by Faubion on David Koresh and the
Branch Davidians), we wish mainly to deepen and amend Hofstadter's study
precisely by coming to terms with the paranoid style, not as distanced from the
"really" rational by exoticized groups with which it is usually associated in
projects of targeted critique or expose, but *within reason,* as a "reasonable"
component of rational and commonsensical thought and experience in certain
contexts. For us, a paranoid understanding of a social field as operating in terms
of conspiracy, while it may always be seeming to move toward the extremist
pole that becomes the target of critics like Hofstadter,[1] need not go that far. The
paranoid style in this fin de siècle is both detectable and manifest in different
ways and with different intensities across a wide spectrum of situations. And
in some of these, paranoia and conspiracy theories are quite unexpected tendencies. This volume is a casebook of these situations.

Indeed, we believe that there are at least two broad contexts or conditions of
contemporary life that make the paranoid style and conspiracy theories an eminently reasonable tendency of thought for social actors to embrace. The first
derives from the fact that the cold-war era itself was defined throughout by a
massive project of paranoid social thought and action that reached into every
dimension of mainstream culture, politics, and policy. Furthermore, client
states and most regions were shaped by the interventions, subversions, and
intimidations pursued in the interests of a global conspiratorial politics of the
superpowers. The legacies and structuring residues of that era make the persistence, and even increasing intensity, of its signature paranoid style now more
than plausible, but indeed, an expectable response to certain *social facts.*[2] That
is, the effects of decades of paranoid policies of statecraft and governing habits
of thought define a present reality for social actors in some places and situations that is far from extremist, or distortingly fundamentalist, but is quite rea-

sonable and commonsensical. In this volume, the palpable legacies of paranoid histories can be found most strongly in those pieces that deal with actors who have experienced changes in governing regimes in places where cold-war disciplines and interventions shaped the experience of civil society—that is, the meditation of Andrea Aureli on his generation as political actors in cold-war Italy under the specter of an era of terrorism of murky origins; the related interpretation by Robin Wagner-Pacifici on the symbology of the conspiratorial edge to contemporary Italian politics; the stories by Luiz Soares on complicities during and after the military governments of Brazil; and representing the paranoid legacy of the cold war in the former Soviet empire in transition, Bruce Grant's probing of the conspiratorial climate of Russia's wild capitalism, and Tatiana Bajuk's elicitation of an alternative account of Slovenia's transition, steeped in the facts of cold-war intrigue and more compelling, or at least more vivid and comprehensive, than the rhetoric of Slovene professional economists and planners remaking themselves to fit into the victorious global market economy.[3]

The other important and perhaps more subtle way to take note of the present paranoid style as a kind of pervasive cold-war legacy is to indicate the extent to which highly influential frameworks of social theory have this potential within their conceptual rhetorics. Frameworks that have at their core notions of game, self-interested motivation, fields of contest and struggle, and generally a valuation of cynical reason (Sloterdijk 1987) as the most reliable posture from which to interpret human action are ones in which the reality of conspiratorial activity is well within reach of their common sense. The most influential forms of strategic thought during the post-World War II period, such as game theory and the Prisoner's Dilemma (Poundstone 1992) have the paranoid style close to their surface, but a paranoid potential is at least legible in some of the most prominent brands of contemporary social theory as well.[4]

Finally, one might say that all elite politics—high-level power games in any institution—to some degree share the same intellectual capital with the language of strategic policy and prominent social theories. But as working models for action, these elite models in use inspire even more paranoia and conspiratorial thinking by the very subcultural atmospheres and assumptions of elites (Marcus 1983). The mere conceptual language, then, of the transaction of interest in a field of politics makes paranoia reasonable and legitimate, as long as it is restrained, and distinguishable from its exotic, excessive other—the extremist or fundamentalist paranoia of the kind Hofstadter skewers, given free rein by a panicked sense of clear and present danger to a valued or privileged way of life. Of course, the whole strange history of nuclear diplomacy was given its utmost rationality by its thinking through the controls on the potential excesses of an inherently paranoid era (Marcus 1998a). This volume registers the very real legacy of that era in various places facing new circumstances and changes for which the cold-war verities will not do, but in which its deeply embedded consequences and modes of thought still have their unpredictable impacts.

The second broad context that defines a contemporary paranoid style within reason arises from the much discussed crisis of representation—also a base rationale for the entire Late Editions series—keenly experienced over the past decade, and not only in academic life but in many other realms of professional middle-class activity. We have held that this problem of the felt inadequacy of metanarratives and conceptual frames to explain the world as it has historically emerged and is currently changing is generated not so much by the radicalized intellectual fashion of the critique of knowledge of recent years as by the rapidity and extent of actual changes themselves—by the social and ethnographic facts of the world if only they could be apprehended by large theories and concepts in which one still had faith.

In his book *Metahistory* (1973), Hayden White spoke of a similar moment in European historiography, at the end of the nineteenth century, as an ironic mode—a time of saturation of descriptions, diagnoses, and analyses of social change, either among literati or as experienced in everyday life—in which there were a number of equally comprehensive and plausible, yet apparently mutually exclusive, conceptions of the same events. Now, there remains a healthy respect for facts and evidence, but accompanied also by a high tolerance for speculative associations among them—an impulse to figure out systems, now of global scale, with strategic facts missing that might otherwise permit confident choices among competing conceptions.

The specifically postmodern version of a contemporary crisis of representation as the opportunity for the proliferation of paranoid mode of social thought is expressed in John McClure's study of the novels of Don DeLillo, whose work has most evoked a contemporary atmosphere of institutions and systems sustained by powerful, invisible conspiracies. McClure connects the pervasiveness of conspiracy theories to the contemporary predicament of the romance genre in a time when the exotic places—the "dark places of the world," as Conrad called them—on which the latter has depended have been overtaken by global capitalism. He notes Fredric Jameson's assertion that the postmodern period begins when such places are abolished: "The 'prodigious expansion of capital into hitherto uncommodified areas,' Jameson writes in *The New Left Review* (1984), 'eliminates the enclaves of precapitalist organization it hitherto tolerated and exploited in a tributary way.' The result is the 'purer capitalism of our own times' and the eradication of those cultures and professions from which modernists extracted romance" (1991, 102). McClure goes on to argue that DeLillo refuses to despair about "the intolerability of the world" as a result of the eradication of the precapitalist sanctuaries of the Western imagination. Instead, DeLillo "focuses his attention on sites within capitalism, and discovers there the materials of new forms of romance. It's true, he suggests, that capitalism has penetrated everywhere, but its globalization has not resulted in global rationalization and Weber's iron cage. It seems instead to have sponsored a profound reversal: the emergence of zones and forces like those that imperial expansion has erased: jungle-like techno-tangles; dangerous unknown 'tribes'; secret cults with their own codes and ceremonies, vast conspiracies. 'This is the age of conspiracy,' says a character in *Running Dog,* with the mixture of wonder and revulsion that is everywhere in DeLillo's work. This is the 'age of connections, links, secret relationships' " (1991, 102).

So in this version of the crisis of representation the plausibility of the paranoid style is not so much in its reasonableness, but rather in its revitalization of the romantic, the ability to tell an appealing, wondrous story found in the real.

Either version, then, of this condition of the inadequacy of established genres and forms of narrative in the face of watershed changes such as the full globalization of capital in its own changing forms creates the space for a kind of paranoid reasoning that can be entertained as plausible. As Jamer Hunt remarked in our collective editorial meeting, "It could be argued that conspiracy itself revolves around a contestation over the presence and/or verifiability of an explanatory, or causal point of origin. Paranoia, to use one obvious example, becomes a relative category of description based in part upon the question of whether in fact there is something 'out there,' or whether the paranoiac is simply delusional." In the domain of paranoia within reason that we are probing here, there is no question that there is something "out there." The paranoia arises from expert desire or duty toward knowledge in the absence of compass. With just enough of the facts missing, what is speculative in every project of reason, as Hunt's essay argues, becomes distorted, even playful, and stays this side of delusion. In paranoia within reason, more play is given to what is finally constrained in every reasoning process. Here the stakes are the large ones of defining and affecting the real, again, without a compass (as in the pieces of this volume, the real of climate change, the real of the fragmented self in therapy, the real of open markets for the Securities and Exchange Commission regulators, the real of the physics of teleportation, and the real of scientific truth in Imre Lakatos's skepticism).

Paranoia, positing conspiratorial agency, can emerge with different intensities, in diverse forms, and across domains of knowledge and politics. Moreover, when this paranoid tendency within scientific, expert, or bureaucratic practice circumstantially makes connection with more outlandish, extremist forms of conspiracy theories, it creates strange bedfellows indeed. The pursuit of knowledge and the politics of knowledge become blurred, and are played in a broader field of associations and alliances. The sense of this is communicated most tellingly by the essays of the first section: in John Kadvany's piece, the brilliant skepticism, powering Imre Lakatos's sociological understanding of science, becoming entangled with cold-war phantoms in the crossing of the boundaries of both national and academic communities; in Mike Fortun's piece, the paranoid associations—experienced as the "willies"—that spur physics at the lines of science fiction; in Myanna Lahsen's piece, in the domain of trans-science—where science is forced to address issues of broad public interest that it can't answer—the paranoid potential of scientific controversy rapidly aligns with more extremist versions that take this paranoia association-ally into full-blown conspiracy theories about arguments concerning the extent of global climate change; in Michael Brown's piece, the appeal within therapist communities of hidden causes, abuse lost to memory, healing by recovery; and in Michael and Kim Fortun's piece, an in-depth look at the pursuit of real con-spiracies in legal definition by an SEC official and the resulting chimeras within this solid domain of reason.

All of these are examples of how, in the gap between the aspirations of pro-fessional analysis and description to understand and solve social problems—tied to historic engines of reason and progress in modernity—and the world of immense change that undermines assumptions and techniques, the paranoid potential is drawn upon in many forms—as speculation, as skepticism, as curing—most often short of its suspect and extremist forms, but sometimes, surprisingly, even shockingly, in alliance with them and their promoters.

The Organization of the Volume

Following this introduction are two associated discussions that are intended to provide a specifically conceptual introduction consistent with the above con-temporary sense of a paranoid style developed in this assemblage. While nei-ther mentions Hofstadter, they are important contemporary revisions of his classic statement. Kathleen Stewart's essay, though tending to focus on the paranoid style in the condition of extremis, elegantly creates a sense of it none-theless coming within the ken of reason in the post–cold war era of mistrust of government and the emergence of "risk society" (Beck 1992) in which always incomplete understandings of the causes behind and consequences of complex events are normal. Her essay resonates with many of the pieces of this collec-tion, but for an immediate connection, I would suggest reading Kim Fortun's interview with a Gulf War veteran in conjunction with Stewart's essay.

By reviving, through Rem Koolhaas, an interesting and very relevant per-spective of Salvador Dalí, Jamer Hunt's essay most cogently explores the ar-gument that paranoid speculation is at the heart of every theory, eventually revised and made consistent with the norms of reason in the "conquest of the irrational" as Dalí describes this process. This archaeology, so to speak, of a paranoid potential at the heart of processes of rationality—from science, to government, to architecture, to therapy—stands as an effective conceptual statement of the main provocation of this volume. As with Stewart's essay, Hunt's resonates with many of the pieces in this volume, albeit from a distinctly different angle. As an immediate exemplar, I would suggest reading in conjunction with his essay Michael Fortun's account of the theoretical plausibility of teleportation in the uncanny ruminations of physicists that give rise to paranoia, or "the willies," as it is referred to in Fortun's piece.

Before proceeding, it should be noted that the subject position within most of these pieces is defined by a point of view and experience that is always in relation to conspiracies elsewhere, lurking, or surrounding. These, then, are not pieces that interview self-determined conspirators, although some of the subjects move from a sense of being completely outside a world in which conspiracies operate, perpetrated by others, and of which they are victims, to the more ambiguous situation of suddenly discovering oneself implicated in or complicit with conspiratorial processes and movements emanating from a mysterious elsewhere.

The empowered, middle-class, professional persons who have most often been subjects of pieces in this series find themselves unexpectedly caught up in something that defies their commitments to the rational and the commonsensical. This is the paranoid style in its most atmospheric sense, in which detachment or a sense of victimage by others' conspiracies is overcome by an evolving feeling of involvement and complicity. The strongest resistance to this is in the interview by Michael and Kim Fortun with the SEC hunter of real conspiracies in markets, who tries to make others' paranoia and imputations of conspiracies a matter of certainty in legal regulation. In contrast, the sense of the rationalist being "drawn in" is strong in the piece by Myanna Lahsen on the global warming debate, in the assessment of Imre Lakatos by John Kadvany, and again in the state of teleportation physics, treated by Michael Fortun.

The first section, "Paranoia within Reason," collects the essays that show the working of the paranoid style in a variety of specific rhetorics within otherwise very rationalist discourse. The movement is from the flickering of the paranoid and the conspiratorial in the career of Imre Lakatos, associated generally with skepticism as a mode of philosophical inquiry, to a demonstration of Dalí's paranoid-critical method at the edges of theoretical physics, to the case of trans-science, where the paranoid potential in the politics of knowledge surrounding scientific controversies sometimes aligns with full-blown paranoia in extremis, of the sort Hofstadter reflected on, to the ironically paranoid within therapeutic doctrines trying to grasp new manifestations of "shattered" subjectivity, to, finally, the severe rationalist judgment and control of the notion that there are conspiracies "out there" by the SEC lawyer.

The second section, "Paranoid Histories," traces in Italy, Slovenia, Brazil, and Russia cold-war histories and their continuing legacies in the politics and cultures of transformed or transforming regimes. What comes through strongly in each case is the plausibility and reasonableness of thinking of the social predicaments of these places in terms of conspiracy theories and a paranoid style.

The third and final section, "Paranoid Presents," emphasizes the near normality of a paranoid style of thought in more visceral and immediate responses to contemporary events and experiences—responses of anxiety and fear to a still evolving chain of circumstances and associations. Here the emphasis is less on the past than what may be emerging, indicating that in this temporal posture regarding the present, paranoia is sometimes just as reasonable (and appealing) as it is in confronting very real historic legacies in the present, as in the pieces of the preceding section.

This section touches most directly on the kind of paranoid social thought that, while still "within reason," moves most closely to paranoia in extremis, as the familiar ideology of politically marginal, fringe groups. Robin Wagner-Pacifici shows that a kiss is distinctly not just a kiss in Italian politics. In this case, an alleged kiss in 1987 between Giulio Andreotti, a major figure in postwar Italian politics and a several-time prime minister, and the boss of the Sicilian mafia served as the symbolic centerpiece of the state prosecutor's corruption case against Andreotti, in a remarkable wave of such cases in Italy in the 1990s. In a companion piece to Aureli's, Wagner-Pacifici works at the level of cultural analysis to expose the particular symbols and associated allegories in Italian life that trigger characteristic paranoid, cynical responses by a broad public to political events.

Holmes's piece might be read as a companion to his interview in Late Editions 1 with Bruno Gollnisch, an academic and a close associate of Jean Marie LePen. It offers a vision out of fin-de-siècle working-class resentment in which Richard Edmonds, an organizer of the British National Party, accounts for the dramatic changes in the East End of London through a classic (à la Hofstadter) discourse of the paranoid style. Conspiracies of unknown proportions have filled the space of failed empire and failed liberal, as well as moderate conservative, social policies at home. The result is the present situation of a polyethnic London in which the traditional white working class has been forsaken. Strong exclusionary measures to correct the situation are required from denial of rights and opportunities to certain categories of residents and citizens, to forced repatriation. But what is marked about Edmonds's discourse is his care and belief in being reasonable, using language and turns of phase that are difficult to distinguish from political discourse and opinion as usual in Britain.

The last three essays focus on reasonable contexts of a paranoid style in the contemporary United States. All three evoke a palpable atmosphere of paranoia, reminiscent of a Don DeLillo novel. Peck, the Gulf War veteran, makes paranoid good sense of his relations with the government in establishing the disease "syndrome" that resulted from the war. (This piece should perhaps be read alongside Kim Fortun's interview with environmental activist David Henson, appearing in Late Editions 5 [Marcus 1998b].)

Jim Faubion brilliantly interprets the figure of David Koresh, the deceased leader of the Branch Davidians, in his very contemporary reading of the Book of Revelation. In a sense, his piece brings together in confrontation the paranoid styles of government in its avid function of surveillance and of cult religion in its millennialism.

Finally, after reading Scott Lukas's noirish memoir of working in the backstage management of an amusement park, one is unlikely ever to feel the same about patronizing this American entertainment. Lukas's piece works not by convincing one of what had never occurred to one was there; rather, it puts a paranoid edge to what is frequently sensed on visits to theme parks but lacking in definition. He thus makes the paranoid visible in that which is taken for granted, in the background of what is produced as most nostalgically pleasurable in American life. What better way to conclude a volume that has sought to slide the paranoid, the conspiratorial, into everyday effects of the expectable and reasonable?

Notes

1. For example, James Bowman, reporting in the *Times Literary Supplement,* notes that the current update of Hofstadter is the notion of "fusion paranoia" (coined by journalist Michael Kelly) "to describe the way in which the complementary paranoias of the extreme Left and Right in America are becoming indistinguishable, involving many of the same elements and always including a prominent role for the security forces of the federal government" (1996, 16).

2. John Borneman, one of the reviewers of this manuscript, makes the fascinating suggestion of comparing the paranoid legacy of the cold war with other kinds of legacies of contemporary historical events such as the trauma in the aftermath of holocaust (or The Holocaust) in order to see if they "contaminate," as he says, or leave deep traces in the same way.

3. The contemporary paranoid style "within reason" as a cold-war legacy in various places could also be read into many of the pieces appearing previously in this series. In particular, the pieces of Late Editions 1 (Marcus 1993) and Late Editions 4 (Marcus 1997) can be interestingly reread in terms of the concerns of the present volume, especially the pieces on Russia, Poland, Germany, South Africa, Colombia, and Argentina in those volumes. It has been our persistent hope in developing this series that as volumes appear, readers would indeed come to make backward and forward connections among the pieces according to the array of concerns that have emerged cumulatively from the series' collection of interviews and reflections. The present volume, especially, seems to lend itself to this sort of exercise in cross-volume associations.

4. Take for example the ambitious and comprehensive corpus of Pierre Bourdieu, which makes visible through an elegant and complex framework a kind of politics of

value and status that could appropriately be understood in a paranoid atmosphere and through conspiratorial causation by social actors caught in games that they hardly understand in terms of their larger stakes (something that Bourdieu's framework purports to describe—something inaccessible to the embedded practical consciousness of actors). In *Distinction* (1989), particularly, class conspiracy seems to be behind the hierararchy in the habitus of taste. There is conceivably a paranoid atmosphere for someone who wants to understand the prestige of cultural forms without the models or frameworks to do so, but when that someone also knowingly believes that behind these forms are cynical and systematic class games of self-interest. In the face of impenetrable works of culture that are nonetheless marked with prestige, the petit bourgeois experiences a paranoid moment well within the limits of his reason. While never explicitly conceived in such terms by Bourdieu, the paranoid style is thus a reasonable mode of social thought either for those experiencing the hierarchy of taste or for those theorists trying to explain it with Bourdieu's conceptual scheme.

With regard specifically to the discipline of anthropology, both of the press reviewers of this manuscript, who are anthropologists themselves, had very interesting points to make about the practices of this discipline in relation to paranoia. John Borneman notes the effect on the explicit moral economy in which anthropology operates of anthropologists *not* having been that much concerned with the cold-war context of their work. As he says, "I think something could be made of the fact that most anthropologists have been concerned with colonialism and not the cold war, and have therefore had an easy time using realist styles of reporting and critique. (How bad we were back then!) If they had been more concerned with the cold war, the modes of reporting would have been more reflexive, less confident, and perhaps more paranoid."

The other press reviewer makes the very interesting point that the ordinary experience of quite conventional ethnography (whether in contexts of colonialism or the cold war) has often involved charges and suspicions among their subjects that anthropologists were spies of some sort. A kind of paranoia thus has frequently attached to the very process of initiation of standard fieldwork, and in some unfortunate cases has plagued it to its very end. By extension, then, it is even interesting to speculate about the often unreflected-on paranoid dimensions of the fieldworklike interview situations that have produced the pieces of this volume (but see Holmes's piece, where the atmosphere of suspicion and deceit in the interview situation is palpable).

References

Beck, Ulrich. 1992. *Risk Society.* London: Sage.

Bourdieu, Pierre. 1989. *Distinction.* Cambridge, Mass.: Harvard University Press.

Bowman, James. 1996. Commentary. *Times Literary Supplement* 3 Apr.

Hofstadter, Richard. 1967. *The Paranoid Style in American Politics and Other Essays.* New York: Random House.

McClure, John. 1991. "Postmodern Romance: Don DeLillo and the Age of Conspiracy." In *Introducing Don DeLillo,* ed. Frank Lentricchia; 98–115. Durham, N.C.: Duke University Press.

Marcus, George E. 1998a. "Postmodernist Critique in the 80s, Nuclear Diplomacy, and the Prisoner's Dilemma." In *Critical Anthropology Now: Unexpected Contexts, New*

Constituencies, Shifting Agendas, ed. Marcus. Santa Fe, N.M.: School of American Research Press.

Marcus, George E., ed. 1983. *Elites: Ethnographic Issues.* Albuquerque: University of New Mexico Press.

————. 1993. *Perilous States: Conversations on Politics, Culture, and Nation.* Late Editions 1. Chicago: University of Chicago Press.

————. 1997. *Cultural Producers in Perilous States.* Late Editions 4. Chicago: University of Chicago Press.

————. 1998b. *Corporate Futures: The Diffusion of the Culturally Sensitive Corporate Form at Century's End.* Late Editions 5. Chicago: University of Chicago Press.

Poundstone, William. 1992. *Prisoner's Dilemma: John Von Neumann, Game Theory, and the Puzzle of the Bomb.* New York: Doubleday.

Sloterdijk, Peter. 1987. *Critique of Cynical Reason.* Minneapolis: University of Minnesota Press.

White, Hayden. 1973. *Metahistory.* Baltimore, Johns Hopkins University Press.

1

Conspiracy Theory's Worlds

There's so much to say and so little time. I hardly know where to begin. Things are already out of hand.

Maybe I should start with the world that has made conspiracy theory not only possible (and popular) but ever present, unavoidable, pervasive, compulsive, fun, frightening, and fascinating often to the point of a paranoid-mystical urgency. The world that stands as conspiracy theory's condition of possibility. The networked world of system and power, the constant shock waves that never quite wake us from the dream world of late capitalism but replicate states of anesthesia and obsession. The always already replicated, the simulacra, coupled with the suspicion that someone is hiding the REAL behind the curtain. The burgeoning new world order of starkly divided camps where haves and have-nots have become, more simply and efficiently and finally, winners and losers. This coupled with a desire for an Other order of a true US and THEM coming from someplace outside our control. A cultural politics awash in inchoate yet palpable structures of feeling that are themselves peppered with the occasional shock of half-recognition that there is something going on. The sure knowledge (and experience) that everything is interconnected and merging— a seduction, a dreaming, a moving toward and within—coupled with the guilty pang, the moment of terror when something whispers in our ear that the interconnectedness is all controlled by a dark and monolithic Other and we are in it, no exit.

Imagine this world as that moment when the simulated has attached itself to the REAL and overwhelmed it with kindness; the REAL reemerges as trauma and is endlessly repeated without resolution; events and phenomena call to us as haunting specters lodged somewhere within the endless proliferation of images and reports. The more you know, the less you know. What causes cancer? Ozone depletion, smoking, radiation from microwaves, light bulbs, transformers, TVs (and what about heating pads and electric blankets left on all night?), hormone replacement therapy (HRT), the absence of vitamins in the food we eat. Piles of information; it's hard to keep up; you can get paranoid trying. Who can tell the truth from the mistake, the inaccuracy, the flight of fancy, the lie, the cover-up, the manipulation, the disinformation? The paranoid can; that's the point of conspiracy theory—to jump the gun and throw yourself in the line of fire, to call the cards on the table because you've already lost, to find the clarity of the final showdown, to find a focus, to bring things to a head, to realize once and for all that things are even worse than the worst you could have imagined. ("So *shoot* me!" says the one accused and unable/unwilling to respond.)

Constant scanning, writing down the name of the latest cure (to be out in six months), predictions, prophesy, hypervigilance, self-help groups, keeping a diary, recovered memory buffs, history buffs, curiosity collectors, a pathological public sphere focused on trauma, trauma, trauma. The mantra of trauma. The mantra of plots. Conspiracy theory is a skeptical, paranoid, obsessive practice of scanning for signs and sifting through bits of evidence for the missing link. Enter the world of conspiracy theory (as we all do and must) and you enter the world of global systems with missing details. This is a world of hopelessly arcane, obscurantist systems that are expert at leaving a paper trail that cannot track them. The moment of seduction is the moment when the puzzle is almost solved but there is always something more you need, the missing piece. Conspiracy theory dreams of an end point, an ur-text, a pure and stable past, but it never gets there because it is always pushing the REAL to the outer edge of the horizon—a carrot to struggle toward.

Then there's the pleasure of the practice itself. The medium becomes the message and the home base: the speculating, the hypervigilant scanning, the scheming, the meticulous planning, the lists, the inventories of equipment, the clever bricolage of making do, the invention of new tools out of ordinary household products, the research expertise. Conspiracy theory is a hunter creeping through the woods at night on the track of a scent; nose to the ground, armed with a rigged-up spotlight to stop the deer dead in her tracks, it aims for an illuminated object, frozen at point-blank range—bull's eye. It both (a) fixes a final REAL and recreates (or endlessly replicates the fantasy of) a raw agency and (b) builds a spot of mystical merger where the subject gives itself up to the invisible forces of interconnection and merges with the object in a moment of abject communion. (If you can't beat 'em, join 'em.) Concrete objects sing with illumination. (One of the main items in the FBI's profile of a dangerous militia member is an obsessive compulsive attachment to one of a small number of particular makes of older, high-maintenance trucks. Other main characteristics include being a married man with children who has recently lost his job.)

Picture in this world a little man with a big head. I remember first hearing about this guy in Walter Benjamin's story about the storyteller—the guy who finds himself on the side of the road after a world war and suddenly realizes his tiny, fragile human body is surrounded by a world of an overwhelming scale and unthinkable violence. Then picture him some years later when he's gotten caught up in the machinations of that big world, channeling its moves and orders like a spirit medium. Imagine him caught up in the panoptical function of always looking around, scanning the landscape for signs of something out of place or eruptions of the inchoate and at the same time looking for THE missing detail that will stop the merry-go-round.

Try to focus. There are things, details, signs, evidence. What about the brand-name sportswear that was supposed to have KKK symbols and messages sewn into the seams as a plot against African-American pride? Or how did the Heaven's Gaters decide that they needed to wear black Nikes and bring their lip balm and some quarters and take their glasses off and leave them folded by their sides? For some it's in the details.

Others find a monstrous object, an all-consuming pursuit like a Moby Dick. The little man with the big head comes alive against the giant adversary, the dreadful will that haunts him and draws him in. He knows he'll shatter. He brings it on himself; he brings it to a head. The encounter is the way to come to life. Like the guy who started "The Republic of Texas" in Fort Davis and brought things to a head by kidnapping neighbors and by the end of the drama there was a little man lost in the desert shooting guns at helicopters.

Or, to come back to the everyday, take the disorientation of standing in front of one of those maps of a mall where everything is laid out in clear view and the cardinal directions are given (nothing hidden from view) and there's a dot and an arrow pointing out "you are here" and yet the effect is hopeless confusion. You look back and forth between the map and the overwhelming scene around you and you wonder which way to go and how you ever got here to begin with. Some people, of course, are experts and have strategies: they get to know the mall from practice and they arm themselves with a purpose, a search for something in particular; or they make a decision (like the Heaven's Gaters' decision to carry lip balm) that they *like* to wander the malls (it's exercise, it gets them out of the house, they're looking for love). But even for the well-adjusted, conspiracy theories will drift into an ear. Everyone knows about the piped-in oxygen, the music and lighting planned to excite and manipulate, the planned disorientation. The pleasure of the mall is, secretly, the pleasure of giving in and taking things to excess or getting away with something (the tangible object captured and brought home to the drawer, or the price that really *is* a sale price)—if you can't beat 'em, join 'em.

Conspiracy theory, and the mundane practices that root it on planet earth, can become a stable center in itself—the missing detail in a life. The little world of like thinkers one joins, the massive adversary always almost caught, the focus. The subject lurches into a communion with an object world full of tiny details and big structures of feeling. Contamination, communion, hope, fear: politics and feelings grow palpable together. The details create the need for a plot. It's not that for conspiracy theory everything is always already a rigid, all too clear plot, but rather that the founding practice of conspiratorial thinking is the search for the missing plot. Think of it not as a prefabricated ideology (as if abstract, exegetical ideas were what ruled the world) but as a practice. An obsessive and skeptical practice of scanning and speculating from the realm of the concrete, undeniable, tangible detail to the realm of the final word, the system that makes sense of inchoate sensibilities and moments of strange convergence. It's a practice born of a world that cries out for interpretation.

Its goal is to find the traces of a REAL that sticks out of the system and simulacra like a gross protuberance and, at the same time, like a wound. It lives in a world where the line between inside and outside, fantasy and reality, animal and human and machine does not hold. This is a world full of gaps and the urge to find the missing link. It hums with the possibility that the uncanny is real and it hunkers down in fearful but excited expectation. We're waiting for something to happen—a drama, an endpoint, something to break the enclosure of untouchable systems and the drone of an endlessly repeating present.

The scanning gaze finds objects—points of focus—that combine the mechanics of "system" with the mechanics of "eruption" or dramatic "intrusion": the omnipresent unmarked black helicopters that suddenly appear out of nowhere in a shock of noise and speed and looming threat, the international financiers that are taking over the world with untraceable paper trails on the one hand and the universal bar coding of citizens on the other (here the image of the UFO implants), mysterious diseases that come from the ventilation system of a building and suddenly kill masses of people, food additives that systematically sterilize black men but not white men. At moments the system goes too far and gets recorded on the ubiquitous home video whose omnipresent possibility mimics the logic of the seamless system itself. No exit. The constant search for one, for the REAL.

I remember a neighbor on a little lake in Michigan who would walk around the lake with a video camera in the dead of the winter, recording the condition of all the summer people's houses. He'd leave the camera running continuously so much of the time you were just walking along with him, listening to his breathing (like a horror movie) and his unbelievably mundane commentary on banks of snow and someone else's footsteps in the path—"Looks like somebody's beat me out here this morning." Then he'd focus in and zoom close to some kind of protuberance down by the foundation in the front of a house. He'd speculate that there may have been broken pipes, now refrozen into lumps of ice sticking out from the foundation or a wall: there may be damage. Then the camera would zoom off again and we'd be back on the track, looking for the next drama, disaster, trauma that will signal the eruption of the REAL out of the endless loop of sign, simulation, replication, mimicry. At the moment of shock we'd draw close; seduced, we'd lose ourselves in the detail (he would send copies of these alarming shots to his neighbors summering in Florida). Then we'd pull back and get on with the systematic routine that mimics the job of the security guard (which in turn mimics the panoptic mechanism of the "system").

Conspiracy theory repeats itself: it reenacts trauma; it's always returning to something you thought you knew but couldn't quite account for. It looks for the trace and fastens onto it. It's a fascination that quickly turns into horror and that then lends itself to fascination again. It alternates.

Conspiracy theory is a texting of everyday life where everything is connected and the connections are uncanny. There are moments of déjà vu, moments when the sense of overdetermination is palpable. Conspiracy theory lays a claim to a threshold state of consciousness where you are at once connected to the concrete tangible detail and projecting into a future, a higher knowledge, a leading edge, seeking an order behind the visible. It moves between the realms of story and event, the official and the unofficial story, the fantasy and the reality, the subject and the object: caught up in the nervous oscillation of no-man's land, it finds itself fascinated by transformation, encounter, risk. It gets excited and begins to prophesy and name: it cryptically foreshadows; it announces; it channels latent forces; it gives voice, embodies, enacts, creates a density and matter to floating effects. Or it puffs itself up with self-importance, grows big-headed and hot-winded. Or it gets scared and looks for an outside. No exit. It passes judgment, looks for proof, verifies. It gets spiritual and looks for an ur-text. It goes mad and looks for something to happen—drama, trauma, final purifying fire and regeneration out of the ashes. It grows anxious: it anticipates, plans, makes scrupulous lists and inventories, lays up stores for all contingencies. Or it sits in the comfort of a reading chair by the fire sifting through the pleasures of interpretation and the hunt: at moments, it finds itself sublime in its own preoccupations with presenting the unrepresentable.

Conspiracy theory lies whispering under the wallpaper of optimistic modernity. It channels the contradictions of a late capitalist world fueled by difference and uniformity, desire and despair, the bureaucratic self and the romantic action hero, a sudden convergence of "private" feeling with a "public" world, and the sense of being stuck in a moving, exhilarating, but endlessly looping present. Conspiracy theory channels both the up side and the down side of things: progress and abjection, enchantment and disenchantment. It combines radical doubt with the sense that the truth is out there. It knots together knowledge and desire, marginality and the status of being "in the know."

It tracks: it channels as it goes about its seemingly mundane and obsessively focused task of sniffing out the smoking gun. It's prolific: it's caught up in things. It's a way of tracking events and phenomena in an "information society" with (more than) a twist of trauma. It has good days and bad days just like days on the Web. On a good day on the Web you can see forever; on a bad day you can enter a narrative madness, you can find yourself caught up, addicted, at once fixated and disoriented, both maniacally focused and alienated, stuck in an endless loop; you can grow angry, skeptical, suspicious of that "lost time" inside the probe. A good day is a surge of open possibility, freedom, newness. A bad day is abjection at the feet of obsession and the machine. One minute you're lost in space, the next you're the master of the universe. The Internet was made for conspiracy theory: it *is* a conspiracy theory: one thing leads to another, always another link leading you deeper into no thing and no place, floating through self-dividing and transmogrifying sites until you are awash in the sheer evidence that the Internet exists. The medium is the message again. Theory rules.

Conspiracy theory is a tense and twisted gathering of elements that do not meld but only feed on the mutual unsettlings they highlight. That's why conspiracy theory is all over the map: it's right-wing one moment and left-wing the next. It's modernist and postmodernist. It's both an open and closed form of texting. It's heavy-handed master narratives and hopelessly dispersed mumblings about this and that. It's "inside" the system and "outside" it; it speaks from positions of power and powerlessness. It penetrates the subject to the bone and leaves us cold with detachment. It seduces and repulses. In its hermeneutics of suspicion and dream, (a) nothing is what it seems (nightmare forces beyind the scenes), and (b) anything could happen (everything is still possible). It is nostalgic and future oriented. It's precise and hallucinatory, delusional and internally much too consistent; it's as rational as they come and yet its key moments are moments of slippage: a (insane) leap (of faith) is at its core. It is apocalyptic and fundamentally banal, ordinary, and dull. One minute it's drifting over the line into armed violence and the next it's writing detailed recipes for how to build cocoonlike cells of utopian communities in a Robinson Crusoe-like fantasy land made up entirely of the practices of scavenging, cleaning up, ingenious refashioning of matter into useful technology, getting food, making do. Its discipline is both military and aligned with the neatness of the suburban lawn. It believes in experts and mystics; it's cynical and it's into self-help groups and the imagined communities of partial publics and counterpublics. At one moment it's out there investigating cover ups and at the next moment it's seeking cover—cocooning in a little world of its own that has its own headquarters, stores of supplies, uniforms, flags, constitutions, regular gun practice, and last stands. It believes equally in arcane knowledge and common sense. Its signs point at once to the hyperreal and to the inchoate or latent. It twists and turns in its role as the abject trauma and vengeful victor; rather than be reduced to the object of a panoptic gaze, it trains a listening eye on the world.

It shows us something about the nature of power and affect. And it channels something about the nature of theorizing. It throws its cards on the table in order to enter a space vibrant with the foundational anxieties and powerful force fields at work in the act of theorizing itself in moments of dread and desire, unwarranted hope and bitter disenchantment, crazed optimism and deadened cynicism, half-hidden fantasies and half-articulate, mostly unknown truths. It gives us (academics) the willies because it presents, point blank, the abject alternative to our own continuing modernist obsession with "the (pure) idea" and the act of discriminating (reason) that is still our ace of spades, our queen of hearts, our wild card, and our jack of all trades. But it also holds out the fascination with "the real" as an uncanny trace that may (or may not) be "the key" to something else so caught up in the tracks of our droning dualisms (subject/object, real/fantasy, inside/outside, active/passive) that it is no longer satisfied with the daily practice of maintaining the fences but begins to notice things out of the corners of its eyes.

PARANOID, CRITICAL, METHODICAL, DALÍ,
KOOLHAAS, AND . . .

What, in the process of scientific discovery, transpires in the interval between mad imagination and its coalescence into a rational theory? How do ideas that have no objectifying architecture solidify into reasonable certitude? What transpires in the gap, in other words, between conspiracy and theory?

I want to lay the groundwork for a reassessment of the usefulness of a Paranoid-Critical Method (PCM). This notion, brought to life by Salvador Dalí in the 1930s and resuscitated in the late 1970s by Rem Koolhaas, enables one, I will suggest, to open up productive channels between interpretation and theory, paranoia and identity. More than simply giving irrationality a moment in the sun, the Paranoid-Critical Method allows one to reinscribe the temporal and spatial contests that get sloughed off in the agonistic coming to presence of scientific and humanist realities. The Paranoid-Critical Method reasserts an often lost continuity between the delusional and rational—retying the knot of their mutual genesis. In the course of this brief sketch I shall first focus on the Paranoid-Critical Method in order to outline its contours. I will then examine some of the ways in which one can use the PCM to illuminate the surprising proximity of conspiratorial thinking to the production of scientific facts. Finally, I will consider the paranoiac element in all hermeneutic practices, and how subjectivity itself is cleaved by an uncertainty that returns as the "willies."

At its origin, the Paranoid-Critical Method was Salvador Dalí's means of production for the complex, hallucinogenic images that wilted across his visual landscapes. As such, the PCM's applicability was specific to the fabrication of optical illusions, bifurcating doubles, and oscillating images. Dalí—perhaps the most public of paranoiacs—waged a constant and active war on visual reality, substituting his own delusional images for the object world in order to "systematize confusion and thus help to discredit completely the world of reality" (1970, 97). His technique of "forcing" inspiration from images was intended to infect reality with a host of parasitic impostors whose artificial, irrational origins tested the integrity of phenomena both objective and rational. As Dalí puts it in "The Stinking Ass,"

> Paranoia uses the external world in order to assert its dominating idea and has the disturbing characteristic of making others accept this idea's reality. The reality of the external world is used for illustration and proof, and so comes to serve the reality of our mind.
>
> Doctors agree that the mental processes of paranoiacs are often inconceivably swift and subtle, and that, availing themselves of associations and facts so refined as to escape normal people, paranoiacs often reach conclusions which cannot be contradicted or rejected and in any case nearly always defy psychological analysis. (1970, 98)[1]

There are a number of essential features that Dalí describes here that are critical for understanding paranoia as he conceives it. First of all, the observations and connections made by the paranoiac are "swift," "subtle," and "refined." Second, the paranoiac does not loosely knit these associations together but instead systematizes them. In other words, the conclusions are rigid, defensible, and (most significantly) rational. They are built on an original delusion, but that wobbly foundation still supports a rigid structure. Third, they are contagious. The paranoiac conclusions are hard to resist and they spread. Like a conspiracy, they compel others to believe. Last, reality provides "illustration and proof" in the form of readily recognizable objects and observations. Paranoia, in Dalí's version, is not wild irrationality or psychosis, it is a style of interpretation.[2] It is a fine-grained but delusional association of observations that are then tightly and rationally woven together and ultimately substantiated by "objectifying" facts. The small measure that separates it from nonparanoiac knowledge is not always easily discerned. The practice of hermeneutics and the PCM run precariously parallel.

Corrupting interpretation, however, was not Dalí's primary agenda. Instead, he wielded the PCM as an instrument in the service of visual trickery. It was as a faculty of perception that Dalí deployed the PCM, but the results, while mesmerizing, did not explore the full, disruptive potential of the paranoid style of interpretation. Using the PCM to "force" double (and more multiple) images out of his oneiric landscapes, Dalí's method was in fact a visual analog to Freud's notion of condensation. He compressed incompatible images into one, creating, for example, a Venus de Milo that is simultaneously a toreador in *The Hallucinogenic Toreador,* or a bust of Voltaire that is a group of Dutch merchant women in *Slave Market with the Disappearing Bust of Voltaire.* Simultaneously two things—two identities—Dalí's images of a doubled reality, however, rarely transcend optical chicanery; they are domesticated by Dalí's calculated manipulations. Rather than using the PCM to contest the objectivity of interpretive practice, Dalí simply hallucinated with it.[3]

And paranoiacs are everywhere, it seems. In *Delirious New York,* Rem Koolhaas reanimates Dalí's Paranoid-Critical Method, using it to more seductive and subversive ends. His point of departure—the paranoiac's calculus of delusion plus systematic interpretation—is vintage Dalí:

> Just as in a magnetic field metal molecules align themselves to exert a collective, cumulative pull, so, through unstoppable, systematic and *in themselves strictly rational* associations, the paranoiac turns the whole world into a magnetic field of facts, all pointing in the same direction: the one he is going in.
>
> As the name suggests, Dalí's Paranoid-Critical Method is a sequence of two consecutive but discrete operations:
>
> 1. the synthetic reproduction of the paranoiac's way of seeing the world in a new light—with its rich harvest of unsuspected correspondences, analogies, and patterns; and
>
> 2. the compression of these gaseous speculations to a critical point where they achieve the density of fact: the critical part of the method consists of the fabrication of objectifying "souvenirs" of the paranoid tourism, of concrete evidence that brings the "discoveries" of those excursions back to the rest of mankind, ideally in forms as obvious and undeniable as snapshots. (1994, 238)

Again, the same formula: original delusion, systematic associations, rational architecture, and concrete evidence. But whereas Dalí's intention was to radically confuse the real, Koolhaas's is to *produce* the real (in this instance in the form of a theory of Manhattanism). It is this subtle difference that will make Koolhaas's effort all the more effective.

Koolhaas shifts the terrain of the PCM's applicability, utilizing it as an interpretive strategy to reread the history of Manhattan's modern development. With scant attention to the conscious agency of Manhattan's architects, planners, and designers, Koolhaas sifts through the present cityscape of Manhattan, locating in its spasmodic congestion the outlines of a coherent strategy of metropolitan construction. A "retroactive manifesto," as he terms it, *Delirious New York* works through the problem of the death of avant-gardism and the life of the city: "How to write a manifesto—on a form of urbanism for what remains of the 20th century—in an age disgusted with them? The fatal weakness of manifestos is their inherent lack of evidence. Manhattan's problem is the opposite: it is a mountain range of evidence without manifesto" (9). It is, in other words, confirmation in need of a hypothesis. The "evidence" that he collects will guarantee the validity of this theory's existence; the evidence is the "souvenir." It is not so much the *truth* of his theory that he must substantiate, but its *exis-*

tence; its truth is answered by the irrefutable rationality of the argument. The "objectifying facts" that Koolhaas creates—Coney Island, Manhattan's Grid, the Skyscraper—cool, solidify, and coagulate into the concrete manifestations that *prove* his theory's existence.

An example will help clarify: the Skyscraper, one of these "objectifying facts," is, according to Koolhaas, a fundamentally irrational technology. Originally envisioned as a stack of uncoordinated levels, each with a different function, the skyscraper defied a unitary signification. Despite the building's genetic disunity, its developers nevertheless sold it as a powerful, pragmatic, and rational structure. To Koolhaas's mind, however, "the subversiveness of the Skyscraper's true nature—the ultimate unpredictability of its performance—is inadmissible to its makers" (87). Their claims to predictability belied the skyscraper's crazy form: they crammed it full of the "Fantastic Technology" that only recently had been developed at Coney Island to bedazzle the masses; contemporary zoning laws, not architects, dictated its setback shape; its exterior drifted away from any semantic continuities with its interior. Even so, the Skyscraper dominated Manhattan, dissimulating its aleatory origins as the efficient use of space and rational bureaucratic organization. As Koolhaas argues, New York's developers "have developed a schizophrenia that allows them simultaneously to derive energy and inspiration from Manhattan as an irrational fantasy *and* to establish its unprecedented theorems in a series of strictly rational steps" (173). It is Koolhaas the Paranoid who "discovers" the irrational unconscious that others could not detect in Manhattan's delirious development. With a mountain of rock-solid evidence he *proves* the existence of a coherent Manhattanism unknown to the developers themselves. He deploys the PCM to test our own beliefs in conspiratorial theories: isn't Koolhaas's theory simply the fabrication of an overheated imagination? And yet it is so convincing. He has tangible evidence.

It is in this way that Koolhaas cannily updates and sharpens the PCM. Wielding it as an analytic tool, he exposes us to its convincing—near universal—applicability. And in his hands it becomes a means for critically dismantling the transparency of conventional, causal explanation. In the process he reenergizes the field of New York urbanology, creating a new pole of attraction for an alternate hermeneutic grid.

It is in fact the necessary materiality of that evidence that makes the PCM so powerful as an analytical instrument for understanding the magnetic attraction of conspiracy to theory. The PCM helps to refocus attention on the origins and contests that are systematically shed in the coming to presence of "truthful" theories. By offering convincing counterevidence, it calls into question the means (often forgotten) by which certain versions of reality become unassailable. It makes theory look conspiratorial.

Conspiracy, conventionally, is a clandestine effort to effect an outcome. It relies on secrecy and invisibility. A conspiracy theory, then, is simply an alternate explanation for that outcome. Conspiracy theorists, therefore, have the burden of exposing—making visible[4]—the clandestine causal agents. Their interpretation is only as good as the evidence they have to support it, and their interpretive logic is only separated from the prevailing one by the ratio of visibility to plausibility. With enough evidence (here is where the tangibility of the "objectifying souvenirs" is so critical) one can convince a nonbeliever to "see" the connections and thus "see" the occulted agents. It is to this process of "making visible" (or making tangible) and its relation to proof that I want to turn now.

"Making visible" relies on nothing but instruments of measure. That is to say, one must possess testing mechanisms adequate to the reality that one wants to make visible. This process is perfectly illuminated in Bruno Latour's dazzling rereading of Louis Pasteur's discovery of the microbes that were causing anthrax in *The Pasteurization of France*. Latour describes in compelling detail how Pasteur mastered the contests of proof by recognizing the power of visibility to embody truth. According to Latour, the experts of the nineteenth century French hygiene movement had a theory—morbid spontaneity—that effectively explained the seeming random outbreaks of disease. In fact, as Latour argues,

> this doctrine, which is ridiculed today, corresponded perfectly to the style, mode of action, and facts, since disease appeared sometimes here, sometimes there; sometimes at one season, sometimes at another. . . . This strange, erractic behavior was well recorded by statistics, the major science of the mid-nineteenth century, which corresponded perfectly to the analysis of such *impalpable* phenomena. (1988, 21; emphasis added)

The science of statistics had been the first to make visible a causal force of the disease, lifting out from the random data a pattern and a theory that made "impalpable" phenomena knowable. From there, the hygienists developed a social strategy—cleaning out gutters, removing trash, airing out neighborhoods—that would have a profound ameliorative effect. Their statistical instruments had identified a disease and a strategy for its eradication. It might very well have succeeded, except that Pasteur's instruments were more persuasive.

It was Pasteur's ability to make manifest the invisible microbe that overwhelmed their weak, statistical instrument. His competing theory of contagion—almost ludicrous at the time—vanquished morbid spontaneity in part because, as Latour argues, Pasteur's "proof" was there for all to see. Its near delusional hypothesis was transformed into concrete certitude with the addition of the "objectifying facts" of halos and spots:

> They [the microbes] grow enthusiastically in these media. . . . They
> grow so quickly that they *become visible* to the eye of an agent who
> has them trapped there. Yes, a colored halo appears in the cultures. . . .
> This event completely modifies both the agent, which has become a
> microbe, and the position of the skillful strategist who has captured
> it in the gelatine. Without this transformation's being made on the
> microbes, the Pasteurian would have been without a fulcrum. (82)

> If they still disputed our findings, we would get them to examine the
> curves and dots and ask them: Can you see a dot? Can you see a red
> stain? Can you see a spot? They would be forced to say yes, or aban-
> don the profession, or in the end be locked up in an asylum. They
> would be *forced* to accept the argument, except to produce other
> traces that were as simple to read—no, *even simpler* to read. (83)

Latour's accomplishment here is in reconstructing the process by which Pasteur
manufactured irrefutable proof. He demonstrates exactly how it is that Pasteur
made a wild set of associations convincing by using the objectifying souvenirs
of halos and spots to make the enemy palpable and his theory invincible. Pasteur's theory was hardly more rational than the hygienists' (to the nineteenth-
century scientist), he simply had a better instrument for making it so.

Latour's analysis of Pasteur is helpful because it acts like an ethnography of
laboratory proof. That is to say, Latour refuses to accept scientific testing as an
act of pure knowledge production. Instead, he enmeshes Pasteur's laboratory
discoveries in the webs of power and proof; he demonstrates how competing
theories—often each irrational—come to rely on the fabrication of concrete,
visible evidence to establish the real on their own terms. Because he situates
his analysis in the nineteenth century, Latour enables us to see the irrationality
of both hypotheses: Pasteur's "crazy" contagion theory and the hygienists'
wild ideas of "morbid spontaneity." Pasteur, in the end, is much like Koolhaas.
Both insinuate their (delusional) hypotheses into the real, create the real, and
then leave the erasure of their traces to others.

The use of the PCM as an interpretive instrument is hardly limited to artists,
psychotics, and the occasional intellectual eccentric. It is far more pervasive
than that. In several of the contributions to this present volume, in fact, one can
see a variety of contexts in which the PCM proves itself useful for demonstrating the contact points between conspiracy and theory. Once again, what de-
limits delusional ideas from verifiable facts in these cases is often nearly inap-
preciable. In the following instances we will be looking for the competing
interpretations of events, the "objectifying facts" that are produced, and the
instruments of measure that make visible the substantiating "souvenirs."

*If declining worker productivity is bringing down both management and
worker morale, recalibrate your instrument for measuring it.* This is the happy

conclusion that the operations manager reaches in Scott Lukas's theme park article. Few instruments are more freely readjusted than statistical measures; and few instruments are more powerful in the creation of a new sense of the real. This malleable tool can produce nearly infinite truths, sealing each with the stamp of scientific rigor.

Paranoiacs do not look, they find. Michael Fortun's essay on the willies even further implies a tight compatibility between science and the PCM. Here we see that even high-level physicists do not experiment on some known phenomena called "reality." They do not simply weigh and measure it, but they *create* it with their instruments. Herb Bernstein admits as much: "the properties of the other one [particle] are kind of predetermined by what you choose to measure. But they're unknown until that measurement is done"; "when you look at an object at the microscopic scale—when you take physics down to where it's at its roots, its reductionist roots—it seems like the phenomena that you study are being created"; "when you look at something, you create what you're studying." This last phrase truly captures the productive potential of all paranoid-critical investigations, for how can one look at something that only gets created by the act of looking? Or, as Rem Koolhaas phrases it, "the paranoiac always hits the nail on the head, no matter where the hammer falls" (1994, 238).

Why trust instruments anyway? A telling detail in Kim Fortun's essay on the Gulf War syndrome asks as much. The Department of Defense admits that their sensors for chemical warfare agents have a high rate of "false positives." This is a peculiar and murky observation. It seems to be an admission that instruments are as inventive in their identification of empirical certitude as humans. The sensor detects the invisible agents; however, we know that the sensor is mistaken. If indeed these agents are undetectable by human actors, how precisely do we justify that conclusion? It is difficult not to conclude that a "false positive" is the *aporia* that marks the limits of instrumental certitude. For what could be more conspiratorial than a scientific instrument that deceives?

The conceptual black hole of the "false positive" is radically unthinkable; indeed, it is incommensurable with scientific reality. It is, I would argue, the *aporia* that produces the willies. Its incommensurability suggests an alternate reality, a different explanatory model. It is this radical doubt that fuels conspiracy and feeds the willies. To conclude, I want to address this point by asking what compels conspiracies. What makes them irresistible? One answer to those questions is perhaps best indicated by the phrase that lingers as the opening title sequence to the television program *The X Files* disappears: "the truth is out there."

This mantra—which could just as easily be the disciplinary slogan for all ethnographers and scientific investigators—is potent because it knots together knowledge and desire, the self and the other. It illustrates, by extension, that subjectivity is haunted by a truth that always comes from somewhere else. It is a presumption that innervates the subject's interpretive faculties to continue their fine-grained search for likely correspondences, objectifying souvenirs, and an alternate explanation.

Freud's notion of the uncanny is helpful here. Taking the reader through the vicissitudes of the German term for the uncanny *(Unheimlich)* in his essay (first published in 1919), he stumbles upon a surprising fact: *Heimlich,* it seems, means something that is familiar, congenial, and comforting; but it can also mean something hidden from sight, concealed, and secreted.[5] The discovery of this paradox is not lost on Freud. In trying to capture the presence of the uncanny in human experience, Freud focuses on one of its most notorious manifestations: the double. Both in the perception that one has seen oneself and in those moments of temporal repetition—déjà vu—the subject encounters the confusion of sameness with difference, self with other. Subjectivity, haunted by its own splitting, encounters the impossibility of two incommensurable explanations: it is real; it was delusion. Put another way, the phenomenal world is familiar and menacing—or haunted. Freud explains this recognition of a double as a repetition of the infant's stage of nondifferentiation from others, a repetition of its own early traumas (1963, 39).

This is an explanation that Jacques Lacan—Freud's double—echoes and then expands on in his work on the Mirror Stage. For Lacan, subjectivity is always split, or alienated, through a process of visual identification with an ego-ideal (its own specular reflection) that the *infans* undergoes in the mirror stage. Trapped in an ambivalent dialectic of desire (for that other, unified self) and aggressivity (toward that other, unified self), subjectivity emerges split from its originary encounter with its own reflection, or double. Lacan suggests in "Aggressivity in Psychoanalysis," "What I have called paranoiac knowledge is shown, therefore, to correspond in its more or less archaic forms to certain critical moments that mark the history of man's mental genesis, each representing a stage in objectifying identification" (1977, 17). In other words, we are all, to varying degrees, paranoiacs; we are all occasionally haunted by the sense that we do not necessarily know the reality that we claim as the anchor of our subjectivity. That reality is buzzing with the currents of desire and danger that recapitulate the subject's originary relationship to its other. Lacan puts it this way: "And the two moments, when the subject denies himself and when he charges the other, become confused, and one discovers in him that paranoiac structure of the ego that finds its analogue in the fundamental negations described by Freud as the three delusions of jealousy, erotomania, and interpretation" (1977, 20). Paranoia is then, in Lacan's analysis, both constitutive of the structure of the ego and generative of the interpretive drives that the ego later manifests. It is a radical uncertainty that compels the subject to search for the "objectifying souvenirs" that will verify experience as real or delusional.

After detours in many different directions, we are right back to Dalí's notion of paranoia as a (delusional) style of interpretation.[6] And so we alight one final time on the twin themes of proof and existence, delusion and reality. A shiver—the willies—is predicated on the suspension of certainty, or more accurately, the possibility of the existence of the uncanny as real. It is a rational interpretation of random occurrences ("objectifying facts") based on a delusional hypothesis. It is strangely reminiscent of the Paranoid-Critical Method. It is the possibility of a real, built by the rational, anchored by the delusional.

Notes

1. If one substituted in this paragraph *scientific investigator for paranoiac,* how far, one might ask, is this from describing the popular profile of the "brilliant scientist"?

2. This is a point for which Nacomi Schor argues convincingly. Linking together the paranoiac symptom that the French term *délire de l'interprétation* with Freud's notion of a "delusion of reference," Schor excavates the forms of interpretation that are bound up with the paranoiac method. To do this she cites this relevant passage from Freud's work, *The Psychopathology of Everyday Life:* paranoiacs "attach the greatest significance to the minor details of other people's behaviour which we ordinarily neglect, interpret them and make them the basis of far-reaching conclusions" (1987, 102).

3. One might argue that Dalí was more successful with the PCM in another realm, however; namely, his own signature. His willingness to attach his signature to all sorts of commercial, insignificant, and fraudulent works has ended up having a disturbing effect. By randomly associating his name with objects unconnected to him, Dalí endorsed the proliferation of (fake) "Dalís" that call into question the status of all "real" Dalís. That gesture (mimicked in the 1980s by Mark Kostabi and other artists) may well be the enduring legacy of his PCM.

4. I use the term "visible" here only loosely. What I mean to describe is the process of becoming perceptible, legible, or meaningful. It is for the coming to presence of the phenomena that I will continue to use the concept "making visible."

5. It is interesting to note that the German term *heimlich* also covers the following two meanings: "Officials who give important advice which has to be kept secret in matters of state are called *heimlich* councillors," and "*Heimlich* also has the meaning of that which is obscure, inaccessible to knowledge" (Freud 1963, 30).

6. This is not coincidence. In a now famous encounter, Lacan went to visit Dalí in the early 1930s specifically to discuss paranoia. At that time, it was a focus of both men's work, and their mutual influence is well documented (see Roudinesco 1990, 110–13).

References

Dalí, Salvador. 1970. "The Stinking Ass." In *Surrealists on Art,* ed. Lucy Lippard, Englewood Cliffs, N.J.: Prentice-Hall.

Freud, Sigmund. 1963. *Studies in Parapsychology.* New York: Collier Books.

Koolhaas, Rem. 1994. *Delirious New York.* New York: Monacelli Press.

Lacan, Jacques. 1977. *Ecrits.* New York: Norton.

Latour, Bruno. 1988. *The Pasteurization of France.* Cambridge, Mass.: Harvard University Press.

Roudinesco, Elisabeth. 1990. *Jacques Lacan and Co.* Chicago: University of Chicago Press.

Schor, Naomi. 1987. *Reading in Detail: Aesthetics and the Feminine.* New York: Routledge.

PARANOIA WITHIN REASON

John Kadvany

János Radványi is a respected Hungarian essayist and critic who was trained in mathematics, philosophy, and engineering, earns his living in Budapest as an environmental risk analyst, and publishes frequently on pollution, risk, and the philosophy of science. During the 1980s Radványi published a series of controversial articles on the Hungarian emigré philosopher of science Imre Lakatos, who had been a major influence in England and America in the philosophy of science debates associated with Thomas Kuhn, Paul Feyerabend, and Karl Popper. Radványi claims that Lakatos, who died in 1974, developed a covert Hegelian-Marxist philosophy within his English-language publications and that his work is that of a "philosophical mole." While he does not consider himself a Marxist, Radványi found himself de facto in the role of intellectual historian of a convoluted, semisecret, and philosophically important strand of nineteenth-century ideas connecting Lakatos, in England, to one of Lakatos's Hungarian teachers, Georg Lukács, perhaps the most influential Marxist philosopher of the twentieth century. Because of conflicts surrounding Marxism during the 1980s arising from both government ideologies and Hungarian intellectuals, and Radványi's need to protect his professional role as a government policy analyst, he chose to publish much of his work on Lakatos through his collaborator John Kadvany, who has lived in the United States since the failed 1956 Hungarian Revolution. George Marcus learned of Radványi's tangled, cross-cultural intellectual life and his theories about Lakatos's covert Hegelianism through Kadvany, who arranged the following interview. The interview was held in February 1996 when Radványi was on a short visit to New York. To facilitate the dialogue, many questions were scripted in advance, and Radványi worked on the final text with Marcus and Kadvany after the interview to clarify his responses.

Michael Fortun

Uncanny correlations: the day on which I sat down to write these framing comments, over two years since I began working on the "teleportation" piece printed here, the *Washington Post,* CNN, and other media outlets were announcing the first experimental achievement of "teleportation." The stories had such titles as "On a Table, 'Beam Me Up Scotty'-Like Experiment," and "Science Fact: Scientists Achieve 'Star Trek'-Like Feat." They were reporting the report in the journal *Nature* by a group of Austrian experimental physicists who had successfully "pulled off a startling trick that looks like . . . the technology of science fiction." The Austrian group, headed by Anton Zeilinger, had "destroyed bits of light in one place and made perfect replicas appear about three feet away" by taking advantage of a quantum effect called "entanglement." CNN reassured the reader of its Web page. "If the notion of entanglement leaves your head spinning, don't feel bad. Zeilinger said he doesn't understand how it works either. 'And you can quote me on that,' he said." End of story.

Citationality, entanglement, the influences of pop culture, spinning heads, incomplete understanding, and remarkable technical achievement in spite of it all. Indeed, technical achievement as an effect of these supposedly undermining qualitities. My piece here circles around all of these subjects. At its center is the theoretical physicist, Herbert Bernstein, with whom I collaborate in a nonprofit organization, the Institute for Science and Interdisciplinary Studies (ISIS). ISIS invents new ways of both questioning the sciences and deploying them to address current problems such as cleaning up the military's toxic legacy, developing aquaculture techniques with the indigenous people of the Amazon basin in Ecuador, and advancing the field of sustainable agriculture. Bernstein is also one of the theorists in a cutting-edge National Science Foundation-funded group of physicists reinscribing the limits of a field called multiparticle interferometry; the Austrian physicist Zeilinger heads the experimental wing of their group.

So this is a piece about multiple entanglements, about the indirect, subtle, and elusive forces that disrupt—without destroying—our conceptions of conspiracies: entanglements between theory and experiment, between pop culture and the culture of science, between "science fiction" and "science fact," between scientist and ethnographer, between "spookily" correlated photons, between judging and recording, between the pure idea and the military application, between funder and funded, between chance and determinism, between words and things, between speakable and unspeakable. Which means it is a piece about an unmasterable assemblage of forces that, while never quite cohering into a full-blown conspiracy, nevertheless *feels* as though it *might* have some "will of its own."

Which means it is a piece about "the willies," Bernstein's term for that feel-ing, that thought that can't yet be thought. It was this haunted sense of uncanny possibilities, a sense that seems to bypass the mind to immediately crawl over the flesh, that has prompted Bernstein's dis-ease with his own theoretical work. Years before any "application" had been achieved in the entangled pursuits of quantum teleportation, quantum computation, and quantum cryptography, Bernstein felt the willies. He sensed, somehow, that the field of quantum phys-ics, which he loved for how it demonstrated the "responsibility" the physicist had in "making reality," was, somehow, being turned to the service of institu-tions like the U.S. Department of Defense and the National Security Agency. The intractable uncertainties of those "somehows" called for an invention somewhat different from other ISIS projects—an invention geared more to-ward questioning, uncertainty, play, and theory than it was toward the practical assertions of policy work or technical assistance. One of these inventions be-came the ethnographic experiment represented here, staging a public "trial" of Bernstein before his former students. We knew in advance that the trial would fail to adjudicate the questions of innocence or guilt, or the existence of a mili-tary or any other kind of "conspiracy" behind quantum teleportation. It did succeed, however, in creating a dialogue about practicing responsible science in entangled states, where uncertainty and indirection are dominant. I hope to extend this dialogic effect in the continuation of the ethnographic experi-ment here.

Finally, then, this is a piece about the ethics of experimentation and experi-mental ethics, another entangled chiasmus. For much of this century, quantum physics has worked not to overthrow but to destabilize traditional conceptions of scientific epistemology and ontology. It has foregrounded chance, indeter-minism, and correlations or forces that so exceed the capacities of our lan-guage—mathematical or otherwise—that many call them spooky. The piece here should likewise destabilize the category of conspiracy, displacing it from a realm of hidden yet direct and specifiable control mechanisms, into a world characterized by indirect, indistinct, and suggestive associations. And while a code of ethics may be appropriate for a hidden but knowable conspiracy, the uncanny entanglements within and around "quantum teleportation" demand something more experimental—something more attuned to inquiry than to as-sertion, to spectral possibility rather than confirmed conviction. There is as yet no ethics appropriate to entangled states, yet such haunting, uncertain entan-glements are for that very reason even more demanding of an ethical response. The trial is one such experiment in the invention and enactment of that open, inquiry-based ethics.

To supplement the experiment with the trial, I've experimented with form here, miming the quantized, disjunctive microworld of quantum physics. The text is itself teleported, suddenly jumping from one site, topic, or time to another. The entanglements between these sites remain allusive. Since some of the greatest physicists in the history of quantum theory have stressed how play, creative experiment, and attention to language are essential to working productively in the quantum realm, I have tried to follow their example. And since even the physicists who are most expert in the field feel free to express their inability to understand perfectly, I thought the effect I wanted this piece to produce in the reader should be less one of understanding and more "leaving your head spinning," if not your flesh crawling.

I'm compelled, by forces that I don't understand perfectly—and you can quote me on that—to end with a few words about my own willies. This piece was written and is being published at a time in which a tremendously resilient conspiracy theory is being articulated by what Bernstein and I, in another of our collaborations, call science purists. Under this theory, there is a growing cadre of postmodern, irrational, relativist, antiscience academicians who practice a phantasmatic charlatanry sometimes known as higher superstition. They lack an understanding of science as well as respect for scientists, and they should be either dismissed as promoters of nonsense or feared as pushers of poison. (Exploring the contradictions there would take too much time.)

Let me clearly state: I've had the pleasure of meeting and talking with Anton Zeilinger, Charles Bennett, and many of the other physicists mentioned here who toil in the teleportation field along with Bernstein. They are admirable people for whose accomplishments I have the greatest respect. Yet I worry that my playing with language and form will be taken as evidence of an unserious attitude toward some of the most remarkable work in twentieth-century physics. I worry that my *questioning* here of the undecidable entanglements between science, culture, spooky language, the military, and ethics will be interpreted as a negative, decisive judgment on these physicists and their work. I worry that my hope for a continuing dialogue on these questions, between scientists and other scholars captivated by the sciences, will sputter rather than fluorish. The odds that these worries will be materialized, despite my best intentions, seem frighteningly high to me.

But I've built this textual experiment and have set it running, and can only accept the risks entailed in it. So all I can do is live with these willies, promise to clean up whatever mess might result from operations of my machine, and express my most heartfelt thanks to Bernstein for helping to make a space for these trial-and-error procedures. I am, as the colloquialism goes, much obliged.

Myanna Lahsen

I came to the focus on climate change research in a roundabout way. It was triggered by thoughts that came to me as I sat on my balcony in warm, muggy

Houston, Texas. I found myself bothered by the pollution I smelled in the air, and began to reflect on the processes—social, political, technological, and economic—resulting in this polluted environment potentially affecting my body and health. My preliminary research into air pollution as a transboundary phenomenon quickly led me to the subject of global warming, an environmental threat the transboundary nature of which expands to the geopolitical level, ultimately involving a debate about North-South relations and global inequity in power and material resources. I chose the National Center of Atmospheric Research, in Boulder, Colorado, as the base from where to do multisite research into the production of scientific projections of human-induced climate change.

Initially intending to study only climate modelers—the scientists producing the climate simulations most centrally informing projections of human-induced climate change—I soon found myself intrigued by the broader range of scientists involved in the often antagonistic debate about the science supporting these projections. I encountered a greater level of scientific disagreement and uncertainty on the issue than I had expected, hearing scientists of various orientations (scientific, sociocultural, and political) question the scientific and environmental preoccupation with it, foregrounding the frequent sensationalism surrounding it, and questioning its reality and potential severity. I found myself confronted with my own environmentalist convictions, assumptions, and values.

The conflicting scientific arguments on the issue also exposed me to a rich complexity of discourses I found unfamiliar due to my upbringing in Denmark and France. I started to focus on the deeper dialogue embedded in the scientific arguments, thereby simultaneously familiarizing myself with American culture, environmentalism, and science, exploring their connections with larger socioeconomic and political processes and transformations related to globalization.

My research exposed me to the impact of broader social changes on the production of scientific knowledge. I witnessed scientists express concern about increasingly becoming "consultants to groups with an agenda," I learned of the tension among scientists around the issue of scientific advocacy, behavior that fits uneasily with traditional notions of the "proper behavior" of scientists in society. I also learned of the federal funding practices promoting "socially relevant" science; of new pressures for scientists to provide answers to policymakers; of widespread dismissals of research "exploring" or "giving in" to pressures to provide "answers" to policymakers in face of great uncertainty, as well the traditional tendency for scientists to attach greater value and prestige to curiosity-driven as opposed to applied science carried out in response to the demand for "relevant" science. All of these issues inform the controversy about the IPPC report's Chapter 8, the subject of my article in this volume.

Michael F. Brown

While undertaking ethnographic fieldwork among Americans deeply involved in New Age spirituality, I had occasion to discuss channeling—essentially a postmodern version of spirit possession—with psychologists at my home institution and elsewhere. To my surprise, mental-health professionals who scoffed at channeling and other New Age practices were likely to defend the reality of multiple personality, recovered memory, and satanic ritual abuse. It occurred to me that it might be useful to compare the utopian narratives of a group of channeling therapists to the dystopian vision of those considered experts in the diagnosis and treatment of multiple personality. Their common cultural logic supports the contention of the late Christopher Lasch, a prophet of dystopia in his own right, that the banality and moral emptiness of modern life create an inner void that desperately seeks to be filled by something from outside the self—in this case, by stories of dark conspiracy or collective ascension that potentiate one another like the ingredients of a terrorist's bomb.

Kim and Michael Fortun

We became interested in the Securities and Exchange Commission as a result of our interest in claims that commercial corporations have become a major threat to democracy due to their "global reach" and "behind-closed-doors" decision making, in the interest of monopolization rather than the public good. Such claims surface often in our primary arenas of research, in debates surrounding the commercialization of biotechnology and in those concerning the environmental effects of the chemical industry. Our initial idea was to interview a practitioner of "conspiracy busting," a lawyer trying to disrupt monopolistic corporate control through antitrust litigation or some other defensive strategy. We wanted to learn how such a practitioner maps the landscape on which corporate conspiracies operate, and devises strategies of interruption. So we went to speak to Michael Mann, a former student of Herb Bernstein's at Hampshire College (see the essay in this volume on quantum teleportation), who was working at the SEC.

We thought Mann could direct us to a sharp-thinking, sharp-talking colleague directly engaged in confrontations with Union Carbide, Eli Lilly, or some other corporate giant. What we soon realized was that conspiracy busting was the mission of the SEC itself, albeit without a defensive, confrontational tone. Moreover, within the SEC, conspiracy busting was configured primarily in terms of information, and the promise that being "in the know" could undergird fair transactions of power within a democratic system. The SEC's focus on information as a social good resonated even more strongly with our interests; information and "the right to know" are frequently offered as solutions to the risks created by hazardous production, and as the chief raw materials for biological research and production. We were also triggered by Michael Mann's role as what we came to call a middleman, responsible for working the crossroads at which *private* corporations disclose their identity and operations to *the public*. This particular interface of the public and the private seemed somehow to embody the ways identity and information about identity are entangled, but separate—providing the stage on which we both desire to know, and fear conspiracy. And Mann, as director of the SEC's Office of International Affairs, worked at a particularly strange intersection, where *the* market confronted *different* trading cultures, and everyday disruptions of its own systematicity.

We liked the fact that Mann's job did not involve flamboyant courtroom arguments or carefully choreographed media interventions. His job did demand rigorous skills of interpretation and translation, coupled with fine-tuned implementation strategies that continually asked him to draw and then walk a line between ideal and practical possibility. Mann, as middleman between that which (possibly) conspires and those who desire to know, could not afford to be dogmatic, or to simply rail against the shifting, globalizing context in which both corporations and information now operate so powerfully. Mann therefore seemed as interesting a "conspiracy buster" as we could hope to find, with the added allure of being a fabulous storyteller.

His engaging stories about the SEC today whetted our genealogical appetite, our desire to know something about how this relatively unsung and unseen institution came to underwrite a system predicated on transparency and disclosure. The interview is prefaced by a brief history of the SEC's creation, and the various conspiracy theories concerning both Wall Street and Washington that circulated in that middled, interwar period of U.S. history. Throughout the interview we've added additional bits of information in the form of notes that suggest additional ways in which Mann's role has been shaped by the institutional culture of the SEC.

The interview itself can be read as an attempt to disclose how the disclosure mandated by the SEC is imagined and realized, by someone working within the system, to facilitate the transparency and fairness of the system itself. At least that's how we initially conceptualized it. After listening to Mann, working with the transcript, and learning more about the SEC, we thought that "working at the limit of the system" would be a better positioning device. Like information itself, Mann and the SEC operate on the border separating (and joining) inside and outside, transparency and opacity, full knowledge and hidden conspiracy. As we elaborate in the postscript to the interview, information is doubled and contradictory: information is both the outside frame of the market system that ensures its transparency and is bought and sold inside the system like any other commodity. As the site of flux, contradiction, trading, and negotiation, the limit is a fascinating place to watch.

While we didn't get our interview with a stridently oppositional figure articulating a conspiratorial outside from within a well-defined inside, we found someone even more interesting. Someone who worked at the limits or the borders of the market system, at a time when cross-border transactions have escalated dramatically, trading has been liberalized, financial and environmental risks have been refigured and delocalized, and limits themselves are said to fade away as the market's horizon becomes globalized. Mann's work takes him to all of these heavily trafficked crossroads, and his words here afford a unique perspective on this incredible rush of forces. Mann is less interested in making conspiracy theories than he is in "taking the chance of making things work," in the words of one of the creators of the SEC in the 1930s. It seemed to us an admirable tactic, and one worth paying attention to.

3

THE EXTRATERRITORIALITY OF IMRE LAKATOS:
A CONVERSATION WITH JÁNOS RADVÁNYI

> Something I owe to the soil that grew
> More to the life that fed
> But most I owe to Allah
> Who gave me two
> Separate sides to my head
>
> —Rudyard Kipling, *Kim*

KADVANY: János, you've written for several years that Imre Lakatos, the Hungarian emigré philosopher of science, was a philosophical mole. What does this mean?

RADVÁNYI: There's a two-fold reading possible of Lakatos's philosophy of science and mathematics. In one, he's the culmination of his mentor Karl Popper's "critical rationalism," and a rationalist defense to the more free-wheeling ideas in philosophy of science of Paul Feyerabend and Thomas Kuhn. In the second reading there is a covert Hegelian at work, creating a historicist response to problems of scientific and mathematical method that is analogous to Marx's historicization of nineteenth-century political economy. This is a type of rationalism, also, but one is that historicized and temporally specific. The methodology of modern science, for example, essentially didn't exist before the end of the Renaissance for Lakatos. At the same time, he gives a characterization of scientific criticism that implies its own historical transience.

KADVANY: Has anyone else noticed the Hegelian side of Lakatos's work?

RADVÁNYI: In Feyerabend's best-known book, *Against Method,* he calls Lakatos a "Trojan horse," and often noted, though without elaboration, strong Hegelian themes in Lakatos's philosophy. After Lakatos died, both Marx Wartofsky and Ian Hacking described Hegelian undercurrents in Lakatos's work. I'm not sure any of them recognized the seriousness of the whole enterprise.

KADVANY: And what enterprise is that?

RADVÁNYI: Lakatos was writing during the 1960s and early 1970s. Anglo-American philosophers, who were Lakatos's main audience in England and the United States, were barely able to deal with the idea that problems of scientific method were problems of history, or that scientific method was intrinsically a historical phenomenon. Lakatos had lots of innovative ideas about how to tackle these issues, but they had to be introduced under a sedate philosophical cover. Popper's "critical rationalism" and his notion that scientific theories aren't justified but rather are subject to "falsification" provided the springboard in England.

KADVANY: Could Lakatos have done this with anybody's ideas? What's special about Popper?

RADVÁNYI: Popper, through *The Open Society and Its Enemies,* along with other works, was a famous critic of Hegel and Marx, but many of Popper's ideas have an inchoate Hegelianism about them. For example, falsification as a fundamental principle implies, as Popper saw, that scientific progress, rather than being due to the inductive collection of facts, is created through a process of "negative" criticism, and theories are potentially always in flux. You quickly are led to expect some kind of temporal view of scientific change, which is absent in Popper, and then to ask what the status of falsification itself is. Is it a historical idea? How would you express that? Popper thought he'd solved the "problem of induction" through the logical asymmetry of falsification—that while you can never prove a theory, you can refute it and replace it with an improved version. That idea turned out to be assailable, as it doesn't say enough about how successive theories cohere or fail to cohere over time, or why some contradictions get ignored while others become refutations. Lakatos saw the technically sweet problem of historicizing Popper and made it his own. There's also the delicious irony of Lakatos building up a Hegelian view of science in Popper's own house, a house that was entirely unfriendly to Hegel and Marx. Popper loved to ridicule Hegel, such as in an early essay called "What Is Dialectic?" in which he essentially says that Hegel believes in contradictions, and logic shows from a contradiction that you can deduce anything, therefore Hegel is nonsense. With Lakatos, the crows come home to roost. Popper, in spite of his antipositivist ideas, made formal logic and the law of noncontradiction sacrosanct, as if people can't function knowing some theory they have of the world contains inconsistencies. It's a refusal to recognize reflection in knowledge, that we can think and talk about our theories even as we use them.

KADVANY: What are the key Hegelian elements in Lakatos's work?

RADVÁNYI: The unifying issue for Lakatos is historiography, whether historiography of mathematics or of science. How we understand scientific or mathematical reason is the historical problem of how to reconstruct these subjects' pasts, and not just for the historian, but for scientists and mathematicians themselves. Whether you're a scientist or a philosopher of science, you are always involved in some reconstruction of the scientific or mathematical past. In Lakatos's principal mathematical work, published posthumously as *Proofs and Refutations: The Logic of Mathematical Discovery*,[1] the goal was to demonstrate the specific historical achievements of nineteenth-century mathematics and how these led to the revolutionary theories of modern logic which we have today. Lakatos accomplished this goal by writing a kind of mathematical *Bildungsroman*, being the historical odyssey of a single famous theorem, Euler's theorem, on polyhedra, through its many nineteenth-century formulations and proofs. The journey of Euler's theorem is intended to be representative of nineteenth-century mathematics as a whole, and recreates, as Georg Lukács might put it, "the mathematical present as history." *Proofs and Refutations* is written as an enormously complex historical dialogue among eighteen characters, each representing a characteristic position mostly from nineteenth-century mathematical method. There's also an elaborate footnote apparatus in which Lakatos uses actual history to provide a counterpoint to the historical reconstruction taking place in the dialogue "above." Historiographically, *Proofs and Refutations* is Hegel's *Phenomenology of Spirit* in miniature, but focused only on modern mathematical history. Hegel's *Phenomenology* is also a reconstructed history based on the *Bildungsroman* form, and makes historical and cultural education not just another category of experience, but the basis for the growth of knowledge. While Hegel's "hero," the subject and object of *Bildung*, or historical education, is a generic philosophical consciousness, Lakatos's "hero" instead is a nineteenth-century mathematical theorem. The bond between Lakatos's historical claims and historiography then is expressed through his remarkable historiographic style, his rewriting of mathematical history. The point is to show how mathematical methods get built up through historical change but in mathematics itself; the book, after all, simply also is just the proof, or proofs, of a single theorem. It's the first sustained account in the history of ideas of mathematical reasoning as a constructive, historical process.

KADVANY: So there's a closer affinity to Hegel than to Marx in Lakatos's philosophy?

RADVÁNYI: Very much so, in that he's trying to explain the historical basis for big chunks of mathematical and scientific methodology, but without a reductive invocation of materialist, psychological, or sociological claims. Not that such categories are historically irrelevant, but that external explanations can be misguided by impoverished theories of mathematical reason. There's a naive response that has to be guarded against here, namely, that this return to Hegel contains the same idealist flaws that Marx criticized. But part of Lakatos's program is to reinvent our ideas about rationalism, by creating a philosophical alternative to both formal logic and social psychology. The autonomy of scientific and mathematical discourse becomes another complex subject in Lakatos, especially when you try to sort out his personal relationship to the ambiguous and diabolical legacy he left behind. He was no naive Hegelian.

KADVANY: What is the method of proofs and refutations?

RADVÁNYI: It's a detailed account of the idea that some mathematical theorems are invented, meaning that informal decisions are made regarding the types of mathematical entities the theorem should be about, the types of restrictions that need to be made to make the theorem true, and the scope of the theorem's applicability. These conditions, according to Lakatos, often come about through a historical process involving recognizable heuristics for changing and modifying a proof in order to improve it, especially by incorporating Popperian counterexamples or potential counterexamples. What's most interesting philosophically is that the method of proofs and refutations didn't exist until about the middle of the nineteenth century. *Proofs and Refutations* is the story of its emergence and the consequences for modern mathematics.

KADVANY: What happens to formal logic in Lakatos' philosophy of mathematics? That's part of modern mathematics, and it's all but taken over analytic philosophy. Is the idea that mathematics is contingent?

RADVÁNYI: *Contingent* may not be the right word, but certainly Lakatos argued forcefully for the historicity of modern methods of mathematical proof, and that they emerged only in the midnineteenth century. My reading of *Proofs and Refutations* is that Lakatos was outlining a historicist position for modern mathematical logic, an historicist account of the skepticism that became explicit in Kurt Gödel's famous incompleteness theorems and their considerable aftermath. It's only an outline in Lakatos, though. *Proofs and Refutations* is mostly about the changes going on in nineteenth-century mathematics, not its sequel. The main idea Lakatos delivers about modern logic is that mathematical logic itself is continuous with the rest of informal, historical mathematical theory; it's not a formal calculus itself, but is an informal mathematical theory about mathematics being a formal calculus, and makes use of the same historical methods used in other parts of mathematics. Perhaps Lakatos's ideas are not so radical now that we have chaos theory, fractals, nonlinear dynamics, and computer-assisted proofs. The four color theorem, for example, which says every map needs only four colors to distinguish adjacent regions, was proved several years ago using computers in an essential way.

KADVANY: Lakatos's philosophy of mathematics is not as well known, though, as his philosophy of science. What's the relationship between the two?

RADVÁNYI: Lakatos turned to philosophy of science after taking his job in the early 1960s at the London School of Economics, through his relationship with Karl Popper. Popper was Lakatos's new mentor, and the LSE was at the center of the philosophy of science debates which changed philosophy, the humanities, and social science as a whole since then. Popper's starting point was normative, like the positivists', in that he wanted to evaluate competing characterizations of scientific practice by asking what should "count" as science and what shouldn't. Again, as he'd done in *Proofs and Refutations,* Lakatos ultimately made the problem into one of historiography: what is your methodological conception of science's past, and how good an account does that give of science's history? Histories of science become "experiments," so to speak, against which philosophy of science is judged. At the same time, philosophies of science, if they are worth anything at all, should provide interpretive heuristics by which to build histories. And if you can't reconstruct "enough" history as science which you think should be science, that's a problem for your methodology. To invoke Lukács again, actual history is the yardstick against which philosophical histories are measured, while philosophy provides normative criteria for evaluating science's past. For Lakatos, methodology becomes wedded to history because methodology is nothing but the rational reconstruction of history.

KADVANY: Isn't this just privileging scientists' accounts with an historicist ideology?

RADVÁNYI: Lakatos, like Feyerabend and Kuhn, wanted to get philosophy closer to scientific practice, so the possibility is there. He also made clear that his role was to criticize science and its histories from a value-laden perspective for "lack of rationality," which he frankly described as how science "ought to have gone"—so Lakatos is not a complete Hegelian, he's quite willing to give critical philosophical advice giving direction to the world. Popper began with what he took to be the scientific pretensions of Marxism and Freud, and Lakatos also takes up this demarcationist starting point, which tries to characterize "science" and "nonscience." But where it ends is different from what Popper envisioned. The projected title of a book Lakatos planned before his death was *The Changing Logic of Scientific Discovery,* instead of Popper's static *Logic of Scientific Discovery.* It wasn't just that scientific "facts" might change because they were theory-laden, which even Popper recognized, nor just that theories were changing through criticism and falsification. Methodological standards for science as a whole were the result of historical developments following the Renaissance, nothing ultimately justified that these standards got you closer to the Truth, and the whole shape of scientific reason itself was subject to change. Making *that* point, and *how* he made that point, is the key to Lakatos's internal attack on Popper. It also shows the importance of keeping friendly with science, since that gives Lakatos's historicist case a kind of empirical corroboration.

KADVANY: What happens to science before the Renaissance?

RADVÁNYI: It's a huge blind spot for Lakatos, one that Feyerabend exploited with impunity. Science before Galileo is almost prehistory for Lakatos. While Aristotle is a first-class methodologist, especially for biologists and even decision analysts, he doesn't fit Lakatos's scheme at all. There's no way out except to accept the limited scope of Lakatos's project in the history of science.

KADVANY: Hadn't Thomas Kuhn essentially established that science was a constructive, historical process in *The Structure of Scientific Revolutions?* Some people see Lakatos as a swan song for Popper's "critical rationalism," a last defense against Kuhn's followers, or at least the epigone.

RADVÁNYI: In its obituary for Kuhn in 1996, the *Observer* of London wrote that Kuhn was philosophically tone-deaf, and that's just right. Kuhn popularized many good ideas, like "paradigm" and "incommensurability," but his philosophy was largely history teaching by example. He never dealt effectively with the enormous problems he raised of language, perception, historical interpretation, skepticism, relativism, and the normative status of science. Feyerabend and Lakatos were all the time building their own historical philosophies and historical vignettes which really addressed these issues. Others in the Anglo-American philosophical community paid scant attention to historical problems, since they were historically tone-deaf, just as Kuhn was philosophically tone-deaf. Lakatos's methodology of scientific research programs, as he called it, was a clever implementation of Hegelian ideas to put reason into historical motion, and his coversion was partly a response to an intellectual immaturity of the philosophical community of the 1960s and 1970s, vis-à-vis history.

KADVANY: Do you mean "covertness"? What's a "coversion"?

RADVÁNYI: It's a shorthand to distance Lakatos the person from the body of work he left behind. The "coversion" is the product itself, the pattern of ideas we observe in his philosophical essays.

KADVANY: How does Lakatos's idea of a research program work? How does reason get a historical character?

RADVÁNYI: First, science is not built up just out of theories, but larger units Lakatos called research programs, which are series of theories evolving in time, replacing one another, and loosely unified through a "hard core" of assumptions at the heart of the program. The hard core provides a kind of metaphysics for the program, without which the program falls apart. A research program at any time has a past which it is trying to improve upon, and competing programs to fend off. It is awash with contradictions, anomalies, and puzzles. Those participating in the program try to make novel predictions, some of these predictions may be corroborated and others refuted. A research program is not also just a series of interpreted observations and theories, there is a "positive heuristic," or set of promising ideas, for generating new models or observational theories which move the program forward; likewise, there is a defense structure of "negative heuristics" for fending off criticism from competitors. Since a research program includes what could be taken as "falsifying" anomalies or contradictions, it already takes a major step beyond Popper by allowing science to progress on inconsistent foundations. A research program usually can't be refuted or proved by an isolated experiment or fact, as the reasons for rejection or acceptance or programs involve a more extensive mosaic of the program's competitors, their relative progress or degeneration, and the changing status of supporting observational and mathematical theories. There's no single refutation or corroboration which makes or breaks a program's success, in direct opposition to Popperian falsification. In this way, research programs become the basic building blocks for science as a holistic and temporal process. Research programs are also science in science's own languages, not the philosophical language of formal logic, what Feyerabend derided as a "pidgin" language as far as scientific practice was concerned. For example, if informal science contains contradictions and you translate these into formal logic, you get garbage; but that's the fault of the translation, not the original informal knowledge. There's a deep point being made here by Lakatos about language and history, that the flexibility inherent in nonformalized discourse is essential for scientific criticism, and for reconstructing progress and degeneration in the scientific past. If you insist on fitting too much into a formal model of theory change, you risk eliminating science at least as we know it. Logical positivism's legacy to always think in terms of formalized and static theories turns out to be an enemy of criticism and the growth of knowledge. Though Lakatos liked to deride Kuhn's "incommensurability" for its "irrational" overtones, he was keen to point out the importance of language change in science, and the impossibility of representing historical science or mathematics in a fixed formal language.

KADVANY: Why wouldn't Popper welcome all this as an elaboration of his idea that you don't prove theories, you propose them and maybe refute them, the winners being the ones which resist refutation the longest?

RADVÁNYI: Once Popper had raised the idea that theory progression is fueled by contradiction, but without wanting to make the next natural step to an historicist approach, he was led to a Kantian defense against dialectical arguments, in which the law of contradiction, of "not: P and not-P," is sacrosanct. For Lakatos, what counts as refutation or "falsification" turns out to be a historical and constructive problem for specific research programs. Research programs have contradictions all over the place, so there's never any simple confrontation of theories and facts. "All theories are born refuted," Lakatos liked to say, which is his sanitized version of Hegel's conception that "the true always contains the false." This means for Lakatos that there can be no genuine "crucial experiments," no single confrontation of a theory with facts implying "accept" versus "reject," so, as Hegel says, "the true is the whole" as well. The temporal perspective is introduced by Lakatos's numerous arguments that criticism often occurs after the fact, with historical hindsight, not through crucial experiments intended to make or break a theory in advance of conducting an experiment or study. Falsification and logic in isolation get a diminished status, and Popper's half-logicist and half-critical position is seen to be not at all adequate to scientific practice. The Hegelian idea that reason is retrospective and constructive, that history is built into scientific practice itself, is anathema to Popper because it makes science depend on so much more than classical logic.

KADVANY: But there still is a strong Popperian side to Lakatos, in that he doesn't reject Popper entirely.

RADVÁNYI: Popper's negative progress of science through criticism, falsification, and the overall evolutionary perspective of science are still there. Lakatos's relationship to Popper is that he doesn't reject anything wholesale, his philosophy is built up dialectically out of Popper's and others' ideas. Lakatos's constructive approach to building his own philosophy is a Hegelian trademark which you also see in a synthetic philosopher like Habermas, but this criticism and elaboration of Popper is intended to illustrate the same transformations of ideas which occur in science.

KADVANY: Even if research programs give science a historical character, what justifies them? It still sounds like you've traded in one Popper for another, even if a more sophisticated and liberal one.

RADVÁNYI: You've repeated one of Feyerabend's criticisms of Lakatos, that he has moved the problem of justifying science without solving it, or accounting for its origins in a noncircular way. There's ultimately no answer to this skeptical attack. Lakatos said himself that modern science is a new way of replacing one body of knowledge, one research program, with another, and that this activity was created after the Renaissance. Ian Hacking says Lakatos tried to create a nonrepresentational theory of scientific progress, but even that's probably too generous. Lakatos was not an epistemologist in the traditional sense of asking how knowledge links up with the world.

KADVANY: What then is the bottom line for philosophy of science as far as Lakatos is concerned?

RADVÁNYI: It's not only that Lakatos argued that scientific methodology was in flux, it's that there is a changing logic of scientific method, and he demonstrated that idea *in media res.* The methodology of scientific research programs itself consists of a series of reconstructed philosophical theories, including several versions of Popper's ahistorical falsificationism; this series culminates in Lakatos's historicized research programs which in turn is applied to various episodes in the history of science; *all* that finally just becomes both more history and a reconstruction of method. You are supposed to see and experience how science's past gets built out of a conception of scientific method, how that conception contains its past, its own contradictions, and positive heuristic, and consequently how Lakatos's theory and reconstructions themselves will become historical moments eclipsed and absorbed by other historical reconstructions. Like Lukács's account of Marxism, or Hegel's account of his own philosophy, the theory of research programs is placed in history as a transient theory of scientific method. This active demonstration of the present in history is more important than the details of Lakatos's historical reconstructions, such as his account of the Michelson-Morley experiment and its role in the theory of relativity, or his account of Newton's criticisms of Descartes, and the rest. Unfortunately, you have to get this from Lakatos's work firsthand, like understanding a mathematical proof; no abbreviated summary reproduces the effect. I believe both Hegel and, later, Adorno, made the point that certain philosophical ideas resist summarization, and Lakatos's changing logic is one of them.

KADVANY: There still must be some basic idea behind his "changing logic." How is it done?

RADVÁNYI: Lakatos developed a historiographic metatheory laying out criteria for assessing the fit of philosophy of science against so-called actual history, which turns out not to be "actual" in a naive sense, but a name for theory- and value-laden history: the theory being your methodological theory of science with an accompanying value structure implied by what's "good" or "bad" science. This historiographic theory is just the theory of research programs itself, but applied to Lakatos's own development in the philosophy of science and his historical conjectures. By applying the theory of research programs to itself, science literally becomes historiography, with its own historiographic refutations, corroborations, theory-laden historical facts, positive heuristic, and the rest. These criteria for evaluating history and methodologies constitute an elaborate self-application of research program categories to Lakatos's own enterprise in the philosophy of science. Lakatos shows himself to have his own historiographic research program, which "progresses" over Popper's implicit program, and is also subject to change and supersession—a type of Hegelian *Aufhebung*.

KADVANY: There appears to be an affinity between Lakatos's ideas and those of postmodern thinkers concerned with history and historiography. How do you explain the late twentieth-century flavor to it all, of Lakatos's reflections on texts and historical discourse?

RADVÁNYI: Feyerabend once made the apt comparison of Lakatos with the famous American philosopher Quine, saying that Quine was to Lakatos what Robert Hooke's "discovery" of the gravitational law was to Newton's.

KADVANY: Meaning?

RADVÁNYI: Meaning that Hooke just guessed at the gravitational law, he had no explanation of why it should be true. Similarly, Lakatos dealt continuously with real historical problems, he wasn't just reciting generalities or reacting against positivism without useful examples or applications. Lakatos didn't just describe the theory-ladenness of all historical writing, he *demonstrated* it through *Proofs and Refutations* and his various "rational reconstructions" of episodes from the history of science, such as whether the Michelson-Morley experiments on the speed of light functioned as Popperian crucial experiments. Ian Hacking has done a good job criticizing some of Lakatos's history of science, including what he wrote on the Michelson-Morley experiments, but it's still important to see how Lakatos writes his vignettes, how ostentatiously he lays out his rearrangement of historical "facts," his "actual history," and the methodological categories he uses to interpret the past. And nobody did this in the history of mathematics, as Lakatos did in the 1950s. Lakatos was way ahead of his time, though many of these modern ideas on historiography are well expressed in Hegel's lectures on world history.

KADVANY: But is there any such thing as "actual history"? That's another positivist dogma.

RADVÁNYI: No, there is no actual history, that's the point; you just aren't hearing the ironic quotation marks. We're always reconstructing the past in a type of hermeneutic circle. But you have to settle conventionally, for some time, on some historical "facts," otherwise you can't write or think, you end up in a skeptical regress, and ultimately a skeptical abyss.

KADVANY: It still sounds a bit like history of ideas spiced up with a lot of clever dialectics.

RADVÁNYI: If you are asking whether Lakatos is just a virtuoso, to a certain extent in the philosophy of science, the answer is yes, without denying a profound pedagogical value. You should keep in mind how forcefully he attacked Popper's idea of crucial experiments in science and argued for the backward-looking, historicist dimension of science itself. On the other hand, in the philosophy of mathematics, since mathematics is not much more than its methods and theorems, being "just" a historical and methodological virtuoso means you're at the center of the subject. Ultimately, Lakatos was a greater philosopher of mathematics than a philosopher of science; the design of his changing logic of scientific discovery is, I agree, overingenious.

KADVANY: Is there a precedent for Lakatos's self-application to create his changing logic?

RADVÁNYI: The idea of changing method was one of Lukács's key ideas about Marxism in *History and Class Consciousness,* that Marxism itself had to be seen as an historical theory, that it had its own history, and was subject to change. While Lukács got into a lot of trouble with Lenin and others for this idea, it was overshadowed by everything else in *History and Class Consciousness* about reification and the role of consciousness in Marx, plus Marx's great unacknowledged debt to Hegel. That was the real beginning of Western Marxism in the 1920s. The skeptical trope of self-application was almost a trivial idea from Lukács's Hegelian perspective, since that's always the Hegelian move, to turn the subject of history into its object, and vice versa. If you see the understanding of these subject-object relations in history as the heart of Hegelianism, then Lakatos takes it to the fore as far as science and mathematics are concerned: whether it's between a theorem and its proof, a proof and its history, scientific theories and observations, research programs and theories, or finally historical reconstructions and research programs. But the difference in Lakatos is a change from *who* is the subject of history to *what*.

KADVANY: Does the critical dimension of Western Marxism have more than a passing relation to Lakatos's criticism of Popper?

RADVÁNYI: Lakatos's sequential critique of Popper is a presentation of a system, and simultaneously through his presentation a critique. The development combines the action of thought with its criticism, so that the forms of thought themselves become an object of investigation. Of necessity, it's a historical approach.

KADVANY: That's nicely put.

RADVÁNYI: I'm quoting Marx or Hegel almost verbatim, I can't recall which. What did Lukács say? "Every quotation is an interpretation." There's no lack of disguised reference in Lakatos, but you find that in Hegel's *Phenomenology* as well.

KADVANY: Is there an "end" to history of science in Lakatos, a Hegelian integration of subject and object?

RADVÁNYI: Definitely not. There's no "true" scientific consciousness in Lakatos, and historical reconstruction is always imperfect. Lakatos knew enough not to repeat some errors of the past.

KADVANY: Is this self-application the central Hegelian theme of Lakatos's research program approach?

RADVÁNYI: The central theme is the retrospective stance of historicism, of methodology as reconstructed history. There is also the wide-ranging holism, and the omnipresence of contradictions. The self-application synthesizes all these ideas and places them in a temporal framework which unifies science and its history. As I said, while you have to read Lakatos's work somewhat carefully to get this entire picture, it's clear that this dialectical construction, in which the theory of research programs becomes self-conscious, so to speak, through its self-application, was deliberately planned from the start.

KADVANY: The start?

RADVÁNYI: In 1965 a conference was held in London featuring Kuhn, Popper, Lakatos, Feyerabend, and other philosophical luminaries. Quine, in his autobiography, presents the conference as a demolition of Rudolph Carnap and late positivism, but he misses the point. It extended the revolution which had started with the publication of Kuhn's *Structure of Scientific Revoultions,* and which was to spread new ideas about scientific method and the role of history into social theory, anthropology, even literary criticism. The conference papers were published by Lakatos and Alan Musgrave in *Criticism and the Growth of Knowledge,* which became a bonfire of controversy. The word spread about incommensurability as an idea associated with Kuhn and Feyerabend, along with new problems about relativism, perception, and language. Lakatos was seen as a major innovation over Popper, apparently not as liberal as Kuhn and Feyerabend, but injecting similar detail about actual scientific practice. But returning to Lakatos's exposition of his ideas, looking carefully at Lakatos's lengthy essay in *Criticism and the Growth of Knowledge,* the objective of creating a reflexive methodology, the changing logic, is apparent in the footnote apparatus. That's always where the action is in Lakatos.

KADVANY: There's something special about his footnotes?

RADVÁNYI: The footnotes are first of all used, when Lakatos is reconstructing some piece of history of science or mathematics, to comment on the problems of the reconstruction and compare what so-called actual history "really did" compared to the reconstruction. That technique is most spectacularly exploited in *Proofs and Refutations.* There's a creative tension created between the historical record and historical interpretation that is one of Lakatos's consistent and most thoroughly worked-out accomplishments. Marx did something similar with his footnotes, too, as noted by Engels in the preface to one of the later editions of *Capital.* Marx uses his footnotes to relate economic history to his dialectical conception of capital, just as Lakatos relates his method of proofs and refutations to nineteenth-century mathematics, or his reconstructed scientific research programs to actual history. At the same time, Lakatos's footnotes are used to carefully comment and modify the text, and to cross-reference ideas without being too explicit. Feyerabend knew what was going on: the title page, of all places, for the first edition of *Against Method* has the title footnoted, which is just another semiprivate joke with Lakatos.

KADVANY: But why isn't Lakatos's covertness—excuse me, "coversion"—just obvious, or obviously not there?

RADVÁNYI: Lakatos was a brilliant and seductive writer, and he uses the footnote apparatus to link essays published in different journals, make oblique suggestions, and carry out subdiscussions. You just have to pay attention, but this is also a coversion, not a hide-and-seek. A concealment fails if there's a definitive clue.

KADVANY: Does someone finally win in the Kuhn-Feyerabend-Lakatos debate?

RADVÁNYI: If the criterion is who had the widest influence, it would be Kuhn, though few people could make complete sense of "paradigms" and "incommensurability," or their variants. Nonetheless, you get 80 percent of the ideas for 20 percent of the effort from Kuhn. It's sort of an engineer's solution to huge philosophical and historical quagmires; that's also why *The Structure of Scientific Revolutions* has sold a million copies. Philosophically, in terms of what is "best" for science, the winner might be Feyerabend. He was most alert to normative and descriptive implications for scientific practice, and really was a champion of science, even more than Lakatos; he just didn't care for its calcified and authoritarian versions. What Lakatos provides is a powerful calculus for reconstructing the history of science, much richer analytically and more carefully thought through than Kuhn's paradigms, or whatever other *Weltanschauung* "unit" you choose. Lakatos also shows you can be "rational" while violating lots of traditional rules—that's why Feyerabend saw him as an ally—which shows the rules are just bad models, normatively and descriptively, of scientific practice. Lakatos wins the debate if the goal is to come up with the most creative and liberating conception of rationality, one that is a changing logic, a self-modifying rationality. It's also relatively straightforward to apply the theory of research programs to history, and that's been done in chemistry, physics, geology, and economics. There really is a positive heuristic in Lakatos's historiography.

KADVANY: Lakatos would appear to be as radical in his own way as Feyerabend, just not as upfront about it. Does their work relate in any deeper way, or are they just both renegade progeny of Popper?

RADVÁNYI: Both make use of the tropes of ancient Pyrrhonist skepticism, and both take refuge in a type of constructive skepticism popular among many scientists from the Renaissance to today. Both use classic skeptical gambits to enforce the position that science has no foundations, while believing that a vigorous historicist sensibility is the best means of coping with radical skepticism; hence both could be great critics and admirers of science. Feyerabend integrated his skepticism with a mix of anthropology and history. The title *Against Method* refers to the Greek skeptics and many "Pyrrhonist" texts of Sextus Empiricus, including "Against the Logicians," "Against the Physicists," "Against the Mathematicians," and so on. Feyerabend wanted to show the varieties of reason and knowledge, and he used skeptical analyses of all kinds of traditions and scientific theories to demonstrate that. Feyerabend's approach didn't add up to anything grander, but that's what he wanted; epistemological options were just all laid out, and it was a value choice of which way a society proceeded. Like a true skeptic, he acknowledged the varieties of epistemologies possible in the world, but he mostly suspended judgment on whether any one was better or worse. For Feyerabend, history plus skepticism did not have to lead to a dialectical approach; an eclectic anthropology was good enough. Lakatos also understood skepticism, and his main use of it was the "self-application" of the methodology of scientific research programs to itself, which is an old skeptical gambit, called the peritrope, or "turning the tables." These skeptical tropes also occur, though, in Hegel and Marx. Hegel designed them into his so-called "phenomenological method," meaning the historiographic rules for his *Phenomenology,* so it's no coincidence that Lakatos can develop an antifoundational and skeptical account of modern mathematics in *Proofs and Refutations.* When Marx took over Hegel's critical-historical method, even as he brewed in a materialist metaphysics, he willy-nilly appropriated skeptical tropes Hegel had used for reconstructing the history of Western philosophy. It's kind of a secret "Pyrrhonism become historiography" that Marxists and many historians don't acknowledge, perhaps because of an antipathy toward even a constructive or mitigated skepticism. Lukács probably knew how his application of Marxism to itself in *History and Class Consciousness* was related to skepticism, but I don't know that he was ever explicit about his use of Pyrrhonisms's dialectical acids. He certainly didn't need to make Marxism any more flexible than he'd done already. At bottom though, the skepticism at the heart of Hegel's historiography is essential to Marxist criticism, and is implicit in Lukács's reinvention. The skepticism built into Hegel's characterization of human consciousness means in Lakatos that skepticism is lurking within every historiographic framework.

KADVANY: Feyerabend and Lakatos, then, take skepticism in two directions.

RADVÁNYI: Lakatos wants a tidy, dialectical structure, something with unity, lots of analysis and synthesis. Feyerabend is an anthropologist visiting cultures and rationalities of the past and present, an historicized Wittgenstein of the *Philosophical Investigations.* Feyerabend and Lakatos were also the closest of friends. They communicated almost daily until Lakatos's death, and *Against Method* was to have been published with a reply from Lakatos which was sadly never written. Some of the Feyerabend-Lakatos correspondence has been published in Italian.

KADVANY: When did Lakatos die?

RADVÁNYI: In 1974. Then Feyerabend died in 1994, as did Popper. Kuhn died in 1996.

KADVANY: Did Lakatos know Lukács in Hungary?

RADVÁNYI: Lakatos was one of Lukács's first-generation students after World War II, when Lukács returned to Hungary after an absence of over two decades. Other students around this time included Agnes Heller and Ferenc Fehér, who became well-known as critical theorists. At a public debate in England with the philosopher of science Jerry Ravetz in 1970, Lakatos said in an aside that it was his original goal to be a successor to Lukács, but such comments were forgotten as Lakatos's fame and influence grew. He took on a partial façade of virulent anti-Marxist rhetoric in the role of Popper's most devoted disciple, liberated by Popper, as he said, from a Hegelian outlook which held him captive for over twenty years. At one point he was wearing "Agnew for Vice President" buttons. He's like a character out of a Graham Greene cold-war spy novel. He may well have been anti-Marxist in terms of hating Hungarian Stalinists, I am sure; but that's not inconsistent with a complete Hegelianism or even Hegelian-Marxism. Something like the Agnew button was worn, no doubt, with ironic bravado, too. Lakatos fought his bitter wars in a Hungarian style, maintaining a joking relationship with all his enemies.

KADVANY: There are some intriguing crosscurrents here. Feyerabend almost once worked for Brecht, while Lakatos was a student of Lukács.

RADVÁNYI: Brecht and Lukács also engaged in a famous debate, with Brecht taking a more tolerant attitude toward aesthetic theory—at least as certain modernist trends were concerned—than Lukács's demand for a more unified and systematic approach, so there's even a superficial similarity between some of the themes of the Brecht-Lukács debate and Feyerabend's criticisms of Lakatos.

KADVANY: Did Lakatos achieve his goal of becoming a successor to Lukács?

RADVÁNYI: Absolutely. All the Hegelian elements that matter in Lakatos's work are present in Lukács: Historical education as *Bildung,* Hegel's *Phenomenology* as a *Bildungsroman,* the central role of historiography in historical philosophy, self-application as a trope to temporalize just about anything, antiromanticism and antielitism, the autonomy of language in exteriorizing human consciousness, the intricate subject-object relations in historical thinking. Regardless of his other ideas, Lukács provided one of the more attractive versions of Hegel to appear in this century, and Lakatos made systematic use of this interpretation in all his work. In English-language countries, Lukács's account of Hegel was popularized through the late Walter Kaufmann, who read Lukács in German before Lukács's books started to be translated into English in the 1960s; so it's not as if these ideas were unknown.

KADVANY: What is the antiromanticism and antielitism you say is shared by Lakatos and Lukács?

RADVÁNYI: At the time the *Phenomenology* was published, Hegel positioned himeslf as a critic of the romantics, mainly Schelling. The *Phenomenology,* with its pervasive idea of *Bildung* as historical self-education, is intended as an exoteric guidebook to philosophy, in opposition to any kind of intuitionist, nondiscursive philosophy. For years, these pedagogical themes in Hegel, which continue earlier ideas of Goethe and Lessing, were used by Lukács as a covert critique of Stalinism. You can see in Lukács's writings over decades an obvious parallel between Stalin's personality cult and the intuition-

ism of romantics, with Hegel's antiromantic critique being a covert proxy for
Lukács's Hegelian Marxism. These ideas came about during the 1930s, when
Lukács lived in the Soviet Union, and then continue after Lukács's return to
Budapest at the end of World War II, and up to the 1956 Hungarian uprising.
Hungary between 1945 and 1956 is known for its own personality cult and a
rigidly élitist political and police hierarchy, which some say was the most Stalinist in its political culture of all the satellite states. Lukács's parallel critique
between irrationalism and Stalinism was not only correct, it was heroic, and
the first suggestion of the idea that Marxism ended up as Stalinism through a
macabre turn of history. In Hungary Lukács wrote at length about the degeneration of Western philosophy into intuitionist irrationalism and even fascism
in his *Destruction of Reason,* published in 1954; Lakatos parrots Lukács's in-
flammatory rhetoric—Adorno spoke of the destruction of Lukács's reason—
almost perfectly in polemical essays written just before his death and in which
he attacks anything in the philosophy of science suggestive of "tacit knowledge" or other nondiscursive practices in science. *Proofs and Refutations* provides a less shrill and more reasoned critique of intuitionist or esoteric ideologies in mathematics, and is right in line with Lukács's and Hegel's account of
the *Phenomenology*'s goal of making philosophy publicly accessible to all,
not just a fortunate élite of initiates.

KADVANY: Something doesn't quite fit here. Lukács was always a believer
in "vanguard" theory, the idea that there was a subject of history whose consciousness and understanding of events was clearer, ultimately more accurate,
and providing a justification for leadership, even perhaps of a dictatorial kind.

RADVÁNYI: You are right, there are two types of "élites" in both Lukács
and Lakatos. Lakatos had to recognize as élite leaders those scientists who
end up leading the development of progressive research programs. How this
vanguard can be identified without circularity, say, for purposes of tabling
a degenerating research program, ultimately brings you back to the same
problem of justifying leadership and choice as raised by Leninism. Lakatos
created a critical theory of scientific discourse through which the value judgments of the "élite" could be criticized by seeing how their research programs stacked up. One could, for example, consider to what extent climate-
change research programs are "progressive" in Lakatos's sense. Nonetheless,
there still is a hint here of one moral and epistemological antinomy embedded
in philosophy of science disputes that gets exposed through Lakatos's
dialectics.

KADVANY: Lakatos's close ties to Lukács and his use of Hegel would put
him in a tradition of covert Hungarian Hegelian-Marxism.

RADVÁNYI: Exactly.

KADVANY: Who else participates in this covert tradition?

RADVÁNYI: I don't know. But Lakatos and Lukács are surely the most important twentieth-century Hungarian philosophers, and through such a strange and convoluted relationship.

KADVANY: What does Lakatos's coversion imply for the history for Marxism, especially the Western Marxism started in part by Lukács? Does Lakatos's work feed back into this tradition?

RADVÁNYI: Regardless of your views on Marxism, there's an important old problem about the relationship between dialectical reasoning and science. Is dialectical reasoning just fluff, or does it have some substantive role in the sciences? Much of Marxism is the story of this debate. Engels, in part following Hegel, devised his famous dialectics of nature as one response, which we even see revived today through reputable physicists such as the late David Bohm, but simultaneously reviled as vulgar Marxism by critical theorists. But Lakatos was not interested in a diamat-style "reason submerged in nature," he showed there was a role for dialectical reasoning in the historical progress of theories of nature. Lakatos completely explains the role of dialectical reasoning vis-à-vis science, in a way that lets you "keep" what you ordinarily recognize as science, and not try to create a specious metaphysics. Lakatos's achievement is considerably beyond what Habermas or other critical theorists tried to achieve in terms of reconciling criticism and positive scientific knowledge. Lakatos showed that science was at bottom historicist and critical; that was his solution avoiding both scientism and dialectics as ornament. In a way, it's an answer to the debate between scientistic and dialectical philosophies of science going back to Parmenides and Heraclitus.

KADVANY: What about Marxian economics? Does Lakatos's theory of research programs say something about whether Marx's economics is "science"? Popper's polemic began when he was a young Viennese arguing that Marxists and Freudians were pseudo-scientists. Did Lakatos ever answer that challenge?

RADVÁNYI: It's well known in the history of economics that Marx—not his successors, mind you, but Marx himself—is the heir to what is known as the labor theory of value, with David Ricardo and Adam Smith as his predecessors. In Lakatos's language you can identify, in nineteenth-century economists, a labor theory of value research program, with Marx as the nineteenth-century culmination. You can identify all the categories needed to reconstruct Marx's work in research program terms, including the labor theory of value as the hard core, Marx's economic predictions, the sequence of economic models he used, his observational data, and so on. Marx also had an extremely clear conception of himself as participating in the same program of political economy as Smith and Ricardo. Lakatos, in short, created a critique of Popper that also leads to a reconstruction of Marxian economics as "science."

KADVANY: You're saying that playing Popper's and the positivists' "What is science?" demarcation game leads to Marxian economics being a "science" after all.

RADVÁNYI: Precisely. Now, you have to be careful in that Marxian economics didn't go far after Marx, but as far as what Marx created, his work satisfies Lakatos's elaborate criteria for "what is science." The approach that Lakatos took, of showing this via what critical theorists would call an "immanent critique" of Popper's philosophy, is just the way to do it. Marx subtitled *Capital* "A Critique of Political Economy," so the way to deal with Popper's challenge that Marxism is "not scientific" is via the same critical methodology, at least from a Marxist perspective. The historical ironies are a delight and an inspiration. Lakatos did what Marx might have done, had Marx come to England as a philosopher of science rather than an economist. Because the theory of research programs itself, with its changing logic, has a historical character, the consistency between the account that's implied in Lakatos about Marxian economics and Marx's own constructive historicism is quite deep.

KADVANY: How explicit is the application of the theory of research programs to Marxian economics in Lakatos?

RADVÁNYI: He doesn't mention a word about it, and numerous economic historians who are familiar with the methodology of scientific research programs successfully manage to avoid the issue. But it's also straightforward historiography that's supported by Marx's own account of economic history in his *Theories of Surplus Value.* Again, the conventional history of nineteenth-century political economy identifies the tradition largely with Smith, Ricardo, and Marx. There was a debate several years back over the labor theory of value prompted by technical work of the economist Piero Sraffa, so the topic still is somewhat alive.

KADVANY: Aren't there still some scientific pretensions here about prediction in economics?

RADVÁNYI: Marx made a number of economic predictions, such as the expected falling rate of profit, and these have been studied empirically. Most were not confirmed, though there's some isolated positive evidence. But remember, the competitors to Marx's research program are other nineteenth-century economic research programs, not physics. Though most of his predictions were not confirmed, Marx was conducting reasonable economic science, if your standard of science is "research program." Marxian economics started degenerating only after Marx; in Marx it still shows its promise and a certain genius.

KADVANY: But almost everyone sees "economics as science" as a deeply suspect claim; the subject is fraught with ideological implications regardless of where you start. No matter what, you just can't take a "rehabilitation" of Marxian economics too seriously.

RADVÁNYI: Marx said that Ricardo was the most "honest" economic "scientist" for rigorously adhering to the labor theory of value, and it was the labor theory that defined Marx's research program. It's what Lakatos calls the "hard core" of the program: it doesn't get refuted or confirmed directly, but it unifies all the detailed theories and models built out from it. Now, how disingenuous is Marx's historical reconstruction of his economic, "scientific" predecessors? How central was the labor theory of value before Marx, or at least Ricardo? Marx wanted to use the labor theory as his central object of critique, to show its internal contradictions, and ultimately all the contradictions of capitalism. So it was only in Marx's interest to define "the science" as he did; it fell into his reflexive scheme of matching economic ideology to class interests, and economic ideology to labor and market practices. It's part of Marx's strategy of combining ideological criticism with participating in the tradition of classical political economy, *and* of being at least as good an economist as his predecessors. If you now buy into Lakatos's conception of scientific progress, you have to accept that Marx's economics, which supports his ideological analysis, is "science." Does that imply that Marx's radical theory of ideology now becomes "science," too, since the former is expressed through the latter, and especially as Lakatos allows for a dynamic, changing logic of science? There's no inconsistency here between an economic science and the idea that it may dissolve into history, along with its facts and the economic form of life constituting them. Is Marx's "critique of political economy," as a historical enterprise, then also "science"? That would all appear to be coherent via Lakatos, and it has nothing to do with the tired old idea of whether Marx was a "determinist" or not; that just is irrelevant. The point of seeing Marxian political economy as a research program is not to rehabilitate Marxian economics, but rather that in one of the most famous episodes in the history of ideas, you cannot separate out ideology, or historical criticism, from science, no matter how good a job you do at "methodology." Lakatos ultimately gives, implicitly, a profound account of the entanglements among historical criticism, scientific method, and ideology in which they are inextricably bound to one another.

KADVANY: That would seem then to undermine the ultimate importance of Lakatos's philosophy of science, if his rationalism is inexorably wedded to ideology.

RADVÁNYI: It undermines the philosophy of science as nonideological, but in a very instructive way. The right word is *deconstruct,* since he has uncovered some persistent contradictions, or "aporias," if contradiction is too logical. Lakatos would, of course, hate the idea of deconstruction, but it's hard to avoid it, given his Hegelian commitments. Superficially, the theory of research programs is a liberal, historicist rationalism trying to avoid the stain of ideology. In the end, Lakatos's philosophy of science turns out to be about the troubling difficulties of that very enterprise; that's the covert lesson.

KADVANY: What is known about Lakatos's Hungarian background?

RADVÁNYI: Lakatos was a Hungarian Jew. He was born Imre Lipsitz in 1922, then, according to some accounts, became Molnar when he joined the Communist underground during World War II. His mother, uncle, and grandmother died in the Holocaust. Various stories abound, including some of Lakatos's treachery in the underground, and these have recently been confirmed by archival research. After the war, Molnar changed his name again and became Lakatos. He published a fair amount, was known as a brilliant debater, and was involved in Stalinist *apparatchik* work for the government on educational issues. In a college yearbook he is called "Mephistopheles" and "a slinking wolf." Interestingly, some of his writing from just after the war shows his inimitable footnote style, like what he used in England. He was imprisoned for four years in the dreaded Resck forced-labor camp during the worst times of the Stalinist "ice age," including, he said, a year in solitary confinement. After Stalin's death and the "thaw," he was released, and supported himself by translating the great Hungarian mathematician George Pólya's writings on mathematical heuristic into Hungarian. Lakatos left Hungary for good shortly after the failure of the 1956 revolution, and after participating with many ex-Stalinist intellectuals in the important Petöfi circle debates, which helped precipitate the revolt. He was a paradigmatic Hungarian élite intellectual of 1956.

KADVANY: Mathematics then was his primary interest when he went to Cambridge after 1956.

RADVÁNYI: Yes. There he was, a superannuated graduate student, fresh from the horrors of Budapest. His age wasn't all that unusual. Francis Crick, who codiscovered DNA in the 1950s, was also older, and the recent Nobel economist John Harsanyi also took an unneeded Ph.D. when he came to the U.S. from Hungary. It was a way of entering the culture. But mathematics, and the complementary roles that heuristics, education, and history would play in *Proofs and Refutations,* could have been in his mind well before he arrived in Cambridge through his work with Lukács and Pólya.

KADVANY: Cambridge was associated with Communism for many years.

RADVÁNYI: Through the Cambridge spies Kim Philby, Guy Burgess, Donald MacLean, and Anthony Blunt, along with Marxists or communists such as John Cornford, Maurice Dobb, and many others. That phenomenon was over by the 1950s, yet at Cambridge, Lakatos was still more openly Hegelian. It was the era of the Moral Science Club, and Lakatos's intellectual differences with his hosts could not have been more pronounced. But once he moved to the London School of Economics and took on the role of Popper's best student, he at least appeared to become somewhat right wing and disowned his Hegelian past. He rightfully criticized student radicals at the LSE, perhaps fearing a repeat of the kind of subversion he fomented himself while a Stalinist, but I cannot believe completely in the innocence of his actions or words. It's almost comic. This is also just what, for example, Philby did, too: an apparent *volte-face* from the well-known leftism of his youth, which is supposedly "forgotten" with "maturity." Lakatos was the ex-commie who flip-flops to its conservative opposite. I think it was at least partly a pose, but we can never know for sure. Lakatos was editor of the prestigious *British Journal for the Philosophy of Science* when he died; it reminds me of Philby being the head of England's MI5 counterintelligence.

KADVANY: But then are you saying he was a mole or not? What finally is your evidence?

RADVÁNYI: We have all the evidence of a mole, which means the evidence can be interpreted in two ways. That's the whole point. I can't "prove" anything, just assemble a body of evidence and draw conclusions which others can reject or accept. Philby, of course, managed to live on in England for several years after Burgess and MacLean escaped to Moscow. English culture at times is just brilliantly naive.

KADVANY: Let's get back to the philosophy of mathematics, which was Lakatos's area of focus in the 1950s. Is there a role for dissembling there? It seems different from the covert battle going on with Popper, the changing logic, and Marxian economics.

RADVÁNYI: The concealment of heuristic logic, or the informal logic leading to a mathematical proof, has a history as old as Archimedes. The seventeenth-century mathematician John Wallis noted of Archimedes' geometrical treatises that they covered up his ideas, and both Galileo and Descartes make similar comments. Partly there is the motive of keeping a good trick to oneself, but there's a methodological issue, too. A formal proof, to be valid, has to start with definitions and assumptions and proceed from there to the theorem proved. What actually is done by the practicing mathematician is often the reverse. A theorem is conjectured, but by working "backward" from the conjecture's consequences (or consequences of assuming the conjecture to be false), the "right" definitions and starting point may be discovered, but this search and its logic is usually concealed in the final proof. The Greeks understood this informal pattern of discovery in their "method of analysis and synthesis," which was an educational tool intended to make proofs easier to create. Remarkably, Marx seems familiar with this tradition, and notes a kindred difference in the *Grundrisse,* the rough outline for *Capital,* between the historical sequence of economic categories, and the inverse logic of their theoretical presentation. This difference is also relevant vis-à-vis Marx's known, even acknowledged concealment of Hegelian ideas "built into" *Capital* and Marx's dialectical "presentation." Popper and the logical positivists rediscovered the contrast between the logic of justification and the logic of discovery, but only Lakatos saw its methodological importance for writing mathematics books and histories. His criticisms of strictly deductive style was influential, and you see today many more mathematics books combining detailed histories of mathematics with its exposition.

KADVANY: Now, in terms of covert method, Marx's covert use of Hegel was Lukács's great discovery.

RADVÁNYI: Lukács showed in *History and Class Consciousness* that it was impossible to ignore the Hegelian influence, and its persistent positive role, in Marx's work: that, against the mechanical Marxists, Marx's conception of human consciousness was directly indebted to Hegel and implied a nondeterministic role for human agency. Lukács had inferred all this through his prodigious knowledge of the history of philosophy, and was proved right with the discovery of Marx's unpublished manuscripts in the 1930s.

KADVANY: So Lakatos in his own way is recreating all of this again?

RADVÁNYI: Yes. The way to read Lakatos is analogous to the way Lukács read and interpreted Marx, as containing a hidden and radically transformed Hegel. We just won't discover any unpublished manuscripts as we did with Marx.

KADVANY: Does this qualify Lakatos's work as Marxism? Where does it stand?

RADVÁNYI: Lukács says on page 1 of *History and Class Consciousness,* that orthodox Marxism does not imply the "belief" in this or that thesis, nor the exegesis of a "sacred book"; orthodoxy for Lukács refers exclusively to *method.* Now, what was Lakatos but a preeminent methodologist, and with all the right historicist claims? He even called his creation the *methodology* of scientific research programs. Not that any methodologist is a Marxist, but that Marxism is not wedded to a single intellectual or practical arena, nor to a uniform approach; you also have to grant that the social content of such Marxism may be indirectly "mediated," as they say. By that criterion, Lakatos is a Marxist, I suppose, in the same way Popper wanted to play the positivist-demarcationist game of setting up criteria of what is or is not science. Certainly the entire covert cavalcade heaps more irony on Popper, who thought he'd excluded Marxism from science. To see Lakatos as Marxist, you do have to use Lukács's general definition of Marxism, which is also the one underlying much of critical theory, because the Hegelian themes in Lakatos are so different from those used by Marx. At a certain point it makes you dizzy, like reading a Borges story. Look at me, I'm just citing Lukács, and *his* "sacred book" to characterize Marxism!

KADVANY: Does the theme of covert method in ideas reinforce the Marxist connection?

RADVÁNYI: As for Kierkegaard, there are layered masks of authorship in Lakatos, and that's something the reader has to grapple with. One of the most important layers is distinguishing Lakatos the person from the author, since the autonomy of language, science, and mathematics is a key problem for Hegel, Popper, and their student Lakatos. Such a maieutic learning experience with the author—in which the reader learns the lesson actively, through Socratic "midwifery"—is slightly present in Marx, though he was trying to be as much of a social scientist as possible. Lukács no doubt went through a revelation when he discovered what was really going on about Hegel in Marx, and his "conversion" to Marxism is the subject of several books. But Lukács's intellectual discovery of Marx's covert method gets confounded with Lukács's social transformation from a privileged member of one of Europe's wealthiest families to one of the twentieth century's leading leftist intellectuals, and the philosophical importance of this incredible covert pattern in the history of ideas, and its intellectual discovery, gets lost. With Lakatos, the arena is shifted to math and science, and the problem of covert education and the subterranean transformations of ideas and their routes to power comes front and center.

KADVANY: Your own publications are somewhat covert.

RADVÁNYI: Not really. Before the collapse of Soviet rule I wrote some English-language work under your name, John Kadvany, but it wasn't much of a secret. It was too close to my real name, for one thing. But it was fun for my friends, who know I'm a real coward. I keep my mouth shut if I possibly can. Hungarians, by the way, find the Hegelian-Marxist reading of Lakatos almost repulsive; it conjures up too many ghosts they still can't deal with intellectually.

KADVANY: Lakatos was a survivor of the 1956 Hungarian revolution. Does that event have a specific bearing on his covert Hegelianism?

RADVÁNYI: The 1956 revolution in Hungary was led by intellectuals, many of them popular Hungarian writers, and many of them ex-Stalinists. They came to see how badly they had betrayed Hungary through their allegiance to Stalin, and they saw how they helped create the prisonhouse of lies and treachery on which Hungarian Stalinism was based. It's well documented that the Hungarian Revolution was about, to use an old-fashioned word, truth, meaning the right to undissembled and free discourse. The novels about the time by Georg Konrád, the memoirs, and all the histories document the paranoia engendered by a total surveillance society, in which nobody knew what was meant in the press, where what you could say in private was a risk, where someone was always watching you visit an apartment, the whole dissembled life. You had to be very, very strong to survive this insanity, much less protest against it. The importance for Lakatos's covert writing is that postwar Hungary was a prisonhouse of lies and covert speech and dissemblance, the writers created it, but also then helped undo it, also as a kind of "immanent critique." Lakatos in this way is a philosopher of the Hungarian Revolution. He shows us in the West what it's like to dissemble in ideas, and the intricate

webs of reason which emerge from necessity to rebuild norms of truth. Lukács, of course, was a master of the dissembled writing which spread more
broadly among Hungarian writers and contributed to the 1956 revolt. Lakatos,
though, unlike Lukács, was a real Stalinist contributing to the perverse *Leben-
slüge* leading to the events of 1956.

KADVANY: But still, your mole metaphor; Kim Philby was a murderer, not
a heroic Hungarian poet.

RADVÁNYI: The mole leads a double life and through this double life becomes involved in all kinds of moral traps, problems of identity, and ultimately diabolical choices. There's also no escape. Once having been a mole,
one is always at best an ex-mole, and never in the clear. Many crack under the
pressure, and Lakatos provides a philosophical window into the logic of these
complexities. While you might not like the mole metaphor, remember what
the Hungarian revolution was about, and all that preceded it, including
Lakatos's Stalinist past. A whole society had lost a workable conception of
truth. About 1960 or so, János Kádár, the leader of Hungary at the time, said
in a moment of reconciliation that "a whole nation cannot be suspect." To
survive in such a world and undermine it, you had to be like a mole. Lakatos
shows how that opportunity and its opposite are built into reason. As far as I
know, though, Lakatos did not become involved with the Hungarian opposition until fairly late; for a while he argued with his friends, after being released from prison, that the regime was the best they could get. You could
speculate that, if Lakatos was not central to the Hungarian ferment of 1956,
his philosophy afterward was somehow denatured because of that lack of engagement. No, his philosophy is all about reason and moral compromise.

KADVANY: Marx made use of the mole metaphor as well, didn't he?

RADVÁNYI: That's in *The Eighteenth Brumaire of Louis Bonaparte,* with
ironic reference to unknowing repetitions of history: "We recognize our old
friend, our old mole, who knows so well how to work underground, then suddenly to emerge."

KADVANY: What does this mean about Stalinism? There's a long debate
about whether Stalinism is the "outcome" of Marxism of not. Even Popper
contributed to that in *The Open Society and Its Enemies.* Popper was also a
hero to many behind the iron curtain, where his books sold by the thousands
in samizdat.

RADVÁNYI: About Stalinism, it means that you can't disentangle "good"
historicism from the "bad," you can't prevent a Stalin with reason, or rule
him out philosophically. A major intellectual dimension of Stalin's pathology
is the Stalinist rewriting of history. In Lakatos, scientific and mathematical
methodology also turn out to be rewritings of history; that's the whole point
of his historiographic theory. Lakatos's troubling lesson is that you can't distinguish these two historiographies in principle. Lakatos's historicized ratio-

nalism becomes a Faustian monster, with a tolerant rationalism bearing underneath a relation to some of the worst excesses we've seen in our century. It's frightening, but that's the final lesson I think we're supposed to get from Lakatos's coversion, his educational message from the Recsk labor camp. I admit, I too read Popper and gained inspiration from him, but Lakatos is showing how naive Popper and his "open society" is in the context of actually existing Stalinism. Sure, Stalinism was the antithesis of an open society, it was a closed society and repressed criticism. But the writers who started the Hungarian Revolution weren't led by Popper. Neither Popper nor most of his English colleagues could help undo Stalinism from within it, especially if they were at least part Stalinist themselves, as were the Hungarian writers. Lukács was one of their intellectual heros, even though he wasn't on the front lines in 1956. He and the writers knew that you had to lie to survive, and they were sick of it, but they would prevail. The story goes that when a military officer asked Lukács to turn over his weapon after the revolution had failed, he handed in his fountain pen.

KADVANY: Yet Lakatos's coversion all occurs in England, or rather, Anglo-American philosophy.

RADVÁNYI: I see it as Lakatos's mission as a cross-cultural educator. How else, except though coversion, might he effectively teach of rationalism, historical reconstruction and rewriting, and the covert dissemination of ideas? Lakatos was an "extraterritorial," one of those writers for whom their political, geographical, linguistic, and intellectual displacement has become an essential element of their work. The essence of Lakatos's extraterritoriality is that he was a philosophical mole. Lakatos shows the subterranean connections in and out of a Stalinist society and an open society. The heroes of Budapest in 1956 showed the way out, and Lakatos takes us back into their world, from the other side, from the open society to the closed.

KADVANY: There's definitely a touch of evil in Lakatos.

RADVÁNYI: This was intimated by George Soros when I wrote him for support a few years back. I was turned down, since my interests didn't match what his foundation was doing, but I think he was also intrigued by what I said Lakatos did to Popper, who was Soros's philosophical model. Soros is a great believer in Popper's idea of an open society and did much in its support in Central and Eastern Europe through his foundation's work.

KADVANY: Now you are talking about the billionaire Hungarian-American financier?

RADVÁNYI: Yes. Soros of course is also a Hegelian, and a Popperian, it's all laid out in his book *The Alchemy of Finance*. It's funny how these Hungarians and Hegelians gravitate to Popper, or vice versa. By the way, Soros's unsparing criticism of orthodox economic theory in *The Alchemy of Finance* is close to Marx's and Lukács's, that economics thoroughly confounds natural and social facts and fails to account for the reciprocal influences between economic facts and our perceptions of them. Soros uses his word *reflexive* to describe the active relation we have in perceiving and changing economic facts, but *dialectical* would do just as well. I suppose Soros, through his work in the Soviet Union, is a bit of what Hegel called a world-historical individual. What a mensch.

KADVANY: János, I'm sorry, I think we're running out of time for George Soros. It's been good talking with you.

RADVÁNYI: *Köszönöm szépen, Kadvany. Viszontlátásra.* [Thanks very much, John. See you again.]

Notes

1. Editor's note: Lakatos's writings have been published as John Worral and Elie Zahar, eds., *Proofs and Refutations: The Logic of Mathematical Discovery* (New York: Cambridge University Press, 1976); Worrall and Gregory Currie, eds., *The Methodology of Scientific Research Programmes: Philosophical Papers Volume 1,* and *Mathematics, Science and Epistemology: Philosophical Papers Volume 2* (New York: Cambridge University Press, 1978).

4

Entangled States:
Quantum Teleportation and the "Willies"

Beam to: Primary Coordinates—ISIS

Scan for: initial disorientation; a purloined letter; the willies

The daily mail arrives. The usual crap, plus one fat envelope from a respected and well-liked physicist colleague. A copy—"FYI"—of a multimillion-dollar grant application to the U.S. Department of Defense, proposing to develop a system for (among other things) more secure military communications on the electronic battlefield of the future/present. Appended is a "theoretical" paper, the subject of which might be called "unitary matrices," but "quantum teleportation" would be only slightly less correct. It is a paper which holds the key, says the grant's author, to making the proposed communications scheme practical. It is a paper with Herbert Bernstein's name on it, and the name of the institute on which we collaborate, the Institute for Science and Interdisciplinary Studies (ISIS); it is a paper for which we are, however indirectly and to varying degrees, responsible. It gets tossed on the desk, and both physicist and ethnographer sit stunned, four hands move to furrowed brows to rub above eyes squeezed shut, bodies squirm and then freeze to chairs and only mouths move to voice a habitual guttural utterance.

A haunted feeling. Something's wrong here, this can't be happening. Is someone watching? Are we imagining things? Can't put a finger on it. A communication returns, read and altered, and desire rebounds as guilt. This is not what we intended. The willies: a palpable, bodily state in which flesh crawls, a chill runs through the blood, a tingle up the spine. The forceful certainty of an adrenaline rush would be welcome, prompting action, but there's only a vague dis-ease.

Beam to: *Scientific American,* **February 1996**

Scan for: scrambled genres; technological promises;
need for ontology

An advertisement from IBM for—*something*—appeared on the inside front
cover in the February 1996 *Scientific American* (fig 4.1). With the right decoding apparatus, one might read here promises for the technological overcoming,
via "quantum teleportation," of the mutating, perilous state, cultural differences, geographical distance, and perhaps even the problems of aging as the
body's recipe begins to become unreadable after so many years of use.

In the following weeks, Robert Park from the American Physical Society
sent out a series of messages on his electronic newsletter *What's New,* covering
developments in science:

> *IBM Science: Beam Me Up Scotty, It's Getting Crazy Down Here*
> "Stand by. I'll teleport you some goulash. . . . An IBM scientist and
> his colleagues have discovered a way to make objects disintegrate
> in one place and reappear intact in another," according to an ad in
> February's *Scientific American.* Tipped off by a *WN* reader, I sent
> an e-mail to "askIBM" requesting more information. "Hello Bob,"
> came back. "This is still under development and no further informa-
> tion is currently available. Thank You for using askIBM. Roseann."
> Are they having trouble with the di-lithium crystals?

> *IBM: Too Much Paprika Leaves Scientists with a Bitter Taste* The
> "goulash" ad (*WN* 26 Jan 96), which ran in magazines ranging from
> *Scientific American* to *Rolling Stone,* claims "IBM scientists have dis-
> covered a way to make an object disintegrate in one place and reap-
> pear intact in another." Do you believe that? Well, neither does IBM!
> An article in *IBM Research Magazine* says, "it is well to make clear
> at the start that teleportation has nothing to do with beaming people
> or material particles from one place to another." So what's going on?
> There are several theories. One reader noted that many research scien-
> tists, disintegrated at IBM labs, have been observed to reappear intact
> at universities.

> *More Goulash: National Examiner Decides to Use Its Own Recipe*
> In an article that raises the important question of what happens to the
> soul when a person is teleported, the supermarket tabloid quotes
> "IBM's top genius, Charles Bennett" as saying, "Mankind is at the
> dawn of a new era, solid matter will be teleported through space and
> time and reassembled." Bennett, of course, said nothing of the sort.
> He told the *Examiner,* "teleportation of macroscopic objects would be
> impossible for the foreseeable future." If an IBM ad can't get it right
> (*WN* 2 Feb 96), why should the *Examiner?*[1]

Park's basic complaint seems to be the familar, truth-in-advertising one: quantum teleportation isn't what the ad says it is. The ontology of "quantum teleportation," what it *is,* appears to have been withheld, if not lied about. So is the true ontology of quantum teleportation lying about somewhere, waiting to be found and uncovered?

Beam to: Author's Brain, Somewhere Near the Fissure of Sylvius

Scan for: authorial intention

So the question, once again, is, What is it? The problem is not one of misleading advertising, however, and this present account takes the perspective that the ontological question about "quantum teleportation" (QT) is not answerable in these authoritative terms. What QT *is* is spectral, spooky, ghostly, phantasmatic, and just possibly ghoulish, if not goulash, and one can read this shaky ontology in every possible register, from the physical to the cultural. What "is" "true" of any of the shifting subjects of this paper—quantum teleportation, conspiracy, moral responsibility—is that "one does not know what it is, what it is presently. It is something that one does not know, precisely, and one does not know if precisely it is, if it exists, if it responds to a name and corresponds to an essence. One does not know: not out of ignorance, but because this non-object, this non-present present, this being-there of an absent or departed one no longer belongs to knowledge. At least no longer to that which one thinks one knows by the name of knowledge" (Derrida 1994, 6). It is for reasons such as these that if we want to learn about QT and how to respond to it, it will be "necessary to learn spirits":

> Even and especially if this, the spectral, *is not.* Even and especially if this, which is neither substance, nor essence, nor existence, *is never present as such.* . . . To learn to live *with* ghosts, in the upkeep, the conversation, the company, or the companionship, in the commerce without commerce of ghosts. To live otherwise, and better. No, not better, but more justly. . . . And this being-with-specters would also be, not only but also, a *politics* of memory, of inheritance, and of generations. . . . It is necessary to speak of the ghost, indeed *to the* ghost and *with* it, from the moment that no ethics, no politics, whether revolutionary or not, seems possible and thinkable and *just.* (Derrida 1994, xviii–xix)

The ghost story here, an ethnographic tale from and of the crypt, a tale of coded messages and haunted remains, is a hurried whistling walk through four ontological graveyards.

One, the model of the physical world which QT employs, a model founded

'Stand by I'll

Fig. 4.1   © IBM. Reprinted with permission.

For years, she shared recipes with her friend in Osaka. She showed him hundreds of ways to use paprika. He shared his secret recipe for sukiyaki. One day Margit e-mailed Seiji.

teleport you some goulash."

Margit is a little premature, but we are working on it.

An IBM scientist and his colleagues have discovered a way to make an object disintegrate in one place and reappear intact in another.

It sounds like magic. But their breakthrough could affect everything from the future of computers to our knowledge of the cosmos.

Smart guys. But none of them can stuff a cabbage.

Yet.

IBM

Solutions for a small planet

on what Albert Einstein over fifty years ago called "spooky action at a distance": a world consisting of what the physicists call entangled states, where the "real" physical properties of particles are muddled with other physical and nonphysical properties (to use very unghostly, quaint, and completely inadequate terms).

Two, the entanglements between these fields of quantum physics and the literary, cinematic, and tabloidish phantasms of popular culture where, as already glimpsed, the stable genres of science and science fiction become transmigrating souls that periodically take possession of more corporeal presences.

Three, the entanglements between these entangled scientific and cultural domains with the ghostly possibility of conspiratorial politics, located institutionally (perhaps) in the National Security Agency (NSA), operating through the disciplines of cryptology and cryptography. In this graveyard one can also find historians and philosophers of science, other wandering mediums trying to establish contact with the spirits that "guide" modern physics, at least since World War II.

The fourth graveyard is called ISIS, the Institute for Science and Interdisciplinary Studies, where the author/ethnographer works with the physicist/institute president, Herbert Bernstein. ISIS invents new ways of both questioning the sciences and deploying them to address current problems such as cleaning up the military's toxic legacy, developing aquaculture techniques with the indigenous people of the Amazon basin in Ecuador, and advancing the field of sustainable agriculture. Bernstein, then, is both informant and collaborator, and it's through him that I keep up with the doings of a group of about a half-dozen scientists working on QT. It wouldn't be wrong to say, "Bernstein works on QT"; he might prefer to say he works on "unitary matrices" or "multiparticle interferometry," but it is the entanglement between these fields that is at issue here.

It's certainly legitimate to say that his work gives him the willies, and I try in this essay to account for how Bernstein—who is, by any definition of the term now available in science studies, a "socially responsible scientist"—arrived at those space-time coordinates wherein his work became of interest to the military, and he got the willies. If something like moral outrage, a change of heart, a new spiritual or political resolve is the response to the presence of a conspiracy, then the willies is the response one has to the presence/absence of conspiracy. In a slightly different articulation, if an ethics answers to the ontological contours of a fully plotted, fully present conspiracy, then the hauntology of a present/absent conspiracy calls for a different kind of response, which for now might be put under the name of a "moral responsibility"—albeit an impossible moral responsibility.

Thus I also try in this essay to account for how Bernstein and the author tried to figure out what might be the "responsible" or "moral" thing to do, through a series of staged events. In one of these events, Bernstein graciously subjected himself to a trial—or rather, a parody of a trial, since what he was charged with was never clear, and the outcomes of "guilty" or "innocent" were excluded from the start.

Beam to: Primary Coordinates—ISIS

Scan for: paralegalism

We staged "The Trial of Herbert J. Bernstein, Physicist" at the Hampshire College twenty-fifth anniversary alumni reunion, 25 June 1995, where ISIS is located and where Bernstein teaches physics, among other subjects. In attendance in this makeshift, parodic courtroom in the "Kiva" in Hampshire's library were about fifty Hampshire alums, many of whom were former students of Bernstein's, including a few who had actually gone on to become certified, working physicists. A cabal of three other alums and former students of Bernstein's presided: the ethnographer cast himself in the role of judge, but his identity multiplied further still when David Gruber (a member of ISIS's board of trustees) was unable to attend and perform his role of prosecuting attorney; Michael Mann undertook the pro bono work of defense attorney.

The intent was to use the trial format as a dramatic device for a public discussion about science and social responsibility. Among the things we hoped to accomplish was a demonstration of the inadequacies of the binary logic of guilt or innocence, and precisely where and how these categories and other similar ones break down in the territory of questioning "pure science."

> *Judge/prosecutor/ethnographer:* This court is now in session. I am the presiding judge, and I have to say I'm also, more or less, the prosecuting attorney *[laughter]*—convenient!—since David Gruber is ill and was unable to come. The defense attorney, some of you may know, is Michael Mann, from the Securities and Exchange Commission *[laughter]*. And we are dealing today with matters of security and exchange.
>
> This is "The Trial of Herbert J. Bernstein, Physicist." We had thought of entering it in the dockets as "In the Matter of H. Joseph Bernstein," but that would have been too close an allusion to "In the Matter of J. Robert Oppenheimer"—and look around you: is this the 1950s? No. Is there a widely perceived communist threat? No. Is there any single, identifiable enemy in what we might call "the military"? No. So the allusion does not quite hold, and we're challenged both to find out exactly what Bernstein is charged with *[laughter],* and once we've established that, whether he, under our judicial system, can be rendered guilty, innocent, or some other third term, perhaps.
>
> Let me tell you what the trial is about. "Experimental Realization of

Any Discrete Unitary Operator": a paper published in the *Physical Review Letters*—very prestigious journal, perhaps the most prestigious journal in physics—Fourth of July 1994, Independence Day. The authors are Michael Reck and Anton Zeilinger, from Austria; Herbert J. Bernstein and Philip Bertani, from Hampshire College—Phil Bertani was an undergraduate at the time he helped write this. The paper comes out of research funded by the National Science Foundation, a grant which Bernstein administers here. This was the only NSF grant that Clifford Shull, the most recent Nobel laureate in physics, was an advisor to, putting Herbert J. Bernstein's face in all the local newspapers. It is an "algorithmic proof that any discrete finite dimensional unitary operator can be constructed in the laboratory using optical devices."

What does this mean? We'll have to ask the defendant to clarify. But this paper does not stand by itself. It is in fact attached to exhibit A: a funding proposal submitted to the U.S. Department of Defense by an electrical engineer in California, for developing "spread-spectrum coding, which presents a new opportunity for optical communications. The huge bandwidth is put to use for security and intercept immunity." It has uses for the intelligent battlefield of the future/present.

The question is, What is the relationship between Bernstein's beautiful piece of pure, theoretical physics, and this submission to the Department of Defense? This is what the charges revolve around.

Beam to: Nature

Scan for: The socio-crypto-logic of error

If the dominant effect of the willies is to leave one's skin crawling, and if the dominant effect of QT comes from the realm of an obscure hauntology, it is appropriate to start again, before we go any further with the seance that would conjure a visage of QT for all of us gathered around the table to see, with an image of what QT might do to the body.

Almost exactly a mere three years before IBM advertised the shape of teleportation-to-come, the scientific paper which announced the theoretical possibility of teleportation was published in the prestigious *Physical Review Letters*. The event of publication was itself covered by *Nature* magazine, and the illustration which accompanied that story demands to be read (see fig 4.2).

How to read this body, misassembled? At first pass, it plays jokingly on the anxiety of the technical error: "Didn't quite get all the sequences matched up properly, heh heh. You know how it is: trying to do several things at once, ignoring those panel lights that seem to indicate something wrong, and pretty soon you've put your foot in your mouth, or at least on your arm. Well, that's life in the age of smart machines. Get Engineering to run a full diagnostic

Fig. 4.2 Reprinted with permission of Andrew Birch and *Nature* magazine.

on the new biofilters, and let's try it again." Such a reading can in fact be quite productive, providing glimpses of the new logics of the body that are the narrative engines not only for *Star Trek* episodes and films like David Cronenberg's remake of *The Fly,* but for the production of science as well.[2]

But read again. Rather than machinic logic, read it for what we might call the socio-crypto-logic. In the following pages we will see how physical research is a process of becoming, and the physicist in process *will be disrupted.* More specifically, we'll see how the physicist's *will* will be disrupted. She didn't ask to have, say, the National Security Agency at arm's length, but there it is, jammed into the socket. Those were supposed to be her feet down there, moving her resolutely across the ground under a solitary sky—but they're the hands of liminal colleagues whose thoughts and acts impel her own, while her own blood circulates through them to flex their distant fingers. In addition to these phantom limbs, time is also out of joint: 1935 is grafted onto 1993, the 1950s and 1960s sink their tendons into the present, and that haunting presence whose best referent is "the future" sends us impossible nonrelativistic signals, faster than light. Employing other analytic phrases that have been conspiratorially spliced into my own neuronal patterns: the physicist is always already teleported; always already an in/appropriated other. The experiment is up and running before we know the outcome, or even how to do it.

Beam to: Primary Coordinates—ISIS

Scan for: enlisting; (pre)science; imperatives and implications

Judge/prosecutor/ethnographer: Let me just read a few quotes from an article by the defendant, from his book *New Ways of Knowing,* coedited with Marcus Raskin—on sale from ISIS after these proceedings are concluded. In Herbert J. Bernstein's article "The Idols of Modern Science and the Reconstruction of Knowledge," he writes as follows: "If the typical scientist were an individual seeker of externally given truth, an isolated genius working alone on his or her specialized problem, then perhaps the moral implications of scientific work would be mitigated. Indeed, the dispensation of knowledge could then be closely controlled by its inventor, and the act of publishing would more fully bear the moral weight. But as we have seen, modern science must always be perceived in the context of a scientific community; that subsociety is supported, nurtured, and utilized by the larger society, or by its ruling elite, for reasons far from those motivating scientists themselves."

In this situation we are presented, as Herbert J. Bernstein goes on to argue, with a number of moral imperatives. "In every case, the motivating human impulse—the childlike wonder of the scientist, the playfulness of the artist—is enlisted for some moral purpose and social good: satisfying people's material needs, organizing our society openly and equitably, even delighting our aesthetic sense. . . . Without requiring perfect prescience or a crystal ball, where purpose intended justifies the search, purpose attained is a legitimate measure of the moral implications of today's science. And while scientists do not believe they steer their research toward production of technology, they are quick to seek new technologies for use in their experiments."

Later in the essay, Herbert J. Bernstein goes on to bust Joshua Lederberg for conducting experiments in 1951 with *E. coli,* which thirty years later would result in great social dilemmas of recombinant DNA research—busting Joshua Lederberg by writing, "If all the considerations of ultimate purposes of biological research had been weighed, perhaps we would all be safer now."

Can we not bust Herbert J. Bernstein for not thinking through the next thirty years to where "Experimental Realization of Any Discrete Unitary Operator," what effects this is likely to have thirty years down the road, once it becomes institutionalized within the U.S. Department of Defense?

With that said, we will now hear from the defense attorney.

Beam to: 1993/96/35

Scan for: science/fiction; long-range correlations

In 1993 Charles Bennett, a physicist at IBM's Watson Laboratory, published a coauthored paper which appeared as the lead article in *Physical Review Letters* (and whose announcement in *Nature* inspired the artist's rendering of fig. 4.2). Titling their paper "Teleporting an Unknown Quantum State via Dual Classical and EPR Channels," the authors—whose corporeal bodies might be located from time to time in Yorktown Heights, Montreal, Paris, Haifa, and Williamstown—explicitly borrow from a genre other than physics: "We call the process we are about to describe 'teleportation,' a term from science fiction meaning to make a person or object disappear while an exact replica appears somewhere else" (Bennett et al. 1993, 1896). Never mind the fact that *Star Trek* viewers or even members of the *Enterprise* crew may not agree with this definition of teleportation as destruction of the original and creation of a replica. We could imagine a more technically oriented term for Bennett et al.'s proposal, such as "remote quantum spin transfer," but we would be deluding ourselves to think that the empirical could, or even should, be stripped of the imaginary. Nevertheless, the authors go on to write that the "net result of teleportation is completely prosaic: the removal of [a particle state] from Alice's hands and its appearance in Bob's hands a suitable time later."

The identities of Alice and Bob will be left to emerge over the course of this writing. Their gendering, however, obeys the same powerful polarities that show up in the "goulash" ad three years later, suggesting that Alice/Bob might be the future anterior of Margit/Seiji. Shortly after the goulash ad appeared in print, Web crawlers could find a "quantum teleportation" page nested within the site coded http://www.ibm.com. This so-called location contains a nice photograph of the six coauthors of the 1993 paper, and a good description of quantum teleportation. Further down the page, quantum teleportation is contrasted to "classical facsimile transmission," which exhibits a Platonic logic: a kind of parallel universe containing an "original" is scanned for data by a photocopy, fax, or more humanoid cave-dwelling machine, which upon further treatment yields a cheesy simulacrum of the intact original (see fig. 4.3, the author's facsimile of IBM's diagram). The page also provides various hypertext links to other information sources, including the "original" paper of which this cyberspace version might be said to be the "approximate copy" and, in a particularly nice touch, a recipe for goulash.

In the middle of the page is a diagram of "quantum teleportation" (reassembled by the author as fig. 4.4) and an accompanying descriptive narrative. Again, the reader is asked to be patient; it takes time to establish communication with such apparitions, and we are still firmly within an hauntological realm.

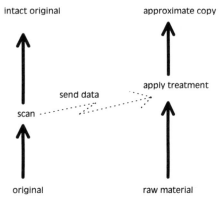

Fig. 4.3   Classical facsimile transmission

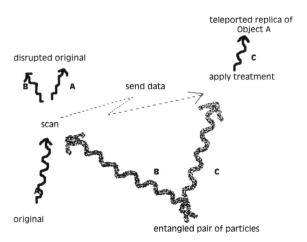

Fig. 4.4   Quantum teleportation

If we have to make the mistake of identifying the "heart" of this scheme, then it lies in the "entangled pair of objects" dominating the lower center of the diagram. These particles exhibit what the text names as " 'Einstein-Podolsky-Rosen correlation' or 'entanglement.' " The name refers us back to 1935, when this trio of physicists coauthored a paper which would haunt quantum theory for the next sixty years.

Beam to: Quantum Litter

Scan for: desiring full presence; living/dead cat;
hidden variables; nonlocality; experimental and cultural
proliferation; zombie kittens

Because this text can't go fast enough for the relativistic time-dilation effect to kick in, what the reader gets here is the table-rapping, cheap conjurer's version of the history of quantum mechanics and its philosophical conundrums.

The 1935 paper in the *Physical Review* by Albert Einstein, Boris Podolsky, and Nathan Rosen (usually collapsed into the initials EPR) can be characterized as the traditionalist, realist response to the radical, constructivist writings/ interpretations of the Copenhagen school, symbolically led by Niels Bohr. EPR maintained that physics had been and should continue to be concerned with developing "one-to-one correspondences" between elements of physical theory and elements of the real physical world; a theory about the physical world had to be *complete,* and the stringencies of such a requirement left little or no room for chance and indeterminism. Bohr and his associates defended just as energetically the view that physics was about the performative acts of measurement and calculation, and that when these acts were performed at the quantum level, language constructions such as "the real physical world" were out of place, and indeterminacy had to be acknowledged as ineradicable.

Each group was probing and mapping the limits of its own philosophical/ physical theories, and would invent elaborate *Gedankenexperiments* to see what contradictions emerged at those limits. Crudely, the EPR thought-experiment involved two correlated particles at some distance; measurement on one particle would, by the new logic of quantum mechanics, exert an unexplainable and therefore unacceptable "spooky action at a distance" on the other particle. The physicist must be missing something, and quantum mechanics couldn't be "complete."

Another quantum conundrum introduced that same year involved Schrödinger's cat, a thought-experiment whose crucial component was the conjunction of the microworld of quantum physics, where information is always incomplete, statistical, and phantasmatic, with the macroworld of the flesh, where information is visibly and grossly final. Like Einstein, Erwin Schrödinger desired a physics whose goal was the perfect and complete representation of the real world. In this thought-experiment, the physicist places a cat into a box which also contains a radioactive atom, a hammer, and a cyanide capsule. This box is closed, so that the physicist has no further information about what goes on inside. If the radioactive atom decays, it triggers a chain of events: a signal is sent, the hammer falls, the cyanide capsule breaks, the cat dies; if the uranium atom doesn't decay, the cat continues to live. When a time corresponding to the half-life of the radioactive atom has elapsed, it has a 50-50 chance of having decayed or of remaining intact. According to quantum mechanics, however, the physicist, without opening the box, can only speak about the probability state of the wave function that corresponds to the uranium atom: in theory, the atom is not *either* decayed or intact, but *neither* decayed *nor* intact, or *both* decayed *and* intact. Which is fine for atoms, or for their wave functions, but not very acceptable for cats. If quantum logic carried the day, crossing the boundary between the micro- and macroworlds, the cat would be a zombie: neither dead nor alive, but both dead and alive, suspended in a twilight zone. More importantly, it seems that what the physicist does with this apparatus makes him "responsible" for whether the cat, in the final analysis, lives or dies.

Since then, theorists and experimentalists alike have been puzzling over these conundrums, taking a number of very interesting and productive tacks which can only be referred to here in shorthand terms. David Bohm, a physicist who was both hero and friend to Bernstein, theorized in the 1950s and 1960s about "hidden variables" in an "implicate order." In the 1960s and 1970s, J. S. Bell did some of the most important theoretical work in this area. "The 'Problem' then," he puts it in one article, "is this: how exactly is the world to be divided into speakable apparatus . . . that we can talk about . . . and unspeakable quantum system that we can not talk about?" (Bell 1987, 171). (In the IBM quantum teleportation diagram introduced above, the dark lines and the acts called "scanning" and "applying treatment" make up the speakable part of the apparatus, while the spooky correlations of the EPR particles in the fuzzy lines represent the unspeakable part.) The early 1980s brought a set of experiments and papers, whose principle author was Alain Aspect, which "considerably diminished . . . the feasibility of bizarre conspiracy theories, designed to salvage the E-P-R reality criterion" (Mermin 1985, 146).

What is the situation in the 1990s? One available tracking device is in the genre of popular physics writings and one of its eminent practitioners, John Gribbin. In 1984 Gribbin wrote *In Search of Schrödinger's Cat* (Gribbin 1984). The title reflects that stage in the practice of quantum theory and experiment in which one could engage in those puzzling metaphysical musings about a single cat, or a superimposition of a number of cat-probabilities, how weird cat-reality was and how the physicist was "responsible" for making a dead or a live cat "real." Gribbin's most recent book is called *Schrödinger's Kittens and the Search for Reality* (Gribbin 1995), and the title effectively captures the changed situation: the cat is out of the bag, it has reproduced, disseminated itself, the subject of an unruly multiplication.

Bernstein is in part responsible for this situation marked by proliferation. He is a coprincipal investigator and the administrator of a National Science Foundation grant that supports one of the more productive groups of physicists working in the field of "multiparticle interferometry." Their work and that of others in the same field was the topic of a *Newsweek* article in 1995, which opens with a scenario of genre scrambling similar to those already cited, and exacerbated by high-speed technological forces:

> Say you're the editor of a science journal deciding whether studies arriving over the transom deserve to be published—or forwarded to "The X-Files." And say that this morning's FedEx delivers a paper reporting that a beam of light traveled faster than—how to put this?—faster than the speed of light. Then your e-mail brings a paper describing how a particle of light—navigating an obstacle course of slits and detectors—"knows" what lies ahead of it. At quitting time, your fax shrieks with an arriving P.S.: in that last experiment, the authors add, you can change the past.
>
> Fodder for "The X-Files"? Not in today's physics. (Begley 1995, 67)

An accompanying graphic suggests that photons possess an anthropomorphic awareness of what to them must appear as a very conspiratorial setup: "It's as if they know they're being watched." The article concludes with a reference to another favorite figure of conspiracy theorists: "For now . . . quantum mechanics is the only game in town. Nonsensical, counterintuitive, crazy—sure. But as Henry Kissinger has said about less abstruse matters, 'It has the added virtue of being true.' "

So in 1998 it seems incontrovertibly true that the physical world is both riddled with indeterminacy and fundamentally unspeakable. In any quantum operation, there are always unspeakable remains, something that continues to be inaccessible, and along with the remains of dear departed cats, these remains go into the crypt. But it also appears that in 1998 that what is so encrypted can be conjured up again, and even if these remains can't be made to speak, they can be made to write.

Beam to: Primary Coordinates—ISIS

Scan for: spreading spectrums; amplifying viruses; getting out of the matrix

Defense attorney: We're here to judge Herbert Bernstein. The charge is treason. Good versus evil, as the prosecutor would make it sound. It's somewhat anomalous to be here defending Herbert Bernstein, because he confessed before he committed the crime, according to my esteemed colleague. The basis for the confession is a paper that he wrote that you've heard quotes from, but the quotes that you've heard are relatively confusing to me because what they really point up is that science is always filled with dilemmas: how far to go, and how science should be used. And I think if you really look at the essence of the paper, and I point to two quotes in particular, you'd see that what Bernstein was getting at is the fact that we've lost the original connection between scientific truth and social good. And he saw a lack of moral inclusiveness in society today, and in science today, and that is the essence of what you the jury must judge Herbert Bernstein for. That is the whole question that's here for us to discuss. The grant paper that we've heard selective readings from—and I'll spare reading you Herb's whole paper, because for all I know, you'd find it really interesting. The description of what a Hermitean matrix is could take us the better part of the afternoon. But the fact is that Herb has found a way out of that matrix, and the result is that today, we can look at a grant proposal that is, granted, something that was submitted to the Department of Defense, but something that created a communications system that was potentially highly secure. Again, turning to Herb's paper, one of the worst evils is when scientists stop communicating. When information is controlled by the government. When people don't have security for their own ability to give their ideas and have a free flow of ideas.

The point here is that the use of a "spread-spectrum" does not necessarily have any effect on whether we strengthen or weaken the military. In fact, and I think you'll see no evidence submitted of this today: one can argue that by making battlefield communications secure, you actually improve the deterrent and reduce the ability of a first strike. And therefore, the invention in fact could be improving security on the battlefield.

Now, I won't belabor this, because we want to get on to the real guts of this discussion. Higher security versus better definition of radio images, versus being able to transmit information over longer distances, is it a military art, is it civilian?—these are questions that we'll leave to you the jury to decide. But before you do, we want you to think about this question of guilt and innnocence. The key questions, and really what makes this not just good theater, but interesting discussion material, that I would posit you have to decide before you decide the guilt or innocence of Herbert J. Bernstein are, Is there any basic research that can't be used for evil? And if you decide that there isn't, then you have to decide: should basic research cease, because it's more important to avoid evil? If the answer is basic research should cease, I offer you Herb Bernstein's head. But if the answer is that you end up with good and evil, and that that is the natural outcome of every scientific discovery, then we're not arguing that science is neutral, but we're arguing that a scientist has a special role in society, that it just doesn't begin and end with basic research, but that it means being involved in the very discoveries and their applications. What was talked about in the essay about mitigation, I think is really wrong; it doesn't go far enough. What we're talking about is amelioration. We're talking about the ability of a scientist to introspectively scrutinize his own studies, his own discoveries, and his own work, and come to a conclusion about how it should be pursued.

I'll give you an example that's very easy to consider, that's outside of physics. We've read a lot about the Ebola virus in the last couple of months. The Ebola virus, obviously, has come out of the jungle and has been found now in cities; in Africa, people worry about it being transmitted in monkeys that are being brought to the United States. A scientist doing research on a vaccine for the Ebola virus is clearly, I would argue, doing something good for society. He or she should also understand that the minute a vaccine is created for that virus, it makes the virus a weapon. Because anybody who holds the vaccine also holds the ability to inoculate themselves and infect others. So there is a clear effect of that good, basic research that's going on, that could end up in the devastation of a population. I would say that person is no more guilty than Herb Bernstein is, for having done work on the spectrum. Herb did not do what others in society are doing today, figuring out how to amplify the Ebola virus. That person is clearly guilty.

So you can't say we haven't given you a standard to think about the problem. The question is, What is the role of a scientist? And the story we think we should tell today is the story of a scientist, and how a scientist chooses their work, but also how magnified the effect can be in a very fast-moving society. So with that, we should move on.

Beam to: The Open Conspiracy

Scan for: patents; corporations; war; secrecy/openness;
moral luck

The ghosts of two other physicists, Leo Szilard and Niels Bohr, deserve at least a brief channeling.

The name of this beam site comes from H. G. Wells's book *The Open Conspiracy: Blueprints for a World,* which, when published in 1928, made a deep impression on Szilard, the nomadic physicist often ranked by his descendants as among the most "socially responsible" because of his ceaseless petitioning, his political activism, and his constant efforts to inject questions of political and moral responsibility into the discourse of physicists (Lanouette 1992, 96). His tactics within particular historical circumstances, however, were not without their contradictions. A staunch advocate of full and open communication (Wells's influence), Szilard attempted to create an agreement among French, British, and American physicists to keep fission experiments secret in 1939. Szilard had also patented his ideas for a chain reaction, without knowing which element could be used in such experiments (he thought beryllium might be the ticket), and tried to get General Electric and the British army interested in supporting his experiments.

Szilard's proposed solution to the social/moral problems created by scientific research—full disclosure—was echoed by Bohr, who, despite his recognition of the failures of language to perfectly describe the world, believed that international openness was the only possible answer to the moral problem of physicist-created nuclear weapons. In an "Open Letter to the United Nations," published in 1950, he wrote:

> Without free access to all information of importance for the interrelations between nations, a real improvement of world affairs seemed hardly imaginable. . . . The ideal of an open world, with common knowledge about social conditions and technical enterprises, including military preparations, in every country, might seem a far remote possibility in the prevailing world situation. . . . In the search for a harmonious relationship between the life of the individual and the organization of the community, there have always been and will ever remain many problems to ponder and principles for which to strive. However, to make it possible for nations to benefit from the experience of others and to avoid mutual misunderstandings of intentions, free access to information and unhampered opportunity for exchange of ideas must be granted everywhere.
>
> Any widening of the borders of our knowledge imposes an increased responsibility on individuals and nations through the possibilities it gives for shaping the conditions of human life. The forceful admonition in this respect which we have received in our time cannot be left unheeded and should hardly fail in resulting in common understanding of the seriousness of the challenge with which our whole civilization is faced. . . .
>
> The efforts of all supporters of international cooperation, individuals as well as nations, will be needed to create in all countries an opinion to voice, with ever increasing clarity and strength, the demand for an open world. (Bohr 1950, 293, 295–96)

These messages are channeled here because their terms–open communication in an open world (but be strategic: patent, persuade, try to cut deals) as the antidote to the destabilizing forces of scientific progress and political conspiracy—will still be seen to operate forcefully in the imaginaries of many people called upon to respond to these questions at Bernstein's trial.

Wait, wait, just a moment. Szilard's spirit has something else to add through the medium of his biographer, something about "moral luck":[3]

> Ironically, he said later, he helped keep Germany from winning World War II. If he *had* raised the money and painstakingly tested all seventy

elements, Szilard concluded, he could have discovered as early as 1935 or 1936 that uranium released neutrons—a fact not recognized until 1939. Such a discovery could not have been kept secret, and Germany, then planning for war, would likely be quick to apply this knowledge to building an A-bomb. After the war, Szilard said jokingly that he, Fermi, and other physicists should receive the Nobel Peace Prize for *not* having conducted uranium experiments in the mid-1930s. Had they done so, Szilard said, Hitler might have conquered the world. (Lanouette 1992, 155)

Beam to: Primary Coordinates—ISIS

Scan for: unitary matrices; perfect secrets; complete security

Defense attorney: I call Herbert J. Bernstein as a witness.

Dr. Bernstein, could you explain this discovery of yours to us in a few words? "Experimental Realization of Any Discrete Unitary Operator"—sounds to me like the breakup of the Baby Bells.

Bernstein: This paper is about—for me—solving a problem in quantum mechanics. It's one very close to a number of the things that I talk about in my class that a number of you have taken, "Quantum Mechanics for the Millions." My esteemed defense attorney has characterized it as a discovery, but that gives you the idea that there's something waiting out there to be found, and I prefer to think of it as something that we "worked out." We played around with ideas about "what can be measured." In the microscopic world, everything that can be measured has to come out with real answers, because when you make a measurement, you get a certain real number. And the mathematics of real numbers are operators that are called Hermitean. So there's a long-standing question: Can you make a measurement for anything that you can write down, that will give you a real number as the answer? Nobody knew if you could or you couldn't. What we "discovered" is that you could take an optical table—a slab of marble—and stack things in there in a triangular array that would take any number of beams in that you wanted, and send them out, and in effect—by fooling around with the devices, putting some glass and mirrors in there—you could make a measurement, in that system, of anything you could write down mathematically. That was one of the fundamental things.

The second fundamental thing that was "discovered" was that you could make any transformation—these two things go together—the same kind of theory of what happens on the microscopic scale. A photon coming in on any one of the beams might change around, might change around as time went on and go out in a different state. That transformation from a single photon coming in, to the possibility of a photon being anywhere along five or six different lines, has to be a unitary transformation. What we "discovered"—that is, what we worked out, is how to put little pieces of glass and mirrors on the table so that you could have any transformation—any possible evolution of the state of the photon—that the mathematics told you of what was going to go on. So we basically solved a couple of fundamental problems in quantum mechanics by giving—and this is the kind of work I like to do—by thinking clearly mathematically, and giving actual experimental details.

And that's where the problem comes in. Since there's no opening statement from the missing prosecutor, I'll start prosecuting myself.

The problem is, when you're working that closely with devices, you have to remember the stuff that I wrote in the book *New Ways of Knowing,* and have to really think through very carefully what the devices can be used for.

Defense attorney: I object!

Judge/prosecutor/ethnographer: Sustained!

Defense attorney: But how can it be used? Because the prosecutor has basically said this is only useful for the military. He's said that the people who really found this and thought it was a good thing were people who were going to go to the defense department for money.

Juror A: Who funded your research?

Bernstein: My research was funded by the National Science Foundation. And also, two of our colleagues were in Austria, and were funded by the National Science Foundation of Austria.

Defense attorney: How can it be used?

Judge/prosecutor/ethnographer: Isn't it true that you also work with people who talk about "quantum teleportation" and "quantum cryptography"?

Bernstein: Oh, yeah. It can be used for quantum teleportation, or quantum cryptography, or quantum computation. Each of those needs some explanation. Basically, quantum teleportation is a set of processes where an unknown state comes in from a hole in the wall— somebody's out there sending the state. Actually, I should introduce new characters: the original story was about Alice and Bob. Alice takes the state that comes through the wall and measures it, together with one of these weird-ass particles in quantum mechanics, where two electrons with opposite spins to each other, or two photons with opposite polarizations. They can fly away from the mutual region where they got that condition, and then when you measure one of the particles way over there where Jonathan is, then where Jeffrey is on this side of the room, the properties of the other one are kind of predetermined by what you chose to measure. But they're unknown until that measurement is done. Anyway, you've probably heard about Bell's inequality, or "spooky action at a distance." You can use that now, through quantum teleportation—we're actually working on quantum teleportation—I'm getting in worse trouble all the time. Anyway, Alice over here captures the particle that comes through the wall, whose state is completely unknown to anyone, except maybe Charles, and Alice measures that: looking at reality, and creating, in my mind, creating the reality by doing the measurement—together with a particle that's one of these spooky ones. So Alice, by measuring the relative state that's coming throught the wall, can determine one of four things to say to Charles, four messages: nothing, *x, y,* or *z.* And Bob over there takes the particle that he has, one of these weird particles that has no properties until you measure it, and if Alice told Bob "zero," he does nothing. And if Alice told Bob "*x,*" then he turns that particle 180 degrees around the *x* axis. And if "*y,*" he turns it 180 degrees around the *y* axis, and so on. So there's only four messages, two bits of information that have to be transferred. And the entire quantum state reappears for Bob. That's quantum teleportation.

The device is very important for quantum computers. Quantum computers have recently been shown, in theory, to be able to solve problems faster than any classical, mechanical problem-solving computer. And quantum cryptography can provide a way, using these same weird-ass particles, to send a secret code, a string of symbols that's identical to Alice on one side of the room and Bob on the other side of the room, in a way where if any eavesdropping is done, it can be detected. And if any eavesdropping is not done, the code that's sent is automatically completely and provably random, and the two codes are guaranteed to be identical. That's why it's a perfect secret code.

Defense attorney: Is what you're saying, I'm not sure I completely understand this: if you want to communicate with another scientist, and the government wants to spy on you, if you're using this code, you can actually have a secure way of communicating?

Bernstein: Well, it probably wouldn't be the first application.

Judge/prosecutor/ethnographer: What *would* be the first application?

Defense attorney: I object!

Judge/prosecutor/ethnographer: Overruled. The witness will answer the question.

Bernstein: Banks in Europe have commissioned a four-year project to implement quantum—it's so silly—quantum cryptography for communications between a teller's desk and a central computer.

Defense attorney: So your account is completely secure?

Bernstein: Completely secure, no problem whatsoever. It's guaranteed by quantum physics.

So basically it has some uses for the cutting edge of technology. By the way, these are three different effects. And teleportation of this kind is not like Star Trek teleportation. *[Groans of disappointment]*

Defense attorney: So basically what you're saying is, this can be used in a variety of ways, but that basically what it ends up doing is enhancing the ability to communicate information, for whoever is using it.

Bernstein: Yeah, with a very heavy dose of the spy metaphor introduced, instead of just privacy.

Juror A: What is the responsibility of the scientist in directing who gets this information? What is your responsibility, given what you can imagine, obviously? What do you feel your moral responsibility is, and what will you do?

Bernstein: What I do is try to work out with my Austrian colleagues how you're supposed to write it up. And we didn't come to complete agreement, so part of the way that I look at this problem isn't totally disclosed by the paper. But the ethics of science, which are really what's under scrutiny today, are to publish fully and frankly and let the other physicists in the world know what it is that you have discovered. And so far I haven't really completely done that, because I've been a little bit—

Beam to: Cryptography's Crypt

Scan for: invisible forces; the moon's other face; Black Chamber; homelessness

At some distant, unknown location a laser scans a rapidly spinning disc and converts the information encoded there into an electrical signal which, again transduced, is beamed into a spreading electromagnetic wavefront, picked out of numerous others by the antenna and tuner in the rental car, and converted to sound waves so that we can hear a track from Pink Floyd's *Dark Side of the Moon,* an uncanny presence as we drive toward the National Security Agency. The quite explicit directions that we downloaded from the World Wide Web would take us there from any direction of the compass: "From Washington, D.C.: take the B/W Parkway (Rt. 295) North towards Baltimore. Take the exit for Rt. 32. When you reach the light at the end of the exit ramp, make a left, towards Columbia. Take the first right onto Colony 7 Rd. Go past the Shell station to reach the museum." After the Shell station the road turns rough, hardly fitting for an approach to a national museum, until it ends a short distance later in a parking lot. The chain link fence has a small sign, Colony 7: we're in the right place, whatever that—Colony 7?—is. We're at the National Cryptologic Museum.

This memorial to the extremes of secrecy, paranoia, and conspiracy may only exist because of a fear of the homeless and the policy paralysis that they elicit. The NSA had bought what was once a small motel, which sat vacant and unused while various factions within the agency haggled over what should be done with it. A new federal policy required any unoccupied government building to be used as a homeless shelter, so the NSA historians, ready with a plan to build the museum, saw an opportunity and took it.

At least, this is what we were told by one of the museum's guides, a woman dressed in simple, everyday clothes, looking ready to jump in the minivan and drive to the PTA meeting or pick the kids up at soccer practice. She had worked at the NSA for ten years, and was now even allowed to say she worked at the NSA; up until a few years ago, she would only say that she worked for the Department of Defense.

She became an intermittent presence as we slowly wandered around the various exhibits. There are some heroes depicted in photographs and print: Herbert Yardley, of course, founder of the Black Chamber, MI-8, whose legacy would become the NSA; William Friedman, geneticist turned cryptologist (a short turn); a number of Choctaw and Navajo Indians utilized as "code speakers" during WWII. There are some villains: Julius and Ethel Rosenberg and Klaus Fuchs, caught sending secret atomic messages to the Soviets; Kruschev with the remains of Gary Power's U2.

And there are a lot of machines, from "primitive" coding machines consisting of wooden or ivory wheels, to modern—well, things seem to stop around World War II. But despite the overwhelming emphasis on displaying machines and information, it's striking how the body always has to be exhibited, too. The absent body: mannequins with a variety of military uniforms. The assaulted body: a poster of a schematic brain inundated by phrases, mathematical formulas, technologies, trying to discern what is secret and what isn't. The imprisoned body: photos of four heads, displayed behind a foreground of steel prison bars, listing the numerous consecutive life sentences they are serving for divulging secrets. The hyperbody: a time-lapse video showing the assembly of a "data storage tower" to the frenetic soundtrack of a classical fugue. Calculated and sacrificed bodies: an old newspaper article tells of how Churchill, having decoded information that Coventry would be bombed, made the difficult decision to do nothing, since evacuating the town or mounting an extraordinary air defense would reveal that the British had cracked the German Enigma code. The state cultivates cryptology so it can know the secrets of other states, but then can't show that it knows these secrets; better for the greater, long-term good to assign other remains to crypts.

We ask about the posters. The NSA, the guide says, has an entire office devoted to turning out these cheesy propagandistic reminders that—she is too young to remember this from direct experience, but who needs direct experience in this area anyway?—"loose lips sink ships." "You don't notice them after a while," she says, "until a new one appears and grabs your attention briefly." Then it, too, will fade from memory, and the security urge must be reinstilled in bodies again. The guide goes on: "There was one at Christmas with Santa Claus with a finger over his lips, checking his list twice"—that primitive code written into bodies at a very early age: naughty, nice. For the fiftieth anniversary of WWII, one poster displays another poster from that time with a new message written underneath: "The message is still the same."

The back wall of the museum is rather enigmatic, until you realize it, too, is about the body. Three large panels taking up a lot of seemingly valuable space relate the episode of the USS *Liberty*, a vessel conducting surveillance in the Mediterranean during the 1967 Arab-Israeli war. A picture shows one wounded NSA employee, and the text mourns another who was killed. The message, says the guide, is that all us spies don't just sit here at Fort Meade, but some of us put our bodies on the line defending the country. (It's also the only part of the museum dealing explicitly with post-WWII events, although this may change as materials become declassified at a faster rate in the next few years. But for now, no Korean War, no Vietnam War, no public key cryptography, no Clipper Chip.)

The exhibits on Enigma are the most compelling. They show the patents for the original German machines, used by corporations and banks, and narrate their modification for military purposes. A small Enigma with a blank white pad stands available for interaction. K. punches in a message on the typewriterlike keyboard, the coded letters light up, the encrypting wheels turn, and K. writes down the scrambled message. Seemingly drawn by this iconic activity, as though tapping on the Enigma machine has created this intense vortex into which swirls the entire museum's tropology, the guide comes to look over K.'s shoulder and asks her if she "needs help." She "helpfully" resets the wheels and then K. types out the coded letters to reveal the original message: Why are—the guide starts to chuckle good-naturedly at the obvious message—we here.

We leave the museum, reeling, standing stunned in a violent wind. A bad, bad case of the willies. The key calls the subcompact Ford Escort into life again, and "Washington's classic rock" station is now in the middle of decoding Golden Earring's "Radar Love" from yet another laser disc:

> When I get lonely and I'm sure I've had enough
> She sends her comfort comin' in from above
> We don't need a letter or phone
> We got a thing that's called radar love
> We got a line in the sky

Beam to: Primary Coordinates—ISIS

Scan for: fooling around with pencil and paper;
splitting beams; megalomania

Bernstein: Some of you were here—John Woodell in this audience is actually working away on this problem. In 1974 I had studied the unitary matrices and looked at a certain way of trying to fool around with them to get them to perform; that had some interest for physics. And I did it because we wanted to find out: if you have a mirror that's only partially silvered, and kind of splits the beam in two—you know those one-way mirrors? They're actually partially silvered—and if you shine light on a partially silvered mirror, some of it reflects and some of it goes through. So if you have it at an angle you can take a beam and actually split it. We were sitting around in my colleague's apartment in Boston one day, with our intoxicants of choice, pencil and paper, and I said, Well, what about a device where instead of being a splitter, it was what we called a "tritter," where a beam shines in and it comes out of three holes? And of course, there'll be two other input holes, and they also split equally. And it also turns out that these devices work backwards, so if you shine it in the output, you get the three inputs. We found, within the afternoon, that there was, and then we asked if there were higher dimensional "critters": I called the four-dimensional one the "quitter"; its name is now the "quarter."

Anyway, we were interested in generalizing the beam splitters.

Juror B: This is where it starts to get—this scene with guys there with intoxicants, raises the question—your example of the virus: there's a clear and present means that causes the question to be asked. But why are you guys asking these questions?

Bernstein: Oh, that's a great question. But I might get in trouble, right? What the hell.

Defense attorney: What he means to be asking is, What did you think this would contribute to society? *[Laughter]*

Judge/prosecutor/ethnographer: Leading the witness!

Bernstein: First of all, a lot of you know that I'm a real cheap date: there weren't a lot of intoxicants involved. The thing that I was after, and I'm always after, and the reason I was playing around with guys doing things maybe closely connected with spies and computers and junk like that, is the whole idea that when you look at an object, at the microscopic scale—when you take physics down to where it's at its roots, its reductionist roots—it seems like the phenomena that you study are being created. And it seems like it's important to know why you study the things you do. There may be even a moral question at the level of what you choose to measure. In the story of Alice, what makes her able to teleport Charles' particle over there to Bob—Alice has to look at the world as if it's totally connected. Even though she knows she's got a particle connected to the one Bob has, she has to imagine that the one coming through the wall is also connected. And when she does that, she creates an image—sets up her apparatus that allows her to teleport a huge and complicated quantum state. So it seemed to me that that was a great place to start. And it's not so— you're right. It isn't practical, like punching a cure for the Ebola virus, or the multiplication of the virus. And this may be a bit of megalomania, but the theoretical physicist today serves our society the way storytellers and mythmakers—in the sense of pattern stories that are summaries of the moral fibers of a nation or a people—the songster of ancient Greece, rather than the philosopher who was the person who gave out the story of the gods and reality—and the theoretical physicist, especially as played by the popular press, serves that function. So that also raises for me the question of what is the moral relevance.

But I'm concerned that maybe I've missed the instrumental truth, the instrumental application. I was thinking about these other things, and how could I get a device that I could study, that would tell you how Alice's looking at the world as connected, ended up with her able to do this powerful trick of teleportation.

Oh, I know what I wanted to say before: this kind of teleportation doesn't go faster than light, and it doesn't go from the USS *Enterprise* down to a specified coordinate. It goes slower than the speed of light, for sure, and it goes to wherever Bob is. You print in the *Daily Hampshire Gazette:* 0, *x, y,* or *z.* And Bob, with his particle in the box, can then turn it into that quantum state. It's very different, and much more possible, in accord with current science, and quantum teleportation will probably take place within the next couple years.

It's really creepy how science fiction can become science, and how theoretical and experimental physicists are involved. And me being sort of right at that juncture of theory and experiment, I want to find out how experiments create reality. And how can I hope, or help, everybody in the sciences and in society recognize that as an important factor in modern science. Both in something as esoteric as quantum mechanics, and also throughout science in a much more generally accessible way. When you look at something, you create what you're studying. When you use science, you set out a field; that field becomes important, it's highlighted out of everything else that's going on, and there's a strong moral implication of what we choose to study becomes the thing that turns out to be most real. If you are guided by the fact that numbers are important, and you throw out the unquantifiable, a lot of stuff that I hold very dear is going to be left out of what we all consider real and therefore important.

Beam to: Aye Spy

Scan for: secrecy; encrypted bodies; nonlocality

A quick check of the computer logs from previous beaming operations: this account has been going back and forth between two papers published in *Physical Review Letters,* trying to map the (possible) entanglements between them. The paper which Bernstein coauthored and which was the focus of the trial dealt primarily with the mathematical properties of "unitary matrices"—properties which could be experimentally realized/verified through an apparatus which splits and recorrelates beams of photons. What is under question is the relationship between this paper and, on the one hand, possible devices with military (and commercial) applications and, on the other hand, to other literature in physics.

The other physics article, the 1993 teleportation paper by Bennett et al., lays out some remarkable accomplishments in physics through the story of its two characters, Alice and Bob. Quite simply, Alice and Bob are trying to communicate clandestinely and accurately. In their most general form, the entanglements of EPR particles "assist in the 'teleportation' of an intact quantum state from one place to another, by a sender who knows neither the state to be teleported nor the location of the intended receiver. . . . Suppose one observer, whom we shall call 'Alice,' has been given a quantum system . . . prepared in a state $|\phi>$ unknown to her, and she wishes to communicate to another observer, 'Bob,' sufficient information about the quantum system for him to make an accurate copy of it" (Bennett et al. 1993, 1895).

We are dealing, then, with neither human bodies, cats, nor tonight's dinner, but only particle states. This is more or less equivalent to saying we are dealing with information. If Scotty, Tabby, and goulash are on the future's distant horizon, what is on the more immediate horizon is simply the Message.

In the diagram of quantum teleportation in figure 4.4 we see that what this turns out to schematize is a method of sending perfectly uneavesdroppable, unbreakably coded messages. This perfect security is an effect of the "unspeakable" part of the apparatus, the entangled EPR particles in the lower center of the diagram. Because these particles are correlated at the "nonlocal" level, and because the particle properties—or, if you prefer, the particles themselves—don't exist in the usual, stable ontological sense, but only in the spectral hauntological sense, they can in theory constitute a perfect signaling system. Somewhat paradoxically, their very spectrality and "unspeakability" results in their being able (with the assistance of the physicist, the experimental apparatus, and perhaps some other terms) to literally write themselves into reality—a writing that is without a trace of difference. A perfect transmission because it's not a transmission at all, but a re-creation of the world, a writing of the real. A perfect code because the only intermediary term, in the gap between the destruction/reading and the making/writing of the world (that is, particle state), is an incommunicable ghost.

But now entangle this reading of the diagram at the level of microphysical processes with another reading at the level of the socio-crypto-logics. What remains outside the frame of this diagram, which may or may not be the space of conspiracy, is the answer to the question, Who prepares the unknown quantum state for Alice? Where does A come from? One possible answer is the National Security Agency, that government agency which has tried the hardest to remain in the spooky realm of the unspeakable, and been fairly successful at it.[4] But as the court transcript shows, other answers cannot be dismissed, such as: banks sending information about *your* monetary transactions.

Because Bernstein's coauthored paper, according to the socio-crypto-logic reading, might be represented by the fuzzy line C in the zone of the unspeakable, it is entangled with these other ghostly presences of the teleportation paper, and by extension, with the fields of cryptography and the out-of-frame workings of the NSA. One of my roles as ethnographer has been to try to help Bernstein communicate with these scary half-presences, and the machinery of this text has been geared primarily toward that more spectral side of the diagram.

But together, at ISIS, we have tried different genres, to see what different effects we would get. The "trial" is the one that this text has been beaming back and forth to, but in each case, the central issue was the problem of what it means to be a socially responsible scientist in this kind of entangled situation. For a variety of reasons, that question gravitated mostly to the zone represented by the upper righthand corner of the diagram, the speakable realm of future application: should Bernstein consult for the Defense-funded engineer? In that more public realm, where time is limited and available discourses leave something to be desired, questions of application, ethical use, control of devices, good and evil, guilt and innocence, and so forth become much more manageable. They seem to make much more sense: "We can understand how you might be worried about how your ideas will get used, but worrying about the theory you're creating, the form of knowledge you're participating in? That's crazy! Those are ghosts!"

The opening section of this essay was drama, a literary device to warm up the apparatus before starting the experiment. While it was not wrong for us to focus in public events on the military application of Bernstein's work as willies inducing, it's neither ethnographically precise nor the entire picture. Long before he was asked to consult on the military grant, Bernstein felt the willies. Not knowing what exactly was wrong or what bothered him about these references to "Alice" and "Bob" cropping up in these papers in associated physics literatures, he could only say, "It just gives me the willies." What makes the willies the willies is that Bernstein sensed something within the most "abstract" theory, with no application in sight. It's as if he knew that his present work was tuned in telepathically to the future—an indeterminate future that nevertheless had some ghostly effect on the past with which it was correlated, just like the EPR particles—and knowing at the same time that telepathy is crazy and impossible, and that he was worried about nothing.

When the trial proceedings strayed more toward this ghostly side, I think the transcript shows (because I perversely preserved it by not cleaning up the transcript) Bernstein's encroachment into the realm of the unspeakable: he stammers, grasps for phrases, falls back on worn and inadequate notions. My own rearticulations here are no less stammering and, ultimately, inadequate. It is, as the saying goes, the nature of the territory.

Beam to: Primary Coordinates—ISIS

Scan for: garbled transmissions; cats out of the bag; patent or lobotomize?

Juror C: I have a question. Your defense apparently is, while you really think there is, or at least the possibility, that the results of your research may be used for military purposes, but your defense is that the scientist's job is just to report the findings in a public way to the rest of the scientific community. Does that defense work for those who discovered the atomic bomb, the machine gun, or any discovery, no matter what the result is?

Bernstein: That's a great question. It comes from my poor presentation. I said that putting your ideas into a paper like this are what the usual scientist would say is their responsibility. I don't believe that, and this stuff about finding out my role as a mythmaker and so on is only part of what the answer is. I believe that we don't know the replacement for the story that your only responsibility is to publish. What we do know—and I don't know whether I would cite the same examples you did—but we do know at this point, so late in the twentieth century, that more has to be done by the scientists, about thinking and doing something with respect to what the applications are. And what I personally do is spend a great deal of my time with ISIS. And it should be no real mystery to the people in this audience, who are so closely associated with Hampshire, that all scientific projects have some kind of social conditions around them, both in the input and in the output. What are the effects going to be, who gets to fund it—when you're taught at Hampshire how to read a scientific paper, you read between the lines: who paid for the funding, where are the people, what are their previous researches, what are the social conditions of science? What I do is I think about that all the time, I work with people who are actually applying science at the same time, and I should be thinking about the applications of my own science. Publication is not the end of it. What I was saying is, that's what is usually presented as the defense of science. For me the real defense is that you don't know what science is going to be used for. If you're really engaged, if you love the stuff and you want to do it, if you want to find out something, you've got to ask, Who are you working with, what are they doing with it, what are you doing with it, what can someone imaginably do with it, and how did you come to it? And you the scientist have to ask it. You can't turn it on and off, like between eight and five you're doing your science and afterward you sign the petitions.

Juror D: I have an objection. I've heard this same line for a long time. And it comes back to this exact same point, right here, where it ends with: "and you have to ask all of these questions." That avoids the responsibiliity of actually *doing* anything. The responsibility, the time wasting, taking you away from the science that you want to do as a scientist. The responsibility of following the path on all the elements that you've developed, developing a corporation to take control of it, and propagate it, and control its use. Which will take over your life.

Bernstein: Not necessarily.

Juror D: How will we know unless we've tried?

Defense attorney: So are you positing that the only way a scientist can really protect his science is to patent it?

Juror D: Not necessarily, but it's clearly not the end of the road when you say, "Aha, it's out in the world." Because there's this other stage that a bunch of people are now going to go through to apply it. You're not divorced from that, you're not powerless, you don't have to sit back and say, "Oh, well, there it goes." Because you have an advantage that no one has: you knew it first. You have a leap. You can exploit it. You may not be successful. But that's not relevant.

Bernstein: But you also have other responsibilities.

Judge/prosecutor/ethnographer: Let me ask this witness a question. Dr. Bernstein has been contacted by the person who submitted this grant, and who actually got this grant from the Department of Defense. He called Dr. Bernstein up, said, "Please come consult with me. There are a few things that I don't understand about your proposed piece of technology. Perhaps you can help me work those out." Do you think Dr. Bernstein should go and consult with this person? If so, how would that consultation proceed? Or if not, what are the consequences of that?

Juror D: Clearly he should talk to him and find out what it is he's actually talking about. And also I would say that the way you have a table-top device which is close enough to an algorithm that you believe it could essentially be duplicated in silicon or in some other medium, then you have a patentable thing. . . .

We have all this marvelous technology, and stories about how people gain control of them and keep control of them through economic means. And I think there are worse—there are times when the cat's out of the bag, and forget it, once it's out, you can't control it. But there are other things where you come very close to designing a piece of technology, you're right there, and you have a lot of options.

Juror E: If you're trying to define the responsibility of a scientist as being held responsible for the applied use, or the potential, I just think that's ultimately impossible. Because you're trying to predict one small factor *[tape ends]* technology. And in genetics alone, it's just not going to happen. So I think trying to take control of that behavior through things like patents—it's trying to control far beyond what you can do. And I also don't think that trying to sift through, predicting that outcome, is doing good science.

Bernstein: But it may be good literary analysis. Maybe you could deconstruct your own paper.

Juror E: Yeah, it may be good literary analysis, and it's good for discussions like this, but it isn't good science.

Defense attorney: Do you think if you do identify some bad use of the information, or some way that you wouldn't be able to control it, you should not have the idea?

Bernstein: Not have the idea!?!?

Judge/prosecutor/ethnographer: The court orders a lobotomy!

Defense attorney: Okay. Do you think you shouldn't write it down?

Juror F: That's the same idea as destroying it by measuring it.

Juror G: A more abstract and concrete example of that is the people who invented group theory, who were very proud of the fact that it had absolutely no conceivable use, or that there would ever be any earthly use for group theory. It turned out to be absolutely essential to crystallography and also to the atom bomb. So you may think that you've explored all the possible uses, but you're guaranteed you won't.

Juror H: [Inaudible] what I was planning to. Some of the things *[inaudible]* you seemed to talk a lot about *[inaudible]* things that are going to be empowering, especially around communications *[inaudible]*, the telephone, and the radio, and the television *[inaudible]*, and all the applications *[inaudible]*. And I was wondering whether, never mind just the possibility *[inaudible]* of something you want to pursue, and on the other hand, it seemed that all of the things, the ability to communicate has become cheaper, now you can get a cellular phone for nothing. The ability tó create a cellular phone has become much more *[inaudible]*—you can't do that anymore: you have to go to Texas Instruments, you buy their packaged chips, you put it on a circuit board. It's very cheap for me to do that, but only Texas Instruments *[inaudible]* created those chips; only AT&T *[inaudible]* have the committee to set the standards for which *[inaudible]*. And now we're talking about quantum mechanic materials that I don't have the *[inaudible]* to create on my tabletop—I know you have, with some help from NSF.

Judge/prosecutor/ethnographer: The prosecution did fail to mention that we've organized this trial around the military as the problem. But in fact, section 5 of this proposal is a commercialization strategy: "it can be used on the information superhighway and multimedia environment, where immense image and video data need to be processed and transmitted in real time." And there are supporting letters from the chief executive officers of various corporations who are ready to commercialize these devices. So perhaps the military is no longer the real evil in the world: it's transnational capital that Herb is aiding and abetting! *[Laughter]*

Defense attorney: Fortunately, that's not what he's on trial for!

Juror I: Did you talk to this guy?

Bernstein: Yeah, sure.

Juror I: And what was the outcome?

Bernstein: It's a little bit scary, actually. There are a lot of people that I like in the world that have no qualms about working for the military or transnational capital or whatever. And I have my own qualms about working for the military. But he's a really nice guy, walked us around campus, made sure my family had some drinks on a hot day, and a place to sit while we were talking. But he is the son of Russian émigrés, and like some of my Austrian colleagues, tends to think that the U.S. Army is one of the world's greatest gifts, because of what its presence did to the social and political structure of their countries: breaking up various forms of tyranny and saving Austria from becoming part of the Eastern bloc, and so on. So he gave me this speech about how great it was that it could be sold as part of the battlefield of the future, to these guys who were so far removed from research that they didn't even have a copy of *Physical Review Letters* in their whole institution—he had to staple my paper on the back, because when he called them while preparing the proposal—he's a physicist, they're physicists, they don't even have the main journal in our field at their fingertips. It was recently published, maybe they get it late. Or maybe they're actually engineers. But anyway, his story was that just like we're discussing now, this stuff is great, as he saw my ideas, in an application that I hadn't foreseen, according to him, which is to do the same thing for lightwave communications that you would do for radio in what is called spread-spectrum communication: you have different channels, each of which is a *combination* of different frequencies, unlike ordinary radio where each channel, each station, is one frequency. You put this stuff in a triangular-array device inputting different colors, it mixes them together, and you have one white-light pipe that holds all the signals. It's called multiplexing. But it's really the same thing as having different radio stations on your dial, making these bits appear more rapidly and having coding for different messages, but you gotta do what you do on the airwaves: mix the frequencies together.

It's really remarkable, in this trial setting, people have come to this: that that's what's behind this, that the patenting is what's important, and the capital flows are interesting, and that the ideas are probably more connected to our current social and cultural environment. Mike alluded to that: this isn't a witch hunt for commies versus capitalist, or militarists versus nonmilitarists. It's more like, What is our current economic and social circumstance going to do with this? And as you probably suspected, it's going to be big-time communications stuff.

And there's always this thing: a lot of my colleagues say, "Look, it's going to be secure"—this is what my defense attorney was saying—"That means you'll have privacy." No, that means the government will want to screw up your idea, don't worry about giving it out to your colleagues. But then the literary analysis is important: when you have a paper that's written about teleportation and it talks about Alice and Bob, and those are characters in all of the spy literature—that is, not spy novels, but in cryptography—you have Alice and Bob instead of A and B.

Did I answer your question?

Beam to: Dear Old DoD

Scan for: driving history, under the influence; nonlocal conspiracy

How massive military funding for basic physical research in the period since World War II has affected the kinds of knowledge produced by physicists accepting these funds, and how it has affected the discipline of physics as a whole, has been subject to more theorizing by historians and philosophers than can be covered fairly here. Again, I select a few examples noteworthy for the force which they have exerted within their disciplines.

Paul Forman, an historian of science at the Smithsonian Institution, has provided one of the most thoroughly documented empirical studies of defense spending in the physical sciences in this, the postwar period. While not explicitly endorsing anything like a "conspiracy theory," its title, "Behind Quantum Electronics: National Security as Basis for Physical Research in the United States, 1940–1960," carries a fundamental conspiracy trope: behind the veil of appearances lies an unseen yet powerful controlling force, which may be an institution or a logic. The basic narrative is that physicists once had "control" of their discipline but, as a result of the political-economic realignments of World War II and new patterns of federal and industrial spending in the sciences, lost control by ceding it to the military (and industry). Thus there is no room for any third or higher term in the analytics of control: it resides either with the physicists or with the military. Even if that latter term is multiplied into the suggestive phrase "military-industrial *complex*," the logic of control still remains at a noncomplex level: if *we* don't have it, *they* do. In terms that physicists themselves have been prone to use: someone had to be "calling the tune," and that someone was increasingly the national security state.

Exactly what methods these songsters employ remains hazy, however. How is the tuning, directing, steering, or guiding accomplished? What, in short, is the conspiratorial *telos* and mechanism for attaining it? The textual presence of Forman's article itself—eighty journal pages crammed with extensive, copious footnotes; an army of charts, tables, and graphs of federal, industrial, and military research and development spending; and numerous quotes from physicists, political figures, and military officials—suggests that an almost obsessive documentary strategy is required if one wants to see what lies behind physics, and particularly its branch of quantum electronics which produced such devices as the laser, the maser, and the atomic clock. It is a noble attempt to *locate*.[5] Forman concludes, however, on a fairly nonlocalizable note: "Though they have maintained the illusion of autonomy with pertinacity, the physicists had lost control of their discipline. They were now far more used *by* than using American society, far more exploited by than exploiting the new forms and terms of their social integration" (Forman 1987, 229).

It appears, then, that if "control" has gone anywhere, we might look for it in something called a form. The term may come from philosopher of science Ian Hacking, whose frequently cited article titled "Weapons Research and the Form of Scientific Knowledge" Forman quotes earlier in his own article. Hacking discusses how what he calls the form of knowledge, as opposed to content, might be connected to military funding. He admits that the concept "form of knowledge" may be too vague to be useful, a ghost that analysts might chase after futilely, but offers it as an experiment to replace the metaphor of autonomous knowledge with one that "admits that possibilities are constrained in a manifold of complex ways at a particular time." At the end of the article, he explicitly disavows any type of "conspiracy theory":

> I would altogether deplore an inference from this paper, that forms of knowledge connected with research that is primarily funded by the military are wittingly created by those who are responsible for weapons research. Such ideological paranoia is absurd, if only on the ground that, contrary to what I write, the concept of a form of knowledge may be either inexplicable or when explained, empty. I am more concerned that we have no idea of what we are doing in the overall directions of our conceptions of the world. There is no monolithic military conspiracy in any part of the globe to determine the kinds of possibilities in terms of which we shall describe and interact with the cosmos. (Hacking 1986, 259)

Such reservations and cautions notwithstanding, the language of conspiracy remains present as Hacking tries to reformulate terms:

> But our ways of worldmaking, to use the phrase of Nelson Goodman, are increasingly funded by one overall motivation. If content is what we can see, and form is what we cannot, but which determines the possibilities of what we can see, we have a new cause to worry about weapons research. It is not just the weapons . . . that are being funded, but the world of mind and technique in which those weapons are devised. The forms of that world can come back to haunt us even

when the weapons themselves are gone. For we are creating forms of knowledge which—spinoffs or not—have a homing device. More weapons, for example. (260)

It would seem that conspiracy theory itself has a kind of "homing device," an internal guidance mechanism which allows it to keep on haunting even after it has been killed and exorcised. There's no need for a "monolithic" military conspiracy because it has been shrunk down and implanted into the body of knowledge, a tracking device that keeps signaling even after the guys in the control room have stopped paying attention or can no longer dominate the complex informatic systems, and even though "we have no idea what we are doing." Along with Hacking we have arrived in a territory of deep paradoxes: "We have no idea what we're doing"—but here are one or two ideas about that. Remote control from an infinite distance—but with no control, exercised by no agent, through the haunting possibilities of "forms of knowledge."

Beam to: Primary Coordinates—ISIS

Scan for: genies; global positioning; timing is everything; ya gotta have heart; dichotomies and beyond

Juror J: What makes you think that you can control information once it's released, whether you have a patent or whether you attempt to control it yourself? Now that the information is out there in a journal, this physicist already saw it and said, "Oh, let's do this with it." He doesn't quite understand exactly how you got there, but can't he figure it out? Once you've let the genie out of the bottle, is it possible to say, "I've got it, don't worry, I've got my thumb on it here."

Bernstein: I like the guy because he's smart; he's definitely going to figure it out whether I go and consult with him or not. But he might not be able to figure out this jumbled mess of physics, and just where the thread that I work on was, that I think is really quite powerful. And I really am in a position where I can try to stop people from doing that particular analysis, rather than going ahead and writing about it in Austria next week or in Italy the week after that. So I do have a decision to make, and I'm kind of leaning to not going out there—the guy got $500,000, and it was nice to talk to him in Baltimore last year, but I don't have to go and talk to him again. I'm concerned that I can't get alignment with him as to how—you see, when you pick a problem to work on, you're steering it. You may not know all the consequences. You may have things that many years later are going to have consequences, and you can't quite foresee it, you may not be able to foresee it at all. But you can figure out where you are now, and who you're working with, and who their allegiances are to. If my program is to investigate reality and morality and all that kind of stuff, then I have to be careful who I work with. I mean, the other guys should be careful if they're in favor of military applications of hardware, that they don't work with peaceniks.

[The Defense calls Aristotle to the stand]

Defense attorney: You have a book with you, Aristotle?

Aristotle: My *Ethics.*

Defense attorney: Aristotle, I know it's been a long time and you've been very patient, and we won't go over many of the things that have already come up at this trial. But it would be very useful if you could talk about your physics, and the types of things that you did in your time, and the observations you made.

Aristotle: Well, way back when, I did a lot of research. A lot of it had to do with everything falling into its natural place. Objects would fall down because it was natural for them to fall down. Likewise, the heavenly bodies would move on these great spheres that they were attached to, perfect circles. Nowadays I'm told you don't believe this anymore. Nonetheless, this was the basic research that I was involved in two thousand some-odd years ago.

Defense attorney: How did people use that research in a practical way?

Aristotle: Well, for example, the applications of my research into the perfect circles that the heavenly bodies traveled on could then be generalized for navigational purposes. One could use the skies to chart where one was going, and where one was. In the short time that I've been here, I've heard about something called the GPS: the global positioning satellite. This is the current result of my basic research into the spheres, mine and Ptolemy's, the founding of the basic science of navigation. The GPS is the ultimate result of what started out as really unapplied, basic research.

Defense attorney: Now, Aristotle, isn't it true that this GPS is also for the precision guiding of missions in our modern battlefield.

Aristotle: Sadly, it is so.

Defense attorney: And when you were sitting back in your shop, two thousand years ago, did you think about this? Did you worry about the fact that attached to some grant proposal that some guy submitted to the Department of Defense of the United States there was the possibility that your very science of those perfect spheres could be used this way?

Aristotle: I didn't know what a United State was back then.

Defense attorney: Well, what impact does it have on your thinking about your science today?

Bernstein: You're making him jump out of character.

Defense attorney: No, he's prepped. Unlike you.

Aristotle: It is troubling to see applications such as these guided missiles being helped by my research. However, there is little I feel I could have done about it. I did not stop doing basic research, because

I thought these weapons would be falling out of the sky. However, I did not just do research. I wrote my *Ethics [slaps book]* and made them available to all. And in doing so, I made a guide which could be used to understand how to best use this research.

Juror K: But what should we do today?

Aristotle: Perhaps the founding of an institute *[laughter]* that combines science and interdisciplinary studies. Perhaps this would be the modern-day equivalent, combining both doing research and attempting to control where it is used.

Bernstein: [reading from ISIS brochure] Military Nuclear and Toxic Waste Project, Seminars on Socially Repsonsible Science, Science for Survival, Scientists' Dialogue Initiative, Science Education Programs, and Foundation of Physics and Biology.

Juror K: I don't think the Romans are going to attend these seminars.

Juror L: Isn't it elitist, in the same way that you publish a book when, what, one-tenth of one percent of your population could read? Isn't it elitist to create an organization that's strictly among scientists?

Judge/prosecutor/ethnographer: Bailiff, remove this woman from the courtroom!

Juror L: —have a responsibility to the general population, instead of being a great white father? *[Applause.]* Sorry, Aristotle.

Juror M: Don't worry; he's been prepped, remember?

Aristotle: I think it might be troubling that such an elitist configuration occurs. However, would one not publish a novel because it might not be accessible to those at an eighth-grade reading level? Is that not elitist? That which is known and is not communicated, that is elitist. Because it is holding to oneself, and that is the greatest elitism of all. If you know it and communicate it with others, then you're spreading the knowledge. If it cannot be spread to everyone, that is not a reason not to spread it to anyone.

Bernstein: Your preparation just fell apart.

Defense attorney: One last question. We've had a lot of discussion about your physics and its use for gobal positioning satellites. Is your physics correct or incorrect by today's standards?

Aristotle: It is incorrect.

Defense attorney: Thank you. Your honor, the two thousand years that it took for the realization of a global positioning satellite was a very long period of time. But in the time of a scientist today, one minute or ten minutes can be the equivalent of two thousand years. You can't predict how your science will be used. You can only try to direct your science so that it's used in a productive way. On that, the defense rests.

Judge/prosecutor/ethnographer: At this point I would normally ask the jury for a verdict, but perhaps they would like to make a few last points.

Juror N: I'd like to ask Herb the question I asked Aristotle, who essentially dodged it. Could you, realizing what you wanted the conclusion of the experiment to be before you attempted it, could you from that point analyze and determine if it could be used for illicit purposes? And if so, did you make that attempt before you began the experiment?

Bernstein: Boy, that's a good question. I did think about applications, and I did not have the idea of the battlefield of the future in mind, or of spread-spectrum multiplexing. And I don't think I did a great job of thinking that this was going to be an appealing device, and the diagram of the triangular layout was going to attract somebody just because it was so cute. That's probably one thing I could have done, to say, This is a real, new, interesting technological device. What the guy did, actually, was replace the mirrors with fiber optic couplers. And with fiber optic couplers you can just turn a screw and it's like varying how much silver you have on the mirror. And then when he showed me the proposal he said, "I don't want to give you another copy because all of the devices in there are wrong." And he told me basically no light would get through any of these devices, because they're not very efficient.

Juror O: I'm completely baffled by why you think this is even a moral question. I mean, at least take the money off him.

Juror P: Obviously, you're not doing this just to make money, or you would be soliciting grants from the military and build it direct. I think the court agrees that knowledge is power, and that it's dangerous. And yet we also seem to agree that the most moral and conscientious and careful scientist cannot conceivably cover every single base. Forming ISIS is a good step toward that, a good step to communicate, to educate, to share your ideas. But ISIS is a form of communication, not a police force. How do you deal with scientists who are in it specifically for the bucks, who are going to be lurking around the edges of the research, always waiting for the opportunity to take it where you don't want it to go? And in the middle of the paranoiac power struggle, how do you do scientific research?

Bernstein: The answer that I would suggest is that science doesn't stay still. It seems to be that every time I talk about this stuff, I learn more about how old and old-fashioned I am and my views are, and how the notion that "you just don't work for the military," which may have been okay even in the eighties, when I wrote that stuff in *New Ways of Knowing*—it really may not be that the military's so bad. Maybe the military is evolving into one of these rapid-deployment humanitarian forces—I doubt it. I still won't take the bucks, but I did when I was a kid work for the Navy for summers in college, and I didn't feel as good, ever, as when I found out that the project I was working on had been canceled. And it was a great project: I got to fly on the centrifuge that was imitating a rocket, and subject myself to five and a half G's, and feel what it was like to be going up in the space shuttle. And I loved that. But the moment I really discovered how I really felt about doing that kind of research was when I read in the paper, about four weeks after I had left, that they had canceled this Dyna-Soar project, the forerunner of the Shuttle, and I suddenly felt tremendous relief. Because the project I was working on was a fractional-orbital bomber.

But I think other people would make very different moral judgments, and I alluded to that. Some of my colleagues have life histories, where they think working for the U.S. Army is great.

Juror Q: Herb, insofar as you didn't look far enough ahead, how do you feel about it, really?

Bernstein: Well, I feel much better, right now, about this, than I did in my senior year, when I found out what it meant to have been working on a weapons system. But I feel really on the edge about what I'm going to do. Because I'm going to these scientific conferences in a few days, and I don't know if I'm going to be talking fully and freely and happily about my research, knowing what just happened to the last piece of it. And knowing that these are the guys, who I'm going to be with, who if I give them the mathematics in the way I would— that is, in the way that *didn't* come out in the paper—it's really going to click and it will take off in a direction *[inaudible]*. I don't know what I'm going to do about it.

Juror Q: Let's just *[inaudible]*—one is, you spill your guts *[inaudible; major courtroom disturbance: laughter, voices, gavel banging]*. On the other hand, if you don't tell them, you only buy a delay, and it ain't that long a delay—I could measure it in hours, but months might be a better frame. So the question is, if you don't tell them, what do you do with the months you buy? That's the real question, that's the only real question here. And obviously my sort of take on that is if you want to buy some months—and that's really all you can do— then you can go out and do something: patent, or take some more control, or follow the research along—if you don't believe you've really found out what's going on here—following along some more. All you need to do is buy time. That's almost the only real practical thing here, because you don't work alone in a vacuum. So what you get is you get these lead times: in practical cases in modern science, what you've typically got is lead times. I mean, you can exploit that.

Juror R: But you do lose something: you lose the high. The high of getting up there and banging heads with people that have the same high as you. I mean, it's part of what you want.

Juror S: We're gathering around a scientist to talk about what scientists do with their work, but I'm struck by that—this discussion is moot, without knowing more about the motivations of other people which you perceive to be evil. And so if you were to disclose to this group here everything you know, and even if we were all physicists, chances are that we wouldn't do anything bad with that information, because we're not motivated to do anything socially unconscious, or unconscionable. And the grist of this entire mill is the motivation of other people to do things which are exploitive or damaging. Yes?

Bernstein: Well, no. If you were in a room of physicists this large, there would be at least one or two totally bought into things that I don't like.

Juror S: My point is only that you're trying to control for something which—which I'd rather sort of intervene on that other variable, rather than try and isolate and control for.

Bernstein: I think this suggestion is right: you work on all of those fronts, but what hasn't come out here is that you actually do start to get transformed when you do a science that involves the other people. When you are working—I haven't made the connection, admittedly, in quantum mechanics, of trying a new thing this year, which is to get students up to speed to have a community that I do trust and talk with about which direction it should go. But ideally, I think having a large variety of people in on the science, and talking about what it might be used for, and more thought in advance about devices and mechanisms *[inaudible]*—that the more people you get to talk to, the less it is just a group of physicists in the room, the more, uh, the, you know, direction you get, the more real connection to, uh, some, uh, better, more complete, more inclusive—

Juror S: It makes it harder to isolate it from the heart.

Bernstein: Yeah, exactly! *[Gradually trailing off.]* The more combination between the heart, the head, and something else.

Juror T: We've been hearing a lot about the reasons that you might not want to let the information out, and about what you think are socially irresponsible misuses. And I'm just curious as to what you consider the socially responsible use is for your research. What's the potential good?

Bernstein: That's a good question. The stuff that I think that device can be used for includes—there are additional transformations of it— it includes ways to change pictures, or information, or images, but what I want to use it for is to investigate these questions about how do you make reality?

Juror T: Pure research.

Bernstein: It's not pure research to me, because that question is a burning social question: How do you make reality when you do science? I want to use the device to think clearly with, to tell people about, to show—actually, what I want to do is to show people how physics creates reality—and that doesn't sound like a practical application, but it might be one of the most practical applications—that this device gets closer to the heart of the things I've been working on, and there's a practical—that's why I look at that boundary between the theory and experiment. If it's a real live device, and you can describe or show something very interesting *[tape ends]*.

Juror U: We've been focusing on what is the potential evil, but we haven't been looking at what the potential good is. And isn't there a responsibility, to the extent that we can predict, shouldn't we be balancing the potential good against the potential evil, rather than just saying, because it's potentially evil we should think about it.

Bernstein: I think we've gotta go beyond these dichotomies. I think the whole purpose of ISIS—the reason for mixing the practical together with the theoretical in such a strong way, is to break that dichotomy. But another part of our program is the whole idea that it can be used for good and it can be used for evil—the use/misuse dichotomy—is going to be superseded, for sure, in fifty years *[inaudible]*—it's under question at this current time. I think it's possible that that's up for grabs right now. If so, we want to work in a much more nuanced, much more complicated way, than to try to predict either of those. And by focusing on "the misuse of Herb's latest paper"—big deal! The point is, we don't know, whether looking at use or misuse and trying to balance it, helps you one whit. We don't know whether looking at the military funding versus the corporate funding—which is good, which is bad? Nobody knows. So you've gotta do something active, you know?—you have to think clearly, and act nicely or purely or goodly or whatever you want to call it. And I think you do that in concert with bunches of other people, including a lot of people who haven't been included—look at this, it's all white males. The idea of decentering the discussion—you know, we picked something you could polarize around: duh, Herb's bad, Herb's good! But by shifting the whole arrangement *[inaudible]*—

Juror V: I mean, maybe this is cynical, but even if you educate 98 percent of the population to be conscious about science, it's still the other 2 percent that's gonna sneak up on you and *[inaudible]*—

Defense attorney: Well, 2 percent is better than 4.

Juror W: People talk about scientists when they want to scapegoat, or otherwise empower a bunch of people with something—I don't know what. The fact of the matter is, the community of so-called scientists which used to in some way exist because it was small, and it came from common roots, no longer exists. And in fact the real problem is not so much how scientists relate to the rest of the world, because they don't relate to each other. And they can't take from their community outward to anyone else, because they don't have a community. And until they do—they don't speak with one voice.

Juror X: I don't know if any of you have heard the story of the Chinese farmer who didn't know the difference between good luck and bad luck. He had a really good ox that he could plow his field with, and one day his ox ran away. And the neighbors came to him

and said, "This is very bad luck; your ox has left you." He said,
"Good luck, bad luck, who knows?" The ox went up in the moun-
tains, the ox came back the next week with an entire herd of oxen, and
he was now rich. And the neighbors all came and said, "It seems like
good luck this time." He said, "Good luck, bad luck, who knows?"
Well, the next week his son was riding on the ox, fell down and broke
his leg. And he said to them again, "Good luck, bad luck, who
knows?" The week after that the army came in and conscripted all the
young men in the village. They went off: all killed in the war—except
his son, because of his broken leg he wasn't conscripted. So that's why
I urge the innocent verdict for Bernstein: he couldn't have known.

   Judge/prosecutor/ethnographer: Well, as many of you, being former students and colleagues of Herb's—I think you probably all knew
coming in here today, as I did, that really the only possible verdict in
this is: not guilty by reason of temporary insanity. *[Laughter,
applause]*

   The case is not closed, but court's adjourned.

Beam Decoherence Approaching Critical Levels

Scanners Off-line

General System Failure Imminent

Conspiracy relies on an ontology, a firm delineation of forces, a clear and present danger that, however remote, however inaccessible, at least suggests strategies of control, however unrealizable and far in the future those might be. It is
a diagnosis. Conspiracy diagnosed allows one to write a prescription, perhaps
for the new genetically engineered drug Will-Ease, the pharmakonic poison/
cure for the willies: "Tired of that nagging conscience? Is your will overexer-
cised, stiff, and aching from an exertion that finds no simple outlet in our
complex world? *[Animated graphic of head slice with throbbing lurid colors
permeating every cerebral fissure]* Try the new night time cold medicine for
today's Cold Night Time: Will-Ease. It knows what ails you. Now with calcium
and vitamin E."

   What have I offered here? A list of symptoms that might or might not cohere
into a syndrome, but certainly holding out no inoculative or curative possibilities. Like those things which are sometimes called "psychosomatic conditions," the willies occupies a half-world, a between-state of undecidability. I
read this in the data present to me, whether empirical or theoretical—but these
terms I know (really, I do *know* this) are fully entangled in a conspiracy of their
own, sending super, natural messages to each other through the medium of the

and: empirical *and* theoretical. It is a conspiracy we locate now, for good reasons, in language:

> It is language that is "cryptic": not only as a totality that is exceeded
> and untheorizable, but inasmuch as it contains pockets, cavernous
> places where words become things, where the inside is out and thus
> inaccessible to any cryptanalysis whatsoever—for deciphering is re
> quired to keep the secret secret. The code no longer suffices. The
> translation is infinite. And yet we have to find the key word that opens
> and does not open. (Blanchot 1986, 136)

The willies can't be fully diagnosed, nor can it be adjudicated. It permits no
final decision, but only a continual deciphering generating more ciphers. When
does randomness aggregate into conspiracy? Where does innocence shade to
guilt? What marks the fall from pure to applied? How does the local harbor its
own outside? Why does the impossible seem possible? How should one respond to the call of responsibility? When does one stop asking the unaskable?
And yet we have to find the keyword that opens and does not open.

* * *

The French poet and novelist Théophile Gautier coauthored the book for the
great classical ballet *Giselle,* inspired by Heinrich Heine's telling of the story
of the Wilis. The Wilis were girls "who were engaged to be married yet died
before their wedding days. . . . Endowed with unearthly gifts of movement,
their ghostly forms seemed never to touch the ground." The Wilis, both "real
and unreal at the same time," are among those entities with the qualities of the
uncanny or sublime: "The Wilis were so beautiful that it was simple for them
to attract young men into their midst. But they were as dangerous as they were
irresistible. They danced with the young men who came only to trap them: their
suitors were compelled to dance until they died" (Balanchine 1954, 194–95).[7]

* * *

Another mail delivery, more recent. An envelope arrives at ISIS, addressed to
Herbert Bernstein. The printed return address reads "Department of Defense,
National Security Agency," penned above in black ink, only what seems to be
a mail stop, "M322." The brown envelope is empty, there's nothing inside.

Notes

1. The *What's New* electronic newsletter is now archived on the Internet at http://
www.aps.org/WN/toc.html.

2. These topics are beyond the scope of this account.

3. On the most fortunate concept of "moral luck," see Williams 1981. As Spivak
points out, moral luck is "an after-the-fact assignment," a transmission from the future

to the past (1993, 296 n. 18). For another exposition on what it means to be "after-the-fact" in the pursuit of the sciences, see Fortun and Bernstein 1998.

4. The sole account of any length and detail remains Bamford 1982. See in particular pp. 344–49 for an account of the history of entanglement between the NSA and IBM, and how IBM turned a cipher system named "Lucifer" into the "Data Encryption Standard" (appropriately weakened to facilitate NSA eavesdropping) for all telecommunications.

5. My ascription of "nobility" to Forman's article is quite sincere. Forman's work and that of other historians, sociologists, and philosophers of science has been an enormously productive and important response to what Forman here calls the "inevitability" argument: that the development of physics follows an inevitable and internal logic, unaffected by funding sources or other external, "conspiratorial" forces. For an earlier attempt to locate the military conspiracy (or "legacy") in such a vein, see Fortun and Schweber 1993.

6. Aristotle was played by Matthew Malek, a Hampshire alum-to-be who was studying physics with Bernstein at the time.

7. Deep thanks to Laurel George for putting me in touch with these spirits.

References

Balanchine, George. 1954. *101 Stories of the Great Ballets.* Ed. Francis Mason. Garden City, N.J.: Doubleday.

Bamford, James. 1982. *The Puzzle Palace: A Report on America's Most Secret Agency.* New York: Houghton Mifflin.

Begley, Sharon. 1995. "Faster Than What?" *Newsweek,* 19 June, 67–69.

Bell, J. S. 1987. *Speakable and Unspeakable in Quantum Mechanics.* Cambridge: Cambridge University Press.

Bennett, Charles H., et al. 1993. "Teleporting an Unknown Quantum State via Dual Classical and EPR Channels." *Physical Review Letters* 70 (29 Mar.): 1895–99.

Blanchot, Maurice. 1986. *The Writing of the Disaster.* Trans. Ann Smock. Lincoln: University of Nebraska Press.

Bohr, Niels. 1950. "Open Letter to the United Nations." In *Niels Bohr: A Centenary Volume.* Ed. A. P. French and P. J. Kennedy. Cambridge, Mass.: Harvard University Press, 1985.

Derrida, Jacques. 1994. *Specters of Marx: The State of the Debt, the Work of Mourning, and the New International.* Trans. Peggy Kamuf. London: Routledge.

Forman, Paul. 1987. "Behind Quantum Electronics: National Security as Basis for Physical Research in the United States, 1940–1960." *Historical Studies in the Physical Sciences* 18:149–229.

Fortun, Michael, and Herbert J. Bernstein. 1998. *Muddling Through: Pursuing Science and Truth in the Twenty-First Century.* Washington, D.C.: Counterpoint Press.

Fortun, Michael, and Silvan S. Schweber. 1993. "Scientists and the Legacy of World War II: The Case of Operations Research." *Social Studies of Science* 23:595–642.

Gribbin, John. 1984. *In Search of Schrödinger's Cat.* New York: Bantam.

———. 1995. *Schrödinger's Kittens and the Search for Reality.* Boston: Little, Brown.

Hacking, Ian. 1986. "Weapons Research and the Form of Scientific Knowledge." *Canadian Journal of Philosophy,* suppl. vol. 12:237–60.

Lanouette, William. 1992. *Genius in the Shadows: A Biography of Leo Szilard.* With Bela Silard. New York: Scribner's.

Mermin, N. David. 1985. "A Bolt from the Blue: The E-P-R Paradox." In *Niels Bohr: A Centenary Volume.* Ed. A. P. French and P. J. Kennedy. Cambridge, Mass.: Harvard University Press.

Spivak, Gayatri Chakravorty. 1993. *Outside in the Teaching Machine.* New York: Routledge.

Williams, Bernard. 1981 *Moral Luck: Philosophical Papers 1973–1980.* Cambridge: Cambridge University Press.

The Detection and
Attribution of Conspiracies:
The Controversy Over Chapter 8

1988 was the year global warming hit the headlines in the United States, when atmospheric scientist Jim Hansen of NASA's Goddard Institute of Space Sciences testified before Congress asserting "99 percent" certainty that human emissions of greenhouse gases already were causing severe changes in the global climate. Other scientists were soon heard supporting his concern about potential future consequences, with statements to the effect that "the problems unaddressed have the potential of turning the world into a chaos not greatly different from that produced by global war" (Lawson 1990). Encouraged by the example of the 1987 Montreal Protocol to reduce global emissions of stratospheric ozone depleting chlorofluorocarbons, or CFCs, many concerned about global warming hoped to gain the same level of public and diplomatic support of action to reduce global emissions of greenhouse gases. The success of influential mainstream scientists in creating concern about the issue soon created a backlash among some scientists, politicians, and socioeconomic forces in U.S. society. The backlash comprises accusations concerning the motives of scientists and environmentalists stirring up public concern, and it has provoked a wealth of equally acrimonious counteraccusations, rendering the scientific controversy—the subject of this paper—bitter and rife with conspiracy theories.

As a result of concern about humans' possible "dangerous interference with the climate system," the United Nations Environmental Program and the World Meteorological Organization set up the International Panel on Climate Change (IPCC). Designed to assess the science of climate change, the IPCC provides the scientific reports informing international negotiations under the United Nations Framework Convention on Climate Change (FCCC) to reduce global emissions of greenhouse gases. The first (1990) IPCC report expressed concern but also uncertainty regarding the reality of human-induced climate change. It was thus a significant new development when the IPCC released their 1995 report (in June 1996), concluding that although observed temperature changes could be due to natural variability, "the balance of evidence suggests a discernible human influence on global climate" (Houghton et al. 1995). This conclusion led many environmental and political leaders, nationally and internationally, to call for controls on fossil fuel consumption in favor of renewable energy sources. The 1995 report was released one month before the first meeting in Geneva of the Conference of the Parties (CoP) under the FCCC to discuss international reductions in greenhouse-gas emissions. Key to the report was Chapter 8, which assessed the science seeking to detect changes in the climate record and to establish whether observed changes can be attributed to humans. The chapter concluded that a "human signal" in the climate record seemed to emerge with recent improvements in the understanding and simulation modeling of the climate system.

Then, on 12 June 1996, the month the IPCC report was issued, an op-ed letter appeared in the *Wall Street Journal* by Frederick Seitz, a now retired scientist with an impressive resumé, including past posts as president of the American Physical Society, president of Rockefeller University, and president of the National Academy of Sciences.

"A Major Deception on Global Warming," stated the large title of the letter. The letter concerned revisions to Chapter 8. Suggestive of his social concerns and values, Seitz feared that policymakers would act to reduce greenhouse-gas emissions based on the IPCC report, something he assumed to have "an enormous impact on U.S. oil and gas prices" and an "almost certainly destructive impact on the economies of the world." He wrote that like other IPCC reports, this latest report is held in high regard because it has been peer reviewed and approved by an international body of experts. But, he warned, things are not what they seem; there is a deception involved on the part of scientists who made final editing decisions of Chapter 8:

> this report is not what it appears to be—it is not the version that was approved by the contributing scientists listed on the title page. In my more than 60 years as a member of the American scientific community, including service as president of both the National Academy of Sciences and the American Physical Society, I have never witnessed a more disturbing corruption of the peer-review process than the events that led to this IPCC report. (Seitz 1996)

The IPCC is divided into a steering committee and three working groups dealing, respectively, with the science of climate change; impacts, adaptation, and mitigation of climate change; and economic and social implications and policy responses. Within each working group are "lead authors" of individual chapters, usually consisting of three or four scientists, plus a dozen or so contributing authors. The chapters are drafted, then sent out to be peer reviewed, a process involving scientists of varied persuasions and affiliations, including national research labs, industrial and environmental groups, governments, and universities. An estimated twenty-five hundred scientists worldwide were involved in the peer review of the 1995 report. The chapters and summaries constituting the report have to be approved at a final plenary meeting where all participants in the process—government organizations, industry groups, and nongovernmental organizations—interact with the scientists to forge the language by which to state current scientific knowledge of climate change. This is where the wording and general presentation of chapters and conclusions are decided on.

Governments participating in the IPCC process had accepted a draft of the chapter at a meeting in Madrid in November 1995, and all participants in the process had accepted the draft at the full plenary meeting in Rome the following month. Seitz wrote in his op-ed that the version agreed upon in Madrid "kept the participating scientists and the IPCC honest," but that this version was changed afterward, without proper authority; fifteen sections had been changed or deleted, he charged, with the effect "to deceive policy makers and the public into believing that the scientific evidence shows human activities are causing global warming." Seitz singled out the chapter's convening lead author, atmospheric scientist Benjamin Santer, as most likely responsible for the changes.

Seitz's charges of deception and conscious plotting for political gain provide a quick introduction to the style of argument that characterizes scientific controversy about climate change—a controversy taking place through the media and involving scientists but also environmental groups, politicians, conservative think tanks, fossil-fuel-related industries, and public-relations firms, among others. A majority of climate scientists express some degree of concern about the possibility of human-induced climate change, and no one disputes evidence that industrialization processes have increased atmospheric concentrations of the heat-trapping greenhouse gases. However, significant scientific disagreement exists concerning the consequences; to the extent that there's agreement that the net effect will be increases in global average temperatures, the size, timing, and impacts are subjects of debate. Seitz is among the scientific factions skeptical of the theory of human-induced climate change, and he is part of a subgroup among skeptical scientists I refer to as the "contrarians" due to their particularly staunch opposition to concern about human-induced climate change, as well as a list of other issues of environmental concern, such as the use of CFCs, the pesticide DDT, and nuclear technology. They have been unrelentingly active, vocal, and high-profile in their attacks of mainstream scientific pronouncements of increasing scientific certainty and concern about the possibility of human-induced climate change. As a result, contrarians have been extremely influential in the U.S., despite the fact that they constitute a group of less than ten in the U.S.

Most broadly, in this chapter, I will (1) show the pervasiveness of conspiracy theories in the debate about human-induced climate change, and (2) render evident the disconnect between such theories—with their suggestions of tightly organized, deliberate, and sinister acts of deception—and the actual complexity of actors and decisions that resulted in the revisions. I will show that the drafting of the report and editorial changes were made in a context of much less clarity and coherence, and with no clear acts of deliberate deception; it was, rather, a context characterized by imprecise and indeterminate knowledge, meaning, and rules, and involving inherently "messy" processes of negotiation of different possible representations, each involving different sets of interests and values. This study identifies among scientists and groups on both sides of this controversy a tendency noted by Richard Hofstadter in his writing on conspiracy theorizing and paranoia in American society:

> The typical procedure of the higher paranoid scholarship is to start with . . . defensible assumptions and with a careful accumulation of facts, or at least of what appear to be facts, and to marshal these facts toward an overwhelming "proof" of the particular conspiracy that is to be established. It is nothing if not coherent—in fact the paranoid mentality is far more coherent than the real world since it leaves no room for mistakes, failures, or ambiguities. (Hofstadter 1967, 36)

In addition to showing the assumptions of conspiracy, this case study shows the ease with which unverified claims and suggestions of conspiracy are disseminated among sympathetic audiences. I suggest some reasons why and how this happens and illustrate how claims or suggestions of wrongdoing are changed and even further exaggerated in the process of their dissemination.

The Marshall Institute

Seitz went straight to politicians and the media without consulting IPCC leaders and rules. Without specifying the source of his understanding of the IPCC rules, Seitz confidently stated in the op-ed that "nothing in the IPCC Rules permits anyone to change a scientific report after it has been accepted by the panel of scientific contributors and the full IPCC." He concluded that "if the IPCC is incapable of following its most basic procedures, it would be best to abandon the entire IPCC process, or at least that part that is concerned with the scientific evidence on climate change, and look for more reliable sources of advice to governments on this important question" (1996). To Seitz, a more reliable source would be the Marshall Institute, of which he is chairman. The Marshall Institute is a conservative Washington, D.C.-based think tank established in 1984 with the objective of influencing public opinion and policy in favor of unregulated free-market forces, national defense technology, and nuclear power (Fleagle 1994, 154; Gelbspan 1997, 52; Seitz 1994, 384). During the Reagan years, the Marshall Institute was concerned to promote Strategic Defense Initiative, also known as Star Wars. The institute has since turned its focus to environmental issues, forming perhaps the most influential—and certainly the most prestigious—faction among U.S. scientists skeptical of the theory of human-induced climate change. It is supported by "private donations," and forms part of the "conservative labyrinth" (Diamond 1995, 205) and "counterintelligentsia" built by political and economic elites in the U.S. since the 1970s in response to social changes, including antimilitarism, and environmentalism, affected by the rise of protest politics after 1968 (Fischer 1991; Ricci 1993). By the early 1980s the right wing had built a strong and broad network of foundations, corporate backers, and organizations, including military lobbies, electoral vehicles, media watchdogs, and campus outreach (Diamond 1995, 205).

The most high-profile Marshall Institute scientists are part of the generation of physicists traditionally privileged among U.S. scientists and politicians due to their importance for military defense during most of the twentieth century. Their status and influences waned some with the end of the cold war, but they formed an important source of scientific advice on the climate issue during the Bush administration. They also continue to influence important members of Congress, especially Republicans, including Dana Rohrabacher, chair of the Subcommittee on Science and Energy within the Science Committee, a Republican representative from California, and vocal critic of environmental regulation and global warming theories.

The Newness of the Process and Imprecise Rules

Traditional conceptions of the function and role of science as objective, establishing "truth," and able to bring order to political emotion and factionalism, were shattered in the "environmental era" by scientific controversies revealing disagreement within the scientific community (Hays 1987). Climate change is one of the new frontiers of science that environmentalism has pressed forward, and the ensuing debates to which these new frontiers generally have given rise has put intense pressures on the traditional methods of fashioning agreements—methods consisting in the give-and-take of open discussion in journals and meetings, and in more private interchanges in peer reviews of research proposals and results.

The IPCC represents an effort of cooperation and consensus formation unprecedented within the scientific community in terms of its size and scope, and pressures to form consensus position within the community are new to the climate change community as a whole; prior to the recent surge in concern about climate change, climate research was not associated with such urgency and policy relevance, and the impact of this change within the atmospheric sciences has been profound. An apparent result of the newness, large scope, and complexity of the IPCC process, the rules guiding the formation of the 1995 IPCC report were imprecise, sufficiently ambiguous to enable different persons to draw markedly divergent conclusions based on the same formulations. Seitz's charge that the editorial changes were unauthorized was not based on precise knowledge of the IPCC rules; the editorial revisions were neither in clear conformity with nor in violation of the rules, which simply weren't precise with regard to the point in the process after which authors must not make more editorial chanages. A certain confusion reigns among participants and critics of the IPCC process due to partial knowledge of existing rules, the imprecision of the actual rules and procedures guiding the process, and the almost overwhelming complexity of the processes, procedures, and competing claims involved.

The confusion is only heightened by the involvement of strong vested interests in the climate debate. For example, some fossil-fuel industry groups have created organizations and "front groups" with green sounding names and, sometimes, the appearance of being grassroots organizations, obscuring the fact that they are in fact established to counter environmental concerns. Oil and coal companies have spent millions of dollars to hire public relations groups to orchestrate such efforts as well as aggressive media campaigns seeking to undermine public concern about global warming (Gelbspan 1995; 1997). An early example of such campaigns was the Information Council for the Environment (ICE). Run by the Washington, D.C., public relations firm Bracy Williams and Company, ICE was established in 1991 by twenty-four coal companies, mining associations, and public-utility corporations at a time when legislation was being proposed to impose energy taxes and regulations on fossil-fuel use and industries. The explicit aim of ICE was to persuade the government and the public that global warming is a myth, and to thereby undermine conversion to less-polluting alternative energy sources. "If a slick ad campaign can cool Americans' enthusiasm for controls on greenhouse warming, stand by for a big chill," wrote *Science,* describing the scientific inaccuracies of the ICE ads (*Science* 1991). Upon further examination of the controversy over Chapter 8, it became clear that fossil-fuel industries also were involved in the creation of this controversy.

The Global Climate Coalition Report

In his op-ed letter, Frederick Seitz suggested that he had "witnessed" what he considered a "corruption" of the IPCC peer-review process. Though this wasn't clear from his letter, Seitz was not part of the IPCC process; he is not a climate scientist but a retired physicist whose scientific contribution has been mainly in the field of solid-state physics. Seitz himself learned of the charges from elsewhere; they had circulated in informal networks between scientists, industry groups, and politicians before their debut in the mainstream media with Seitz's op-ed letter in the *Wall Street Journal.*

I first learned of the charges two weeks prior to Seitz's letter when interviewing another Marshall Institute-affiliated scientist, physicist William Nierenberg, director emeritus of the Scripps Institute of Oceanography in California. Nierenberg was coauthor with Seitz and Robert Jastrow of a 1989 Marshall Institute report (Jastrow, Nierenberg, and Seitz 1990) that centrally informed the Bush administration's position on human-induced climate change (Rowlands 1995, 80). In his interview with me, Nierenberg referred to a document about the changes to the IPCC report that he had received through two different channels. He had not yet carefully read the document, but he relayed with confidence what had happened: the changes had been made by people in the highest echelons within the IPCC, without the knowledge and consultation of the lead authors of the chapter.

NIERENBERG: What it is, there is a chapter of which Tim Barnett, Wigley, Santer, and four or five others were authors, and about twelve people were advisors. It is a standard procedure. And what they were writing about was the detectability of—I forget the exact details about that chapter. And they finished it, and they sent it in. It had been reviewed, and so on. And the editors that finally put it together—they have done it before, but not in this way—they went ahead and edited it, to take out just about—I don't know how to put it; it just altered the *whole meaning* of the document. *Without* permission of the authors. In fact there is an editorial in the *Washington Times* about this. *[He finds the document, leafs through it]* They call it scientific cleansing now. It's got a new name.

LAHSEN: And the changes, you feel, really change [the meaning]?

NIERENBERG: Well *you* can decide. It's—*[scoffing laugh]* people think that it is just *outrageous!* What is more, it was done without—they are not grammatical changes—it was done, they never consulted the authors. Anything that would imply that the current status of knowledge is so poor that you can't do anything is struck out.

Nierenberg's rendition contradicted that of Seitz, who speculated that the convening lead author likely was responsible for the changes; by shifting the responsibility for the changes from the lead authors to unnamed and unknown people with no official editorial authority, Nierenberg added a new, more conspiratorial twist to the story. Nierenberg's rendition suggests the role of misunderstanding and misinformation in the dissemination of conspiracy theories surrounding Chapter 8. It also suggests the role of trust in the sources of information; how such charges of conspiracy can be accepted as valid and based on clear facts without being verified, as long as the source is trusted. When I asked who the report was by, Nierenberg suggested that that was irrelevant: "Oh—it just—it doesn't matter by whom! All they did was, they took the final report and compared it with what was sent in for publication."

The source of the charges, I later learned, was the Global Climate Coalition (GCC), a Washington, D.C.-based lobby group formed by about sixty companies and trade associations from energy and manufacturing sectors, including ARCO, Amoco, Texaco, Phillips Petroleum, BP America, Shell Oil, the National Coal Association, and the American Petroleum Institute. A GCC document, entitled "The IPCC: Institutionalized 'Scientific Cleansing,'" was sent to reporters, congressional representatives, the White House, and certain scientists. The document outlined the revisions and compared the draft of Chapter 8 that had been accepted in Madrid to the final, published version. Like Seitz, the GCC identified not unnamed high-ranking officials but the lead authors of the chapter as the ones most likely responsible for changes, similarly alleging that the changes were unauthorized and "politically motivated," intended to suppress scientific uncertainties and to thereby increase scientific support for attribution of changes in climate to human activities. As a lobby group for fossil-fuel industries, the GCC does not hide its resistance to greenhouse-gas emission reductions. Prior to the meeting of the Conference of the Parties (CoP) under the FCCC in Geneva, officials associated with the GCC publicly expressed concern that the 1995 IPCC report would result in regulations to reduce greenhouse-gas emissions from fossil-fuel combustion (Feder 1996).

Reflective of the role of trust and of convergence of views in the dissemination of conspiracy theories, the charges by the GCC traveled unchanged and unverified through politically conservative channels receptive to the GCC's antiregulatory, probusiness point of view, appearing in publications such as *Energy Daily* and the *Washington Times* (Wamsted 1996). The charges were given credibility without verification and without consultation of alternative sources for perspective, defense, or deeper knowledge about what happened and about the actual IPCC rules and procedures. Within a short period, other articles appeared in the fossil-fuel industry-underwritten *World Climate Report* (1996), in the *Financial Times, Energy,* and the *Economist* (Feder 1996). Articles about the controversy that did present alternative perspectives appeared in other publications, including *Science* (Weiss 1996), *Nature* (Masood 1996), *Physics Today* (Feder 1996), and the *New York Times* (Stevens 1996).

Mobilization of the Defense: Consequent Letters, e-mail, and Exchanges

The evening of 12 June, the day Seitz's op-ed appeared in the *Wall Street Journal,* convening lead author Benjamin Santer (of the Lawrence Livermore National Laboratory's Program for Climate Model Diagnosis and Intercomparison) sent out an e-mail message appraising some eighty-two colleagues around the world of the developing controversy and urging everyone to write letters of protest to the *Wall Street Journal* and *Energy Daily*. The defense machinery set into motion. The day following Seitz's op-ed, the Union of Concerned Scientists (UCS) distributed through their Sound Science Initiative (SSI) an e-mail message with the subject heading: "SSI Alert: IPCC under attack!" Describing the charges as an "extremely serious challenge to the integrity and credibility of the IPCC," the UCS message, like Chapter 8 convening lead author, Ben Santer, urged all recipients to write letters to the *Wall Street Journal*. They called upon everyone to monitor their local newspapers for other attacks on the IPCC and to respond to them in defense of the IPCC. The e-mail message asserted that Seitz's allegations were categorically false and that "there has been no politically-motivated doctoring of the IPCC report, and the [IPCC's] own procedural rules have not been violated." The UCS did not describe how it could ascertain the motives of the lead authors responsible for the changes. Moreover, again reflective of the role of social networks of trust in the circulation of information and of the potential for unchecked information to be widely distributed (this time on the side of "the defense"), the UCS message did not specify the source of its rendition of the IPCC rules. Yet it provoked a stream of letter writing.

Several scientists who wrote letters in defense of Ben Santer conceded, upon my questioning, that they had not checked the draft version against the published version to verify the nature of the changes, nor were they entirely clear as to the actual IPCC rules and procedures. Similar to Nierenberg on the side of the IPCC critics, many scientists supportive of the IPCC took their position in the controversy—and acted in the form of letter writing—primarily based on personal acquaintance with Ben Santer. Actors on both sides are often influenced by the mutual dislike and distrust that has built up since 1988 between the two opposing "camps" of scientists, organizations, and political actors and groups around the issue of human-induced climate change. Also shaping responses in support of Santer was the knowledge among scientists involved in drafting Chapter 8 that Ben Santer had fought during drafting sessions to retain passages emphasizing difficulties and uncertainties associated with detection and attribution of a human influence on observed temperature changes.

Official responses by IPCC scientists to the charges were soon published in *Energy Daily* (3 June) and in the *Wall Street Journal* (25 June). The 25 June issue of the *Wall Street Journal* included letters of response by Santer and thirty-nine other IPCC lead authors, plus a letter expressing full IPCC support of Santer's revisions by the top-ranking leaders of the IPCC: Bert Bolin, Sir John Houghton, and Luiz Gylvan Meira Filho. "No one could have been more thorough and honest in undertaking that task," they write, emphasizing that,

as the responsible officers of the IPCC, we are completely satisfied that the changes incorporated in the revised version were made with

the sole purpose of producing the best possible and most clearly explained assessment of the science and were not in any way motivated
by any political or other considerations. It is, of course, easy to take
isolated sentences from the earlier version that have been deleted or
replaced to bolster arguments or suspicions such as those presented
by Dr. Seitz. But that is to misunderstand the nature of the science
with which we are dealing and the very open IPCC scientific assessment process.

The officials do not specify what the nature of the science is, perhaps a way for
them to suggest that the science is sound *and* to suggest—without having to
expand on this—that the IPCC process also requires IPCC scientists to operate
in untraditional and, in the words of an IPCC scientist quoted below, in a
"slightly non-scientific mode."

According to the IPCC and associated scientists, the changes were authorized, the rules observed; the authors of Chapter 8 only acted as required by
making changes in response to written comments from scientists, governments,
and nongovernmental organizations (NGOs) before, during, and after the plenary meeting in Madrid. They also referred to the official demand of the United
States in a letter from the U.S. Department of State (dated 15 November 1995)
that IPCC chapters *not* be finalized prior to Madrid. The letter stressed that it
is "essential," and "in keeping with past practice . . . that chapters not be
finalized prior to the completion of discussions" at the IPCC plenary meeting
in Madrid, and that "chapter authors be prevailed upon to modify their text in
an appropriate manner following discussion in Madrid." It is unclear, however,
that a government can unilaterally dictate IPCC procedures.

The defense by Santer and other lead authors in the *Wall Street Journal*
(25 June) pointed out (correctly) that the changes did not alter the conclusion
of the report that "the balance of evidence suggests that there is a discernible
human influence on global climate," nor the conclusion of Chapter 8 that,
"taken together, these results point towards a human influence on climate";
both conclusions in the final report were entirely consistent with those in the
draft and were unanimously approved at the Madrid meeting by delegates from
nearly one hundred countries. Santer et al. stressed that uncertainties were not
deleted, which my analysis below confirms. They also pointed out that some
of the deletions were made in response to criticisms of "overlap" between
Chapter 8 and other chapters in the same report, an issue that was raised often
during the three drafting sessions prior to Madrid. The authors wrote that about
half of the information in the concluding summary was integrated with material
in another section within the chapter (section 8.6); the section containing the
passages declared by the GCC, Seitz, and others to have been deleted did not
disappear completely. I will return to this below, showing that the statements
Seitz highlighted as deleted indeed can be read into the last section of Chap-

ter 8. However, I will also point out that certain wording in the chapter did subtly change the presentation of the state of scientific knowledge concerning climate change. Rather than conspiracy, this highlights the unavoidable role of language, judgment, and representation in assessment reports of this nature, and the insensitivity to this on both sides of the controversy, at least in their official rhetoric. The question of bias aside, the difficulty of accounting for editorial changes in this kind of scientific assessment, involving fluid processes of judgment and negotiation of meaning, is already apparent.

Analysis of the Revisions

Seitz claims that widespread skepticism among scientists about the theory of human-induced climate change is reduced to mere "hints" already in the draft, with the final version deleting even these—in Seitz's view—too-faint expressions of uncertainty. Yet analysis of the revisions shows that the changes are not as dramatic as claimed by Seitz and the GCC, and that uncertainties are given substantial treatment throughout the chapter. Allegations that uncertainties were downplayed have to be considered in light of the chapter's actual detailed description of current limitations of the science of detection and attribution of climate change. Simply checking the table of contents of the chapter shows that mention and treatment of uncertainties were not deleted, nor even reduced to "hints"; two entire sections out of the six that make up the chapter address uncertainties. One is titled "Uncertainties in Model Projections of Anthropogenic Change," with the following subsections: "Errors in Simulating Current Climate in Uncoupled and Coupled Models," "Inadequate Representation of Feedbacks," "Flux Correction Problems," "Signal Estimation Problems," and " 'Missing Forcing' and Uncertainties in Space-Time Evolution of Forcing." The other section devoted to uncertainties is titled "Uncertainties in Estimating Natural Variability" and covers the difficulties of estimating natural variability based on instrumental data, paleoclimate records, and numerical computer models.

Analysis of the statements Seitz listed as deleted shows that the deletions were not as clear-cut or complete as he and others suggested. All three examples provided by Seitz to suggest deletions and deception can be found in, or inferred from, different sections in the final version. Whether the sentences in the final version form a satisfactory equivalent is open to interpretation, however. Seitz offered the following examples of deleted sentences to make his strong allegations of wrongdoing and deception:

- None of the studies cited above has shown clear evidence that we can attribute the observed (climate) changes to the specific cause of increases in greenhouse gases.

- No study to date has positively attributed all or part (of the climate change observed to date) to anthropogenic (human-made) causes.

- Any claims of positive detection of significant climate change are likely to remain controversial until uncertainties in the total natural variability of the climate system are reduced.

Though Seitz provides no examples of sentences possibly replacing the deleted sentences, such examples can be found in the final version, including this statement: "Finally, we come to the difficult question of when the detection and attribution of human-induced climate change is likely to occur. The answer to this question must be subjective, particularly in the light of the large signal and noise uncertainties discussed in this chapter."

The recognition that there are only "subjective" answers to "the difficult question of when the detection and attribution of human-induced climate change is likely to occur" implies that there is no conclusive evidence linking observed climate changes to human activities. The references in Seitz's examples of deleted sentences to lacking conclusive evidence—"None of the studies cited above has shown clear evidence;" "No study to date has positively attributed all or part;" and "Any claims of positive detection of significant climate change are likely to remain controversial"—are also arguably summed up in a sentence in the final version not quoted by Seitz that "few would be willing to argue that *completely unambiguous* attribution of (all or part of) this change has already occurred." (Seitz 1996)

The following example also shows that substantive changes to the chapter are not demonstrated through Seitz's examples of deleted sentences. The final version included this segment: "Some scientists maintain that these uncertainties currently preclude any answer to the questions posed above. Other scientists would and have claimed, on the basis of the statistical results presented in Section 8.4, that confident detection of a significant anthropogenic climate change has already occurred" (Houghton et al. 1995, 439). Ending the quote here, one could arguably consider the division of views represented (that is, into those held by "some" versus "other scientists") to be potentially manipulative, failing to specify the relative representativeness of the different views. It would have shifted the emphasis from the strong statements listed as deleted by Seitz ("No study to date has positively attributed all or part;" etc.) to sentences that might give the false impression that as many scientists maintain that confident detection of human-induced climate change has been made as maintain that it hasn't. This would have been problematic, since very few scientists consider human-induced climate change to have been detected unambiguously; the only claim to that effect I know of was made by Thomas Wigley in a quote in *Nature* described further below (Masood 1995). Even the studies that have come out with the greatest statements of confidence about having detected a human influence on the climate have not been unequivocal; for example, the statistical study by Hasselman et al. (1995) found the human signal in the climate record with 95 percent certainty—which still leaves a possibility of being wrong.

But the chapter doesn't end on the "some vs. others" argument; it goes on to acknowledge precisely this—that "few would be willing to argue that *completely unambiguous* attribution of (all or part of) this change has already occurred, or was likely to happen in the next few years."

There are, however, some subtle shifts in meaning between the draft and the final version. The word *completely* in the above sentence tilts the interpretation toward attribution rather than away from it. Had it been left out, leaving only "few would be willing to argue that unambiguous attribution of (all or part of) this change has already occurred," it would have incorporated the opinions of more atmospheric scientists.

The editorial changes arguably resulted in other subtle shifts in meaning. For example, the change from "we do not know" when unambiguous detection and attribution might occur to "the answer must be subjective" changes the assertion of unanimous recognition of uncertainty to simply describing this point as debatable. That can be taken to suggest that some scientists do claim to know. In e-mail correspondence responding to the charges of wrongdoing, one lead author explained that the replacement of "we do not know" with "the answer must be subjective" was made in response to criticism during the plenary meetings of the "we do not know" statement. Once again, it is very difficult for outsiders to know whether this is true. The importance of personal judgment in deciding whether these editorial changes are satisfactory should be clear to readers, along with the difficulty for outsiders to know whether the changes were or were not justified by the input received at the plenary meetings.

Of importance for this analysis is recognition of the subtlety of the changes in meaning resulting from the revisions—whether or not the revisions are perceived to be justified, which remains open to interpretation. The subtle changes between the draft and final version of Chapter 8—at least some of which might have been made in response to the criticism and peer review built into the IPCC process—constitute the foundation from which the critics derived their strident claims of "scientific cleansing" [1] and "major deception" on the part of IPCC affiliated scientists and bureaucrats. Hofstadter has written, "If for every error . . . one can substitute an act of treason, we can see how many points of fascinating interpretation are open to the paranoid imagination: treason in high places can be found at almost every turning" (Hofstadter 1967, 25). *Error* in Hofstadter's quote might in this case be replaced by "subtle editorial change."

Industry Involvement: IPCC Reports' Multiple Influences

Critics tend to represent the IPCC reports as one-sided documents with an environmentalist activist point of view excluding contesting perspectives and interests, but the reports involve significant ambiguity. In her study of the IPCC, political scientist Sonja Boehmer-Christiansen refers to the reports' summaries as "skillful exercises in scientific ambiguity" using "language which simultaneously allowed Greenpeace to call for a target of reducing emissions by 60 percent, and the UK Treasury to conclude that no action was needed until more scientific certainty was available—each citing the same source" (1944, 402) Also left out of contrarian renditions in the Chapter 8 controversy is the significant role of fossil-fuel industries among other antigreenhouse interests in the drafting of the reports and the fact that concessions also are made by groups who would like the wording to be more forceful.

Ben Santer commented on the role of such interests in drafting of Chapter 8:

> We tried to represent the science in an accurate and balanced way. We did not shout, "Eureka! We have found the answer!" It became evident during the course of our work on Chapter 8 that powerful interests were intent on skewing the "balance" of the chapter, and on accentuating the uncertainties rather than what we had learned in the past five years. Such interests would have preferred us to attach three or four caveats to each statement documenting progress in our field. An extreme case of this was the view expounded at Madrid that there were no scientific bases for any statement made in Chapter 8, and that the entire chapter should have been deleted.[2]

The important role of fossil-fuel interests in shaping the report is also described in a *Nature* article about how Kuwait and Saudi Arabia, with clear interests against curbing fossil-fuel consumption, held up the three-day IPCC meeting in Madrid. They insisted on modification of the report's conclusion that "the balance of evidence suggests that there is a discernible human influence on the global climate," and that the evidence of detection and attribution of a human influence on climate be described as more uncertain than suggested by the draft. Suggestive of the importance of words and representation in the IPCC process, they based their argument in part on the word *preliminary* used in Chapter 8 to describe new climate model-based evidence important for the chapter's conclusions, interpreting this word as suggesting more uncertainty than reflected in the concluding statements. Thomas Wigley, a lead author of the chapter, later objected to the two countries' take on that word: "This word," he is quoted as saying in *Nature*, "implies that evidence for a human effect on climate change is initial, but clear and unambiguous. It does not mean that evidence of human influence on global climate is uncertain. We did not realize how this word could be misinterpreted" (Masood 1995). Due to loss of time resulting from such resistance at the plenary meeting, entire sections of the report, though published, remained unapproved and hence less authoritative.

In a document distributed through e-mail, Greenpeace complained that these same delegates worked to "weaken" or "over-qualify" many of the IPCC conclusions. One of the examples it provides concerns the overall IPCC 1995 conclusion:

> Industry attacked [Chapter 8] all the way through the review process and then at the IPCC plenary. Without those attacks the conclusion would have been stronger, not weaker, as industry alleges. The conclusion that "the balance of evidence suggests a discernible human influence on global climate" was adopted under extreme duress at the Madrid IPCC plenary, with Saudi Arabia threatening to block the meeting and with only a few hours time left to complete the adoption of the IPCC report. The lead authors present wanted words that were significantly stronger: "The weight of evidence [strongly] indicates a significant human influence in global climate." At least one wanted the word "strongly" inserted. Lead authors were increasingly sidelined during the final stage of the negotiation over the summary. Their preferred version clearly conveys more force than the finally agreed-upon text, which was very much a compromise pulled together at the last minute.

The Charges are Repeated and Increased

The IPCC responses in the *Wall Street Journal* provoked another set of letters on 11 July by Seitz and Fred Singer and Hugh Ellsaesser, two other contrarian scientists, repeating the charges and furthering the theme of secret, self-interested plotting and mystery. Singer is a solar physicist who designed the first satellite instrument for measuring atmospheric ozone. Besides several professorships, Singer has held positions with the U.S. Department of Transportation and Environmental Protection Agency. He abandoned such positions to establish—with mainly private donations—the Science and Environmental Policy Project (SEPP), over which he presides. Concerned to disseminate his views, Singer, like other contrarians, has established ties with groups of the political and religious Right in U.S. society. Singer has received material support from a conservative religious group led by Reverend Sun Yung Moon (Deal 1992, 89) which since the early 1980s has worked to build organizations promoting far right-wing politics. He has become a key organizer for scientists skeptical of the theory of human-induced climate change, often orchestrating letter-writing and petition campaigns against remedial action on behalf of human-induced climate change. Hugh Ellsaesser is now a retired meteorologist and guest scientist at California's Lawrence Livermore National Laboratory (LLNL). He is isolated at LLNL, where he occupies an office in a trailer all by himself, immediately behind the trailer shared by Ben Santer and dozens of other atmospheric scientists. Communication between the two trailers has broken down and now takes place mainly through letter writing in major newspapers and journals.

In this second letter, Seitz repeats his allegation that the changes were unauthorized and suggests again that the IPCC is not to be trusted by the government. He writes:

> Of course [IPCC procedures require changes in response to comments], but not after the governments have accepted the final draft. The fact is that someone connnected with the presentation of the published version, presumably Dr. Santer and others, rewrote basic technical material in Chapter 8 with the result that scientific doubts about man-made global warming were suppressed.

With the vague "someone connected with," Seitz evokes conspiracy through the theme of not knowing precisely who made the changes. And he repeats his pitch for alternative scientific authorities on the issue: "Clearly, governments will have to look elsewhere than the IPCC for sound science on climate change."

Singer's letter contains even stronger suggestions of secretive plotting and corruption, with the words "revealed" (that is, something was hidden) and "tampered with for political purposes" in the introductory sentence, simultaneously bolstering Seitz's scientific authority: "Dr. Seitz, former president of the U.S. National Academy of Sciences, has revealed that a UN-sponsored scientific report promoting global warming has been tampered with for political purposes." Evoking detective imagery, Singer delineates the time frame within which the act of changing the chapter had taken place: "A crucial chapter of the IPCC's report was altered between the time of its formal acceptance and its printing." The theme of not knowing is evoked again when Singer makes a point of the fact that IPCC officials mentioned in a *Nature* article about the controversy (*Nature* 1996) were "quoted (but not named)." At the time of his letter, official responses by *named* IPCC officials had already appeared in the *Wall Street Journal* and elsewhere, rendering unnecessary his reference to "unnamed" IPCC officials, which works to further envelop the IPCC in an aura of secrecy and unaccountability. A similar suggestion of inherent untrustworthiness of the IPCC is made when Singer calls IPCC officials' denial of wrongdoing "predictable," implying that the IPCC can be expected to put up a front of denial in the face of such charges: "Predictably, there have been protests from officials of the IPCC, claiming that the revisions in their report, prior to its publication, did nothing to change its emphasis. They also claim that such unannounced changes of an approved draft do not violate their rules of transparency and open review."

The words *claim* and *unannounced* similarly cast doubt on the reliability and transparency of IPCC officials' statements and actions. Yet the rules do not specify that all editorial changes have to be "announced."

Both Seitz and Singer emphasize the point that the chapter was altered. Seitz calls the changes "unauthorized," considering his initial editorial letter to have presented "facts" indicating that Ben Santer "and possibly others" made "major unauthorized changes" to the chapter. Importantly, and by contrast, Singer acknowledges that it is unclear whether the changes were or were not in accord with IPCC rules, but then quotes a *Nature* article (1996) about the controversy which wrote that "there is some evidence that the revision process did result in a subtle shift . . . that . . . tended to favor arguments that aligned with the report's broad conclusions." Singer's recognition that the changes might be in accordance with the rules is likely lost on most readers, however, surrounded as it is by suggestions of wrongdoing. Thus, immediately following this recognition, Singer proceeds with more of the same subtle but pervasive accusatory rhetoric, suggesting secrecy, conspiracy, and repression; he calls the IPCC summary a "political document" that is "economical with the truth" and that "has problems with selective presentation of facts."

Singer's criticism of the IPCC's presentation of facts suggests that *unselective* presentation of facts is possible; in reality it is the nature of representations to select and highlight certain things over others, and particularly so when what is requested in this interface between science and policymaking is an *assessment* of the science, an evaluation, that is, which by nature involves judgment and selection. The following excerpt from an interview with one of Chapter 8's lead authors reveals the considerations and difficulties that are part of drafting the IPCC reports. The lead author conceded in a personal interview the difficulty of the science-policy interface:

> this is meant to be not a review of the science but an assessment of the science, and the audience is the policymaking audience, so it is a case where an international group of scientists is operating in a slightly nonscientific mode. And most of the people are not experts in communicating scientific knowledge or scientific uncertainty in a way that can be understood by policymakers or policy advisors. So, boy, the number of reiterations that individual sentences can go through in order to express a particular concept in a way that doesn't overstate but doesn't totally diffuse the issue by stressing the uncertainty. It is a very difficult road to tread, I think. What policymakers want to know is, Have we detected the greenhouse effect or haven't we? Black or white. But it is not black-and-white. So it is very difficult to word an assessment of the problem in a way that will provide useful

information to the people who need the information without completely discrediting the scientific approach to the problem.

IPCC officials' defense above that the final version of Chapter 8 represented
"the best possible" and "most clearly explained" assessment of the science,
and that the changes "were not in any way motivated by any political or other
considerations," is not directly contradicted by this lead author's articulation.
Their defense does, however, reveal a lack of self-reflexivity and recognition
of the role of interpretation, judgment, and of extrascientific considerations in
representations of climate change research. Recognition of the role of such
factors in this fierce political debate is rare, and individual scientists who have
acknowledged the role of values and beliefs in their scientific positions have
subsequently suffered attacks on their scientific authority by opponents wanting to subsequently discredit them as too biased to offer credible scientific input on the subject.

Suggestions of Political Repression Connect with the Right

Themes of political repression and even of totalitarianism are evoked by the
above critics of the IPCC through references to "unauthorized" deletions,
"suppression of dissent," "political manipulation," "scientific cleansing," and
the like, furthering suggestions of deliberate and organized plotting, intimidation, and abuse of power. These themes also constitute a shared discourse between contrarians and right-wing groups in U.S. society.

The theme of political repression is evoked repeatedly in Singer's letter, as
in his reference to the IPCC's "selective representation of facts" and his claim
that "politicians and activists striving for international controls on energy use
(to be discussed in Geneva in July when the parties to the Global Climate
Treaty convene) are . . . trying to marginalize the growing number of scientific
critics." It is not clear that the number of critics is either growing or diminishing, but describing the momentum behind opponent groups as diminishing in
size—and implying the force and numbers behind their own position to be
growing—has obvious rhetorical gain. This strategy is found on both sides, as
are suggestions of marginalization and even persecution; in the quote included
above, Greenpeace described the Chapter 8 lead authors as "sidelined" at the
Madrid meeting by industry lobbyists bent on weakening the IPCC report's
conclusions. The large number of scientists involved in the IPCC, and the increasing confidence of the conclusions of their reports concerning detection of
a human influence on climate, is often presented as illustrative of a growing
consensus among scientists. Thus a June 1996 editorial in *Nature* characterized
the contrarians as "a dwindling band of skeptics," asserting "growing support
within the scientific community" for the IPCC view that "the balance of evidence suggests a discernible human influence on global climate" (*Nature*

1996). Of course, consensus knowledge is not immune to error, and it can discourage or deemphasize articulations and knowledge of alternative views.[3] Even so, it requires perceptions of organized and sinister plotting on the part of a coherent group to perceive such processes as due to conspiracies rather than the diffuse working of multiple, ad hoc social processes and interests; as Hofstadter writes, conspiracy theories exceed the real world in their coherence, leaving little room for mistakes, failures, or ambiguities (1967, 36).

Each side in this controversy has its martyrs. Santer is described among IPCC scientists and supporters as victimized by the critics' charges of professional irresponsibility and violation of procedural rules, at great personal and possibly professional cost. In contrarian renditions, the alleged political repression by the establishment is painted as a defensiveness that becomes increasingly oppressive as the oppositon to its "regime" supposedly mounts. Discourses by contrarians and their supporters frequently describe dissenters of the dominant view as righteous victims persecuted by powerful, repressive forces. (For examples, of this pervasive tendency, see the *Wall Street Journal* editorial [Jenkins 1993] as well as Singer's 11 July letter described here, both of which also manifest anticommunist rhetoric. With the decline of the cold war, actors from the Right have shifted their focus to environmentalist activists, identifying the former reds in the greens. Thus the late *Forbes* writer Warren Brooke, whose 1989 article was part of launching the backlash to scientific and public concern about climate change, wrote that "just as Marxism is giving way to markets, the political 'greens' seem determined to put the world economy back into the red, using the greenhouse effect to stop unfettered market-based economic expansion" (Brooke 1989, 97). Singer's suggestions of conspiracy graduate into theories in other writings, where his strong anti-regulatory views are expressed with anticommunist rhetoric. For example, in a piece called "Global Warming: Do We Know Enough to Act?" Singer writes on the "hidden-agenda problem," asking,

> Why do so many different groups focus on greenhouse warming? Because the issue provides a wonderful excuse for doing things that they already want to do, under the guise of saving the planet. . . . More dangerous are those who have a hidden political agenda, most often oriented against business, the free market, and the capitalistic system. Of course, after the collapse of socialism in Eastern Europe it is no longer fashionable to argue for state ownership of industrial concerns. The alternative is to control private firms by regulating every step of every manufacturing process.

Singer then mentions those using global warming as a vehicle for international action, "preferably with lots of treaties and protocols to control CO_2 or perhaps even methane," or who view the issue as "a launch platform for an ambitious foreign aid program" (1991, 45–46). Singer sees the IPCC as an institution aiding such efforts, and he has suggested elsewhere that climate change is a plot by "Third World kleptocrats" to find new excuses to demand money from the West (1992). More details outlining how such leaders of less developed countries have managed to enlist the international community of scientists.

The letter by Hugh Ellsaesser similarly exhibits the tendency of assuming great orchestrating powers on the part of opponents. Adding his own twist to the story, Ellsaesser considers the whole controversy around Chapter 8 unfortunate and attributes it to the manipulating powers of the opponents; Ellsaesser suggests that the controversy was masterminded by IPCC scientists and supporters through conscious plotting by which to divert attention from the weak basis for their conclusions regarding climate change: "By concentrating on IPCC rules and procedures, IPCC writers and supporters *have managed* to avoid the more important scientific debate as to whether 'the balance of evidence suggests that there is a discernible human influence on global climate' " (Ellsaesser 1995; emphasis added). Ellsaesser does not specify how IPCC writers and supporters masterminded the GCC's charges.

Like other contrarians, Ellsaesser has established ties with right-wing political groups; for example, he has associated with *21st Century,* a magazine by followers of Lyndon LaRouche, his name appearing on the list of fifteen people comprising the scientific advisory board. *21st Century* has published a number of articles by Ellsaesser,[4] including at least one specifically criticizing the IPCC (1995). As Chris Toumey has described, LaRouche's ideology is strongly conspiratorial, believing the world is threatened by evil orchestrated by, among others, the London Financial Center, the Swiss and Venetian insurance cartels, the Soviet and U.S. governments, the Anti-Defamation League, Jesuits, European royalty, Socialist International, and communism generally (Toumey 1996, 85). In their publications, including a report titled *The Greenhouse Effect Hoax: A World Federalist Plot,* LaRouchies express their belief that the greenhouse theory is a plot by the above groups, centrally orchestrated by British royalty and communist forces, who, by means of the UN and environmentalist dogma, infiltrate and undermine the United States (Executive Intelligence Review 1989).

While there are significant discursive convergences between contrarians and political groups such as the ones described here, it is important to not simplistically lump together scientists like Singer and Ellsaesser. For example, in a November 1996 interview with me, Ellsaesser himself expressed that although he "occasionally contacts them and sends them his papers when he comes up with them," he is "not too sympathetic with a lot of the ideas LaRouche has." There are also instances where scientists do not realize or care to probe the points of views of particular groups soliciting their expert advice, sometimes simply reflective of the tendency for scientists to blind themselves to the "hermeneutic larceny" and cultural turmoil surrounding science in society (Toumey 1996, 161, 164). For the purposes of this essay, the point of noting these connections is to show how contrarian suggestions of deception and conspiracy are amplified by political groups with even greater inclinations toward conspiracy theorizing.

Contrarians often explain their associations with extrascientific groups by means of their marginalization by the mainstream scientific community, and by what they portray as suppression of dissenting views. Exhibiting worldviews largely challenged by those shaped by the protest politics of the 1960s and 1970s, contrarians find themselves increasingly alienated from society, an alienation manifest in their opposition to main tenets of present-day environmentalist beliefs, which they consider economically dangerous and rooted in incomplete scientific understanding and irrational emotionalism (see for example Seitz 1997 and contributors to Lehr 1992). According to Hofstadter, perceptions of marginalization heighten tendencies to perceive social and political processes as conspiracies:

> The situation becomes worse when the representatives of a particular interest—perhaps because of the very unrealistic and unrealizable nature of their demands—cannot make themselves felt in the political process. Feeling that they have no access to political bargaining or the making of decisions, they find their original conception of the world of power as omnipotent, sinister, and malicious fully confirmed. They see only the consequences of power—and this through distorting lenses—and have little chance to observe its actual machinery. (1967, 39–40)

Seitz's charges of deception might thus in part reflect the fact that he was not part of the IPCC meetings, "witnessing" the process only indirectly and through the mediation of accounts by the GCC and other interested parties. Despite their strong influence outside the scientific community, signs of disempowerment pervade contrarian discourses, a reflection of their marginalization by mainstream scientists, many of whom deny contrarians scientific authority on the issue of climate change and care little to engage with them in discussion.

Suggestions of conspiracy is also occasionally found among IPCC affiliated or sympathetic scientists, as in the following e-mail message circulated at a U.S. climate research lab: "Ironically, the people who are conducting these attacks and accuse the scientific community of belonging to some sort of 'global conspiracy' are themselves part of a conspiracy, funded by the oil and coal industry, to discredit any scientist or piece of evidence that supports the hypothesis that humans are causing a detectable change to global climate." Conspiracy theorizing on the IPCC side of the issue is perhaps most obvious in the discourses of environmental activists. Greenpeace, for example, suggests that the critics actually believe that scientific evidence proves the reality of dangerous human-induced climate change. "Greenpeace believes that this is a *deliberate and blunt attempt to distort* the nature of the climate threat. The evident intention is to force policy-makers to ignore the science, and disagree over CO_2 emissions reductions" (Greenpeace 1996; emphasis added). By contrast, my research suggests that critics of the theory of human-induced climate change sincerely believe that there is no demonstrated scientific basis for current concern about the issue.

Finally, with regard to several of the assertions of conspiracy by scientists on both sides discussed above, including that by Singer concerning other political agendas at work (since environmentalists undeniably would like to see pollution reduced, regardless of global warming) and the one immediately above by Greenpeace (given my earlier description of industry creation of green sounding "front groups" and questionable ad campaigns),[5] one might mark Hofstadter's words that

> paranoid reasoning begins with certain defensible judgments, and nothing entirely prevents a sound program or a sound issue from being advocated in the paranoid style. . . . What distinguishes the paranoid style is not, then, the absence of verifiable facts (though it is occasionally true that in his extravagant passion for facts the paranoid occasionally manufactures them), but rather the curious leap in imagination that is always made at some critical point in the recital of events. (1967, 37)

Ellsaesser's argument that IPCC scientists and supporters orchestrated this controversy to divert attention from uncertainties in the science is the mirror opposite of that found on the other side of the controversy; here accusations suggest that the GCC and Seitz et al. raised this entire controversy to "divert attention" from the strong conclusion of this new report that the evidence suggests that humans are changing the climate. These arguments by both sides can be read as conspiratorial, with their attributions of deliberate plotting for political gain on the part of their opponents. From another vantage point, these arguments are little more than legitimate political differences expressed through conspiratorial rhetoric—easy point-scoring, based on apparently heartfelt disagreement and dislike.

Whether meant seriously or simply used as means of achieving political gain, attributions of conspiracy are unhelpful for constructive discussion about the state of scientific knowledge about climate change and about possible "no-regrets" policy action (policy responses related to energy consumption that have environmental and economic benefits aside from reducing the potential risk of global warming). The vilification inherent in such attributions of sinister motives rarely resonates with the self-perceptions and intents of the accused, and hence further polarizes the groups involved in this already frequently antagonistic debate. One lesson to draw from this case study is the care with which charges of conspiracy must be received and their factual basis examined for assumptions of sinister plotting applied to a reality of much more complexity and much less coherence. Charges and suggestions of conspiracy spread with little resistance among sympathetic audiences in a social and scientific context characterized by uncertainty, fragmentation, complexity, and competing interests; who was who, and who said or provoked what and with what authority and expertise, is not always easily established. As a result, most controversies around human-induced climate change—including this one concerning Chapter 8—remain unresolved, competing claims rarely verified but allowed to fester, with the general effect of reinforcing preconceived suspicions and positions.

The influence of the conflicting claims around this and other controversies concerning human-induced climate change is not easily measured. The GCC originally called for an investigation into the propriety of the revisions, as did Singer in a 9 August letter addressed to all recipients of Santer's informal e-mail messages concerning the controversy. Dana Rohrabacher, Republican chairman of the House Subcommittee on Energy and Environment, initiated an investigation into the extent to which U.S. scientists within the Department of Energy have spent time and resources on the IPCC process. The controversy fit his view of climate change research as a "liberal claptrap" and his anti-regulatory values. However, none of the above were followed up by significant action, and the charges against the IPCC did not surface significantly outside of the U.S., where the report heightened concern about climate change. Several Global Climate Coalition member companies, including British Petroleum left the GCC immediately after the Chapter 8 controversy, apparently because they disagreed with the GCC actions surrounding it. But the GCC claims that other industries joined as a result, so the net effect in terms of the organization, force, and strategies of fossil-fuel-industry lobbying efforts is unclear.

The charges did not appear to influence the Clinton administration, at least not in an immediately obvious way. The Clinton administration strongly supported the 1995 IPCC report and now considers global warming "no longer a theory" but a "fact" (U.S. Government 1997), a sufficient basis for policy action. However, Clinton's Climate Action Plan presented at the FCCC meeting in Kyoto in December 1997 was sharply criticized by European leaders as too weak (Stevens 1997), and the relative modesty of the U.S. commitment to reduce its greenhouse-gas emissions are often attributed to the existence of strong industry pressure in the U.S. against such reductions.[6]

As we have seen, conspiracy theories in this study span a full range of uses. Moving away from the political fringes of the U.S. political landscape occupied by groups such as the followers of Lyndon Larouche, conspiracy theories amount to little more than rhetorical means by which to cast suspicion on scientific and political opponents; they constitute one tactic among many at play between conflicting interests and views concerning what kind of society and future is wanted, a simple strategy by which to advance interests, including environmentalism, unregulated capitalism, and partisan politics.

Notes

1. The charges were advanced during the height of the "ethnic cleansing" in former Yugoslavia, creating a discursive link between those atrocities and the revisions to Chapter 8.

2. E-mail communication with colleagues.

3. See Fuller (1988, 214) about the "spiral of silence" possible in "suboptimal essential consensus" when those who either disagree with a standing belief or have no strong views simply remain silent. The IPCC forms a suboptimal essential consensus insofar as each member of the group does not know the justificatory standards and current beliefs of all other experts and members of the IPCC.

4. Source: Hugh Ellsaesser, Nov. 1996 interview.

5. For example, the above mentioned ICE campaign included ads asserting that the theory of human-induced climate change was proven wrong by local instances of colder than usual temperatures. The big print of one ad read: "Some scientists say the earth's temperature is rising. They say that catastrophic global warming will take place in the years ahead; Yet, average temperature records show Minneapolis has actually gotten colder over the past 50 years. . . . Facts like these simply don't jibe with the theory that catastrophic global warming is taking place." Yet, as also explained by the above-mentioned *Science* article on the subject, scientific arguments supportive of the theory of human-induced climate change hold that temperatures in any one place have little bearing on the global-warming question, rises in the average global temperature believed likely to simultaneously involve local instances of average cooling.

6. Both President Clinton and Vice President Gore have modified their public statements of commitment to strong preventive action on the issue. See media analyses (Birnbaum 1997) of Al Gore's attempt to appease both environmentalists and industrialists around the Kyoto meeting and his more moderate statements at the Kyoto meeting compared with statements in his book (Gore 1992).

References

Birnbaum, Jeffrey H. 1997. "A Cloud on Gore's Horizon." *Fortune,* 8 Dec., 122.

Boehmer-Christiansen, Sonja. 1994. "A Scientific Agenda for Climate Policy?" *Nature* 372 (1 Dec.): 400–402.

Brookes, Warren. 1989. "The Global Warming Panic." *Forbes,* 25 Dec., 96–102.

Deal, Carl. 1992. *The Greenpeace Guide to Anti-Environmental Organizations.* Berkeley, Calif.: Odonian Press.

Diamond, Sara. 1995. *Roads to Domination.* New York: Guilford Press.

Ellsaesser, Hugh W. 1995. "An Open Letter to the IPCC." *21st Century.* Summer.

Executive Intelligence Review. 1989. *The Greenhouse Effect Hoax.* Washington, D.C.: Executive Intelligence Review.

Feder, Toni. 1996. "Attacks on IPCC Report Heat Controversy Over Global Warming." *Physics Today* (Aug.): 55–57.

Fischer, Frank. 1991. "American Think Tanks: Policy Elites and the Politicization of Expertise." *Governance* 4(3): 332–53.

Fleagle, Robert G. 1994. *Global Environmental Change.* Westport, Conn. Praeger.

Fuller, Steve. 1988. *Social Epistemology.* Bloomington: Indiana University Press.

Gelbspan, Ross. 1997. *The Heat Is On.* New York: Addison-Wesley.

———. 1995. "The Heat Is On." *Harper's,* Dec.

Gore, Al. 1992. *Earth in the Balance.* Boston: Houghton Mifflin.

Greenpeace. 1996. *The Scourge of the Skeptics: Industry Attacks on the IPCC Second Assessment Report.* E-mail, July 1996.

Hasselmann, K., L. Bengtsson, U. Cubasch, G. C. Hegerl, H. Rodhe, E. Roeckner, H. V. Storch, and R. Voss. 1995. *Detection of Anthropogenic Climate Change Using a Fingerprint Method.* Vol. 168. Max Planck Institut fur Meteorologie.

Hays, Samuel, P. 1987. *Beauty, Health and Permanence.* Cambridge: Cambridge University Press.

Hofstadter, Richard. 1967. *The Paranoid Style in American Politics and Other Essays.* New York: Random House.

Houghton, J. T., L. G. Meira Filho, B. A. Collander, N. Haris, A. Kattenberg, and K. Maskell, eds. 1995. "Climate Change 1995." In *Contribution of Working Group I to the Second Assessment Report of the Intergovernmental Panel on Climate Change.* Cambridge: Cambridge University Press.

Jastrow, Robert, William Nierenberg, and Frederick Seitz. 1990. *Scientific Perspectives on the Greenhouse Problem.* Ottawa, Ill.: Jameson Books.

Jenkins, Holman, Jr. 1993. "Al Gore Leads a Purge." *Wall Street Journal.* 25 May.

Lawson, Hilary. 1990. *The Greenhouse Conspiracy.* BBC, channel 4.

Lehr, Jay H., ed. 1992. *Rational Readings on Environmental Concerns.* New York: Van Nostrand Reinhold.

Masood, Ehsan. 1996. "Sparks Fly Over Climate Report." *Nature* 381 (20 June): 639.

———. 1995. "Climate Panel Confirms Human Role in Warming, Fights Off Oil States." *Nature* 378 (7): 524.

Nature. 1996. "Climate Debate Must not Overheat." *Nature* (13 June): 539.

Ricci, David M. 1993. *The Transformation of American Politics: The New Washington and the Rise of Think Tanks.* New Haven, Conn.: Yale University Press.

Rowlands, Ian. 1995. *The Politics of Global Atmospheric Change.* Manchester: Manchester University Press.

Santer, Ben, et al. 1996. *Wall Street Journal,* 25 June.

Science. 1991. "Can PR Cool the Greenhouse?" *Science* 252 (28 June): 1784.

Seitz, Frederick. 1997. Foreword. In *Hot Talk, Cold Science: Global Warming's Unfinished Debate.* Ed. S. Fred Singer. Oakland, Calif.: Independent Institute.

———. 1996. "Major Deception on Global Warming." *Wall Street Journal.* 12 June, editorial.

———. 1994. *On the Frontier: My Life in Science.* New York: American Institute of Physics.

Singer, Fred S. 1992. "Warming Theories Need Warning Label." *The Bulletin of the Atomic Scientists* (June): 34–39.

————. 1991. "Global Warming: Do We Know Enough to Act?" In *Environmental Protection: Regulating for Results.* Ed. Kenneth Chilton and Melinda Warren. Boulder: Westview Press.

Stevens, William K. 1997. "Talks on Global Warming End on a Pessimistic Note." *New York Times,* 1 Nov., A6.

Stevens, William. 1996. "U.N. Climate Report Was Improperly Altered, Underplaying Uncertainties, Critics Say." *New York Times,* 17 June.

Toumey, Christopher P. 1996. *Conjuring Science.* New Brunswick, N.J.: Rutgers University Press.

U.S. Government. 1997. "Opening Remarks by the President and the Vice President at Discussion on Climate Change." 24 July.

Wamsted, Dennis. 1996. "Doctoring the Documents?" *Energy Daily,* 22 May.

Weiss, Peter. 1996. "Industry Group Assails Climate Chapter." *Science* 272 (21 June): 1734.

World Climate Report. 1996. "Santer Springs Forth." *World Climate Report* 2(1): 1.

The New Alienists:
Healing Shattered Selves at Century's End

Anita Sanderson shares a thriving psychotherapy practice with several colleagues in an affluent New England suburb. A licensed clinical social worker holding degrees from two reputable colleges, Anita radiates the self-confidence of a single mother who successfully provides for a family of four. In the comfortable office where she meets clients, she describes the techniques that she now uses to address her clients' emotional pain, much of which originates in what Anita refers to simply as "trauma," professional shorthand for deeply repressed episodes of childhood abuse, often incestuous. As she gestures, her permed black hair sweeps dramatically over the violet shawl gathered around her shoulders. "I was learning about trauma back in the 1980s and realized that talk therapy wasn't going to hit trauma memory for lots of reasons," she explains. She studied techniques of hypnotic induction and began to explore her own trance states for insight into the recovery of buried pasts. This led to workshops in hands-on healing, aura visualization, and what she calls energy work, the manipulation of a client's energy field to recover hidden memories and achieve emotional equilibrium. Today, about half her clients, the majority of whom are women, receive some form of energy work in her therapy sessions.

Anita describes a client's recent breakthrough:

> Sometimes my guides decide that I should start working with a person. That's what happened last week with a client whom I've been seeing for about six months on a straight trauma contract. She came in and said, "I've looked at this and looked at this for a long time. If there are other ways to get to this material I'd like to try them today." That's all it takes—a direct request like that and the energy shifts. So we channeled the session. I work with Pleiadian energy primarily. That's my home frequency. With this woman, the session consisted of working half with the Pleiadians and half with one of her personal guides that began to come through.

Anita explains that as she barraged her client with spiritual energy from the Pleiades, the woman's newly discovered spirit guides helped her to pinpoint memories of childhood abuse that had stubbornly resisted discovery. Such painful memories, Anita insists, must be confronted and healed, a process that in her practice involves the production of piercing "energy tones" that she focuses on her clients like an auditory laser.

The circumstances in which I first met Anita Sanderson and her close friend Katherine Reynolds, also a therapist, were singular. I had been invited to offer a workshop on the social meaning of channeling at a large annual meeting devoted to spirituality and alternative healing. To give the audience a sense of the range of contemporary channeling, I played brief excerpts from channeling sessions recorded across the United States. After a question-and-answer period, the session ended, and most of the conventioneers moved on to other workshops. One woman, however, remained seated. The abstracted look on her face marked her as someone in the throes of personal crisis. Anita and Katherine, who had stayed after the session to chat about channeling, immediately offered spiritual first aid.

Anita took up a strategic position in front of the woman's chair, facing her. Katherine stood behind, moving her hands gently on the woman's back, neck, and head. Sobbing loudly, the woman began to rock back and forth. A falsetto wail, abrasive and sustained, exploded from Anita and was echoed by Katherine at a slightly different pitch. The resulting interference pattern set my teeth on edge. The few people remaining in the small conference room watched as if mesmerized. A hotel employee opened the door from the hallway, surveyed the unfolding drama, and quickly retreated. Occasionally Anita halted her toning long enough to whisper assurances that everything would be all right. Slowly the target of this sonic blast went from weeping to quiet laughter, although tears continued to roll down her cheeks. After ten minutes of Anita and Katherine's ministrations, she recovered her composure.

Katherine later provided an explanation. For months the woman had been communicating with spirits, but she had no sympathetic friend with whom she could share the experience. Apparently, energies from the tapes played in the channeling workshop pushed her even closer to the edge of spirit communication, causing her to shake uncontrollably. "Basically, the guides came and told her that she wasn't crazy." Katherine, a veteran of this sort of crisis, was confident that she and Anita had rebalanced the woman's spiritual energy, thus averting a more serious emergency.

Anita and Katherine are core members of a group of therapists who use these methods to treat a growing clientele, especially among Baby Boomers confronting the dislocations of middle age and the disappointments of corporate downsizing. This small collaborative, informally called the Energy Group, is part of the nation's expanding network of freelance counselors and therapists who confront the fragmentation of their clients' sense of self. Although the Energy Group's therapeutic strategies appear unorthodox, the issues around which it is organized—the exploration of memory, an awareness of internal voices struggling to break through to consciousness, and a conviction that the everyday self disguises underlying personas—are shared by thousands of therapists in the clinical mainstream.

If, as Anthony Giddens has asserted, "therapy is an expert system deeply implicated in the reflexive project of the self" (1991, 180), then emerging therapies directed to fragmenting selves offer an ideal opportunity to explore the contours of the self among middle-class Americans. The pervasiveness of self-fragmentation has been celebrated by postmodernists, who cheerily point to the ludic possibilities of decentered subjects. Nowhere is this more evident than in reports from the on-line frontier, where personal identity has become infinitely malleable. The players in multiple-user fantasy games, for instance, take on identities that are, in the words of Sherry Turkle, "not only decentered but multiplied without limit," an experience that many find more fulfilling than their everyday lives (1996, 152). Nevertheless, although some welcome the collapse of the great metanarratives of our time and experience self-decentering as a form of personal liberation, many others hunger for over-arching narrative frameworks. And these narratives are hardly difficult to find: increasingly segmented communications media offer a perfect breeding ground for apocalyptic or millenarian enthusiasms. Eschatologies that once would have been dismissed or shouted down in public forums now unfold in their own special-interest niches, unchallenged by alternative views.[1]

The continued vitality of apocalyptic, conspiratorial, and millenarian views of the world would have surprised the major social thinkers of the immediate postwar era, most of whom were convinced that American society was heading inexorably toward secularization. Philip Rieff's *The Triumph of the Therapeutic* (1966) argued prophetically that institutionalized psychotherapy was steadily taking over the counseling function formerly associated with religion. Rieff predicted that therapists, experts in the technologies of self, would provide the means of adjusting to the impossible demands of modern life.

Much of Rieff's vision has been realized. Therapeutic idioms now inform the central institutions of American society, from politics to family life, while therapists and counselors of every conceivable variety proliferate at a remarkable pace.[2] Survey data show that 40 percent of Americans participate in support groups of some kind (Wuthnow 1994, 47). Although many of these groups are closely connected to religious denominations, the therapeutic language that characterizes them—for example, their emphasis on "recovery," "personal healing," and "self-empowerment"—draw heavily on the secular ideals of the human potential movement. When communities experience natural disasters, they are today as likely to seek the intervention of psychotherapists and sociologists as they are the counsel of priests and rabbis.

Secular therapies have hardly overwhelmed the power of religion, however. If anything, religion and therapy have begun to converge, heading toward a synthesis that has more in common with the shamanic healing of tribal societies than with the rationalist psychoanalysis envisioned by Freud and his followers. Appropriating the metaphors of contemporary psychotherapy, for instance, American evangelicals are likely to stress human potential and the manifold possibilities of self-realization through the acceptance of God's message (Hunter 1983, 97–98), even as a small but growing number of therapists move steadily in the direction of spiritualized treatment strategies. Despite concerted attempts by psychologists and clinical social workers to police their professions through the imposition of rigorous certification procedures, even a cursory glance at regional journals devoted to alternative healing reveals a burgeoning informal sector of self-identified therapists, many of whom offer quasi-religious treatment modalities. Healers in my staid corner of western New England, for instance, offer such services as "past-life regression therapy" and "cosmic cellular clearing." Far more exotic therapies can be found in Santa Monica, Sedona, and Boulder. Growing demand for explicitly spiritual brands of psychotherapy has begun to affect the practices of conventional therapists, who struggle for professional survival at a time when cost-conscious HMOs are downsizing their counseling staffs. Many clients willing to pay out of pocket for psychological services are no longer satisfied by simple empathy or the healing powers of talk. Instead, they seek holistic healing that addresses the needs of their bodies, souls, and minds. Amid this scramble for spiritual meaning, it is hardly surprising that therapists have begun to weave together notions of self-fragmentation and dramatic theories that attempt to explain and counter it.

A narrative of splintered selves that has edged into the psychotherapeutic mainstream is associated with the condition known as multiple personality disorder (MPD). In clinical terms, MPD is defined as "the presence of two or more distinct identities or personality states . . . that recurrently take control of behavior" (American Psychiatric Association 1994, 484).[3] Clients are typically diagnosed as "multiples" when they exhibit sharp changes in expressive behavior that segregate into distinct, consistent personalities or "alters." Oscillation among different alters is regularly accompanied by amnesia, such that the victim's original self (variously referred to as the "birth person," "main alter," or "core personality") cannot recall events that occur while a secondary alter is in charge. Prior to 1980 only about two hundred cases of MPD had been documented anywhere in the world psychiatric literature. By 1991 a clinician could propose in a respectable journal that as many as one percent of North American adults suffer from MPD, implying that undiagnosed cases number in the millions (Ross 1991, 506). The average number of alters increased even faster than the number of diagnosed MPD sufferers. A document posted on the Internet by a self-identified multiple notes matter-of-factly that "it is rare to have less than five alters . . . [and] there are a number of multiples that have a count in the lower hundreds" (Discord and Sapphire Gazelles 1994).

For an anthropologist it is hard to see multiple personality as anything other than a culture-bound syndrome analogous to *amok,* magical soul-loss, or the *windigo* psychosis. Of recent origin, it is widely diagnosed in the United States and Canada but virtually unknown in most of Europe and Asia. Beginning with a few highly publicized cases, it has ballooned into an epidemic that spawns clinics specializing in its diagnosis and treatment. About 90 percent of multiples are women, mostly well educated and working in service professions (Nathan 1994, 79). This unusual epidemiology has led to heated debate about whether MPD exists as a real malady or instead represents an iatrogenic condition—that is, something induced by therapists who unconsciously encourage expressions of multiplicity in emotionally fragile clients. Philosopher Ian Hacking makes the sensible observation that multiple personality provides "a new way to be an unhappy person" (1995, 236), to which one might add that the specific form of this new manifestation of unhappiness—the fragmentation of the self—is surely a symptom of the powerful cultural forces that increasingly threaten self-integration.[4]

As important as the social meaning of MPD's signs and symptoms is its presumed cause: childhood trauma, often sexual in nature. The etiological model favored by therapists holds that multiples are created when children are repeatedly subjected to abusive treatment: a combination of hyperarousal and absolute helplessness leads them to dissociate, producing a sense of detachment, repression of memory, denial of the abused self and its rage, and eventually the kind of personality fragmentation that leads to the production of alters. Because 90 percent or more of MPD patients are thought to have been victims of childhood sexual abuse, typically incestuous, such abuse is now presumed when patients exhibit symptoms.

MPD is thus thoroughly intertwined with one of the major moral panics of our era, the problem of childhood sexual abuse. A controversial diagnostic category that might otherwise be dismissed as one of psychology's fads becomes in this context a political force with far-reaching consequences in American law, workplace relations, and domestic life. If 90 percent of MPD victims are women, the argument goes, then it is because childhood sexual abuse affects girls far more frequently than boys, a pattern carried on into the life-cycle as rape and domestic violence. Because psychotherapy and social work are now among the most feminized of professions, it is largely women who treat the victims of incest and physical violence. Many come to see their work as a form of warfare in which their role is to believe the abused and punish the accused.

The tendency to demonize, to answer the rallying cry of "Believe the children!" by declaring war on the unspeakable evil in our midst, causes the narratives of MPD and sexual abuse to skid swiftly toward conspiracy. In the 1980s grass-roots and professional organizations began forming to share stories about the nation's alleged epidemic of satanic ritual abuse. These tales emerged as therapists mined the childhood memories of sexual abuse victims. By 1991 reports of cult abuse had increased so dramatically that an organization in Maine could claim that 40 percent of the fifteen thousand incest survivors for whom it provides services reported that their abuse had been ritualistic in nature (Bennetts 1993, 46). In 1993, to considerable fanfare, *Ms.* magazine published a horrifying autobiography of intergenerational cult abuse, including ritual rape and cannibalism. While acknowledging that "the secretive nature of the abuse eludes accurate statistics," the author subtly implies that cult violence is far more common than readers imagine (Rose 1993, 45). At their most florid, the recovered memories of cult victims coalesce into a pattern of worldwide satanic organizations that breed children for torture and sacrifice. Cult members include doctors, lawyers, and other respectable members of society; victims are subjected to sophisticated mind control of the kind portrayed in the film *The Manchurian Candidate.*

The seductiveness of this dystopian vision is seen in the work of Robert Friesen, a licensed psychologist and pastor with a practice in California. In his book *Uncovering the Mystery of MPD,* Friesen argues that the increase in reported cases of MPD is a warning of evil's gathering momentum. "As psychology becomes increasingly willing to accept the emerging data about MPD," Friesen writes, "it is getting ready for the next phase of the rollercoaster ride. . . . More than a hundred preschools in California have been reported to the police on charges of grotesque abuse, and that represents only the tip of the iceberg of evil allegedly perpetrated against young children. Adult survivors have told therapists of identical abuse practices in more than forty of the United States and across Canada!" (1991, 207–8). For Friesen and others who identify multiple personality with satanism, treatment of MPD is more than psychotherapy, it is "spiritual warfare."

Views such as Friesen's, which one might be tempted to dismiss as those of an extremist minority, find support in unlikely places. Growing interest in ritual abuse has produced alliances between feminists and the religious right, a notable example being Gloria Steinem's financial backing for an investigation of alleged "molestation tunnels" under the McMartin Preschool in Manhattan Beach, California. (No such tunnels were found.) Law-enforcement officials have proved willing to act on allegations of ritual cult abuse, perhaps because of the Manichaean nature of their occupational world. As of 1995 fifty-seven people, many doubtless innocent, were known to be serving long jail sentences for these crimes, and scores more have suffered unspeakable humiliation until declared innocent by skeptical juries.[5] Amid the high drama of this moral panic, two themes stand out in high relief: the metaphor of self-fragmentation (and, by implication, its obverse, self-integration or holism), and the tendency of reflections on multiple personality to move in an eschatological direction, taking on the cadences of dystopian conspiracy.

At a cultural moment when trained professionals, drawing on the institutional support of a technically advanced society, are willing to accept the reality of recovered memory, multiple personality, and satanic cult conspiracies, the healing techniques of Anita Sanderson and other members of the Energy Group seem less idiosyncratic than they otherwise might. When I met members of the group on a grey January afternoon in 1995, they proved disarmingly thoughtful, hardly fitting a stereotype of New Age vacuity. The five women and two men sitting around a conference table shared Anita Sanderson's educational background, and they took pride in their formal training as psychologists and clinical social workers. As we talked through the lunch hour, I found myself thinking that they were as smart and likable a group of people as I'd met in some time.

In their clinical practices they wrestle with the problems and possibilities of dissociation, a psychological process that, as the name implies, entails a splitting, severing, or uncoupling of consciousness. As clinical interest in multiple personality and other so-called dissociative disorders has grown, therapists routinely confront dissociation in their patients. The Energy Group has taken this to the next logical step by using their own dissociation to help their clients come to terms with emotional distress.

Karen Smith, one of the most talkative members of the group, explained that therapist and client both radiate a field of energy. "All we're doing is trying to gain some mastery of what we're putting out in our energy field. Any therapeutic interchange, or any other human interchange, is energetic," she said. Karen described a gathering at which she and some colleagues had experimented with hypnosis, dissociation, and channeling. They took turns sensitizing themselves to changes in the auras of hypnotic subjects and of the hypnotist himself. As their sensitivity to these energy shifts increased, they found they could apply them in therapy sessions with clients. "Most people with trauma history dissociate very easily, and when you watch their dissociation, it's a leaving of the body," she noted. This phenomenon apparently refers to a movement of energy, perhaps even of the soul, that takes place as clients enter trance. "If people can be helped to be aware that that's what they're doing, they have some choice about bringing themselves back into their body." This awareness, she explained, can lead them to self-mastery impossible to achieve by more conventional methods.

The Energy Group slowly coalesced as its members met and came to know one another at various healing workshops. "The group started with the purpose of integrating energy work into clinical practice," Anita explained. "It was much like a counter-transference supervision group. We met to talk about our gifts as they were expanding and to practice them with each other." They regularly devote part of their meetings to dealing with their own spiritual crises, including problems that arise in therapy sessions when they marshal powerful forces to heal their clients. Anita described an encounter in which she was adversely affected by what she called dark energies. "I got one of those energy critters, an octopus, stuck on my third chakra," referring here to one of the body's seven energy centers. But she was rescued by other members of the group at their weekly meeting. "One of the things that's wonderful about this group," another woman emphasized, "is that we're good enough that if one of us gets stuck, there are at least three or four who can help."

When asked what their colleagues in psychotherapy would think about such stories, the group burst into laughter. "We're sitting here talking about things that most of our colleagues would think were reason for commitment," one woman admitted. From an outsider's perspective, the members of the Energy Group are ambivalent about their professional training and credentialization. Don Burke, one of the two men present, voiced the opinion that university degrees serve a gate-keeping role, providing clients with a competent and responsible therapist. "There's some quackery out there," he cautioned. Another therapist added that she appreciated her rigorous scientific training because it helped her to "know what the ground rules are." At the same time, however, members of the group chafed at the limited options offered by conventional talk therapy. Katherine Reynolds made the case for their unorthodox methods in practical terms: "The amazing thing is that people get better a lot faster. There's stuff that would have taken me a couple of years that I now do in a much shorter period of time because I can read my clients' energy fields. These methods *work*. People feel better. They have more joy in their lives."

Later Anita added detail to Katherine's explanation of their success. By opening herself to high energies, Anita said, she makes it possible for clients to dislodge emotional blocks that harm them—blocks that simply aren't responsive to standard talk therapy. She likened herself to a kidney dialysis unit: "My energy field literally will merge with people's energy fields and begin to pull things through," she insisted.

The group's commitment to therapeutic channeling and other unorthodox healing potentially puts members beyond the pale of accepted professional behavior. In the New England states licensed psychologists and clinical social workers bill insurance companies and HMOs for services provided to clients, but therapy must conform to standard protocols. Although the members of the Energy Group maintain that much of their practice is still conventional talk therapy, a growing proportion of clients request hypnotic induction and even channeling, techniques that are clearly outside the bounds of approved procedure and which, if paid for by insurance companies, would constitute malpractice and possibly fraud. All are aware of the risks they run by moving into these areas. But Karen captured the sentiments of the group when she declared that she was ready to lose her license if it came to that: "This work is important. It feels to me like it's what I'm intended to be doing by whatever the higher power is."

Katherine is confident that she could make an adequate living by providing such services. She now regularly receives referrals from other therapists unable to help clients wrestling with spiritual crises. When asked to give an example, Katherine described clients who arrive at her office saying, "I'd like to explore my spiritual journey with you," or "I'd like to know how to feel God's presence in my life," or even "I'd like to get in touch with my spirit guides." By their own estimation, as many as 80 percent of their clients are women. The clients of James Borden, a therapist who is gay and HIV-positive, are the exception: most are HIV-positive men. By his own admission he was heavily invested in his identity as a professional psychologist, and it was harder for him to come out as a channel—a term that he and many others involved in such work use in preference to the more familiar *channeler*—than as a gay man:

> I was afraid that clients were going to think that I'm nuts—you know,
> if I start to tone in their presence, even if I explain what I'm doing.
> But in fact their response has been the opposite. They express gratitude at being able to integrate whatever happens into their greater understanding of themselves, their family background, or whatever issues that they're working on.

Anita explained that she has been using energy tones to treat her clients for two years. When she broaches the subject to clients, most readily agree to participate. "Ten percent of the time the guides decide it's the right moment," Anita said. "They say, 'Start working with this person.'" Once the process is initiated, clients begin to perceive the energy fields around them and how these can affect their self-understanding. One of her spirit guides explained, "It's like an eye chart. At first you can't see the chart, and they keep putting on lenses, and eventually you can see the letters. It never occurs to you that the letters aren't there just because you can't see them." Once patients acquire the "lens" that allows them to see the energy forces impinging on the human spirit, they apprehend the world with greater acuity and understanding.

Anita Sanderson and several other members of the Energy Group also participate in a weekly meeting devoted to the exploration of channeling's spiritual implications. Three months after interviewing Anita and her colleagues, I attended an evening event organized by the larger channeling collective, their first attempt to introduce this work to an audience of family and friends.

About sixty people, mostly middle aged and apparently successful, gathered in a circle on the polished floor of a church activity room. As the event unfolded it became obvious that Anita was the group's guiding force, although perhaps a dozen others also contributed to the event by producing energy tones or acting as mediums themselves. Anita explained that their goal was simply to help us "follow the energies," a process that would aid us to "listen deeply inside in a different way and to bring forward what you hear there." All that was needed was an open mind. She assured everyone that no harm would come to them. After a few minutes of silence, Anita made sibilant whooshing sounds that stabilized into a constant, uninflected tone. Her voice was quickly joined by others. At first the intervals were fourths and fifths, reminiscent of Gregorian chant. The sonority was soon replaced by ascending and descending pitches that shot off into spiraling waves of dissonance—Elliot Carter on peyote. Somewhere in the room, a male voice boomed out a Tibetan rumble with parallel overtones. Periodically, Anita punctured the wall of polyphony with electric-sounding squeaks and pops.

The next two hours alternated between periods of toning and brief spoken passages, mostly channeled by Anita. She spoke first in her slow, modulated Pleiadian voice. The Pleiadians assured us that exposure to their energies would clarify the meaning of the turbulent age in which we live, an age that makes many feel sad and dislocated. "Move forward with hope," they said. "We have been working with many groups around your country and countries around your world to begin what is considered a transitional time on your planet." This transition is not, they insisted, a time of "doom and desolation and destruction." It will lead instead to a "restructuring of the energetic being" in which the "illusion of separation simply falls away."

Later Anita slipped into an entirely different voice, the stage Southern accent of a being named Belle. Belle, who was as folksy and informal as the Pleiadians had been dignified, explained that her job was to prod Anita's channeling group into paying attention to the voices that they resist hearing, presumably the wise counsel of their spiritual guides and allies: "I'm also hoping that you're willing to let yourself listen a little bit to some of the things that go on inside your head. Are you willing to listen to that voice telling you something important? Are you willing to change a decision based on that voice?" A willingness to heed those voices, Belle insisted, would help to accelerate the transition to another way of being, another era:

> Now, there isn't one of you here who hasn't noticed that things are a little different inside and outside, and it's coming through in lots of different ways. But y'all have noticed it, and if you're honest with

yourself, you've noticed it pretty regular. So we're all hoping that you can be a little more open to what you *know* is really going on around you. You'll notice that you are actually up to the point where you can let yourselves believe that you're hearing the beings from other dimensions communicating with you. Because they do, all the time.

The event continued for another hour. There was more group toning and a hand-holding ritual to bring the evening to a close. But the gathering's central message was that we should welcome our own multiplicity, the presence of internal voices that can, if we are only willing to attend to them, bring happiness, broader understanding, and a new stage in the human passage to the divine.

The ideas of mediumship expounded by Anita Sanderson and her colleagues draw on themes elaborated by other Americans involved in channeling, a spiritual practice that has been part of the New Age movement since the 1970s (Brown 1997). Unlike the American and European spirit mediums of the nineteenth century, who generally thought of themselves as making contact with the dead and thus confirming the reality of Christian visions of the afterlife, contemporary channels see their mission as that of helping others to recognize their own spiritual multiplicity. "You are," one channel told a small crowd in Santa Fe in 1993, "multidimensional beings living simultaneously on all dimensions back to God-All-That-Is." Channels look forward to a time when everyone will be able to make personal contact with their spirit guides and with the past-life experiences that run through each of us like a vast, silent river. At the very least, the dissociative processes of channeling allow one to contact the "higher self," a transcendent, eternal core that links each of us to other places and times, other planets and dimensions. For channels, then, dissociation is a doorway to the grandeur of the self.

As one might expect from a highly improvisational practice, beliefs about channeling differ among its advocates. Some subscribe to the idea that the entities for whom they speak are separate, named beings who bring their wisdom to earth for complex, though always benevolent reasons. Others think of channeled voices or energies as expressions of the collective unconscious. All agree that the messages, whatever their source, convey crucial information that can transform the world by accelerating humanity's spiritual evolution or even by bringing about a "mass ascension," the collective achievement of divinity.

The occasional apocalyptic rivulet surges forth from this flood of cheerful prophecy. J. Z. Knight, a controversial channel from Yelm, Washington, has published works that drift toward right-wing conspiracy theories, complete with references to the Rothschilds, impending world takeovers by international financiers, and the universal bar coding of citizens (Koteen 1989). Yet even Knight insists that a global change in consciousness can avert this impending age of darkness. Most channels prefer to see ominous prophecies as useful lessons in each person's spiritual journey. As a Massachusetts woman involved in channeling explained, "I'm not into fear myself, but some people need to go through fear modes in order to come up out of them." When the predicted disasters fail to occur, she said, followers of J. Z. Knight and other New Age prophets of doom learn that they must exercise their own judgment rather than accept uncritically the beliefs of others. The "fear mode" is thus a necessary step on the road to personal autonomy and spiritual growth.

Although channeling still lies on the cultural fringe, its idioms have percolated into the self-help movement, including motivational training courses sponsored by some of the nation's largest corporations (Rupert 1992). In 1995, for instance, the Federal Aviation Administration admitted paying $1.4 million for sensitivity training classes administered by one of Knight's disciples. The growing plausibility of ideas of self-multiplicity among the general public suggests that channeling encapsulates key aspects of the postmodern *zeitgeist*.

Particularly striking is the overlap between the discourses of channeling and multiple personality. Psychiatrist Bennett Braun, a prominent figure in the diagnosis and treatment of MPD, regards the alters or personality fragments of MPD sufferers as having an ontological standing not unlike that which channels attribute to their spirit entities. For instance, Braun recommends that therapists treating cases of MPD should diagram the names and interrelationships of each patient's alters. Treatment includes "communicating with each personality state" and "working with each personality state's problems" (1986, 9). He goes so far as to caution therapists against medicating their MPD patients, because "different personality states [in the same patient] have been observed to have different responses to, as well as different tolerances of, the same amount of a given drug" (24). Braun envisions the resolution of MPD not as the elimination of alters but as the achievement of "co-consciousness and integration." Alter personalities are likely to fear for their death when therapy is initiated, leading them to resist the measures that may produce recovery. Braun reminds his fellow clinicians that these nervous alters "need to be reassured that they all will contribute to the remaining whole" once the client's personality fragments have been reintegrated (15–16). The healing process that he advocates, then, simultaneously affirms and domesticates self-fragmentation.

Self-help publications written by and for MPD sufferers pursue the theme of internal multiplicity far beyond the limits of Braun's clinical language. In sometimes heart-rending prose, multiples describe the practical problems caused by the warring personalities inside them.[6]

> Things are already complicated as soon as we get up in the morning and go over to the stereo to put on some music. The hand reaches out for a tape and we all sternly state our requests. Personally, I'm really into alternative rock, but our younger parts think it's too loud

and want their nature/instrumental music. Our teenagers fight over
pop/dance music and our feminist folky tapes. The olders want to put
on the classical music radio station and end the whole ordeal. (*Many
Voices* 1995, 5–6)

Others describe problems associated with dressing (male alters, for instance,
object to wearing skirts), romantic relationships (alters with different sexual
orientations may take over at awkward moments), and even driving an automobile (when alters who know how to drive unexpectedly turn over control to
those who don't). Multiples whose therapists haven't succeeded in recovering
memories of sexual abuse fret about their second-class status.[7] They and their
therapists write frequently of a key alter called the inner self-helper (ISH), a
wise personality state who acts in the best interests of the whole patient. Accounts of the role of the ISH sound remarkably similar to the descriptions of
guardian angels or spirit guides offered by channels. James Friesen describes
an ISH named Socrates whom he discovered in a patient named Beth. Socrates
"was one of Beth's intellectual alternate personalities," Friesen writes. "He
was also wise and terribly honest. He called things as he saw them, and he
talked to me as though we were equals. Socrates and I could work well together" (1991, 44).

Both channels and believers in multiple personality assert the central role of
memory in defining the self. The treatment of multiple personality focuses on
the evocation of memories of past abuse, the events that gave birth to the personality fragments which define the condition. Channels often use dissociation
to help themselves and their clients uncover similar memories of abuse, in this
life and in previous ones. Increasingly, channels also explore what I would call
(with apologies to the writer Charles Bowden) memories of the future: visions
of lives waiting to be lived in parallel dimensions, of narratives to be recovered
from the ether of what was and what is to be.

The literature of multiple personality depicts the family as a site of (mostly
patriarchal) cruelty and betrayal. Channeling and related New Age therapies
share this picture, although they tend to give it a less sinister cast: the family
denies the individual a personal authenticity that can only be restored by peel-
ing off accumulated layers of parental influence. The reinvention of the family
as a hotbed of pathology—or, among conservative ideologues, as the most
sacred of human institutions—reflects the impossible demands placed upon
families by the economic and social realities of our time. The last site of diffuse, enduring solidarity left in our society, the family is simply not up to the
task of resisting the centrifugal forces that tear it asunder.

Resemblances between channeling and multiple personality break down
over the issue of control. Channels usually describe themselves as active seek-
ers of contacts with entities, which they feel free to continue or abandon according to their personal needs. Multiples, in contrast, do not welcome the

intervention of novel personality fragments, and the mental health community regards the presence of alters as an affliction. Yet even here there is ambiguity. Some multiples resent assertions that they suffer from a disorder, arguing that this view "disempowers" them. A volume of essays and poetry published by multiples includes a Bill of Rights, which asserts that each alter self has a right to be happy, to be respected by others, and to express its views freely (W. 1993, 56). Advocacy publications even celebrate the alleged advantages of multiple personality. "We do like some aspects of MPD," writes one multiple. "We can be interested in many things that we share with various friends and family because any personality is welcome to join in" (Many Voices 1995, 5). Multiples and the therapists who treat them are quick to point out that the condition is most likely to strike those who are unusually gifted. Their ability to dissociate creatively has become a problem only because they had the bad luck to find themselves in abusive situations as children.

The assumptions that underlie channeling and MPD have been subjected to sustained assault by debunkers of various persuasions. Because critics see channeling as little more than a giddy form of mass entertainment, their attacks favor the light irony of the cartoon strip Doonesbury, which in the 1980s amused readers with the escapades of a being named Hunk-Ra, an obvious spoof of Ramtha, the Atlantean warrior channeled by J. Z. Knight. Debates over multiple personality and recovered memory, in contrast, have provoked far heavier fusillades—hardly surprising in view of the institutional resources at stake and the potential harm to psychotherapeutic clients and the unfortunate family members typically named as the cause of their affliction. Although critics both within and outside of psychiatry make a convincing case that MPD will eventually join frontal lobotomies and the doctrine of signatures in the annals of medical fallacy, they express little curiosity about why this particular way of understanding emotional distress has proven so plausible to contemporary therapists.[8] Why are notions of personality fragmentation so intuitively satisfying? What are their connections to the convergence of psychology and spiritualism exemplified by Anita Sanderson's Energy Group?

To answer these questions one must consider the conflicted status of the self in conditions of advanced modernity. Because the bureaucratic and market-driven institutions of our time advance forms of utilitarianism notable for their moral emptiness, the self becomes the sole remaining site where moral meaning can be sustained. Yet the quest for meaning in the self creates profound dilemmas, especially in a society as focused on consumption as America has been since the end of World War II. When identity is closely linked to the kind and quantity of goods we possess, how do we maintain a sense of personal authenticity? How can we reconcile the pursuit of happiness with the needs of significant others? These dilemmas, challenging enough in settled times, have become even more difficult to resolve as modern social forms give way to post-modern ones. Individuals now face a "pluralization of life-worlds" (Berger et al. 1973, 64) such that in a single day they routinely encounter many different social settings, each of which may force them to assume a different persona. It is no exaggeration to say that never before have human beings been forced to exhibit such malleable behavior or to redefine themselves so frequently. One needn't appeal to our Paleolithic genetic hardware to make a convincing case that the postmodern self is stretched in ways for which we as a species are poorly equipped.

Mediating between the individual and the social world is the therapist, tech-nomancer of the soul. With their formal education, clinical apprenticeship, and state-sanctioned licenses, therapists embody the bureaucratic cult of expertise. Some, defining their mission narrowly, strive simply to restore damaged selves to full functioning. Since the 1960s, however, many therapists have embraced a more exalted goal, namely, guiding clients toward self-realization and a vaguely specified, if deeply felt, authenticity—meaning, among other things, that they use therapy to uncover the "true self" by stripping a client of harm-ful emotional baggage acquired from parents, marital partners, and society as a whole.

Within this social context we can comprehend the advent of diagnostic and therapeutic frameworks preoccupied with self-fragmentation. Clients come to therapists troubled by "the voices inside their heads," to borrow a phrase from Anita Sanderson's channeled entity Belle. The accounts provided by multiples express the anxieties faced by those who must choose from among a continu-ally expanding range of products to consume, places to live, values to uphold, and identities to take on. Like the disoriented characters who populate post-modern novels, they ask, "Which world am I in and which of my personalities do I deploy?" (Harvey 1989, 301). Although some, particularly in the on-line community and the arts, apparently experience such polymorphism as a kind of liberation, for others it is deeply unsettling.

The marked overrepresentation of women among therapists, channels, and victims of multiple personality suggests that they bear a disproportionate share of the burden of this fragmentation. The attraction of channeling for women is fairly straightforward: it offers an alternative to mainstream religious de-nominations, within which women continue to be marginalized from posi-tions of power. Channeling, in other words, carries on the feminist tradition of nineteenth-century American spiritualism and illustrates the key social role played by female spirit mediums in societies around the world. But what connection, if any, is there between channeling and the current epidemic of multiple personality among middle-class women?

Janice Haaken, a feminist psychoanalyst, finds the answer in the links be-tween gender and the historical emergence of capitalism. She observes that

Freud's focus on repression emerged in a phase of capitalism when "the push toward capital accumulation required renunciation and sublimation of desire" (1994, 134). In a postindustrial economy, in contrast, "repression of impulses is less dominant than chaotic expression of alienated, commodified desire." Because women are still less free than men to respond constructively to "fragmenting discontinuities," Haaken contends, they are more likely to express their distress through the dissociation characteristic of multiple personality. Multiples turn dissociation into heroic stories of survival, but for Haaken this comes at a high price: perpetuation of the "wounded feminine object" instead of the development of an "active, desiring feminine subject" (142; see also Nathan 1994). Perhaps channels such as Anita Sanderson have successfully transformed female subjectivity from passive victimhood to the kind of active desire and fantasy-play admired by Haaken.

One thing is certain: Sanderson and her colleagues in the Energy Group enthusiastically embrace their own multiplicity, seeing it as a resource for healing. This signals to their clients that multiple inner voices are an acceptable, even desirable part of self-understanding and personal growth. Such inner voices are not the alters of multiple personality, fragments of the self born in pain and helplessness, but instead hidden facets of a grander self whose threads reach out to other places, times, and dimensions.

If one attends to the discourse of channels and psychotherapists, it becomes evident that both groups attempt to heal the self's essential emptiness by splintering it into a simulacrum of community. A common feature of treatment for multiple personality is the preparation of diagrams tracing the links between a client's personality fragments, noting their names, ages, and social statuses (see, for instance, Friesen 1991, 52). The alter map offered by a multiple named Kristin shows her diverse personalities clustered in a large residential unit labeled "our internal home." Kristin depicts an inner world from which loneliness has been banished. "We have different groups who work to get tasks done during dissociative periods. . . . We have specialists and helpers who rally together to deal with crisis," she writes. Kristin is especially pleased that therapy has "brought cell groups closer together in their group, and has built bridges from group to group, making it easier to be multi-conscious" (*Many Voices* 1995, 8). These harmonious inner villages remind me of the channel who explained that when he makes contact with his spirit entity—actually a spiritual collective called the Clan—"it's as though I'm immersed in water and the Clan is the water in which I'm immersed. We join in a cooperative venture."

No matter how much we expand the boundaries of self or repopulate it with colorful fragments, however, it proves to be lonely place. Trapped in solipsism, postmodern selves reach out for narratives that bind the individual to others moving in a common direction. For channels and their clients, the story is one of collective ascension and the establishment of a spiritual utopia. Victims of multiple personality and the therapists who care for them, in contrast, tend to see the future in the darker hues of conspiracy. Although public belief in the specific eschatologies offered by channels and ritual-abuse alarmists may be on the wane, the social conditions in which these narratives have arisen are unlikely to disappear anytime soon. In the face of new manifestations of self-fragmentation, most therapists will, as Anthony Giddens claims, content themselves with reducing their clients' anxiety and guiding them toward greater self-control, "thus confirming, and even accentuating, the separation of the lifespan from extrinsic moral considerations" (1991, 180). But others will find themselves drawn to powerful narratives of millenarian renewal or dystopian conspiracy that can account for life's vicissitudes and provide shattered selves with a master plan.

Notes

My research on channeling and alternative psychotherapy, conducted between 1990 and 1995, was supported by Williams College, the School of American Research, and the Wenner-Gren Foundation for Anthropological Research, Inc. I am grateful for bibliographic help and constructive criticism from Frederick Crews, Andrew Crider, James Faubion, Laurie Heatherington, Peter Just, and James Nolan, some of whom, it should be noted, take strong exception to the argument advanced here.

1. In a study of the rhetoric of apocalyptic thinking, Stephen O'Leary argues that apocalyptic and conspiratorial discourses implicate one another: "While conspiracy strives to provide a spatial self-definition of the true community as set apart from the evils that surround us, apocalypse locates the problem of evil in time and looks forward to its imminent resolution" (1994, 6). On the persistence and growth of apocalyptic views of history in the United States, see Boyer 1992.

2. James Nolan (1998) offers a provocative analysis of the infusion of the therapeutic ethos into various American institutions. Occupational data strongly support Nolan's institutional analysis. The number of degree programs in clinical psychology approved by the American Psychological Association, for instance, increased sevenfold between 1948 and 1989 (Nietzel et al. 1991, 29), and the number of licensed psychologists more than doubled between 1975 and 1985 (Manderscheid and Sonnenschein 1990, 199). At the master's-degree level there was a more than threefold increase in the number of degrees awarded between 1966 and 1990 (American Psychological Association, personal communication). Information on growth in psychotherapy's unregulated, informal sector is difficult to obtain, but presumably it constitutes a significant part of the estimated $10–14 billion spent on "alternative healing" in the United States each year.

3. The *Diagnostic and Statistical Manual of Mental Disorders,* 4th edition (known as the *DSM-IV*), published in 1994, reclassifies multiple personality disorder as "dissociative identity disorder." This change reflects the concern of therapeutic professionals that the label MPD places too much emphasis on multiplicity rather than on the central problem of the condition's victims, which is maintaining a sense of psychic

integration (see Hacking 1995, 18–19). In this essay, however, I use MPD because it is a term more familiar to readers outside of clinical psychology; it continues to be used by multiples themselves in their own advocacy and self-help writings.

4. The debate about the scientific status of multiple personality is too voluminous to review here in detail. Key sources for a social analysis of MPD included Kenny 1986 and Hacking 1995; see also Merskey 1992 and Saks 1994. Experts such as Saks argue that even if multiple personality remains controversial among professional psychologists, it is now widely accepted as a legitimate dissociative disorder.

5. Information on the McMartin Preschool case and on the number of individuals convicted of ritual-abuse charges is from Nathan and Snedeker 1995. Debate on the validity of recovered memory and allegations of ritual abuse have generated a literature as vast as that dealing with multiple personality. In developing this brief summary of the issues, I have drawn on Crews et al. 1995, Hacking 1995, Nathan and Snedeker 1995, Ofshe and Watters 1994, and Wright 1994. Readers interested in exploring the problem of ritual abuse from the alleged victim's perspective may consult the Ritual Abuse and Healing Home Page on the World Wide Web, http://www.xroads.com/rahome.

Because of the polarized nature of current debate on these themes, I am obliged to state that I do not rule out the possibility that children are sometimes abused in ritualized ways or that formerly repressed memories of psychological trauma may, under certain clinical conditions, be "recovered" by a skilled therapist.

6. The self-help writings of multiples echo contemporary debates about multiculturalism in curious ways. One self-identified multiple, for instance, encourages nonmultiples to treat different alters courteously when they express themselves in a person with MPD. This writer also notes that many multiples experience real distress because their distinct alters are of different religions, races, or sexual orientations that cannot coexist happily because of mutual intolerance (see Discord and Sapphire Gazelles 1994).

7. "Other DID's [dissociative identity disorder, now the preferred term for MPD] I know have full-fledged symptoms, complete with memories and histories of big-time abuse. This makes me feel like a phony, a fraud, like maybe I jumped on the DID bandwagon to get attention, or to justify or rationalize my polarized behavior and feelings" (*Many Voices* 1995, 4).

8. This chapter was drafted in 1995. By the time this volume went to press in 1998, lurid exposés of medical abuses associated with the treatment of multiple personality and ritual abuse had begun to appear in the popular media with increasing frequency, suggesting that we are about to witness another of the reversals characteristic of modern psychiatry.

References

American Psychiatric Association. 1994. *Diagnostic and Statistical Manual of Mental Disorders,* 4th ed. Washington, D.C.: American Psychiatric Association.

Bennetts, Leslie. 1993. "Dispatches: Nightmares on Main Street." *Vanity Fair,* June, 42–62.

Berger, Peter L., Brigitte Berger, and Hansfried Kellner. 1973. *The Homeless Mind: Modernization and Consciousness.* New York: Random House.

Boyer, Paul. 1992. *When Time Shall Be No More: Prophecy Beliefs in Modern Ameri-can Culture.* Cambridge, Mass.: Harvard University Press.

Braun, Bennett G. 1986. "Issues in the Psychotherapy of Multiple Personality Disor-der." In *Treatment of Multiple Personality Disorder.* Ed. Bennett G. Braun, 3–28. Washington, D.C.: American Psychiatric Press.

Brown, Michael F. 1997. *The Channeling Zone: American Spirituality in an Anxious Age.* Cambridge, Mass.: Harvard University Press.

Crews, Frederick, et al. 1995. *The Memory Wars: Freud's Legacy in Dispute.* New York: New York Review of Books.

Discord and Sapphire Gazelles. 1994. *Dissociation: An Informal Look from an Insider.* FAQ document, UseNet newsgroup alt.support.dissociation, unpag. Accessed 19 Nov. 1995.

Friesen, James G. 1991. *Uncovering the Mysteries of MPD.* Nashville, Tenn.: Thomas Nelson Publishers.

Giddens, Anthony. 1991. *Modernity and Self-identity: Self and Society in the Late Mod-ern Age.* Stanford, Calif.: Stanford University Press.

Haaken, Janice. 1994. "Sexual Abuse, Recovered Memory, and Therapeutic Practice: A Feminist-Psychoanalytic Perspective." *Social Text* 40 (Fall): 115–45.

Hacking, Ian. 1995. *Rewriting the Soul: Multiple Personality and the Sciences of Memory.* Princeton, N.J.: Princeton University Press.

Harvey, David. 1989. *The Condition of Postmodernity.* Cambridge, Mass.: Blackwell.

Hunter, James Davison. 1983. *American Evangelicalism: Conservative Religion and the Quandary of Modernity.* New Brunswick, N.J.: Rutgers University Press.

Kenny, Michael G. 1986. *The Passion of Anselm Bourne: Multiple Personality in American Culture.* Smithsonian Series in Ethnographic Inquiry. Washington, D.C.: Smithsonian Institution Press.

Koteen, Judi Pope, ed. 1989. *Last Waltz of the Tyrants: The Prophecy.* Channeled by J. Z. Knight. Hillsboro, Ore.: Beyond Words Publishing.

Manderscheid, Ronald W., and Mary Anne Sonnenschein, eds. 1990. *Mental Health, United States 1990.* National Institute of Mental Health, U.S. Department of Health and Human Services. Washington, D.C.: U.S. Government Printing Office.

Many Voices. 1995. Vol. 7, no. 2 (Apr).

Merskey, H. 1992. "The Manufacture of Personalities: The Production of Multiple Per-sonality Disorder." *British Journal of Psychiatry* 160: 327–40.

Nathan, Debbie. 1994. "Dividing to Conquer: Women, Men, and the Making of Mul-tiple Personality Disorder." *Social Text* 40 (Fall): 77–114.

Nathan, Debbie, and Michael Snedeker. 1995. *Satan's Silence: Ritual Abuse and the Making of a Modern American Witch Hunt.* New York: Basic Books.

Nietzel, Michael T., Douglas A. Bernstein, and Richard Milich. 1991. *Introduction to Clinical Psychology,* 3rd ed. Englewood Cliffs, N.J.: Prentice Hall.

Nolan, James L., Jr. 1998. *The Therapeutic State: Justifying Government at Century's End.* New York: New York University Press.

Ofshe, Richard, and Ethan Watters. 1994. *Making Monsters: False Memories, Psycho-therapy, and Sexual Hysteria.* New York: Charles Scribner's Sons.

O'Leary, Stephen D. 1994. *Arguing the Apocalypse: A Theory of Millennial Rhetoric.* New York: Oxford University Press.

Rieff, Philip. 1966. *The Triumph of the Therapeutic: Uses of Faith after Freud.* New York: Harper and Row.

Rose, Elizabeth S. (pseud.). 1993. "Surviving the Unbelievable: A First-person Account of Cult Ritual Abuse." *Ms.* Jan./Feb., 40–45.

Ross, Colin A. 1991. "Epidemiology of Multiple Personality Disorder and Dissociation." *Psychiatric Clinics of North America* 14(3):503–16.

Rupert, Glenn A. 1992. "Employing the New Age: Training Seminars." In *Perspectives on the New Age,* Ed. James R. Lewis and J. Gordon Melton, 127–35. Albany, N.Y.: State University of New York Press.

Saks, Elyn R. 1994. "Does Multiple Personality Disorder Exist? The Beliefs, the Data, and the Law." *International Journal of Law and Psychiatry* 17(1):43–78.

Turkle, Sherry. 1996. "Who Am We?" *Wired,* Jan., 149–52, 194–99.

W., Lynn, ed. 1993. *Mending Ourselves: Expressions of Healing and Self-integration.* Cincinatti, Ohio: Many Voices Press.

Wright, Lawrence. 1994. *Remembering Satan.* New York: Knopf.

Wuthrow, Robert. 1994. *Sharing the Journey: Support Groups and America's New Quest for Community.* New York: Free Press.

Due Diligence and the Pursuit of Transparency: The Securities and Exchange Commission, 1996

Capital and its markets have long been the object of great conspiracy theories. As a "breathing together," conspiracy (or at least the possibility of conspiracy) seems particularly fitted to the world of money and finance—a world which has long challenged political economists to theorize the vitality that results from the impossible conjunction of spectral, shady, breathlike "value" and the more corporeal, exchangeable, transformable "commodity." In addition, the very "shadiness" of value seems to allow and even promote the kind of shady deals that characterize conspiracies—the con's piracies. Indeed, while the term *conspiracy* itself has a long history, the first conjunction of "conspiracy" and "theory" is located by William Safire (in cahoots with Merriam-Webster) in talk about the workings of capital:

> In the Oct. 22, 1945 edition of *The New Republic,* Henry Morgenthau Jr., the Treasury Secretary, was quoted predicting "the end of heavy industry in Germany will permit transfer of factories to the very places where they would have been located in the first place, if access to raw materials, markets, labor and power had been really decisive factors in European development." Heinz Eulau, assistant editor of *The New Republic,* waved this idea off: "Mr. Morgenthau's conspiracy theory simply does not hold." (Safire 1995, 24)

By the 1990s it almost goes without saying that capital and markets have become globalized, and while conspiracy theories may "hold" no better, the embrace of cooperation has certainly been tightened. Lord Kingsdown, governor of the Bank of England from 1982 to 1993, recently explained the growth in the volume and global integration of financial transactions in *The Banker's Magazine,* noting how such dynamic growth has "required monetary authorities to cooperate ever more closely," to maintain orders of risk management appropriate for an intensely entangled financial system:

> What lies behind this extraordinary growth? First, of course, has been the continued growth of international trade and investment flows.

> This, and the global reach of major multinational corporations, have called for a comparable growth in the provision of financial services. Even more important has been the tide of liberalization that has affected the financial services industry. In particular, controls over cross-border transactions among industrialized countries have been almost completely eliminated. Also, the evolution in information technology has dramatically reduced the cost of financial transactions and made possible the development of markets in sophisticated derivative instruments. A fourth development with far-reaching implications has been securitization. As the range of financial instruments has grown, so has the share that is marketable as securities.
>
> These developments have made the distinction between the three main areas of financial activity—banking, securities business, and industry—harder to define. New forms of maturity transformation, and the desire for liquidity on both the liability and asset sides of balance sheets, have created new orders of risk management that cross traditional boundaries between financial institutions. (Kingsdown 1994, 34)

Conspiracy theories about the market may hold no better now than they did in 1945. But they nonetheless seem particularly evocative, as a way to organize the extraordinary density of linkages which characterize contemporary global order, and its "market system" in particular. To the sober banker's description circulated by Kingsdown, however, one must add John McClure's commentary on the novels of Don DeLillo, whose texts convey a world in which

> capitalism has penetrated everywhere, but its penetration has not resulted in global rationalization and Weber's iron cage. It seems instead to have sponsored a profound reversal: the emergence of zones and forces like those that imperial expansion has erased: jungle-like techno-tangles . . . secret cults with their own codes and ceremonies, vast conspiracies. "This is the age of conspiracy," says a character in *Running Dog,* with the mixture of wonder and revulsion that is everywhere in DeLillo's work. This is "the age of connections, links, secret relationships." These zones and forces—the various computer circuits, multinational business networks, espionage agencies, private armies, and unconventional political players—make a mockery of the collective desire of democracy and social justice. . . . Conspiracy theory, on which the thriller is based, replaces religion as a means of mapping the world without disenchanting it, robbing it of its mystery . . . . It offers us satisfactions similar to those offered by religions and religiously inflected romance: both the satisfaction of living among secrets, in a mysterious world, and the satisfaction of gaining access to secrets, being "in the know." (McClure 1991, 102–3)

DeLillo's novels begin to provide a language of description for the "age of conspiracy" in which we seem to live—which cannot be captured in the dry tones of the business press. To accomplish this, DeLillo depends on the allure of mystery and biting cynicism about social justice. In his account of the techno-tangles of contemporary capitalism, democracy has little room to breath, and satisfaction comes from being "in the know" about this brutal fact. In this essay we, too, seek a vocabulary and conceptual scheme for understanding a world of complex cross-cutting linkages. Our tactic is ethnographic rather than fictional, and overtly works to locate spaces within contemporary capitalism where democracy is pursued, even if never perfectly realized. Thus we choose to interview Michael Mann, who then was director of the Office of International Affairs at the U.S. Securities and Exchange Commission; he has since moved into private practice in a Washington, D.C., law firm.

We first approached Mann to discuss our interests in changing perceptions of the role of commercial corporations in national welfare, hoping he could connect us to interviewees involved in antitrust legislation, consortium busting, or some other idea of work linked to the control of corporate activity. We wanted to learn who was "taking on the giants," and then ask them how they were doing it. By the time we had gotten through preliminary discussion of Michael Mann's own work, we knew we needed to refocus. If we wanted to learn how "new orders of risk management," capital's crossings of "traditional boundaries," and the "far-reaching implications . . . of securitization" occur in practice, within the dynamic change of globalization, we needed to talk to Michael Mann himself.

While conspiracy theories are not an overt part of Mann's rhetoric, he nonetheless was involved on a daily basis with work which many would consider conspiracy busting. Mann's main mission, institutionalized by and through the SEC, was disclosure. By SEC logic, corporations cannot hide secrets, or trade them internally; corporations cannot obscure important information and thereby fraudulently deny risk; corporations cannot hide their crossholdings and thereby cannot restrain the impetus of the venture capitalist, who, according to Michael Mann, "at least consents to the risk, placing it where it belongs, where it can be valued." Furthermore, by Mann's system of accounting, the SEC gives corporations incentive to adhere not only to legal practice, but to "best practice." In short, corporations must be transparent, to the letter of the law, and beyond. The basic equation in this geometry is money, information, and the "right to do business," exchanged for each other, with a middleman to oversee the transfer.

If conspiracy theories hold because they religiously set up two separate worlds, this one of appearances and that other one of secrets, then Michael Mann is an interesting ethnographic subject because, in his role at the SEC, he was a middleman, situated in the rushing traffic between these realms. And in that sense he serves as a metonym for the SEC itself, an organization very much in the middle; what kinds of middles, and what happens in them, will emerge below.

1. An Ethnogenealogy of the SEC

Prior to 1933, securities market regulation in the United States existed primarily at the level of the states, which had passed "blue sky" laws of varying degrees of strength to protect individual investors from fraudulent stock sales. Interstate traffic in securities was not regulated, and the securities industry's own internal regulations "were designed to protect the exchanges and their members, not necessarily investors" (Khademian 1992, 25). A growing national economy and the forceful opposition of Wall Street kept federal securities regulations from being legislated.

But following the 1929 crash of the stock market and the onset of the Depression, "Wall Street had neither the economic stamina nor the political clout to prevent the passage of the Securities Act of 1933." Hearings of the Senate Banking and Currency Committee, begun in 1932, became "a public display of Wall Street's dirtiest dealings" (Khademian 1992, 26–27).

In addition to such "public display," events were moved by a powerful alliance of political figures. Franklin Roosevelt had made securities regulation part of his campaign; in office, he commissioned former Federal Trade Commission chairman Huston Thompson to draft legislation. Thompson's draft was criticized in Senate hearings both for its "lack of clarity," and particularly for "its provision that the FTC . . . should judge the solvency of corporations issuing stock" (Khademian 1992, 27–28). Rep. Sam Rayburn (D-Texas) was enrolled to keep things moving in the direction Roosevelt desired; Rayburn's own motivations stemmed in part from a desire to forestall a clear conspiracy: "When a people's faith is shaken in a business the business becomes halting and lame . . . only one thing can follow in the wake of this destroyed confidence . . . the evils that attend socialism, bolshevism, and communism" (quoted in Parrish 1970, 42).

It may have been Rayburn who recommended that Roosevelt enlist Felix Frankfurter, "a Harvard law professor and a longtime friend and associate. Frankfurter responded by coming to Washington with three former students to redraft the bill: James Landis, Benjamin Cohen, and Thomas Corcoran" (Khademian 1992, 28). The relatively new involvement of this kind of "unelected expertise" in the federal government in the New Deal period would in turn become fodder for conspiracy theories of yet another stripe. Such theories were advanced by "captains of industry" such as Raoul Desvernine, president of Crucible Steel and a prominent figure in the right-wing Liberty League, who pointed to vague but ominous hidden forces in his 1936 book *Democratic Despotism:*

> We have seen that our traditional democratic ideas have been violently distorted, and our constitutional concepts manhandled, by a coterie of visionaries, appointed to non-elective key positions, and that the

President himself has progressed under their tutelage to a practical ,cceptance of their "professed objectives." We have seen that the New Deal was not included in the Democratic platform of 1932. It was rather evolved from the motives and ideals of those who sprang out of the unknown after the election. We are now confronted with a universal belief in the philosophy of the "New Order" by all those composing the directive force of the New Deal. . . .

To gain power by a cunning misuse of democratic methods is the most generally adopted technique of all politicians, who are planning to destroy, for their own self-seeking purposes, cherished governmental theories and institutions, and history proves it to be more efficacious, and certainly less perilous, than violence. . . . The party names, platforms, and principles, which were utilized as a means to gain power are remolded to fit the real motives and ideals of the incipient usurpers. (Quoted in Davis 1971, 270–71)

But the conspiratorial vision of a cunning New Deal cabal conjured up by Desvernine seems to have had little tangible effect. The rush of events and the flush of Roosevelt's first hundred days conspired to push through the massive legislative reforms of the early New Deal. Frankfurter and his Harvard "coterie" rewrote the Thompson securities legislation in a matter of days. The problem of reconciling it with the original Thompson bill that had passed through the Senate was settled by Rayburn's power: "As Chairman of the conference committee, Rayburn immediately called a vote on the Senate version— producing, as he had anticipated, a tie. He then declared the House version the winner by default" (Khademian 1992, 28). So passed the Securities Act of 1933.

Coexisting with the exercise of such singular power was a more subtle and ironic force, the effects of which can still be felt today. When the redrafted bill passed in the House, Cohen told Landis that Rayburn had made the comment (we are firmly within the realm of rumor here) that he "did not know whether the bill passed so readily because it was so damned good or so damned incomprehensible." [1] The origin of the SEC's mission of transparency and disclosure of information thus appears to have depended on the lack of these very qualities. The "incomprehensibility" of securities regulations will come up again in this history, continually destabilizing the opposition between disclosure and secrecy, between what's available to the knowing subject and what isn't.

But the overt logic "underlying the Securities Act was the premise that an *informed* investor was an investor protected from the fraudulent sale of new securities" (Khademian 1992, 29). This would become the logic of disclosure that would underwrite the regulation of the securities industry. At the time it was theorized that one of the things that would give the SEC leverage to enforce disclosure was timing. If a filing was incomplete or incorrect, the agency (at that time, the Federal Trade Commission) could place a stop order on the

sale of stock, and since "time was money," it would be in the economic interests of the industry to comply with disclosure requirements.

After securities became regulated in 1933, attention turned to the exchanges
themselves. Where the Securities Act of 1933 was marked by haste, force, and
incomprehension, the Securities and Exchange Act of 1934 would be shaped
by the politics of resistance and the spirit of compromise—and incomprehension. Resistance was led by the president of the New York Stock Exchange,
Richard Whitney, who believed that the free market system was a "perfect
institution" which the federal government should not be permitted to regulate
or otherwise interfere with (Khademian 1992, 33). It was rumored in a later
letter to Landis that Whitney, "desperate . . . to unite his constituency," returned to New York during the period in which the legislation was being negotiated in Washington and "began to circulate the idea that the legislation had
been written 'by a bunch of Jews out to get [J. P.] Morgan.' " [2]

It would be more productive and more historically responsible to trace the
operations of a more subtle kind of shared spirit than a Jewish one: a spirit of
compromise and reluctance to invoke the powers of written law, a spirit which
in fact breathed through both Whitney and these New Dealers. "Whitney and
the governing cabal of the New York Stock Exchange" (Parrish 1970, 130) did
not want statutory restrictions on securities and their exchange to be part of a
"fixed rule of law," but instead wanted authority to reside in a commission,
which could invoke as well as revoke rules and regulations. The drafters of the
legislation were split: some of them advocated "explicit statutory prohibitions
and requirements," while the others "preached more administration and less
legislation." It was the latter faction, closer in spirit to Whitney and Wall
Street, which would prevail. Landis was the key figure.

> "The problem is very complex," Landis said, "very delicate, very
> technical. . . . Flexibility and the opportunity to move rapidly, to ex-
> periment, as the exchange itself experiments . . . is imperative in
> legislation of this type." To individuals like Whitney, discretion and
> flexibility meant little more than yawning statutory crevices where
> one could place more than enough legal dynamite to demolish a regu-
> latory structure. Landis's pleas sprang, in part, from genuine uncer-
> tainty about effective regulatory techniques and from an unwilling-
> ness to limit administrative resources. But Landis and others also
> recognized the desirability of compromise. The bill needed new polit-
> ical allies and they could be recruited only by real concessions. (Par-
> rish 1970, 124–25)

Thus began a lengthy and tumultuous period of compromise between New
Dealers (who had lost the momentum of the first hundred days) and Wall Street,
compromises which resulted in what many actors at the time and historians and
commentators since have argued was a securities regulatory apparatus that was

weaker than what, ideally, might have been obtained. But if there is one thing that good history or good ethnography shows, it is that the ideal (and "conspiracy" is certainly an ideal concept) never in fact occurs, especially in the muddled affairs of politics. Historian Michael Parrish provides ample detail of the pragmatic and cultural context in which Landis and others had to work on their way to the eventual enactment of the Securities Exchange Act of 1934, and the creation of the SEC. One residing feature was "incomprehension." To quote but one brief passage from many pages describing the months-long process:

> The Seventy-third Congress was not inclined to radicalism. While Roosevelt went fishing for seventeen days in the Caribbean, the revised bill encountered major difficulties. . . . Taken as a whole, the Interstate Commerce Committee of seventeen Democrats and seven Republicans was distinguished by its mediocrity: one tobacco farmer, one dairy farmer, one automobile dealer, one independent oil producer, one railroad engineer, four small manufacturers. . . . Like most House committees in 1934, it was Southern in leadership, pedestrian in temperament, and provincial in allegiance. With [a few] exception[s], . . . members of the committee were not intellectually equipped to evaluate the details of exchange legislation. They were capable, however, of accepting at face value the anguished cries of exchange presidents, brokers, dealers, floor traders, specialists, and businessmen who predicted increased unemployment and financial chaos if the bill became law. Sensitive to these pressures and to the limitations of his fellows, Rayburn . . . ordered revisions . . . that would anticipate objections and avoid a committee imbroglio. These defensive alterations further weakened the measure. . . .
>
> Even these concessions did not satisfy the full House committee. Members denounced the margin ratios as excessive. . . . "There will be a statutory formula for margins," Rayburn said after [a subcommittee] meeting, "but it is not fixed yet." He denied, rather sheepishly, that there was a conspiracy at work to mutilate the legislation. "That," he said, "is just so much tommyrot." (Parrish 1970, 131–33)

Pragmatic compromises, always subject to second-guessing and the apparent clarities of hindsight, continued to characterize the early history of the SEC. One result was the agency's emphasis of "disclosure" as its primary mission:

> The acquisition of the FTC's rule-making authority gave the SEC a mandate to make sweeping changes in the reporting of financial data, the structure of the markets, and trading practices. . . . However, in a precedent set by the first members of the agency, the SEC chose to use its rule-making authority sparingly, to *structure* the reporting of data and to *structure* the trading activities on an exchange. Instead, the enforcement of disclosure became its central objective. This

approach was determined as much by the commissioners' desire to
see the agency and the New Deal succeed as by congressional and
presidential concerns that the agency maintain a balance between the
interests of public investors and those of Wall Street. (Khademian
1992, 37)

Another part of such a balance was the appointment of Joseph Kennedy as
the first chairman, which "sent a signal to the financial industry: the administration sought to work with Wall Street to restore investor confidence in the
market and to speed economic recovery.... Had Roosevelt selected a chairman
with a strong interest in reforming the markets, Wall Street might have reacted
adversely, and the New Deal recovery plan could have fizzled as public issues
of securities dwindled" (Khademian 1992:39). Kennedy was appointed, and
the system was made to work.

2. The Lure of the SEC, and Some SEC Lore

M. FORTUN: Can you give us a brief version of how you came to work at
the SEC?

MANN: I went to Antioch Law School. Antioch required you to take a full
semester and work somewhere in the government, or in public service. I had
always been fascinated with the role of the SEC as a disclosure agency, in
giving just raw information out about companies. I had used the information
at one time during a campaign to stop the B-1 bomber, to write an article
about the B-1's prime contractor, Rockwell International, and how Rockwell
had placed its B-1 subcontracts in every Congressional district in order to
build vested interests in building the B-1. All that information came out of
SEC filings. This experience showed me that the SEC was really the place
where all the information about corporate America resided. The SEC's mission was neutral: it didn't matter whether it was during Nixon or Ford or anyone else—the information was out there, it had to be disclosed, and that's
what the SEC stood for. So I was fascinated by this concept of the SEC and
what its role was. The head of the enforcement division at the time, Stanley
Sporkin,[3] taught a securities class at Antioch, and the SEC was very open
to having Antioch students, unlike a lot of other, more mainstream organizations and law firms. So I was able to get an internship here in the Division of
Enforcement.

During the internship I was assigned to work on a case against a company
called Occidental Petroleum, that had purchased Hooker Chemical—a company best known for its poisonous waste dumps all over the United States,
including one called Love Canal. The question arose in this case: when did
Occidental know of the problems, and when did they tell their shareholders? I
got involved at the very end of this investigation as a student, and as with a

lot of the things at the SEC, people left and by the time the investigation was over, I was the only living person at the SEC, at a staff level, who knew anything about it. So when Occidental said they wanted to settle the case, the crux of which was that Occidental had failed to disclose that they had contingent liability for its environmental dumps of over a billion dollars, I was assigned to it. Other things that had come up in the course of this case were that Armand Hammer, who had been the chairman, had required every director at the time that he became a director to give him an undated resignation letter. They had made illegal campaign contributions, they had done many things that should have been disclosed. There were many memos in many files about the toxics, because everybody who was doing anything was sending them and they kept a copy, by the by. It's impossible to destroy a memo today, because once it is delivered to a third person, there are copies left all over the place. And that's what this case built on.

This was a very complex settlement, because it involved not only these waste dumps, and stating what we had found, but also what their remedy would be, since the SEC at that time had no power to seek monetary penalties. It was more a remedy of trying to fix the process for considering and disclosing these types of problems in the future. The SEC used a rather novel approach to try to achieve an equitable result.

The settlement discussions went on for a long time, my internship finished, and the case wasn't done, so they asked if I would come back in the summer. I came back in the summer, the case was settled that summer, and at the end of the summer I was trying to figure out what I would do for a law job, because I had just another year of law school. And they said they'd be pleased to have me come back, I said I'd love to come, so I got a job offer and came in the fall of 1981 in the Division of Enforcement. I worked there for the next eight years.

K. FORTUN: The perception of risk in this story—"we might be doing something bad, so I'm going to save the memo so I'm not the only one caught doing it"—that leads to people keeping things that are incriminating, if they're kind of stuck in the middle of collective culpability: has perception of individual responsibility for decisions within these commercial structures changed, so that this kind of data is around more now than it would have been twenty years ago?

MANN: Organizations are much bigger today than they were. But I think there are so many things that have changed, I don't think it's any one particular aspect. First of all, we have the ability to gather and manage data in a way that we've never been able to do it before. So how much is saved is a quantum greater, because we have Xerox machines, we have fax machines, we have computers that hold the data. People's productivity is greater also. People today put in a memo what they otherwise would have said orally. People need to put it in a memo, because there are more decision makers involved. So part of this is proresponsibility, where you can actually filter something out—I can send an e-mail to fifteen colleagues to let them know what's going on, and then I get their input and I do a better job because of that. The fact that one of my colleagues saves that, for any number of reasons, is not terribly material to whether there's culpability or not. Also, I've seen people who keep this because they just love to see the stuff they've written.

At the end of a negotiation, I have a practice where I throw away most of the drafts, other than the things that are meaningful for understanding the negotiation. I do a memo that says what the basis of the deal was, but I don't want somebody confused about what was going on. It's not helpful. What's helpful is the fact that we thought this was the good deal, and that's the only thing that really matters. So I believe it's important to have a practice of destroying drafts, not retaining things that aren't meaningful for a hundred years, other than things that are historically significant for understanding the deal.

K. FORTUN: When the Occidental-Hooker case was settled, what did it do? If the SEC was good for you when you were working on the B-1 bomber because it made information available, what was the function of this settlement?

MANN: There were a lot of different functions. First, that was settled in 1979, and I think the State of New York just finished their case against Occidental and Hooker last year. So one thing it demonstrated was that the SEC as a disclosure agency was able to get information—our files became the files that were used by the State of New York, and the State of California, for their cases. We investigated that case very fast, we resolved it very quickly. We didn't get huge penalties or anything else, but what was put into place were procedures for considering and disclosing environmental information. The market got information about what had happened, right away. It was done by consent, it wasn't litigated. So it was negotiated.

And some people said, "well, you know the SEC got sort of half a loaf"— no penalties. The fact was, we put the story out, we put out the documents, the relief we got was not just responsive to what had happened but what could always happen in a boardroom on an environmental case. And it was done by consent. There were reports done by specialists that were required by our settlement, not just to deal with these dumps, but to deal with their whole practice of dealing with dumps. And it brought to the public attention— obviously, the whole Hooker Chemical thing had brought it to the public— but it also showed that there were ways of dealing with this.

So to my mind it showed, if you want to have markets, you can't dilly-dally around with always having criminal prosecutions that take a decade. Sometimes it's better to get in and get out, get the information to the market, try to make the system run better. Because there's no question there's corruption in the world—there are bad people, they do bad things. But you can't stop the music and just wait, until you prosecute every bad act. So if you're going to have a system that's going to be responsive—everybody read that case and said, "Holy smokes! The SEC will bring an environmental case?" Because that's what it did.

K. FORTUN: Was that the origin of environmental reporting requirements?

MANN: Well, there were no environmental reporting requirements. Those are all based on the SEC disclosure requirements. There are now some guides that have been done since then. But that was one of the first environmental cases that was done. This was a good idea that somebody had, and here's something that you can do, and our laws are flexible enough that the SEC can do it.

I wasn't involved in this, but the SEC did a case where there was a huge scandal—the Salomon Brothers treasury notes scandal. There were a hundred firms that were alleged to have traded illegally. There was no way the SEC logistically could have brought every case. So what the SEC did was craft a global settlement with the one hundred firms. The Foreign Corrupt Practices Act era was the same way: there were hundreds of companies that were found to be paying illegal bribes in the 1970s. The SEC said, if you do a report on what you've been doing, and what controls you will put in place to prevent them from recurring, we'll give you a pass if you make it public. And so in the seventies, most of the Foreign Corrupt Practices Act "cases" were reports by these companies. It was a way of trying to deal with a problem that was identified, and get it over with fast. Still, it was really an important set of issues: governments fell as a result of the information that was disclosed—in Japan, for example, in the Lockheed scandal.[4]

I think the point is, keep your objective in mind. The SEC doesn't exist just to punish people, but as a forward-looking force for getting information to the market. And that means sometimes leaving something on the table to obtain agreement regarding this prior conduct. Because if you're telling somebody there are no compromises possible, they're then fighting for their life, and it will be impossible to address the broader issues.

I'll give you another example. An investigation I worked on when I was a very junior staff attorney, involved a company that said, publicly, we will go bankrupt if the labor union doesn't submit to our terms. We all agreed that this was a great case to investigate, because it seemed clear that the company was not going to go bankrupt. So we did a very fast investigation, about a week. And it appeared that it was a lie. But we needed something else, the "dispositive fact." In the course of the investigation we learned that the company had gone to the banks to borrow more money. So we wanted to find out what they told the banker, about whether they were solvent or not. It was just an investigation to determine whether they really thought they were insolvent or not.

To get the banking information we needed to get authorized by the SEC to compel the banks to answer our questions. The commission, however, was very wary of getting involved in what was a huge labor dispute, and other things. We argued very hard about how to proceed, and the solution was to put out a release that identified the bad practices without identifying the company, with the conclusion that such practices would be punished in the future. So instead of a protracted investigation and litigation, we put this release out the next week. And while no case was ever brought, the practice was never used in the same way again.

Indeed, I would argue that it would have made no difference for the outcome if we'd investigated it forever, and named the company. The release was put out, and it really was noticed and written about, and it got out there. In three weeks we were done, it was over. And it was a great victory for us. We didn't have any scalps, we didn't have any money, we didn't have anything else. But it affected conduct immediately.

3. Analytic Communities, Trading Cultures, and Paper Tigers

MANN: What really became interesting for me was this whole concept of integrity. When you look at Germany, you see an incredibly strong economy, and no securities market of any size.[5] You ask people, what's the difference? They say, well, insiders trade in Germany; everything's cross-held; all the boards are cross-held; and there's no confidence that I, as a smart person, can get access to the information that I need to profit in the market. In the United States there's much more of a belief that you can get the information. So one out of every three households holds mutual funds today. There are over sixty million individual investors here. In Germany, people buy stamps, they buy other stuff. I remember being in Switzerland, at a very big private Swiss investment bank, and I was talking to the head of the bank. He said, "We gave bonuses last week." I asked what happened. He said, "Well, you know, it was really amazing. I was sitting in my office, and an armored truck pulled up, and they started carting in all this cash. So I said to my managing director, 'We're not a bank, what's all this money for?' And he said we're giving out bonuses. And I said, aren't people going to deposit it? And he said no, we gave them the option of cash."

And so I asked if this was to avoid taxes, and he said "no, they report it all. People just feel more comfortable with the cash." And these were people taking hundreds of thousands of Swiss francs in cash, a very profitable bank. They wanted the cash to salt it away here or there, they weren't going to buy stock with it.

K. FORTUN: What is the benefit of Americans holding mutual funds and having faith in the market, instead of holding all this cash?

MANN: My view is that if you look at the structure of our market—look at a company like Microsoft. It didn't exist ten years ago. Netscape, a $2 billion company, it didn't exist two years ago. They got all this capital from the market, to develop their products. And they returned it tenfold to the people who put the money in. So it not only makes capital available for long shots that end up being huge corporations, but they also have returned something to the people that have invested in them.

If you have a disclosure system that makes information available, that does a couple of things. First, it creates an analytical community that's highly sophisticated. A venture capitalist who has the ability to look at an industry and say, Okay, these ten companies, I think one of them has a concept that will do well, I'm going to invest in the group. The reason why he'll do that is because he knows that if one of them does develop the idea into a viable concept, he can sell it in the market, and he can sell it rather quickly. That kind of market opportunity creates the ability to fund ideas. In contrast, the bank loan officer only cares about one thing, whether the loan's going to be repaid. He doesn't care about his equity stake in it because he doesn't want an equity stake. He wants his money back with interest and he wants his fee for making the loan. Well, that's not going to stimulate someone to either analyze or try to identify whether a company has the potential to be the next Microsoft. If you look at markets like those in the United States, what you see is investors willing to risk their money for an equity stake rather than a fixed, albeit guaranteed, interest rate.

Money, in terms of loans in the United States, is also available through the securities markets via money markets. Japan, until recently, hasn't had money markets. Money markets allow the individual investor to put their money directly into the commercial paper market. When I buy a money market fund, I'm loaning money to GM or some other highly rated borrower. No middle man, other than a broker that's putting together the instrument. And GM is borrowing at a lower rate than they would from the bank. That means that GM can loan money to somebody to buy a car, at a lower rate than that of a bank. The U.S. market for securitization of debt is unique. We securitize uniform contracts, credit card debt, and almost anything else. Through securitization, Fannie Mae or Ginnie Mae drive down mortgage rates for home ownership, and our rates are far lower than in most countries in the world. And it's long-term loan money, not like in Mexico, where it's every six months. Even bank loans don't stay in a bank for long: they get packaged and sold into the securities market—where, I would argue, they belong. People are then valuing the time-value of money and what kind of risk they want: interest rate risk, term risk. That's what markets are great for. And so if you have really good, functioning markets, you create all these opportunities. Sure, you have businesses making money packaging it, but you're taking risk and putting it where it belongs, in a place where people can value it. And you're giving them the information to value it. And you're making more capital available for business, making people compete for the capital on the basis of the information that's made available.

If you compare an offering in the United States to an offering, say, in the Eurobond market, with the same company doing the offering, you'll pay more in the Eurobond market for the money. It's true that in Europe you won't have to give as much information, but you'll pay more, up to a hundred basis points for a large offering. If you're talking about a billion-dollar offering, that's a hundred million dollars. That's a lot of money.

K. FORTUN: If you take the example of something like the Barings deal, where basically one trader destroys an entire corporation, does the greater likelihood of risk crossing borders stem from simple fact that there's more transborder activity? Is it just volume that increases the risk?

MANN: It's volume—the instruments have gotten more complex—and the nature of the markets have become more complex. The kinds of derivatives that Barings was trading didn't exist in 1975.

M. FORTUN: What allows them to exist now?

MANN: The market is just very dynamic, and people have created instruments that are synthetic, that are designed to deal with particular needs of particular companies.

M. FORTUN: The National Association of Securities Dealers (NASD) talks both of technological change, and changes in economic and financial theory, that allows the creation of things like derivatives—both responding to change and creating further change.

MANN: And also, higher math and computers have added to the ability— one of the issues in creating an exotic new instrument, is valuing it. Figuring out how you value it and how you sell it. And that is a big issue with any of these new instruments, because they may not have trading markets.

M. FORTUN: But is that your job or their job?

MANN: That's their job. It's the SEC's job to make sure that they're telling all the information they should tell. For example, look at the Bankers Trust case, where Bankers Trust wasn't really telling Gibson Greetings the information they needed to know to understand the way it was being valued, and as a result Gibson was taking risks that it didn't understand.

M. FORTUN: So how do you figure out new disclosure mechanisms for these new processes?

MANN: We have a very broad law: it requires full disclosure—the truth. Some of it is accounting, and there's a huge debate in the accounting world over what the appropriate disclosure is. I remember talking to our chief accountant a few years ago about the difficulty of valuing new instruments. He said, You know, I was an accountant in Houston when the oil boom came to an end, and he recounted that people told him it was impossible to figure out the value of one of these "see-through" buildings—the overbuilt and vacant office buildings. He said, You offer a low enough, and you'll find the value! You start at zero and start working up! So that's one approach; I don't necessarily suggest it here.

But I think that if you recognize that the market's dynamic, it means that your regulation has to change. The SEC has a rule concerning net capital: it requires a firm to have at least 15 percent. It's a clear rule but it's awfully arbitrary and probably not right, in the kind of market that we have today, where you can lay risk off in a variety of ways. You have to allow for some netting of positions, you have to allow for giving credit to different kinds of instruments, and so forth, that didn't exist at the time the rule was written. This is exactly what the SEC is now studying; it's allowing more modeling to take place, where the modeling is based on prior trading experience, and so on.

So the problem for the SEC is trying to figure out how you get to that new answer. In an internationalized marketplace, where a firm can keep its books in London, and hold 3 percent or 1 percent in capital—or it can keep it in New York, where 15 percent is required: the SEC has to deal with that competitive reality. The way to deal with it is not just to say, Our rules are the best and therefore you should just want to be here. The way to deal with it is to deal in the international marketplace and talk to people, talk to the other regulators, and try to find rules that can be applied as consistently as possible, so that you don't have a race to the bottom.

K. FORTUN: With this fast-paced change, does the burden of producing the analytic tools for disclosure lie more with the SEC because there's not an internal production of them by accounting departments?

MANN: No, I don't think so. What's interesting is, when you look at internal controls, you see that they aren't just for SEC compliance—you have to have them if you want to be in business next year. You've got to have them. One of the amazing things about American firms is that they have great internal controls. I wouldn't endorse everybody's by this, but it's really interesting to see how well controlled most of the American trading firms are by comparison to their counterparts, and how well-thought things are. Because they want to be in business tomorrow. This is their business. If you look at the profitability of the American firms in Japan during the last ten years compared to any other country, it was huge. And if you ask them why, they'll tell you it was because we were selling derivative instruments to the Japanese, and nobody else had the capabilities that we did. And it was just a technological-human brain power that they had, and they want to safeguard that. So it would be foolish for them not to want and develop the best controls. They make money doing it. The SEC can't rely on that solely, but it is something. It is working to create a culture, and a legal system that endorses a culture in which these controls are seen as important. These guys have been successful because they live in a culture that allows them to innovate. If they want to stay in business, there's no reason for them to act irresponsibly.

Now, that may be a sort of pie-in-the-sky statement that I wouldn't endorse across all boundaries. One of the backbones of our system, however, is that it endorses a system of self-regulation. But unlike many other markets, where self regulation means letting the industry take care of itself, self-regulation here means everybody looking over everybody else's shoulder. So you have the broker who is regulated by his employer, regulated by a self-regulatory organization (SRO), and regulated by the SEC. If the broker screws up, first he'll be in trouble with the SEC. Second, he'll get fired. If he gets caught by the SEC and not the brokerage firm, the brokerage firm may be in trouble for failing to supervise him. They'll get sanctioned by the SEC. So they have every incentive in the world to be watching the broker and to be regulating his conduct. If the broker gets caught by the SEC and not by the self-regulatory organization, because the SRO isn't doing a good job of overseeing him, the SRO will be in trouble with the SEC. And so it's an inverted pyramid. The negative spin on it is, everybody's looking over everybody else's shoulder. The positive spin on it is, what you're doing is creating a culture whereby compliance with rules of fairness is something that is encouraged and makes sense.

M. FORTUN: Robert Reich and others make the argument that because of the wave of mergers and acquisitions, in part because the SEC changed its rules on the fees that brokers could collect, that you get these "paper tigers" that don't serve John Doe. While you have these companies that are doing great because of these mergers and acquisitions, it results—we saw *Newsweek* in the airport, with a cover story on how all these corporations are downsizing. So that the market reinforces that kind of asymmetry.

K. FORTUN: It's partly predicated on the argument that if you're not making pipes, you're not being productive. So the question is, is capital or the market productive in a generalized way?

MANN: First of all, I've never heard the argument that you just stated about deregulating commissions. Basically, when commissions were regulated, you were guaranteed a 5 percent profit on everything you did. So generally the industry hated deregulation of commissions, because it was a gravy train: you just got it, all the way down the line.

But there's an aspect of it that's true: deregulation created and reinforced a trading culture. I think if you look back, people would say the industry was wrong to have opposed deregulation of commissions. Deregulation created enormous competition, and discount brokerage firms were established and access for individual investors to the market at a lower cost was possible. By increasing the liquidity and depth of the market, prices are better suited to value—because liquidity tends to create higher price-earnings ratio—or at least valued more fully. I don't think that means that companies are more susceptible to being acquired. Without question, Michael Milken is the perfect example of somebody who made billions of dollars buying companies and creating different kinds of structures, but not because of deregulation. I've never looked at the social effect of deregulation because I've tended to think that the government shouldn't really be involved in deciding the terms on which a company should be taken over, and when not. There's no question that people lost jobs as a result of some of those restructurings. There's also no question that American business is structured completely different than it was in the 1980s as a result of it. Some of the strength of the market and the economy today is a result of the fact that all this overcapacity in business has been wiped out. Companies just operate in a very different environment than they did in the early 1980s.

I don't know enough to say that it was because the market structure changed. I think that it's a truism, though, that if you compare the United States to France, that we have more capital available for investment here by many, many times. And if you look at the companies that have securities traded in the market, especially new technology companies, you see that their seed capital comes from the securities markets. If you look at the strength of the American economy today, it's not the manufacturing sector as much as it is the technology sector whose innovation has been funded by the markets.

K. FORTUN: Let me ask you about another argument: many now claim that the corporation, rather than the state, constitutes the main threat to freedom and prosperity. And access to capital is one way that the supposed power accumulates. Do you hear that argument anywhere in the world that you move in, and does it make any sense to you?

MANN: This is just my own bias, but there is an aspect of the truth of this in universal banking. Where you can have one institution that controls all access to capital on its own terms. Securities markets are democratizing, because anybody with an idea—he doesn't have to have gone to Harvard, he doesn't have to be from the right family, but he has to have a good idea—can get access to capital. If you believe the vision of power that you just described, then we wouldn't have desktop computers today. IBM would never have allowed it. So I think securities markets are generally democratizing, because they create the opportunity for more merit to rise up.

K. FORTUN: One argument that you hear from the grass-roots environmental movement is that it's much worse than it was ten years ago. We never had any power vis-à-vis DuPont down the street, and now we have even less because there's the possibility of plant flight. So globalization, aided by all these new forms of capital, has exacerbated the problems of democratic participation when corporations are your neighbors.

MANN: There's no question that plant flight is something that's affected by people who are investing, because people who are investing are looking for return. On the other hand, I think shareholder activism, and the activism of pension funds in particular, has very much changed the way companies run themselves in terms of their responsibility to their community. That doesn't mean that they leave a plant in a place that's unprofitable, but it does mean that the board can't sit around and do whatever it wants without fear of a proxy fight. So it's very hard to imagine a situation where you can actually change a plant closing, I think; I don't disagree with that, and that as these companies have gotten bigger, they're looking at a global marketplace.

But the question—and maybe this sounds too free-market even for me— but one of the questions is, a plant moves out of Lynn, Massachusetts, because it can make fluorescent bulbs cheaper in Thailand. What kind of business is going to be able to raise capital to go into that factory in Lynn, Massachusetts, and employ people? And where is that going to come from, where are those possibilities going to come from? Is it worth it to keep the price of fluorescent bulbs high, or is it more worth it to have a plant in there that's doing something else? And I think that it's in some respects cruel, but in other respects, if you look at the companies that are coming in, that's where the focus should be. And the capital market should be worrying about those companies much more than worrying about the company that's moving out, and should be providing capital to those companies. I'd be much more upset with the charge that our market's not accessible for small venture firms, than I would be about the charge that people can't really affect decisions at the corporate level in a large Fortune 100 company.

4. The Office of International Affairs

M. FORTUN: Tell us about the creation of the Office of International Affairs.

MANN: Because we're a disclosure agency, and we're only concerned with the United States market, it might seem somewhat anomalous to have an Office of International Affairs. The way the international program really grew was out of the Division of Enforcement and problems surrounding the internationalization of the U.S. market.

For example, in October 1981 the government of Kuwait announced a tender offer for a company called Santa Fe International. Coincidentally, this is the day I arrived at the SEC. Santa Fe International was trading at about $22 a share, and the offer was a preemptive offer at $51 a share. There were options traded on Santa Fe stock, and the options, exercisable, were traded at $20, $25, $30, and $35. They expired on the third week of the quarter, which happened to be the third week of October. Santa Fe had traded as high as $25 during this quarter, and was trading down at the time the announcement came. So as a result, an October $25 option was worth almost nothing, because the stock was trading down, not up, and there were only three weeks left. Just before the merger announcement, four Swiss banks came in and bought three thousand call options, which is the right to purchase thirty thousand shares of Santa Fe stock, and they purchased them for about a sixteenth of a dollar per share. So for a minuscule investment per share, they made the difference between $22 and $51, approximately. It was not a bad investment.

The SEC sued the Swiss banks and froze all their profits. These were not small Swiss banks: Swiss Bank Corporation, Credit Suisse, Lombard Odier, which is the largest private Swiss bank, and the Swiss office of Chase Manhattan Bank. We froze all the profits here, and then fought over whether they would tell us who their customers were. In the course of this there had been another tender offer where the same thing happened, and the SEC went in front of a judge about two weeks after we had filed the Santa Fe case and argued that people shouldn't be able to trade in the U.S. market, and violate U.S. law, and then hide behind another foreign government's law—that they had basically waived their right. A federal court judge, Milton Pollack in the Southern District of New York, agreed. It was a fantastic argument: the banks said such a judgment would be extraterritorial, and argued it wasn't fair. The judge listened to arguments and when everyone was finished he looked up and said, Okay, do you have anything else to say? The SEC said no; the banks said no; and he then read about a twenty-five page opinion he had written prior to hearing the argument, in which he said it would be a "travesty of justice" to allow this conduct to go forward without knowing who the customer was, and he said to the bank: I'll give you ten days; come forward with the name, everything will be fine; if you don't, it'll be $50,000 a day until you do. And $50,000 a day, for even a large bank, over eternity, is a pretty substantial amount of money. The next thing we knew, the customer "voluntarily" came forward. We're not exactly sure why or how, but he did, and he was culpable.

This sent a shock wave of enormous proportion through the foreign banking community. The result of it was that over the next year (1982) we negotiated an agreement with Switzerland where, notwithstanding the fact that insider trading wasn't against the law at the time, all the Swiss banks agreed as a matter of contract to give up customer names in insider trading cases.

K. FORTUN: Is that an example of a memorandum of understanding?

MANN: Yes. This was the first memorandum of understanding we ever negotiated. It was an agreement with the government of Switzerland that blessed a private convention among the Swiss banks whereby they got waivers from their clients to turn over the information, in this very narrow circumstance. It was another example, I think, of going for the objective—dealing with insider trading—rather than the kill—assistance in all SEC cases. There were a lot of other areas where we knew we would need assistance, but this was the one that we could get. So this agreement was made very, very quickly—it was not a treaty, it was just an understanding. It required people to act in good faith. The price of not acting in good faith would be a disaster for them.[6]

K. FORTUN: Did they have to submit to your sense of good conduct, or did they say, "It's our culture, we inside-trade," and you had to go halfway with them?

MANN: The last clause of the agreement said that when insider trading was against the law in Switzerland, the agreement would terminate, because then we could use a treaty on criminal matters. So this was an accommodation based on a recognition by the Swiss that if they wanted to do international business, this was one of the norms, and they were going to have to change. And it wasn't "Lex Americana," it was "the law of the market is different than just being a little Swiss bank." And I think it really was a recognition by the Swiss, very forward-looking and something they deserve a lot of credit for—they want to be, not Swiss banks, they want to be international banks. They want to be able to do business in any market in the world. That means not condoning conduct that makes them pariahs. And they would rather not have the illicit business than have to deal with being seen as protecting bad actors.

K. FORTUN: The perception of the need for an Office of International Affairs, does it come from individual cases like this, or from a larger sense that there's a whole lot of different stuff going on out there now?

MANN: What happened was, from 1982 to 1988, we began developing some of these relationships. And all of our relationships were based on the need to cooperate for cross-border enforcement issues. And in 1989, when Richard Breeden became chairman, very early in his tenure we signed agreements with the Netherlands, France, and met with the U.K. And he came back and said to me, it's bizarre that our international policy is guided by the associate director of enforcement. There are so many other things we should be doing in this area, and I want to have a more neutral approach to it. You can handle international enforcement matters out of your office, but I want more. We've got to deal more with these countries, we've got to worry more about regulating an internationalized market.

That's really when the office was created. I would argue that it really was the perfect way to establish the function, because the SEC is principally a domestic securities regulator, and is about preserving the integrity of the American markets from threats, whether they originate in the U.S. or abroad. The other aspect, thinking of the competitiveness of U.S. markets, and safeguarding that, has only come about later, as we started to deal with the fact that there are other markets out there, and that there could be a race to the bottom. We recognized that the SEC can't be so cavalier as to say we have the best markets, the best standards, and we're never going to listen to anything else that's going on in the international environment. Because you could have the best markets in the world, and if nobody comes to them, it's not going to work. So the SEC needs to be responsive to the competitive pressures of the international market as well. We can't just say, No, we're going to do it our way because our way is best. We need to know what's going on out there.

In addition, the thing that's really changed is, because of the interconnections in the markets, you can now create risks in one market that affect another market in a way that you never could ten years ago. If you look at the Barings case, it's a perfect example of one crazy trader basically sinking a pretty large bank. That can happen more, and you need to have the ability to stay on top of cross-border business.

M. FORTUN: But Barings would argue that they didn't have enough control over this trader. Are you suggesting that there's something structural that makes that kind of thing possible?

MANN: Structural in that you have banks trading on a cross-border basis. I would argue that there's nobody in Osaka that didn't know that Barings was going over the edge. The fact is, the regulators in Singapore didn't know, and the regulators in London didn't know. But the regulators in Singapore and London knew there was a controls problem. They never talked to each other or to Osaka. And there's a problem when people aren't talking to each other. One of the things that regulators spend a lot of time worrying about today is, how should people be talking to each other? You don't want to be in a situation where you've got a concern about an entity, and therefore you put it on the Dow Jones wire: we're really concerned that XYZ corporation doesn't have capital to stay in business—because you know that in about two seconds, they'll truly not have any capital left. On the other hand, you want to be in a position where if you've got a concern, because you're seeing things happen, that regulators can talk to each other and try to resolve the problems before a crisis develops.

K. FORTUN: And the appropriate people to talk to are the regulators in the other country?

MANN: That's right.

K. FORTUN: The challenge of making the U.S. market more accessible to a foreign company: how does that serve the American populace? Why is that a good thing?

MANN: There's one very general way, which is, you project into the future where capital will go. Having it go to New York for investment elsewhere is better than having it go to some other country, because it means there's more capital in the United States available for investment. So it means the expertise stays here. It means we are the capital for capital, and it's accessible and abundant when a Microsoft and the other companies need it.

I think that increasingly in the next decade there will be a real competition for capital. There are more companies out there than capital. And having a capital market that's capable of sustaining itself, and that's viewed as a place to which the capital goes, means something both for the American investor and American companies. The more capital that's in the market, the easier it will be to raise it, and the easier it is to raise it, the less you have to pay for it. So I think there's a "cost of capital" aspect to having the predominant market in the world be in the United States, that will redound to the value of American companies, American entrepreneurs, American investors, and American workers.

The other thing is that as a matter of just investment, having more companies available in the U.S., using U.S.-style disclosure, is better than having people investing abroad. There's no question that as you have a global marketplace, you'll see diversification of investment. You'd be stupid not to have that kind of diversification. And if you have the choice of buying a stock that's listed on the New York Stock Exchange, and that's registered with the SEC, or buying one that's listed on the Egyptian market registered with the Capital Market Authority, I would say, as much as they're trying in Egypt, our system is better developed and works better. The information you'll get will be higher quality, it will be more promptly provided, and it will be more rigorously overseen than in most any other market in the world. So from a U.S. investors standpoint, if you can do your international investing here, I think you're just going to be better off in the long run. So having the companies come here is better.

K. FORTUN: Does it do any good for the noninvesting strata of the population? In the international relations literature, there's a lot of talk about globalization serving the American economy but not John Doe, suggesting an increasing disjuncture between corporate interests and citizen interests?

MANN: I don't specialize in empirical data, so I really don't know the answer. But I would say we have a mortgage market here, and there's money coming into the American market because it's a market with high integrity, on which people expect good returns. And there are more French and German and Japanese investors buying in our mortgage market. That means mortgages should be cheaper.

I'm not sure what the argument would be against this, other than that you are assisting in the export of American capital to foreign companies, and therefore that's bad, I suppose. But generally speaking, I'm more laissez-faire. I believe that money's going to go out there anyway, and it might as well be via a better vehicle. It's really a matter of seeing a few markets in the world developed, and what we are going to do to see our market develop as a competitive market.

There's another aspect to this that probably will show my own xenophobia: I think our rules are the best, and the best way to defend our rules is to have more people use them. There's nobody who doesn't think that it's not expensive to comply with the U.S. system. Would GM or some other company rather not have to make all the disclosure we require, and that they sometimes criticize us for? I would guess that the answer is probably yes. If we think our rules are so good and so appropriate, the place they have to exist is not just in the national marketplace, but in the international marketplace. So it's a challenge to stay relevant, and that's why the SEC is spending so much time trying to help develop international accounting standards that are rigorously applied and high quality. Because we know that just as sure as there's internationalization of marketplaces, there's got to be internationalization of rules. And the SEC has to be proactive in trying to have good rules.

5. Technical Assistance

K. FORTUN: The technical assistance program, how does it work and not work? How did you get the U.S. Agency for International Development to fund it?

MANN: From my perspective, technical assistance is motivated by two things. The SEC views its technical assistance program as a vehicle for exporting the best of its regulatory practice. We only provide technical assistance where we think this effort is clearly in the interest of the United States. Americans are investing abroad all the time; there is an enormous amount of American capital going out. And there's a lot of companies coming in to raise capital here. We spend a lot of money sending all kinds of other things to foreign countries—why not strong markets? It's in our direct interest. Cross-border trading is taking place. Having the markets be more like ours is good for American investors, because they're investing there anyway because their economies are becoming more involved in our economy, because these countries are looking to link somewhere.

This is a hodgepodge of ideas, but if there's a choice between an emerging economy having a trading system that's more like the U.S. system, with rules that are more like the U.S., or having it more like the Europeans, from a competitive standpoint, it's better to have them look more like the U.S. Because the chances are they'll do more business here: they'll do their capital markets business here, they'll do their business deals with American firms. American brokerage firms and American businesses will have an easier time doing business there. Just because the system will be more like ours, it'll be something they're more familiar with. So there are enormous payoffs—when a country is interested in trying to develop the interrelationship, and where they're coming to the U.S. market and looking to the U.S. market as a financial center— to help them develop their markets in a manner that's consistent with ours.

We believe our rules are the best and our effort is motivated by the fact that we recognize these interconnections, and we recognize that American investors want to access foreign markets. How do you talk to people about their restrictive trade practices? How do you talk to them about the fact that Americans want to do business there and can't get access? Technical assistance gives us a platform to develop enormously constructive vehicles for raising these issues.

K. FORTUN: Is this due to expanding demand for places where Americans can invest? I've read that the overall increase in trading can partly be attributed to the Baby Boomers. They've come of age financially, and need these places to put their money.

MANN: No. I think there's a motivation, in that there is more investment taking place abroad, but it's not that specific. It's more of a general belief that this is the appropriate thing to do. And frankly, if there's any general point, it's that if New York is going to remain the center of the financial universe, one of the things that will help it do that is this kind of outreach. And it would be foolish for us not to do it, because people can look anywhere for capital, since it's a global market, and having them look more to New York is in our interest.

M. FORTUN: So what are some of the places you've gone into, and what have been some of the differences and problems in different places?

MANN: We have a substantial technical assistance program for all of South America. We worked with the Mexicans to create an organization called the Council of Securities Regulators for the Americas [COSRA], with the idea that the best way to try to influence the development of high-quality standards would be to try to build consensus over principles of markets throughout the region. There was a real receptivity throughout Latin America to look toward what you'd call "neutral principles of law" that could be implemented—depending on their legal system and so forth—in various different ways, but there would be principles that would be consistent throughout the markets.

One example is transparency. In the securities markets there's a huge debate. In Europe transparency is seen as a competitive issue. Transparent markets mean that people know the size of the transaction, and when it takes place, and they have an idea of who bought and sold, in terms of at least the brokerage firms. That's terrific in a highly liquid market, because people can price better and it allows options to trade better—because if you see the underlying trading, the option will follow the underlying. In Europe, where trading firms are not as well capitalized as they are in the United States, transparency is viewed as working against the firms—they take positions they can't hold, everybody knows they don't have the capital to hold them, and so the price goes down. And so you have a different approach to transparency than you do in the American market.

In an emerging market there is a lot of attraction to opaque markets, because the markets aren't highly liquid. But the best example of what happens in a nontransparent market is what happened to the peso in December 1994. The lack of transparency created suspicion, which tended to push things down, not up. The ultimate example during the peso crisis was that the markets of Southeast Asia fell in sympathy to the crisis. But there was no structural reason for them to fall. Everybody knew there was no reason. But if you look at the one thing that wasn't out there, it was that there was no transparency of what their national banks' reserves were, because they never made them transparent. In response, and in recognition of this point, the economic ministers met last spring and agreed to put out the information to alleviate the pressure on their markets created by the uncertainty.

So in making a decision about transparency there are lots of people who are going to say they don't want it because there could be risk for them as brokers, and all the rest. But having an open discussion of those issues and creating some understanding of its effect was COSRA's goal. This effort created momentum throughout the region to improve their markets and market transparency. The result was improving their stocks' ability to finance in their home market and in the U.S.

K. FORTUN: So you argue that while transparency may not be an obvious good at the local level, looking at the broad system shows how it serves long-term interest? You seem to be asking people to shift their sights from the micro to the macro.

MANN: That's right.

K. FORTUN: Is that hard, especially for people with experience in relatively closed economies?

MANN: I think it's hard to figure out how to make the transition. What the SEC is trying to do is work with a select group of people—the securities regulators, or people from the finance ministries, or the central banks—who may be from emerging markets, but remembering the fact that just because these markets are emerging doesn't mean their officials are unsophisticated. The SEC and these regulators are working together as a unified force to influence the governments, saying this is the way we think the markets of the region should run, and how they should run together.

K. FORTUN: And is the forum for doing that the Institute for Securities Market Development?

MANN: No, the forum for doing that in Latin America is COSRA, where we have these principles that we try to work on every year. We created the Institute for Securities Market Development to try to bring together, more from a training standpoint, all of the emerging markets globally. We normally get attendees from about fifty-five countries, maybe a hundred people a year. It's a two-week training institute, held in the SEC's basement, where we talk about market theory, regulatory theory, how a commission can be set up and how it works, and what from a U.S. standpoint the fundamental features of it are.

The interesting thing about it is not only do they get to hear what we think, but they get to meet each other and hear each others' experience. It becomes quite a cohesive graduating class after two weeks. We've learned that every one has something to learn and something to teach. Sometimes it's more appropriate for the Mexican to tell the Russian how to build a securities market than it is for us. Because the SEC staff has never built one—we already have one.

K. FORTUN: At these forums, you're in a teaching role. When you're dealing with COSRA, that's as colleagues. Is your style of engagement different?

MANN: No, because when you're in a teaching role, you're really not teaching. You're just sort of percolating issues up, and telling them how we do it. We don't presume that we know how anybody else should do it, but we have some experience in this area. There are some things that I feel deeply about, where I tell people, If you don't do this we think you're really going to have a lousy market, or You're making a big mistake. But generally, it's more talking about just how we do it, and exploring the issues with them. Sometimes it's talking about the strategy of how you get to where you want to do it right.

K. FORTUN: Do people feel like they're being told that they have to restructure? Do they think of you as being in cahoots with the IMF?

MANN: No, because everything's free. We don't charge for the advice, we don't charge to come to the institute. They have to figure out how to get themselves here and pay for their room and board. If they want to come, they can come; if they don't want to come, they don't have to come. We are lucky that we have a market that people want to emulate. Our market works pretty well, and people recognize that. There's a lot of pressure to try to figure out how to create institutional investors, how to use markets for savings, and so forth. We have a commodity that people want, and so we try to figure out how best to deliver it.

AID [Agency for International Development] generally likes to send out long-term advisors who sit in an office and are the font of wisdom. The SEC doesn't do that, and told AID that SEC contracts are somewhat different than the average contract. The SEC bills AID for its time, on an hourly basis. The SEC has a contract now for Russia and the NIS [New Independent States] where it provides very specialized assistance, but the SEC decides what it's going to be, and negotiates it with the Russians or the Ukrainians or whomever. There's a group of thirty Russians coming next week for a week-long training program on enforcement. We've translated all the materials into Russian, we'll have Russian translators because they don't have enough English speakers. And sitting in a hotel room for a week, there's going to be this group of thirty Russians, Moldovans, Ukrainians. That is something that we think we do reasonably well. Having somebody go out for six months to sit around and talk to them about enforcement, I don't think works terribly well.

K. FORTUN: If they're having trouble with enforcement there, how far does your expertise go? Aren't whatever problems they're having with enforcement partly grounded in local-level, political-economic dynamics, or in local socio-cultural dynamics?

MANN: A lot of times it's as simple as, What do you do when you find this problem? We were in one country, and they were having trouble getting people to pay for securities. People weren't paying. And they said, What do you do about it? Our response was, Make them pay. This is serious, not paying! That's the foundation of a market, you know, buy and sell. It's just one of those things that you're supposed to do. And you've got to create the understanding that if you do this and you don't pay, you're going to have serious legal problems.

K. FORTUN: And they said: it would be reminiscent of the old regime.

MANN: Exactly. Their reaction was, Gee, isn't that harsh? And we said, Well, it may be harsh, but there's a reason for it, and it's connected with building the market.

K. FORTUN: But if they were concerned that the market would be associated with oppressive regimes that people wanted nothing to do with, it does seem that promoting investor confidence in the market would partly rely on it not being associated with the old regime.

MANN: Yeah, but the old regime was sort of considered to use its power gratuitously. You have to explain what you do. One of the things that is remarkable about the SEC is, here's this agency of 2,700 people worldwide, and if you open the *Wall Street Journal* on any day, there will be an article in the front column on every action the SEC has taken that day. It's a little agency, but our message is sent out clearly every day. There are reporters assigned to this agency that sit down in our basement for the *New York Times,* the *Washington Post,* the *Wall Street Journal*—all they do is consume the news that we create here. So everybody knows and understands what we do, every day. The business community knows, Wall Street knows, and they pay attention to it. So that's not gratuitous. People may say that some of our actions are wrong, but they fully understand what we did and why we thought it was right. So half of what market regulators need to do is to be able to figure out a way to have that kind of credibility, that the message gets out. What we said to this country was, Look, guys, you just need people to understand why you're taking such strong, and appropriate, action.

A much harder example is with some of the Ponzi schemes, the pyramid schemes that have taken place internationally. A regulator is very unpopular when it breaks up a pyramid scheme, because people have been making money—the people at the top of the pyramid. And they're all saying, "You're taking away my gravy train." And what the regulator is saying is, "We're smarter than that; we know this is a pyramid, eventually you're going to lose." But the evidence for it is just information. And so there's really a great reluctance, especially in emerging markets, to break up pyramid schemes. It's difficult enough to do it in the United States; there are people who are complaining here. But the SEC says, We're smarter than that, and we go ahead and do it anyway. Somebody is taking in ten dollars, and then distributing it to people who paid something less, and they're looking to broaden out—just being able to explain the Ponzi scheme is all you have to do. So it's not like it's that complicated. You get five people to pay a dollar, and then you say to them, you get two people to pay a dollar. So then you have ten more people paying a dollar. So you give a dollar fifty back to the first five: they're all happy. You say to the next ten: get me a dollar, and you do the same thing. You're creating a return, but what you have to do is explain that they're not making a return, but they're just taking the money from the guy below them in the pyramid.

K. FORTUN: Is the sense that future predictions can be made, and made reliably, dealt with differently in different cultures?

MANN: I think—no. If you start from the assumption that people are generally greedy, and that greed can be good or greed can be bad, and that greed for bad reasons is bad and for good reasons is good, you have all the people in the world. And really, that's all it is. There's nothing bad about investing in the stock market because you think you're smart and the stock's going to go up and you're going to make a lot of money and be able to buy a new house.

6. Good Faith, Best Practice, and Due Diligence

K. FORTUN: Do you think we have the expertise or personnel right now to keep up with this? It seems we're going to need whole cadres of people to come up with accounting mechanisms, and so on, so you can make them disclose, and that they have mechanisms to disclose with.

MANN: But that's my point: we have very general rules. The most powerful tool in the securities laws is one sentence long. Section 10b says *[walks to bookcase]—*

K. FORTUN: But doesn't disclosure get complicated?

MANN: Disclosure's very complicated, but 10b says *[reading]:* "It shall be unlawful for any person, directly or indirectly, by use of the mails, by any instrumentality of interstate commerce or the mails, or of any facility of an exchange, to employ or use in connection with the purchase or sale of a security," so on and so forth, "any manipulative or deceptive device or contrivance, in contravention of such rules as the Commission may make." *[Snaps book shut]* That's it. That is *the* sentence under which every securities law violation has been prosecuted. We've got reams of rules and guides to try to help people understand it, but basically it's against the law to commit a fraud.

K. FORTUN: But fraud seems to frame the easy ones. I read in your annual report about the cases that were prosecuted. My sense was that old-fashioned lying is definitely still at work, but aren't there new things happening, new financial mechanisms that are much grayer?

MANN: Well, everything's much grayer! But until there's a case brought—

K. FORTUN: But terms like *risk:* how do you assess it? What constitutes risk? What constitutes fair dispersal of information on risk?

MANN: See, our answer has nothing to do with that. Imagine you're the chairman of company X, and you get a report that says, "We found leaching of poisonous chemicals ten feet away from our factory and we better worry about that because we're liable." Unless you've got something telling you that report's wrong, you've got a risk you have to disclose. It's much more objective in our business, in that sense.

K. FORTUN: But twenty years ago, would a report on leaching have been considered a financial risk, when there was little threat of regulatory or legal liability?

MANN: If there was none, no. And we didn't sue Occidental for what Hooker Chemical did in 1956, when they didn't own them. We sued them for what they knew was happening in that waste dump at the time that it happened. We sued them on 1978 disclosure, not on 1970 disclosure. One of the things they said was, Wait a second, we just bought Hooker, we didn't put this stuff in the ground. And the answer was, Well, that doesn't matter, you own it now—the ground, the plant, and the liability.

So I'm not saying it's simple. But there really is a pretty reasonable approach here: if you know there's a problem or think there's a problem, that's what you have to disclose. And that's what due diligence is all about, when companies go to market. That's what people worry about. Before you go to market, the underwriter will require what's called a 10b5 letter from the lawyers that basically says we've looked at this and we think the disclosure is accurate. People spend millions of dollars for that one-page piece of paper.

One of the interesting things is, in transactions in the United States that don't fall under these laws, that are exempt: most underwriters will still ask for the 10b5 opinion. And they won't take it from a foreign firm. They like it from American law firms, because they view their processes as being more rigorous. They know the way it's done in the United States. There are a lot of these practices now that have become "best practice," not just legal practice.

M. FORTUN: So are people going to have to pay more and more just to get that statement, because ideas about what constitutes risk and about what you have to disclose are going to keep escalating?

MANN: You're now driving into one of the conservative arguments of the day: litigation reform. They're saying it's costing too much, the possibilities of litigation cost too much, and therefore we should scale it back. And I'm in the camp that would argue, Don't scale it back, the possibility of litigation for false and misleading statements promotes responsibility. But there are a lot of people who believe that it's gone too far and it should be scaled back.

M. FORTUN: Does the SEC have an opinion in that matter? Where they say that it's important for the transparency and integrity of the market, and market confidence, that liability be in place? Would you go to a congressional committee and testify for that?

MANN: The SEC did go to a congressional committee, but we didn't testify for it. The chairman testified that there should be some scaling back. So this is a debate: how big a safe harbor do you have for people who are involved in the markets? Should the accountants be liable for everything that they do the accounting on, and how does that work?

M. FORTUN: There are interesting parallels in so many domains. Nobody seems to understand what accountability means in the contemporary economy, particularly within these massive corporations. Do you pin it on accounting firms, or on individual accountants, or on the CEO? What constitutes negligence within these incredibly complex, interconnected structures? But the people that are creating these disclosure reports: what is their training?

MANN: They tend to be lawyers or businesspeople. All they're doing is making sure that what's in the prospectus is what's true.

K. FORTUN: I noticed in reading the annual report that sometimes individual heads roll, and sometimes it's more institutional. How hard is it to trace the line of liability back from the bad conduct?

MANN: I think what's complicated is trying to find out how broad it is. The decision-making chain makes people responsible for certain things in a company. In a complex financial fraud, there may be a lot of characters involved in it, some of them knowing and some of them not. The question can sometimes be, At what level of fraud should the board be liable? At what level is the CEO liable? At what level was the head financial person liable? And those are the kind of things that would come out in the SEC's investigation.

K. FORTUN: An interesting initiative in the environmental movement is attempting to criminalize managerial decisions. But it's usually just assumed that it should be the CEO who should be held responsible. And whether that's right or wrong, these activists don't have access to information which would tell them who actually made decisions. So the possibility of SEC disclosure material providing material for activists working on corporate accountability is interesting.

MANN: I would argue that the biggest positive that we have is that it's not just criminalized. The SEC can get other sanctions. Because when you have a criminal case, you have to prove willful intent. You don't just have to prove that it happened, or that it's more likely than not that it happened. Willful intent is a really high standard. And you can spend ten years dickering around over that; because of the penalties people will argue harder, and it's not possible to settle the case.

One of the things that I think makes the SEC such a great agency is that it has this really simple mission: tell the truth. Disclosure, period. No matter what your political bent is, no one can disagree with the proposition that information is good.[7] So all the SEC does is set rules to ensure the information is put out. And when somebody doesn't put it out there, when somebody does a manipulation that creates artificial information, when somebody trades on inside information—which is trading on information that's not out there—when somebody doesn't disclose information about bad earnings or whatever that affects the market artificially: the SEC goes after them. No other value judgment is made. People are supposed to deal fairly, and if they don't, they get sued. I believe that as a result of those efforts, the market is better for it.

Postscript

That the SEC doesn't make "value judgments" is clearly one of its strategic strengths. "We are taken seriously because we have no ax to grind," says another SEC staff member, quoted in another account of the SEC. "Our work is more respected than, say, FERC [the Federal Energy Regulatory Commission]. They are industry driven. When we send a bill [to Congress], from a technical standpoint, no one would suggest anything [about the SEC's motives]. We are a cleaner agency. I say cleaner, I mean less industry-dominated" (Khademian 1992, 156).

This does, however, raise the question of other places where value judgments might in fact occur, and one key location is in the realm of accounting. A return to the early days of the SEC is instructive.

"Accountancy lacks definition. Unlike the law, it has no high court." [8] These words from an editorial in *Accounting Review* in 1929 suggest some of the problems confronted by the early architects of disclosure. Although the legislation of 1933 and 1934 gave the SEC broad statutory control over accounting methods, the SEC "allowed corporations abundant accounting flexibility" and "insisted only on full disclosure" (Parrish 1970, 205). Attempting to promote economic recovery in the midst of the Depression, pressured by Wall Street, fighting the public utilities industry, trying to maintain the interest of a Congress whose capacities for understanding these issues may have been strained: the first SEC commissioners found themselves with their hands full, and split along idealist and realist lines. Some commissioners like Robert Healy felt that the SEC "should have entered the accounting area vigorously by demanding more than full disclosure." Landis's more pragmatic sensibility became the majority opinion, and much of its flavor can still be sensed in Mann's articulation of the SEC's strategy today: "If [Healy's] viewpoint had carried in several significant instances," Landis later wrote to Roosevelt, "the work of administration would have been seriously clogged due to his failure adequately to appreciate the exigency for practicable and workable methods of control. Part of that attitude springs . . . from an unwillingness to sacrifice certain ideal qualities and take the chance of making things work" (quoted in Parrish 1970, 208). To make things work, the SEC turned the authority to create accounting standards over to the American Institute of Accountants, now the American Institute of Certified Public Accountants. As one of the "self-regulatory organizations" that the SEC oversees, the AICPA retains much of the power to define the standards of disclosure.[9]

In the view of critics such as Ralph Nader, "this was a great opportunity lost. The idea that the accounting profession was self-regulating became fixed in the Commission's imagination." If disclosure is a good in itself, consumers interested in "taming the giant corporation" (as the title of one of Nader's books phrases it) need more kinds of it than the accountants are willing to provide. "The more inclusive public interest in an efficient economy, good health, and full employment mandates disclosure of market structure, industry-wide competition, the control exerted by dominant firms, freedom of entry for potential competitors, the true cost of products, product quality, product safety, and the social and environmental effects of production" (Nader, Green, and Seligman 1976, 162, 158).

From the other side of the corporate spectrum, chairman and CEO of Bankers Trust Charles Sanford Jr. finds reason for extreme optimism in the growth of a "science of markets" that is "radically improving our comprehension and management of risk." We are currently in a "Newtonian" era of "classical finance," "in which we tend to look at financial instruments—such as stocks, bonds, and loans—in static, highly aggregated terms. . . . These models have great difficulty dealing with the multitude of underlying critical risk factors . . . such as changes in financial-market volatility or global product, transaction processing volumes, an earthquake in Japan or California, consumer confidence in the United Kingdom, or a change in our corporate strategy." This is a promised disclosure of a different sort: the science of markets will march on, integrating broad intangible forces via chaos theory, "fuzzy logic," and other tools of an emergent "Theory of Particle Finance." And although, "just as today's man on the street does not practice particle physics, he will not practice particle finance in the next century," there will be a cadre of experts in whose scientific hands he can place his trust and his money (Sanford 1994, 30).

The desires of Nader and Sanford rely on a similar structure: critics such as Nader suggest that the "neutral" methods by which information is produced for SEC requirements have themselves been produced and certified by nonneutral professional accountants who are beholden more directly to industry and investors rather than to the public interest. Nader retains faith in reaching a sufficient quantity of information dispersal, once vested interests are overcome. He wants to fix our macroaccounts of corporate enterprise, fixing the world by extending disclosure to realms where the work of corporations interlink, and possibly conspire. Sanford's promise moves in the other direction: honing our understanding of microrealms with the tools of a science which, by grasping ever smaller atoms of information, will eliminate the opacity of the market and its mysterious ways. Sanford believes that all that is unknown can, in fact, be known, and all risks, chance occurrences, and collusions fully accounted for from within.

Albeit from different locations, both Nader and Sanford want fullness, completion, plenitude—they want it all. Both Nader and Sanford imagine an outside, inaccessible yet controlling, that must be brought inside the system, across the border between what is secret and what is information. The line of disclosure must be pushed completely outward or inward, eventually incorporating everything within the transparent domain of information.

The problem in each case is both conceptual and practical. Conceptually, neither viewpoint comes to terms with the fact that, as legal scholar James Boyle argues, "the implicit frameworks within which the regulation of information is discussed are contradictory—or at least aporetic—and indeterminate in application" (Boyle 1996, 34). Boyle identifies the aporia haunting the conceptual and social regimes of "information" by describing how "the analytical structure of microeconomics includes 'perfect information'—meaning free, complete, instantaneous, and universally available—as one of the defining features of the *structure* of the perfect market. But the perfect market must also treat information in a second way: as a good *within* the perfect market, something that will not be produced without incentives. . . . This dual—and contradictory—incarnation of information reappears in the *actual* market" (29). Information, in other words, must be both outside the system, guaranteeing the transparency and fairness of the market, and inside the system, bought and sold like any other commodity. Information is the limit of the system itself, that place where inside and outside spill into each other, and create each other. It is the place of change and growth, that might also be called the "dynamism" of the market.

Boyles's explanation points to structural limits on what information is and can accomplish. These limits can also be thought of in practical terms. Nader wants corporations to tell so much that they would end up disclosing, and thus critiquing, capitalism itself. Imagine a disclosure form accounting for "true cost," social effect, and total market structure, to serve "inclusive public interest." Imagine the collected works of Marx, Weber, Durkheim, and even

Lyotard, signed off by the CEO of Union Carbide. And just as the particle physicists never reach a level that might be termed "fundamental," but always (with the aid of bigger, faster, more powerful machines) encounter another level of complexity, Sanford's particle financiers will only encounter new effusions of the dynamic markets which their tools help to produce. Nader, Sanford, and others less embroiled in the actual traffic of information tend to romanticize what information is, how it is produced, and how it circulates and what it can become: a universal, all-telling language that can integrate the micro and the macro into one narration.

Michael Mann speaks from and works in a different place than either Nader or Sanford: the middle space of the SEC, where people wrangle with the powerful forces of vested interests, local ignorance, chance conditions, dynamic markets, human uncertainty, and motivating ideals. His descriptions suggest that while "information" is an aporia, generating contradictions, its incessant demands can be met, even without disclosing everything and even if something is lost in the translation between words and practice. Mann and the SEC invent and enforce new ways to enact disclosure through highly contextualized, culturally laden vehicles, subject to continual evaluation, documentation, and re-negotiation—information is both a vehicle and a result. Mann and the SEC do desire full disclosure, but within a sharp sense of the necessity of indirect tactics, negotiations, and compromise enabling them to "take the chance of making things work," in the words of their predecessor Landis. They make decisions and take actions, often quickly, based on their readings of the law, the market, available administrative resources, and what is within the realm of pragmatic possibility: being "responsive," in Mann's words, when one "can't stop the music and just wait." They pursue the promise of information as a social good, knowing full well that the utopian desire to be "in the know" can never be fulfilled.

Notes

1. See Parrish 1970, 70; see also Khademian 1992, 28, who ascribes the comment directly to Rayburn.

2. Parrish 1970, 130, quoting a 1940 letter from William Harris to James Landis.

3. Stanley Sporkin was director of the enforcement division from 1974 to 1981, when he left to become general counsel of the CIA under William Casey. The figure of Sporkin has been textually inscribed in somewhat conspiratorial fashion. Ronald Reagan's transition team had written a report highly critical of the SEC's enforcement division and recommended replacing Sporkin who, "perhaps more than any other representative of the agency . . . had been closely identified with SEC activism throughout the 1970s. Former members of the SEC staff referred to the 1970s as the era of 'Sporkinism.' One even commented that under Sporkin 'the enforcement staff was very— I don't want to say religious—but very committed.' "

The series of connections and events that led to Sporkin's new position provide fodder for a number of conspiracy theories: "Sporkin was offered the position by the director of the CIA, William Casey. It was reported that when Casey was chairman of the SEC (1971–72), Sporkin saved him from being implicated in a White House scandal. When the Nixon administration attempted to delay an SEC investigation of New Jersey financier Robert Vesco, Sporkin advised Casey to let the investigation continue. Vesco, a contributor to the Nixon presidential campaign, was later indicted for defrauding mutual fund investors." See Khademian 1992, 167, 246 n. 5.

4. It was in the 1970s that critics of the SEC charged that the commission veered from the enforcement of disclosure toward trying to impose standards of "corporate responsibility." When SEC investigations revealed that companies like Exxon, Gulf, and Lockheed were bribing officials overseas (investigations which led to the Foreign Corrupt Practices Act of 1977), the commission used "consent decrees," in the view of such critics, to force corporate change. SEC Commissioner A. A. Sommer Jr. responded with a nuanced line about "collateral consequence": "The commission . . . is not concerned with remaking the world in its own image and likeness. We're not trying to extrapolate out from our notions of morality as it should govern the conduct of American businesses, or the way in which business is done overseas. If, as a collateral consequence of the policies that we are pursuing with regard to the requirements of disclosure, there are changes in the practices of American business, I would suggest that while that is not our objective, it may be one of the happier results." See Khademian 1992, 150.

5. For example, Germany's Deutsche Bank in the 1980s "dominated the German capital market, led nearly half of all new mark-denominated Eurobond issues, underwrote 90 percent of new West German equity issues, and accounted for nearly one-quarter of all trading in German securities" (Goodman and Pauly 1995, 307).

6. Compare this with the comments of another SEC official, quoted in Khademian (1992, 106): "There is a wide divergence in the industry. The commission [uses] restraint. There [is] an awareness of institutional boundaries. . . . There is a difference between taking the initiative and ramming a rule down people's throats. When the SEC does take the initiative, it takes comments, questions. . . . There is an exchange of ideas . . . a willingness to give and take."

7. Other literature shows that this sense of being "outside" of partisan politics is a dominant part of SEC culture. A former House staff member who dealt with the SEC put it, "There is a consensus that the markets should be fair, and that the individual investor should have confidence to invest. That's not a partisan issue. Everyone sympathizes with the investor who does not want to be out technologied, or who doesn't want to play with a stacked deck. . . . Bottom line is, it's good politics to catch the rich crooks. The Ivan Boeskys . . . the rich inside trader who manipulated the market, epitomizes the evil character" (Khademian 1992, 17). Even members of the securities industry support strong SEC enforcement for similar reasons, as suggested by an official of the Securities Industry Association: "Absolutely! Our entire business is entirely intangible. It is dependent on conditions being honest and above board. Every day, trillions of dollars change hands on word of mouth. Securities . . . is a business where belief in the system is critical. . . . There needs to be a timely review of disclosure, and there needs to be strong enforcement" (99).

8. Eric L. Kohler, editorial in *Accounting Review* 4 (Sept. 1929): 192, quoted in Parrish 1970, 200.

9. The SEC, particularly through its chief accountant, continues to issue guidelines and impose standards when necessary; see Khademian 1992, 108.

References

Boyle, James. 1996. *Shamans, Software, and Spleens: Law and the Construction of the Information Society.* Cambridge, Mass.: Harvard University Press.

Congressional Record, 73rd Cong., 1st sess., 77. 2919, 2983.

Davis, David Brion, ed. 1971. *The Fear of Conspiracy: Images of Un-American Subversion From the Revolution to the Present.* Ithaca, N.Y.: Cornell University Press.

Desvernine, Raoul E. 1936. *Democratic Despotism.* New York: Dodd, Mead.

Goodman, John B., and Louis W. Pauly. 1995. "The Obsolescence of Capital Controls? Economic Management in an Age of Global Markets." In *International Political Economy.* Ed. Jeffrey A. Frieden and David A. Lake. New York: St. Martin's.

Khademian, Anne M. 1992. *The SEC and Capital Market Regulation: The Politics of Expertise.* Pittsburgh: University of Pittsburgh Press.

Kingsdown, Lord. 1994. "Toward Greater International Stability and Cooperation." *The Bankers Magazine,* Jan.-Feb.: 34–38.

McClure, John A. 1991. "Postmodern Romance: Don DeLillo and the Age of Conspiracy." In *Introducing Don DeLillo.* Ed. Frank Lentricchia. Durham, N.C.: Duke University Press.

Nader, Ralph, Mark Green, and Joel Seligman. 1976. *Taming the Giant Corporation.* New York: W. W. Norton.

Parrish, Michael E. 1970. *Securities Regulation and the New Deal.* New Haven, Conn.: Yale University Press.

Safire, William. 1995. "Conspiracy Theory." *New York Times Magazine,* 5 Nov., 24.

Sanford, Charles S., Jr. 1994. "Global Financial Markets in 2020." *Bank Management,* Mar.-Apr.

U.S. Securities and Exchange Commission. 1994. Annual Report. Washington D.C.

Zizek, Slovoj. 1992. *Looking Awry: An Introduction to Jacques Lacan through Popular Culture.* Cambridge, Mass.: MIT Press.

PARANOID HISTORIES

Andrea Aureli

Is it only me? Or is it everybody else's hidden temptation to endlessly rewrite to exhaustion what he has written? Deadlines have the undeniable virtue of checking the "Sisyphus-compulsion" which so much informs the process of writing. Picture yourself sitting at your desk in Houston, Texas, 90 percent humidity. You are sweating your brains out trying to write about an exotic and bewildering subject such as Italian politics. It may not be exotic to you, a balding Italian anarchist, but it definitely is for your (potential) readers. So you are faced with the task of translating your "commonsensical" understanding of the topic for those who have not "been there." You may turn to the literature on the topic searching for inspiration but you find precious little. However informative and carefully researched, those thick books and scholarly essays do not really satisfy you. There is something missing. You ask yourself what is missing. You are about to get lost in your mental meanderings when you come to suspect that the authors you have been reading maybe were not looking for the things you are so keen to narrate. If conspiracies lie in the eye of the beholder, then writing about them immediately implies the acknowledgment of the writer's situatedness. Then you realize that there is no objective stance you can take; you either explain them away as delusional or end up entangled in the webs of their plots. For unlike what special agent Fox Mulder may believe, the "truth" about Italian conspiracies is not "out there" in some hidden archive but in the truth-effects their "revelation" produces. To unveil plots somehow allows the possibility for "providential" events to occur. Their success is paradoxically tied up with their localized publicity. Their far-reaching influence can only be perceived through idiosyncratic events. Thus we are back where we started, in my Houston apartment. Viewed from afar, Italian conspiracies may seem the product of a paranoid imagination. If a highly—perhaps disturbingly so—partial account of the "Italian case" such as the one I have written may be of any value it is because it consciously takes sides.

Luiz Soares

In 1972, when I began my undergraduate studies in literature, in Rio de Janeiro, the Brazilian dictatorship was at its darkest moment. Some of my colleagues and teachers were being arrested and tortured, accused of "crimes of opinion." Some were murdered by the military. Any outspoken comment about freedom and democracy could be overheard and labeled communist propaganda, which meant severe penalties, from electric shocks to death. In this oppressive atmosphere I decided to postpone my literary projects and dedicate myself to the cause of political resistance. But to do that I needed to choose among several options, tools, paths, and utopian horizons. Which underground party should I join? How could I contribute to the building of what kind of political institutions? What should I do? What should I wish for my country's future? The magnitude of the questions and their urgency led me to the social sciences. To me as well as to many in my generation, studying social sciences meant a lot more than choosing a profession and becoming an academic.

But life is much more tricky and unpredictable than idealistic youngsters can imagine. Brazil became a democracy—even if our enormous social problems are far from being solved, we are now in a free country—and I became a professional academic, a professor. Social sciences became my language and my home. Nevertheless, I've never been able to outgrow the spirit of the sixties. In other words, although my home is the language, the community or small world of the social sciences, political engagement as well as literature still mean a lot to me. I understand engagement as civic commitment, as sharing national and global political responsibilities, but also as getting a kick out of creative experiments of sociability. And I think of literature as aesthetic production, but also as a way of life devoted to self-transformation and cultural critique.

My life requires a bit of unity for pragmatic reasons. This has inspired my intellectual work and led me to explore the connections between social sciences, literature, and ordinary lives of self-fashioned subjectivities, under the assumption that such self-fashioning implies interactive experimentation and performative cultural critique—or reframing, or recontextualizing, or relativizing, or distancing oneself from one's beliefs and opening up new spaces for new potentialities, or politics.

"A Toast to Fear," as I read it, is a quasi-ethnographic experiment or a short-story quilt which, far from defending a thesis, proposing an interpretation of life under the dictatorship, explaining Brazilian politics, analyzing its culture or describing its society, and far from achieving a mimetic picture by narrative means, simply describes some episodes that might be suggestive of a general atmosphere—part of which, as will be shown, can still be inhaled. (Well, in fact, I have to admit it: living in Brazil in that dread period, I did inhale it.) Another way to put it would be, conspiracy was at large throughout those hard years. Conspiracy and fear: a fever of imagination; oppression spilling over its dark spirit. "A Toast" tries to capture the spirit, or should I say, pursue it? Or perhaps better yet, translate? Share? Exorcise its enigmatic and fierce bite? Pour its poison into language?

Bruce Grant

There is nothing magical about living in a country that recently reported forty thousand murders and seventy thousand disappearances in a single year. Yet an almost gritty magical realism suffuses daily efforts by Russians in conversation and in the press to normalize lives made ever more absurd and unpredictable by the collapse of the USSR. In Russian business, circa 1996, with state taxes often demanding over 100 percent of gross earnings and the widespread understanding that crime was essential for almost anyone to get ahead, the concept of the normal seemed in for a tough ride, with the mafia emerging as a powerful idiom for a world of invisible hands guiding markets no one could entirely see.

In interviews with three Russian businessmen, my interest was to shed light on some of the new market's murkier practices, and perhaps to humanize the more sensational stories of Russian gangland lives that fill the press each day. The first two interviews, with a professional Soviet-era trade magnate and a most erudite former antistate conspirator, were disarming to me for their blithe portraits of sense and sensibilities at the highest and lowest rungs of the Soviet trade ladder. Yet the third session, with a Soviet foreign agent turned public relations consultant, was in many ways the most telling, reminding how easily the predatory aspects of capitalism can be masked by the imprimaturs of power and distinction.

Tatiana Bajuk

Slovenia had declared its independence from Yugoslavia between my first and second years of graduate school, in the summer of 1991. I watched those historic events on CNN with great interest, for all of a sudden Slovenia took on a new relevance in my life. The faraway place where my parents had been born and from which they had fled after the Second World War suddenly became a nation unto itself and claimed for itself a place on the map of Europe. Furthermore, the events that held the interest of the international community as the disintegration of Yugoslavia progressed spurred me to shift my site of fieldwork to Slovenia. I had been preparing to conduct an ethnographic study of the culture of economists as a means of analyzing the authority of discourses of economic development, and the transition that Slovenia embarked upon seems a place in which the issues that I wished to explore had taken on a new significance.

When I came to Slovenia I was surprised at the extent to which discourses of economics and of economic reforms set the terms in which debates about the transition were discussed, including debates about Slovenia's communist past. The stories about postwar repression at the hands of the Party were "rationalized" away, glossed over by the apparent success of Slovenia's economic transition from which position Slovenia's history was being recast. When I began reading Edo Ravnikar's book I became intrigued by the way in which his story about Yugoslavia's parallel economy engaged debates about the past and about the economic transition in productive ways, opening a space to speak about other issues, a contested space with a particular sort of terrain which Ravnikar began to map out in our interview.

I met with Ravnikar in late November on two snowy afternoons in his architecture studio in the heart of Ljubljana's old town. Our meetings took place in the weeks after Slovenia's parliamentary elections, which had not provided a clear advantage to either political bloc, and political parties negotiated among various configurations that could result in a parliamentary majority. That very parliamentary ambiguity that defined those weeks fueled new speculations about who was (going to be) guiding Slovenia's future in the years ahead.

The Usual Suspects

The Spider's Web[1]

I can thus positively state that I am not aware of the existence of a security structure parallel to the official one, and made up of civilians in support of the armed forces, being it either a deviation in favor of anti-Communist political groups or of non-official and secret initiatives aimed at the creation and maintenance of an efficient anti-Communist apparatus. . . . On the other hand—though I would be surprised to learn that such an organization and deviation on the part of members of the armed forces and of the intelligence does exist—my experience leads me to maintain that it would be absurd if it did not actually exist. . . . What I am saying is that I would be surprised that a parallel and secret organization with a specific anti-Communist function did not exist; moreover, I would tend to believe that such an apparatus would not run along the official intelligence chain of command, for were this the case, the risk of it being uncovered would be enormous. . . . Furthermore, if one formulates the hypothesis, itself highly probable, that the leadership of such an organization is either part of or dependent from an international force, one could then logically think that the recruitment of its members is related either to their having held official positions or their entertaining contacts with members of the official structure. For similar reasons I believe that this secret and non-official organization could take advantage of the official security structures connected to the multinational defense organization that may exist. In theory I would believe that any official security organization of this sort, especially if we attribute to it a certain political intent, could have had the initial function of selecting those individuals eligible to become members of the above mentioned organization. General Miceli,[2] if he has indeed done something, and if what he has done is not the result of misjudgment on his part, of his desire to "wash his dirty laundry at home" or to minimize the responsibility of others, could only have acted upon request or stimulus derived from foreign and superior centers of power. Thus, we are not dealing with the leadership of the structure but with an intermediary leading to another. It is my opinion that the organization is such and is so large that it is capable of operating in the field of politics, of military affairs, of finance, of organized crime.[3]

I cannot say whether the security structure and its parallel hierarchy are part of the SID [Servizio Informazioni Difesa, the Italian army intelligence] nor can I say that it is the old organization led by [De] Lorenzo.[4] In order to become a member of this parallel organization one has to share specific feelings and one has to have performed specific intelligence activities in the military. One has to be anti-Marxist. One does not apply to become a member, such a request would imply that one is aware of its existence. One is observed, evaluated, especially in reference to certain past activities one may have been engaged in.[5]

Upon reading the above excerpts, we are immediately thrown in the arcane world of (cold-war) conspiracies. A world whose characters may well be created by the fertile imagination of spy-story writers. Yet they come from official records of one among many unresolved investigations into the Italian intelligence's role in support of attempted coups and bombings aimed at preventing an electoral victory of the Left.

Different stories could be spun out of records such as these: one could put the blame entirely on the CIA, the National Security Council, and Italian right-wing military; one could historicize those events as the unavoidable result of cold-war geopolitics; one could even blame the Italian communists for having been so prominent in post-WWII Italian politics. Each of these stories would have its own specific moral: the devious character of foreign forces encroaching upon a national community; the amoral character of international politics; the ominous consequences of "ideology." One could even assign to each story a specific slot in the political spectrum: extreme right (or left), center, center-left, and so on. Granted, the differences are not clear cut, and there are a lot of intermediate positions. Yet the issue is not the definitive allocation of responsibility (or agency), for if it's true that U.S. national interests played a major role in allowing a bomb to go off in a bank in Milan in 1969, it is also true that the people who placed it, and the organization(s) they were members of, were also articulations of Italian political history; the cold war construct can serve well to evoke the ruthless and "inevitable" features of post-WWII geopolitics, but this does not account for the different way of dealing with the "reds": foreign intervention (Greece in the late 1940s); indiscriminate bombings and elaborate plots (Italy 1964–84); military dictatorships (Chile, as an example); and, of course, the organized left was "unusually" strong in Italy. Yet to claim that it was preparing the revolution is at best ridiculous, even without reading its internal documents (admittedly boring) one needed only to wire-tap the offices of the high-ranking party officials to understand that the last thing they were thinking of was storming the Winter Palace.

Learning and reading about Italian conspiracies was immediately connected to my relatively brief, yet extremely important, militancy in the Italian anarchist movement. When I first joined the movement I was also joining an imaginary historical subject, or rather subjectivity, connecting the French revolution to 1848 and to the Paris Commune, the October Revolution to Kronstadt, to the Spanish Civil War, Joe Hill, to Joan Baez, to Woodstock and Wounded Knee, the Clash, to Brixton, to Nicaragua. I could go on for ever. Of course, I did think that one day or other we were going to storm the Winter Palace (today such thoughts occur to me only when I am overcome by optimism). One problem was clearly how to avoid the hidden cameras that we thought controlled the whole area where the parliament and the key government buildings were. During rallies against the deployment of cruise missiles in Sicily I would look up in suspicion wondering whether that strange-looking device on the pole was an exotic light or an extremely sophisticated surveillance camera.

And yet, the connection linking my political militancy and conspiracy goes well beyond the liberal caricature that likes to picture anarchists as fanatics who while away the time placing bombs wherever and whenever they can in the hope of bringing about the final revolution. Indeed, the first major event that revealed the conspiratorial character of Italian politics marks the inconsistency of this image. On 12 December 1969 a bomb placed in a bank in Milan exploded killing sixteen people and wounding eighty-seven. The bombing, soon to be referred to as the Piazza Fontana Massacre, triggered an attempt to criminalize the radical left movement then on the rise.

At the time I was four, I cannot recall the event. What I do recall is watching the news on our black and white television, I guess my generation is the last to have witnessed the transition from black-and-white to color TV, to this day I am still fascinated by color TV, its hyperrealism, its tricky resemblance with reality. The news I remember was reports on clashes between students and the police emphasizing how many people were injured (especially the police). I remember wondering why people could not avoid violence. Sitting at our dinner table in our safe middle-class attic in Rome, I would listen to my mother reproaching the violence and unruliness of what was going on. I never heard an explicit condemnation, but then again the middle classes are not prone to explicit political commitments, and my father was always furious for the widespread corruption of the government and the bureaucracy. I felt sorry for the police.

Now all the journalists in the world are licking your arses. . . . but not me, my dears. You have the faces of spoilt brats, and I hate you, like I hate your fathers. . . . When yesterday at Valle Giulia you beat up the police, I sympathized with the police because they were the sons of the poor.[6]

To juxtapose Valle Giulia and Piazza Fontana is not to imply the contagious character of political violence. If Valle Giulia symbolically marked the emergence of a radical movement of predominant middle-class origins which will soon manage to forge an alliance with an increasingly active labor movement, Piazza Fontana soon became a symbol of the antidemocratic tendencies present within the state apparatus, a reminder for the students, the radical intellectuals, and the progressive sector of the public opinion of the inherent subversive character of the Italian ruling classes. A symbol that has survived to this day:

> We would like to stress that *La strage di Stato* was dedicated to an anarchist machinist, Giuseppe Pinelli, and to a magistrate, Ottorino Pesce. . . . From the legalized killings derived from the Reale law[7] . . . to the obscure death in 1984 of the Roman anarchist Marco Sanna while he was in jail, to the arms trade with South Africa during the Apartheid, to the emerging naziskin electronic network. There are many incidents the magistrates did not want to or could not even begin to investigate. While remembering Ottorino Pesce one has to underscore some long-forgotten judiciary truths regarding all the trials that have been hindered, regarding all the conspirators on the loose, regarding the intelligence service that have been always accused yet never challenged. With the exception of the Peteano killings, nobody has been convicted for terrorist events connected to the "Strategy of tension."[8] All this notwithstanding the fact that—from the political point of view—the magistrates themselves acknowledge that the responsibilities of these events are clear enough (fascists and intelligence service, and/or the other way around) . . . , if one has not yet been able to uncover the culprits—ten, twenty, twenty-five years after the events—the reason is that state apparatuses have gradually destroyed the evidence.[9]

The day Marco Sanna was picked up by the police was exceedingly cold, it had snowed—an extremely rare occurrence in Rome. According to the official version Marco, in a deranged state was throwing snowballs in a park, one of his snowball hit a patrol car, the police said he would not answer them, they searched him and found a knife, he was brought in. The morning after, he was found dead, hanging from the window of his cell, the official version claimed that he had committed suicide. The autopsy revealed bruises on his body and a head trauma. Nobody knew he had been held in custody. The day after, I received a phone call from a comrade, he told me what had happen to Marco and said that he could not talk over the phone and that he was going to pick me up later that afternoon. It was already dark when we met. I got into his tiny Cinquecento and we drove away. He said that we had to go somewhere quiet where we could talk, a place where we could not be overheard by the police. We parked at the Gianicolo, a hill overlooking Trastevere, Rome's historic district, with the huge statue of Garibaldi on his horse hovering behind us. I was thrilled. I expected the revelation of some dangerous secret at the same time I was enjoying the thought that the government could consider us dangerous enough to tap our telephones and shadow us in a cold winter afternoon. I was disappointed, I did not learn any frightening secrets, nor was I able to spot any suspicious car tailing us. I returned home with little more than an appointment for the next day to organize a public initiative on the incident and a faint anticipation of the possible intimidations from the police that never occurred. But then fifteen years had passed since that bomb went off in Milan.

State Terrorism

Immediately after the blast, the investigators pointed to the anarchists as the perpetrators of that bombing as well as of others that had taken place that same day in Rome. Three days after the bombings, anarchist Giuseppe Pinelli, who had been brought in for questioning, committed "suicide." The official version claimed that Pinelli, during a break in the interrogation, had raced to the open window and had jumped crying "this is the end of anarchy!" The reason for his actions, the police claimed, was that seeing his plot had failed and that his alibi regarding his whereabouts on the day of the bombing had been proven false, Pinelli had decided that his life was not worth living anymore. In the meantime Pietro Valpreda, another anarchist, was indicted for the bombing. As the investigations progressed, it soon became apparent that "the red trail" was highly inconsistent. Soon, investigative journalists and left-wing militants uncovered clues pointing at the involvement of radical fascists and of members of the Italian intelligence in the bombing. The results of their investigation were published in a book entitled *La strage di Stato* [The State Massacre].[10] In it the authors uncovered evidence of the existence of an hidden plan whereby fascists were attempting to infiltrate groups of the radical left and act as provocateurs; moreover, they were able to discover a network of organizations and groups whose activities were funded, and supported not only by conservative sectors of the bureaucracy, of the military, and bankers (Sindona), as well as junior members of government at the national level but also by the Greek intelligence[11] and the CIA.[12] Among the people involved in the bombing there was a well-known fascist, Prince Julio Valerio Borghese.

In 1967 "The Black Prince" had founded a right-wing organization called Fronte Nazionale, whose aim was to "pursue all necessary initiatives for the defense and the renewal of the supreme values of Italian and European civilization." Borghese had been an officer of the Italian navy during WWII. He had been a war hero and had carried out sabotage operations against the British navy in the Mediterranean. After the armistice in 1943, he had joined the Salò regime in northern Italy and at the head of an army unit he had specifically led a ruthless fight against the antifascist partisans. At the end of the war he was convicted as a war criminal but was pardoned in 1949. His social background (the Borgheses are an old aristocratic family) and his military past granted him the respect and support of the upper classes, the military, and the clergy, as well as the radical rank-and-file members of the neofascist movement.

On 7 December 1970 a fascist coup attempt, led by Borghese, failed. Up to this day it is not clear why the coup failed. On the night of the seventh Borghese and his followers, among whom were members of the military and of the intelligence services, had occupied the Ministry of Interior. Apparently the plan was not aimed at establishing a military dictatorship, but to offer the possibility for a military counterinsurgency plan to come into effect thus facilitating an authoritarian political environment to be created.[13]

> Once right-wing armed groups, . . . together with some units of the armed forces, had managed to take control of some centers of power (RAI [the national television network], the presidential palace, the Ministry of Interior, etc.), a counterinsurgency plan was to come into effect. Such a plan existed in the safe of the Carabinieri High Command. According to this plan the Carabinieri were to arrest labor leaders, politicians and military officers. . . . The coming into effect of this plan would have allowed the establishment of a military regime supported by sectors of the establishment that had already expressed their implicit agreement.[14]

Yet somehow other groups who were to go into action did not. The sympathy, if not explicit support, granted to Borghese by high-ranking officers and members of government circles can be fully appreciated if one considers that his attempt was not revealed until some months after it took place, even though the Minister of Interior himself had been immediately informed of what was happening. The intelligence had informants among the conspirators and they—as was their job—had informed their superiors, yet nothing was done to stop them. That night, while the group of neofascist militants that had entered the Ministry of Interior received the order to return home, military units that were moving toward their assigned positions received orders to return to their barracks,[15] as did police units that had started to seal off Rome. Later investigations revealed that someone had instructed the conspirators to withdraw. It was not until three months later that news leaked out regarding the coup attempt. Borghese had had time to flee the country while the establishment tried to banalize the incident as a disorganized and isolated attempt of old retired fascists whose lack of organization only matched their delusional view of reality.

Yet the counterinsurgency plan the Carabinieri kept in their safe was basically the same plan drafted by Giovanni De Lorenzo, commander in chief of the Carabinieri in the early 1960s, that had been recently uncovered. The plan, to be carried out by the Carabinieri alone, had been scheduled to come into effect in June–July 1964—though this of course did not happen.[16] The scheme and its failure were only to be made public in March 1969. In the meantime, De Lorenzo had in 1965 risen to the rank of chief of staff of the army. Born in 1907, De Lorenzo had fought on the Russian front during WWII. Back in Italy in 1943 he had been a member of the antifascist resistance until the early months of 1944. He was the appointed vice-commanding officer of the underground military intelligence in Rome during the German occupation. He was later a senior NATO officer in southern Europe, and in 1955 became commander of Italian military intelligence. He was forced to leave the army in 1967, and later joined the MSI, Italy's neofascist party.

On 17 May 1972 Luigi Calabresi, head of the Milan police political-affairs bureau in charge of the Piazza Fontana investigations, was shot dead by unknown killers.[17] A year later, during a ceremony in commemoration of his death, Gian Franco Bertoli threw a bomb killing four people. He was arrested immediately. Though he claimed to be an anarchist, investigators soon found out that he had worked for the Italian intelligence and had collaborated with the CIA. A year before, a photocopy of his passport had been discovered among Calabresi's papers.[18] The ensuing investigations revealed that Bertoli, as well as being on the payroll of the Italian intelligence, was also a member of a right-wing secret organization called Rosa dei venti [Weather vane]. This time, though, the plot did not seem to be that of establishing a right-wing military government, but to coordinate right-wing terrorism in order to "stabilize" the Italian political scene against the increasing electoral support enjoyed by the Left. Such a plan was to be uncovered only some years later (1974), yet the politics of stabilization had already been hinted at in November 1972 by Arnaldo Forlani, a prominent Christian Democrat, during a speech in La Spezia:

> An attempt has been made by the reactionary right, which is probably the most dangerous ever since the Liberation. [. . .] Such a disrupting attempt, carried out by means of a plot with relevant organizational and financial capabilities, has probably enjoyed the support not only at the domestic level but also at the international level. Such an attempt is still a present danger: we know in well-documented fashion that it is still going on.[19]

Thus the code name Rosa dei venti had to be interpreted as evoking the network of twenty secret organizations involved in the project (*venti* in Italian is the plural of *vento,* "wind," but also means twenty). Later investigators noted that the weather vane is also the symbol of NATO.

Among the leading figures of this project was Edgardo Sogno, a former leader of the monarchist wing of the resistance movement who had later served

as an ambassador in Latin America; Randolfo Pacciardi, former leader of antifascist militias who had fought for the Spanish republic in the thirties; and
Luigi Cavallo, a well-known provocateur.[20]

In the 1950s Edgardo Sogno had also been a leader of the anticommunist
organization Pace e libertà, whose aim was to gather information on militants of the Left and to establish a nationwide intelligence network. Financial
backing of this organization had come from Fiat and Pirelli, as well as from
NATO.[21] Later he had been asked by the Ministry of Interior to organize a
secret structure of civilians to be trained in antiguerrilla warfare in case communists came to power. Apparently his career as a diplomat had consequently
suffered, and in 1969 he had to write to Aldo Moro, then minister of foreign
affairs, a letter lamenting how he was lagging behind colleagues that had his
same tenure but had not been engaged in the fight against communism as
he had.

> As early as 1949 Mr. Scelba, at the time minister of interior, contacted
> me to learn if I were willing to accept a position that would have
> entailed my temporary transfer to the Ministry of Interior. . . . I re-
> fused in order to accept the position of vice consul in Paris. . . . In July
> 1953, as a result of an initiative of the premier (Scelba), I was again
> offered a position of exceptional and classified nature (I was to orga-
> nize the psychological defense of our democratic institutions). . . . I
> accepted such a position after I had received formal guarantees that
> my advancement in the service would not be hindered. . . .[22] What I
> have summarized above does not intend to question the position of
> my colleagues, I only want to underscore the serious discrimination
> to which I have been subject.[23]

In Italy the period from 1969 to the early 1980s was marked by what has
been defined as the "strategy of tension"; a sequel of "failed" conspiracies and
bloody bombings aimed at stabilizing the country in a period of widespread
left-wing activism.[24] The overall political consequence of these events was to
secure the Christian Democratic Party's role as the centerpiece of any coalition
government in a period of shrinking political support. During this period, the
rise of the Left (the 1976 general elections marked the highest level of left-
wing electoral consensus: all parties combined harvested 45 percent of the
votes) was thus accompanied by widespread terrorism leading to the bombing of the main train station in Bologna that killed eighty-seven people and
wounded two hundred. This was to be the last and the bloodiest massacre since
the end of the war, "symbolically" marking the end of Leftist political initiative. Bologna, the capital of Emilia-Romagna, was (and still is) the symbol of
leftist government. At the heart of that central region of the country comprising
Tuscany, Emilia-Romagna, and Umbria, where the Left enjoyed wide electoral
support, Bologna has been governed by the Left ever since the end of the war.
As was to be expected, investigators were soon to uncover a network connect-

ing right-wing terrorists to Italian intelligence. Yet the more they revealed the involvement of state agencies in the bombing, the more these agencies refused to help them, either by claiming that the information they were requesting was classified or by giving them partial or totally fabricated accounts.

What the Bologna investigators managed to uncover was the involvement of freemasonry in the bombing and the existence of a "plan of democratic renewal," drafted by members of the secret lodge P2, headed by Licio Gelli, aiming at stabilizing Italian politics by a global reform of the state along authoritarian lines. As already mentioned, members of this secret lodge were the "Gotha" of the political and economic elites. The P2 soon appeared to be the master planners behind the "strategy of tension," yet the high status of the majority of the conspirators prevented any initiative against them to be taken. The paradox was that while the existence of this secret lodge confirmed what had been suspected regarding the Rosa dei Venti conspiracy, there was little that could be done about it short of putting all the upper echelons of the state in jail. The dimension of the network was only partially revealed when, in 1981, the police searched Gelli's villa and discovered part of the lodge's membership records, which included the names of ministers, high-ranking officers of the military, of the police, of the intelligence service and industrialists. These documents also revealed that many of those who had been investigated in connection with conspiracies were P2 members: Edgardo Sogno, Michele Sindona, Siro Rossetti,[25] and others.

In his youth, Gelli had fought in the Italian expeditionary force during the Spanish Civil War (1936–39). Later he was in Albania, where he collaborated with the Fascist intelligence and made contacts with British intelligence. In 1943 he was back in Italy, where in the aftermath of the armistice he managed to become a liaison officer for the Germans while at the same time maintaining his contacts with the U.S. 5th Army counterintelligence corps and with members of the antifascist resistance.

The last major conspiracy was revealed by Andreotti himself in the context of an investigation on arms smuggling that involved, as is only natural, members of Italian intelligence. The name of this last secret organization was Gladio. This time there was definitive proof of the existence of an international counterinsurgency plan supported by NATO involving all postwar members of government and the armed forces. Yet, one more time, the uncovering of a master plan connecting all past events did not result in any intervention because of the sheer dimension of the network involving major politicians of the postwar period.

To violate the rules of parliamentary democracy appears then to have been the inherent vocation of the Italian ruling classes. Indeed, one might well view this as a major historical trait in post-WWII Italy. Again, depending on the perspective one chooses to take to make sense of these events, the ensuing analysis will lead in different directions. On the one side one could say that the violent and unstable character of Italian democracy is in the end an aspect of the uneven development (modernization) of the country, of its being a "geographical expression" bringing dangerously together industrial modernity (the north) and agrarian traditions (the south). Another perspective would be to look at these same events as the expression of the bipolar international order that emerged after WWII. Regardless of the perspective, it would be difficult not to acknowledge that the fall of fascism and the antifascist struggle mark a watershed in the Italian national consciousness. In a sense, fascism and antifascism have defined the ways post-WWII Italians conceived their country as a nation and as a democracy.

A Nation Under Siege [26]

The date 8 September 1943 best symbolizes the ambiguous origin of Italian democracy. On the evening of that day, Italian radio broadcasted a recorded message of the prime minister of the provisional government announcing Italy's unconditional surrender to the Allies. Mussolini had been arrested as a result of a coup. More concerned with their political survival, the same forces that had supported twenty years of fascist rule and that had brought the country to war had turned their backs on Mussolini and were pulling out without taking any responsibility for their actions, leaving ordinary people to fend for themselves.[27] The tragic irony is that an armistice, instead of bringing peace to a country impoverished by war, brought with it an even crueler civil war. Overnight the enemy turned into friend and the friend became the enemy. Out of this total collapse the armed resistance was born; militarily and politically hegemonized by the Communist Party, it combined socialism and antifascism with ideals of national renewal. At the time, such a mixture did seem to work. After all, the provisional government had fled, the fascist state had collapsed, and fighting the Germans could very well combine social revolution with national independence.

At the end of the war Italians had both lost (if they were Fascist) and won (if they were antifascist). The antifascist front soon lost much of its political viability, and the provisional government lasted only a couple of years. As early as 1947 the communists and the socialists were excluded from government, and in the 1948 elections the Christian Democrats gained the absolute majority in parliament and were thus able to form a government; it was the beginning of their political hegemony. This electoral victory also put an end to any attempt to reform the state structure, which of course had been molded by the previous regime; indeed, the reluctance to confront the presence of fascist elements within the state had been sanctioned as early as 1946 by Palmiro Togliatti, the secretary of the Italian Communist Party, and at the time minister of justice, who pardoned fascists regardless of their crimes.[28]

The predictable consequence, though, was that senior members of the civil service, the police, and the military who were either fascist or monarchist remained in office. Indeed, as soon as the Christian Democrats gained control of government, they excluded most of the left-wing personnel who had been active in the resistance. In doing so they had to take into account the political allegiances dominant in each sector of state institutions. Police forces are a case in point. In Italy there are two major police forces: the national police, which is a body of the Ministry of Interior, and the Carabinieri, which is part of the armed forces. While the former's personnel was dominated by fascist elements, the latter's allegiance was to the monarchy; as a consequence the Carabinieri, though not leftist, had nevertheless participated in the fight against fascism, and this made their members "unreliable" for anticommunist purposes. Be that as it may, the national police was entrusted with the control of urban centers, while the Carabinieri were to have jurisdiction over the countryside and small towns; at the same time, though, it was also agreed that the latter were to reorganize army intelligence.[29] When Italy joined NATO the Carabinieri found themselves in a position that allowed direct contact both with NATO structures and with the CIA. In this context a secret agreement was signed between the two agencies binding them to share intelligence as well as draft plans to counter communist expansion.[30]

Christian Democracy's hegemony went unchallenged for over ten years. By the end of the fifties, though, it became apparent that this "golden age" was coming to a close, for by now the Christian Democrats were unable to put together a stable government, and their attempt to seek support from the Right (neofascists and monarchists) was highly unpopular. The sensible solution was then to form an alliance with the socialists. Though sensible, such a move was unpopular among the right-wing sectors within the party. These groups (that had connections with the CIA and the Carabinieri) began to contemplate a coup.[31] In 1956 Giovanni Gronchi, a Christian Democrat who favored the move to the Left, was elected president, while Giovanni De Lorenzo,[32] who did not favor such a move, was appointed chief of Italian intelligence. During his tenure, De Lorenzo went into a wire-tapping and information-gathering craze; he not only managed to bug Pope John XXIII's private study, but he also managed to put together over one hundred thousand files containing personal information about left-wing politicians, trade union leaders, political activists, and priests. By now, 1962, Antonio Segni has succeeded Gronchi to the presidency, and De Lorenzo has risen to become commander in chief of the Carabinieri. Segni, a Christian Democrat, shared with De Lorenzo his dislike for the center-left.

The first coalition government took office in 1962, and though the socialists supported it, they had no active part in it. The problem was to break their alliance with the communists and to draft a viable reformist program. This they managed to do a year later, in time for the second center-left government. Yet De Lorenzo and the CIA were not losing time: while the latter was putting together a counterinsurgency plan that was to be put into effect by the Carabinieri to the point of constituting an armored brigade capable of carrying out such a plan, the CIA bankrolled right-wing organizations with the help of Italian intelligence. The network thus created included among others the group led by Borghese.[33] The network was ready, yet there was no need for it actually to carry out the plan. It was sufficient to let the socialist leaders know that such a plan did exist (and the meeting between Segni and De Lorenzo was one way of doing it indirectly) to limit their reformist intentions. What this scheming accomplished was both to isolate the communists and to galvanize right-wing elements present in the army and the bureaucracy, and in the process to forge a network connecting neofascists to sectors of the state institutions and industrialists. Such a network, as dispersed and far-reaching as it now was, constituted the organizational context in which the sequence of bombings and coup attempts were planned and carried out. The decentered character of such a network allowed it to enjoy a partial though effective autonomy in relation to individual governments.

As the findings of thirty years of parliamentary investigations testify, such a network soon became a useful tool of social control within Italian civil society, especially in the period following the late sixties.

I first met A. in 1984 at the University of Rome. We were protesting against yet another bill that was going to raise university tuition. Ephemeral as it was, the movement soon subsided. Some time afterward, I ran into A. again. He was desperate because his father, an officer, wanted him to spend his draft period in the air force. He did not know what to do. He also told me that he had a friend in the police archives. If I wanted him to, this friend could check to see if the police had a file on me. I was both thrilled and almost flattered at the possibility that the authorities could consider my political activity worthy of their attentive surveillance.

As in other parts of the world, the late sixties saw in Italy the emergence new social movements.[34] Though unlike what happened in other parts of the world, in Italy this new wave of widespread social and political activism coincided with a radicalization of large sectors of the working class, in turn the consequence of a vast urbanization process generated by the economic expansion of the previous decade. The radical and the long-lasting character of Italian social movements can be understood as the combination of two elements. On one side, the increased upward social mobility of the middle classes who, having gained access to higher education, not only found these aged institutions unable to deliver high-quality education as they were supposed to, but also that once they graduated they could not be absorbed by the economy.

On the other side, the changed composition of the working class, a relevant part of which was made up of immigrants from the countryside. The combination of failed social mobility (students) and harsh working conditions (immigrant labor) allowed the emergence of radical social movements and their persistent presence in Italian politics for over a decade.

By the mid seventies Christian Democrats faced another crisis. On one side the development of social movements brought to the forefront of the political scene, or rather politicized, issues which had previously been relegated to the private sphere of everyday life. In 1974, against all expectations, the referendum to repeal the divorce law that had been recently passed by parliament, was defeated.[35] The referendum had been supported by the Christian Democrats and by the neofascists. This defeat revealed to what extent Italian civil society had changed. The extent of this change not only surprised both the Christian Democrats and the communists, who had reluctantly campaigned against the referendum, but also proved that the majority of Italians were increasingly questioning traditional political allegiances. This period saw the emergence of new radical movements that sought to politicize everyday life: on one side, the feminist movement emerged, questioning not only gender inequalities but the concept of political action in itself as it was expressed by traditional notion of militancy dominant on the left;[36] on the other, a youth movement which was not restricted to university students anymore but also involved working-class youths and that put into question not only class inequalities but the traditional work ethic dominant in the traditional Left.[37] In short, the new social movements of the seventies developed a radical critique of capitalism both as a system of production (economy) but also as system of reproduction (culture).[38] The ongoing crisis that characterized Italian politics in the 1970s, enhanced by the oil crisis of 1973 and the ensuing economic slump, was marked by a legitimation crisis of the political sphere as such.

In this context, the solution sought by the Christian Democrats was to seek an alliance with the left, this time with the Communist Party and again the same problems emerged. Yet the situation was far more volatile: the internal divisions of the Christian Democrat leadership were the same as the previous decades, but the difference was the persistence of social movements, and the usual parallel structures which, though once politically useful, were now extremely dangerous, even more so considering that the alliance this time was sought with the communists. Such a project called for careful maneuvering both by the Christian Democrats and by the communists. The communists sought to reduce and constrain the autonomy of social movements which they had difficulty in understanding in the first place. On the side of the Christian Democrats there are the first (limited) breakthroughs in the investigations of past plots. Both parties are now joined in the fight against terrorism whereby they identified both right-wing bombings and radical social movements which were accused of being supporters of the Red Brigades. The "historical compromise," as it was called by the communists, resulted in an indiscriminate wave of arrests and in a militarization of society.

The Bologna bombing in 1980 marks symbolically the beginning of the crisis of the social movements of the seventies and left-wing politics in general. On another level, this bombing becomes the expression of the militarization of Italian political scene, and it seals off the possibility of alternative "postpolitical" politics. As mentioned earlier, investigations into the bombing revealed the usual conspiratorial network of neofascist militants, intelligence, and sectors of the bureaucracy and yet, though the actors appear to be the same, the plot seems to be different, rather nonexistent. The reasons for the bombing are utterly unclear, for if investigations on previous plots had uncovered some "straightforward" strategic plan underlying each specific incident, a similar plan has not been uncovered behind the Bologna bombing. As the chairman (a former communist) of the last parliamentary commission writes in reference to this bombing, "the strategy underlying [the bombing] is yet unclear. . . . the role of [the various conspirators] points to a "grey zone," . . . whose existence cannot be denied, . . . nor can it be denied that its internal dynamics are yet to be fully understood." [39]

Whatever the strategic plan accounting for the bombing, its interpretation by mainstream politicians (Christian Democrats and communists alike) was that the country was facing an attack by hidden forces and that the solution was a vast national alliance calling for all citizens to rally in defense of the state. Parliamentary democracy was thus conceived as the only legitimate framework of social activism and the only legitimate political activity was that which recognized the institutional order of society as the only legitimate social order. The fight against terrorism in defense of the democratic institutions was compared with the fight against fascism in WWII. From this perspective, the alliance between the communists and the Christian Democrats had the effect of recreating the heroic times out of which the republic, indeed the nation, had emerged.

Intermezzo—Fascism 1

For me, much of the difficulty in writing and thinking about politics in Italy is the difficulty in coming to terms with biographical frustrations, ethical concerns, and intellectual responsibility. Intertwined as these levels are with one another, their unsettled—and unsettling—effects, their coming together generates, enhances the blind spot around which any reflexive account first emerges. Here I am, sitting in front of my computer trying to weave my reflexivity into a radical critique of the state and yet, on second thought, the locus of my writing, the reflexive springboard that grounds it, is a trace of

past I have not lived. The perspective underlying this account rests on a conception of social and political involvement practiced by the movement of the
seventies that was disappearing when I got involved in politics. The people I
met in the early eighties were veterans of the seventies who often looked to
the past with a mixture of cynicism and nostalgia. Caught between the impossibility of autonomous political intervention, the disarticulation of the collective identities which had been the strength of the movement and the distrust
of institutional politics, they embodied the vacuum created by emergency
politics.

Much of my militancy has thus been characterized by a keen interest in the
past. I was extremely attracted to the "heroic" past of revolution, "the way
we were." There was a longing to appropriate events, tensions, and passions
of the past. In a way it was an attempt to reexperience those recent and not so
recent years, a way to ground a present commitment in a past I had not had
the possibility of experiencing. It was a past "before the deluge," if you will,
a period when the spell of defeat had yet not been cast. I would then picture
myself attending those meetings, participating in those marches. "Things"
had already happened, but they had happened before my time. And yet, now
that I look back, I realize that my reading about the recent and not so recent
past was only a nostalgic enterprise, a recapturing of a past "we," but also an
attempt to reconstruct an alternative tradition (genealogy) that would enable
me to bridge the gap that had opened up between the "now" and the "then."
I believe that for an Italian the reconstruction of an alternative past cannot
ignore the fascism-antifascism divide. To some it may appear to be an issue
for historiography, but to me it is a way to come to terms with my own background. My parents were never fascist, indeed they have never considered
politics as something more than the idiom of corruption. And yet since they
had grown up during the thirties, their youth had been defined by the war.
They had different stories to tell. For my mother, fascism evoked a happy period of her life, especially after 1943, when to avoid the air raids her family
had fled to the countryside. For my father, fascism was the "opportunity" his
father grasped to lead the "adventurous" life of the fascist soldier. For me,
then, fascism evoked the romanticized version of my parents' youth, their de-
politicized intimacy with a cruel period of Italian history, but also the banaliz-
ing rhetoric of mainstream politicians legitimizing emergency laws, as well as
the trace of an enemy whose presence could be perceived but that I had never
faced.

> I believe, I truly believe, that true fascism is what sociologists have
> too good-naturedly called "consumer society." An apparently inno-
> cent, merely indexical definition. It is not so. If one were closely to
> observe reality, especially if one is capable of reading into objects,
> into the landscape, into the urban planning, and most of all, into

people, then one could perceive that the results of this thoughtless consumer society are the product of dictatorship, of true fascism. . . . This new fascism, this consumer society . . . has deeply transformed the younger generations, has deeply influenced them, has given them other sentiments, different modes of thoughts, different ways of life, different cultural models. It is not, as in Mussolini's time, a matter of superficial and spectacularized ordering of a people, but of a real ordering that has stolen and changed their soul. What this means, basically, is that this "consumer civilization" is a dictatorial civilization. In other words, if the word *fascism* means the arrogance of power, then "consumer society" has succeeded in realizing fascism.[40]

It was only recently, as I was reading Pasolini's editorials, that I understood Italian fascism as a folk category. I realized that the way I was using the word implied quite a different meaning than the historical movement of the twenties and thirties. However, related to the historical movement, fascism was for me a shorthand way to refer to a structure of power that not only excluded conflict but banalized democratic competition. A structure of power whose legitimacy or, rather, hold on society could not be explicitly connected to overt repression or otherwise explicit authoritarian practices but to an eerie feeling of oppressive "friendliness," smothering understanding. In other words, what I was evoking, as I still do, with the word *fascism* is that aspect of any structure of power that constructs it as a destiny, the feeling that things can only be as they are, and that the objectivity of the bottom line can never be questioned because it is beyond the control of everybody, especially of those in power. No wonder that when I talked about fascism to non-Italians I felt that they could not understand what I was talking about.

Here is where "enchantment" comes in, for reading about Piazza Fontana, Borghese, and the sequence of bombings that had characterized so much of recent Italian history not only testified that the marginalized minority of today had indeed challenged the dominant social and political order but also that an enemy had been violently manifested itself.

What now was conceived as a past of defeats, of hopes that had not been fulfilled, was a past of loss, and a present enchantment with failure.

> Umberto Eco has recently maintained that the reason why Italian Fascism has become a synecdoche, able to define and evoke totally different authoritarian regimes, is its "fuzzy" ideological character, its being at once "philosophically out of joint" but emotionally "firmly fastened to some archetypal foundations."[41]

> The notion of fascism is not unlike Wittgenstein's notion of a game. . . . Games are different activities that display only some "family resemblance." . . . Fascism became an all-purpose term because one can eliminate from a fascist regime one or more features and it will still be recognizable as fascist.[42]

One could argue that the rationale of "urfascism" functions by dissolving antithetical features in a totalizing synthesis neutralizing the (politically) conflictive nature of differences without eliding their distinctive features. It could also be argued that the conspiratorial character of post-war Italian politics is a continuation of fascism through different means. This is not to say that the new democratic regime was fascist; rather, that the power relationships whose stalemate had resulted in the establishment of the fascist dictatorship reemerged after its fall. The continuation of fascism has in Italy been more subtle than any cynical or sociological and political narrative is able to represent. What needs to be acknowledged is that fascism as the historically circumscribed experience that collapsed at the end of WWII was one of the expressions of Italian national identity. Its chauvinism and its authoritarian character were a result of the historical exclusion of the lower classes from the formation of the nation-state in the nineteenth century.

In the interest of national capitalism, fascism performed a "preventive counterrevolution" against the socialist project of liberation. But this was not accomplished by establishing an "ethical" state (both in the sense of condition as in the sense of bureaucratic institution) as much as by creating/enforcing a community of pure tradition.[43] Yet such a tradition was itself ambiguous: on one side, it was the "cosmopolitan" narrative of imperial Rome and of the Renaissance which exalted military expansion and cultural chauvinism and ignored the question of national solidarity; on the other, it was also the tradition of an agrarian society with its encapsulated communities and atomized municipalities. Thus fascism was riddled with an inherent contradiction: it enjoyed the support of the economic elites (industrialists as well as landowners), the army, and the monarchy who sought to put an end to social unrest; of the lower middle classes (bureaucrats and professionals) who sought protection from the economic elites as well as from the working class; and by a Vatican that feared the secularizing effects of modernization. Fascism's appeal to its constituencies resided in its negative ideology,[44] negative not for its ominous effects but because it defined its political project along the irreconcilable enemy-friend dichotomy. Fascism subsumed society (conceived as a mere collation of isolated corporate groups) into the state (conceived as the sovereign body whose task was to enforce homogeneity within its borders by eliminating opponents). It thus appealed to sectors of Italian society for totally different, irreconcilable reasons. The elites saw in fascism an instrument to curb the growing militancy of the working class. For the nationalist middle classes, fascism represented the possibility of revenge against plutocrats and politicians whose bickering and private interests had deprived the nation from fully enjoying the spoils of victory. Thus for the conservatives fascism meant internal peace, and for the nationalists it meant external war.[45] Both exalted authority and favored a hierarchic social order, the former as a means to discipline society, the latter as way to total mobilization against an undifferentiated enemy.

Torn between two conflicting tendencies, fascism was thus incapable to pursue the same political project it claimed in its official rhetoric. Twenty years of fascism produced a proliferation of bureaucratic bodies but was unable to produce a fascist nation.[46] While monopolizing the means of control, fascism never managed to be hegemonic. It was a mode of governance whose power of absolute decision, of life and death, resided in the immanence of its imposition onto reality rather than in the carrying out of specific policies. "Italian fascism was certainly a dictatorship, but it was not totally totalitarian, not because of its mildness but rather because of the philosophical weakness of its ideology. Contrary to common opinion, fascism in Italy had no special philosophy. . . . Mussolini did not have any philosophy: he had only rhetoric." [47]

Antifascism as a Moral Category

The negative and contradictory features of Italian fascism, its "fuzziness," leads to the acknowledgement of the existence of a plurality of fascisms which in turn resulted in the emergence of different forms of antifascism. In arguing in favor of the actuality of antifascism in Italy, Marco Revelli distinguishes three different antifascist "paradigms" which not only refer to the different interpretations of fascism in Italy but also have different historical and political life spans.[48]

The military paradigm limits the validity of antifascism as political identity to the political struggle against the fascist regime. According to this interpretation, the fall of the regime in 1945 relegates antifascism in the historical (and heroic) past out of which the new republic emerged.

A second paradigm, which Revelli calls constitutional, conceives antifascism as mediating the mutual recognition of all political parties binding them to pursue their political projects within the institutional frameworks of parliamentary democracy. Such an agreement of mutual recognition exhausted its validity at the beginning of the eighties and was substituted by the joint effort of all parties in the struggle against terrorism.

One last paradigm conceives fascism as the cultural and political expression of the unresolved contradictions of the Italian nation-state, as the "autobiography of the nation." [49] By interpreting fascism as a recurrent aspect of Italian national character, this paradigm is able to grasp aspects of cultural continuity embedded in Italian national culture. From this perspective, being antifascist implies that political engagement goes hand in hand with a cultural critique of Italian public culture that aims at developing an alternative worldview.[50]

Among the features that the cultural antifascism paradigm considered to be responsible for the emergence of fascism in Italy was the commonsensical view that access to power (political or otherwise) can only be gained through cooptation from above and that those in power do not need to be accountable for their actions. The corollary of this was that holding power did not mean carrying out a project, taking initiatives, or promoting change, but accumulating resources that the single power holder could distribute to his supporters.[51] The allegiance to a hierarchical view of society was thus combined with competition among peers for the acquisition of a larger share of power. Furthermore, this continuous struggle by emphasizing the ability of power holders to hold on to their positions devalues the idea that politics and power need to be informed by some sort of national political project. Thus politics as usual had the paradoxical consequence of *depoliticizing* political struggle. Of course, this ethos of Italian ruling elites was an effect of their historical failure to develop a national popular culture, and thus failing to acquire a hegemonic role in Italian society.[52]

These historical and cultural traits did not disappear with the fall of fascism. If anything, the Christian Democrats and the postwar geopolitical order allowed these historical tendencies to prosper.[53]

Thus cultural antifascism combines an indictment of Italian power structures, as inherently (historically) authoritarian and shortsighted (and morally corrupt), with a positive view of social movements as agents of democratic change (the autonomy of the social) and democratic politics as personal commitment. Cultural antifascism can function also as a "countermemory" and as a critique both of the military and of the constitutional antifascist paradigms. On one hand, by emphasizing the role of social movements, it conceives the resistance period as not just a period of armed minorities fighting each other, but as a broader movement of popular democratic renewal;[54] on the other, by viewing fascism not as a break in Italian history but as a development of the historical bankruptcy of Italian ruling elites, cultural antifascism is capable of seeing the elements of continuity which connect the fascist regime with the postfascist republic.[55]

The Uncanny—Fascism 2

The continuity of fascist power structures and personnel, as well as the re-emergence of progressive social movements, are two central elements that can contextualize (even emplot) the politics of conspiracy that has characterized the past fifty years of Italian democracy. The institutional continuity and the *recycling* of elites are among the key feature of Italian conspiracies.[56]

A relentless return of the repressed that had an ironic twist. Like in the case of Julio Valerio Borghese and his attempted coup; here we have a true fascist (in the historical sense) who had distinguished himself for his ruthless repression of partisans and who was later pardoned by a law drafted by Palmiro Togliatti—one of the founders of the Italian Communist Party—when he was serving as minister of justice in the provisional government, who twenty years later, enjoying the ambiguous support of the military, tries to overthrow democracy.

In other instances, the recycling of the elites has paradoxical features which are all the more dangerous, as in the cases of General De Lorenzo (Solo plan) and Edgardo Sogno (Rosa dei venti). Both had actively participated in the resistance (the former as officer in the monarchist army, the latter as one of the leaders of the National Liberation Committee in northern Italy), both, as early as the late fifties, are—*as public officials*—busy hatching plots against the same democracy they established. General De Lorenzo was able to devise his plan by being able to pool resources and support from conservative sectors of the military, the Christian Democrats, and the CIA. Sogno, by mediating conservative sectors of the Christian Democrats, moderate politicians, and NATO counterinsurgency structures with neofascist terrorist groups.

Licio Gelli is yet another example. His life resembles scheming characters worthy of Balzac. After some years of apprenticeship as a petty official under the fascist regime, he joins the winning side as a liaison officer for the Allied Office of Strategic Services, and over the years he works his way up, bribe after bribe, plot after plot, to fulfill his dream of "democratic renewal."

> I know.
>
> I know the names of those responsible for what has been called *coup* (which in reality is a series of *coups* that have developed into a system whereby Power protects itself). . . .
>
> I know the names of those who, while going to mass, have given the orders, while guaranteeing political protection to old generals, . . . to young neofascists, . . . and to common criminals whose names are today unknown and will probably never be known. . . .
>
> I know. But I have no proof. I do not even have circumstantial evidence.
>
> Power and the world that, though not being part of it, has practical ties with power, has excluded—because of it inherent characteristics—free intellectuals from the possibility to acquire proof and circumstantial evidence. . . .
>
> Yet, there is not only power, there is also an opposition to power. In Italy such an opposition is so large and strong that it constitutes a power in its own right; I am referring to the Italian Communist Party. . . .
>
> The Italian Communist Party is an uncorrupted country within a corrupted country, it is an honest country in a dishonest country, it is an intelligent country within an idiotic country, it is a cultivated country within an ignorant country. . . . The Italian Communist Party has thus become a "separate country," an island. And this is precisely the reason why today it can have close relationships with real power, which is corrupt, inept, degraded; but those are diplomatic relations, as two different countries may entertain with each other. . . . An op-

position thus conceived identifies itself with *another* power, which is
power nonetheless.

    As a consequence, politicians, members of such an opposition, can-
not but behave as men of power.[57]

The metaphor of two separate countries is employed by Pasolini to describe
the split between politics and ethics, or, in Gramscian terms, the split between
coercive power and its legitimation through hegemony,[58] whereby the exercise
of power, through the monopolization of violence, is an end unto itself. The
split between the coercive moment and the hegemonic moment can then only
be conceived as a friend-enemy dichotomy whereby "diplomatic" relations
can easily be overturned into violent antagonism. By defining power as that
from which society is excluded, Pasolini seems to evoke an image of power as
an intrusive monster generated by the sleep of reason, its finger constantly on
the trigger, its hands relentlessly manipulating a fuse.

    Constantly on the verge between patronage and aggression, the Italian power
elites seem to be caught in a repetition compulsion; constantly switching from
trasformismo[59] to repression, they end up reproducing Italy's long-standing
traumatic ambivalence regarding the fall of fascism. "Apparently, the double-
bind of the message Enemy-Liberator (the Americans) and Friend-Assassin
(the Fascists, the Germans) can neither be read nor elaborated in all its complexity and heterogeneity, and must remain as an experience repressed from
the collective memory." [60]

    By mediating the state-civil society dichotomy with the friend-enemy di-
chotomy, fascism opened up the way to the *de facto* institutionalization of state
terrorism. The cold-war anticommunist paranoia became not only the excuse
for the Christian Democrats to conceive all challenges to "their" institutions
as external and disruptive attacks on democracy whose institutions, but re-
newed the cosmopolitanism of the Italian elites that had been one major historical factor that had prevented them from constituting a national-popular
bloc. Their new allegiance to transnational forces hindered them from a national democratic project, thus renewing the conditions out of which fascism
had emerged.[61] At the same time, the institutionalization of the resistance
stressed its characters of a movement of national liberation while underplaying,
indeed repressing from national consciousness, its aspects of civil war, thus
virtually effacing the Italian origins of fascism. The reemergence of a social
movement which, however fleetingly, posed the problem of a democratic historic bloc (the students' movement plus the workers), which combined the autonomy of the social with political initiatives, was inevitably framed as a military attack according to the friend-enemy dichotomy. The challenge to expand
the limits of parliamentary democracy was then mystified as an attack to democracy *tout court*. The state apparatus thus readily reverted to its fundamental
violent character whereby its monopoly on violence functions as pure menace.

In his "Critique of Violence,"[62] Benjamin distinguishes between violence that opens up the possibility of transcendence in the midst of history, that is, violence as the midwife of justice whereby power is dissolved, and violence as instrumental device legitimating power understood as positive right. The latter form of violence is a constant threat, a fateful force inscribing domination onto the present as inescapable presence. The present as a projection of "natural history," wherein the "objectivity" of its limits curbs any possibility of its transformation; indeed, where possibility and transcendence are locked away in a past conceived as mythical.

In Italy the resistance being officially conceived as national liberation, as military struggle, constituted precisely such a foundational event. Framing away political and social opposition as an enemy the militarization of Italy's immediate past legitimated the militarization of the present whereby Italian democracy was permanently conceived as being permanently under siege. A situation where the past is conceived as heroic, as an epic, and where individual choice can only be framed as a fateful reactualization of total destruction, where political militancy falls prey to military aggression: this can be a way to conceive Italian conspiratorial politics, a sort of time machine that shapes the present as "state of emergency," where revealing the arbitrary and contested character of Christian Democracy's monopoly of power is converted into its legitimization.

Coda

In April 1995 prominent politicians were on trial; the neofascist party MSI had changed its name and was declaring itself postfascist; the Italian Communist Party had also changed its name, now it was post-something; Christian Democracy was pulverized into three parties, all of which had different names; Andreotti was facing trial for his connections with the Mafia. Commenting on yet another investigation on Piazza Fontana, Rossana Rossanda, cofounder in 1969 of the independent communist newspaper *Il Manifesto,* wrote:

> I look at the names of [past] prime ministers, and I shudder at the fact that Andreotti is indicted for an improbable kiss with Riina and not for having tampered with the intelligence files on the 1974 massacres. I think [of] all the ministers of defence and . . . the ministers of interior, whom the intelligence services gave explicit reports. . . . In Italy, it was obvious, it was tacitly understood, it was admissible to do anything in the name of anticommunism, including killing citizens unfortunate enough to be in a bank, in a square, on a train. . . . I hear people full of wisdom cautioning me to forget: once cured, one does not linger on the illness, life must go on; what do you want to tell the young? That the governments of the republic had some agreements

with the Mafia, that they have also stolen, and, finally, that they had also been assassins? Better to look to the future. . . . They have shot at us, they have annihilated us with bombs, plots, and lies. Those who will come after us will build their own destiny, but we owe them the truth.[63]

Notes

I would like to thank James Faubion, George Marcus and Julie Taylor for their comments on the previous drafts of this paper.

All translations from the Italian are my own.

1. Roth 1988. Written in 1923, the book narrates the story of a German army officer, a WWI veteran. Of lower middle-class background, Theodor Lohse, his dreams of social mobility shattered by the defeat and the collapse of the German Empire, joins a right-wing terrorist organization whose members are veterans, high-ranking officers, bureaucrats, and police officials. The more he gets involved in the terrorist activities of the organization, the more he becomes hostage to its secrets and pervasive network.

2. Head of Italian intelligence from 1970 to 1974, indicted in connection with the Rosa dei venti affair.

3. General Siro Rossetti, cited in De Lutiis 1996, 60–61. De Lutiis has been an advisor to the parliamentary commission investigating terrorism. This book is an abridged version of his report.

4. Giovanni De Lorenzo was head of Italian intelligence from 1956 to 1962.

5. Lieutenant-Colonel Amos Spiazzi, cited in De Lutiis 1996, 59–60.

6. Pier Paolo Pasolini, cited in Lumley 1990, 74. The events that were soon dubbed "the battle of Valle Giulia," where the school of architecture is located in Rome, took place on 20 March 1968; they marked the turning point when the student protest acquired a more aggressive character against the police.

7. The emergency legislation drafted in 1975 specifically targeted to political violence and which often resulted in widespread abuse by the police.

8. On 31 May 1972 three Carabinieri were killed by a car bomb. Later investigations revealed a network connecting Italian intelligence and neofascist groups.

9. Daniele Barbieri, "Quel 1969, questo 1993," in Di Giovanni and Ligini 1993. This book is a reprint of the collective book documenting the involvement of the fascists and the Italian intelligence in the bombing; it contributed to the acquittal of the anarchists the authorities claimed had planted the bomb in the main hall of the Milan branch of Banca Nazionale dell'Agricoltura in Piazza Fontana.

10. Ibid.

11. In April 1967 a right-wing military coup had successfully overthrown the Greek government establishing a military dictatorship. The Greek regime soon became a major supporter of Italian neofascism that in turn considered the military regime as an example to imitate. Cf. Di Giovanni and Ligini 1993; Barbieri 1976.

12. Cf. Di Giovanni and Ligini 1993; see also Stajano and Fini 1977, and Pellegrino 1996. Gianni Pellegrino has been the president of the parliamentary commission mentioned above.

13. Cf. De Lutiis 1996, 53.

14. Paolo Aleandri, neofascist militant, cited in De Lutiis 1991, 102.

15. Lieutenant-Colonel Spiazzi was one of the commanders involved.

16. The public perceived that something strange was going on when on 5 July 1964, during a round of consultations between the president (Antonio Segni) and leading political figures in the context of the negotiations for the country's second center-left government, Segni had unexpectedly summoned De Lorenzo. Nobody was able to learn what the two talked about, yet it was also common knowledge that the president did not favor a coalition government with the Socialist Party.

17. The Calabresi affair is yet another example of Italy's unsolved political mysteries. As late as 1988 the affair reemerged when Leonardo Marino, a former militant of the leftist organization Lotta Continua, claimed that he had been an accomplice to the killing that had been planned by members of the organization's Central Committee. The leader of the organization, which had long been disbanded, Adriano Sofri, was indicted, spent two years in prison, and was later acquitted. The irony was that by now Adriano Sofri had distanced himself from his "revolutionary" past in favor of a far more moderate liberal perspective. The whole event acquired the characteristics of a Freudian intrusive memory, both biographically and nationally, whereby the past, the historical past, truly appeared as a "foreign country." It is then of no surprise if Carlo Ginzburg, both as historian as a longtime friend of Sofri, seized the opportunity to reflect on the politics of the inquisitorial paradigm in the writing of history (Ginzburg 1991).

18. Cf. *Maquis dossier* 1982, 27.

19. Cited in De Lutiis 1991, 106.

20. In 1937 Cavallo had been arrested for stealing books from the national library in Turin. Later released, he had won a scholarship allowing him to study German. He remained in Germany until 1942, when he married the daughter of a high-ranking officer of the German intelligence. On his return to Italy he worked for the Wehrmacht engineer corps while at the same time becoming a member of the extremist leftist group Stella Rossa. After the war he became a journalist of the Turin edition of the Communist Party newspaper *L'Unità*. In 1949, upon the discovery of his past involvement with fascism, Cavallo was expelled from the party. He immediately traveled to the United States as a foreign correspondent for the Italian newspaper *La Gazzetta del Popolo*. In 1954 he was back in Italy and was an active member of the anticommunist organization Pace e libertà, led by Edgardo Sogno.

21. Cf. De Lutiis 1991, 143ff.

22. The organization was Pace e libertà. The decision to constitute it had been made after a meeting of the Atlantic Council (a body which brings together the foreign ministers and defense ministers of all NATO countries) held in Lisbon in 1952. Cf. De Lutiis 1996, 197.

23. De Lutiis 1996, 189–91.

24. I make a distinction between right-wing violence and left-wing violence, that is, between the generally offensive character of the former and the initial defensive character of the latter. It is not only an ideological claim I am making here, for it is also confirmed by the chronology of the events. Left-wing armed struggle (of which the Red

Brigades are the most famous example) appeared *after* Piazza Fontana; it was a reaction to what was perceived as the first sign of an imminent right-wing coup. This of course does not entail a generalized advocacy of violence. Yet one needs to note that this tragic mistake split the movement, thus preventing further democratization of the country, which, after all, was the aim of the strategy of tension. Moreover, it is also necessary to stress the autonomous character of leftist armed struggle, to claim that formations such as the Red Brigades where fanatics totally isolated from the Left, or, often a corollary of this thesis, that they were merely pawns in game played by the state, amounts to a misrepresentation of the specific character of Italian politics in the sixties and seventies. Cf. Silj 1979; Mafai 1984; and Moretti 1994. For a more global perspective, see Negri 1988.

25. See note 3.

26. The following narrative may appear to be a cynical analysis of Italian politics, yet, as I hope will become clear, it is written from the perspective of radical social movements that view parliamentary democracy and liberal political institutions as inherently authoritarian and conservative. In writing this paragraph I have drawn heavily from Moroni 1991. Primo Moroni has been a leading figure of the "autonomia" movement, a loosely connected network of groups active in the seventies who saw social movements as the main driving force for a global transformation of society and that developed a brand of revolutionary Marxism which refused all forms of bureaucratic leadership. See Moulnier 1989, and Negri 1994.

27. Zangrandi 1971.

28. Indeed, it was in this climate of "reconciliation" that Prince Julio Valerio Borghese was pardoned and released in 1949.

29. Cf. Moroni 1991.

30. Cf. De Lutiis 1991, 42; De Lutiis 1996, 5ff.; and Pellegrino 1996, 28ff.

31. This is also the same period that the Italian intelligence signed a secret agreement with the CIA to form a secret structure (under the code name Gladio) whose task was to train guerrilla units to be employed in the case of foreign invasion as well as against "internal subversion."

32. See previous paragraph.

33. See previous paragraph.

34. Cf. Lumley 1989.

35. The referendum had been conceived by its proponents as a major cultural and political showdown against the Left. They were convinced not only that the vast majority of Italians, modernization notwithstanding, would rally to uphold traditional family values, but that the victory of the referendum would isolate the Left and reveal the minority status of social movements.

36. Cf. Rossanda 1989.

37. Cf. Negri 1988.

38. Cf. Moulnier 1989.

39. Pellegrino 1996, 149.

40. Pasolini 1990, 233. My translation.

41. Eco 1995.

42. Eco 1995, 14.

43. "Italian fascism was the first to establish a military liturgy, a folklore, even a way of dressing—far more influential, with its black shirts, than Armani, Benetton, or Versace would ever be" (Eco 1995, 13).

44. Cf. Bobbio 1990. See also Revelli in Giovanni De Luna e Marco Revelli 1995.

45. Cf. Losurdo 1994.

46. Cf. De Luna and Revelli 1995.

47. Eco 1995, 12.

48. Cf. De Luna and Revelli 1995.

49. De Luna and Revelli 1995, 48.

50. This also implies the possibility of understanding to what extent Italian politics is prone to be conspiratorial in character. In this sense, conspiracy loses its Anglo-Saxon sense of a delusional and simplifying narrative of alien forces secretly influencing the everyday life of a community and becomes a critical assessment of the Italian ruling elites.

51. Such a view of power was, of course, and is male centered.

52. Cf. Gramsci 1977; vol. III.

53. Cf. Galli 1991. For an example in the anthropological literature, see Stirling 1968; Stirling links the development of what one could call conspiratorial reasoning (ex post facto reasoning, in his terminology) to the development (indeed, modernization) of clientelistic power relationships in post-WWII Sicily. His argument being that the momentous proliferation of complex bureaucratic structures targeted encapsulated communities. In this context, "conspiratorial" reasoning becomes a way to make sense of the processes that excludes certain individuals from access to resources and services while including others. The bureaucratization of Italian society is one major accomplishment of the fascist regime and has continued in the postwar years. If under fascism such a process had disciplinarian ambitions, after the war, state agencies became means to distribute resources in return for electoral support. See Ginsborg 1990; Schneider and Schneider 1993; and De Luna 1995.

54. Cf. Bobbio 1990; Rossanda 1989.

55. Cf. De Luna 1995 and Rossanda 1989.

56. George Marcus notes that in democratic regimes, elites face a constant deficit of legitimation, and that this in turn facilitates their tendency to develop a conspiratorial mentality and practices: "Elite organization accomplishes the reconstitution of one kind of rules (bureaucratic codes and procedures that are publicly available) though the creation of other rules of a different type in order to make formal organizations serve the interests, however defined, of the members of the elite" (Marcus 1993, 42).

57. Pasolini 1990, 88–91.

58. Cf. Gramsci 1977a.

59. *Trasformismo* is the parliamentary tactic whereby governments coopt parliamentary support to stay in office. Thus the parliamentary majorities vary according to the policies pursued and are quite independent from any global political project. In return for support, the individual representative (or the political group) gains access to resources that can be distributed to supporters. *Trasformismo* emerged in the 1880s and has characterized much of Italian political elites' behavior ever since.

60. Pandolfi 1995.

61. Cf. Gramsci 1977b.
62. Benjamin 1978.
63. Rossanda 1996.

References

Barbieri, Daniele. 1976. *Agenda nera: Trent'anni di neofascismo in Italia.* Rome: Coines.

Benjamin, Walter. 1978. *Reflections: Essays, Aphorisms, Autobiographical Writings.* Ed. Peter Demetz. New York: Harcourt Brace Jovanovich.

Bobbio, Norberto. 1990. *Profilo Ideologico del '900.* Milan: Garzanti.

De Luna, Giovanni, and Marco Revelli. 1995. *Fascismo/Antifascismo: Le idee, le identità.* Florence: La Nuova Italia.

De Lutiis, Giuseppe. 1996. *Il lato oscuro del potere.* Rome: Editori Riuniti.

———. 1991. *Storia dei servizi segreti in italia.* Rome: Editori Riuniti.

Di Giovanni, Eduardo M., and Marco Ligini, eds. 1993. *La strage di Stato: Un libro che ha fatto epoca.* Rome: Libera Informazione Editrice.

Eco, Umberto. 1995. "Ur-Fascism." *New York Review of Books* 92(11), 22 June.

Faenza, Roberto. 1978. *Il malaffare.* Milan: Mondadori.

Galli, Giorgio. 1991. *Affari di stato: L'italia sotterranea 1943–1990: storia politica, partiti, corruzione, misteri, scandali.* Milan: Kaos.

Ginsborg, Paul. 1990. *A History of Contemporary Italy.* Harmondsworth: Penguin.

Ginzburg, Carlo. 1991. *Il giudice e lo storico: Considerazioni in margine al processo Sofri.* Turin: Einaudi.

Gramsci, Antonio. 1977a. "Quaderno 13 (XXX): Noterelle sul Machiavelli." In *Quaderni del carcere* 3. Turin: Einaudi.

———. 1977b. "Quaderno 19 (X), Risorgimento Italiano." In *Quaderni del carcere* 3. Turin: Einaudi.

Losurdo, Domenico. 1994. *La seconda repubblica: Liberalismo, federalismo, postfacismo.* Turin: Bollati Boringhieri.

Lumley, Robert. 1990. *States of Emergencies.* London: Verso.

Mafai, Miriam. 1984. *L'uomo che sognava la lotta armata: La storia di Pietro Secchia.* Milan: Rizzoli.

Maquis dossier. 1982. "Il conflitto segreto." No. 2, June.

Marcus, George. 1993. "Elites Communities and Institutional Orders." In George Marcus (ed.), *Elites: Ethnographic Issues.* Ed. Marcus. Albuquerque: University of New Mexico Press.

Moretti, Mario. 1994. *Brigate Rosse, una storia italiana.* Milan: Anabasi.

Moroni, Primo. 1991. "Quel ferrovecchio di 'Gladio.'" In *La notte dei gladiatori.* Padua: Calusca.

Moulnier, Yann. 1989. "Introduction." In *The Politics of Subversion,* by Antonio Negri. Cambridge: Polity Press.

Negri, Antonio. 1988. "Do you Remember Revolution?" In *Revolution Retrieved: Writings on Marx, Keynes, Capitalist Crisis and New Social Subjects 1967–83.* London: Red Notes.

————. 1994. "The Physiology of Counter-Power: When Socialism Is Impossible and Communism So Near." In *Body Politics*. Ed. Michael Ryan & Avery Gordon. Boulder: Westview Press.

Pandolfi, Mariella. 1995. "Facts of Rhetoric/Rhetoric of Facts: In Between Mediterranean Representations." Paper presented at the 94th annual meeting of the American Anthropological Association, Washington, D.C.

Pasolini, Pier Paolo. 1990. "Fascista." In *Scritti corsari*. Milan: Garzanti.

Pellegrino, Gianni. 1996. *Luci sulle stragi*. Lecce: Lupetti/Pietro Manni.

Rossanda, Rossana. 1996. "Stragi." In *Note a Margine*. Turin: Bollati Boringhieri.

————. 1989. *Le altre*. Milan: Feltrinelli.

Roth, Joseph. 1988. *The Spider's Web*. London: Chatto and Windus.

Schneider, Peter, and Jane Schneider. 1993. "The Dissolution of the Ruling Class in Twentieth-Century Sicily." In *Elites: Ethnographic Issues*. Ed. George Marcus. Albuquerque: University of New Mexico Press.

Silj, Alessandro. 1979. *Never Again without a Rifle! The Origins of Italian Terrorism*. New York: Karz.

Stajano, Corrado, and Massimo Fini. 1977. *La forza della democrazia: La strategia della tensione in Italia 1969–1976*. Turin: Einaudi.

Stirling, Paul. 1968. "Impartiality and Personal Morality." In *Contributions to Mediterranean Sociology*. Ed. John Peristiany. The Hague: Mouton.

Tarrow, Sidney. 1989. *Democracy and Disorder*. Oxford: Oxford University Press.

Zangrandi, Ruggero. 1971. *L'Italia tradita*. Milan: Mursia.

Luiz E. Soares
Translated by Paulo Henriques Britto

9

A Toast to Fear: Ethnographic Flashes and Two Quasi-Aphorisms[1]

From calculation to conspiracy is only a short step. There is a thread running through realism and utopianism, and its opposite ends are strategic reasoning and outright paranoia. So it is that game theory and psychoanalysis converge, in spite of the chasm that separates them, when it comes to tacitly acknowledging that the difference between reason and paranoia is no more than a matter of degree. They are points along a continuum, and it is not at all easy to draw the line between them. Paranoia is the exacerbation of rational calculation by a troubled psychological economy. It must be placated, or else domesticated into political agencies, giving rise to the formulation of strategies or defensive anticipation. In either case, imagination and deductive reasoning are fused together. In the individual, it induces fear and feelings of omnipotence, vulnerability, and arrogance.

Conspiracies and their complex alchemy are to be found in the tragic fabulations of classical Greek drama and in Shakespeare's plays, in Homeric mythology and modern allegories, in the Machiavellian scheming of Florentine princes and in the revolutionary plans of the Soviet vanguard, in the moderate constructivism of prudent liberals, and in the populist virtues of Jacobinic radicalism.

The rise of social science itself was based on the unveiling of the covert, the disclosure of deception, the revelation of what is hidden behind the masks of ideology. Elias Canetti, with irony and revulsion, saw all such subjective leanings and the theories they resulted in as paranoid. He was skeptical about the compatibility of this paranoid view and the disarmed openness that was supposedly required by democratic pluralism. The specter of conspiracy haunts the halls of academia. Canetti may have a point here; there may well be elective affinities between paranoid action and thought, on the one hand, and authoritarianism in its countless manifestations on the other. The very idea of critique, often associated with libertarian rebellion, partakes of the authoritarian spirit whenever it is expressed as an investigation aiming to unmask, expose, disclose, bring to light. The critical theory of the Frankfurt School, Marxism, even Foucault would all fall into the trap set by the wise and lamented Canetti.

What about politics? How to differentiate it from conspiratorial theories and practices, even (and particularly) in modern, post-Machiavellian times, after the creation of nation-states? Norbert Elias has shown how the transition from feudal wars to state monopoly on legitimate violence that arose in tandem with the modern nation-state led to a number of changes. One of these was the replacement of war strategy by games of persuasion, dissuasion, and dissimulation, the establishment of alliances, the isolation of adversaries. Psychology—the art of deciphering covert intentions— replaced bravery and force. The theater of politics became the arena of modern heroism. Conspiracy is the prolongation of war by other means—means that are compatible with the institutions of modernity, and that would have become increasingly common and intense not only in politics but also in social life, as expectations grew less stable, if conspiracies and conspiracy theories did not have the effect of stabilizing expectations by generating Manichaean arguments for the legitimation of national power.

So pervasive is the presence of conspiracy that the danger is not that of overestimating its importance, but rather that of dissolving the concept into the unlimited repertoire of its meanings and historical configurations. Since Thomas Hobbes the social order has been seen as a set of expectations concerning the behavior of others. Such expectations encourage action that tends to confirm them; they are self-fulfilling prophecies. Predictability is no more than the expression of the stability of expectations, as David Hume has taught us. In social life, the substance of expectations is as ethereal as expectations themselves. That is why trust is so decisive. And trust is immediately associated with belief and faith—or, on the other hand, with mistrust and defensive forethought. We return to Hobbes and the means of anticipation: calculation, fear, imagination; strategy and paranoia. When trust in institutions, in the action of others, in the effectiveness of the morality in force, is undermined, when expectations are shaky, conditions are favorable to the exploitation of conspiratorial theories, to active or preventive conspiracies—even, I insist, if only to stabilize them again. Or, conspiratorial paranoia is part and parcel of the process of stabilization of expectations, creation of legitimacy, consolidation of identities. The two readings are possible and provocative. We may explore both.

In situations of crisis, Jacobinic voluntarism, ingenious schemes to overthrow the government, and paranoid fantasy replace routine and the generalized belief in the stability of the status quo. Conspiracy, fear, and conspiratorial speculations take the place of trust. Are they symptoms of crisis, typical signs of the weakness of political institutions with no roots in the people's tradition, no historical depth, insufficient social grounding and inclusiveness, precarious legitimacy? Or, on the contrary, are fear and paranoid fantasy, as expressed in conspiratorial theories, a precondition for routine and a credible order?

If paranoia and conspiratorial theories are a symptom of crisis, they are typical marks of Brazilian society, where in the twentieth century there has been democracy in only two periods: from 1945 to 1964 and since 1985. Our present democratic constitution dates from 1988. The first direct, democratic elections for the presidency held since the 1964 military coup took place in 1989. Thus Brazil would seem to be a good testing ground for a study of "conspiracies" and conspiratorial theories. That is what I have attempted to do, indirectly, by focusing on various aspects of the "culture of conspiracy," in different configurations, from the viewpoints of different characters, in diverse contexts. In many cases I have stressed the bizarre nature of certain situations or accusations, or the humorous and ludicrous character of anecdotes. Is there an element, a sort of conspiratorial spirit, common to all the fetishes, episodes, fabulations, to the speech of all the characters I evoke?

But maybe it just isn't so. Conspiratorial paranoia is probably not the characteristic disease of fragile institutions, analogous to pathologies of the mind. Perhaps it is an integral part of the contradictory process by means of which political institutions are legitimated. The case of the United States is exemplary, as Richard Hofstadter observed long ago. The cold war played an important part in the construction of the American national identity, at a time when it had become necessary to adapt traditional values to the country's new historical circumstances and international role. It was also a decisive factor in the preservation of the cohesion of the Soviet empire for decades. International bipolarity was the backdrop that gave ultimate meaning to the major conspiratorial adventures and tragedies of the postwar period. Today, the meaning of narratives relies on new contexts, with countless references and motivations whose nature is religious, ethnic, and so forth.

It might be wiser, then, to see these stories set in Brazil not as pointing to the weakness of Brazilian political institutions but as contextualized experiments in the conspiratorial imagination, which cannibalizes icons, heroes, exemplary dramatic plots, all sorts of ideological vocabulary. Seen in a positive light rather than as symptoms of weakness, these Brazilian cases may seem less parochial, topical, and singular than one might expect, although there is indeed local color, and the characters, political contexts, and consequences are all local. Most of the stories involve not grand conspiratorial theories but individual reactions to conspiratorial contexts, beliefs, or discourses.

These brief stories are all true—that is, to the extent that one may properly speak of a "true" narrative. Some names have been changed for ethical reasons; a few incidents have been summarized and edited so that the context could be more easily understood; but all the essential and relevant aspects have been preserved. Two of the fragments are not really narratives—they might perhaps be described as ethnographic insights or quasi-aphorisms. Here is the first one.

Go, Go, Native!

The anthropologist, writes Clifford Geertz, reads the cultural text over the native's shoulder, interpreting native interpretations. The native has learned to turn around. He fears capturing the voyeur's vanishing presence. At any time he may feel the hot breath of the scholar on the nape of his neck. He already senses the anthropologist's vague, ethereal presence inside the closet, or under the bed: cowardly lover, treacherous danger—serial reader. The native makes great fun of this alien shadow and plays pranks on him; he reads to the intruder a fake version of his fundamental truths—his ultimate practical joke, the innermost pleasure afforded by his cunning.

Premonitions

Conservatives—industrialists, landowners, respectable middle-class families —anticipated a reformist, protocommunist coup in Brazil in 1964. Determined to resist it, they enacted their own coup. The military, protectors of fatherland, family, and private property, found it prudent to remain in power for twenty-one years.

The Corpse Thrown into the World, or Fake *Dasein* in the Tropics

It's summer in Rio; the year is 1989. At the bank, people stand in line and argue over politics. An elderly gentleman is a passionate follower of the populist leader Leonel Brizola, a bugbear of the Brazilian elite who was persecuted by the military in 1964 and remained in exile for fifteen years. Every Brizolista is, above all, a fiery believer. The wild-eyed little old man with grandiose gestures, faced with a captive audience, seems to be illuminated by a sort of cosmic wrath as he denounces Roberto Marinho, the Brazilian Citizen Kane, owner of a media empire, the Globo television network, the fourth largest in the world, always the defender of whatever conservative government is in power, and the archenemy of Brizola. "If Brazil is the way it is now," fumes the old man, "it's because of Roberto Marinho. Globo is the devil. But listen to me: all of you are being fooled. The whole thing is a big hoax. A huge hoax. There's no such man as Roberto Marinho. Not any longer. He's been dead for years. What you see on TV is just a stand-in for him, shown for just a few seconds and from a distance. This double was artificially made. Plastic surgery. He's an American.

He speaks Portuguese with an accent. But every time he speaks, the voice is dubbed in. For a long time now, U.S. corporations and the CIA have been directing the Globo network, with a dead man's double for a front."

Scruples (1990)

The meeting of the Department of Social Science of a Rio de Janeiro university dragged on, monotonously and inevitably, like a procession in the desert. It was necessary to develop research projects and increase fundraising efforts. Individual suggestions were pooled; lists of possibilities were drawn. The air conditioning was out of order. This provided a good excuse for the teachers to set aside their scruples and smoke without guilt. So serious was the agenda that every vice could be overlooked. Though the windows were open, the whole laborious, circumspect, dedicated setting still reminded one of Camus's remote beach, where the stranger was about to commit his unlikely, unmotivated, uncalled-for crime. Sunlight, glazed eyes, gleaming surfaces, a gun. Suddenly, a shot, flashes of light, a body. Suddenly, the only professor who had been silent until then, his face as hard as the cold marble of national heroes, bared his blameless heart and shouted, "You can count me out! I'll have none of this! I'm unfundable, do you hear me? Unfundable!" And he stalked out of the room, slamming the door behind him. To this day he remains proud of his gesture; better to do no research, to publish nothing, than to run the risk of involuntarily reproducing the ruling ideology, the spirit of which is a living presence in money and the pleasures it makes possible.

An Underground Statesman on the Tightrope

Statements about international politics always came first in Brazilian Communist Party meetings, congresses, and documents: "The forces of peace and progress are advancing around the world!" The forces of peace and progress were always advancing. There might be a setback here or there, but such obstacles were to be expected in an inexorable historical process. Any contrary impressions were instances of petit-bourgeois illusion or ideological deviation.

This was particularly true of the Polish crisis in 1981. By then there were anti-Soviet dissident tendencies within the Brazilian Communist Party, influenced by the democratic initiatives of some European communist parties during the seventies. The Italians, heirs of Gramsci and Togliatti, were particularly prestigious among non-Stalinist and non-Maoist communists in Brazil. The idea of dictatorship was increasingly unpopular—even the dictatorship of the "proletariat" advocated by Lenin and his followers. At long last, Brazilian communists had learned the hard way to value democratic freedoms, which at the time they still referred to as "bourgeois freedoms."

In order to preserve their hold on power, the pro-Soviet communists, whose leader had been Secretary General Luis Carlos Prestes since the thirties, had no qualms about resorting to the perverse combination of clandestineness and Leninist organization. The basic idea behind this model of organization was that every member had the right to express his or her opinions in Party meetings, but once the different proposals were voted on, he or she had to accept the victorious proposal and to defend it publicly. In order to enforce Party discipline, a monolithic, unitary practice, there had to be a single command, the Central Committee. Lenin conceived this model—known as democratic centralism—in military terms, since the Party was to be seen as a revolutionary vanguard, a machine of war, ready to resort to violence in order to impose on history the "necessary" corrections. The Jacobinic voluntarism of the enlightened vanguard was, ironically, the instrument by means of which the "inherent laws" of history were to be implemented. Now, being an underground organization, the Central Committee had the power to produce as many grassroots delegates as it found convenient, since—for obvious security reasons—no one could question the existence of the grassroots units the delegates were supposed to represent. Thus the Central Committee could never be defeated, as long as democratic centralism and clandestineness were combined.

But the result was not always easy to control or predict. For instance, sometimes intermediate-level leaderships reacted against the Stalinist authoritarianism of the Central Committee, and held regional or sectorial congresses that were more democratic, without the usual manipulations. A significant case occurred when a certain intermediate-level leadership summoned delegates of grassroots units to discuss the Polish crisis, when a coup by General Jaruzelski or a Soviet invasion seemed imminent. The most prominent "democratic" leader listened in silence as the delegates unanimously criticized the threats of Soviet imperialism. Though the wording and the values expressed were not always the same, the disapproval seemed consensual.

When the intermediate-level leadership, which had organized the meeting, retired to deliberate and draft a document expressing the position of that particular sector of the Party, the "democratic" Party leader was furious with them. He had sat through the meeting with the grassroots delegates in silence, but now he vehemently attacked, using all the devices of his passionate rhetoric, the "liberal" positions that seemed to be consensual among the leadership. Before an astonished audience he gave a lesson in Russophile geopolitics, denouncing the conservative and pro-American character of the Polish democratic resistance. Once again, he was defeated; his harangue had failed to convince his comrades. At last he conceded his defeat, under one condition: he himself would read, in the plenary session with the grassroots delegates present, the anti-Soviet manifesto that had been drafted by members of the majority.

From a Friend's Letter (Posted in Rio de Janeiro, 20 September 1994)

You can't imagine what it was like. The media was determined to assassinate the governor's character, exploiting the population's fear of unchecked urban violence. And all of a sudden I was in the eye of the storm simply because I had written against media manipulation and tried to encourage a public discussion that was less passionate, more analytic, more positive. Because of this, he's been phoning me, to talk. Perhaps he likes me personally. As you know, the governor was active in the resistance against the dictatorship. He stood up for human rights at a time when many were silent. In a certain sense, we belong to the same group, in spite of the difference in age. I'm not sure he actually listens to what I say, but he does like to talk. Maybe he doesn't listen to me at all. He's a man of strong convictions, if you know what I mean. This doesn't affect my admiration for him; I like him. But he has all these unshakable beliefs.

Well, you know David is an important man now, don't you? You remember David? We're very close. I've been close to him throughout his public career. Now he's all over the media. They ask his opinion about everything. And he's a leader of civil movements. He loves grassroots politics. But he's reinventing popular politics. He's got the elegance of an ambassador, even though he wears sandals. The man is a force of nature; he can't be stopped. He could sell sand wholesale in the Sahara, to say the least. He's articulating civil society from top to bottom. He speaks as an equal to the president or to a housewife in a favela—or, for that matter, to a Pentecostalist, a follower of an Afro-Brazilian cult, a politician, or a community leader. He's all piss and vinegar. With his prestige and his ability, you can imagine the envy, the suspicion, the resentment he arouses. Suspicion most of all—both from the Right and from the Left. And from the center as well, of course, if there's such a thing as a center. Since David has no ties to any party or group with a clear ideological identity, and since his discourse doesn't fit into any of the usual pigeonholes, there's plenty of confusion, and suspicion abounds.

You know how it is: he likes to talk about "partnership." In this way, he can't be branded as an adversary of the government or of any particular sector of society or political tendency. Little by little he opens every door. He's able to get a union leader, a big-shot industrialist, a police chief, and a hip-hop fan to sit at the same table and talk. His tool is the pacifist movement he helped create and now coordinates. Since the movement threatens or opposes nobody, it grew unexpectedly and began to take over public spaces. David avoids accusations and complaints, which worked during the dictatorship but now, when the democratic rule of law has been fully reinstated, seem outdated, ineffective. He prefers to say things like, "Let's get together and try to find a feasible solution for each problem." This has none of the epic glamour of denunciation, but it works.

Then the inevitable happened. The movement had to talk to the governor, whose political fate was at stake. The elections were coming; there was a smell of gunpowder in the air; there was talk of a coup; there were bogus shots in the favelas. Just loud pops. Drug traffickers, armed to the teeth, fired rounds of shots into the air all through the night. In the morning the headlines were "Another Night of Violence and Terror in Rio." As authorities sit on their hands, the editorials proclaimed, organized crime is taking over the city. But the drug lords were shooting into the air, financed by the governor's opponents, in order to generate panic and mistrust in the state government. The problem was that the governor needed a reliable police force if he was to act effectively. But there was no such thing. Criminals and policemen were part of the same world. Since he trusted practically no one, the governor had no means to pick out the bad apples in the police force, or to persuade the press to give him a break.

In such an atmosphere of fear and sham, obviously the governor was afraid of David and his movement, particularly because they had the media on their side. This, the governor believed, clearly indicated that there were vested interests behind them. I tried to convince him that the movement against violence, though backed by the media, was also supported by the Left, and by grassroots leaders as well; all to no avail. His convictions remained as strong and unshakable as ever. What was I to do? After much urging from David for me to talk the governor into receiving a delegation of the movement (how *can* one refuse him anything?), I finally managed to persuade the governor. The delegation was headed by David himself.

I don't think I've ever seen David as nervous as he was that afternoon, in the waiting room of the governor's palace. He knew what was at stake: should it prove impossible to arrive at some sort of understanding with the governor, to work out a common project with him, David would have to assume an adversarial position; he could no longer talk about "partnership." If he turned against the governor and abandoned his earlier language, he would inevitably help the opposition gubernatorial candidate, a conservative who was allied to the corrupt and procoup groups active in the police. Or else he would have to give up the movement, or his leadership of it. In addition, the only person who could possibly succeed him as leader of the movement and keep up its momentum was precisely the most influential representative of the local elite, a man whose democratic convictions were questionable, a former ally of the right-wing military during the period of dictatorship, and an outspoken supporter of the opposition gubernatorial candidate. To the governor, however, this was also a turning point. He would not be able to find another way out of the predicament he had got into, or been driven into. If he joined forces with a comprehensive, nonideological, nonpartisan movement, he might come out of his isolated corner and revive his political chances. But to do this he needed trust, he had to overcome his own suspicions. What if the whole thing was just another trap, like so many others he had stepped into lately?

David chain-smoked and walked back and forth, like a stereotypical character in a bad novel. In his mind he went over every argument, every proposal. David and the governor knew each other. Did they like each other? I think David was fond of the governor, for all their differences. But a man who is cornered and isolated, who sees his great political opportunity slip through his fingers, cannot really be expected to be trusting or affectionate. Why then did he listen to me and seem to like me? Perhaps because I couldn't be thought of as a potential rival. I was just a college professor, a researcher like so many others. The waiting room was thick with journalists. The leaders of the movement huddled in small circles, which the most daring and curious journalists would sometimes elbow their way into. There were secretaries and security guards galore, newspapers piled up in corners, and dozens of phones. Everyone, as is usual in such situations, was late.

Finally, the governor's aide opened the door and announced that his boss would now see David and me. We asked whether there was some misunderstanding; after all, the governor was supposed to talk to *all* the leaders of the movement. There was no mistake; the governor had made himself perfectly clear. We hesitated for a second; we looked across the room at the opposite wall and then the two of us marched into the labyrinth of the palace, behind the impeccably uniformed aide. Labyrinths, indeed: a succession of halls and rooms, most of them deserted. The tension had been increased by the governor's rather inelegant exclusion of the others, you see. We walked in silence. High doors, large bare rooms, drenched in colorful light from the gardens. Finally, the last door was opened before us: the governor's office. The aide introduced us and retired. At the far end of the long central room of the palace stood the governor, leaning on a dark desk covered with sheets of paper and phones. By his side, the Evangelical minister who had recently converted him—much to the dismay of the governor's Marxist friends. This clergyman was a childhood friend of David's, and had always been one of his closest friends; a leftist, a charismatic man, who honored his calling.

David walked fast, breathing audibly, sweating profusely. I remember well the heavy black bag he carried in his hand, and the almost visible, contagious way he trembled. Calculation gave way to rhythm. For a few seconds everyone was motionless; against the dark background of the wall David's quivering figure and the governor's severe presence were sharply drawn. All of us stood before the desk and looked at one another, in silence. Somewhere in the depths of soul, a remote chord was struck and resonated across the room, driving David into the governor's arms. Then the two men, amazed with themselves, poured out their feeling in copious tears. The minister put his arms around us and prayed for peace in the city. The late-afternoon sun deadened the colors in the room. For some time we stood there, dumbfounded and elated, drawn into an inconceivable ritual, in the most unlikely of temples.

The circle broke up and we looked at one another. We felt a sweet, out-of-place, mischievous joy. The governor, relieved, one arm on my shoulder, the other on David's, asked, "Can I let those people in? You guys sure?"

Going Native

Nineteen seventy-two. The military dictatorship is at its most violent and repressive moment. The press is censored, people are arrested and tortured, no elections are held for any executive posts. The young Marxist hesitates on the threshold of a new existence. He is about to give up his petit-bourgeois life, his status as a college student, the comfortable apartment where he lives with his parents. Tomorrow he will turn into a worker. He will no longer see his family and his friends. He will leave a vague message for his girlfriend, striking a romantic, heroic attitude: "We shall meet again on the first day of the future." The brave young priest of socialism will live among the people. He will learn from the oppressed, and offer them in return class consciousness, the treasure that exorcises alienation and frees the spirit. The young man is anxious and excited, on the eve of the day when he is to sacrifice his own identity. The Party will furnish him with a new name, a new home, a job, a fake ID card, a life story to tell his neighbors—and his fellow workers. Tomorrow he will learn about his own past. The past, as everyone who has lived underground knows well, is always uncertain and unpredictable in such situations. About the future, however, there can be no doubt. No member of the socialist resistance harbors any doubts concerning the future.

At night, as he finishes packing his well-worn suitcase with his new old clothes, he bares his heart to his closest friend, thus breaking the number 1 rule of life underground. "What if it turns out I just can't do it? That the historical nature of my class is inbred in me, and there's nothing I can do about it? What if I, if I'm an enemy of the working class? A petit-bourgeois forever, beyond hope of any change? An unconscious, unwilling tool in the hands of the ruling classes? What if all of us are traitors of the people at heart?"

A Quasi-Aphorism by an Obscure Brazilian Poet

If your wife loves another, do not worry. Remember that you may be at the far end of the affair, so that, by loving another, she will find that her own soul is imprisoned by your fear of losing her, my friend.

Crime and Slander: Treason

To Luis Carlos Prestes, Brazil's foremost Communist leader, it was a self-evident truth, and so it remained to his death: the Soviet blueprint was the only one to follow. He never wavered in his convictions since his own conversion in the thirties. To the end, he was sure that Arruda—the dissident who was to found another Communist Party, thus creating a Brazilian version of the USSR-China conflict—was a traitor on the payroll of the CIA. The final proof came in 1956.

I quote from memory what he told me soon after he returned from exile, in 1979: "Arruda represented the Brazilian Communist Party at the twentieth congress of the Communist Party of the USSR in 1956. During the congress and in the months to follow, the bourgeois press published alarmist and slanderous reports about the 'crimes of Stalinism.' We denied everything and denounced the political scheming of the press in Brazil and elsewhere. But we had no firsthand information, because Arruda and his groups had decided to travel around Europe after the Moscow congress. For months we were in a fix. Finally, Arruda arrived in Brazil, and presented, in the name of our delegation, his report to the Central Committee. He had the nerve to trot out the same malicious fabrications that had been published by the bourgeois press, making a deep impression on a number of comrades, some of whom broke away from the Party. Ever since that day I've been absolutely sure that he was being paid by the CIA to divide and demoralize us."

Compromising (Phone Conversations, 1976)

Young, intelligent, a leader since she was a little girl. People called her a natural-born leader. At an early age she rose in the hierarchy to become one of the first and only women to occupy the dangerous and enviable position of a member of the leadership of the Brazilian Trotskyite Communist Party, a clandestine organization ever since it was founded. She was admitted into the Central Committee in the seventies. Those were days of suffocating oppression, when paranoia was necessary for survival, when it was hard to tell the difference between fanciful conspiracy theorizing from realistic prudence.

But even leaders have birthdays. Many enjoy the privilege of communicating with their families regularly. They are underground only on a part-time basis. They lead a phony normal life as a cover for their clandestine activities. Some of these leaders had loving mothers. Such was her case:

"No, Mother, thanks, but no. I know you mean well, and I'm really moved. I mean, thank you very much, Mother. But I *don't* want a TV set. No, Mother, please, don't insist. I positively refuse to have a TV set in my apartment. Can't you understand? You know very well how I feel about television programs,

Mother. Yes, I know, but how old was I back then? I was only a child, Mother. I've changed since then. You know that. Please, Mother, you're placing me in a very awkward position. Look, just buy me a book. Or a record. I swear it'll please me a lot more. Okay?"

Some Brazilian communist leaders had dedicated, loving mothers, even in the darkest years of the seventies. These mothers were also stubborn, mothers who just wouldn't give in. And, come to think of it, what's so terrible about having a color TV set?

"Color? No way, Mother. I know, I know everyone is buying a color TV these days. That's just the point, Mother. Can't you see that. Well, I think we should discuss the, uh, the sociology of television as a status symbol. I mean, we ought to get together and talk it over, Mother; it's not the sort of thing you can discuss on the phone. And it's not just that, Mother: think of what, what my friends would think if they found I have a TV set in my place? And a *color* TV, too?"

It's not just members of the resistance who must be bold and persistent. Real adoring mothers never rest, never give up, either.

"Look, Mother, for Christ's sake. Don't cry, Mother. No, it's not that. Of course I do. Mother, listen: I give up. You *can* give me that TV. Yeah. You're happy now? Sure, I'm happy too, Mother. But there's just this one thing. Please listen, Mother. Let's not argue over this; will you promise you won't argue? Okay, Mother: no remote control. You hear me? Absolutely *no* remote control!"

Garrincha

He was a genius. Everyone who knows the history of international soccer would be hard pressed to say who was the greatest: Garrincha or Pelé. A simple-minded, half-literate young man, he concocted the perfect antidote to the Jacobinic omnipotence of planners and conspirators—one that is also effective against all who fabricate, infer, or anticipate enemy conspiracies. Just before a major match in the 1962 World Cup, in Chile, Garrincha listened dutifully to the coach, who presented a detailed, blow-by-blow explanation of how the Brazilian team was to confuse their opponents and score a goal. The skull session presentation was perfect, precise, elegant. The heavy silence that followed was broken by Garrincha: "What about the guys in the opposite team? You've talked them into it, too?"

Hot Line (Summary of a Statement
by a Participant in the Meeting)

Nineteen ninety-four. That night I was late. I parked my car in front of the building where the secretary of justice lived, and looked at the sea for a while. I was calm. Everything seemed to be under control; the federal government had made it clear that, contrary to current rumors, there was to be no intervention in Rio de Janeiro State. I took in the breeze and the smell of the sea. Then I greeted the doorman, who knew me. Rumors and speculations were some of the weapons used by those who wanted to overthrow or sabotage the state government and hurt Leonel Brizola, its candidate for the presidency. Nothing could be more annoying in these days of neoliberal policies than a populist leader, a political dinosaur like Brizola, who still stands for the same nationalist causes he defended back in the fifties. But none of those rumors made much sense. The federal government about to send in the army to contain the wave of violence—just a few weeks before the elections? Who could ever take this seriously? As I stepped into the elevator, I thought how unlikely this scenario was. Such a precedent might jeopardize Brazil's brittle, hard-won democracy. And what would the army do? Take over the favelas, as in the bad old days of the military regime and the struggle against the guerrillas? The military wouldn't do such a crazy thing. A stray bullet, a provocation, a single casualty would be catastrophic. Also, there was the danger of demoralization. No, the federal government couldn't possibly do that—even if the elections were just around the corner. Or *because* of the elections, perhaps.

In the living room, I found the atmosphere strangely oppressive.

"The intervention has been decreed," somebody told me, laying a hand on my arm.

A journalist had called from Brasilia and given the news to the secretary of justice, asking him how he felt about it. This was a major journalist, a reliable source.

It felt like a blow in the pit of the stomach. Everyone in the room was broken, shattered; they shook their heads in disbelief. All except for the secretary's wife, who kept repeating what we knew, trying to convince herself that if reality isn't rational it can't be real. Wishful thinking. She reminded us of each fact, to comfort or to shake us out of our passiveness. I found I couldn't sit down. While the secretary talked with the governor on the hot line, I paced the large living room, with its view of the Atlantic. The television was on; at any time we expected to hear an official announcement, followed by the joyous comments of the opposition.

Why hadn't the minister called the governor? None of us could answer the question. I began to think of what we could do to resist the federal government. Which civil-society organizations could we count on? How would the parties react? They wouldn't be able to join forces in defense of the state since the elections were just around the corner and they were all busy attacking one another. What to do about the probable news blackout? Which legal and constitutional arguments could we rely on? What exactly did the constitution say about the federal intervention in states? Who was orchestrating the federal strategy? Who were the conspirators?

The ghosts of coups past haunted the room; memories of other resistance movements mobilized everyone.

An hour later, the secretary finally managed to contact the minister of justice. There was to be no federal intervention, after all. It was just another rumor. We toasted the rationality of the real. We exorcised ghosts and paranoias. It seemed that times had indeed changed, and for the better. The power of rumors, even among us, was the scar of old wounds. Twenty years living under a dictatorship will leave a mark on you.

Two weeks later there was a sort of disguised federal intervention: the state government was forced to sign an agreement under the terms of which the army would be allowed to help control violence in the city of Rio de Janeiro. The governor found it more prudent to accept this agreement to avoid intervention pure and simple, with all its institutional consequences. The opposition won the 1994 elections in Rio de Janeiro State. Leonel Brizola suffered his worst political defeat ever, in a forty-year-long career, in the presidential elections. The army invaded favelas in Rio, but retreated a few months later. During the period of military control, opinion polls showed that the population felt safer, more protected. On the other hand, the homicide rate rose dramatically: never had so many cases of murder been recorded in Rio as during these months. The newly elected government nominated as secretary of public security an army general who had been associated with repression during the military regime (1964–84). The new secretary implemented a system of productivity bonuses by means of which police officers could double or treble their salaries. Ever since, police action has resulted in an increasing number of deaths. The secretary and the governor who came into power in 1995 have stated that human rights do not apply to criminals, who ought to be seen as animals or monsters, not as human beings. When asked what methods of identification are used to allow police officers to make sure that they always lay their hands on the right culprits, even before any trial takes place, the secretary usually replies that the entire notion of human rights is a communist idea.

A Cop in New York, or 1994: Brazil Celebrates Ten Years of Democracy (Excerpts Adapted from a Friend's Account)

"Fan-*tas*-tic, Professor. Fan-*tas*-tic." My friend the colonel was infatuated with the Big Apple. He turned around on his heels, admiring the tallest buildings, basking in the city lights. He looked forward to his future memories. So far his life had been restricted to a provincial country in the periphery of the capitalist world, south of the equator. Until then, all he had was his Saturdays at horsemanship school in the hot, empty suburb, his medal for horsemanship, his pride in his equestrian skills, his close-knit, well-behaved family. The very stereotype of the Brazilian nice guy, a man with no ambitions, but eager to get to know the capital of the empire, delighting in the gadgets he had acquired on 46th Street—but, above all, a man who took pride in doing his job, in showing off the signs of his rank, the colors and icons of his avocado-green uniform. And so my friend turned around and around, basking in the bright lights, proudly packaged from top to toe in his uniform of a military police colonel, resplendent with golden braid and bronze medals and brass buttons. Since on a New York street anything is possible, his unlikely appearance was the object of no particular attention: perhaps someone was shooting a film set in some faraway republic. The camera hanging from his neck was just another military decoration. Fan-*tas*-tic, Professor.

Of course, after we were through with the official visits, the interviews, our observation of the activities of the New York Police Department, as required by our mission, which was to prepare a plan for democratizing Rio's military police, I invited my traveling companion to an evening in the Village. The colonel was willing to put off his well-deserved rest. I found it prudent to suggest, diplomatically, that he don civilian clothes for the occasion. After the Chick Corea concert at the Blue Note, which left us ecstatic, we found a good Italian restaurant still open. Now it was my turn to say: "Fan-*tas*-tic, Colonel."

Two Brazilians at a restaurant table inevitably wax sentimental, particularly in the wee hours, drinking margaritas, Chick Corea still echoing in their minds, away from home. We couldn't help getting emotional. We were both inwardly inclined to celebrate our unlikely comradeship, which only a few years before would have been unthinkable. One of us dared evoke the past: Where was the professor when the colonel was repressing the resistance, on orders from the military government? Where was the colonel when the professor was chauffeuring for a leader of the underground resistance? Where were the two of them when, in the seventies, on the narrow, steep streets of Santa Teresa, a hilltop neighborhood in Rio de Janeiro, a military police jeep was tailing the suspicious-looking car?

"Professor, I trembled and hesitated as I raised my machine gun and took aim, ready to shoot if the driver did anything unexpected. I ordered the soldier driving the jeep to step on it, so that we were side by side with the Volkswagen. I pointed my flashlight at the car and looked inside. I never felt so scared in my life."

"Why didn't you shoot, or order me to stop?"

"I don't know, Professor."

And we toasted our own fears.

Notes

I would like to thank a number of friends and colleagues for the raw material on which some of these stories are based, in particular João Trajano Sento Sé and Silvia Ramos.

10

The Return of the Repressed:
Conversations with Three Russian
Entrepreneurs

In his 1925 film *Strike!* the young Soviet director Sergei Eisenstein plotted the progress of the revolutionary proletariat against four bourgeois captains of industry. Obese, cigar-smoking, and impervious to the suffering of others, the four men personified the evils and excesses of Russia's late imperial merchant classes, whiling away their evenings over expensive trifles while their henchmen brutally quashed strikers' revolts. This telling of the decline and fall of Russian capitalism, similar to many other Soviet films of the 1920s, bid farewell to the epoch of the *shkurniki,* greedy profiteers interested only in themselves, and heralded the age of *udarniki,* shock-workers of the new classless society.

Much political history in the Soviet period, as in czarist Russia before it, hinged on the repression of the powers that had been: Lenin lamented the capitalist degradation into which Russia had fallen and exploited the exploiters, Khrushchev denounced Stalinism's excesses in his famous "secret speech," Brezhnev sent Khrushchev into early retirement, Gorbachev set out to revive communism, and Yeltsin shed his own communist past in order to renounce it. Hence, in the current post-Soviet age, many see poetic justice in the return of capitalist entrepreneurs after seventy-four years of socialist rule. However, a closer look would seem to dispel the romanticism of such a return. Here I present interviews with three Russian businessmen of varying backgrounds, taken during the summer of 1996, which call into question the kinds of labels so often used to explain Russia's postsocialist terrain, the country's transition to free market economics, the democracy taking hold, and the emergent "New Russian" populace. In the contemporary Russian economic landscape, capitalists and communists are two categories that are far from mutually exclusive.

Limited private enterprise never entirely disappeared during the Soviet period. Lenin's New Economic Policy (1922–28) temporarily loosened the initial claims of the state over the means of production, and Stalin soon after denounced the "leftist" practice of wage equalization that had been favored early on. In the agricultural sector, small plots of private land became one of the few ways for collective farmers to sustain their households during the economy's dimmest years. The system of perks and privileges that emerged under the Soviet socialist banner became legendary, as did the trading strategies of Soviet factory managers who routinely overordered supply goods in order to participate in expansive circles of barter and influence. Nonetheless, a generalized ambiguity about the culture of material gain, long prominent in Russian society, endured. As historian Jeffrey Brooks wrote of the Russian middle classes of the late nineteenth century, "Money [gained from business or commerce], although clearly sought after . . . was regarded with ambivalence and hostility by much of Russian society, both because it was not old . . . and because commerce and industry were associated with the exploitation of others" (quoted in Pesmen 1996, 4). The same sentiment, nurtured under Soviet tutelage for decades, is witnessed still in the marked distaste so many Russians have for open discussions of money and property.

In December 1993, when the new constitution of the Russian Federation asserted that "every person has the right to freely use his abilities and property to engage in entrepreneurial and other economic activities unrestricted by law," few might have gauged the extent or irony of the "unrestrictions." By 1996 the federal government had transferred over 100,000 commercial entities, large and small, to private ownership. The ultimate privatization of over 15,000 factories affected more than 60 percent of the industrial work force (Stanley 1996, A1). But the move toward privatization, or *privatizatsiia,* was quickly likened to "grabification," or *prikhvatizatsiia.* The most common scenario was for managers of state firms to install themselves as *de facto* owners, using their influence to run their new companies as small satrapies which often buckled from the weight of their inherited debt loads. The more spectacular robber baron successes have led men like former auto dealer cum auto potentate Boris Berezovskii to insist that he and six other men control over 50 percent of the Russian economy (*Forbes Magazine* 1996). The loosening of state controls all around has also heightened rates of violence, with almost anyone doing business in a major city the potential target of extortion. In 1995 over forty thousand murders took place in Russia (an additional seventy thousand people disappeared), making the country's per-capita murder rate three times higher than that of New York City.

At the forefront of Russia's postsocialist merchant classes are a group known, appropriately, as "New Russians" *[novye Russkie].* In Moscow perhaps more than any other city, they have come to personify the nouveaux riches lifestyle that has transformed the grey capital into a sea of fur coats, Mercedes, Rolexes, protection services, nightclubs, and casinos. Such sudden rises in fortune illustrate how high the stakes can be. In 1996 one British investment prospectus for a Russian satellite telephone company opened with an array of caveats so dizzying it was difficult to imagine how investors could have proceeded. On the one hand, the promise of investment was evident: Only a few years before, the company had been a wing of Soviet satellite military surveillance and it was able to enter the market with considerable inside influence over radio frequency regulators. But among the risks potential foreign partners faced were nationalization and expropriation of property, the instability of market legislation, the falling value of the ruble, limited repatriation of profits, the inexperience of the Russian courts in commercial and corporate law, the frequent legislative contradictions between different levels of government, the near impossibility of honoring erratic tax regulations, the absence of insurance on bank deposits and, finally, the high cost of bodyguards. Yet upon their opening on the foreign stock exchange, the company's stock tripled almost overnight.[1]

During the 1996 presidential elections Communist politicians got a good deal of press by reminding the electorate that the simultaneous rise of New Russians and the Mafia was not a coincidence. Here New Russians appeared as the hidden class of capitalist conspirators who had brought about *perestroika* and the eventual ruin of the country. Conspiracy discourse has long been a popular gambit in Russian politics, and between the folklore for all things Decembrist, Masonic, Bolshevik, and Stalinist, it would seem at times that Russia invented the genre. When consulted for an example of the use of *conspiracy,* even the Oxford English Dictionary offers up, "He had a Russian face, strong and conspiratorial," as if Russia and conspiracy were apposites. But conspiracy also simply can mean "breathing together," or "concerted efforts toward common ends." With the stunning, if forced pace of market reforms and the simultaneous rise in organized crime, it is this second moment that returns us to the predatory aspects inherent to capitalism, the conspiracy at the heart of Russia's sober, law-abiding return to the fold of civilization so often heralded in the world's popular press. The attention to Mafia affairs becomes all the more relevant when one reasons, as Katherine Verdery has from her work in postsocialist Romania, that "Mafia is a symbol for what happens when the visible hand of the state is being replaced by the invisible hand of the market. The image suggests that there is still a hand, but it has disappeared into the shadows" (1996, 219). Indeed, the mafia has all too appropriately become a key symbol in postsocialist Russia where few other links between signifiers and signifieds—between socialism and the social honor it was meant to uphold, between market relations and the rapacious path of the government, between New World Orders and organized crime—have been managing to hold up. In the frighteningly blank space of explanations, the Mafia have emerged as one of the few persuasive emblems of a political economy no one entirely sees.

Capitalist conspirators from Sergei Eisenstein's 1925 film *Strike!* (Stachka!). Courtesy of the Museum of Modern Art Film Stills Archive.

With the realm of the public so routinely conflated with the private, and with words like *capitalism* (and *socialism*) so seemingly emptied of commonly held meaning, Russian entrepreneurs, embraced by the state for the second time in this century, are left to do business in an environment where all manner of persuasion, benign, bellicose, and baroque, is king. This lends an added import to the Russian word for conspiracy, *zagovor,* meaning both "magical words toward a desired end," and more plainly, "the start of talk."

Rafael Pavlovich Khakopian

A Russian citizen of Armenian descent in his early seventies, Khakopian rose to prominence in the aluminum industry before undertaking professionally what many state managers did privately throughout the Soviet period, the re-distribution of state-owned commodities. He was in the unusual position of representing Soviet trade interests abroad, and now pursues several large-scale resource development projects. We met for the first time at his home outside of Moscow through a friend who tutors his children in music.*

KHAKOPIAN: So what, start with a biography?

GRANT: Right.

KHAKOPIAN: I was born to a relatively well-off family. My father fought as an officer in the White Army before the Revolution, became a prisoner of war in World War I, and then left for Europe for a short time before returning. My mother, in her later years, worked as the first secretary of our local Party Executive Committee in Uzbekistan. You know what this means—she was part of a very elite caste for her time. Growing up I had everything. I finished school with a medal. I entered the law faculty so that, upon finishing, I could enter the Moscow Institute of Foreign Relations. But life took its own course. In 1949 I was named in a lawsuit for anti-Soviet agitation and a host of other small fabrications of a political nature. For this they gave me twenty-five years, and for this I came to know the entire archipelago of Stalinist camps. Although in 1947, before this, I had been given the high honor of attending a banquet in Stalin's personal chambers in the Kremlin. This was in Moscow, in 1947. I had won an all-Union prize for mastery in boxing and attended a sporting banquet given by Stalin. In 1949 they turned on me.

Nonetheless, I understand that this wasn't so much against me as against my father and mother. It was all such political intrigue.

GRANT: Were your parents still living then?

KHAKOPIAN: They were, though shortly after my arrest, my father became bedridden and soon died. My mother lived until 1978, though she had long before been cast from Party offices given my status as a political criminal. This is how it works.

GRANT: How dreadful.

KHAKOPIAN: Yes, it was dreadful. I went through dozens of Stalinist camps. They arrested me in Tashkent, where I was living at the time, and initially sent me to Kazakhstan. From Kazakhstan they sent me to Siberia. There is a city there called Angarsk. Not far from Irkutsk. Earlier it had been named after the river Kitoi, so Kitoi-Lag it was called. From Kitoi-Lag they sent us to Bukhta Vanina. From Vanina they sent me to Kolyma. From Kolyma to Chukotka.

GRANT: What would the point be in moving people so often?

*All names are pseudonyms. What follows are three interviews of the eight I conducted for this project in June and July of 1996 in Moscow and St. Petersburg. Of the three printed here, roughly half the conversations have been used since I excluded the more particular talk about presidential elections going on at the time. The internal sequencing of the conversations themselves has been retained. All conversations were conducted in Russian, except for the interview with Aleksandr Malyshev, who is fluent in English. All translations from the Russian are my own.

KHAKOPIAN: People were being moved about all the time. All the time, so that people couldn't form into special groupings or get too accustomed to one area and become too knowledgeable about their surroundings. It was very important for camp psychology that no one know each other very well. This was all done very brilliantly. During the Khrushchevian thaw, there was a Central Committee commission that traveled directly from place to place, examining people's documents and reviewing their cases. They freed some, left others, and sent new prisoners still off to more camps, but in general, they cleaned the camps out. And so, finally, in 1960, by request of the solicitor general of the USSR, the Central Committee reviewed my case and pronounced me innocent of all charges and I was rehabilitated. But of course, I'm just giving you the most general outline. I don't see why I should go into the horrors and the details of camp life. It should be clear in and of itself.

GRANT: Twelve years?

KHAKOPIAN: Almost. Well, what do you do? You have to start your life again from scratch. I had no one left in my family except my mother, and so I headed back to mother's home. This was back in Tashkent. I was offered a permit to live in Moscow, but I declined and asked to stay in Tashkent. I finished one more institute, to get a formal education in engineering and construction. I was in my thirties, but my health had suffered greatly. I had had one heart attack while in the camps, and then a second, but I was eager to begin another career. Through this I again became involved in the work of the Party.

In 1964 I was asked to move to a new enterprise in Dushanbe, the former city of Stalinopad. Why? The republic of Tajikistan is relatively small, and was largely agrarian at that time. But at the same time Tajikistan is rich in certain resources, especially hydroelectric resources. Work began on the construction of an enormous natural gas project, Norekskii-Gaz, an enormous well of energy. And in connection with that the government decided to create one of the largest aluminum factories in the country. So I was sent there to work in connection with the factory. The factory was built in conjunction with a French firm, Aluminum S.A. This was the 1960s and the French Socialists somehow made headway with this. As a result, we built one of the most modern aluminum plants in the country in Tajikistan. This is where I worked for many years, well, until 1984, when I had my third heart attack. By that time I was already part of the *nomenklatura* of the Soviet industrial ministry. And in 1983 they had offered me a new position in Moscow, with a quite high position as the senior assistant to the minister, a certain Lomakh, Petr Fadeevich, a very smart man. We were in charge of absolutely everything, do you realize? There was gold, and aluminum and silver—basically, all of the precious metals. I had this offer from Moscow, but by the time I had my third heart attack, I realized that I had to take on a less demanding pace of work and I declined. I decided to retire where I was already living, in Dushanbe.

GRANT: What came next?

KHAKOPIAN: In a word, *perestroika* began. Cooperatives became in fashion again. I had a lot of enterprising friends, colleagues, and comrades who had a good amount of experience in the existing hierarchies. And so, with a number of these friends, I founded a firm called Kontakt. I became its president, and by association, its principal executive. All of my colleagues were formally listed as contract workers. That is, no one else bore legal responsibility for the firm, no one else purchased stock or that kind of thing.

At the time, Gosplan [the state planning ministry] controlled—as it does to a certain extent still today—how much various firms could be allocated and could produce. It was a rigid system of limits on various sides. As a result, every manager looked for any way to organize reserves, to have a set of reserves beyond his limits. However they did it, legally or illegally, spending weeks in Moscow restaurants plying clients with cognac and expensive food, most people got what they wanted. What happened of course, was a situation where thousands and thousands of enterprises had accumulated a great deal of goods they eventually had no idea what to do with. That is, goods, equipment, machinery that were all excess, just piled up in a warehouse waiting to be traded over another bottle of cognac.

GRANT: Very smart.

KHAKOPIAN: Yes, but what to do with all these things? Because during *perestroika* everything had to be counted. The government started demanding inventories. What kind of situation were you left with? You have one fellow who suddenly is supposed to be paying taxes on his warehouses, on his inventories, and has no idea what to do with these enormous loads of goods. And then you have another guy who is searching the country high and low for these very products. So you start to get the picture. I became involved in the redistribution of state property.

We made our own kinds of advertisements, but mainly we worked through friends. I went to all my old colleagues and comrades and acquaintances and I said, "Tell us what you need, and tell us what you want to get rid of." That's how it worked. And once we started to get this database together, it couldn't have been more simple. Well, look, he needs this, and he has this. Let's move it, and let's get our commission. It couldn't have been easier.

The firm started to grow, and it grew quickly. I opened some extra branches outside of Moscow. One in Kaluga, another in Rostov-on-the-Don, another in Sochi. Eventually Gorbachev announced the formal end to the Afghan war. Soviet troops and all their equipment had to be evacuated from the country. When I heard this news I got very excited and I knew that I had to act quickly.

I flew to Alma-Aty, which had been the main shipping point for goods to the Afghan front, and there I got permission from both the Alma-Aty and central Moscow governments to ensure that all equipment returning to the country via Alma-Aty would be realized only through our firm, Kontakt.

GRANT: Good idea.

KHAKOPIAN: It wasn't just a good idea, it was a monopoly. We made a killing. It was a very big deal. Literally, day after day, we did nothing but receive convoys of equipment and send it off in all directions around the Soviet Union. Some of it we bought ourselves and then sold later on. Some of it we bought and remantled. It was a very big leap and very big money. By 1990 the accounts for Kontakt held over 450 million rubles.

GRANT: That was an enormous amount of money.[2]

KHAKOPIAN: It was a ridiculous amount of money. It was literally half the budget of the entire republic of Tajikistan! Their annual budget was 800 million rubles at the time. And the thing is, once we reached that level, we were playing in a completely different power structure. The same year, we set up an agreement with an Italian partner involving a $300 million contract. But the nature of the contract, very unique for the Soviet Union at that time, because it was declared a federal contract, was such that the republic of Tajikistan didn't receive a single lira.

The Italians were very interested in aluminum. Indeed, all of Europe was interested in aluminum. Processing aluminum, as I already mentioned, was very harmful. So I made them a proposal: we would produce aluminum foil from our factory—and incidentally, Tajik aluminum is some of the purest in the world—and alongside that, we would produce specially lined boxes for long-term storage, like the tetra bricks you use for juices or long-life milk. Meanwhile, in Dushanbe, we had an enormous factory that produced refrigerators. It worked with very old technology and hadn't been doing very well. So in return, our plan was that the Italians would completely renovate the factory using the most modern new methods, producing new refrigerators as well as refrigerated shipping containers. On top of that, the Italians were able to provide us with entire new conveyor systems for fruit and vegetable processing for dozens of plants. This was and still is a particular problem in Tajikistan, as all around the USSR, where you have enormously rich produce and up to 30 percent goes to waste for want of adequate processing facilities. The Italians were ready to guarantee us full processing for all we harvested. So in return for the aluminum we set up the refrigeration plant, and the tetra bricks, and the food-processing units. In and of itself this kind of deal wasn't unique, but we added in an extra clause. From the new fruit and vegetable processing lines, the Italians agreed by contract to purchase 30 percent of our projected output, that is, 30 percent of all the packaged fruits and vegetables we projected for a three-year period, paying in hard currency. This was, indeed, hundreds of millions of dollars. Staggering! We worked out our schedule, the Italians sent their engineers to lay the ground. And then, the war in Tajikistan began.

Naturally, I wasn't without influence in Tajikistan. I had opened up an entire line of plants myself and directed an enormous amount of funds in and out of the republic. I was a middleman as well as an industrialist. What can I say? I had everything. I had transport, I had my own airplane. I spent most of my time between the car and the plane. It was commonplace for my wife to wake me at three in the morning to say, "Tel Aviv is on the line." It was not an average Soviet life. We had an apartment in Moscow, an apartment in Dushanbe. But when the war started, I realized, I had to get out quietly. Money was not that difficult. Most of my money I was able to redeposit in a Moscow bank. There was other money that I redirected to Belgorod, just over the border from Ukraine, where we also had a branch. And I started a new firm, Rafik, in order to move things around. But one day I knew it wasn't going to work. I had sent a convoy of trucks, eight trucks, and they got stopped at the border. The drivers called me from Moscow and said, "They're not letting us by." And I said, What can you mean? Remember, this was still all the same country, one Soviet Union. How can you not let something by? But I knew what was happening, and I said, "What do they want?" They said, "They want one of the eight trucks." And I said, "Okay, let them have it." I knew that it was over, and it would go on like this until they stopped asking permission. Next I sent off thirty train cars. Next I sent off five more cars filled with refrigerators, and what's more, with enormous security provisions. But this was only a fraction of what could be done. In 1992 I went back into Dushanbe to relocate my family. The day we left we had machine guns in our laps as we drove through the center of town to the airport.

So what is this to say? You have to start over. We had lost over half of our assets in one fell swoop, more. The hydroelectric equipment was there. The air conditioning plant was there. The food-processing plants were there. My apartment! It is not an apartment but a museum. In every room there was a different museum-quality parquet, just like in the Hermitage. Carpets! I did it all for the children. I know who is living there now—friends of mine—but it's all fallen apart. It's effectively still a war. I have constant connections. I know what's going on, but it was the end there for me.

So that was the twenty-fourth of October [1992]. In four days we were back in Moscow. My wife is German, and I am Armenian. A purebred, as they say. By the same token my wife is, according to state criteria, a pure German. She has a number of relatives there and they were all calling her. That very day, on the twenty-eighth, her last relatives were leaving to go live there. Her grandmother, uncle. And while we were in our apartment, we get a call. "Rafael Pavlovich, are you home?" someone asks. I said, "I'm home." And they said,

"Okay, we'll be right over." I have no idea who these people are. Who? What? Where?

I am sitting in one of the back rooms of the apartment with an employee of mine from the Sochi office. We're sitting over a bottle of cognac and talking. And there's a knock at the door. My wife goes to answer, and Boom! OMON [the Russian alpha security force]. There are eight agents, two in fatigues with machine guns. Everyone is armed. And they march in quickly to seal the apartment. Someone produces a warrant. The Moscow attorney general had signed an order for a search. You can imagine what my wife had to watch. They turned the entire house upside down. Everything. Finally, they looked at me and said, "You'll have to come with us." And I said, "Well, if I have to, I have to." And my wife said, "And you're going to bring him back." They looked at her in this funny way and shrugged their shoulders. "Sure, probably. We're just taking him in for questioning." You can imagine this after ransacking our entire apartment, with our relatives and guests watching in horror.

We got into the car and that was that. The fellow turned to me and said, "Okay, we're going to Belgorod."

GRANT: Isn't that a long way?

KHAKOPIAN: Seven hundred kilometers. At night. We drove at night and arrive in Belgorod and they put me into prison. What are the charges? Well, they say, 214 million rubles have arrived via the bank. What are they for? I explained that I had been moving my capital from Dushanbe because of the tensions, that it had all gone through a government commission in Moscow which had approved the transfers and taken the tax. It wasn't as if I did it in the dark of night. I had trainloads of equipment arrive. I had over a dozen employees relocated there. We purchased apartments for them. We were organizing new production. They said, "What about the arms?" And I said, "What arms?" And they said, "The bodyguards that came with the trains?" And I said, "Well, that's obvious. It's an official protection service." But they said, "Exactly. You got permission for those weapons there, in Dushanbe. And you transported them over the Russian border." Well, what were the border guards doing, among other things? In short, they made me out to be a heavy mafiosi. And they held me for seven months.

GRANT: In prison?

KHAKOPIAN: Yes. But I was literally being held. Nothing more. There was no violence. No brutality. Occasionally they would call me in the middle of the night for "conversations," but even then they served me coffee. It was very unusual. And every time I said to them, "Look, you know better than anyone that you have no shred of proof and you won't find any. I am not a criminal and you won't turn me into one. So what do you want?" They said, "Rafael Pavlovich, have you ever seen in the West that someone takes out a big mafia kingpin for big crimes? They're always held up on minor charges and kept in prison while their organization falls apart without them." And that was it. In seven months, they let me go, as if it was the most natural thing in the world. Poof. That was it.

GRANT: It sounds like old Soviet times.

KHAKOPIAN: Yes, but it wasn't. This was May 1993. The sad irony, of course, is that, though I wasn't a mafiosi, half of my organization did fall apart while I was gone. Some people thought I would simply never get out of prison. Others thought I would even die there, and they started to carry things off.

So again, I had to start over. One way or another, we put our lives back together. While I was away, my wife gave up our Moscow apartment on Prospekt Mira and moved here to the suburbs. It was only a year later, the summer of 1994, that they tried again. We were at the apartment in Belgorod, planning to leave to go on to Sochi. It was around six o'clock at night, and we were preparing to leave the next day. There's a ring at the door. My wife answers the door, and again two men in fatigues. With weapons. And they say, "You'll have to come with us." My wife doesn't even say anything this time, nor do I. It is all beyond belief. We get in the car and arrive at the station and they look at my passport. They announce, "You're under arrest." And I say, "Are you out of your mind? Do you have any idea what you're doing? Do you even have a charge?" He pulls out a piece of letterhead from the solicitor general of Tajikistan which says, "Arrest and extradite." When my wife found out she practically fainted.

The next day they took me from the station to the prison, but at the prison they wouldn't admit me. They needed something from the Russian solicitor general, and of course they didn't have anything. The next day they tried again and got the same response. And so on. In the meantime they were keeping me in a cell in the basement of the local militia office. A vile place.

On the one hand, it was fine because I knew I had done nothing wrong, but by the time they had kept me for three months, I began to get worried. In the first place, staying in the cellars of a militia office was not pleasant. It was extremely damp and cold, there was no bedding—they were clearly trying to make it difficult for me. After the first two months I began to get sick and doctors arrived to have me transferred to a military hospital, but the militia wouldn't give me up. Finally, it was the doctors who got the most exercised at the criminality of it all and they were the ones to call in the state's attorney himself. He came to me and said, "Rafael Pavlovich, the state of Russia has no charges against you, but we have this letter from Tajikistan." I said, "Do you have any idea what Tajikistan is right now? If you hand me over, I won't even make it between the plane and the airport when I arrive because they will shoot me the moment I touch the ground." He said, "We don't want to give

you up, but we don't know what to do." I said, "Well, at least send me to
prison, because in prison at least they have normal conditions. They feed you,
they let you bathe, they give you sheets." And this is what happened. I went
on to spend another month in the Belgorod prison.

It was another month until one day, a special affairs agent from the Tajik
government came into my cell. He was wearing this special uniform and I had
to keep myself from smiling because it was the same man who used to be one
of my deputy directors, Vadim Vladimirovich Chekhov. He came in and said,
"Raf Pavlovich, it's time to pay up." He held out a piece of paper which said
that the Tajik government had no claims against me, but said he couldn't sign
it until he left with money. I said that I had nothing to give him but that if he
wanted to contact my wife in Moscow, that was his prerogative. That was the
entire conversation. He smiled at me and said, "All right. I'll go to Moscow."
And that was that.

They asked for neither a lot nor a little. Fifty thousand U.S. dollars. My
wife called in dozens of debts and liquidated some of our holdings quickly. In
the presence of some of the security people who still work for the company,
she handed over the money and got a signature. Two days later, I was released. You have to realize the condition I was in when I got out. I looked
terrible, and was taken directly to the hospital. I stayed there another month,
began to get my strength back, and look around me. It was a strange feeling
because, you know, I wanted to toss it all. I wanted to give it up and just turn
my back on the whole thing. But it's strange, you know, because you have
to work.

GRANT: You're an existentialist.

KHAKOPIAN: But you also have to realize what kind of time it is for Russia
today. Let me give you an example. I remember a conversation I had with my
wife, in 1988 or 1989. We had a balance in our bank book of fifty thousand
rubles. And my wife said, "Let's stop. This is enough. We could retire on this
now." I wasn't sure, and I said, "Wait until we get to one hundred thousand."
Think of that! Can you imagine what one hundred thousand rubles is today?
Barely twenty dollars. And we wanted to retire. For me to feed my family
and live normally today, I need something in the order of 5 million rubles a
month. A thousand dollars. That is for a plain existence. And I still need to
raise my children. The twins are only nine. I married very late, my wife is
much younger than me. I could go abroad, my health would permit that. But
what would I do? I can't get my pension there. Which means I have to stay,
and I have to start something new once more.

Democracy is a word people use to describe Russia all the time these days,
but it's not a democracy. Today we are closer to anarchy. It's true that you can
say anything you want and you can protest anywhere you want, but you can
also kill anyone you want, which incidentally is taking place, left, right, and
center. In business—I will speak openly—every single person, and I mean

every single person who has achieved a thing in Russia today, has done so through some criminal activity. I could give you such a list—banking criminals, trade criminals. Everyone is lying to everyone. The government lies to everyone that has money, and even those that don't. Everyone else lies to everyone else. It is complete corruption from top to bottom. When you go to the city offices downtown, the first words out of every single low-ranking bureaucrat you speak to are, "What will I get out of it?" If he gets paid, then fine, if not, then that's that. I'm not even talking about the outrageous system of taxes. Outrageous.

What are we left with? No one is investing anything and no one is producing anything. So instead we have a massive exchange of debts and services. Every single enterprise is in debt to a dozen other enterprises and no one has a single dime in their accounts. For example, I recently negotiated for and received the rights to harvest an unusually high quantity of natural gas. This was for sale since it went above someone else's limits, and it's easy to see since Russian natural gas is so inexpensive. The sites are not far from Nizhnii Novgorod. I found a major company there to harvest the gas, the automobile company Gaz. But rather than pay me, they offered instead to pay me in Volgas, in automobiles. All of Nizhnii Novgorod needs this gas desperately. Industries are suffocating without fuel. And yet we are still working within this ancient primitive social formation of one good for another, a moneyless economy, barter. I am overseeing one of the largest business transactions in Nizhnii Novgorod there is, and yet I may never see a single ruble from it. There's no promise that I won't be lost in an endless cycle of one good promised for another. What do I need thousands of automobiles for? And yet somehow we are working.

Think about where this leaves me, however. On the one hand, it's not so bad because I have a very wide network. I have a friend who works with the governor's office in Nizhnii Novgorod who has been looking out for me, and he can probably help me find a buyer for the cars. We might end up selling them for the lowest price going, but we'll sell them. Yet imagine—I've never bought or traded automobiles before in my life. I know a lot about natural gas, but somehow now my fate hinges on how well I can represent the auto industry to another buyer. It puts anyone in a very tenuous position. That's only the beginning.

Of course in this kind of situation it's difficult to work. But if you want to live, and not live badly, you have to be sharp. You have to analyze, you have to think, and you have to try to figure out what will come around the bend tomorrow. What disturbs me the most is not the whole system itself. The system itself hasn't changed. It was the same system we had before and I fear it's the same system we'll still have tomorrow. It's really not a question of politicians or parties. It's a battle over power, and power can be a terrible thing. You realize—crime exists everywhere. But what kind of crime? Can you compare it to the all-consuming crime we have here? The level of crime in our country today means horror—complete horror. Add to that the psychology of a country that permitted Stalinism in the first place.

And yet having seen all of this, I still can't describe to you what it's like to live today. To imagine that Russia could have arrived at the situation it's in today, to see the economy on the verge of collapse—indeed, to see it collapse—this is something I could have never imagined. And to even think of what would be required to remedy this. Look, in the past there have been mistakes, lots of them. And even me, with all of my contacts in politics—I was in the middle of a business deal three years ago and pledged to someone, "I'll lay my head down on train tracks if the government should raise prices again. They won't!" And this fellow just looked at me and said, "That train's already left."

Valerii Shchipok

Shchipok, 47, was a graduate student in Sanskrit philology in the 1970s when he was arrested for theft of state property. Though he admitted to the crime, he refused to name his coconspirators and served ten years in prison. We knew each other through a close friend in common, a woman with whom he had begun in graduate school. We met at her home in St. Petersburg.

GRANT: Let me start by asking what you're doing now.

SHCHIPOK: Formally, I'm the director of a firm. So far we haven't had any actual business, so it doesn't really exist. We have some thoughts of working with some people in Finland, but that's up in the air. That would be good. A kind of joint venture. Before that I was selling lottery tickets on the street, but it was too much hassle. I gave it up. In the first place, there was too much competition, but I also got tired of having to deal with the police all the time. With Mafia it wasn't so much of a problem because no one really takes lottery tickets seriously. The small Mafia concentrate on the street vendors selling vegetables and coffee and stuff, but for some reason they kind of leave the lottery people alone. But the problem is—then the police decide to go for you because the Mafia haven't. And the police would hassle us all the time for our profits. I know how bad it was getting since I had started selling tickets years ago, right on Nevskii Prospekt. I thought it would be better there since it was more crowded but they hassled us just as much as before, so I gave it up.

It's a shame, since lottery tickets used to be such a good racket. That's why I got into it. Just three or four years ago, for example, I could go to Moscow and take out a million rubles' worth of lottery tickets. Because I was a state employee, I was entitled to large loans, and they would loan people just enormous sums. So I could take out a million rubles. The point was that hard cash was a huge problem around Leningrad in 1992, as it was almost everywhere.

Stockbrokers clambering at the steps of the Petersburg Stock Exchange, 1917. From Vsevolod Pudovkin's *The End of St. Petersburg* (Konets Sankta-Peterburga, 1927). Courtesy of the Museum of Modern Art Film Stills Archive.

Almost anywhere in the country you could get two rubles credit on paper for every real ruble you had in your hand. So all I had to do was get a million in cash in Moscow, take it to Leningrad, take half of it and send it back to the bank as one million, and pocket the other half. Get it?

GRANT: Wow.

SHCHIPOK: It's all in the double accounting. In Russia it's one of our specialties. Cash-flow problems had crippled the country and the left hand never knew what the right hand was doing. I took the money back to Petersburg and handed half a million rubles in cash over to a company I had registered. Then, in turn, acting for the company, I deposited it as one million rubles in the bank since the government had decreed banks could give double credit for actual cash. It was completely criminal and it was very easy. I was left with half a million rubles in my pocket. It's just one moment out of many.

GRANT: I know that it's called "criminal"—

SHCHIPOK: It's criminal but it has also become the very ground on which the whole society works. It leaves the whole government in a double bind. On one hand, the government knows that it has to combat crime. But surviving today means breaking the law, plain and simple, and government officials know this better than anyone. For a clerk or a policeman to make enough money to feed their family—and I'm not even talking about people getting rich and taking it all to Spain—they need to be taking part in the very crime they are meant to resist. In the end, it's very profitable for everyone involved.

GRANT: You hear all the time about taxes.

SHCHIPOK: Let me tell you, if I tried to pay my taxes honorably, I physically could not have a cent left. They are literally above the level of gross earnings.

GRANT: What kinds of taxes did you pay?

SHCHIPOK: Personally I've never paid any. I've never even gotten into that. Honestly, I planned on paying taxes when I started, but after consulting with accountants, I understood that it wasn't feasible.

GRANT: Russian accountants today have to be either walking computers or sorcerers, or both.

SHCHIPOK: Fraud artists would be closer to it.

GRANT: We hear about these things all the time, but how does it actually work? You said that policemen gave you a hard time, but did they just walk up and ask for money?

SHCHIPOK: Sure. Lottery salesmen are easy targets since they are normally part of small operations and policemen guess that they won't be taunting too large a group if they cart off one or two guys. When I was selling, I had a group of four or five guys working under me, and they were always getting put in prison for no reason. We had registration papers and everything, but the police would just shrug their shoulders and hold them there until I gave them money. After a while, I learned to buy them off in advance, because paying by the incident just became too expensive.

GRANT: Was it called a penalty, or was it openly just called a bribe?

SHCHIPOK: Once or twice they claimed we had not properly filed our papers, which wasn't true. But after a while there was no point in pretending. It happened too often for them to even register the arrest.

GRANT: I'm curious about what this meant financially. Was it a big sum for you to pay?

SHCHIPOK: It was a lot of money. Eventually, as I said, it became too much money to even stay in business. I was working, and I was losing money on top of that, so what was the point? But initially, it was better to pay the policeman than have them invent a crime you would have to somehow pay for. It was always easier to pay the policemen.

The only thing that helped from time to time is that lotteries all used to be controlled by the state, and sometimes that made the policemen standoffish. They didn't want to get involved in taunting other state workers. But the irony was that lotteries have all been privately owned for the last five years. You can even buy the rights to call your lottery a state lottery, since that makes people think they are somehow investing in state welfare even if they lose. Most call themselves charitable lotteries, but in reality the money just becomes a feeding trough for the people that run it. As ticket sellers, we were at the very bottom of the totem pole. We got to keep 10 or 15 percent of the money, and the rest we were supposed to pass up the hierarchy.

Besides, once you get into this kind of crime—and almost everyone in business is— it's very hard to get out of it. Everyone has something on someone else. Everyone knows too much about everyone else. These days I don't even come to the phone anymore. Half the time it's someone trying to get money out of you—bandits or militia calling you into their offices under false pretenses.

GRANT: Like something out of the Wild West?

SHCHIPOK: People say that all the time, as if that's supposed to make it better. "The West did it, so now we can do it too." The problem is, it makes it look like there's some kind of real logic to how all this works, because sometimes people do things that are purely Soviet. Once, one of the tax inspectors who knew me came up to me on the street and said, "I sent you tax forms to fill out so don't go pick up your mail. If you don't pick up your mail we can't prosecute you for having failed to pay." The strangest part was, this guy was probably the only person I *hadn't* paid off. What do you say when even the informers start to inform on themselves!

GRANT: Do you think there are any people who have gotten rich honorably?

SHCHIPOK: I don't know. Maybe people like artists, who make careers out of their talents. But in principle, the famous performers already lived pretty well, even under Stalinism. Although, of course they received a lot less. For those people who actually pay the taxes, I mean. I don't know, I couldn't say. I'm not sure I've ever met anyone who paid all the taxes.

GRANT: I ask because I'd like to move away from stereotypes and yet, when you do meet very rich Russians, most of the reaction is, "Slippery."

SHCHIPOK: Naturally. But that's also our mentality. The reaction of any simple Russian when they see a successful person is, "What a swine." It's the typical response of someone from below looking up. But I would also have to say it has been validated, since the kinds of people that have gotten ahead in the last few years have been the least honorable, by my experience. I think that any form of business, in principle, requires a craftiness. How one walks the line between craftiness and fraud—between, for example, commercial common sense and crime—is always up in the air for us. Where is that line?

GRANT: So do you think the idea of wealth is changing?

SHCHIPOK: Yes, and I think there's a clear logic to the kind of robber baron phase we're in. It's not any different from the age of Henry Ford or J. P. Morgan. The period of capital accumulation, the initial phases of capitalism, are always dominated by semicriminal elements. But even now you start to see a certain change. It's almost as if some people have accumulated so much they start to suffer from a stress of excess. They don't know what to do with all this money and they finally just want to invest it somewhere, just to get rid of it.

On the other hand, with all the competition at the lower levels, the trading networks have gotten stricter. Much stricter. The low-level profiteers now, the ones who work in larger protected networks, they have become like voiceless drones. But I'm talking about real bandits. Most of them have been in prison once or twice. He's a typical *baryga* and he gives himself over to the business. He won't serve in the army, he won't be allowed to marry, he will only see certain friends. Some of these groups are really severe. It's like a sacrifice, a sacrifice to the bandit ring.

GRANT: And *baryga* means?

SHCHIPOK: *Baryga,* from *barysh, baryshnik. Barysh* is income, profit. *Baryga* is a person who—it's like a *fartsovshchik,* a speculator, but that's all the old terminology. Today we'd call him a *kooperator* or an entrepreneur. But it's one of the lowest rungs on the totem pole, even though he's the person that handles most of the money.

GRANT: What about the idea of *blat,* having pull? It was such a key term in Soviet stories of reciprocity and influence.

SHCHIPOK: *Blat* is kind of on its way out. Market relations have started to supplant it. But you have to remember that communism was largely a feudal system. Now the obligations are more strictly economic than symbolic. There was also a lot less money in circulation before and it didn't play such a crucial role because it was much harder to get your hands on. It was funny a while back, because you would never hear people talking about *blat* so much as *sviazi,* connections. Someone would say, "Everything's okay, I have a connection," and you would laugh, because it sounded so Soviet. It's kind of on its way out, but to a large extent we still live in a Soviet system, so you can't observe its demise yet.

GRANT: When you look at the very wealthy around you, is it obvious that many of them are former Communist Party figures, or is that just a stereotype?

SHCHIPOK: Absolutely. Of course! They were the leaders of the society at the time of the transition. They were a state mafia before and there is little difference now. One of the most outstanding things that sets them all apart is the famous inability to listen to anyone else's opinions. It's purely Bolshevik thinking, almost a genetic inability to listen to someone else. That's why it's so interesting to think about New Russians because you find almost the same leveling process [*uravnilovka*] you saw under communism. Before, if you didn't smoke or you didn't drink, then you stood out too much. Either you had to be a stoolpigeon, an informer, I don't know what. For Russia, this is especially widespread. And you notice it the second you leave the country. If you go to the Baltics and look at someone building a house, no one pays any attention. If you build a house in Russia, every single one of your neighbors will just stand at their window, gawking!

GRANT: What else can you say about New Russians?

SHCHIPOK: Oh, who even wants to talk about it? It's such nonsense. It's the story of any simpleton who gets rich overnight, who flags down cabs, slams the door, barks at the cabdriver and then says, "I'll pay for it all." Extravagance, distinctiveness in all things, but not distinction. Basically, it's barbarism. But on the other hand, maybe it's necessary for us to overcome the decades of dull greyness. It's like [Valerii] Briusov, our famous nineteenth-century symbolist. Once he went off to Tallinn and wrote letters to a friend in Petersburg making light of all the delicate fineries of the Baltic lifestyle. Going for little walks, admiring the lawns, having breakfast brought to you! An average Russian just shakes their head at all of this. It's just beyond us. It is very funny.

GRANT: The kind of leveling you were talking about reminds me of how odd it was when I was first learning Russian to get used to the prevalence of expressions like *nash* and *vash* [ours and yours], signifying huge groups of people you putatively were included or excluded by.

SHCHIPOK: The only time I really felt that kind of leveling powerfully was when I was in prison. From the very first day, you're obligated by other prisoners to act exactly the same as them. Drink tea with them, although I never drank tea before. To smoke with them. The majority are real polytechnical dropouts, working-class masses. Whenever anyone different fell in among them, it could be very cruel. I remember one older man who had been director of a state enterprise. People mocked him savagely. And there's no way to get away from it. You're obligated to spend all your time together. That's when the leveling was the most intense.

I think, in fact, that the greatest tension in prison didn't come from the guards or the amount of time you had to spend there, but the constant psychological friction with the other inmates trying to draw you into whatever it was they were doing. Even when you got moved around from city to city. I was transferred once from Leningrad to Sverdlovsk and then from Sverdlovsk to Krasnoiarsk. And even when you would have all these guys in a holding tank in a new city, up to fifty, and none of them have ever met, that's when this grouping mechanism was the most obvious. The second we were all put in one of those tanks, people would start forming into small circles, usually for drinking tea. Usually there weren't enough cups and so you'd have four or five persons sharing the same cup of tea. But the ritual was always the same— once you got to the fifth person, and they drank up, the first question was, "Who else do we draw in?" That was the most difficult part for me since I obviously didn't fit in. I wasn't exactly from the intelligentsia, since I never finished my degree. But everyone knew I was different.

GRANT: So how did you deal with it?

SHCHIPOK: Well, I'm a very cautious person. It's hard to draw me into things. And I used to box before I got into prison, so I fought when I needed to. No one in prison ever liked to fight one on one. It was more common for whole groups to attack someone while they were sleeping. It's the lowest kind of psychology, and this criminal mentality finds its way through the whole society. For starters, you have to remember the number of people who went through the gulag system. A very significant portion of the society either went through it or had relatives who came back and influenced them.

GRANT: It's interesting—would you say that the time you spent in prison helped you when you started in business, the kinds of things you learned?

SHCHIPOK: It's hard to say, because on a very plain level, prison life put me behind in so many aspects of social life. There are hundreds of things still today that I just don't understand because I wasn't reading the newspapers, I wasn't watching television. But in other ways, sure. It's very easy for me to defend myself against competitors, to show them who's boss, because I have more practice at standoffs than they do.

What struck me the most in prison, though, was how much people could reinvent themselves. You have to in order to protect yourself. You become someone new, someone tougher when you get in. Then you pass yourself off as someone new, more respectable, when you get out. I think about this all the time for business now, because everyone I know is changing their skins like clockwork. One day they're in a suit and smiling at you. Then, the next moment, they're roughing someone up.

Once when I was in prison, I knew one fellow named Kalinin. Initially he was hired on as a carpenter at the camp, and eventually he trained to become a guard. That is, he became an officer. Then he became the director of the camp, then the director of all the camps in the zone, and so on. Over the course of ten years he became a colonel and a very highly placed figure in the entire camp system. He was both severe and cruel. That is, he beat people himself. He punished transgressors himself, and did it with some pleasure. Then when *perestroika* came, I used to see him on television. He was advertised as a leading light of democracy and *perestroika* and all the rest. And so I decided to write a letter. I wrote the prison commission and they actually came and interviewed me. They pulled me out of the camp one day and came to interview me. And they kept stressing, "Did he personally beat people?" And I answered, "Yes, I know a list of people who he absolutely beat, who

---

"No Worse than Others"
by Iurii Alekseev
from the newspaper *Evening Moscow* [Vecherniaia Moskva], 12 November 1977

I saw my friend Paramon Petrovich the other day on the street, looking gloomy, and carrying an object whose purpose was unknown to him. I asked him what he had bought.

"What do I know? A pickle dish, maybe?" He shook his head, "I waited in line three hours for it, like a dog, but managed to make off with the second to last one. I was incredibly lucky."

Luck comes incredibly and daily to people besides Paramon Petrovich. Where does this fairy tale passion for crystal come from? Perhaps a certain part of the population has taken to enjoying not only the contents of their wine bottles but the musical tones of their Baccarat followed by the obligatory finger washing in the "pickle dish"? Unlikely! Paramon Petrovich squirrels away his crystal while he pours all manner of drink into his unbreakable, 23-kopeck tea glasses. . . . The same could be said for the carpets he hangs on his wall, eager to have his home look mystically Eastern, though he himself has never been further east than Moscow.

I asked him, "Was it worth digging through the rug store, as if it were Troy, to find such 'wall art'? Was it worth busting your gut for a 'pickle dish'?"

He looked at me as if wounded and parried, "What, am I worse than others or something? The Migunovs have a rug, the Drovunovs have a rug, and the Karaulovs have an entire set of cut-glass goblets. I'm a person too!"

Such is the fate of the Paramon Petroviches. They are naively convinced that without rugs on their walls and their crystal deposits, someone will take them for a pterodactyl rather than a human being. From this, the Migunovs rate the Drovunovs and the Drovunovs rate the Karaulovs. They work to create completely identical homes, and together plan assaults on stores which are naturally unprepared for such invasions. But then, who would have guessed that in Paramon Petrovich a love of eastern aesthetics would blossom? Who would have guessed that the Migunovs, musically illiterate, would go for months without the proper winter clothes in order to haul a piano up the stairs to their apartment, fearing that one day they might be seen wanting were Richter himself to drop by and need to compose a prelude. All according to the sly observation of Oliver Wendell Holmes—give us the superfluous, and we'll get around the necessities.

Go without necessities they do. In all these piano-filled, rug-laden homes there is not a single book or a newspaper. Nothing but Press Attaché suitcases and a Eureka typewriter, upon which, after an entire year, nothing has been typed but "asdfghjkl" and "Paramon Petrovich." There is no way for the Paramon Petroviches to understand that being no worse than others does not mean being better, and that the urge to acquire is no more effective in life than "asdfghjkl."

---

could confirm it." And they kept saying, "But it's not possible. He's the kindest person you could ever meet. The finest we know." And I realized, that's possible, too. I mean, we all know stories of the officers from fascist Germany who played the violin while thousands died in their camps. A lot can fit into one personality. A lot.

Ivan Andreevich Malyshev

Now thirty-nine years old, Malyshev worked abroad for several years as a high-level Soviet diplomat before becoming a foreign investment consultant. I met with him and his wife late one afternoon in the lobby of a luxury hotel in Moscow, where they were attending a formal reception. They were elegantly attired and spoke flawless English.

GRANT: Can you tell me a little bit about yourself, about your biography?

MALYSHEV: I am naturally concerned about anonymity, obviously, because of the client base and for other obvious reasons. But, well, I graduated from the Moscow University of International Relations, majoring in economics and politics. Then I entered the foreign service. Since 1991 I've been in private industry—that's a short summary.

GRANT: What kind of work have you been doing over the last four years?

MALYSHEV: I've been involved in consulting, in explaining how to do business in Russia. We've been representing a couple of vendors here, major oil companies, and also we've been promoting a system of communication between the congress and the parliament. So this is kind of what we've been doing. We work with a lot of companies who don't know a lot about Russia but are excited to do something. So we offer representational services, logistical support, visa services, and over time, if things go well, we can start establishing rep offices for them. With time, either we are working in depth with them or we're out.

GRANT: What's the most interesting part for you?

MALYSHEV: For me, I'm always amazed at how much can be lost in translation. You'd be completely amazed at how much can be lost in day-to-day interaction between Russians and Westerners. You'd be amazed at how tension can be built around something that never took place, you know, just because of perceived attitude to something. Such as thinking, "Hey, he meant that he was really upset," when someone wasn't. Russian body language is much more explicit, while English language, English English, and even American English, is much more subtle in many ways. Very often there are misunderstandings that come from this subtlety that are universally accepted in the West but have more difficulty being accepted here.

GRANT: So, for example?

MALYSHEV: Oh, it's very easy. When somebody is coming from the West and tells you, "I'm not sure I can do it," the way a Russian will often interpret this is to think that maybe you can, but you just don't want to. Whereas in real life, the speaker really meant that he's absolutely sure he can't do it, but doesn't want to be impolite by putting it directly. You are being mildly rejected, and rejected probably forever. There you have two absolutely different takes. Or you have more basic questions of literal translations. When an English speaker uses the phrases, "That will work," the most common assumption among Russian translators is that a specific mechanical aspect of some operation will function, whereas what it really means is, "Let's go for it."

GRANT: It's such a tricky game when so much of foreign investment has to do with trust and confidence in the first place.

MALYSHEV: Obviously. I mentioned before that Russians are very shy to ask questions. They so often can just think that you think something you don't. My job is to sit down and explain to people that Russia is not as difficult and complicated as many people believe. And yet they are allowed to believe this by so many other consultants who insist on how difficult and enigmatic the Russian soul is. While in real life, it's simple, it's down to earth, it's all very simple. Once you know what's going on, then you can go in and walk the walk and talk the talk. Then you're on the map. But before that you're wasting your time trying to find your way. And many people are deliberate about making this more difficult for you so that they can stress their usefulness. Which is, of course, a good thing for the consultant because if anything goes wrong, they can just say that Russians are bad. So, you have a situation where most Russian businessmen indeed lack basic business knowledge, but more importantly, you get a great deal of distortion from consultants themselves.

GRANT: Is there a sense that foreign investors as a whole have changed in the last five years? Such as the people you've been working with?

MALYSHEV: Well, I'm very privileged. I've been working with real high fliers. But, you know, four years ago, five years ago, maybe even three years ago, there were no high fliers in Moscow. There were a lot more cowboys, you know, like some guy from Minnesota who heard about Russia and thought, "Wow, let's go!"

GRANT: It's supposed to be really cheap there.

MALYSHEV: Exactly. And it was cheap. Also, that created an image of American businessmen as smelling of lots of greenbacks and making fast decisions, while in real life the guy wasn't risking anything. He wasn't even putting his reputation at stake because he never had one in the U.S. in the first place. He came from somewhere in the Midwest, a very small town, a very shallow background, no track record, nothing. He would be asking hundreds of questions, you know, he would be spreading and maybe even burning lots of cash, but at that time everything was so cheap so that, you know, burning 1K was a big deal here, in Moscow. But now with more political stability and more serious players involved, Moscow has become more expensive. And in a way, I think it's good because it's a barrier that prevents small fish from coming to town. Because if you're serious, and you're ready to invest a certain amount of money into a project, that means you're more professional. My experience is, unless you're committed to spending a certain amount of money, you're not a player. Because at the first obstacle, people get scared and then go back to London and just bitch and moan about everything that's wrong in Russia. And Russia's a difficult place.

GRANT: It's rare to hear someone say that business in Russia really isn't that complicated, but do you think that might also have something to do with the level of finance? I mean, for someone trying to sell coffee out of a kiosk on the street, someone who has to pay taxes of 80 percent or higher, I mean *that's* complicated.

MALYSHEV: I'm talking about serious investors that can really shape the future of this country, bringing this country into the civilized part of the world, if you wish, just making it a more open society. I'm talking about vendors with international names, major oil companies, because they're the real players. Because if we're talking about someone selling coffee, that's great, but it doesn't automatically affect the life of the country. There are some current deals underway right now in the oil sector that could do great things. From a strategic point of view, that could change the shape of the country in the future. They are really investing in infrastructure, they come with really big money. Look at the major oil projects like Sakhalin. We are having a party this afternoon in the hotel later, and probably the prime minister will join us for a drink—this is a very serious transaction. So, I would say, yes, the foreign investors have changed. The cowboys are out. Forget it. And they were selling such stories about Moscow, being taken advantage of, always getting mugged. It's not all B.S., largely, because you can get into trouble. But how? I mean, what happens to half of these people? They go to a seedy nightclub after a day at the office, they meet some nice girl taller and better looking than them, they get into a fight with her boyfriend. You can get into trouble anywhere in the world. I mean I haven't heard too many stories of serious companies doing business and getting into trouble with anybody. Because if you're transparent, if you follow the rules, if you pay the taxes, nobody will come to you. As soon as you're in the grey zone, you're in trouble, but as soon as you're out of the grey zone, nobody will touch you, because no fish is big enough, at least here.

GRANT: What about the evolution of the high-level Russian business community? How have they changed over the last five years?

MALYSHEV: It's hard to say. At first there was a milestone of making your first million U.S. These are very wealthy people, very wealthy by any standards, and oftentimes Russian businessmen who are much wealthier than their counterparts in the West. But this commercial success leads them to believe that, "Hey, I've made so much money, they should listen to me." What they don't understand though is that, basically, you just made money because you've been redistributing the property, not really making it. You are not adding any value. If you want to be in this for the long term, to be on the map, you need to understand how to make money, not by redistributing but by bringing new value to the table.

GRANT: Shifting gears a little bit, I wanted to ask after the idea of New

Russians. If you had to choose a few adjectives to describe the New Russian community, what might they be?

MALYSHEV: The problem is that the *real* New Russian rich are people you would never see at all. These are people who have been very smart, who have educated themselves to international ways very quickly, and who have amassed tremendous wealth very savvily. But you never see them because they are discreet. When people talk about the vulgar New Russians on the street, I just laugh, because they are just the tip of the iceberg, and the [biggest part of the] iceberg is something you will never see.

The backbone of this country is the same as in the United States, and that would be the middle class. The New Russians are out on the streets and getting all the attention, but I feel that they are a very small percentage of the population. What people are missing is a very different layer of people that are making less than the so-called New Russians, but they are involved in more serious work to make themselves stable and comfortable. I think you can say the same thing in almost any market. This is the reason why we don't deal with New Russians. They are classless. They don't have our background, they don't have our education, so we don't mess with them. It's not really money, and maybe it's my snobbish attitude, but they haven't read a tenth of the books that we have, they haven't been to the places we've been to before it all started, they haven't been exposed to culture. I mean, we met a couple of New Russians on a recent foreign trip and it was an embarrassment to be around them. They're very loud, they're very free with their money.

GRANT: They're very stereotypically American?

MALYSHEV: I would say it's very like an American you see on a plane who spends his time talking about his hometown which you've never heard of. So it's a different kind of ballgame, it's a different kind of league. Russian people have to make a decision when they get started in business: do they want to be exposed to that kind of world or not? There are some dangers, among other things. Just how much money do you want to make? We're just not part of it.

GRANT: Clearly you lead a very international life, and the hotel we're in for example, could really be a hotel in almost any city in the world. What are the moments when you stop and think, "Wait, this isn't any city in the world. This could only be Moscow."

MALYSHEV: There are hundreds of things you could mention, the kinds of bureaucratic obstacles that have nothing to do with business but everything to do with daily life. Like phoning someone to get information and never getting anywhere. You just need a bit of help and instead you get routine antagonism from people working in stores or offices. But I have to say that with time we have come to feel more and more comfortable living here. Much more so than before. So, basically, I think we're in pretty good shape. We are less irritated by Russian life, for example, than we were one year ago or two years ago.

GRANT: But I was talking to a fellow yesterday who described his elite neighborhood growing up, with the children of the party at the top, the children of diplomats second, the children of the foreign trade office third, and then going down from there. Is there any way you could still point to those kinds of structures surviving today?

MALYSHEV: I think that there is something to that. I mean, there is some kind of concern among those people. I really don't enjoy pointing this out, but I went to the same school with the grandchildren of Brezhnev and Sholokhov and so on.

GRANT: In Europe or even the States, there are lots of ways of identifying people with old money. But in Russia, who's old money?

MALYSHEV: Old money in Russia today, like abroad, doesn't so much refer to who has money but people with social background, people who come from good families, who have good education, people who have been exposed to culture, who have done a lot of traveling. It's very difficult to get into that league. In many ways, we are part of this world. We don't advertise who we are, we don't advertise our class, we don't care, we don't try and get large flats, because in some sense we will be there always. We work very hard to stay in this league, but we've been there as long as we can remember. We will be successful for any occasion.

It was inviting to be mesmerized by Malyshev's crisp analysis of Russia's business prospects, but it was also a signal of how easily large fortunes explain themselves. Smaller firms clearly had fewer choices: the previous day I had sat with a friend for two hours while she explained the labyrinthine strategies she used to fix accounting books at her store so as to reduce the tax burden from a vertiginous 90 percent. Her company hadn't ventured into grey areas, to use Malyshev's terms, so much as they discovered that Russian business was grey to begin with. It was a moral haze embodied.

The maw of analytical categories returns us to the invisibility of power itself, the invisibility of benevolent hands guiding economies after Adam Smith, the invisibility of Mafia, or the invisibility of Malyshev's elite strata, earnestly possessed of distinction, but never distinctiveness. It is a system where New Russians, whoever they might be, are continually denied a valid role in the social fabric because of their very visibility.

For those who lack the easy social status of someone like Malyshev, the current field is also a setting where narratives of loss can mask gains of a different kind. I thought of the algebra of fortune as I listened to Rafael Khakopian, who looked back on his career with a flourish reminiscent of Omar Sharif at the close of *Dr. Zhivago*. What he seemed eager to impress on me was never so much the remarkable heights to which he rose as much as the stunning and repeated drama of his falls. His was an ethos of sacrifice ironically redolent of the Soviet Union's regular invocations of its own spectacular losses in the struggle against czarist oppression, in the October Revolution, the civil war, and World War II. "Out of sacrifice come sacred things," to echo French essayist Georges Bataille—new values to be recirculated in fresh cycles of expenditure. For people like Valerii Shchipok's local tax inspector, denying the state's coffers by tipping off truants can be an invisible gain against an unpopular and uncertain present.

Of the three portraits presented here, Malyshev's perhaps best symbolizes the fact that any form of power, asserted through loss or gain, is about representation—or, to return to the Russian idea of the conspiratorial, *zagovor*—mystical words working toward desired ends. Though people use phrases like "market reform," "transition period," and "the spirit of capitalism" every day, few still are clear on what such a spirit world looks like. Against such dramatic sea changes in political economies, such words may make little more sense than "asdfghjkl," but they sometimes work with the power of a spell.

Notes

1. Correspondence from a principal of the British investment house concerned.

2. To put the sum in context, 450 million rubles was formally equivalent to $700 million at official 1990 Soviet exchange rates. The average professor's salary at that time was 120 rubles a month.

References

Forbes Magazine 1996. "Godfather of the Kremlin?" 30 December.

Pesmen, Dale. 1996. " 'Do not have a hundred rubles, have instead a hundred friends': Money and Sentiment in a Perestroika-Post-Soviet Siberian City." *Irish Journal of Anthropology* 1(1): 3–22.

Stanley, Allesandra. 1996. "Russian Banking Scandal Poses a Threat to Future Privatization." *New York Times,* 28 Jan., A1, 8.

Verdery, Katherine. 1996. *What Was Socialism, and What Comes Next?* Princeton, N.J.: Princeton University Press.

Udbomafija and the Rhetoric of Conspiracy[1]

I don't remember exactly when I first came across the term *Udbomafija*. Yet I do remember when I first saw an advertisement for Edo Ravnikar's book. It was on the third or fourth page of *Delo* [Work], Slovenia's largest-selling newspaper. The advertisement read: "Do you want to find out who are the real godfathers of Slovenia? *Udbomafija: A Handbook for Understanding the Transition.*" There was a picture book with an ominous shadow slanting over it, and a smoking cigar lurking in a corner. I became even more intrigued when I began to read excerpts of the book published daily on the bottom of page 3 of *Delo* over the next few weeks.

When I began to ask around about Edo Ravnikar, I was told that both he and his father were well-known architects, that they had a studio in the old part of Slovenia's capital city, Ljubljana, and that Edo's father had designed Cankarjev Dom, the modern concert hall close to the national assembly downtown. However, when pressing for more than a family genealogy, I was told by many that they did not "know" him, that they only knew "of" him. I was inquiring this of persons whom I had met in my first months of fieldwork, persons I knew through family connections. I was surprised that they did not know him, especially upon learning that Edo Ravnikar was one of the founding members of Civilna Iniciativa, a group of persons dedicated to investigating and disseminating information about the injustices of the transition process—one of the very few organizations of civil society that openly engaged these issues. It seemed logical to me that those persons whom I had met in my first months in Ljubljana—ones who were also engaging in critiques of the past system— would know him, or at least I thought they should. Instead, after asking around, I received a secret dossier from various sources, one that was to be passed on only from person to person (I was to forward it to as many people that I deemed were reliable, particularly to Slovenes abroad). This dossier was published by another group, Civilna Inicijativa, that amassed information about the speaker of the assembly of the time, Herman Rigelnik. The dossier spoke of Rigelnik's secret position in the inner circles of the Party, his political affiliations during the time that he was manager of one of the major Slovenian companies, and his present connections to Milan Kučan, president of Slovenia and the last leader of the Communist Party of Slovenia. The dossier related a campaign that was carefully planned to launch Rigelnik as the next presidential candidate. When this dossier was made public, it provoked reactions of official outrage and every effort was made by the state to track down the members of Civilna Inicijativa and prosecute them. (After his dossier was made public, Rigelnik resigned from his position as speaker and retired from the political sphere and into the retail automobile industry.) However, Civilna Inicijativa remains a secret organization, one that has yet to be uncovered. When the members of the Ravnikar's group, Civilna Iniciativa, were questioned as to their participation with this secret organization, they denied any sort of relationship.

Ravnikar's *Udbomafija* is an extensive presentation of the parallel economic system that existed in Yugoslavia, an analysis that is focused on relating the way that this system continues to exist in symbiosis with the present economic system. Ravnikar draws a continuity between his work and that of Yugoslav dissident Milovan Djilas, who wrote about the practices the Party employed to siphon funds and invest them abroad in the mid-1950s, practices carried out in secret under the supervision of the state's secret-service agencies.[2] In Ravnikar's book, he relates the continual operation of the relationship between the secret service's foreign business networks abroad and the Yugoslav economy during the process of Slovenia's independence from Yugoslavia. While Ravnikar does not draw a straightforward continuity between the past and the present, he does portray how business practices and networks adapted to the circumstances of Slovenian autonomy after independence from Yugoslavia. He maps out how a similar relationship of interdependency with the Slovenian state was set in place, with the majority of key positions being once again occupied by members of the previous system.

Ravnikar's account is interesting because while his main thesis—an argument that all foreign business practices were supervised and controlled by the secret services—does seem exotically conspiratorial by almost anyone's standards, the implications of his argument engage the constructed debates about the past and the present in very productive ways. Engaged as I am in analyzing of the rationalizing power of economic discourse in the Slovenian transition, I have been exploring what allows for a certain interpretations of events to be coded as rational and acceptable, and for other accounts to be relegated to the realm of the irrational, paranoid, or irrelevant in cultural terms. This is particularly pertinent in Slovenia, where, as in other countries across Eastern Europe, the "softness" of the transition has allowed for ambiguities that do not map neatly upon any one set of discourses, particularly economic ones. Ravnikar's analysis recodes the history of the Yugoslav socialism as primarily a history of economic domination that was articulated in political terms, thus questioning the very categories upon which the operation of the "rational" discourses are based. Basing my approach on works such as that of Doug Holmes on illicit discourse (Holmes 1993), I will explore when and why Ravnikar's discourse of critique is identified as illicit and conspiratorial.

Ravnikar is of a well-established middle-class family that has owned land in various regions of Slovenia. While Ravnikar would reject being classified as left-wing or right-wing—his work focuses on deconstructing the operation of the system of political categories—he and his family members historically have allied themselves with the communists. As in the case of the Ravikar family, many who resided in the Slovenian region of Primorska aligned themselves with the communists when Primorska came under Italian rule between the two world wars. Slovenes became communist insofar as they were antifascist and later joined the partisans (who later came under the direction of Tito) as one of the antioccupational forces when Italian occupation expanded eastward all the way to Ljubljana in World War II; the land east of Ljubljana was occupied by Germany. Present-day Slovenia reaches all the way to the Adriatic Sea, yet borders around Trieste.

BAJUK: I understand you are an architect by trade. How did you become interested in these sorts of organizations and when did you begin writing about them?

RAVNIKAR: It was all very strange. My father was also an architect, and right after the war, people looked for work everywhere. As a result we also put in bids for international projects. How did I become interested in this mafia? Two reasons: first was the family connection. My uncle, my father's brother, began working in Trieste after we won the war. During the war, World War II, each in Yugoslavia fought their own war with the Germans. It was only after 1945 that this was all brought together under the Yugoslav Army. Until then Slovenia was on its own, Croatia was on its own, and so on. When the Slovenes won on their own territory, they took Trieste. Maybe you do not know, but Trieste was liberated—as we referred to this—and my uncle was among those partisans who afterward organized Trieste. He was actually from Trieste. This is why I know so much about the Slovenian organization in Trieste. I know that they were the ones who set up the foreign business connections and that the Serbs then took this over. I know these stories from my aunt, about how the Serbian women came in rags and in two weeks they were already walking around in fur coats. The Serbs killed my uncle and destroyed the Slovenian organization, replacing the whole thing with a Serbian organization. This amounted to the Serbian takeover of Yugoslavia. This is one of my "inside" views on this whole affair, firsthand.

BAJUK: When did this happen?

RAVNIKAR: 1945, 1946.

BAJUK: So soon after the war?

RAVNIKAR: Immediately after the war [the Serbs] intervened, because if they had let this go on for another six months, we would have begun to negotiate with the British, and maybe—there was no Yugoslavia at that time as of yet—and maybe Slovenia would have made a deal on its own. This was why it was necessary that this whole organization be destroyed immediately. Yet this was a question of business, people think that they were persecuting some class enemies. This was a business problem. It began with the smuggling of cigarettes. No one explains this properly. Yugoslavia smuggled cigarettes into Italy. This is important, though it might not seem so at first. Italy had a monopoly on cigarettes, and the first source of foreign exchange for Yugoslavia was American cigarettes they smuggled into Italy. This was the first financial basis for what I later call the *Udbomafija*.

Then in 1963 there was an international architecture project to be held in Venice, and we—that is, my father, my wife, and I—won the project. At that time my wife and I were still students at the university. We worked with an Italian group Olivetti—Adriano Olivetti—who then went into business with typewriters and computers. His daughter was also in our group, as well as others from Venice and Florence. Together we formed a group selected by the municipal authorities who published the official call for applications. The municipal authority at that time was communist. Venice was communist always, from 1947 to 1963. The communists were important only insofar as they had an anti-Mafia concept of governing the municipality. They kept the Mafia out of the municipal government. The opposing side, the right wing, this was a combination of quasi-fascists, Christian Democrats, and Mafia. In Italy, the Mafia and the Christian Democrats—the Americans brought them together, this is a well-known thesis. And it is true.

[The Mafia] began to drain the lagoon, and this is when real estate speculation began. They got permission from the urban planning office and they began to drain the lagoon between Venice and Malviro. This meant that they gained land! *[Laugh]* This was dishonest, this was an obscenity, a proper Mafia operation. Those who drained the lagoon fought against us, and we—my father, my wife, and I—worked for the municipality for almost two years and listened to the heated debates between the Mafia and anti-Mafia. That was my introduction to Mafia techniques. Then came this Di Michelis—the one who much later became minister for foreign affairs—who at that time became *assessore* of the municipal minister for urban affairs, and he replaced us with Craxi's people, who then stayed on. During two years we fought for our jobs, our work, and there we met these new socialists. This lasted until 1965 or 1966. We did very little, but this whole operation was crystal clear to me. Then I traveled to London, where I began my Ph.D. in economics.

BAJUK: In economics?

RAVNIKAR: Yes, but the economics of urbanism. I paid my way with the money I had saved from our job in Italy. I didn't have a scholarship or a stipend or anything like that. This became a problem later on. I was in London for two years: first I studied the economics of urbanism, then I transferred to philosophy, and then back to architecture. My mentor was Reynard Banham. He was the one that convinced me to go back to architecture, and he had invited me to work with him in Los Angeles. Only in 1972–73 I went back to Yugoslavia, to Slovenia, on vacation—we had agreed with Banham that I would finish my Ph.D., defend it, and I would go to the United States to work with him. Yet at that time, they took my passport away. This was during the transition from liberalism back to this.

I came back here in 1973 and then could not leave again. My studies fell apart, everything. I had money saved away in London, invested in a partnership with two other architects, but when I never returned it was as good as gone. That was that. But then I began to look around me in Yugoslavia, what was going on at that time. I wrote about this in my book, so I will not go into detail here.

My family is an old—at least two hundred years, if not more—land-owning family. Yet before the war they were all with the communists, though it is a long story. This was a national question, and a fervent Slovene was with the communists. And then there was this foreign capital. Slovenes were sick of this. The story is repeating itself, if we connect this to the present. This is roughly my personal background, why an architect like me deals with the topic of mafias.

Ravnikar's equating being Slovene with being communist points to a certain configuration of political identities that does not overlap with present post-communist ones. Slovenian leftist—formerly communist—intellectuals are wary of nationalist sentiment and regard them as excessive. They also ascribe this sort of nationalism to the right-wing (some of which insofar as they were anticommunist were anti-Yugoslav and thus pro-Slovene), which they in turn label as extremist and even primitive. However, before World War II, communism was aligned with national sentiment among those who were opposed to the Kingdom of Serbs, Croats, and Slovenes formed from the remains of the Austro-Hungarian empire. While at first this formation was generally welcomed as a move toward greater autonomy within a Slav state, the price that Slovenia had to pay to form part of the kingdom became to be seen as excessive. For Slovenia, this had entailed conceding substantial amounts of land to Italy and Austria (including Primorska, where the Ravnikars had lived) as well as being relegated to second-class citizenship in relation to Serbia. According to Ravnikar, communists before World War II were advocates of greater Slovene autonomy.

RAVNIKAR: At that time, around 1968, communism was already exhausted. Though to the West—to the Americans, for example—it seemed really strong. This was rotten by 1970. They had already rebelled in Hungary in 1965, and in 1968 in Czechoslovakia. Russia was able to quell these movements with such brute force only because the West feared Russia so. Now you look at the rusted submarines, and see that the Russian army cannot do anything against Chechnya, a small country within Russia. But in 1970 we already knew about the corruption in the army. There was no military strength remaining anywhere in the Eastern bloc. Of course, the regime was the first to recognize that the whole thing was a facade, and at that time began to open up to the West. Then they had liberalism in Croatia, and the liberal movement swept all the way to Serbia. Slovenia had Kavčič. Yugoslavia could have at that time turned into a moderately liberal—I don't know how I would characterize this, we referred to this as "liberal," but this word has a different meaning in every country—more free, more entrepreneurial, yet nothing extraordinary. Everyone could do what they wanted. During this time I had an office in Ljubljana, at the same time I also had one in Milan and in London. It was very nice, there were no obstacles of any kind. In 1973 this became criminal offense and for this reason they took my passport.

Ravnikar had been part of a generation that benefited from the market reforms that were implemented in the 1960s across Yugoslavia, and by Stane Kavčič in the capacity of prime minister in Slovenia. However, in the early 1970s, Tito cracked down on the economically liberal movements which had by then become quite powerful. Threatened by them, Tito set in motion both political and economic measures to counteract these liberalizing tendencies. The system of self-management (contractual socialism) replaced the market socialism introduced by Stane Kavčič (who "resigned" in 1972), which spelled the end of the economic freedom which Ravnikar enjoyed in the 1960s. He equates this economic freedom with political freedom, and ascribes his experience to all Slovenes. However, there were Slovenes in the 1960s who were considered politically threatening to the regime and did not enjoy the economic freedom which Ravnikar clearly missed. For those who did not have access to (or lose) this economic freedom in the past or memories of it, such freedom— and knowledge that came with it— is coded as suspect. In any case, while Ravnikar does not question why he is able to consider these liberal practices as normal, his experience of liberalism allowed him to evaluate the operation of Yugoslavia's economy and to track the continuity of these liberal practices on another level.

RAVNIKAR: The regime did away with liberalism, it forbade liberalism, but then went into liberalism for its own benefit. And here a division was formed between the ideological—are you acquainted with Kardelj's legislation on self-management?[3]

BAJUK: Yes, I am.

RAVNIKAR: One line went into self-management. This was only on paper; we referred to it as a ritual. The English word for this is very apt, *ceremony,* self-management *ceremony*. We managed something, yet how did this work in practice? Two days a week you implemented self-management by means of a ceremony that made it appear that you decided to do something which you were told beforehand that you were required to do. That is how this worked. This was wearisome, unpleasant. You had to wash out your mouth afterward.

At the same time—and this is very important—an unrefined Mafia organization was being set up, an extremely liberal—no, that is not the right word—wild capitalism—I do not know what the proper word is these days— but that most brutal system, the kind that Nigeria now has, Burma and Turkey. This is now coming to light, only yesterday Clinton made a comment about Burma. A regime maintains itself with drug trafficking and with slave labor. Then it provides concessions to companies like Shell at a low price— that is wild capitalism. This began in Yugoslavia in 1973.

In my architecture firm we had a big project every other year, a project valued between $10 and $30 million dollars. We designed a great many houses. Not in Slovenia, but elsewhere in Yugoslavia and in the world. When you build a house you come to work with the financing of the project because you have to explain what you will do, and a loan has to be taken out. We designed hotels, public buildings, infrastructure. It was rather funny, but if you knew something you would invariably be able to find work. However you always had to find—this is called a cap—a figurehead company that was of the regime. They hired you for your technical expertise and for this you were paid 10 percent. *[Laugh]* You had to do everything for only 10 percent and we had a hard time making ends meet. Yet in these projects we saw everything: the financing, marketing, production, the factories that worked on these projects. I believe that in the Yugoslav situation the architect was one of the most strategically placed persons because he was able to see the whole complex operation, from the political level on up. This might sound strange in America, but maybe not so strange. Let's say that if in America you work in Washington, close to the channels of power, and that when you get work through those channels you then also learn how these channels of power operate. And being an architect has a bit of glamour; a great deal of money is turning over in the project and in the office itself. The whole affair has an aura about it, and the whole thing is considered to be quasi-artistic *[laugh]*. The regime tolerates architects because they are crazy artists.

So, the regime set up heartfelt business relations with the West. Yet so that this would not be apparent, they did something very simple: they established a bank in Frankfurt. They set up a bank in Frankfurt, sent their Slovene people there after enrolling them in the best schools. When they finished their training in, say, America or Germany, they were stationed in Frankfurt, not in Ljubljana, nor in Belgrade. They remained in Frankfurt. This was how they established an elite, a clique—how should I say this—ex-patrio, who managed the whole foreign business operation. This was the same in Russia as

well as across the whole Eastern bloc. And now this is occurring in these
African countries.

It is very simple: from Yugoslavia you exported anything, from pigs to
manufactured products. This all sold quite well due to the cost of the labor
force, and the profits were considerable—a profit of, let's say, 20 percent on
Yugoslav products. But this profit never made it back into Yugoslavia. We
called them the great export companies: these were Genex—we know them
by name—another was Inex, then there was Energoinvest—that was the Bos-
nian company—the Macedonians had one whose name escapes me at this
moment. Each republic had one. Slovenia had Slovenijales, Lesnina, Metalka,
these sorts of companies.

This was apparently distributed in the self-management fashion across
Yugoslavia, but as soon as you went over the border in Trieste, the whole
operation was linked together. These last three years I have worked in Podobnik's parliamentary commission as a mafia expert in these sorts of investigations, particularly those involving Ljubljanska Banka.[4] The whole thing is
very clear to me. The Serbs were the majority owners of all these operations.
Then you had the Croatians and the Bosnians. Majority ownership was given
to the Serbs, and then ownership by percentage for the rest of the republics.

By means of the majority ownership of the foreign business operation, Serbia, or better yet, Belgrade, robbed the developed republics: these were Slovenia and Croatia. The things that I am explaining to you are facts; they still
stand today. It is the same with the LHB Bank in Frankfurt where our esteemed central bank director France Arhar was director for twelve years—
during the worst years. And even today the Slovenes are minority shareholders, despite the fact that formally speaking LHB is a Slovenian bank.
Adria Bank Vienna is the same: the Serbs always had a controlling majority
and the Slovenes were minority owners. And this sort of operation continues
unhindered.

The whole thing is so simple! That 20 percent on Slovenian products stayed
outside, and we Slovenes got all the costs. These costs included wages, school-
ing, medical services, roads, infrastructure. We had all this, except for the
profit on our products. With that profit Slovenia would have been able to develop economically—albeit a few steps behind the developed economies—
but instead the profits remained in foreign banks for that mafia. And now they
have invested these profits in Germany and America, in companies and in
banks as well as in drug and arms trafficking.

These operations were directed outside Yugoslavia by the intelligence services of the regime. There were three different agencies. One was UDBA: this
was the secret police, an FBI of sorts.

BAJUK: For national operations?

RAVNIKAR: Yes, national. Then there was KOS, the counterintelligence
agency. This was the military intelligence agency, like a military CIA. They

were involved because a great deal of the business overseas was in the sale of arms. Yugoslavia had a lot of dealings with both Iran and Iraq. Most of this was produced in Slovenia. Even that tank which the Serbs sold the Iranians and the Iraqis was almost entirely produced in Slovenia: from the motor to the artillery shells and the electronics. Yugoslavia worked a great deal with foreigners, especially Slovenia: 60 percent of Slovenia's production was for export. The U.S. exports only 5 percent. Of course, the situation is different as much of U.S. production is for internal consumption. Yet Slovenia exports a great deal just the same. And they supervised all this export, partly because some of it fell under the military program and partly because some of it was intelligence oriented: UDBA, KOS, and the diplomatic intelligence service were involved.

My thesis is very straightforward. These things that I am telling you now, they are true. In my work in Podobnik's investigative commission I have seen evidence in black and white. As members of a parliamentary commission, we had the authority to demand documents from anyone, and we also got them. Of course, now I am talking to you off the top of my head—something for which many have criticized me—but I know what I am talking about.

In analyzing Ravnikar's writings and the way he operates as a social actor, I have debated the usefulness of Richard Hofstadter's notion of the renegade. In his essay, "The Paranoid Style in American Politics," Hofstadter outlines the special significance of a "renegade from the enemy cause": "In some part the special authority accorded the renegade derives from the obsessions with secrecy so characteristic of such movements: the renegade is the man or woman who has been in the secret world of the enemy, and brings forth with him or her the final verification of suspicions which might otherwise have been doubted by a skeptical world" (Hofstadter 1965, 35). In evaluating his own motives for writing, Ravnikar himself recognized that at first he did not realize the uniqueness of his knowledge of the system's business practices (Ravnikar 1995, 44). He did not consider his experiences with the system constituted an understanding of a secret world which was unknown to others, but instead thought that others either considered this knowledge to be irrelevant or chose to keep quiet. Upon asking some of my friends about their reactions to Ravnikar's first articles published in *Delo,* some went so far as to say that they read like science fiction. Ravnikar's account was definitely a change from the sorts of discourses that one heard used to describe the operation of the Party by those who had been continually against it. As opposed to Ravnikar's depiction, these discourses of critique could be defined as conspiratorial insofar as they ascribe extraordinary powers to one central power or person:

> Decisive events are not taken as part of the stream of history, but as the consequence of someone's will. Very often the enemy is held to possess some especially effective source of power: he controls the

press, he directs the public mind through "managed news"; he has
unlimited funds; he has a new secret for influencing the mind (brain-
washing); he has a special technique for seduction (the Catholic confessional); he is gaining a stranglehold on the educational system.
(Hofstadter 1965, 31)

For me these discourses constituted an impenetrable discourse that would recount the omnipotence of the Party: that "they" still controlled everything, that
they had infiltrated "their" people in every political party, "they" owned all
the media, "they" still tapped phones, "they" were the ones that had the
connections, "they" were always one step ahead of the game. Going back to
Ravnikar, his discourse of critique is extrapolated from his business practices
abroad that maps out a description of the regime as an operating system. His
portrayal of an organization seems to be more "rational" than accounts of the
Party as an omnipotent Big Brother.

Ravnikar had mistakenly believed that if he simply wrote about his experiences that the information would stand on its own (Ravnikar 1995, 45). Yet far
from rendering Ravnikar "a renegade from the enemy cause," this information
was categorized as suspicious because he "knew too much" in the eyes of
those who would have been his potential political allies. By those he criticized
he was considered as not "knowing what he was talking about" because he did
not have the empirical evidence to back up his interpretations, nor was he a
specialist in economics or international finance. As a result, Ravnikar's narrated experiences as a historical subject were generally not recognized as culturally valid. While Ravnikar does not seem to fit the role of the renegade, his
writings and the reactions they provoke beg the question as to why critical
discourses about the regime's past—in light of a strong tradition of critique of
the system in the years before the transition—are coded as conspiratorial and
irrational, or as dealing with the secret and the unknown.

RAVNIKAR: Why did I begin to write? When 1990 came around, and we
had the war, I was convinced that people knew about this—and this was my
great mistake, for I believed that everyone else knew what I knew. It turned
out that due to my background I knew a great deal more. I also was very interested in these things, from the experiences of my uncle to my own experiences in Italy and France.

In 1990 I became panicky when I realized that in Slovenia people don't
know anything about this. Those that came to power, the DEMOS coalition, they didn't understand anything. This became clear to me all of a sudden around 1990. Then I began to write articles in *Delo*—this was 1991,
1992—while the war was still going on. Then the Yugoslav Army retreated
from Slovenia, and the media interpreted this as evidence of Drnovšek's diplomatic capabilities.[5] This infuriated me because until six months before then,

Drnovšek had been the president in Belgrade, and had arranged everything with Kadijević. And Kadijević, he was the real KOS, that Yugoslav Mafia. *[Laugh]* Drnovšek really aided Belgrade because he didn't want to know anything, and he helps himself that way today. He doesn't know anything about anything; it is better that he does not know. Yet he returned to Slovenia, having already agreed with Kadijević that the army would leave Slovenia. And the Yugoslav Army left Slovenia because the Serbs needed a military base. They had UN sanctions and they were at war. And no one knew at that time where the war would spread, if it was to remain in Croatia or if it would move to Bosnia, Macedonia, Kosovo. No one knew. That war was utterly vile. I know Yugoslavia quite well, and I did not expect this war to be so loathsome, but now we all know.

Yet the Serbs knew perfectly well that they could not foresee what would happen. Their only oasis was in Slovenia: to the West they had sanctions, they had war at home. Even in deep Serbia the unimaginable was happening. Slovenia was their base. And during this time Yugoslavia still controlled its intelligence agencies, so it still controlled Slovenia as well as the operations across the border: Trieste, Frankfurt. This was an ideal situation for them. And they placed—not actually placed but simply maintained—their cadre in their positions. If you wanted to be the director of Metalka you had to get the approval of Belgrade. If you wanted to be the director in Frankfurt, you had to get the approval of Belgrade. They even had their network here.

Let's take the case of Tam, which is very interesting. The SDK has reviewed it, we reviewed it in the investigative commission, the national assembly reviewed it in its own fashion, and we now know exactly how this worked.[6] Tam was a company that was part of the military program. This included the production of cannons, motors, tanks, and trucks. Tam provided a great deal for the military program for Iraq, Iran, and Russia. How did this operate? Belgrade established a company—Tam Deutschland—in Germany, put in position a Slovene whose last name is Tavčar, who at the same time worked for Belgrade counterintelligence. They hired a Slovene who speaks Slovenian and understands the situation in Slovenia but that is their agent in—

BAJUK: Tam Deutschland—

RAVNIKAR: Exactly, and they did the same in Czechoslovakia and in Russia. Tam sold its products to Tam Deutschland and was compensated for them, but from then on Tam did not know what happened with the products or with the money. They didn't even know to whom they sold the products. Tam did business with Tam Deutschland, and as far as Slovenia was concerned, the deal finished there. They sent the car or truck there and got money in return, though only enough that they could produce the next car. Ljubljanska Banka would cover any losses incurred. This was taken care of in the bank itself where this network had someone who could assure the credit if necessary so that the company had enough to pay its workers. The interesting thing is that up until last year this operation had worked without any problems. The director is still the one that Belgrade assigned there in 1985, and in Maribor the director is still the one that Belgrade placed there, Andrej Hazabent.

BAJUK: Isn't he the one who is now head of the Credit Bank of Maribor?

RAVNIKAR: Yes, now he is in the bank *[laugh],* the one who in 1986 was the director of the military program in Tam, assigned there by the counterintelligence agency in Belgrade. And this is how it remained, absolutely nothing had been changed. And when Tam went bankrupt—I saw the documents, I have them, they are in my file cabinets, there is no problem if you need evidence. They simply established a company in Bermuda and invested the budget funds that they received from the Slovenian government for Tam's rehabilitation: for the preservation and restructuring of jobs for workers, the money for wages, for the social programs, and for the sale of their products. They simply funneled this into that company in Bermuda and then came on the scene as a foreign buyer who wanted to put in a bid for Tam. If this transaction had succeeded, then this Serbian network would have become the legal owner of Tam in Slovenia, Tam in Germany, and its entire business network.

I saw this in Venice in 1963, and I saw something very similar in France later on. Then I saw this happening in Yugoslavia in 1973, and in 1980, and then I saw the same thing in Slovenia in 1992. The same thing, nothing had changed, the same people were in the same places, I recognized them and know who they were. We always knew who was who. And that is what upset me, and that is the reason why I began to write.

One of Ravnikar's central arguments in his writings is the emphasis on the implications of a continuity with the past. Ravnikar's particular point—one with which most other critics disagree—is to question Slovenia's independence from a still-active Yugoslav system with its established system of colonizing networks.[7] This is the point which one could define as a "curious leap in imagination" in Hofstadter's terms (1965, 36). Hofstadter argues that what characterizes paranoid scholarship is a conscientious accumulation and argumentation of facts and careful attention to rational discourse. It is this very attention and rational presentation of evidence that is to make this "curious leap" defensible. I would argue that the implications that Ravnikar draws from questioning of Slovenia's independence—particularly the criteria he employs to evaluate the complicity of persons with the present system—render this a "curious leap" that for many is irrelevant, impossible, or unacceptable. Yet it is also this turn which gives Ravnikar's argument its coherence. While I would argue that his account does not have the perfect coherence that characterizes paranoid scholarship for Hofstadter, Ravnikar's analysis of Slovenia's past within Yugoslavia, and as such within the larger international sphere in which Yugoslavia did business, develops from this central question of independence.

RAVNIKAR: I wanted to show what we could expect, now that we are approaching the West. This is very important. The West has been collaborating with the Mafia since 1946. Those very cigarettes which we smuggled into Italy were provided by the Americans. This is strongly connected to the Italian Mafia and the Christian Democrats. The Americans stationed themselves in Sicily and began their progress northward. And Mussolini—we also in effect fought against Mussolini in Italy, that was what OZNA was all about. But Mussolini also persecuted the Mafia; we knew this. This was one of his key mottoes: the train will run, there will be order, and there will be no Mafia. He really clashed with the Mafia and managed to weaken it considerably.

The first thing that the Americans, or, more specifically, the U.S. intelligence services, did was make contact with people who were connected to the Mafia and who came from America to Italy by way of family relations. There is evidence to support this, this is true. In New York City, the Americans began to select a cadre to run postwar Sicily. And they already made the deal in New York. And so they sent them: go to this person in Palermo. In this fashion they had an American administration in Sicily, or better said, an Italian administration under American occupation that was truly a Mafia operation.

Political power also developed in this Mafia-like fashion. The communists came on the political scene as a serious party in 1947, 1948. They would have won easily if the Americans had not prevented it. And the Americans also established the Christian Democratic Party and connected it to the Mafia. They said, "We already established certain things here, we have set up a network of people, now you are a party and here you have some friends to work with. Here you have an industrial base, we have already set it up. You will get two and a half billion dollars, and let's go. Just don't let the communists get involved.

This group—some adventurers, some Mafia, some Americans, and some others—began to work together. And if the Americans gave some cigarettes to the Yugoslavs and they knew that the others were smuggling them into Italy, they considered it something that occurred in the Italian civilian sphere and they did not care about it one bit. They did not care that an Italian administrator in Rome is worried because some people are smuggling something over the border on him. They dealt with it this way, the Mafia way: You will do this, I will do that, and that Yugoslav will also get something out of it because we are expanding our operations against Stalin. The relationship between Yugoslavia and the West goes back to 1945, 1946. It was fortified after the fall of liberalism, when they really began to set up their companies over the border.

When communism fell in the East, the West—and this is what I believe to
be perverse and also dilettantish from a civilization point of view, a dilettan-
tism which the West had not committed in three hundred years. That it depended on the *Udbomafija* to penetrate the East. This is a mistake that will
turn out to be catastrophic in proportion. I wanted to at least tell some Slovenes about this, and I think that some—the delegates read this, except for
the hard-core LDS members who were not allowed to read it.[8] *[Laugh]* They
all read it, and later I was astounded at the number of people in the legal
offices—judges, lawyers, high-level officials—who I heard that they agreed
with my interpretation of things.

BAJUK: They agreed, but this is not explicitly recognized at an official
level.

RAVNIKAR: Yet it is.

BAJUK: How?

RAVNIKAR: For example, Drnovšek publicly said that they sold the foreign debt to Genex; they officially recognized this. No one denies that Adria
Bank's majority owners are Serbs. No one denies this, instead they all argue
that this is not relevant. This is the main defense that I have detected. I began
to make fun of this. Once they sent me some reporters, right at the beginning.
A girl from *Mladina* came, asking for an interview, and then she tried to interrogate me a bit. And I said, If they—the opposing side—were smart, their
reaction would be to agree with me that what I wrote is true, but so what if it
is? I suggested this a bit, but then this really took hold. Everyone began to say
that everything is okay, that is just the way things operate. I have a few quotes
about this in the book, though not many. It is clear that the UDBA established
a company in Frankfurt—we all know this happened, but what is wrong with
it? These are qualified people; we have to maintain this and forge ahead. It's
much harder to explain why something is wrong than to simply define it. This
is relatively simple, to describe a phenomenon: this is like this, this is how it
came to be, it operates like this. This is what I write, the description of a
parasite. This is not hard. The problem lies in explaining what is wrong about
it. "There is nothing wrong about it. These are well-trained people, good
people." They did not let me write any more when I began to explain what is
wrong. I couldn't get published.

Ravnikar's strategy of critique entailed portraying how the operations he
witnesses were normal, in the sense of them being the normal operating practices of the previous system, not sporadic anomalies. However, here he identifies another "normalizing" strategy: the depoliticization of those practices by
recoding them as business practices within the context of a market economy.
Far from being condemned as economically colonialist practices—as Ravnikar
would refer to them—these practices and the persons who implemented them

are identified by the establishment as having the know-how and connections to give Slovenia a head start in its transition to a market economy.

This neutralizing strategy spurs Ravnikar to evaluate Slovenia's (and Yugoslavia's) business relations with the West—narrating them within a context of Italy's and Yugoslavia's roles as buffer states between the West and the East—and in so doing drawing out a set of complicities between both sides. In aligning his discourse against depoliticization with the complexities he charts, Ravnikar taps into arguments identified as leftist in the West.

RAVNIKAR: Let's take Boeing's story, the company that now works in China. There are now allegedly three thousand workers who were laid off by Boeing in California. Let us look at how Boeing became what it is today. First some people came from Europe. In the U.S. they were able to find work in a field that didn't have such opportunities in Europe. They tried to develop the technology and know-how to improve. Then the war came. People were mobilized to work in their factories. They were required to become part of their labor force and they had unlimited money from the government: Just build the airplanes in six months; it doesn't matter how it gets done, you will have all the money you need. You will get everything, raw materials, everything. This is what put Boeing on its feet. The advantages that Boeing was able to carve out for itself during the war became advantages on the world market as well. Boeing dominated the world market for thirty years because of this. Boeing was able to milk California and the government for its own benefit, and now it is transferring its operations to China, leaving behind unemployment, poverty, and, in the end, hunger. And why? Because Boeing is managed by scoundrels who see a greater profit in China.

And this becomes our official response to why we don't want this. We don't want this sort of economic system. How can Drnovšek justify this? By simply saying that this is the same sort of economic system. That these two things, a mafia economy and a healthy economy, are one and the same thing. Our response to this is, This is not true, gentlemen. These are two different things.

Then there is the problem of continuity. If there is no continuity of Serbian domination in Slovenia—finance, foreign business—then there is no continuity of Drnovšek and Kučan. They could then join the unemployment lines—the West supports them only insofar as they cooperate with this Serbian connection and aid in maintaining it in Slovenia. Drnovšek can stay as long as this continues. If you remember all those heavy-duty scandals that went through parliament—Tam, Genex, UDBA, KOS, and now the Trieste Credit Bank (TCB).

Drnovšek doesn't know anything. They asked him about Tam, and he was not informed, he didn't know anything. They asked him about the banks, and he didn't know anything. Tam cost him Tajnikar since Tajnikar had signed

those documents, and now Thaler signed these.[9] Yet Drnovšek is clean. If you
know a bit about the Mafia, you know that Al Capone is always clean. He is
always five minutes away from wherever anything is going on. This is the
same technique. You never have anything on Drnovšek. As long as you don't
have anything on him, he is here working for them. The moment that you put
Drnovšek behind bars, everyone would drop him. The same goes for Kučan.
This is the continuity of the political system that ensures the continuity of the
economic system.

Like many of those who attempt to analyze the events in Slovenia on their
own terms, Ravnikar focuses on analyzing the role of the political and economic elite in the transition process. In this manner he touches on a topic that
has been greatly debated, namely, the fact that the overwhelming majority of
Slovenia's elite has maintained its positions of power (Iglič and Rus). For some
this in itself is the cause of continuity—that is, that these elites exercise the
necessary power to maintain themselves in place from certain positions within
a structure. Yet Ravnikar points to another level of complicities in which the
continuity of these elites in positions is the effect of a continuity of the parallel
structure of power. The power of these elites does not stem from their formal
position, but instead from their position in an informal, unseen structure. The
colonization of Slovenia is maintained by networks of parasitic elites, forestall-
ing the possibility of autonomous political and economic development. Thus
Ravnikar defines a set of criteria that does not map onto the political definitions
of Right and Left upon which discourses of political continuity and disconti-
nuity are based.

BAJUK: Who recognizes this continuity and who does not?

RAVNIKAR: Those in the business sphere all know this. Those who are in
the state administration don't, but many have come to me privately to tell me
that they agree with me. It is unbelievable how highly placed in Drnovšek's
administration were the people who came to shake my hand and tell me that
they agreed with me. Only that I wasn't supposed to say anything! *[Laugh]*
This is that continuity among Slovenes, the Slovenian tragedy. Maybe another
anthropological problem. Slovenes are left-wing, because they were oppressed throughout their history. Slovenia did not have its own feudal lords.
From Charlemagne onward, we had Germans. Slovenia was part of the kingdom of Charlemagne. Croatia was not. From within the kingdom, Slovenes
fell under the feudal lords of Bavaria. Slovenia has not had its own aristocracy
since the twelfth century. Then they did not have their own bourgeoisie because it was Austrian, and then under Yugoslavia it was Belgrade's.

There is no interest. A French capitalist, for example, would have an interest in resisting the American influence. The Italians as well. We don't have
this sort of self-interest. A Slovene does not know how to depend on oneself,

does not understand that it is in his own self-interest to fight against Genex. He doesn't see the difference because things haven't changed. Genex shaved 20 percent off the top before and continues to do so now. He isn't doing much worse in the transition, and doesn't want to hear about this. You see the irony of all this? *[Laugh]*

This is a tragedy. On the one hand you have an independent state that came to being because something else fell apart. They had some lawyers who knew how to write a constitution; law and medicine have been traditionally strong in Slovenia. Slovenia has had them for three hundred years. Yet on the other hand, there are no businessmen in Slovenia. That someone would develop a company like Siemens or Westinghouse. Westinghouse was developed by the person who invented the vacuum brakes for trains. That has now become Westinghouse. Siemens has a similar story. This does not exist in Slovenia. We did, however, have some companies after the war whose development was based on Slovene brains such as Sava, Tam, the shoe industry. These all developed from small companies, even Elan, but they soon fell into the Yugoslav operation, that foreign trade network, and never got out. And now they don't see why they should make any fuss about it. "We always sold our goods to that strange company in Klagenfurt and we still do today, what is wrong with that? Nothing has gone wrong! He has everything, we sell everything, why should we worry?" I respond that if we had those 20 percent we would have economic growth and we wouldn't have unemployment. Now we don't have [those 20 percent].

Nothing, no conspiracy. A Spomenka always lived off—this is true, I call them parasites, a parasite of the parasite.[10] It is important to know that I do not hold them in any esteem. I have contempt for them. They help the regime live off the workers. Because Slovenian workers—Mencinger and those others argue that wages are too high.[11] Gross wages are high, not net wages. Net wages are miserable. All the parasitic operations live off what is taken out of gross wages. It is then obvious that someone comes from the United States and tells us that our wages are too high. What the American does not say is to force down the gross wage and to leave the workers alone. *[Laugh]* That would be interfering in local affairs. The gross wage includes smuggling, the cost of filling in holes like the one in TCB, old debts that we don't need to pay, the foreign debt because Genex has bought part of it on the secondary market.

BAJUK: Yes, I heard about that.

RAVNIKAR: All this comes out of the workers' gross wages. The parasites of this parasitic system are the intellectuals. What is the job of Spomenka's husband, Tine Hribar? He is a philosopher, he translates Heidegger. Heidegger isn't modern any more. No one has ever translated Popper; I think the best of Popper. No one has ever translated these modern philosophical movements into Slovene: Feyerabend, Kuhn, those Americans. Mr. Hribar translates

Heidegger; these big fat books, and he lives off them for ten years. He receives funds from the cultural budget, meaning that the gross wage of the
worker allows Mr. Hribar to translate slowly, extensively, and very expen-
sively. He travels to Germany to conduct research and every year or two a
new book is produced, which he then pompously presents. He receives a huge
amount of money, only that I call this being a parasite of the parasite. If I were
in power the first thing I would do is take that money away from Mr. Hribar
and give it back to the workers so that they would have enough money for
potatoes. *[Laugh]* Because people are hungry. Why would I give the workers
money for potatoes? So that they could have some children since the birth rate
is dropping; so that they would feel like working and not simply work around
the system; so that the wives would be more content; and so that they would
raise their children instead of beat them—all this. So you have to take this
away from Mr. Hribar and return it to some poor worker somewhere in Carni-
ola. But Mr. Hribar will not allow this. That is why his wife writes books
against Janša.[12]

In employing what ironically seems a Marxist critique against the former
system's avant-garde, Ravnikar engages in a condemnation of intellectuals,
whose significant roles in Slovenia's independence are also being recoded as
duplicitous as the transition is being continually reevaluated.

On 10 November 1996 Slovenia held its third parliamentary elections.
Ravnikar, along with other members of Civilna Iniciativa, decided to form a
political party that later formed a coalition with a right-wing party, SLS (Slovenska Ljudska Stranka, the Slovenian People's Party). I interviewed him approximately two weeks after the elections, and the situation was still quite
tense. SLS had come in second, behind LDS, but the right-wing coalition of
three parties SLS-SDS-SKD had received exactly half of the seats in the national assembly: 45 out of 90.[13] The election resulted in a draw. When I came
to interview Ravnikar, he gave me a copy of Civilna Iniciativa's election program, and the interview inevitably led to a discussion about the present political situation. I know through his writings that Ravnikar did not evaluate all
parties equally. He had been very critical of the role of the Christian Democrats
in the first government as well as of their decision to enter into a coalition
government with the former communist parties in 1992, which, in the eyes of
many, accorded these parties at least a formal political continuity. I was, however, interested in his reasons for entering explicitly into the political arena
with SLS.

RAVNIKAR: SLS, as you know, began as the Farmer's Association. Farmers
were a breed apart in Yugoslavia as well. They were those that received very
little support, virtually no social support, they received nothing. They sent

their children to bad schools, but at least they had land. If nothing else they
had land that they could farm so that they would have something to eat. The
farmers joined together and formed a political party. The regime looked upon
them as stupid farmers that would not be interested in such business operations. They were not interested in farmers, they never had been. And as such
the regime did not send its agents into SLS as it did with other parties. On the
other hand, the Christian Democrats were traditionally important because the
Church was always important in Slovenia. This is also very important. The
Christians, we always called them the clericalists, this was the Church. They
always knew how to collaborate. When the regime would distribute benefits
in Yugoslavia, first it would distribute them among its own—the communists—and then to the Church. They looked upon this pragmatically: we are
the strongest, but right behind us are the other ones. They are our opponents,
but you have to keep them in check. And when we, dissidents, came on the
scene, at first the regime paid us no attention, and then they marginalized us.
Those who were the most critical of the regime were the Christian Democrats.
But the regime founded the Christian Democratic Party. When new parties
were being formed, everyone knew that there would be one important Christian Democratic Party. Everyone knew that it wouldn't work without them.
The regime also trained them, even before, in a state or administrative organization. The most important person in an organization was always a Party
member, then someone who went to church. The Party member was first, the
other was second because he was hard-working and loyal—the regime was
able to form an administrative structure in the times of Yugoslavia from the
present Christian Democrats. And as such SKD doesn't have anyone who
didn't have some sort of position in the previous regime.

    In attempting to rationalize SKD's political collaboration with the former
communists, Ravnikar draws a history of complicity and collaboration of the
Christian Democrats, of clericalists, that does not allow for any ambiguities or
duplicities, a narrative that he weaves from the time between the wars. However, such a history does not recognize the overlaps between farmers and clericalists that do not map neatly onto the political distinctions between these two
right-wing parties in the present.
    Ravnikar's deconstruction of the political dichotomy between Right and Left
is one of the major reasons why I would regard Hofstadter's notion of a renegade as too simplistic for this case. The critique which allows him to provide
an alternative vision is based on breaking down the very terms that would allow
him to "switch sides."

    BAJUK: As you know, I am analyzing how interpretations such as yours
are being publicly evaluated. On the Right, such books are read and are the

basis for condemning the previous regime, communism, but in a wholesale fashion. The kind of distinctions and ambiguities that you have been describing and writing about get lost. The red-black distinction that you argue is artificially maintained.[14] These kinds of wholesale readings of your work actually strengthens this distinction instead of question it.

RAVNIKAR: The Left-Right distinction, this is that "cover-up." They quarrel terribly on an ideological level: who killed the *domobranci,* who was on which side, communism is dreadfully dark—dreadfully ugly, not dark, because it is red![15] *[Laugh]* But this is exaggerating the ideological conflict, because there is none. This is also interesting: this ideological conflict was artificially maintained. With my father I used sometimes to watch the preparations for the Party congress which were held every four years. Three months before the congress they would "work up steam" for this ideological conflict. One month before the congress they were terribly ideological, but right after the congress they all worked together again and there were no—that artificial ideological conflict is not the same today. When I see these ideological leanings in politics today, something begins to smell. I smell a smoke screen, that something is being covered up with these ideological differences.

At one point in his book Ravnikar described his term *udbomafija* as being a term that one could employ to sort out duplicity, to categorize people who otherwise seemed politically ambiguous. One need only observe the reactions to this term to recognize "who is who." It is here that I would point out that any argument can shift from being critical to being conspiratorial: when it cannot recognize anything outside itself as valid or true, when its discourse is totalizingly coherent so as to preclude any ambiguity or deviation.

On the other hand, I must add that Ravnikar's aim, far from conspiratorial, seems to entail bringing about a political consensus necessary to decide upon measures that would engender change. In this context, Ravnikar's notion of *de facto* independence entails Slovenes attaining a degree of self-determination through elections that would grant Slovenes the political power that could allow for the implementation of technical reforms according to a set of agreed-upon aims. According to Ravnikar, this is the sort of change that needs to come about from inside Slovenia, and not according to certain universal technical guidelines.

RAVNIKAR: I am also vigorously fighting against the idea of anyone coming from America and being placed in a key position in Podobnik's government. It would be wonderful if he would come as an expert in any capacity, but not to take charge of an executive position. The other side thinks that they can do anything with someone from the outside. They are sure of this. And if you begin a bank rehabilitation by American standards in Slovenia—why shouldn't Voljč be director of Ljubljanska Banka?[16] Why? Because he signs anything they put in front of him. Not because he is ugly *[Laugh]* or anything else, but because he clearly knows that he is occupying this position so that someone else is holding the reins of power. He will remain in this position only so long as he keeps signing. If he does he will remain in position in Zurich, in Frankfurt, in all the branches with Serbian majority ownership. He is basically an employee for the Serbs, not for us.

If he wanted to work for us, he would have to take money away from the banks and invest it in companies. This is government money, budget funds, and the government decides whether it allots funds for the banks or for the companies. Drnovšek's government decided that it will give money to the banks. Why? Because there they have the power of decision making. In companies, they have no such power. That is why they do not care much about companies, but when a company is going under, they will lend it money from the banks. But the company has to come and ask for the money, and in the bank they will have their own people who will determine the conditions under which the loan is given to the company. They don't plan to destroy the companies, but simply make them dependent on the banks. Maybe some assets stripping—but in the end they will let them keep exporting. If they put all the government funds into banks, they make the banks dependent on the government, and they do whatever they are told. If they put money in companies, then the companies would become independent. When companies are independent, there is no more political interference in companies. At that moment a Western form of economic system will be attained. We would have capitalism.

But this talk of capitalism—because formally speaking they have a stock exchange and some stocks and bonds and joint-stock companies and they manage business by investing money into banks—this is real socialism, nothing else. This is simply real socialism and this means that companies will never develop themselves because each will work first and foremost to put money in his own pocket; the money is then piled up somewhere across the border. He has branches in Zurich and Prague.

If someone else would come from the outside and would realize that the other ones are right, that they are doing okay, then that will be catastrophic. It would be wonderful if everyone would come help with the technical rehabilitation of the banks. But not to take an executive function, for God's sake. Because you will need someone at the executive level that will wipe out the upper-level officials of Ljubljanska Banka—fire them, if need be. This won't be someone who came from America who doesn't know how things are done here. This has to be a local ruffian who will take care of things. A scoundrel. And we need an outsider who will come and help do the fine-tuning on this bank. A political decision has to be made that half the money goes from the banks to the companies. This will strike at so many interests that the easiest path by far will be to leave things as they are and ask, "So what is so wrong with all this? It doesn't matter if you have a company in Trieste. There is nothing wrong with that." It does matter!

In late January 1997, after approximately two and a half months, Slovenia finally formed a new government without having to resort to new elections. SLS, the right-wing party with which Ravnikar's party was in coalition, joined with left-wing LDS. Yet far from decrying this as another collaboration in line with the historical Right-Left coalitions in his narratives, Ravnikar instead became the personal advisor to SLS leader Marjan Podobnik, who is now the vice president of the Slovenian government.

Notes

1. I would like to thank Edo Ravnikar for his generosity in granting me an interview for this project. The interview was conducted in Slovene; all translations, unless otherwise noted, are mine. I would also like to thank Laura Helper for her comments on a previous draft of this piece. Finally, I would like to acknowledge the support of the National Science Foundation that made it feasible for me to conduct my doctoral fieldwork in Slovenia.

2. "All the years after the war investment funds were deliberately 'exiled' in accord with the policies coordinated in Belgrade. Djilas wrote about this as early as 1955, and few people now know that it was because of this very revelation that the regime held such a grudge with Djilas" (Ravnikar 1995, 45).

3. Edvard Kardelj was one of the leading figures of the Communist Party of Slovenia, known primarily as the main person behind the 1974 constitution which introduced the decentered system of self-management.

4. Marjan Podobnik is the head of the People's Party of Slovenia, Slovenska Ljudska Stranka, and a member of the national assembly. As leader of a party in the opposition, Podobnik was instrumental in bringing many financial scandals to light during his term as head of an investigative commission of the national assembly.

5. Janez Drnovšek is the present prime minister of Slovenia and the head of the Liberal Democratic Party of Slovenia (LDS).

6. The SDK [Sluzba Družbenega Knjigovodstva] is the office of social accounting responsible for conducting audits of all socially owned companies until they are finally privatized. Tam was one of the major industrial companies in the Maribor region, and special legislation was drafted for its rehabilitation and privatization. However, Tam was ultimately declared bankrupt due to an unsuccessful rehabilitation of the company (millions of DEM of state funds were invested, yet to no avail). Maks Tajnikar was the minister of economic affairs at the time that Tam ran into its biggest problems, and resigned amidst charges of corruption.

7. For example, journalist Danilo Slivnik in his work *Kučanov Klan* [Kučan's Clan] addresses the networks of old elites reestablishing themselves, marking them as part of a Slovenian elite led by Milan Kučan, the president of Slovenia (and last president of the Slovenian Communist Party).

8. LDS, or Liberalna Demokracija Slovenije [the Liberal Democratic Party of Slovenia] is the main coalition party in the government led by Janez Drnovšek.

9. Maks Tajnikar is a professor at the Faculty of Economics in Ljubljana and the former minister for economic affairs who resigned due to the scandal that erupted concerning the company Tam.

10. Spomenka Hribar was one of the main dissident intellectuals of the 1980s, playing a central role in the political liberalization of Slovenia. She was the first intellectual to call for a public discussion of the atrocities committed by the Party after the war on its political opponents and called for national reconciliation. She became one of the mediating figures between intellectuals of the Left and the Right until the publication of her essay "Stop the Right," which many interpreted as a betrayal.

11. Jože Mencinger is one of the foremost economists of Slovenia and head of the Economic Institute of the Faculty of Law. He was also Slovenia's first vice president, 1990–91.

12. Janez Janša is head of SDS, Socialdemokratska Stranka Slovenije, or the Social Democratic Party of Slovenia. SDS is one of the parties designated as right-wing to the extent that it is anticommunist and against the political continuity of the former communists.

13. SKD, Slovenska Krscanska Demokracija, or Slovenian Christian Democratic Party.

14. Red = Left = communist; black = clericalist = Right = anticommunist.

15. The *domobranci* were an anticommunist guerrilla group formed by clericalists and farmers whose aim was to defend themselves from the OF—Osvobodilna Fronta, or the Liberation Front, headed by the Communist Party, also known as the partisans. In May 1945, when the Germans surrendered and retreated from Slovenia (Slovenia was occupied since 1941, partly by the Italians, partly by the Germans), a great number of those who opposed communism fled Slovenia and into Austria. This included approximately ten thousand *domobranci*. They were returned unarmed by the British military forces to Yugoslavia, and were then killed and dumped in mass graves across Slovenia. All those killed after the war are still not recognized as legally dead by the Slovene government.

16. Marko Voljč is the present director of Ljubljanska Banka.

References

Hofstadter, Richard. 1965. *The Paranoid Style in American Politics and Other Essays.* New York: Knopf.

Holmes, Doug. 1993. "Illicit Discourse." In *Perilous States: Conversations on Culture, Politics, and Nation.* Ed. George Marcus. Chicago: University of Chicago Press.

Jančar, Drago. 1991. "Memories of Yugoslavia." In *The Case of Slovenia.* Ed. Niko Grafenauer. Ljubljana: Nova Revija.

Ravnikar, Edo. 1995. *Udbomafija: Priročnik za Razumevanje Tranzicije.* [Udbomafija: A Handbook for Understanding the Transition.] Ljubljana: Založba Slon.

Rus, Andrej, and Hajdeja Iglič. Forthcoming. *Dinamika sprememb v. egocentričnih omrežjih slovenskih elit v obdobju 1988–1995* [The Dynamics of Change in Egocentric Networks of Slovenian Elites during the Period 1988–1995].

Slivnik, Danilo. 1996. *Kučanov Klan* [Kučan's Clan]. Ljubljana: Promag.

PARANOID PRESENTS

Robin Wagner-Pacifici

For me, Italy has always been more Heaven than Purgatory, though I have not been immune to its tendency toward *logoramènto* (a wearing out of the nerves). Tragedy, irony, and a generalized sense of aesthetics have characterized the Italy I have known, lived in, and studied, on and off since the late 1970s. This piece operates with a combinatory principle: Italian literature, religion, art, politics, Mafia, and mass media collude to generate an effect at the level of lived allegory. The Andreotti trial and Andreotti himself are situated at the hub of all of these discourses and influences. As to the centrality of the image of Purgatory, Andreotti himself says he may not live long enough to see the end of the trial. In a certain sense, he is just waiting.

As a scholar, it is sometimes perplexing to find oneself drawn to certain themes or ideas that have no obvious connection to what it is that one thinks is one's area of research interest and/or expertise. Purgatory was like this for me. The oblique structure of this piece has allowed me to pull my perplexing obsession with Purgatory into a kind of colloquy with those things that I know I am normally inclined to study: Italian politics, the link between language and violence, and the aesthetic dimensions of political life. I hope the end result has been both revelatory and nearly poetic.

Douglas R. Holmes

The text of my essay, "Tactical Thuggery: National Socialism in the East End of London," is part of a broader project that cuts across Europe starting in the Friuli region of northeast Italy, moving to Strasbourg and Brussels, the two venues of the European Parliament, and finishing on the Isle of Dogs in the East End of London. At the core of the project are 140 interviews that I conducted since the early 1990s with a broad spectrum of political leaders, technocrats, community organizers, and streetfighters. My interlocutors ranged from the former prime minister of Belgium to neo-Nazis in inner London.

A decisive series of events intervened during the course of the research unleashing a discordant set of possibilities. In the aftermath of 1989 and the retreat of the Left from its classic engagement with society, there arose the prospect of an *alternative* configuration of socialism predicated on invidious cultural distinctions and unsettling moral discriminations. I followed the emergence of these peculiar cultural anxieties and aspirations in the last decade of the century and examined their potential to sustain a political imaginary within which a volatile synthesis of nationalism and socialism have taken form.

The conversation that follows contrasts in important ways with my earlier essay "Illicit Discourse," a contribution to Late Editions I. In that piece I examined an emerging discourse on race and culture interleaved in the project of European integration. My interlocutor was Bruno Gollnisch, a Member of the European Parliament representing the French Front National who shrewdly delineated the intellectual foundations of a contemporary radical nationalism. In the following exchange with Richard Edmonds, the issues of racial and cultural pluralism emerge in very different form. Mr. Edmonds's politics coalesce at street level. He sees the East End of London as a site where the contours of a multiracial and multicultural Europe are contested; where cultural discourse becomes social drama. He discriminates acutely the geographies of inclusion and exclusion. He is inspired to confront physically those who embody the contradictions of *his* Britain; those who transgress its racial hygiene, its moral economy. He is an organic intellectual, with a taste for streetfighting, whose vision skirts the paranoid and the delusional. His vexed actions splice the political and the criminal.

Kim Fortun

To claim that my research has focused on the Bhopal disaster is somewhat paradoxical. The Bhopal disaster involves so many issues and provokes so many different kinds of questions that it may be more accurate to claim that it has oriented my gaze and tuned my ears in ways which confound concentration. Rather than resist the distraction, I've tried to keep up with it—allowing the Bhopal disaster to operate like a vortex which draws many opposing currents into its powerful critique of established ways of ordering the world. Thus I have become interested in Gulf War Illness, the subject of the interview here with the pseudonymous Peck. Links to the issues and questions of Bhopal are multiple. Like the Bhopal disaster, Gulf War Illness is an effect of technological interventions intended to protect human welfare; the technologies relied on far exceeded their promise—exploding into threats which designers failed to anticipate or guard sufficiently against. In Bhopal, a pesticide plant was established to serve the promise of Green Revolution agriculture; in the Gulf War, drugs now considered a potential source of malady were administered to protect soldiers from chemical and biological weapons. In both cases, the straight shot between technological intervention and prosperity was tragically detoured, obliging us to reconsider entrenched visions of a world made better simply by injecting it with technoscientific solutions.

Another link between the Bhopal disaster and Gulf War Illness is related to loyalty, trust, and doubt about the validity of established configurations of nationalism. In both cases, there is an external enemy: Union Carbide and Saddam Hussein are key points of reference in how blame is imagined. More striking, however, is how the Bhopal disaster and Gulf War Illness have invoked accusations of governmental disloyalty and even collusion with the enemy. In Bhopal, victims argue that the Indian government has covered up indicators of continuing morbidity to legitimate a legal settlement of the case which ensures that foreign investors continue to feel "at home" in India. In the wake of the Gulf War, veterans have accused the Pentagon of covering up indications of exposure to chemical and biological agents, then "writing off" indications that veterans may be sick, even if a definitive cause cannot be located. The effect of these accusations is profoundly unsettling; the role of trust and loyalty in the organization of personal identities as well as nation-states seems to be shifting. At least in some cases, patriotism is giving way to conspiracy theory and established ways of knowing ourselves and our world are rendered obsolete.

If one reads the interview with Peck with the Bhopal disaster as a backdrop, Gulf War Illness is located within a terrain which foregrounds the inadequacy of established ways of ordering the world. Like the hot spots on a polluted piece of property, where the accumulation of toxins is high enough to provoke recategorization of the entire site, the terrain of Gulf War Illness can serve as an index of contamination which demands reconceptualization of an entire system of knowledge and politics. Like the Bhopal disaster, Gulf War Illness is difficult to locate via origin, end, or territorial boundary. The social processes and cultural logics from which these disasters originated can be traced to too many point sources to count; no end is in site, as victims struggle to rehabilitate both their bodies and the institutions on which they depend for resources, while not knowing exactly what they need; national boundaries no longer delineate shared interests or justify adequate plans of action. The challenge is to recognize that subjects of toxic exposure are confronted with problems which profoundly unsettle how and what we know. Conspiracy theories and other ways of noting "unseemly concurrences" once would have been written off as paranoia; now they operate as locational devices, signaling social, cultural, and conceptual shifts which established technologies of knowing cannot register.

James D. Faubion

During the month of February 1993 I was busy preparing a lecture on early Christian millennialism for the Humanities Program at Reed College, Portland,

Oregon. Two days before I was scheduled to present the lecture, violence erupted at the Branch Davidian compound known as New Mount Carmel, several thousand miles away. Unsettled, or seduced, by the coincidence, I paid somewhat more than passing attention to the events that ensued. In April I unexpectedly found myself invited to take a position in the Department of Anthropology at Rice University. In August I moved to Houston, but did not work up the nerve to travel to Waco until the following spring. Upon arriving at New Mount Carmel, some ten miles distant from Waco's center, another round of surprises: a tangle of scorched metal and broken concrete decaying under a bright prairie sun, a brigade of bulldozers, and a revolving sentry of security guards, all enclosed within a chain-link and barbed-wire fence; on a nearby bluff, a makeshift building housing the new offices of the Branch Davidian Seventh-Day Adventist Church (or to be more precise, of one of its surviving factions), a scattered display of religious pamphlets and gruesome souvenirs of catastrophe, and a gregarious woman, Amo Paul Bishop Roden, whose life, whose calling, and whose voluminous writings have preoccupied me ever since. Call it "research."

Scott A. Lukas

The burning theme park, the ride out of control, the failure of entire computer or operational systems like plumbing and electricity, as commonly happens in the Theme Park, all suggest a metamorphosis of both the potentiality of the environment of fear and the ability of its creators to control its energy. The helpless amusement worker and patron are possessed; their fears and repressed thoughts are recycled in what is less a democratization of their trembling than a complete reversal of the pleasure economy they had helped to create. The Theme Park is now in ruins, both in writing and embodiment.

As a child I had been fascinated by the nature of theme parks—their combinations of speed, velocity, angular momentum, fantastic geography, and odd juxtapositions. My Ph.D. studies took me through a number of theoretical and ethnographic venues, from Berlin city planning to industrial performance art and back to U.S. consumerism and "American spaces." While in graduate school I had the opportunity to work in a major U.S. theme park for two years, partially for the purpose of making summer money, mostly out of curiosity. As a trainer in the park I had the fortune to observe interactions, incidents, and crises which left permanent marks in my memory; it was an experience that was both enlightening and frustrating. After taking that position I began to read all sorts of sources on theme parks and the history of popular amusements, from the accounts of Coney Island, to the histories of various Ohio and Pennsylvania theme parks, as well as the numerous discussions of Disney parks.

Some issues began to congeal for me: architecture, use of space, the narrative qualities of rides and attractions, as well as the psychophysical experiences of patrons and workers. I also explored popular accounts of the theme park industry, looking at sources from the archives of ride and attractions manufacturers, and groups dedicated to the theme park business and experience, like ACE (American Coaster Enthusiasts). At some point I decided for myself that there was much lacking in the popular and academic accounts of the theme park industry, and I also realized that the theme park, as an object of ethnographic inquiry, would become an important site of personal recollection: I saw the theme park as intersecting with various trajectories in my life, and I eventually took this enthusiasm to the writing of my dissertation, an ethnography of the U.S. theme park industry. In the course of my research on theme parks I taught a course on American spaces. Students in the course had the opportunity to create popular "sacrificial"/excess spaces as a way of personally and theoretically reflecting on the spaces significant to their own lives. What emerged was an interesting collection of "antimalls," absurdist theme parks, high-tech convenience stores, and alternative national parks. An interesting outcome of the exercise was the fact that so many of these spaces relied on a generalized ethos of fear as a problem; one student discussed the contemporary shopping mall and gangs, and on various forms of surveillance, from cameras to computer chips, as a "solution." This class ultimately flowed into a follow-up course the next semester: "Risk, Fear, Surveillance," which dealt with the ubiquity of fear and paranoia in American society and suggested technologies of their measurement and "control."

THE JUDAS KISS OF GIULIO ANDREOTTI:
ITALY IN PURGATORIO

*"Italia mia, benche 'l parlar sia
    indarno
a le piaghe mortali
che nel bel corpo tuo si spesse veggio,
piacemi almen che miei sospir' sian
quali'spera 'l Tevero et l'Arno,
e 'l Po, dove doglioso e grave or
    seggio.
Rettor del cielo, io cheggio
che la pieta che Ti condusse in terra
Ti volga al Tuo dilecto almo paese."*

—*(Francesco Petrarch,
    "Canzone XVI", 1345)*

"O my own Italy! though words are
    vain
The mortal wounds to close,
Unnumber'd that thy beauteous bosom
    stain,
Yet may it soothe my pain
To sigh forth Tyber's woes,
And Arno's wrongs, as on Po's sadden'd
    shore
Sorrowing I wander, and my numbers
    pour.
Ruler of heaven! By the all-pitying love
That could thy Godhead move
To dwell a lowly sojourner on earth
Turn Lord! on this thy chosen land
    thine eye."

—(Petrarca 1983, 124)

*"Ahi serva Italia, di dolore ostello,
nave senza nocchiere in gran tempesta
non donna di provincie, ma bordello!
... E se licito me'e, o sommo Giove
che fosti in terra per noi crucifisso,
son li giusti occhi tuoi rivolti altrove?
O e preparazion che nell'abisso
del tuo consiglio fai per alcun bene
in tutto dell'accorger nostro scisso?*

*Che le citta d'Italia tutte piene
son di tiranni . . ."*

—*(Dante Alighieri,* Purgatorio,
    Canto VI, 1319)

"Ah, slavish Italy, the home of grief,
ship without a pilot caught in a raging
    storm,
no queen of provinces—whorehouse of
    shame! . . .
"O Jove Supreme, crucified here on
    earth
for all mankind, have I the right to ask
if Your just eyes no longer look on us?
Or is this part of a great plan conceived
in Your deep intellect, to some good end
that we are powerless to understand?

For all the towns of Italy are filled
with tyrants."

—(Alighieri 1981, 59–60)

Prologue

How else to approach conspiracy in Italy than by way of symbolism and allegory? Only by sifting through the blood-drenched layers of this palimpsest of
a country can you feel the corruption, the intrigue, the crooked smile, the
knowing shrug of the shoulders. Somehow, body parts always enter the scene
of politics and crime in Italy. Hands gesture in exorcism, making the sign of
the horns *[cornuto]*. Italians recall a famous photograph of former President
Giovanni Leone, forced to resign in a bribery scandal, making the sign of the
horns behind a lectern while giving a speech. Hands can also purify—the recent judiciary campaign against corruption is called "Clean Hands," *[Mani
Pulite]*. And eyes—for every Petrarchean or Dantesque imprecation to God to
turn his beneficent eyes on Italy, there is an analogous underworld curse of the
evil eye *[malocchio]*. Mouths kiss in Mafia codes of recognition and betrayal.
Knees are shot at by terrorists aiming at literal and figurative crippling. If you
follow the trail of hands, eyes, mouths, and the knees, the body politic of contemporary Italy begins to take shape.

Purgatory

During the second week of April 1996 a half-hour television program called (after Petrarch's lamenting sonnet, I would discover later), *"Italia mia benche . . ."*
kept me riveted to the screen. The show aired daily during the week and
mirrored, though only faintly, the Phil Donahue talk show. On from 1:00–
1:30 p.m., on the culturally highbrow state-run RAI Tre channel, it featured
the bookish and peripatetic host Giordano Bruno Guerri. Guerri, a young man
in his midthirties, fielded questions on the topic of the day which he addressed
to the in-studio experts while pacing back and forth on a video-screen paved
runway. The experts were invariably academics, politicians, and priests. Guerri
also took questions from people calling in from all over Italy and, occasionally, from the small studio audience which rotated on a moving platform. Each
day presented a new topic, among which were "The Neutrality of Science,"
"People Who Practice Religion but Are Not Believers," "The Relationship
between Religion and Science," and "Italian Solidarity and the Family." Thus
the show typically selected topics that drew out institutional worldviews and
conflicts between doctrine and practice across a wide array of social relations.
On the day I was so riveted, the designated topic was Purgatory.

Among the many shows I watched, it was the show on Purgatory that most
captured the imaginations of Guerri, his expert guests, the studio audience,
people calling in from Sicily to Milan, and me. The designated experts on that
day included a priest, a historian, and a literary critic. The conversation oscil-
lated back and forth between statements of faith and expressions of skepticism,
between literal descriptions of Purgatory—what it looked like, what one had
to do to shorten one's stay—and historical deconstructions of its timely "emer-

gence" in 1254 when the Catholic Church struggled to devise new ways of raising funds and tying the future-dead to the Church.

The show hung between faith and skepticism, between literalness and allegory—and nobody seemed to mind the cohabitation. The slide from realism to metaphor was seamless. Poignant descriptions of Purgatory abounded. Dante's striated mountain was described, with its layers that corresponded to specific sins and its long and sometimes lugubrious march up and around its sides. And then there were the punishments ranging from the overly proud forced to wear giant stones around their necks and the overly envious sentenced to suffer their eyes being sewn shut for thousands of years. Others on the show compared Purgatory to a giant waiting room where, as in a rain-streaked train station, individuals wait alone even as they are surrounded by thousands of others. Information about the who, the why, and the how long of Purgatory revealed that everyone who was not damned to the everlasting Inferno, everyone who might eventually be saved, except the Virgin Mary, must go first to Purgatory, even the saints. For even the saints have, in the words of the show's priest, *"i piccoli peccati"* [little sins]. And then, in some sense the punch line: only the living can redeem the dead from Purgatory and send them to heaven. The shades must be helped by relatives and friends still alive to shorten the glacially long sentences. Dependency continues; we all must wait, even after death. The talk was vivid and passionate, the long years of waiting assessed by audience and experts alike. I had never encountered anything like this in the United States. I had never given a thought to Purgatory. I awoke now to its power.

As I listened to the talk of the seeming endlessness of waiting, the bus-station boredom and fatigue, the terror of endurance commingled with the hope of salvation, or at least change, I began to think about Italy as a kind of late twentieth-century Purgatory. An entire populace waits. At the level of the everyday, the banal, it waits for trains and buses to run again after improvised strikes, for bureaucratic clearance to install a computer in an office, for a book to be located in the underground archives of the library, for a sofa to be delivered. At the national level, it waits for a change, for release, from the nightmare of corruption scandals (secret Masonic lodges networking the powerful; subterranean paramilitary organizations alert to possible Soviet invasions of Western Europe; politicians simply on the take) and violent episodes (terrorists of Left and Right; Mafia assassinations of investigating magistrates). It goes way beyond the wish for a governmental *alternanza* [right and left alternation]. It seemed to signify both a wish for redemption and, simultaneously, the knowledge of an *almost* eternal and punishing deferral. And this is where Giulio Andreotti comes in.

Testimony of Mafia witness, Gaspare Mutolo, 30 May 1996: "I didn't immediately speak [to the prosecutors] about the relationship between the Mafia and politics, because Andreotti was still in a position to send all of us collaborators to Hell. If he wanted to, he could have changed the law and create difficulties for us . . . when I spoke about the Mafiosi, nothing happened, when I began to speak about the [corrupt] judges and politicians—that's when my troubles began." [1]

"And my religion is of great comfort. Everything considered, I have been very fortunate in life—I've experienced glory and red carpets—and I think that in order to merit the next life one must undergo a severe trial. I would rather have had a trial of a different nature. But I believe in the justice of the afterlife and not just on earth, and that gives me a lot of serenity." (Giulio Andreotti, in Stille 1995b, 70)

"The particular form of judgment that allows for the existence of a Purgatory is quite a novel one. In fact two judgments are involved: one at the time of death and a second at the end of time. In between—in the eschatological interlude—every human soul becomes involved in complex judicial proceedings concerning the possible mitigation of penalties, the possible commutation of sentences, subject to the influence of a variety of factors. Belief in Purgatory therefore requires the projection into the afterlife of a highly sophisticated legal and penal system." (Le Goff 1981, 5)

April 1996: "La politica e' l' attivita religiosa piu alta dopo l'intimo communione con Dio" [Politics is the highest religious activity after the intimate communion with God].[2]

June 1996: Italy comes in 34th (behind, among others, Turkey, Greece, South Korea and Chile) on the list published by "Transparency International" and the University of Gottingen ranking countries according to levels of honesty.[3]

Kisses and Handshakes

> It was grisly, the way the betrayer made himself irresistible, wreathed and coquetted with his crooked shoulder, languished with puffy eyes, and showed his splintered teeth in a sickly smile. And alas, at his beguiling words, what was come of our Mario. . . . "Sylvestra!" he breathed, from the very depths of his vanquished heart. "Kiss me!" said the hunchback. "Trust me, I love thee. Kiss me here." And with the tip of his index finger, hand, arm, and little finger outspread, he pointed to his cheek, near his mouth. And Mario bent and kissed him. . . . That was a monstrous moment, grotesque and thrilling, the moment of Mario's bliss." (Mann 1963, 179–80)

The year 1992 marked a watershed in the relations between the Italian state and the Mafia. In January the Supreme Court upheld the convictions of over three hundred Mafiosi. Later that year, the fury of the Mafia was unleashed in the killings of the two leading Mafia prosecutors, Giovanni Falcone and Paolo Borsellino, and in the killings of Salvatore Lima (a powerful Sicilian Christian Democrat and friend of Giulio Andreotti) and Ignazio Salvo, a Sicilian Mafia businessman.

The criminal convictions and the retaliatory Mafia killings occurred in the national context of the first round of judicial investigations of bribery among the established political power elite, with the entire political map of Italy shifting in unpredictable ways. The heightened public awareness of widespread corruption was fueled by an aggressive investigatory campaign on the part of a newly independent and activist judiciary (this judicial campaign, led by Milanese judge Antonio di Pietro, is known as the campaign for "clean hands"). That such corruption was present was no surprise for Italians used to writing in their "special candidates" on their electoral ballots; those candidates, that is, who would secure their patronage jobs.[4] That the corruption was as ubiquitous and ramified as it has been revealed to be was a surprise to even the cynical Italian public. Many of the most powerful and long-lasting politicians would lose their jobs, their parties, their freedom and, in a wave of suicides, their lives as the corruption trials began.

Thus, these latest and most vicious Mafia killings faced a radically new legislative and judicial scene. In fact, due to a newly established witness-protection program, prosecutors in Italy were beginning to receive circumstantial reports from Mafia sources (*pentiti,* or "repentant ones") about the involvement of a high-level Italian politician, namely Andreotti, in the Mafia. The most indicting claim, at the level of symbolism at least, was that in 1987 a certain kiss had been exchanged between two powerful Italian men. The men were Giulio Andreotti, a dominant figure in postwar Italian politics, several-time prime minister among other governmental posts, and a fixed power in the Christian Democrat party, and Salvatore (Toto) Riina, the *"capo di tutti i capi"* [boss of all the bosses] of the violent and powerful Sicilian Cosa Nostra. The kiss, alleged by several Mafia informants to have occurred in the Palermo apartment of a certain intermediary, the doomed Ignazio Salvo, in 1987, was to become the symbolic centerpiece of the state prosecutor's corruption case against Andreotti—the smoking gun, as it were.

Of course, a kiss is just a kiss—but it pointed to an intertwining of legitimate government (however disorganized and revolving) and organized crime in postwar Italy, with Andreotti implicated between the two. On 13 May 1993 the Italian Senate gave the Palermo magistrates the authority to proceed with the criminal trial of Andreotti, and the first of several trials against him began in Palermo on 26 September 1995 with prosecutors indicting him for thirty-six episodes of collusion with the Mafia. While Andreotti is currently (as of fall 1997) on trial in Palermo, Rome, and Perugia for such crimes as doing favors for the Cosa Nostra, accepting illegal campaign contributions from corrupt bankers, and even ordering the assassination of the scandal-sheet journalist Mino Pecorelli in 1979 (around the time that Pecorelli was preparing a cover story "All the President's Checks" about this illegal campaign financing), it was the kiss itself that originally drew my analytical interest.

When the pinnacle of legitimate government and the pinnacle of illegitimate crime meet together and, in a ceremony of recognition, deference, and honor, kiss, something important and complicated is going on. The kiss involved a breaching of boundaries that, while physical, were clearly not *just* physical. This boundary crossing seems to have startled even the jaded Italian public itself, habituated as it is to political corruption and Mafia violence. The kiss struck the Italian public as a symbol of a qualitatively different level of betrayal and all of Italy speculated about whether, indeed, it had happened.

Why was this kiss so remarked upon in Italy, a country in which men kiss each other in greeting all the time? Certainly, such domestic kisses are much more the norm in European countries as Italy and France than they are in the United States. But that kiss alleged to have transpired between Andreotti and Riina stood out from the normal run of kisses for two reasons. First, it was a kiss that was understood to have constituted both a greeting and a ceremony. It was a kiss that referred to Italian culture generally, to Italian postwar political culture (dominated as it had been by the Christian Democrats, of which Andreotti had been so long a leading figure) and to the symbol-rich Mafia culture where, as Diego Gambetta (1991) notes, reputation is everything. Thus the ceremonial referent would be one of recognition—Andreotti recognizing Riina as much as Riina recognizing Andreotti. The Christian Democrats recognizing the Mafia and the Mafia recognizing the Christian Democrats. And while for so many years Italians were resigned to living with the reality of the Mafia, they had also been, for so long, in a general state of denial about it. This kiss seemed to have signalled an end to that denial.[5] The Italian public immediately began to speculate about the likelihood that this kiss had occurred. On the one hand, Andreotti had for some time been suspected of corruption and illicit relations with such shadow governments as the notorious P2 Masonic lodge. But no direct links had ever been established. On the other hand, many commentators could not accept the fact that the cold and dour "Count Dracula," as Andreotti was often depicted in cartoons, was capable of kissing anybody (though if one thinks of the kissing symbolism of Count Dracula, it actually makes it seem more, not less, likely). Journalist and author Alexander Stille speculated that Andreotti's coldness could be attributed to the austerity of his youth and wrote that, "His mother squeezed by on a small pension in an unheated apartment, and Andreotti once admitted in an interview that he could not recall her ever having kissed him." Stille then notes the response of Andreotti's personal confessor: "Nonsense!" Father Mario Canciani said in a recent interview. "Andreotti doesn't even kiss his own children" (Stille 1995b, 70). Thus the

Detail from Giotto's Kiss of Judas, in the Scrovegni Chapel, Padua. Reprinted with permission from Nicolas Perella, *The Kiss: Sacred and Profane* (Berkeley: University of California Press, 1969), © 1969 The Regents of the University of California.

righteous maternal, and paternal kisses are withheld and the corrupt, betraying kiss is granted—fearful symmetry indeed. No kisses where they should rightfully be, and kisses where there should be none.

Upon our arrival, the persons who were present, among whom I recognized without a shadow of doubt, the Honorable Giulio Andreotti, the Honorable Salvo Lima, all rose and greeted each other. In particular, I shook hands with the two deputies and kissed Ignazio Salvo, even as I had already greeted him upon my arrival. Riina, on the other hand, greeted all three people (Andreotti, Lima and Salvo) with a kiss.[6]

As if there were not symbolism enough, one of the corruption trials of Andreotti (now ongoing) was temporarily moved in December 1995 from Palermo, Sicily, to Padova, in the north. Padova is the home of the remarkable Arena Chapel where Giotto painted his famous Judas-kiss fresco in 1304. The great Italian painter captured the intense anxiety of this treasonous kiss in his rendering on the chapel wall. Here the Bakhtinian grotesque is in full flower, as Judas and Christ stand eye to eye, mouth to mouth. Judas himself seems to belong to another, more simian, species—as if he had shrunk and deevolved in the process of planting a kiss on Christ's mouth.

During the interim period, as the trial changed locale, Andreotti was invited to the Vatican to meet with Pope John Paul II. Not only did the Pope meet with Andreotti, but he symbolically gestured his support to him. He publicly shook his hand. Thus, as betrayal was committed through a kiss, blessing would be salvaged with a handshake.

There were immediate grumblings about this handshake, but it wasn't until a few days later that an overt critique was launched against the Pope. And, as should be no surprise by now, that critique engaged ritual gestures as well. In the words of the December 13 edition of *La Repubblica* (a national daily newspaper):

> It had never happened before: the Pope protested in Saint Peter's. The motive: the recent handshake with Giulio Andreotti. During a mass for Roman university students, one young man approached the altar and, before reading the text of the oration, turned to the Pope and criticized him for offering solidarity to Andreotti by receiving him in the Vatican and shaking his hand a few days earlier. "Your holiness, why did you shake the hand of Giulio Andreotti?" The young man then went on to refer to Andreotti with the words of Aldo Moro written during Moro's sequestration by the Red Brigades in 1978: "Indifferent, livid, absent, closed off in your dark design of glory. . . . You are missing that combination of good will, of wisdom, of flexibility, of clarity that the few real Christian Democrats in the world have without reserve." [7]

Several levels of betrayal are compressed in this university student's intervention. Most proximately, he accused the Pope of a betrayal of Italian civil society with its values of legality and due process. Andreotti, in his turn, is being accused of having betrayed the sequestered former prime minister of Italy, Aldo Moro. (In 1978, when the Christian Democratic politician was kidnapped and ultimately assassinated by the terrorist group the Red Brigades, Andreotti, along with other key political players, refused to negotiate for Moro's release.) He is also accused here of betraying the fundamental principles of the Christian Democrat Party. That night, a national radio call-in show I listened to overwhelmingly supported this student's critique. Andreotti's attempt to undo the kiss with the handshake had not, it seemed, worked.

Erminia Artese, a freelance journalist working in Rome, wrote to me in October 1995:

> Andreotti represents *the* Italian political power *par excellence* of the period after the Second World War. He has known how to stay afloat across dozens of governments, coalitions, crises, etc. Thus his fall has an *enormous* symbolic value vis-à-vis Italian postwar politics. It is largely due to the work of the courageous judges and prosecutors who uncovered a boiling pot of horrors and corruption, a real devil's pot. This uncovering was initially facilitated by the Lega's protests against

the extraordinary power of the political parties—of course, the Lega as a movement has now exhausted this protest function.

The mafia is not a clandestine criminal activity that is independent of the political power with, however, its occasional connivance. IT WOULD NOT BE ABLE TO SURVIVE if not with the connivance of the political power, or at least with its active tolerance. Napoleone Colajanni senior said this long ago regarding the Notarbartolo trial at the end of the nineteenth century.[8] If Andreotti represents Italian political power *par excellence,* and the mafia cannot survive without this connivance—or tolerance—of the political party, it goes without saying that Andreotti cannot *not* be responsible for the flowering of the mafia, whatever might have been his real or pretextual initiatives against the mafia.

PROCESSO ANDREOTTI
Le curiosita, le battute, le polemiche del processo a Belzebu.
Piccola guida a quarantacinque anni di segreti. . . . .
Partecipa anche tu al Processo Andreotti.
Hai già una idea in merito?
Registra la tua opinione
Colpevole o Innocente?
Innocente 6347
Colpevole 7098
Ultimo aggiornamento 6 Ottobre 1996

ANDREOTTI TRIAL
The curiosities, the witticisms, the polemics of Beezelbub's trial
Quick guide to forty-five years of secrets. . . . .
You too can participate in the Andreotti trial
Do you already have an idea about it?
Register your opinion
Guilty or Innocent?
Innocent 6347
Guilty 7098
Last update October 6, 1996[9]

Chiaroscuro

Between the darkness of Hell and the illumination of Heaven, Purgatory is a study in chiaroscuro in which the light steadily drives out the dark. (Le Goff 1981, 354)

By June 1996 it began to seem as if everyone who was anyone in Italy was standing trial or about to be brought to trial. Entertainers (Pipo Baudo), industrialists (Fininvest executives, including former prime minister Silvio Berlusconi's brother), politicians (Andreotti, Craxi in absentia), Mafia bosses

Giulio Andreotti (center), surrounded by paramilitary police, leaving the court in Palermo, 29 May 1996. AP/ Wide World Photos.

(Riina, Mafia hit man Giovanni Brusca), former Red Brigades members, ex-Nazis (Priebke), and judges (Squillante) all joined the ranks of the accused. The corruption of the past and the ongoing present bore down on the newly exposed body of Italy like a nightmare that couldn't be resolved or forgotten. Like a fine net flung over the country, the trials involved everyone. Even the family of the slain Christian Democratic former prime minister Aldo Moro's family was continuing, some eighteen years after his kidnapping and assassination by the Red Brigades, to make statements to the press about finding those who are "truly responsible." They, like so many Italians, seemed to want to find the magic thread and pull and unravel the whole nasty skein.

The problem with so many judicial defendants is that their individual and collective legitimacy (or innocence) becomes not just problematized, which would be obvious, but more, it becomes something in suspended animation. Thus a whole cadre of significant and powerful people float in and out of focus—now as the arbiters of Italy's political and economic and cultural life, now as coconspirators of mis- and malfeasance at every level.

The Christian Democrats

Whoever was a young child between the years of 1945 and 1948 saw the sudden appearance of a never-before-heard-of race: the Christian Democrats. Even now, after so many years of trying to fix their appearance in my memory, I am not able to remember anything really precise about them. I confuse them for each other. They had soft and somewhat shapeless faces, on which one could hardly distinguish the features: their noses melted into the cheeks, their jaws were never clean, the color of their hair dallied between brown and blondish, their eyes were dull, on their lips, an indecisive smile wandered. They didn't look one in the eyes. They never declared a peremptory truth: their words would lose themselves in a maternal and reassuring whisper that made you daydream and feel sleepy. (Pietro Citati) [10]

In order to define the "strategy of slaughter" *[stragismo],* the concept of the extremism of the center has been recalled, in order to demonstrate the paradox of a state, eternally occupied by a moderate force such as the Christian Democrats, contaminated by similar subversive tendencies. (Lupo 1996, 12)

March 1996: the Telemontecarlo channel's news show presents an interview between Giulio Andreotti and Indro Montanelli. Montanelli is a respected conservative journalist and elder-statesman. For many years he ran his own newspaper, *Il Giornale,* in which he generally supported the Christian Democrats. Now in his late seventies, he is viewed as having transcended party politics and, as further legitimation, he carries the scars of a Red Brigades kneecapping from 1977. The interview covers Andreotti's political career, particularly those parts of it that involved him in the life of the Christian Democrats in Sicily, and returns over and over again to the question of Andreotti's general responsibility for the decades of political corruption.

The interview is shocking for its banality. Two old political warhorses quietly and casually speaking of the necessary compromises, the factional disputes, and the status quo of a series of governments that tolerated the living presence of the Mafia. All Montanelli/Andreotti dialogues quoted below come from this show.[11]

MONTANELLI: When it comes to power, you have had everything.
ANDREOTTI: Certainly.
MONTANELLI: You have had everything. Who could want anything more?
ANDREOTTI: Yes, much more than what I probably deserved.
MONTANELLI: Let's leave that aside, that's very subjective. You've had everything, so if you are called today to answer for everything, it is because you've had everything. . . . I would be proud of that. So why not assume

responsibility for everything once and for all? We're simply seeking a scapegoat here, the scapegoat Andreotti. . . .

ANDREOTTI: Right. Faced with the public opinion, it is necessary to put
these forty, thirty, fifty years on the table—that which was good and that
which wasn't, and create a balance.

Italian Words in Purgatory

Chiaroscuro, "clear and dark."
Pianoforte, "soft and loud."
Bagnoasciuga, "wet and dry."
Dolceamaro, "sweet and bitter."
Altopiano, "high and low."

Exaggeration

MONTANELLI: I don't know how many votes are controlled by the Mafia,
how many they can control, or if all of the Mafia always supports one or another political party. No one has ever been able to explain this point to me.
But the question I am asking you, Senator, because, whether you want it or
not, you are ultimately responsible for the last thirty years of Italian political life. If something could have been done to purge Sicilian politics of the
Mafia—and somewhat in all of Italy—was this something done?

ANDREOTTI: I believe that at least one thing was done very seriously, that is
whether on an internal level, or more importantly on the international level,
there has been a very strong fight against drugs and narco-traffic, and Italy is
at the vanguard of that. . . . What is more . . . when my last government in '89
*noticed a particularly cruel Mafia situation with an exaggerated number of
deaths* [emphasis added], truly, even in relation to all the other moments of
the past, we adopted the emergency measures . . . which certainly, in terms
of *garantismo* [individual freedoms], were questionable—so much so that in
Parliament we had difficulty passing them. . . . But balancing the two things
together, it seemed right to us.

In the past—I don't want to over or undervalue my role in all this—I was
never Commissar. There has always been a government, a structure of state,
so if there were eventual deficiencies, let's each accept a certain part of it. . . .
Even when we spoke two years ago in Milano, if you remember, at the beginning [of the prosecutor's case against Andreotti] when they said that I had
intervened to affect the outcome of trials . . . this is finished. Now [the accusa-
tion of the Palermo trial] is "association." There is no need for facts . . . and
so from this, the famous kiss, because this would be a substitute for a whole
series of things that [the prosecutors] have tried to show . . . they make up
things, really extraordinary things. For example, it now seems as though the

Mafia was such a helpful organization that it wanted to save Moro, whereas I, or the party, or really me personally, who knows why, but we didn't want to save him, and so on. . . .

MONTANELLI: Let's leave Moro out of this.

ANDREOTTI: My fear is that if we continue with these rhythms—in January I'll be seventy-seven years old, and I hope to have a long extension, but it's not as though I can calculate this as if I were only twenty-one.

MONTANELLI: No, certainly not, Senator, and I believe you will have a role to play in time, to see the end of this trial. I surely won't see it.

ANDREOTTI: I hope so.

MONTANELLI: No. I won't see it.

> "Please do not ask me," said our Mantuan guide,
> "to lead you down to where you see those souls,
> until the sinking sun has found its nest; . . .
> "The one who sits the highest and who looks
> as if he left undone what was to do,
> and does not join the others in their song."
>
> —(Dante Alighieri 1981, canto 7)

Double Lives and Betrayals

> It is not unreasonable to conjecture that there was originally no Judas at all; that he entered the story for the first time at the moment of the Arrest, and was expanded backwards. Paul Winter, in his book on the trial of Jesus, ponders the name of "Iscariot." No one has ever been sure what it meant. . . . Winter thinks it derives from an Aramaic word meaning Betrayal; I have no competence to judge this derivation, but you can see why I find it so attractive. A function develops into a proper name; so it becomes a character, whose life and death have a narrative; and then the function is lost in the character. In the first extant account it has already been forgotten that Judas Iscariot was Judas the Betrayer, and, before that, simply Betrayal. (Kermode 1979, 94)

Six June 1996. "Telegiornale" TG1, 1:50 p.m., afternoon news show. There is a short segment regarding Andreotti's trial in Perugia for the murder of the journalist Pecorelli. A reporter at the trial asks Andreotti a question as he enters the courtroom: "From the demonstrations and parades in Rome, celebrating the fifty years of the Italian Republic, you come as a Senator For Life to this courtroom where you are a defendant in this trial. It's almost as if you are split in two."

Andreotti: "No, I'm not split in two. This is just an ugly period that I hope will pass soon."

> As for the politicians of the past, of the period from the end of World
> War II to the beginning of the seventies, it is important to deal with
> the problem of their eventual double loyalty—to the rules of the
> Mafia and to the procedures of democracy. (Arlacchi 1995, 14)

MONTANELLI: So . . . at a certain point in your political life, you became
aware of the Sicilian reality. Let's describe this reality. Directly after the war,
you are perfectly right, there were these forces in action. There was also this
involvement of the Americans through the worst elements possible, Lucky
Luciano and his friends. Good, there were these centrifugal forces, that is
the Sicilian independent movement, and there were the somewhat centrifugal
forces, the autonomists, that had serious *padrini.* One of these *padrini* was the
great Don Sturzo, Loggia, Alessi, etc. . . . You know, because this is historically true, that at a certain moment the Christian Democrats, *had* to make a
choice. And there was an accord with the Mafia immediately after the war.

ANDREOTTI: Right, a relationship [established] that attempted to break this
triangle [Italo-Americans, *banditi,* Mafia]. The Mafia would kill Giuliano so
that *banditismo* would disappear.

MONTANELLI: Yes, I know something of this because—

ANDREOTTI: This is an aspect—

MONTANELLI: —because Don Carloggio Rovizzini, when he told me a
month before that this slightly too lively Sicilian was done for. So I understood that for Giuliano *[laughter]*—

ANDREOTTI: Let us hope that you will not, yourself, now be bothered now
that you have said this, that the prosecutor won't interrogate you.

MONTANELLI: I am ready. I am ready.

ANDREOTTI: I'm kidding. I'm kidding.

> "Thus the heterodox interpretive schema of Norberto Bobbio is jus-
> tified, as when he refers to a power [in Italy] that is divided," no
> longer in a vertical or horizontal manner, according to the classical
> distinctions, but in levels of deepness. That is to say, in power that
> emerges (or that which is public), that which is half submerged (or
> semipublic) and that which is deeply submerged (or occult). (Lupo
> 1996, 29)

Screens: Contiguity, Contamination, and Trials

This section begins with the image of several kinds of screens in Italy. One is
the screen of the confessional box, latticed and filigreed and dark. The penitent,
the sinner, the petitioner leans in close, whispering the intimacies of body and
soul to the receptive and admonishing prelate. Another is that of the video
screen in the courtroom, imaging the disguised faces and altered voices of the

Mafia *pentiti*. A third is the screen of the television, bright and clear, *almost* transparent. In the glow of the television screen the viewer leans back against the sofa of the living room attracted and distracted by the flow of products and celebrities. In the aura of the video screen, the defendant leans forward on the hard chair of the virtual courtroom, trying to decipher the what and the why of the testimony.

Aldo Moro, the kidnapped and assassinated former prime minister of Italy sits forever in the confessional box, leaning toward the screen, absolved with the words he himself crafted from the Red Brigades "People's Prison": "And *even with my many sins* [emphasis added], I believe I have lived with hidden generosity and delicate intentions. I die, if so decides my party, in the fullness of my Christian faith and in the immense love for an exemplary family that I adore and hope to look over from the heavens." [12] Silvio Berlusconi, another former prime minister of Italy, stands forever in his own television studio, smiling, telling stories, warning of communism and, with the soccer slogan of "Forza Italia," selling himself on the bright living room television screens. Giulio Andreotti, another former prime minister of Italy, sits almost motionless in the courtroom, watching the Mafia informants on the video screen give testimony against him, or staring at the hospitallike white screen behind which another quasi-incognito Mafia informant weaves a narrative of favors and gifts and trials undone.

> Palermo—"One of the judges, [in Andreotti's Palermo trial] Vincenzina Massa, has been stricken with a hematic tear in her eye and is at risk of a retinal detachment. She has also recently had a frightening accident in her armored car. Giulio Andreotti's trial, delayed for the fourth time, has been halted since 11 January. It now risks exploding altogether. The misadventures that have struck Vincenzina Massa are not isolated and there are many, in the Palermo Department of Justice, who speak, between smiles and muttered exorcisms, of the curse of the Andreotti trial. [13]

> Rome—Giulio Andreotti is not able to look his accuser in the eyes. The accuser—Gioacchino Pennino, doctor, Mafioso, and Christian Democrat—is seated in the witness chair, sideways and behind a white screen, in the "bunker" courtroom of Rebibbia [a maximum security prison outside of Rome]. Andreotti seems to stare into the empty space before him, muscles of his face under control. Cold as a marble statue, he doesn't miss a word. [14]

> Palermo—The session of the trial opened with the defense attorneys immediately expressing their "concerns" about the "remote" interrogation. Speaking for the team of lawyers, Franco Coppi stated: "We maintain that the person giving evidence should be able to be looked in the eyes and that the video conference, to the contrary, removes the

witness from the physicality of the debate. . . . The direct examination
of the witness is a central moment in the trial.[15]

The district attorney exhibited photographs, which had originally appeared in newspapers, in which the great statesman appears standing
next to Nino Salvo during an election campaign trip to Sicily in 1979.
Some witnesses saw them chatting together amiably during a party
held in a Palermo hotel owned by the financier [Salvo]. Andreotti
responds that in those occasions, many people were standing near
him—and evidently Salvo among others—of whom he didn't know
their names—then or later. (Lupo 1996, 54)

Agrigento—The beast is in the cage. The number one "most wanted"
member of the Cosa Nostra, Giovanni Brusca, thirty-six years old,
was arrested yesterday evening at 9:00 in the suburbs of Agrigento.
He, his brother Vincenzo, their two wives and children, were surprised
by the police while they all watched the television movie about the
assassination of Falcone [which Brusca, himself, had carried out in
reality].[16]

Life and Art

Petrarch laments the woes of the rivers Tiber, Arno, and Po. Umberto Bossi,
leader of the upstart Lega Nord, in his fury against the South, conjures up a
mythical northern Italian land of Padania. Postwar secessionist Sicily threatens
to float off into the Mediterranean Sea. Italy vibrates and shudders with corruption and separatism. And Giulio Andreotti, in some interstice of politics and
art, travels from Palermo to Rome to Perugia to Padova, the ubiquitous defendant of simultaneous trials.

Six August 1995: Giulio Andreotti defends the late thirteenth and early
fourteenth-century figure Pope Boniface VIII (condemned by Dante to one of
the lowest circles of the Inferno) in a public debate: "The debating point was
that classically studied and discussed in high school—if the spiritual power
[of the Pope] should have prevailed over the temporal power [of the nobility]
or if there should have been a clear separation between the two. . . . Andreotti
defended Boniface, expanding on the themes of the external politics of the time
at the level of Europe. Misserville [the Senator taking on the role of defending
Boniface's enemy, Sciarra Colonna] referred to the historical in-fighting among
the nobility of Lazio, which had been precipitated by the Pope's plundering of
their wealth. This professorial debate was introduced by a more theatrical moment of the festivities in which Mario Scassia read some verses from Dante
relative to Celestino V and Bonifacio VIII. Besides that, Andreotti had cited
Tertullian and the Catholic Encyclopedia in order to recall how Bonifacio, *even*

with his many defects, had attempted to represent a point of clear reference in an Italy that was divided and prey to thousands of internal conflicts." [17]

MONTANELLI: But where could [Sicily] have gone—the separatist movement? What would Sicily have done without Italy? No one wanted it.

ANDREOTTI: But [allowing the separatist movement to continue unabated] could have accentuated the difficulties . . . the Mafias had never fought among themselves and we probably would have had that—

MONTANELLI: But excuse me Senator, Alto-Adige knew where it wanted to go—the Austrians wanted to return to Austria. But the *autonomisti,* the *separatisti,* the secessionists of Sicily, where were they going to go?

> Perugia/Rome/Palermo—After the authorization to proceed [with the indictments], the Prosecutor of Palermo unfurled a vast investigative program, proportional to the delicacy and complexity of the evidentiary verifications and to the necessity of maintaining connections to the public ministry offices in Rome and Perugia. The Roman prosecutor's office, in fact, is investigating the alleged crimes relevant to the first penal section of the Supreme Court, while that of Perugia is dedicating itself to the murder of Pecorelli. (Arlacchi 1995, 25)

> Everything is more uncertain than ever but I feel I've now reached a state of inner serenity: as long as we can check our telephone numbers and there is no answer then we will continue, all three of us, speeding back and forth along these white lines, with no points of departure or of arrival to threaten with their sensations and meanings the single-mindedness of our race, freed finally from the awkward thickness of our persons and voices and moods, reduced to luminous signals, the only appropriate way of being for those who wish to be identified with what they say, without the distorting buzz our presence or the presence of others transmits to our messages.
>   To be sure, the price paid is high but we must accept it: to be indistinguishable from all the other signals that pass along this road, each with his meaning that remains hidden and undecipherable because outside of here there is no one capable of receiving us now and understanding us. (Calvino 1969, 136)

Life and Death

Excerpt from a conversation between the monk Peter and one of Purgatory's medieval founders, Gregory the Great, recorded in his *Dialogues* about a ship to Sicily signifying death and voyage to a place between:

> PETER: But I ask you, why did a ship appear to the departing
>   soul, and why did he say that after death it would take
>   him to Sicily?

GREGORY: The fact that he told this man that he would be taken
             to Sicily can mean only one thing: more than any other
             place, it is in the isles of that land that the fire-spitting
             cauldrons have opened up. These, as the experts tell it,
             expand with each passing day, for, as the end of the
             world is drawing near, and as the number who shall be
             gathered there to be burnt, above and beyond the number
             already there, is uncertain, these places of torment must
             enlarge themselves to receive them all. It is the will of al-
             mighty God that these places be shown as a corrective to
             the men living in this world, so that incredulous minds
             [mentes infidelium] who do not believe that infernal tor-
             ments exist may see the place of torments, so that those
             who refuse to believe on the basis of hearsay alone may
             see with their own eyes (Le Goff 1981, 206)

MONTANELLI: But this is very serious.

ANDREOTTI: Why?

MONTANELLI: Serious because if there wasn't even a need to do this [the
Mafia actively controlling votes in Sicily] . . . because electoral interest, I understand, can overcome the barriers of principle. But if there wasn't even this,
if it isn't true that the Mafia controlled so many votes . . . why the accords?
Why the leniencies toward the Mafia?

ANDREOTTI: The leniency—what was it? Probably a live and let live.

MONTANELLI: A live and let live?

ANDREOTTI: But certainly I must say that there were certain moments in
which the Sicilians also demonstrated a sense of responsibility, the time of
Comiso [a town in Sicily where NATO missiles were installed] . . . the population expressed a notable heroism.

MONTANELLI: A notable heroism or a notable indifference?

ANDREOTTI: But an indifference in this case, in regard to a fairly strong
political polemic. . . .

MONTANELLI: Yes, yes. I am an admirer of Sicilians. I am fond of Sicilians.
And I recognize in them a certain gift which is rare in Italy. They know how
to die. They know how to die. And this is not common in Italy.

             Now I must leave you. I have lost much time,
             walking along with you at your own pace,
             and time is precious to us in this realm.

                              —(Alighieri 1981, canto 24)

Notes

1. "Cosi' chiedevano aiuto ad Andreotti: Il pentito in videoconferenza: sei ore
d'accuse contro il senatore," *La Repubblica,* 31 May 1996, 15. All translations, unless
otherwise indicated, are mine.

2. Handwritten note affixed to the external wall of the Church of Saint Antonio Abate, on Via della Repubblica, Parma, quoting Giorgio La Pira, Christian Democratic mayor of Florence in the 1950s.

3. Classifica degli onesti: Italia è maglia nera," *La Repubblica,* 6 June 1996, 20.

4. Cf. Robert Putnam's acute analysis (1993, 93) of the meaning of such votes, as contrasted with the meaning of votes in referendum-based elections.

5. Obviously, I'm referring to the level of symbolism here. The instrumental wake-up calls were issued by the newly independent and aggressive Italian judiciary of the late 1980s and early 1990s. These judges and prosecutors were the ones who broke open the code of *omerta* and developed the cadre of *pentiti*—and they often, as in the cases of Falcone and Borsellino, paid for such successes with their lives.

6. Testimony of Baldassare Di Maggio, government witness, follower of Riina, indicating the secret hideout/apartment of Riina for the investigators (Procura della Repubblica presso il Tribunale di Palermo, Memoria Depositata dal Pubblico Ministero nel procedimento penale n. 3538/94 NR instaurato nei confronti di Andreotti Giulio, 2:59–63).

7. "Il Papa contestato per Andreotti," *La Repubblica,* 13 Dec. 1995, 1, 14.

8. The Notarbartolo trial was the first national criminal trial in which the defendants were understood to be members of a Sicilian Mafia. The charge against these defendants, among whom was Raffaele Palizzolo, an exponent of the Regionalist political party, was the murder of Emanuele Notarbartolo, a nobleman and reformist director of the Banco di Sicilia. The defendants were absolved for "insufficiencies of proof."

9. Firenze online Web Server: www.fionline.it/informaz/giulio/ga-home.html.

10. Pietro Citati, "Elogio Funebre Della DC," *La Repubblica,* 14 June 1996, 1.

11. Archives of Telemontecarlo, Mar. 1996.

12. Letter to the Christian Democrat Party, 30 Apr. 1978.

13. Giorgio Lo Bianco, in *Espresso,* 16 Mar. 1996.

14. Giuseppe d'Avanzo, "Il medico mafioso: I cugini Salvo e lo zio Giulio," *La Repubblica,* 16 Dec. 1995, 11.

15. Andreotti e Mutulo e' il giorno del tele-duello," *La Repubblica,* 30 May 1996, 21.

16. "Preso il killer di Falcone," *La Repubblica,* 21 May 1996, 1.

17. "Andreotti fa 'assolvere' Bonifacio VIII," *L'Unione Sarda,* 6 Aug. 1995; emphasis added.

References

Alighieri, Dante. 1968. *Purgatorio.* Italian text with English; trans. John D. Sinclair. New York: Oxford University Press.

———. 1981. *Purgatory.* Trans. and ed. Mark Musa. Bloomington: Indiana University Press.

Arlacchi, Pino. 1995. *Il Processo: Giulio Andreotti sotto accusa a Palermo.* Milano: Rizzoli.

Calvino, Italo. 1969. "The Night Driver." In *Tzero.* New York: Harcourt Brace

Gambetta, Diego. 1991. " 'In the beginning was the Word . . .': The symbols of the Mafia." *Archives europennes de sociologie* 32:53–77.

Kermode, Frank. 1979. *The Genesis of Secrecy: On the Interpretation of Narrative.* Cambridge, Mass.: Harvard University Press.

Le Goff, Jacques. 1981. *The Birth of Purgatory.* Trans. Arthur Goldhammer. Chicago:
   University of Chicago Press.

Lupo, Salvatore. 1996. *Andreotti, la mafia, la storia d'Italia.* Roma: Donzelli.

Hall, Peter M., and Dee Ann Spencer Hall. 1983. "The Handshake as Interaction."
   Semiotica 45:249–64.

Mann, Thomas. 1963. "Mario and the Magician." In *Death in Venice: and Seven Other
   Stories.* Trans. H. T. Lowe-Porter. New York: Vintage Books.

Perella, Nicolas James. 1969. *The Kiss: Sacred and Profane.* Berkeley: University of
   California Press.

Petrarca, Francesco. 1983. *The Sonnets and Other Poems of Petrarch.* London: George
   Bell and Sons.

Procura della Repubblica presso il Tribunale di Palermo, Memoria Depositata dal Pubblico Ministero nel procedimento penale n. 3538/94 NR instaurato nei confronti di
   Andreotti Giulio. Vol. 2, 59–63.

Putnam, Robert. 1993. *Making Democracy Work: Civic Traditions in Modern Italy.*
   Princeton, N.J.: Princeton University Press.

Stille, Alexander. 1995a. *Excellent Cadavers: The Mafia and the Death of the First
   Italian Republic.* New York: Pantheon.

———. "The Fall of Caesar." *The New Yorker,* 11 Sept., 68–83.

Douglas R. Holmes

Tactical Thuggery: National Socialism in the East End of London

Richard Edmonds is the national organizer of the British National Party, a truc-ulent, openly racist, and neofascist movement.[1] He was interviewed in July 1994 at the BNP's "bookstore" or "headquarters"—its function is disputed—in Welling, southeast London. It is a pale-blue, steel-clad rowhouse along a nondescript street of small retail stores and residences. One enters the struc-ture through a heavily bolted door. The interior has the subterranean feel of a fortified bunker. Publications of the BNP line the walls of the main, window-less room.[2]

Mr. Edmonds is tall, intense, and articulate. He speaks with a driving ca-dence. He has the habit, while answering questions, of making extended pauses, during which he thrusts his face very close to the listeners, extending his lower lip and glowering. He paced and circled around me as we talked.

The crucial labor Mr. Edmonds performs is to translate illicit discourses into the vernacular of an urban landscape. His métier is "tactical thuggery." He embraces a theory of exclusionary welfarism as a basis of his nationalism. It is a theory woven through a parochial politics of experience. What is at stake in his account is the social reproduction of white working-class household and community. What is resisted is the pluralist theory of nation which aligns the polyethnic boroughs of London.[3]

Mr. Edmonds's politics coalesce at street level. He discriminates acutely the geographies of inclusion and exclusion of inner London.[4] He is inspired to physically confront those who embody the contradictions of *his* Britain, those who transgress its racial hygiene, its moral economy. He is an organic intellec-tual, with a taste for streetfighting, whose vision skirts the paranoid and the delusional.[5] His vexed actions splice the political and the criminal.

The East End is a site where the contours of a multiracial and multicultural Europe are contested, where cultural discourse becomes social drama.[6] Europe is inexorably on the path to racial and cultural pluralism. The inability of main-stream political leaders to render this transformation meaningful, let alone to intervene and regulate it, risks shifting the struggle into the hands of thugs. Those illicit questions, which conventionally oriented political actors will not or cannot address, have the potential to breed violent action on the streets of East London. The results of failed or inept politics are visceral: split heads and battered bodies.

The leaders of the BNP have reclaimed a decisive ideological position. They have identified the instrumentalities of the welfare state as the contemporary social embodiment of community and nation. Fast capitalism with its ideological underpinning in neoliberalism is the dark force they seek to combat. They revile Margaret Thatcher. They believe that the concepts of nation and citizen are in disarray, but the battle, in their view, is being fought not in an abstract discourse on "rights" but over basic human needs: access to public housing, education, health, social welfare, and control of the streets. They are convinced, like Charles Maurras, that "a socialism that has been freed of democratic and cosmopolitan elements can fit nationalism like a well-made glove fits a beautiful hand." [7]

Isle of Dogs

There are few more incongruous places in Europe in the last decade of the twentieth century than the Isle of Dogs.[8] On the northern end is the partially completed Canary Wharf Project, with twelve million square feet of new offices, hotels, and shops, as well as the tallest building in Britain, Canary Wharf Tower, designed by Cesar Pelli. It is the focus of the enormous Docklands Redevelopment Scheme, the most extravagant expression of the real-estate construction and speculation that swept London during the late 1980s.

The project aimed at attracting the burgeoning financial services industry from the City of London, as well as newspaper publishing from Fleet Street, to new facilities in and around the Docklands. The *Times,* the *Guardian,* the *Financial Times,* the *Daily Mail,* and the *Daily Telegraph* have relocated all or part of their operations. By the early 1990s, however, Olympia and York, the developer of Canary Wharf, was in receivership in the face of a real-estate glut and a major economic downturn in Britain and the rest of Europe.

In the south of the Isle of Dogs is Mudchute Park, with a small working farm; Island Gardens, with a pleasant view across the Thames and entrance to the Footway Tunnel under the river to Greenwich; Cubitt Town, an old industrial area with housing built for workers ringing now abandoned factories, shipyards, and docks. Crisscrossing the island are the great basins, slipways, and channels of the West India and Millwall Docks, monuments to the area's maritime past.

A new elevated light railway stretches two and half miles or so from north to south. A link road connecting the island with Limehouse and the rest of the East End was also recently completed. It is reputed to be the most costly roadway in Europe. Renovation and conversion of the old warehouses that line the waterways and docks has created new outposts for London "yuppiedom."

The Isle of Dogs in the nineteenth and early twentieth century was the center of shipbuilding and related industries along the Thames. In 1857 the *Great Eastern*, the largest vessel of its time (630 feet in length) was launched here by Isambard Kingdom Brunel. The Millwall Iron works alone employed four thousand men and boys in the 1860s. Labor activism made the island an important setting in the founding of British trade unionism. It was also an area in which Oswald Mosley found sympathetic listeners in the 1930s. The Docklands were bombed intensively during the Second World War. In early 1996, the Irish Republican Army chose Canary Wharf as the site to recommence a bombing campaign in Britain after an extended cease-fire.

The postwar decline in the British maritime dominance led to the close of the docks and the end of the island's industrial base. The displaced workers and their offspring still inhabit the poor council estates. They identify themselves as islanders. Since the late 1950s new waves of immigrants from Asia and the Caribbean have arrived, creating a sense among islanders of competition for limited public housing and jobs.[9] Millwall was, however, one of the least affected areas of the borough. By the early 1990s the minority character of the ward was 13.5 percent Asian and 6 percent black. This compares with the 27 percent Asian and 7 percent black for the borough of Tower Hamlets, with a total population of 161,000. Unemployment in the borough was over 26 percent in 1994. Of 67,581 dwellings under the borough's housing authority, 45,475 were judged as unfit or in need of repair.[10]

Thus the East End of London is a locale swept by the full force of late-modern, fast capitalism. Within its council housing reside new arrivals dislocated by the insensate force of global markets and pressed against "indigenous" residents who themselves struggle with novel forms of alienation and exile.[11] An enfeebled welfare state mediates the material conditions of a multiracial and multicultural Britain. In the absence of a comprehensive public consensus on the legitimacy of a newly defined British society—managed through democratic means—an incendiary politics materializes with race and nation at its core.

Election and Aftermath

There were a series of violent skirmishes in the East End just before and immediately after the election of Derek Beackon on 16 September 1993 to the Tower Hamlets Borough Council as the candidate of the BNP. In a number of these confrontations Richard Edmonds appears to have been a participant, in one case a principal.[12]

On the evening of 8 September, during the England vs. Poland football match, a grievous assault on a seventeen-year-old student, Quaddus Ali, took place and commenced the period of unrest. Quaddus Ali was brutally attacked by seven men and one woman—alleged to be members or supporters of BNP—while returning a video rental with three of his friends. The attackers pounced on Quaddus in the street and dragged him into a nearby pub, where he was beaten repeatedly. His mates escaped. Quaddus sustained severe injuries to the head, which left him in a deep coma at the Royal London Hospital. A series of clashes among antifascist groups, local Asian residents, and the police ensued in the area along Brick Lane and Bethnal Green Road.

Two days later a vigil by a large, peaceful crowd in sympathy with Quaddus Ali turned violent and nine Bengali youths were arrested. The police were accused by supporters of Quaddus Ali of provoking the fracas. This was followed on 11 September by an incident in which "50 BNP supporters," according to the account in *Searchlight* (Oct. 1993), rampaged down Brick Lane breaking windows, damaging retail stalls, and terrorizing residents. Hundreds of Asians marched down to Cable Street in response protesting the inadequacy of police protection and the lack of arrests.

The clashes culminated in a protest organized by the Anti-Nazi League (ANL) on the morning of 18 September 1993, the Sunday after Derek Beackon's election.[13] Members of the ANL and local residents attempted to dislodge BNP members trying to sell their nationalist broadsheet from their usual corner location on Brick Lane. At the time, an unusually large number of BNP supporters were in attendance to celebrate Beackon's election. The confrontation was bloody, with the BNP denied access to its traditional territory. This particular spot on Brick Lane was considered the BNP's "pitch." Since the 1930s, fascists had regularly congregated on Sundays at that same location to peddle their publications.[14]

There was one more serious incident that took place subsequent to the confrontation on Brick Lane. Shortly after BNP supporters were dislodged, an attack took place on a black and white couple outside the Ship pub on Bethnal Green Road, an establishment regularly frequented by BNP followers. Four men attacked the couple, roughing up the woman and brutally cutting the man's face to the bone with a broken beer bottle.[15] Due to the significant police presence in the area at the time, officers were on the scene quickly, capturing the alleged attackers in the pub. One was Richard Edmonds. The four assailants were identified by the woman, arrested, and the next day all were charged with "grievous bodily harm" (GBH). Edmonds was subsequently convicted of violent disorder and sentenced to prison for three months.[16] In the following account he vehemently denounces the conviction.

HOLMES: What do you believe?

EDMONDS: There are two strands to our beliefs. The first strand concerns the here and now; the problems of Britain. But we see these same problems duplicated in most other white communities of Germany, France, and even the United States. In the here and now, Britain has problems of immigration which are more or less without control. I was born in 1943 and I've spent most if not all my life in London. London of the 1950s was a happy, homogeneous society insofar as any society can be. One could leave one's door key in the front door and leave the house unlocked. An old person could walk the street safely. The schools I went to were 100 percent British. One hundred percent.

HOLMES: When did things begin to change?

EDMONDS: You're jumping in now. We don't want to jump all over the place. When does anything begin? When is the beginning of anything? Beginnings are very complicated things.

But, to answer your question now you've raised it: prior to 1947, only people of British origin—British Canadians, British Australians, South Africans, New Zealanders, and British Rhodesians—had the right to come and go in and out freely; overseas British, one might say. Then, the Labour Party, the Socialists, came to power and introduced the British Nationality Act.[17] This gave British nationality to every citizen, subject, or individual who lived in the British Empire and Commonwealth. So, approximately one-quarter of the worlds' population received British citizenship and had the right to come here. It only took a few weeks for the Jamaicans to start arriving.

However, it wasn't until ten years later, when some prosperity returned to Britain, that the process of immigration really started. You see, Britain in 1945 was technically a bankrupt nation; there was food rationing, electricity was turned on and off because there was no power to generate it, and factories worked three-day weeks. Then, in the middle to late 1950s, some prosperity returned. Factories had big adverts saying, "Labour wanted." The Conservatives were in power and it was then that immigration really took off.

Initially it came from the West Indies, and continued throughout the 1960s. In the 1970s we had immigration of Asians, including Asians living in Africa, Uganda and Kenya. In the 1980s, again under the Conservatives, immigration came in from the Vietnamese boat people, Chinese. In fact, most of the immigration has come under the Conservative government for the simple reason that the Conservatives have run this country for most of the time since the fifties. But, in practice, it makes no difference; Socialists or Conservative, we get immigration and it now seems to be totally out of control.

I might say, for your interest, "officially," immigration stopped in 1961. I remember the newspaper headlines: "Immigration Stopped." However, it doesn't feel like that to the ordinary person.[18]

HOLMES: I'm sorry I interrupted you but can you tell me more about London of the 1950s and how it has changed?

EDMONDS: It was a very happy city. I remember the word *mugging* only coming in to London vocabulary in 1974 or 1975.

HOLMES: Did it come from the United States?

The Sunday *Times*. 7 August 1994
Blame Complacency not Churchill

IN HIS extract from Eminent Churchillians (News Review, last week) Andrew Roberts loads on to Churchill the responsibility for the group of problems which goes by the name "immigration."

I would like to set out briefly what did happen and who, consequently, was to blame. What actually happened was the British Nationality Act 1948. That was legislation of the Attlee Labour government, though it had the support of the Conservative opposition. So both sides in politics were responsible.

When the war came to an end in 1945 two things took place. First, the Canadians passed a law defining a Canadian citizen. Secondly, it became plain that before long every part of the British Empire would be an independent, self-governing country.

Until then all the inhabitants of the Empire had been subjects of the British Crown, and thus all possessed, though very few exercised the right to enter the United Kingdom and live there. If they became independent countries, and especially if they became independent republics, as Burma did in 1946, that would stop.

The prospect horrified the British parties and the British public, who at the time were being persuaded to contemplate with great complacency the transformation of the British Empire in to the British Commonwealth of self-governing independent nations—a piece of contradictory nonsense indeed, but a splendid salve for dented British pride. So what we did was to make a list of Commonwealth Countries and say that all their citizens were to be equivalent to British subjects, no matter whether they became republics or not.

Air travel and private enterprise did the rest. Through the open door, a door which always had been open, there nor surged a great mass of citizens of independnet nations, India and Pakistan in particular.

Shocked by what was happening, the Conservative government in 1962, against frantic Labour opposition, passed the Commonwealth Immigration Act, which gave Britain for the first time what all other countries take for granted—a definition of its own citizens—and confined to them the rights of entry and residence here. But it was already too late. An ethnic minority had come into existence, of which the age structure decrees that it must increase steadily in relation to the rest of the population.

So when we contemplate the consequences of what we call "immigration," we are contemplating the consequences of our own determination to take refuge from reality in pretence. So great a catastrophe does not happen unless a whole people wills it upon itself. That is what we did.

Enoch Powell
London SW1

EDMONDS: Without any question; from New York, in fact.[19] London, as I said to you earlier, was happy and homogeneous insofar as human society can be. We've always had Europeans here and, after the war, in 1956, there were Poles and Hungarians; but they all melted in. Sometimes they anglicized their surnames, sometimes they didn't. But, it didn't matter. There have always been Europeans in Britain. It's not a problem. We are a European people.

But, in addition to immigration, we now have an appalling crime situation. Take the police: the police in London are regularly getting killed by criminals, stabbed to death, shot to death, hacked to death with axes. But, when I was a child, a police officer very rarely got killed. I might also say our police officers are unarmed because Britain has traditionally been a stable, law-abiding society. Our police officers don't carry guns as do police officers in the United States and practically every other country in the world. As an Englishman, to go abroad, whether it be the United States or even Calais, it's a shock to see police officers with a gun or a pistol at their side. You think that man could take that gun and shoot me dead. That's a very shocking experience for an English person. We are not used to it. Now, with law and order collapsing, police officers in London are armed more and more. In fact, now they have squads of police who have machine guns as a matter of routine. Our society is collapsing.

But as I was saying; when I was a child, a police officer was murdered, shot actually by two young juvenile delinquents who got hold of a pistol from the Second World War. The whole country was absolutely shocked. A police officer shouldn't be murdered in the course of duty. But now, police officers in London are murdered about once every three months. We find that very shocking.

As well as immigration and problems of crime, there are problems of unemployment. Again, in the 1950s and the 1960s, we were told the problems of immigration were solved, the problems which caused the [economic] slump in the 1920s and 1930s were solved and politicians had now worked out the solutions to the problem of unemployment. We were guaranteed jobs. By American standards, British wages were not very high, but one could have a pleasant standard of living because we had a sort of socialist state with free education and welfare. So, life was quite pleasant, I would say; stable and pleasant. Certainly, I find this idea now very desirable indeed. There was full employment.

Unemployment in Britain first passed the million mark in 1975 or 1976, under a socialist government, by the way. Out of a male workforce of about twelve million, one million were out of work. It's male unemployment which hurts, you know. Women can always get part-time employment as shop assistants or whatever. It's men that need to work. Since then it has climbed to approximately three million. In fact, it's probably more, but the government can manipulate and "massage"—I think that's the term they use—the statistics. We've had over three million unemployed for about twelve or thirteen years now, so it's quite clear that this unemployment problem will never go away. Chronic unemployment is here forever.

So, you see, these are the problems—simplified greatly—of Britain in the here and now. Our solution, summed up in one word, is nationalism. We value the community above everything else. We see man as a social creature who needs a community. Without a community, literally to be alone, most men would go mad. Robinson Crusoe is probably the exception, but that was a fictional story. Men need community in all senses of the word. They *need* to be *needed.* They need to play a useful role, which certainly must include having a job, having useful employment. This particularly applies to young people. We see young people going "off the rails"—sorry for the English expression—I mean, degenerating. We see chronic unemployment lead to drug addiction, which is quite a problem here. Young people feel unwanted by society, abandoned by society, so they turn inward and start killing themselves with drugs. You may think it a bit rude and take offense: I have lived and traveled around the United States and I've seen what's happened to the American Indians. Life is life and all that, but all the males you see are drunk and disorderly. Now, without turning to the history of it, passing no value judgments and just looking at them as an observer, they are a people who feel finished. They have no future, they have no present. They are just drunk all the time. We are seeing the same phenomenon in sections of our youth today. Chronic unemployment leads to drug taking. They feel finished.

So, how do we solve all this? We make the community the priority. We believe British people have to safeguard their community. In practice, it means this: we want to stop immigration. The motivation behind immigration is largely the search for cheap labor. Somebody decides, Let's employ cheap labor, let's haul that labor in from the Caribbean, Africa, Asia. Let's haul in labor. It is all about the forces of economics and it's a pretty strange force—to simplify this greatly—one can look at United States or Western European wages and compare them with the wages of Shanghai: roughly about a cent to the dollar, a penny to the pound. Approximately a ratio of one to a hundred. So, economically speaking, the thrust and the drive and the power of the one world order is to sack the white man and ship the work to the cheap labor countries of the far East, or, on the other hand, to exploit the cheapness of overseas wages and import labor: be it from Mexico into the United States, from the Caribbean into Britain, from Africa into Britain, or from the Far East into Britain. The same thing happens in France, Germany, and all the other Western European societies as well.

We [the BNP] are totally opposed to all of this. We will put *our* people before the power of money. We will employ British workers even though, economically, it would make more sense to sack the lot of them and transfer all the industry "south of the border," whether that means Mexico or Africa or the Far East. We see whites as, not only having a right to live, but a duty to live. I might also say, I'm an engineer and I admire technology, and I believe all this technology today is a product of *our* genius as a people, a white people. The Far Easterners, the Japanese, the Chinese, are very intelligent people, and are good managers. Not only that, but the Japanese are known to be formidable soldiers. There is no question about their military prowess. But having said that, they have no genius for creating technology. Everything they make is a direct copy of what we have created earlier.

We intend to safeguard the white race, we intend to safeguard the white workers, and we intend to do that by stopping immigration into Britain from the Third World. We want to stop the importation of goods manufactured in the Third World. We want to stop the export of technology, insofar as we are able, from the West to the Third World. We want to stop the export of capital from Britain to the Third World. We want to do all this because they are all to our detriment. We are just building up our competitors. Of course, the people who run the new world order gain, politically and economically, when they sack the white worker. They stop paying a dollar out and start employing the coolie labor of China. They pay a cent rather than a dollar and make the ninety-nine cents difference. That's not in our interest. It's *not* in our interest seeing our people just exterminated. Inevitably, this is where this process will head.

HOLMES: So what would a "British" community look like as opposed to the multicultural community you currently have?

EDMONDS: Well, I've seen one quite recently. I will tell you in a second where, quite to my surprise, I might add. The multiracial and, in particular, the multicultural society just does not work. In Britain there are, perhaps, a million or two million Muslims. I don't know the exact figure because no one will produce them. Whether it's because they're not known or whether it's because the government is too afraid of the enormity of these numbers, I don't know, but either way, they don't produce them.

Now the Muslims have a strong faith in their beliefs, in Allah, and best of luck to them. We have such enormous problems thrust upon us that we need as much strength as possible; and if the Muslims, the Pakistanis, or the Arabs find strength in Allah, best of luck to them. But we now have a situation where they are building mosques all over the United Kingdom, where, in the name of their religion, they are issuing death threats against British citizens!

I'll give you an example. You may be aware there is a British citizen who is in fact of Asian origin, but ignoring that for a moment; a British citizen by the name of Salman Rushdie, who printed a book, written in a secular vein, criticizing Allah. Now if he had chosen to criticize the Christian religion and questioned the existence of Jesus Christ, no one would have blinked. We are so used to looking at the world with secular eyes now. But because he chose to apply these secular values to the Muslim religion, there have now been death threats against him *in Britain.* In addition to that, when the Gulf War was fought—three years ago, I think it was—Muslims in Britain chose to support Saddam Hussein and had a march in London against the involvement of British troops in the Middle East. Then at the termination of this public march and rally there were public calls for the assassination of our prime minister, Mr. John Major.

My point is, all of this is inevitable when you have a multicultural society. Cultures are going to clash. I might just add too: there is going to be a rally in a large arena in London next month, in Wembley Arena, which, apparently, tens of thousands of Muslims are going to attend. I don't know if you have seen the *Jewish Chronicle,* but it's on the front page.[20]

HOLMES: No. I haven't seen it.

EDMONDS: There's going to be a formal call for a "Holy War" against the Jews. The organizers of this rally have already sold over ten thousand tickets and there will be calls for the murder and assassination of Jews! This is where the multicultural society leads—to *clashes* which are impossible to resolve.

HOLMES: So you see [multiculturalism] leading to a radical sectarianism?

EDMONDS: Yes, without a doubt. Without a doubt. Without a doubt. This is not in the interest of the British people. It is not in our interest to have all these religious-political tribal disputes forced out on our territory; here, in London. The sort of society we want is racially homogeneous, a society free of class conflict, a society where all members are cared for and looked after and—I hope this is not too shocking for your American ears—with a degree of socialism, whereby you have a national health service, a national education service so the poorer members of society have a decent basic level of life. If a young chap is intelligent but of poor parents, he will be able to go to the best universities in the land even if his parents can't afford to send him there. We see the people, particularly the young people, as the stock and trade, if I may use a commercial term, of the nation.

HOLMES: So you focus your efforts on young people?

EDMONDS: Young people are important.

HOLMES: Do they find your message compelling?

EDMONDS: I think everybody finds it appealing.

HOLMES: You know your ideas sound like those of Oswald Mosley?

EDMONDS: I think he had similar ideas, but I have never studied Mosley very much.

HOLMES: You are deeply disenchanted with the British political establishment, whether it be Labour or Conservative?

EDMONDS: Yes, the whole lot of them. They are a bunch of traitors. A whole bunch of traitors. Socialists, Conservatives, the whole lot of them. Actually, they are defeatist, sour losers. Defeatists. They should be swept away with a big broom.

HOLMES: So you want to establish a British moral community even if, in so doing, it has negative economic consequences?

EDMONDS: Even if it makes us poorer, I would sacrifice some of our wealth for a stable society. Yes.

HOLMES: You feel nostalgia?

EDMONDS: I don't like the word *nostalgia.* It's a weak word.

HOLMES: A longing then, a sense of loss?

EDMONDS: Yes, we have lost. Yes, we certainly have and all through our own fault. We followed wrong policies.

HOLMES: You would seek a more advanced social-welfare system than the one which exists in contemporary Britain?

EDMONDS: We would just reinforce it. At the moment, the present government is demolishing our social welfare [system]. We would reinforce it.

HOLMES: Is there a problem of public housing on the Isle of Dogs?

EDMONDS: The problem on the Isle of Dogs, as in East London and the poorer parts of London in general, is *all* the available housing, the new housing, is just going to Asians all the time. You may have seen Asian women voting wearing Yashmacs. It is utterly alien to us. Now, there have always been foreigners in Britain, but to see women wearing yashmacs, voting in our elections, who can't even speak a word of English and their numbers are sufficient to decide which candidate wins. That's not participating in Britain, that's simply monopolizing power, albeit in a small area. It was the Asian vote which decided the election [on the Isle of Dogs].

HOLMES: But I have also seen young Asians in London who have assimilated to Britain and the East End. They have cockney accents.

EDMONDS: Well, they were born here.

HOLMES: So what does that make them?

EDMONDS: I'll answer that question. We believe in the sense of duty. We believe British people should have a sense of duty to Britain. For example, Britain does or should provide the British with the bread and butter, the wherewithal to exist in this world. Our "British" community will be built on strong community values. There won't be any place for thieves or criminals in our society. As far as immigrants are concerned, particularly young people of immigrant origins, whether it be West Indian, African, Asian, we can't understand why they think they wouldn't *want* to go back and build up their own countries, especially when every television program you watch, every advertisement you see—it's called Oxfam over here—shows the poverty, the ignorance, and the squalor of the Third World. We believe these young people, specifically the Asians, have had the benefits of a Western education, who may have made a little money, accumulated a bit of capital, *should want* to go back, should have a sense of duty to their own kith and kin. Instead of living a life of quasi-luxury over here, swanning around in cars and such nonsense, they should want to go back to their own countries.

This whole immigration thing is an extension of the idea of empire. I am now fifty-one years old and I remember the whole history of this from A to Z; except, of course, I was four years of age when the Nationalities Act was passed. I remember the first immigrants and the practical consequences. I remember the West Indians coming to London in the 1950s. I was a schoolboy and we wondered what it all meant. The English working class, of which I am a part, had to live and work with these newcomers and, at the time, we didn't understand it. What are they doing here? We wanted to know. I remember clearly, as a young teenager maybe thirteen years old, 1956, 1957 maybe, discussing with my parents what all this meant. Our newspapers would tell us not to worry about immigration. The immigrants would only be here for a short time. They were just learning a trade and then they would be going home.

HOLMES: The sentiments of an empire.

EDMONDS: The empire is finished. We are not interested in empire. We want them to improve their own countries. The West Indies are entirely independent and the best of luck to them. We're not a mean-spirited people. We're a generous people. We don't have a problem with students or apprentices who come here on a short-term basis. That's what we understood it to be [in the 1950s]. That was what it was supposed to be. We were utterly, completely, and absolutely lied to!

HOLMES: There is no lingering obligation between Britain and former members of the empire?

EDMONDS: Zilch. Zilch.

HOLMES: But the Conservatives have, from time to time, addressed or flirted with the issue of immigration.

EDMONDS: The only man who was any good was Enoch Powell. He was good because he paid the price. Look, anyone can talk pretty, meaningless words, but the way to judge a man is by the price he paid. Nietzsche said, "Something is only good if written in blood." I don't know if you've read Nietzsche. A dramatic phrase. In other words, unless you have suffered, [what you say] is meaningless. Now, Powell spoke out about immigration. Until then, nothing had been said. He broke the veil of silence, the conspiracy of silence, and for that, he paid the price. He was immediately thrown into the political wilderness. All his chances and ambitions of being a government minister, possibly the prime minister of Britain, went out the window. He was treated as a total outcast.[21]

HOLMES: There is an effort to portray the tactics of the BNP as thuggish.

EDMONDS: That's true. I don't take offense.

HOLMES: But what do you make of it?

EDMONDS: For a start, our society is falling to bits, it's collapsing. You Americans are a frontier people, a rough and ready people. You built a civilization out of wilderness. And even though your roots are in Britain, you are very different from us. One thing you *must* understand is we are very, very law abiding here. Our policemen are unarmed for very practical reasons: until recently, we had no serious crime. Now, our society is falling to bits.

Our ideal is a Britain, law-and-order-wise, which we had in the 1950s; a Britain with very, very little serious crime. However, our image has been tarnished by the media who are in the hands of the internationalists, in the hands of the one world order, in the hands of the liberals; and all the problems

I have been describing, from an ideological point of view, are ones which have arisen through liberalism: liberalism toward immigration, liberalism toward criminals. We would bring back the rope, capital punishment, but the liberals pat them on the head and send them out again to commit more crimes. We are very much opposed to liberalism. The liberals are our enemy. They use their power through the media, to blacken our good name so we won't get any votes. It's black propaganda. It's all a pack of lies.

HOLMES: The Britain you seek is, above all, respectable. Yet you let yourselves be portrayed as thuggish.[22]

EDMONDS: I understand your question entirely. But you see, no newspaper will give us friendly coverage, no TV studio will invite us in for a nice friendly interview. We have to campaign ourselves. We have to put our leaflet into mailboxes, go out and sell our newspapers and march in the streets. When we campaign we are physically attacked by our political opponents; confronted and attacked. In this last election, one of our candidates lost an eye. [He was] knocked to the ground and kicked in the face with a steel boot and blinded in one eye. That received a little bit of publicity, but had it been a Labour, Liberal, or Conservative candidate who was blinded, you would still be hearing about it now.

So, in practice, we find that we have to physically protect ourselves if we are to survive. So we have to be robust in our manner of campaigning. But we always stay within the law. We always attempt to maintain discipline.

HOLMES: But sometimes the discipline breaks down.

EDMONDS: Nothing is perfect.

HOLMES: Were you arrested recently?[23]

EDMONDS: Listen, if you want to talk about me, then yes, I have been charged and found guilty of a very serious offense of which I will go to my grave absolutely denying. I know I am 100 percent innocent! It is to my misfortune that I was charged with an offense that I did not commit and the jury chose to believe the prosecution. I have no doubt the jury was influenced, in part, by the portrayal [of the BNP in the press]. It's a vicious circle.

I would never compare myself to Jesus Christ because he was the son of God and I'm not even, strictly speaking, a Christian. But I am well aware that Jesus Christ was persecuted and condemned to death by the political authorities of his day. Yet our whole society is based on the idea that Christ was *not* a criminal. On the contrary. He was the son of God who came down here to save mankind. Now, like I said, I wouldn't compare myself to God, but in a zillionth part of a zillionth part, if I may say so, I am attempting to do something for the most honorable of motives. But, my political opponents have very great power: the power of the media and the power of the police.

Don't think we are blowing this out of proportion. We had one of our candidates, Derek Beackon, elected as councilor last September and within forty-eight hours, on the television, the prime minister, the home secretary who is responsible for law and order, the Archbishop of Canterbury, who is the head churchman in England, and the head of the metropolitan police condemned the electorate for voting for the BNP. Now, for this to come from the prime minister and the home secretary is very, very bad because they, as politicians, only hold their positions because they were elected in. So who are they to criticize the electorate? What right do any of these four gentlemen have to criticize a legal, law-abiding party like the BNP? They have no moral right to criticize us.

The London police put out a statement condemning racism. They are correct to do so when, by such condemnation, they mean racial attacks. We don't want any crime either. But the metropolitan police condemned racism *full stop*. Thus they have defined racism in these terms: a racial incident. They make no distinction between a racial incident and a racial attack.

HOLMES: What do you mean by *racist?*

EDMONDS: When we describe the term *racist,* we mean someone who attempts to maintain the British race, i.e., the white race here in Britain. Now, we use that term, *not* in a pejorative sense, as do our opponents, but in a positive, indeed factual sense. Thirty years ago an "Englishman" was taken to be a white man. He was neither a Jamaican, an Asian, a Chinese, a Hottentot, nor a bushman from the Kalahari Desert. We use the term *racist* in a factual, what we would say a positive, sense. We describe a racist as someone who attempts to maintain Britain as racially white.

Now, when the police condemn racism, they describe racism in its literal definition, which is the most open-ended definition you can get. As far as they're concerned, a racial incident can be any incident if *any* person describes it as such. So they log every one of them. In other words, if someone scratches up on a wall "KBW," which is presumably meaningless to you, then it's described as a racial incident. It falls in the same category as if a white man murdered a black man because he hated the *color* of his skin.

HOLMES: What does KBW mean?

EDMONDS: It stands for "Keep Britain White." It was a Mosley slogan. Not many people know it, but you do see it painted on walls.

HOLMES: Technically?

EDMONDS: It falls within the police definition. The theory is that any black person seeing "KBW" written on an English wall might feel affronted or psychologically hurt.

HOLMES: So it's about sensitivities?

EDMONDS: It's just all balls. There's a *plan* to exterminate the white race.

HOLMES: From where does this plan emanate?

EDMONDS: You want to know the name of the enemy?

HOLMES: Who are they?

EDMONDS: More importantly, what are they? They are greed, stupidity, selfishness, and weakness. There are people out there who will say they don't want a multiracial society, but they still want to drive their Japanese cars. That's a contradiction in itself. If we want to be British we will have to be poorer. In terms of the Bible, we are selling out our birthright for a mess of pottage. I'm not a Christian, but there's a lot of wisdom in the Bible, particularly in the Old Testament. We are selling our whole birthright for material comforts.

HOLMES: Your views on international capitalism sound a little like those of people on the extreme Left whom I interviewed.

EDMONDS: Yeah, but we don't *hate* businessmen like the communists. We just want to control them. Let them use their energies, their talents, their experience, and their capital, but only within a framework whereby community values are supreme.

HOLMES: A member of the French National Front [Bruno Gollnisch] suggests the French Left is taking on the antiracist, antifascist struggle because their traditional agenda has been discredited with the collapse of the Soviet Union.

EDMONDS: I think you've got it slightly wrong. I think the drive of these socialists, the Left, the hard Left, is *not* to latch on to us [the BNP]. Their raison d'être, their job, and their whole purpose is to destroy tradition. So because the National Front, in their eyes, stands for some kind of idealized past, they (the Left) hate it. But traditions are very important. Without them—

I've lived in North America and I've lived in Canada. I thought Canada was an ideal combination of Britain and America. It doesn't have the class boundaries like Britain and yet it has all the opportunities of American cities but without violence. It seemed like a very good sort of country. I like Canada. But still, I do think we can sort out the problems we have here.

HOLMES: You think so? How long would it take?

EDMONDS: Time isn't a linear thing. It's not like water pouring into the bath, flowing so many liters per minute. Time. Very, very little can happen in a long period and a great deal can happen in short period. *[He snaps his fingers]* Now, I saw the Berlin Wall come down. I see the problems of the Western world accelerating at an enormous rate: all this immigration, all this crime in New York City, blacks and Jews killing each other, this huge meeting in London where all the Muslims want to kill the Jews. The chickens are coming home to roost.

You know, the Wall Street crash came very quickly, didn't it? The stock exchange crashed in 1929, but it took another three years before the mass unemployment really hit in the U.S. What's going on?

Take the Isle of Dogs. Forget the yuppies for a moment because they have these [affluent] enclaves on what used to be the docks and could be on the moon as far as the locals are concerned. As far as the locals on the island are concerned, the local [council] housing belongs to them as a community. In a council estate the housing is owned by the council, so you might say it's owned by the community, right? So when Mr. and Mrs. Smith's son gets married, the son expects to have a house or a flat somewhere in the neighborhood.

HOLMES: But wouldn't a son have a right to his parents' house?

EDMONDS: Yeah, if they die. It's not written in the law but by tradition. But now all these Asians are pouring into England and have been given the right to demand housing. Did you know that? Immigrants come into Britain and demand to be housed. It's incredible. They can come here illegally and they still have the right to be housed.

HOLMES: So how does this affect your native-born sons and daughters?

EDMONDS: Because there is a queue. It is assumed that the native-born son lives with his mother and father, that he has a bedroom. The Asians, with their suitcases, haven't got anywhere, so they immediately go to the top of the queue. Meanwhile, the young [native] people in reality have nowhere to live. But that's not what you read in the newspapers, is it? Shocking isn't it?

HOLMES: I can see how it is troublesome for the people on the Isle of Dogs.

EDMONDS: Not only do they have to compete with these people for work, which is very scarce, but also they are literally having their houses taken from them. Instead of the house going to the next generation, when someone dies it goes to Asians who could be illegal immigrants. Now, you know the paper called the *Independent?*

HOLMES: Yes.

EDMONDS: It's a serious paper, right? It's not a Nazi paper. I got this fact from the *Independent:* it has been estimated that half the Asians living in Tower Hamlets are illegal immigrants. Yeah. Half! No one throws them out. Listen, listen: until recently, the London borough of Tower Hamlets was controlled by the Liberal Party. Did you know that? And did you know that the Liberal Party in Tower Hamlets is a secret racist party?

HOLMES: Yes.[24]

EDMONDS: All those snobs who live in the countryside with their elegant houses and laid-back attitudes. The London borough of Tower Hamlets used to be run by the Liberal Party, by local people. They didn't call themselves the National Front and hit you over the head. They called themselves liberals, right? Their policy was to try to house the local people. If you were born in the area you got priority over the low-incomers but the low-incomers still got housing because the borough owns massive areas [of council housing]. You can see they are housed all over the place.

Then about two years ago, the London borough of Tower Hamlets wanted to test every Asian applicant for a house to determine if they had a legal right to be in Britain. But the home office told them they had no right to make that determination. They were told to house everybody who turns up.

HOLMES: By securing housing they are also put on the electoral rolls.

EDMONDS: No problem. If you live somewhere, you get on the electoral rolls. Since they [immigrants] have a right to an abode, they are put on the rolls automatically. Listen, this whole society is falling to bits. If you raise these questions they call you a Nazi, Nazi. Perverse. It's the same in France and Germany, too.

HOLMES: These questions cannot be raised? If you do—

EDMONDS: —you get hit over the head. I've a great scar on the back of my head. Hit with a bottle. No warning. Smash.

HOLMES: But the English, the degree—

EDMONDS: Listen! If you know so much—do you know what Voltaire said about the English two hundred years ago?

HOLMES: Tell me.

EDMONDS: He said, "The English are the hardest people in Europe." At that time it was only Europe which mattered. Americans were mere colonists; out there chasing beavers or whatever else they were putting on their heads. Scalping Indians. Sorry about that, my American listeners. No offense *[laughter]*.

HOLMES: So Voltaire?

EDMONDS: "The English are the hardest people in Europe." Have you heard of Admiral [John] Byng [1704–1757]?

HOLMES: No.

EDMONDS: You haven't heard the expression "To encourage the others?" Well, I'm going to tell you a true story. The English spent the whole of the eighteenth century fighting the French, and Admiral Byng was put in charge of an English fleet; so many marines, so many soldiers, etc. He was given the task of capturing a fort in Spain [Minorca] garrisoned by the French, right? Well, his attack failed and the admiralty in London considered Admiral Byng to be 100 percent at fault. He had been given enough ships, enough men, enough marines, and he should have captured the fortress. So the word came down from the admiralty: for dereliction, Admiral Byng was to be punished by execution. He was shot, actually, Admiral Byng was. But there is an interesting twist: Byng was the senior officer present and protocol required that he give the order for execution. And this is all true. So being an English gentleman and officer, he stood in front of the brick wall, held up his silk handkerchief and said to the sergeant in charge of the marines, "Are you ready, Sergeant?" And the sergeant said, "Yes, Sir, I am ready." Then Byng said, "When I drop the handkerchief, fire. Do you understand, Sergeant?" And the sergeant said, "Yes, Sir, I understand." So Byng drops the handkerchief, the sergeant orders "Fire," and the men shoot Byng dead. That's how we ruled the world.

Voltaire picked up on this with the catchy little phrase, *"Dans ce pays-ci il est bon de tuer de temps un amiral pour encourager les autres."* To encourage the others, the English shoot their generals or admirals who botch it up.

Okay, so we want respectability. But it is more important to be respected. Respect is higher up the ladder than respectability.

HOLMES: And that [respect] is being debased?

EDMONDS: Indeed. Liberalism automatically debases it. Automatically.

HOLMES: Above all, you must be committed to certain values.

EDMONDS: Exactly, exactly. Think of Admiral Byng out there. "Are you ready, Sergeant?" "Yes, Sir." *[Laughter]* The English maintain standards.

Exclusionary Welfarism

Mr. Edmonds makes a series of assertions which disrupt what are presumed to be the fundamental political distinctions separating Left and Right. In so doing, he articulates how a core agenda of the nationalist Right in Europe—not just in Britain—is taking form. He starts with a classic assertion of a primal community or nation without which "men go mad." It is an indivisible, racially homogeneous community existing in memory and integral to "identity" which he values above everything else. What gives his vision of community incendiary power is its linkage to the social apparatus of the state. He predicates regimes of community and nation on the political economy of the welfare state—regulated by a racialized delimitation of citizenship—to yield an exclusionary welfarism. The pursuit of a radically discriminatory social contract establishes the basis for a resurgent British national socialism.

Public housing encompasses the ambiguities of community. It has become a setting where social justice is contested, where the social reproduction of the white working-class family is in jeopardy. For the East Enders, the local council housing belongs to them as a community, manifesting their sense of belonging. In Mr. Edmonds's equation, estate housing is owned by the council, so it is owned by the community. The right of newly arrived immigrants to England to petition for public housing disrupts the moral economy of the white working-class estate violating the traditional practices of succession. Under these customary arrangements, flats were transmitted within families from one generation to the next, or preference was granted to young couples seeking housing in close proximity to their parents. The administrative priority given to housing homeless, immigrant families with numerous members, newly arrived to Britain, pits their legal claims against the traditional, moral claims of islander families.

It is "defects" in the legal application of citizenship which creates the mechanism by which a multiracial and multicultural Britain is created and Mr. Edmonds's deep sense of estrangement is instilled. Again, public housing is the crucible. If you live somewhere, you get on the electoral rolls. Immigrants have a right to an abode, even if they are "illegal," and once housed they are put automatically on the electoral rolls conferring on them a basic right of citizenship. The fact that they are voting in numbers sufficient to win local elections, wearing yashmacs, and not speaking a word of English is intolerable to Mr. Edmonds. It confirms his portrayal of an embattled "white" community whose economic and social reproduction is threatened. It is a story which he believes power brokers in Britain, committed to neoliberalism and multiculturalism, will not allow to be narrated. From his plausible account of an encroaching exile in his homeland, Mr. Edmonds goes on, through cascading paranoia, to envision a plot to exterminate the "white man," and hence the rationale for his lurid, "factual racism."

Extermination

There is a tyranny to Mr. Edmonds's memory which juxtaposes a childlike vision of London in the 1950s as a happy city within a law-abiding society, against a middle-aged vision of the present rife with invidious differences, cultural clashes, and societal decay. These same reveries oblige him to project cataclysms into the future. Despite gross distortions in his analyses, in one important way he engages in an acute assessment of contemporary circumstances. He is willing to frame his local predicament in global terms, within a wider critique of political economy.

Mr. Edmonds sees motive in the drive and the power of transnational capitalism—to sack the white man. Its mechanism is obvious; jobs are exported to the Third World, to zones of cheap labor. With three million Britons unemployed for each of the last twelve years, chronic unemployment is the permanent outcome. But the external threat is matched by an internal moral vulnerability: greed, stupidity, selfishness, and weakness. Britons, as representatives of the white race, are selling their traditional birthright—technological prowess—for material comforts.[25] The solution for these challenges is nationalism, a nationalism mediated through authoritarianism and corporatism. This means putting white people before the power of money: stop the export of technology, stop immigration, stop the export of capital, stop the importation of goods manufactured in the Third World. Mr. Edmonds has *no* rancor for the businessman. Let them use their energies, their talents, their experience, and their capital, but community values must be supreme in his corporatist scheme.

Mr. Edmonds asserts that the program of the Left, promoting multiculturalism, destroys the traditional social consensus which made Britain, as he describes it, a sort of socialist state in which life was quite stable and pleasant, where the police were unarmed. He argues that the path to multiculturalism annihilates the social contract which sustained his memorialized Britain. Few are willing to narrate this ruinous progression. For Mr. Edmonds, the proliferation of crime, the murder of police officers, the turning of young people to drug addiction are the consequences of a pluralist society which subverts the traditional social order. Threats to the reproduction of the white working-class family and community posed by immigrants are a "life and death matter." Militant Muslims make direct threats against the lives of British Jews, the British prime minister, and British citizen Salman Rushdie with impunity.[26] It exemplifies a whole society falling apart. He sees the problems of the Western world accelerating at an enormous rate as multicultural principles come to dominate. He predicts cultures will succumb to clashes which are impossible to resolve. The "alien wedge" of nonwhite immigrants threatens the existence of the white race in Britain.[27] Mr. Edmonds "knows" that if you raise these views, they call you a Nazi and you risk attack without warning.

Factual Racism

What poisons Mr. Edmonds's critique of neoliberalism is its identification of nonwhite immigrants as the agents, indeed, the *embodiment* of global capitalism. Each aspect of their difference—skin color, language, religion, dress— conjures the grim battle with "dark" global forces igniting Mr. Edmonds's racist fury. Each encounter with these differences ratifies his sense of exile. The elites of post-World War II Britain conspired to disguise the struggle through the "veil of silence." Politicians lied while the press reported that the presence of nonwhite immigrants was temporary. Only Enoch Powell depicted the confrontation "truthfully," in a virulently nationalist idiom. Mr. Edmonds's sense of betrayal and outrage have been rendered illicit, his claims have no "respectable" means of societal redress. He is left in a world devoid of mediating forms of political expression.[28] His only recourse is to tactical thuggery, to streetfighting. The South Asians he confronts are *not* the victims of a transnational capitalism, they are, in his view, its physical incarnation, its substance. His racism is factual and militant. Repatriation is the only answer.

Notes

1. The BNP is the successor to the (British) National Front. There are a number of journals which have chronicled in great detail all the events covered in this chapter from an antiracist and antifascist stance. The most important and most thorough is the London based *Searchlight,* which carefully monitors and interprets neofascist activity in Britain and Europe. *CARF: Campaign Against Racism and Fascism* also provides a coverage of the struggle against the BNP. See also the collection edited by Mike Cronin, *The Failure of British Fascism: The Far Right and the Fight for Political Recognition* (London: Routledge, 1996).

2. According to *Searchlight*, no. 229 (1994): 3, Mr. Edmonds is the owner of the building.

3. In "Managing a Polyethnic Milieu: Kinship and Interaction in a London Suburb" (*Man* 1, no. 4 [December 1995]: 725–41), Gerd Baumann argues that the complexities of the urban districts of London must be seen as going well beyond mere distinctions between and among "ethnic" groups or "cultures." "What is interesting about urban 'ethnicity,' and in particular its discursive devices of 'ethnic' and 'community,' is its capacity to hide the very multiplicity of linguistic, regional, national and other cultural cleavages that cut across each other. Any of these cross-cutting cleavages, and several others such as religion and caste, can take on the significance of ethnic or community boundaries, depending on context" (738). Abner Cohen's *Masquerade Politics: Explorations in the Structure of Urban Cultural Movement* (Berkeley: University of California Press, 1993) provides an excellent depiction of the Notting Hill Carnival as a vehicle for transformation and integration within a multicultural district of London.

4. See the texts by C. T. Husbands, *Racial Exclusion and the City: The Urban Support of the National Front* (London: George Allen & Unwin, 1983) and David Sibley, *Geographies of Exclusion: Society and Difference in the West* (London: Routledge, 1995).

5. The notion of the organic intellectual comes of course from Antonio Gramsci. "Mr. Edmonds is not only one of the better educated, though nevertheless crazy, BNP leader. . . . His wife is a former Oxford student with a good job in computing at London University. She . . . has been openly critical of the 'Jew-obsessed losers' with whom he has surrounded himself" (*Searchlight* no. 229: 3).

6. See Paul Gilroy's *"There Ain't No Black in the Union Jack"* (Chicago: University of Chicago Press, 1991); and *Black Atlantic: Modernity and Double Consciousness* (Cambridge, Mass.: Harvard University Press, 1993); and Dilip Hiro's *Black British White British: A History of Race Relations in Britain* (London: Paladin, 1991).

7. Quoted in Eugen Weber's *My France: Politics, Culture, Myth* (Cambridge: Cambridge University Press, 1991), 264.

8. Henry VIII kept his royal dogs and visited for hunting trips from Placentia Palace across the river, hence the name.

9. The history of Afro-Caribbeans in London dates to 1555. The most recent wave of immigration dates from the arrival of five hundred immigrants aboard the S.S. *Empire Windrush* in 1948. A small community of Indian seamen was already present around the Docklands in the mid-nineteenth century. See Nick Merriman, ed., *The Peopling of London: Fifteen Thousand Years of Settlement from Overseas* (London: Museum of London, 1993). The most important phase of recent immigration to Tower Hamlets commences with the arrival of around five thousand migrant workers between 1954 and 1956.

10. As of April 1992 (*Communities of Resistance 1993/94*, annual report of the Newham Monitoring Project, 47).

11. This should by no means be construed as a full ethnographic account of the political life of the East End. Although leaders from the major antiracist groups in Tower Hamlets as well as leaders of major Bengali community organization were interviewed, their accounts are not included herein. To do justice to the rich political life of these variously constituted community organizations requires a fuller ethnographic

treatment, which is beyond the scope of this study. Fortunately, John Eade has published in a series of fine-grained analyses of these issues. This body of work constitutes an excellent introduction to the political anthropology and history of the Bangladeshi community in Tower Hamlets. See in particular his essay "The Political Construction of Class and Community: Bangladeshi Political Leadership in Tower Hamlets, East London," in Pnina Werbner and Muhammad Anwar, eds., *Black and Ethnic Leaderships in Britain* (London: Routledge, 1991).

12. I have accounts of eight individuals who participated in the confrontations described in this section. I have drawn heavily on the narrative of these events as reported in *Searchlight,* no. 220 (Oct. 1993).

13. "The Anti Nazi League (ANL) was launched on 10 November [1977]. . . . The League was launched as a broad initiative, drawing together sponsors from right across the spectrum of radical politics. . . . The League's founding statement drew attention to the electoral threat posed by the NF and their associates. The danger they represented was once again conveyed by reference to the Nazism of Hitler" (Gilroy 1991, 131).

14. The events of September 1993 are reminiscent of an earlier election, punctuated by violence, which first galvanized the Bengali community to political mobilization. "Active involvement in local political institutions and policies was encouraged by the events surrounding the 1978 borough election which involved opposition to the National Front and the murder of a young Sylheti garment worker, Altab Ali, on the night of the poll" (Eade 1991, 86). The murder was followed by a rampage by members of the National Front down Brick Lane (Eade 1991, 88). It also recalls a now mythologized confrontations between Oswald Mosley's "Blackshirts" and antifascists which took place around the corner from Brick Lane on Cable Street, the "Battle of Cable Street," on 4 October 1936. Oswald Mosley arrived for a march through the East End "with a motor-cycle escort and standing up in the open Bentley doing the fascist salute in his new uniform—he walked up and down the columns of Blackshirts inspecting them while the crowd, beyond the lines of police, began to charge, were here and there broke through." The march was delayed while the police—six thousand were present—tried to push their way through Cable Street. A melee ensued between the police and the various antifascist groups defending their barricades on Cable Street. Mosley was ordered by the police to halt. He complied and had his men march away from the fray. Thus this famous "battle" was, in fact, a confrontation between the police and antifascists, of whom eighty-three were arrested. See Nicholas Mosley's (1991) *Rules of the Game, Beyond the Pale: Memoirs of Sir Oswald Mosley and Family* (Elmwood Park, Ill.: Dalkey Archive, 1991), 377–78.

15. This is known as "glassing."

16. See the 1994 article entitled "Demands for Action After BNP Boss Walks Free," *Searchlight,* no. 229: 3–5.

17. For an overview of the British Nationality Acts of 1948 and 1981, see Hiro 1991, 198, 259–60.

18. There is a substantial literature on the "official" and "unofficial" immigration and its control. Again, for a general overview, see Hiro 1991: 200–203, 250–51, 257–58. For an analysis of the government's role in this process, see the recent text by Kathleen Paul, *Whitewashing Britain: Race and Citizenship in the Postwar Era* (Ithaca, N.Y.: Cornell University Press, 1997).

19. Mr. Edmonds's view of the history of this terminology is, perhaps, authoritative given that the leadership of the National Front played a direct role in the first panic over "mugging" and its linkage to the discourse on race. "The neo-fascists had organized a 'March Against Mugging' in September of 1975 under the slogan 'Stop the Muggers. 80% of muggers are black. 85% of victims are white.' This was significant not simply for its open defiance of the laws on incitement to racial hatred and the new tactic of provocative marches through black areas but for the convergence it represented between the respectable politics of race signaled by the authoritative official crime statistics and the street level appeal of the neo-fascist groups who had seized the issue of black crime and begun to refine it into a populist weapon which could prove the wisdom of their distinctive solution to Britain's race problem—repatriation" (Gilroy 1991, 120).

20. He is referring to a conference held at Wembley Arena in August 1994 organized by the Muslim Unity Organization, a coalition led by *Hizb-ut-Tahrir*. It is believed to be the biggest gathering of fundamentalists outside the Middle East, with eight thousand in attendance. The conference called for the establishment of Islamic schools in Britain and ultimately the establishment of an Islamic state (*Independent,* 8 Aug. 1994).

21. This is in reference to Enoch Powell's incendiary speech in Birmingham on 20 April 1968. The speech is filled with carefully crafted phrases and images to engender, if not ignite, white fear. "Under the circumstances, to enact the 1968 Race Relations Bill (then before Parliament) was to 'risk throwing a match on to gun powder.' " Concluding, he saw ahead, like the Roman, "the River Tiber foaming with much blood" (Hiro 1992, 246–47). Enormous public support followed in the wake of the speech, as did calls for censure. Ultimately, Edward Heath dismissed Powell from the shadow cabinet. Nevertheless, Enoch Powell continues, as the letter quoted above suggests, to be the most important critic of Britain's immigration and race policies.

22. Bill Buford's account of his participation at a social gathering of the National Front captures the popular view of the style and the temperament of supporters of the extreme Right (*Among the Thugs* [New York: Vintage, 1992], esp. the chapter entitled "Bury St. Edmunds"). See also Alan Clarke's 1983 film *Made in Britain*.

23. "[Richard] Edmonds was remanded at Thames magistrates' court in September 1993, accused of a violent assault on a black man" (*CARF* no. 17 (Nov./Dec. 1993): 12).

24. It was widely reported in the press coverage of the campaign that the Liberal Party's practices regarding the housing of immigrants were highly questionable, if not racist, in Tower Hamlets.

25. Liah Greenfeld argues eloquently in her *Nationalism: Five Roads to Modernity* (Cambridge: Cambridge University Press, 1992) for the crucial role of science in the formation of English nationalism through the work of the Royal Society of London.

26. Ironically, it is precisely Muslim militancy which he seeks to emulate to protect "his" community and nation.

27. A term coined by Enoch Powell.

28. Paul Gilroy has probed this "crisis of representation": "The Right has created a language of nation which gains populist power from calculated ambiguities that allow it to transmit itself as a language of 'race.' At the same time, the political resources of the white working class are unable to offer a vision, language or practice capable of providing an alternative" (1991, 29).

LONE GUNMEN: LEGACIES OF THE GULF WAR, ILLNESS, AND UNSEEN ENEMIES

> From outside, the evil that has invaded Carrell and Shana Clark's home is invisible. Set on a modest plot in a San Antonio subdivision, equipped with a doghouse and a swimming pool, the house is a shrine to the pursuit of happiness—a ranch style emblem of the good life Darrell and 700,000 other U.S. soldiers fought for in the Persian Gulf four years ago. Inside, the evil shows itself at once. It has taken up residence in the body of the Clarks' three-year-old daughter, Kennedi.
>
> — "The Tiny Victims of Desert Storm"
> (Miller, Hudson, and Briggs 1995, 46)

In November 1995 *Life* magazine published the results of its own special investigation of the problems faced by children born to veterans of Operation Desert Storm, the code name for U.S. operations in the Persian Gulf. The cover of the magazine is a portrait of U.S. Army Sgt. Paul Hanson, and his three-year-old son Jayce, who suffers from a syndrome similar to that of the thalidomide babies of the 1950s. His mother, Connie, took no drugs. But his father did. During his service in the Gulf. The drugs were administered with a special waiver from the U.S. Food and Drug Administration, to provide protection against Saddam Hussein's arsenal of chemical and biological weapons.

The drugs taken by Sergeant Hanson were only one component of the concern which motivated *Life*'s investigation. According to a 1994 report by the U.S. General Accounting Office, a key reference throughout the *Life* article, American soldiers were exposed to twenty-one potential "reproductive toxicants." They used diesel fuel to control flying sand, and handled ethylene glycol monomethyl ether, a nerve gas decontaminant which is itself toxic. They doused themselves with bug spray containing DEET, which may multiply in toxicity when combined with pyridostigmine, given to most Americans in the Gulf as protection from nerve gas. They may even actually have been exposed to nerve or mustard gas, supplied to Iraq by U.S. companies, eighty of which have faced a class-action suit filed by two thousand veterans. (Miller, Hudson, and Briggs 1995, 54)

Life conducted its inquiry into the plight of the "children of Desert Storm" for two specific purposes: it wanted to determine whether U.S. policies put these children at risk and therein incurred responsibility for their welfare, and it wanted to determine "whether, as some scientists and veterans allege, the military's own investigation is deeply flawed." The stakes of the investigation were said to be high. "The future of this country's volunteer armed forces— institutions dependent on citizens' willingness to serve, and therefore on their trust—may rest on the answers to such questions. Certainly, soldiers expect to forfeit their health, if necessary, in the line of duty. But no one expects that of a soldier's kids" (ibid., 51).

Life's coverage of the aftereffects of Desert Storm points to many of the themes addressed here, in an interview with a veteran who goes by the name of Peck. The interview is about shifting understandings of responsibility and validity. It is about a social context in which there is an abundance of infor- mation, yet also abundant suspicions that available information is incomplete or even fraudulent. It is about extraordinary desire for understanding, coupled with keen awareness that the complexity of the issues defies the possibility of expert comprehension.

Precision, clarity, "knowing all the variables": these were qualities Peck learned to valorize while he was in the service. They don't seem as promising as they once did, as Peck tries to deal with his concerns about the lingering effects of toxic exposure. Entrenched emblems of excellence, "the good life," and loyalty have become either beyond reach or suspect. Children like Kennedi Clark haunt his decisions, and profoundly unsettle what counts as trustworthy knowledge, and as trustworthy behavior.

Peck is a pseudonym, believed to be necessary, even though it is not clear who would find identification significant, or how repercussions would materi- alize. We chose the name Peck to remind readers of the acute disjuncture be- tween contemporary and classic, often filmic, portrayals of how the military is served, and, in turn, protects. Peck is aware of these disjunctures, noting often how images from *The Guns of Navarone* (starring Gregory Peck) and *The Dirty Dozen* inform, and confuse, his understanding of the military and its alle- giances. These films follow a linear plot, underscored by a clear enemy, a clear mission, and clear possibilities for heroism. Peck's experience in the Gulf War followed a different script, and has lacked climactic conclusion.

For Peck and other veterans, Desert Storm continues. The images and bodily effects of this continuance lack both clarity and any sense of when and how boundaries have been breached and harm inflicted. The medium of remem- brance is not the classic war story narrating horrific eye-to-eye encounters in which blood flowed, limbs were lost, and comrades were pulled to safety. For Peck there are no war stories. While deployed in the Gulf, little, recognizable, happened. The effects of service in the Gulf nonetheless persist. The medium of remembrance is not the story but the sound byte, the Web page, and occasional coverage by sources taken as "grains of salt."

Instead of artillery battery, Peck has been hit by media fire, the Internet, and myriad other inexplicable forces. Like others threatened by the strange logics of toxic exposure, Peck has been hit with what I think of as "the aleatory effect." The aleatory, often associated with the music of John Cage, has an effect of "alloverness." It is produced by an underdetermined deluge of stimuli lacking any syntax or hierarchy of significance. The deluge is scrambled, overtly marked as contingent, and at obvious odds with hegemonic logic. The deluge of stimuli comes as scattershot. The random news story recounting how a baby was born without an ear, and with a heart in the wrong place. The headache, that once would have been ignored. Reference to a report from the General Accounting Office, about the use of a new kind of ammunition in the Gulf: shells jacketed with depleted uranium. The skin rash that one thinks one sees, lurking beneath the surface. The Web site found while surfing, linking without connecting. The glossy magazine cover, asking if our country has abandoned them. The photo: U.S. Army Sgt. Paul Hanson and his three-year-old son Jayce, who has no arms.

For many vets the aleatory effect began as a dribble shortly after the war. Things escalated quickly. By May 1994 the *Journal of the American Medical Association* published an article on a workshop at the National Institutes of Health which was "supposed to reassure Persian Gulf veterans that everything that can be done is being done to investigate their mysterious health complaints." The title of the article: "Veterans Seeking Answers to Syndrome Suspect They Were Goats in Gulf War" (Cotton 1994). A lead sentence explains that "even giving the military full benefit of the doubt, it is hard not to conclude that its efforts to date have created a candy store for conspiracy buffs." The metaphor of a candy store is apt, albeit by way of the negative. The article is about missing information, about a candy store stocked with luring signs of knowledge products which should be available but are, as yet, nowhere to be seen. The lure comes from stories told by veterans and health professionals which indicate an overwhelming lack of explanation—other than coincidence. Herds of dead animals that flies wouldn't touch. Reports of nerve and mustard gas detections by Czech forces that were never confirmed. Repeated "assertions, steadfastly denied by military officials, of mass burials of thousands of Iraqi bodies allegedly contaminated by chemical or biological weapons—what some call Operation Desert Sword." Missing medical records, including accounts of adverse reactions to anthrax vaccinations—which, according to some, "were in fact experimental recombinant DNA products and not the standard preparations that the Food and Drug Administration approved for use without informed consent" (Cotton 1994, 1561). Reference to Desert Storm as a "living laboratory" in which veterans were used as guinea pigs, in a way comparable to the secret radiation experiments by the U.S. Department of Energy.

In isolation, any one of these "grains of salt" would not seem significant. It is the cumulative effect which is powerful, provoking new mappings of how the world works and new logics for explicating where trust should be located. One potent projection: theorization of conspiracy. Conspiracy theories about Gulf War Illness have not been provoked by any one traumatic or especially noteworthy incident. Instead, veterans have heard news stories, exchanged memos across the Internet, and, occasionally, met other vets with whom they could share stories. Theorization of conspiracy has thus been gradual, cumulative, and often via indirection. Here I illustrate the aggregate effect on one individual, exploring how conspiracy theories have been provoked, produced, and made to function, within efforts to respond to the strange circulations of information which shape concern about Gulf War Illness.

Peck's World

FORTUN: So did you want to be a Marine when you were three years old?

PECK: I always had my little army figures that I played with . . . when I got older I'd throw firecrackers at them, make piles. My parents grew up in the fifties and sixties; they still have Christmas ornaments with peace symbols; we lived right in the Woodstock area. . . . So it was a conflict when I wanted to enlist. I was in the top quarter of my class in high school, so they knew I could go on to college, and they were afraid I would never go.

FORTUN: Do you remember why you wanted to enlist?

PECK: I was a typical gung-ho Reagan-era teenager. I grew up with the Iran hostage situation, a very pro-American time in American history. I was always very shy, never talked much, so it seemed quite out of character. I still wanted to deal with the environmental field, eventually go to college, become a forest ranger or a wildlife biologist. But I wanted to do the Marine Corps first. I had American flags all over my bed room. . . .

FORTUN: Were you too young to think about getting shot at?

PECK: No, I knew it. Actually, to be really honest, I was planning to go into the Marine Corps and not come back alive. That was my goal in life. I thought it would be the most honorable thing: to die, in the heat of battle, jumping on a grenade. And it lasted well while I was in. Probably until the last unit I got stationed with, which I wasn't really crazy about. Until I was about twenty-one. A very patriotic attitude.

FORTUN: Did you watch movies, or read novels, that loaded you up with all these military dreams?

PECK: I wasn't really into reading, but I watched all the movies. *The Guns of Navarone. Dirty Dozen.* I watched all of them.

FORTUN: Did they prepare you in any way to question the military, like you do today?

PECK: Back then I still questioned individuals, and individual decisions, but I thought the Marine Corps as a whole was kind of immune. I didn't know if I thought there was some kind of council or something. Not that it didn't ever make mistakes, but that it was always working for the good of the country. And people have to die; that's a fact of life. And I was ready for that. I almost got my recruiter thrown in the brig because I caught him in a lie, and I told someone about it, not knowing that I had caught him in a lie. I thought this guy was an exception, an individual who was bad, since his supervisor responded right to the letter of the law. And my faith in the system was restored.

FORTUN: Was there a reason you joined the Marine Corps instead of the navy, army, or air force?

PECK: It was supposed to be the best. The biggest, the baddest, the toughest. And everything I've done in my life I've tried to do a little bit more than the average.

FORTUN: You got recruited right out of high school?

PECK: I was only seventeen, so I had to get my parents' permission. It was 1987 when I first signed the papers. Then I left for boot camp, at Paris Island, South Carolina.

FORTUN: Was it bad?

PECK: I was disappointed. I thought it was going to be tougher. It wasn't a picnic, but I was disappointed.

FORTUN: Anything like *Full Metal Jacket?*

PECK: A lot like that. The first part of that movie, especially. Almost exactly. I can name people in my platoon who corresponded to people in the movie—we had a Private Pile—

FORTUN: Were you like Joker?

PECK: No, I was one of the ones that they never noticed. That was one piece of advice that really held: don't be on the top, and don't be on the bottom. Just be somewhere in the middle, so that they don't even know your name when you graduate.

FORTUN: Was there humiliation, like in the movie?

PECK: Exactly like the movie. Worse. There were a lot of things that went down.

FORTUN: The idea was that humiliation was productive, because it prepared people to be subservient to command?

PECK: I couldn't tell you exactly, but soon after I went through boot camp there was a restructuring, a revamping of the system, and the people that came out lacked the discipline that I and my peers had.

FORTUN: Does having discipline mean that someone does what they are told?

PECK: Doing what you're told, without being belligerent to your superiors.

FORTUN: Was belligerence a big problem?

PECK: It was a problem when it was my turn to bark out the orders and people didn't jump as high.

FORTUN: Was it respect that was at issue, or the possibility that people could get killed?

PECK: Getting killed was what I was worried about. Granted, cleaning the head doesn't involve life and death, but it was part of the whole process of accepting the decisions of your superiors.

FORTUN: Where were you stationed, what were you doing, before you were sent to the Gulf?

PECK: My official position was as a combat engineer. First I was assigned to a combat unit, then to an antiaircraft battalion, which was structured very differently. The combat unit was all combat engineers; we all practiced techniques of patrolling, explosives. When I got switched to the antiaircraft unit, I was one of only three combat engineers. We were kind of like extras; we picked up the slack, what they didn't want to do. Mess hall duty, things like that. So it was a big disappointment for me.

FORTUN: What is a combat engineer?

PECK: It's very low. There are highly skilled, intelligent people—electronics, intelligence-type people on the top. Combat engineers are about as close to the bottom as you get. We did land-mine detection and installation, explosives, basic construction—bunkers, antimine traps, booby traps.

FORTUN: When you got transferred to the new unit, was there any reasoning behind it?

PECK: The Marine Corps tries to keep you moving. They don't keep you in one place all that long. And, usually, in a four-year hitch, you'll spend one period on an overseas tour, or with a deployable tour. That was my first year, in Okinawa. Then it was time for me to come back stateside, and I got reassigned.

FORTUN: All these stories about the Marine Corps daring—they aren't pulled off by a group of close-knit guys, who have been together a long time?

PECK: It all depends on the job you're in. Combat engineers move around a lot. A friend of mine, in a helicopter repair unit, he pretty much stayed with the same group the whole time he was in.

FORTUN: This friend, did you see him often?

PECK: We were friends at the base school, but didn't see each other much afterward. It's been hard to stay in touch, and hard to really get to know new people. Now I'm almost totally isolated from others with similar experiences, except through the Internet. Online, that's where I meet my neighbors.

FORTUN: While you were in, who did you talk to if you were worried about something, or had something to complain about?

PECK: There's one thing that's true. A marine is never happy unless he's bitching about something. You'll hear that at any base you go to. Bitching all the time, especially about the Marine Corps itself.

So you do have to take what I'm saying now with a grain of salt. I've been out four years now, and am living on idealized memories that leave out the really stupid, stupid things we had to do. Only good memories stick with me. Things that seemed ridiculous at the time. Hike fifteen miles to have breakfast. Get up, hike fifteen, have an MRE [meal ready to eat], go back. Yes, it was for training, but. . . . We'd cover around five miles an hour. With everything on your back. Your feet blistered and swollen. One hundred ten degrees.

FORTUN: What if something came up, and you were unsure about the decisions being made? Could you voice your concerns or fears?

PECK: We knew enough to keep it among ourselves. We knew who we could bitch with. We talked among ourselves, as we were filling sandbags, "until the desert has no sand." But no, not to the commanding officer.

FORTUN: You haven't told me anything that was very exciting. What was the lure that kept you walking all those miles?

PECK: The possibility of being deployed. I just waited for it. Before the Gulf, there was only one time when it seemed a real possibility. Tiananmen Square. We were on a ship en route to mainland Japan, from Okinawa. We were tugging along just like normal and all of a sudden the engine was cut. We were just sitting in the middle of the ocean and two seconds later the commanding officer came on the announcement system. I can almost repeat verbatim the words he used: "A crisis situation has arisen in the People's Republic of China. We're prepared to go in." I guess we were to go and get the Americans out. It was exciting. That was what I was waiting for. Then they announced that they had decided to use aircraft. Decisions were made so fast. Then we were back on course.

This is what's made me want to go back in, after college. Finally, it's fading off. Just for the excitement. Really. Now my biggest thrill comes from a surf on the Internet. That's about as fast as it gets. Being out in the thick of it, adrenaline flowing, doing what you do well.

Here, maybe because I'm in college, I'm so aware that I don't know what I need to know. There's only so much you have to know out in the field. When you get back, there's Physics 101. One class that could occupy your whole life, just trying to understand a little part of it. In the Marines, I felt in control. I like it. That's what would take me back in.

It's easy to forget all that time spent cleaning the head, washing the parking lot with a toothbrush, thirty-mile marches. Imagine flying in a plane. The back door is open as you're landing. You jump out of the plane as it's still moving down the runway. It's great. You know, my wife loves rides at the amusement park. I hate them. She says it's a thrill. There's too much safety involved for it to be a real thrill.

FORTUN: So you equate excitement with what is unsafe?

PECK: It's a performance thing. It's safe, if you totally push yourself to the performance level that's required. That's the key word: *yourself.* I can jump off a moving plane safely, if I plan it correctly. If I don't, I'm going to get hurt. I'm not relying on anybody or anything else to do it for me. I'm in control. Precision. Doing something exactly right. Clarity. Knowing where the weak spots are. Knowing what conditions you can't anticipate. Knowing all the variables, all the uncertainties. The call is mine. Now I rely on somebody else's imprecision.

FORTUN: Tell me about hearing that you might be sent to the Gulf.

PECK: I was on a beach in North Carolina, standing on the back of a truck. Someone came up to me and said he thought we were moving out.

FORTUN: Was this pretty close to the end of your hitch?

PECK: Nineteen ninety-one. Around the two-thirds mark. I was in the middle of the field, doing maneuvers. We had no radio, so we still didn't know much when they said to pack up so that we could get back to base. Someone said that Iraq had invaded Kuwait. I knew where Iraq was. And I kept telling myself that I had heard of Kuwait. I was so excited. I really, really wanted to go.

FORTUN: At this point, did you still want to die in the service?

PECK: I was gung ho and ready. Already I had been trying to get switched to another unit, a combat unit, where I would be with my own kind.

Ready to Roll

FORTUN: So you are in South Carolina, and you hear you are moving out, and you don't know where Kuwait is. What happens next?

PECK: We went back to the base. Less than a month later, half the unit goes, and the other half stays. I was with the half that stayed. And I was really disappointed. I was practically on my knees, begging the noncommissioned officer who was making the decisions. I remember knocking on his door, asking to talk to him, going into his office. Saying that I really wanted to go. Then, it was a waiting game. Every week they would say we were going. Practically every week between August and 2 January. We were told we'd be gone by Halloween, by Thanksgiving, Christmas, by New Year's. Then, all of a sudden, we were gone.

FORTUN: During the wait, were you getting briefings, or special training, on chemical warfare?

PECK: Oh, yeah, lots of extra training. I was given classes on Iraqi land mines. We had a lot of biological and chemical warfare training. A lot of work with MOPPs—Mission-Oriented Protected Posture. It's a suit made out of charcoal. A giant charcoal filter. The suit is very thick, very warm. It's almost like wearing a wet suit. You really sweat. You're covered from head to toe. We did everything from play volleyball in it to go on extended marches.

FORTUN: Did you get freaked out by this? You dreamed of dying because you had jumped on a grenade. Dying from exposure to bacteria or viruses is a little different.

PECK: That's a good question. I had no doubt that the Iraqis were going to use chemical weapons. No doubt. I was 100 percent positive.

FORTUN: Because you were told this in the briefing?

PECK: No, I think it was more my own judgment. I had looked at the situation. They had used chemical warfare agents on their own people. Why wouldn't they use them on us? Maybe I wasn't a 100 percent sure. Just 99.99 percent sure. That .01 percent was because President Bush had said that we would use nuclear weapons against them if they did.

FORTUN: Did chemical weapons seem a less heroic way to die?

PECK: No, not at all. I was just as excited about it as ever; it just made it more of a challenge. To be honest, the only thing I thought about was that I have a harder time aiming my rifle with a gas mask on. It's harder to aim when you've got this flat lens in front of your eyes. That was my mentality.

FORTUN: Did they tell you what it was like to be exposed so that you could understand what was happening to you?

PECK: There was a lot of preparation. We had a lot of medical briefing, from navy personnel, since the marines don't have their own medical unit. Briefings on what you could expect to happen, since there was an antidote, for nerve gas, which everyone carried on them. You were supposed to recognize some of the symptoms and administer your own antidote. Whether it would have worked or not, I don't know. I don't know anyone who actually took it. It was a series of three shots.

FORTUN: Did they tell you what to expect of things they didn't have antidotes for?

PECK: Before we left, the only thing I was thinking about was nerve gas. I didn't even know what anthrax was. I didn't know it was biological, micro-bacterial.

FORTUN: When did they administer the drugs?

PECK: Once we got over there, I think. We were given a series of shots before we left but, as far as I knew, they were for things like typhoid. This wasn't unusual. We were always getting shots; we were human pincushions the whole time we were in. We had flu shots every year. AIDS testing every three to six months. Urinalysis all the time. We used to joke that they were shooting us up with water, just for practice. So nothing seemed unusual, beforehand. I didn't question anything, before we got there.

FORTUN: But now you know that you were given different drugs than other units?

PECK: That's just hearsay. Hearing from people once we got back. When we got over there, I remember taking two specific pretreatments, for nerve gas and anthrax. And a lot of people questioned it. I dealt with it myself, and decided I would take it. A lot of people weren't taking it. They would announce over the loud speaker: "the time is now 1600, it's time to take your nerve agent pretreatment pill." And they wouldn't take it.

FORTUN: Why not?

PECK: After all the drugs we had taken, it does seem surprising. Partially, it might have been the unit I was with. It wasn't a direct combat unit; things weren't quite as strict; people seemed to question things a little more. They weren't constantly told that their lives depended on the discipline, like in my previous unit. This unit was a group of generator mechanics. They had something technical to do. They were pretty much left alone to do their jobs. A friend of mine told me something similar about aircraft mechanics: the pilots knew that if they put a lot of stress on these kids maintaining the engines, they would probably mess up.

FORTUN: The guys who didn't take the drugs—were they just being belligerent, or were they really worried about the effects?

PECK: I think they were worried about the effects. I just made the call that it was the better option. I was 99.9 percent sure we were going to get gassed. And the equipment we had wasn't rated to last very long. I thought my chances depended on taking the chance. I was so sure that we were going to get gassed. I thought it better to take my chances with the pills than with nerve gas.

FORTUN: You think the others didn't really think you would get gassed?

PECK: I think they just said, "I ain't taking these things"—but just to themselves, not out in the open. Once word started filtering around that people weren't taking them, they started having formations. Inspecting each person's mouth.

FORTUN: Standing there and watching you swallow?

PECK: Yeah. Get in formation and bring a canteen. They'd walk up and down, look in your mouth, tell you to lift up your tongue.

FORTUN: I still don't understand why these guys were so worried about the pills.

PECK: I can tell you why I was concerned about taking them. The date on the package. That's what worried me. The things were less than three months old. And in the military you never get anything that's less than three years old. Even our food. How could these things be developed, manufactured, and distributed to us, out in the middle of nowhere, in a matter of months? To this day I don't know how they did it. This was the nerve agent. The anthrax, I can't remember what the packaging looked like.

FORTUN: Do you know for sure that you took the anthrax treatment?

PECK: Yeah, it was a big, orange-looking pill.

FORTUN: Is this recorded on your medical records? Do you even have these?

PECK: I have a certified copy. When you leave the military, they're considered your possession, but you have to get them on your own. I took a day out to get them, went and got a certified copy of every page. Someone suggested I do it, in case I ever have a problem later that's connected to my years in the service, so that I can walk into the Veterans Hospital and be eligible for care. Just because I'm a vet doesn't mean I can go there for anything.

Encountering the Other

FORTUN: I want to go back. You arrive where—Saudi Arabia? You get off the plane?

PECK: It was strange. It was cold. I was really tired. We'd been on the plane for over twenty hours. I hadn't gotten a good night's sleep in at least a week. We were on a runway. The lights were really bright. It seemed like forever before we got to a place where I could sleep. We drove to a place called the Scud Bowl, the nickname for a soccer stadium that we commandeered as headquarters for the entire operation. Supposedly, this is where the bigwigs were. We were there for about a day. Then we got shipped up north. But I got to sleep, and they had hot food.

Then we drove for hours in a truck. And got dropped off in the middle of the desert. A pile of sand, a few guys who had gone up the day before. Less than twenty of us.

FORTUN: They left you there all by yourself? What were you supposed to do?

PECK: We were getting ready for the rest of the battalion to come up. Building preliminary fighting holes, doing security checks of the area. Not much sleep. Probably about an hour a night. There was no one in front of us. We were one of the forward-most troops. Completely isolated. Our defenses were minimal; anyone could have snuck over the berm at night. We had a couple of machine guns. That was about it. We were the front line.

FORTUN: Was it like those films about being scared of Indians, worried that they were going to sneak up at night? You were supposed to be ready to shoot at them?

PECK: That's pretty much what I was waiting for. We would just sit there at night. Waiting. It's pretty much what we did throughout the whole war. Once the holes were built, you sat there, looking out. People here probably knew more what was happening elsewhere. We just saw our own little world. That was it. Jets would fly over, and we would hope they were ours. We kinda assumed because of the direction they were flying.

FORTUN: You were using DEET by this point? I've read that some people are concerned that it could have reacted biochemically with the drugs?

PECK: As far as I remember, we didn't use DEET. I don't remember using any bug spray. There were lots of flies. You couldn't eat without getting one in your mouth. But they didn't bite, so far as I remember.

FORTUN: Sand fleas?

PECK: Not a one. In South Carolina, I was covered by them. But not out there. They did spray the heads with some type of insecticide. I don't know what it was, but it killed everything in there. But we never sprayed anything on ourselves.

FORTUN: When did the sky darken?

PECK: I woke up one morning—thought I was totally out of it, that I had lost my mind. We slept in these holes in the ground. It was completely dark, whatever the time of day. I went outside thinking it was morning and it was totally, totally dark. The oil fires had been lit. That was just before the ground war, if I remember correctly. The days kind of escape me.

FORTUN: Weren't you afraid you'd been bombed?

PECK: Someone told me that the wells had been lit. It was nasty, but I just went back to work. It wasn't difficult to breathe, but you could feel it on you. It did finally clear up.

FORTUN: Did you continue to worry about the effects of the drugs?

PECK: I hadn't yet thought that we might be guinea pigs. And I couldn't really imagine what they could possibly do to me. I didn't wonder if I was going to go into convulsions in the middle of the desert. I thought about it as I was taking them, but that's about all. At that point.

I had faith in the system. I had faith in myself. I was really arrogant. I knew my job; I made a point to know it better than anyone I was with. Unlike the others, I had just come back from a whole year of being in a direct combat unit. And I was still up for the test. I thought I knew what I was doing.

But being in the particular unit I was in was a big disappointment. It was an antiaircraft unit. Very high-tech. I was supposed to protect them, keep them from getting shot at. They were book smart, but little common sense. Before, I felt like I was part of a team. I was with other combat engineers; we had a job to do that we all knew well. These guys were generator mechanics and circuitry technicians. They called the rest of us "combat rocks." The four of us didn't have any skills which they thought were worthy. They thought just anybody could pick up a rifle and shoot someone. I felt very restricted; they didn't let me do my job as well as I could have.

FORTUN: Weren't they scared? Didn't they take the need for defense seriously?

PECK: I think they were more scared. I don't want to sound like I was Mr. No Fear, already ready to charge into battle. But compared to the guys I was with, I didn't feel any fear at all. When the Iraqis did come across the line, an antiaircraft unit would be one of the first things they tried to destroy. But I resented being huddled up in the bunker when the air raid sirens went off. I wanted to go outside and do my job. Maybe I was just stupid.

FORTUN: How old were you at this point?

PECK: Twenty-one. Most everybody was between eighteen and twenty-six. Most closer to twenty.

FORTUN: Some of the material you've given me suggested that some people were aware that there were chemical agents in the air during the war. Was there talk of this in your unit?

PECK: To be honest, I don't even know if we had a chemical detection device in our compound. I have absolutely no idea.

FORTUN: So how were you supposed to know if you were under attack?

PECK: Someone turned on the siren. I don't know who's job it was.

FORTUN: Did they ever put it on?

PECK: Yeah, they put it on. When the first Scud missile got launched, it was about two o'clock in the morning, I think, and I was sleeping. The siren went off, and they started announcing that we had to put our suits on, because there's a Scud missile on its way and we don't know what's on it. So I put my suit on and I went back to sleep. And I woke up and they told me I could take it off.

But the thing that was kind of funny with that was that the suits come sealed in this bag, and once you open the bag, the suit's only good for *x* number of days—I wish I could remember for the life of me what it was. Forty-five seems to ring a bell, but it couldn't have been. It must have been shorter. Because I remember that the time came up that these suits ran out, and we were like, Okay, the war's not over yet, can we have another set of suits? And they said, Oh, the, uh, scientific people said that now they're good for twenty days instead of two weeks, so just keep them. And we were like, Yeah, sure, it's just because you guys don't have any more. And then when that time ran out, they said, again that they've been extended to forty-five days.

FORTUN: People weren't outraged?

PECK: What were we going to do? We couldn't pick up our rifles and start charging the commanding officers. I mean, we could have, I guess, but there was still a sense of discipline and integrity. You had to abide by the code. So we laughed about it, said, Well that's typical. We couldn't do anything but laugh about it.

It's a risky job. When you sign up they say you sign your life away, and you do. Your body is actually considered government property, to do with what the government decides to do. A friend of mine got thirty-days' restriction for getting a sunburn: damage to government property. He was fined for destruction of government property, and suspended for thirty days. It was a bad sunburn, but—

FORTUN: You haven't told me, did you ever even see an Iraqi?

PECK: Quite a few. They were looking pretty bad. Really, really sad shape. Happy to eat the food we were griping about.

FORTUN: Did you ever have to shoot at one?

PECK: I think only one guy in our whole unit had to shoot someone. And it was over, that fast. This was after I had left. After the war was over. Someone was trying to steal something. And an officer walked up to him and said, "Shoot that man." So he did.

FORTUN: Did he kill him?

PECK: No. He shot him; I don't know where, but he didn't kill him. The lieutenant walks up and tells you to shoot someone, you do it.

FORTUN: When did you come home?

PECK: On 5 April. I was just there for three months, shorter than almost anyone in the whole theater. We were the last ones over, and the first ones back.

FORTUN: Tell me about getting back.

PECK: The glory days? I was on top of the world. I didn't really feel like I was put to the test while I was there, but everyone else thought so. It was a wave and I rode it. It was great.

We stopped in Ireland on the way back. Drank beer. I talked to a stewardess and she told me we would be stopping over briefly at JFK [International Airport, in New York], so I called my family. All fifty of them drove down. A few beers and pizza at the airport. It was really good. When we got back to the base there was a marching band.

For Memorial Day my home town threw a big party, on the baseball field. Held an awards ceremony for the four or five of us who went to the Gulf. I had just gotten out of surgery for a hernia. But they insisted I come anyway. So I took a few extra pain killers and hobbled up, still all bent over. They gave me a standing ovation. They announced that I had just gotten out of surgery and that it would take a minute. The whole crowd went ballistic. Girls I went to high school with were crying. It was great. For the Fourth of July parade, I was the grand marshall.

Most of these girls had written to me. Just about everyone I went to high school with. Guilt letters. I could tell. They thought that if I died and they hadn't written to me, they would feel guilty for the rest of their lives. When I read them I could tell. A great bunch of letters. And I wrote everyone back.

Grains of Salt

FORTUN: The year after the war, when you were still in: did you start hearing about people getting sick, or people telling war stories and asking questions about what went on there?

PECK: Well, I was still in the same unit, so I didn't have a lot of interaction with other people. The first time I heard about people getting sick was on CNN. I didn't really hear anything out of the military. And I remember being home and almost getting into a fight with my brother over it. On CNN there was a guy laying in a hospital bed; he had complete memory loss; his hair was falling out; he was really sick. My brother turned around and said, "Look, Peck, it's you!" And I almost punched him right there. He was eighteen at the time, had just gone to his first semester of college; he thought he was on top of the world. So he was really arrogant at the time, and I almost put him out for making a joke of this guy who was sick. He put himself on the line, and now he's dying, and here's my brother making a big joke out of it.

FORTUN: When you saw that, was your first sense that whatever happened to him didn't happen to you?

PECK: Even on CNN they said it was such a big question, they had no idea what it was. And I just figured that if there were chemical weapons there, we would have all died right away anyhow. I thought it was clear-cut: either you're dead or you're not, and there wasn't really any in-between.

FORTUN: When did that start to seem more complicated to you?

PECK: I don't know. I heard of more people getting sick, I think on the news. I think the news started playing it a little more. And then they told us that we weren't supposed to give blood anymore, because our blood was contaminated. There's always blood drives on military bases, and then they told us they didn't want our blood anymore. I think they said they considered it contaminated, but I don't want to hold that down as the truth. I remember vaguely that it was like, There's stuff going around that we don't know what it is and we want to take precautions. Like when we're overseas, if you take malaria pills, you're not supposed to give blood. So really, there wasn't anything definitive.

So as far as I was concerned, it was just that something was going on. I would have decided on my own not to give blood, just because of all the drugs we took in a short period of time. I didn't think it was fair to someone else, to take that risk.

FORTUN: So you didn't connect the blood ban to the CNN stories?

PECK: Maybe in the back of my mind. But I don't think I actually did. Because at that time—I'm trying to remember—no, I don't want to say that either. Because there's still not a blaring outcry. It's more like I've been doing my own research, and I'm finding these things out on my own. So it's really not like they're being made aware to me; I'm finding this information out for myself.

FORTUN: Also, during that first year, most everything was probably presented as short-term stuff. It would have been before birth defects started showing up.

PECK: I didn't know about that until I saw that *Life* article. I was down in the basement of the library, saw the magazine, and I picked it up and I read it. I had questioned all the time—my wife really, really wants to have children. And we've always talked, I've always said, You know, these chemicals that I've been exposed to, we need to go and have some kind of test or something done. I said, I don't know what, but we need to. And then I read that article, and it really brought it home to me, that I really need to weigh the risks.

So the blood thing was the first indication. I thought if there's something wrong with my blood, what's to say there isn't something wrong with the rest of me? Not necessarily that it was something individual with my blood, but, as a group, we had been labeled contaminated.

But of course it was way in the back of my mind. I'd watch something on CNN—they were reporting at first that they thought it was petroleum poisoning. And so in the back of my mind I was thinking, That could be it, I guess. And it would go on the back shelf.

I came up with stuff on the Web. I typed in "Gulf War" and up came this page, and I started reading it. So it was that late in my life that things really started to come home.

I read this article in the *American Legion* magazine while I was in the barber shop. It was about evidence that the Russians had sold a secret biological weapon to the Iraqis just prior to the war, and that it was undetectable by all Allied detection methods, and that it was an engineered virus whose purpose was not to hurt the soldiers directly, but to affect their reproductive systems, so that when they went home they wouldn't be able to rebuild the population. It was meant for a long-term type of thing, so the population would become nothing.

It made a lot of sense. I thought it was strange being in the *American Legion* magazine, which is a very promilitary magazine. But it kind of made me think all the more. If I had seen that in *Covert Action Quarterly* I would have taken it with a bigger grain of salt. But I saw it in the *American Legion* magazine, and that made me think: Why aren't we being informed? Why isn't this common knowledge? What is the big secret holding all this stuff back? If there was a biological weapon used, we should be told about it so that we don't contaminate the population.

FORTUN: You knew it was a risky job; this was what attracted you to the marines. Quite literally, you signed your life away, and were happy about it. Does all this add up to acceptance of whatever was going on, so long as they keep you informed, play it straight?

PECK: I'd like to know what happened. I'd like to know what happened exactly. Other than that, I guess you can't go back and erase the past.

FORTUN: But what is your sense of why you don't know?

PECK: That's my problem. I understand there's a reason for classified information, but as far as this is concerned, I really don't understand the reasoning. Well, I could understand: what if it was a government experiment? They're not going to give the results out to the general public and let everyone know we were purposely contaminated to see how we would deal with chemical agents and pretreatments. They don't want that kind of liability on their hands.

If you had asked me six years ago, I would have said that was the craziest thing I ever heard of. I would have called you a communist or something. But now, after—well, I read an article in *Newsweek,* about the medical experiments using radiation on people without their knowledge. The college review edition of *Newsweek.* That was really humbling. I almost want to believe that in this day and age that kind of stuff wouldn't happen, but—

FORTUN: So what's the craziest thing that you've heard, the one where you would really draw the line?

PECK: I don't think I've seen anything super crazy. Everything I've read has had its legitimacy to it. Even the *Covert Action Quarterly* has had its facts in there, that you cannot dispute. The one I thought was funny was the one about aspartame, that's in Nutrasweet. They were saying that Pepsi donated all these cans of Diet Pepsi, with Nutrasweet, and it sat in the sun at a hundred and twenty degrees, and it turned to formaldehyde, and the guys who drank it were poisoned. But unless you have a study that shows how many people drank Diet Pepsi—because I never had a Diet Pepsi while I was there, I can tell you that—there's no way to legitimate that.

But I don't like to totally rule out anything, regardless of how crazy it sounds.

FORTUN: What if there's nothing wrong with your body? Is there a problem, nevertheless, with the way the government has handled this? Do you feel like they could give you more tools with which to deal with all these weird theories?

PECK: The only tool that would make a difference would be unlimited access to all classified government documents. I don't think anything short of that would satisfy me.

It goes both ways: in some cases, the government seems to be more than willing, and not in other cases. The one that keeps striking me is their blatant denial of detecting any chemicals while in the Gulf. Yet every other country we were there with said they detected chemicals. And the big almighty United States says it was just diesel fuels. I don't know how the alarms work, so for me to make a judgment call on what the Czechs say isn't fair. But I'd like to know how the alarms work, and why the reports are different.

FORTUN: How do you know what you do know?

PECK: Almost everything that I have done is from the Internet. I don't know whether that's good or bad. I take everything I read with a grain of salt, and some are bigger than others, depending on who wrote the article. The one site

I subscribe to regularly has a lot of footnoting, and they're also very neutral: they present the information. That's how I learned about the Diet Pepsi thing. They have short little paragraphs on the current theories, then they have letters written by people in the Gulf, and others involved.

FORTUN: Is this the Gulf War Veterans Resource Page?

PECK: Yeah. There's so much information, it boggles my mind. There's also a page run by the military, a declassification page. I haven't read much of it. There's too much.

FORTUN: When did you first access the Net material?

PECK: It was just luck. A friend had just rigged me up to access the Net from home. I was sitting there with a blank screen, not knowing what I was interested in. So I typed in "Gulf War."

FORTUN: What did you think when you saw all that was there?

PECK: I wasn't completely surprised, but it did seem to bring things together, make it seem more real. It wasn't just stories I was hearing on television. It's happening to a lot of people.

FORTUN: Do you believe the Net more than you believe television?

PECK: I've come to question television a lot. I end up laughing, especially at the local news. Sometimes I just can't get over how they try to play certain things up.

This one page, the Gulf War Veterans Resource Page, is run by a nonprofit group. The Web space that they have is donated by a company. They don't pay for their service. They're more bipartisan. They realize that there is a problem. They don't directly advocate that the government does anything. They present the problem. It's a medium for people to exchange information. A lot of researchers have questionnaires on there, that you can fill out and return. I don't know about the validity of these. I'm not sure you could use the data, in a scientific study. For all you know, some ten-year-old is playing around and sending in fake answers.

FORTUN: Has the Net link affected how you worry about your own health?

PECK: It's so hard to know how to pay attention to symptoms. I'm in college. I stay up late at night. I don't eat healthy foods. My wife works all the time. I forget to drink water. But I have to admit, when I get a headache, I wonder, Is this it, or not?

FORTUN: Do you have a sense that you either have it or you don't? Like cancer?

PECK: I have a sense that something is wrong, or it's not. The statistics are out there. And I think that any I get to see are far, far below what's really going on. Just because of my own experience talking to people. People you meet, when they notice your haircut, or something you say, or the way you always take your first step with your left foot. And nobody has asked me to become data. I'm not in any registry anywhere. So a lot of people aren't accounted for.

FORTUN: There are so many theories. Some say that you all were guinea pigs from the start, that the government was using you to test drugs. Others say you got it from the Iraqis. Are some of these theories easier to believe than others?

PECK: There are lots of stories. I'm not willing to rule anything out. So I appreciate how the Web page handles it. In the first three sentences of their introduction they pose the question: "What is Gulf War syndrome?" Their answer: "We don't know." Then they present their data.

FORTUN: What is it that suggests conspiracy?

PECK: I don't want to point the finger at any one person, or institution. The government has changed its story a few times, which makes me a little curious. First they say the chemical alarms didn't go off. They insisted. Then they say they did, but because of diesel fumes. It makes me curious, but I like to try to stay in the middle. There's so much information out there; it's so big. There are so many different angles, so many different people presenting it. It would be inappropriate for me to cull it all just to make it easier to think about, and talk about.

FORTUN: Would you even bother going to the VA hospital to get an opinion? Would you trust what they told you?

PECK: I would like to hear what they have to say, on some days. Other days, I just want to get on with my life, acting as though I don't know these things. I would accept them saying that there is something wrong, more than I would accept them saying that there's nothing. And, I've heard that they treat everything on a symptom-by-symptom basis, not systematically. One thing people emphasize is that the exams aren't standardized, so it's difficult to make comparisons. But they're also worried about too much standardization.

FORTUN: Do you often get a chance to talk about these concerns, with people who were in the Gulf? Do you test the theories, trying to judge which are more or less convincing? It seems so different from the occupational or residential exposure cases that I've learned about before: the issues are localized, affected people either see each other at work every day or live down the street from each other and meet at little league games.

PECK: Rarely, rarely do I meet another veteran. Even while we were in, we're moved around. Occasionally, you run into people you haven't seen in years.

What's similar is the way veterans who are sick are told they're being hysterical. You have to remember, the DOD's official stance is that there is no problem, that there's only psychosomatic illness. So why would we need further research, or any further information? They say it's psychosomatic, stress induced. But I wasn't stressed, except about the fact that my commanding officer was an idiot. He had us painting the desert with paint, practically. That was the most stressful thing. Otherwise, I was excited; I wanted to be there.

I'm not trying to justify it, but I am trying to rationalize it. I'm a little paranoid, but it would be stupid not to be. But I'm not one to worry about carpet fumes, or new paint.

FORTUN: New paint is one thing; depleted uranium shells are another. What about these theories? If they hold, would it affect you? Are they used in anti-aircraft equipment?

PECK: I've heard two different stories. The first one is that it was artillery shells. The other story was that armor is made out of some kind of uranium compound, and when it's exploded, it turns into uranium oxide, which is toxic.

FORTUN: What about the drugs?

PECK: The FDA had given a onetime waiver to the Department of Defense. We were never told about this. The drugs were not investigated. They were not yet considered safe by the Food and Drug Administration. But they were administered to us, without telling us about the waiver. They claim that they did it in the best interest of the troops. Which I buy, in part. There was a high probability that we would be exposed to either chemical or biological weapons. But, I don't know. Did they do any studies at all? Did they just throw a bunch a things together to make it look like we had some protection when we really didn't? Did they do any studies on side effects? Why is it that never before in history has an FDA waiver been necessary? Even if they thought it might work, it would probably have been best to give it to us. Nobody would want the whole Allied force to be wiped out in a single blow.

The waiver. Forced application of drugs. Denial that chemical warfare was used. One article I read said that captured Iraqis said that they had delivered chemical warfare agents. You have all this conflicting information. I don't want to blame the military, but they do need to tell us what they found. We need something definitive.

FORTUN: But, if they did this, provided "definitive information," would you believe them?

PECK: No. What's to prevent anybody from sitting down at a keyboard right now, and typing up their very own declassified document? Really, nothing would satisfy me, short of having keys to the vault and walking through and reading stuff myself. This isn't going to happen.

FORTUN: Why are you so sure?

PECK: Why am I not the good, believing marine I was six years ago? I think it was gradual, probably starting with the drug packets. I remember looking at them and thinking that I wasn't so sure they were very good for me. Regardless of the military's stance, I still questioned it. Then, the Commanding Officer I had while in the Gulf, I questioned him a lot. My old CO, I would have followed right over the edge of a bridge. This guy, I didn't trust him; I wasn't confident of his abilities. He probably got me thinking.

I doubt there is a single person you could pin all this on. Anyway, how could you track him down? What was the starting point? How could you know? It would be like tracking backward in a sandstorm, looking for the Lone Ranger. How do you track the origins of synergistic effect?

FORTUN: It's impossible to locate responsibility?

PECK: Someone should burn. Whoever made the executive decision to give the drugs without notification. That would be a start, even though notification wouldn't have added up to "consent." They would have had to tell people the risks, then tell them they had to take the drugs anyway. You can't say, "all who want to take these drugs raise your hand." It doesn't work that way.

Stop Gap

FORTUN: Tell me about the genetic counseling.

PECK: My wife went for a checkup, and she got a referral. I was surprised that she even brought this stuff up. The doctor said he didn't know much about it, but he could recommend a genetic counseling center. So he referred us; the form said, "Husband exposed to chemicals." Nothing about the Gulf War.

My wife and I are very different, in some ways. She is willing to believe anyone in authority; if a doctor said she had cancer and was going to die, then that would be it. No second opinions. Nothing. Especially if it's something she wants to hear. Like most everybody. And, she's convinced, or was, that I was looking for a bad answer. That I was going to find out what I wanted to hear.

FORTUN: So she went off to find her own answers?

PECK: Right. So she was all excited to go to the genetic counselor. And, she got what she was looking for. It aggravated me so much. I walked in. I was really excited about it, too. We had already decided that we were never going to find out for sure. But we thought we could get a range, statistically. Fifty-fifty. Ninety-ten. Seventy-thirty. Whatever. That's the best we were hoping for. We would make a decision from there.

We walked in the door and this woman, who wasn't a doctor, who was about our age—she had the answer before I even opened my mouth. She didn't ask me anything. She said we had no greater probability of having a defective child than anyone else in the normal population.

FORTUN: Did she even ask why you were there?

PECK: She did ask what it meant, that place on the form where it said, "Husband exposed to chemicals." She said that, at this point, we have a 3 percent chance of having a child with birth defects. The same chance as anyone in the normal population. My wife, of course, thought this was great. I turned super skeptical—when she had the answer before I ever walked in the door. So the rest of the time, I kept trying to trip her up.

She took a very typical approach; she blanketed everyone. Everyone who served in the Gulf War has the exact same experience and the exact same possibility of a problem. She said that, pretty much verbatim. She said that I wasn't the first Gulf War vet she had seen, and that she had said to all of them that they had a 3 percent chance of having any problem.

FORTUN: Was she suggesting that, by telling you all the same thing, she was the one with the legitimate reading?

PECK: Right. A very medical-type line. She wasn't a doctor, but she had that sense that she was the Almighty, who knew this, that, and could not be questioned. Let me explain it to you. Let me tell you how it is. Let me use these big medical terms, and then have you ask me what they mean. I tried to tell her that she couldn't label everyone who served in the Gulf, that they didn't have the same experiences. You can't do this. Of course, I left without her coming around at all. She didn't ask me where I was, what my job was, how close I was to the oil fires. It didn't matter, whether I was on the front line, or five hundred miles in the rear. Three percent. That's it. Nothing about my family history. Three percent. That's it. What if four of my brothers have brain tumors?

When we left, Audrey was walking on clouds. I didn't want to pop her balloon. It just would have enforced her theory that I was looking for trouble. I just couldn't accept what this woman said for fact.

FORTUN: How do they call these recommendations medical, with no specifics?

PECK: She did have some very good points. She said that she had read a lot of the studies that reported children with defects after the Gulf War. And that most of the articles talked about the same children. I don't know. I've only read a few. And she talked like she had read plenty; it's her job to read this stuff. So she said that you have to be skeptical of the studies, because you don't know the percentages. Are children of Gulf War vets more likely to be born with defects? The articles use phrases like "an overwhelming number." But, since that can't keep track of all the vets, they don't have the numbers to compare the overall birthrate to the number of children with defects. If they could, and they knew how many had children, and how many of these are perfectly fine, maybe it is only 3 percent. Maybe it's 3 percent, or 50 percent.

FORTUN: What about repeated incidents of the same, relatively rare problems?

PECK: Like spina bifida? Babies born without ears? I think that's Goldenhar's syndrome.

FORTUN: I think some argue, using data from the Association of Birth Defect Children, that there is statistically significant clustering of Goldenhar's syndrome. Ten babies with severe Goldenhar's syndrome—which is only supposed to affect one in twenty-six thousand. I think this was reported in the *Life* article, followed by an account of how difficult it is to be "conclusive" given the impossibility of knowing how many babies—total—have been born to Gulf War vets.

PECK: I did have a little bit of an awakening while with that counselor. I went in saying that there is no statistical proof saying that my child is going to come out fine. She got me to think about the fact that there is no statistical proof that my child won't be fine. In all, there is no proof, either way. But there are tendencies. And these articles are out there. Whether it's responsible journalism or not, the articles are there. People are reading them.

FORTUN: I can't quite understand how this counselor legitimated what she was telling you.

PECK: Everything she said was very general; it could be applied to anybody. She said that I had been back for five years, and that sperm regenerate every three months. So some of the kids with problems could have been conceived within the first three months after getting back. If you had any problems, they very well could have already flushed out of your system. As far as genes go. Then she was going on about mutagens and carcinogens, and just because you have cancer doesn't mean your sperm are affected, and just because you have mutated cells doesn't mean anything. Really, she was saying that there is no physical test that can be done. Short of killing a sperm cell and seeing if it has two heads. But you still wouldn't know how many heads the next one has. Motility tests. Can it swim? Does it have three heads? Things like that.

I asked if you could genetically check it out, dissect the DNA or something. She said the technology doesn't exist. We know how to dissect DNA, but since no one has mapped the whole DNA structure, no one really knows the whole thing from beginning to end. So, even if there was a problem, you wouldn't be able to see it.

FORTUN: This would not be an easy phenomena, even if people weren't covering things up. Did you ask what it would take to make it 4 percent?

PECK: I told her I was exposed to radio-frequency radiation, on a daily basis. She said that there is no proof that radiation mutates cells—there's the generator cells, that generate sperm, and then there's the sperm cells. The only way that you would have a problem is if those generator cells were mutated. She said that it's very unlikely that ionizing radiation is going to do this.

But what about nonionizing radiation? I told her, radio-frequency radiation is not ionizing. Have there been studies on nonionizing radiation? I think it does something to you. That's how an MRI works. When you're put in a MRI machine, you're put in a big magnetic field, that aligns the polarity in your body. Then the computer maps how they move back, when you let the magnetic field off. There are magnetic fields everywhere. But, I was standing in front of giant microwaves, every day. We would shoot them into the sky, to guide missiles.

I was digging for things, just to get her to admit that there are some questions. But again and again, 3 percent, 3 percent, 3 percent. I'm not sure if I could have said anything to make her say something different.

FORTUN: Did she have any logic for cumulative effect?

PECK: She kept repeating herself. Three percent. Three percent. As we were leaving she kept asking if we felt better, if we had enough information.

Maybe it was just this counselor. The genetics program we went to is very highly acclaimed. Maybe we should go back, and ask for someone else. Maybe it's just this person.

FORTUN: Sounds like the BB effect. Scattershot, flying at you from all directions. All of a sudden you're supposed to understand what genetic counseling is, as a profession, as a source of authority. Next time you see an article on genetic counseling, you're obliged to read it.

I don't know anything about genetic counseling either. Or very much about how to understand statistics. I just know that I've been in a lot of union halls where it seems everybody has something quite dramatic wrong with them, and the statistics show nothing extraordinary.

PECK: There's counselors for everything. And, for the most part, I don't trust them. I don't want some therapist deciding for me how I should handle my problems.

And, you know, Audrey works in a chemical lab. She's exposed to chemicals every day. We're not talking about cleaning agents. We're talking about methylene chloride, and some pretty good solids. Three percent. She kept repeating. Three percent. That's your chance. Audrey keeps insisting that lots of women in her lab have been pregnant, and have had normal children. But Audrey does the grunt work. She handles the solvents. She thinks she's safe if she wears gloves, which no one else even does. I tell her that just because she's safer than other people, doesn't mean she's safe.

FORTUN: If the counselor couldn't answer your questions, why were you sent to her? It sounds as though she simply contributed to the problem of not understanding what's up. Now you have even more questions for which "I don't know" is the proper answer.

PECK: I was a little mad when I left there. I wanted her to get off her high horse, step down with the rest of the crowd, where we all belong. All her flourishes. Statistics this, statistics that. Standard deviation here, random correlation there. She was kinda caught off-guard when I wasn't as stupid as I was supposed to be.

FORTUN: Why did you feel better?

PECK: I was so stuck on the fact that there is no statistical proof that my kid is going to be fine. At least she reminded me that there is no statistical proof that my kid isn't going to be fine. It brought me back to the middle. I wasn't looking for a bad answer. I was willing to accept whatever the true answer was, but the skepticism really did have hold of me. I was looking for every little loophole, every trace. So, I guess, having a statistic that doesn't really mean anything means that it's in the middle.

I did ask the first doctor I saw what he thought about what the genetic counselor had said. He said he didn't know. He said he couldn't tell me one way or the other, that he couldn't give me any suggestion. He couldn't say have a kid, or not have a kid. It made me trust him a little bit more. A doctor saying he didn't have a clue. He did say that, if it was him, he would try it, but with a contingency plan. Knowing, beforehand, if he would opt for an abortion if the child was deformed.

Official Symptoms

FORTUN: So you found out that the VA was encouraging all Gulf War vets to come in for a registry exam. What happened next?

PECK: I had to wait like a month for the exam; the appointment was made by the social worker. It was the compensation clinic, where you go for worker's comp. I walked in and said I was there for my Gulf War registry exam. They gave me this form to fill out, which was just pages and pages. It seemed to go on forever. All "yes, no, don't know" questions. How long were you in the Gulf? What units did you serve with? Were you exposed to oil fires? Did you take drug "x"? Did you take drug "y"? Did you eat any food that was not supplied to you by the military?

FORTUN: Did they ask you anything that really took you off-guard?

PECK: The food one. That was something I never thought of.

FORTUN: Did they ask if you had any physical contact with Iraqis?

PECK: Yeah, I said I didn't know. I didn't know if they were asking if anyone had slapped me on the shoulder, or if they had been within a hundred yards. I was within a hundred yards, but I wasn't putting handcuffs on anybody. So I put "don't know." I put "don't know" for quite a few.

FORTUN: Funny how often "I don't know" is the most accurate response.

PECK: So I filled out this form, saying that I didn't know a lot. But it did seem very thorough, very objective. When I turned it in I made some kind of joke about the length, and they told me that, in the beginning, it was just one page, single-sided. That's it. But it has developed. To me, it looked like a lot of thought had gone into some of the questions.

Then the worker's-comp doctor did the initial physical. Then, after all this was over, I found out that there is a Gulf War clinic on the first floor. I never saw them, was never even told what they do. I think I'll call and ask if I can come. Ask if they do anything different from these other guys.

FORTUN: Reminds me of Bhopal, where the tuberculosis wards are over-flowing, and the wards for those officially recognized as gas affected are empty.

PECK: Maybe they're just trying to free up space, to focus on people who have been diagnosed. Maybe they don't want to scare everyone who comes in. Seeing a bunch of sick people might not be a good thing.

Anyway, it was a very general physical. Ears. Nose. Throat. Chest. A very typical exam. Then he asked if I had anything wrong in particular. I said I have headaches and a problem with lack of concentration, at times. And I have this little rash on my forehead. So he said he would refer me for a neurology exam, for the headaches. Then I had to go get full blood work, EKGs, chest X-rays. This was all part of the regular registry exam. It was a whole day thing. Waiting in line for EKG machines, X-rays. I finally left, with an appointment for a neurology exam. In the end, the guy from worker's comp will be the one making the conclusions about my case, after the results of the neurology exam are back. He did write a little note about my cholesterol being high, and something else, some kind of chemical that's out of whack. He wasn't there, so the nurse told me. She couldn't tell me what the second thing was, just told me not to worry, that if it was life threatening the doctor calls you right away. The standard procedure is for them to write a letter stating the conclusions and test results. You have to specifically request the actual test results if you're interested in those.

FORTUN: What happened with the neurology exam?

PECK: First, I should tell you, this is where Audrey turned around. After the first exam, when they did refer me to a neurologist, she made a complete flip. It really hit home with her. She said that she finally realized that maybe something, really, was wrong. That I wasn't just making it up, or bringing it on myself—by not eating right, drinking enough water, getting enough sleep. The doctor said it, and she believes those types of people. People with authority, they're almighty to her. When he said that he was concerned, she finally listened. And, for the first time, she said that she didn't care about anything except my being okay. Having children was secondary. She just wanted me to be okay.

It was a big shift, a big thing for both of us. I'm not sure if I've mentioned it before, but I do get headaches a lot. Compared to Audrey, especially. Debilitating headaches, which wipe me out, for whole days. Nausea. Aches. Pains, Fatigue. I just have to sleep. About twice a month. My body just needs to shut down. Most of the time, if I lay down, I don't wake up until the next morning.

FORTUN: How long have you had these?

PECK: Going on four years. Since I started school, which was when I really realized how bad they are.

FORTUN: Has it worried you?

PECK: Audrey would get so mad at me; I would be afraid to say anything. When I was in that condition, the last thing I wanted was to have her yelling at me. Asking if I had drunk enough water, or eaten lunch. Constantly suggesting that it was something I did to bring it on myself. Angry that I would screw up plans we had made. Going to her parents, or out to dinner. When this happens, that's it, it's over. If I get in the car I feel like I'm going to get sick. It's ruined a lot of things for us.

FORTUN: Did she get angry from the start?

PECK: It soon got to be too much, because they were happening kinda often. She just didn't have any more sympathy to give me, because she obviously thought that they were caused by something I was doing. There I was, sleeping on the couch, while she cooked and did the dishes, after working all day. That was the typical scenario. So I just tried to fake my way through it, not letting her know if I had one.

FORTUN: Did you think about going to the doctor?

PECK: At first I never thought of going to the VA. Before the Gulf War syndrome stuff started. She had talked me into it; I figured she was right, that I had done something wrong, that I had brought them on myself.

It ends up I was diagnosed with chronic migraine headaches. After the neurology exam. I was really impressed with the doctors. They seemed to be really listening to what I had to say. Maybe because it was neurological. The exam lasted a while, bending my toes, asking if they were bending them left, right, up, or down. Telling me to close my eyes while they pricked all over my body. Stand on one foot, hop around, close your eyes, touch your nose. But mostly asking questions. About the headaches. Does it travel? Where is it at? Can you tell the difference between this type of headache and a regular headache?

He said I had classic symptoms for a migraine headache. So he scheduled me for a CT scan, and gave me migraine medication. A very site-specific type drug, that only works in your brain, rather like Advil, but just in your brain. If this doesn't work, he says, we'll talk about using an antidepressant, which has more side effects.

FORTUN: Did he link his diagnosis to your service in the Gulf?

PECK: No one made any connections. As a matter of fact, I still have to copay on my prescriptions, because it's not listed as a service-connected disability. I think, though I'm not sure, that this doctor will say that I have been subjected to Gulf War syndrome, in his final report. In his evaluation he'll have to make the conclusion on whether it's service connected or not.

Copayment is trivial. Prescriptions still cost just about $2. But with the compensation tag comes the whole thing of having a service-connected disability. From the point of having priority treatment over other patients at the VA, having your prescriptions paid for, being monetarily compensated. All kinds of things follow. I don't blame them for wanting to be careful. But if they say this isn't service connected, I will fight it. I don't think I would have had the migraines without the Gulf. I'm sure I would be able to fight it.

FORTUN: What kind of data would they need to "conclude" that the migraines are service connected?

PECK: I don't know. That's something I wanted to ask the Gulf War clinic. But I want to make sure that I don't come off as trying to get it connected, right away.

I did, already, talk to the social worker. And she had a whole other exam. Did I have gripes against the government, stuff like that. I went over to her office right after the physical exam.

FORTUN: Her salary is paid by the Veterans Administration?

PECK: Yeah. Pretty much, she could have just asked me if I was a communist. Are you a communist? That would have covered all the other questions. I said that I didn't have any gripe about the government that were out of the ordinary. That I wasn't unreasonable. Everyone has problems with the IRS. It's government. I'm not irrational, or irresponsible. I don't, at all, want to go bomb a federal building. I have no desire to assassinate the president.

FORTUN: Did you tell her you thought there was a conspiracy to cover up information on the effects of service in the Gulf?

PECK: I didn't tell her that. And I wasn't lying. I'm still open. I just think the conspiracy theory is just as valid as some of the other theories. I wanted her, too, to be one more source of information. I want to weigh all that I can get.

She asked if I had any angry feelings. Are you hostile toward anything? Do you feel angry toward society? Do you have anybody you really hate? I said no. She said the reasons she ask is, like, I have this guy who was being shipped out to the Gulf. In the legal system, if he had died, his parents would have gotten everything. And he hated his parents. So he got married, just so they wouldn't get anything. And now he's back, alive, and he's got this wife he doesn't even like. So, the point: people do things for strange reasons.

FORTUN: Do you know if she's held to certain standards of privacy, which would keep her from disclosing your file?

PECK: I don't know, so I was a little careful. Even if I did hate the government, I shouldn't have said it. They could label me, then lock me up as a crazy person. But the social worker seemed really realistic. I tried to remember, that this was the Veterans Administration, not the Department of Defense. They're two different things; they really are.

Contingency Plans

PECK: I'm worried about the implications for the future. The presentation you heard me give; it was a hard decision to decide to do that. Stand before a group of people and criticize the government. I love speaking in front of people, but this time I was nervous. I was letting the cat out of the bag. I was afraid it was going to come back to haunt me. Twenty years from now, someone would dredge it up, tell everyone that I had denounced the government.

FORTUN: I thought you said you weren't trying to blame the government?

PECK: I'm questioning the government; it's almost the same thing. You can get blackballed just for asking. I've heard of that happening. Not just in the military. In industry, in government jobs.

I don't often talk about personal things. I don't express my feelings to people. While in the Marine Corps, I was really proud of this. So, it's a big deal—for me to bring in the personal, to bring in something that means a lot to me as an individual. And, really, this is about myself.

FORTUN: And, really, what do you need? What kind of locational device?

PECK: Really, what we need to do is make up a contingency plan.

FORTUN: How do you do that?

PECK: We've come to the realization that we need one, that's the first thing. Little things, here and there, seem to be coming together. Obviously, something is going to have to give. Either, morally, we're going to feel bad about an abortion. Or, morally, we're going to feel bad about having a child suffer. Then, there's also the middle. There seem to be three major possibilities: we're going to lose the child; we're going to keep the child, no matter what; we're going to have a child that's okay but requires lots and lots of care. We have another child to think of, too.

We're trying. We're dealing with the whole church thing. You know, for the Catholic Church, it's the most wrong thing in the world. So that's one thing. And it's important. Who are we to play God? Deciding that this child can live, and this one shouldn't. You might as well be genetically engineering them. There's that problem. But, also, the other side: is it fair to make a child live her whole entire life struggling, in pain. Once a child is born, the doctors will try to make it live, regardless of whether it is in pain or not. I would like to think that I would insist that they take off life support, oxygen. Let the suffering end. But would we? That's our biggest conflict. We don't know what to do. But we have decided that, before we try anything, we'll have a full contingency plan. Either decide ahead of time that we're going to keep the child, and nurture it regardless of the physical or mental pain it's in.

And then there's our survival. The only thing Audrey and I have, in our life together, is our time. We have, maybe, an hour or two together a day. And, you have to admit, if you have a child that requires that kind of care, that's it. It's over. I'll be working all day. Probably picking up a second job to pay for medical bills. Audrey at home, not leaving the house, not going anywhere. If it's that serious. You have to be ready for that. We don't know. As a couple, could we survive something like that? Would we make it?

FORTUN: Does the Internet have any stories about how people are coming up with these contingency plans?

PECK: I haven't looked at it in a while. It's become like a book. There's so much on there that it's hard to know where to look, where to start. I can only stare at that screen for so long.

The social worker, she's the one who told me about the contingency plans made by other couples, how they decided ahead of time what they were going to do. She said that she was here for me to talk to, to answer questions. She was an older woman. Her office was covered with pictures of her husband, in VFW garb. So, obviously, she has some connection to servicemen.

She kept a file on me. It's her job to keep track of Gulf War vets. She personally follows the cases. I asked her about having kids, that I needed to know. She said that she didn't know, but here's what seems to be working for other people.

FORTUN: Were there any specific steps she encouraged you to take, or things she really thought you should think about?

PECK: First, she suggested genetic counseling. And she suggested that I file a claim against the government now. A worker's-comp type thing. Even if there is nothing wrong, at the moment. What happens is—the government will send you a check for the rest of your life, based on where you are rated on a scale of, like, zero to ten, indicating how disabled you are. So you file the claim and the government says you are 10 percent disabled, or 100, or 0. But, you get in the system. This is what happened with Agent Orange. People who filed immediately after returning from Vietnam, when it came time to really get compensated, they were first on the list. They filed when they got back and the government said nothing was wrong with them. But, when they realized that there was a problem, these people got first dibs on the money, and their claims went a lot faster. If you wait twenty years, you have to prove to the government that your problem is service related.

FORTUN: So, if you filed now, you may get a 0 and no money, but your claim would be registered?

PECK: Maybe 0, or maybe 10 percent? I don't want to feel like I'm taking the government, or the people who are paying taxes, for a ride. Not that fifty dollars a month is that big a deal, but, I don't know.

FORTUN: But, you don't want to be the one bearing the burden of causality in twenty years. The system seems loaded against you.

PECK: I think I've come to the conclusion that I'm not ever going to know. I'm not, within any reasonable amount of time, going to get any more information. Maybe by the time I'm sixty-five or seventy, the truth will come out. But within the next five years, I don't expect any earth-shattering disclosures. Nothing that would affect my decision. Right now, we need this contingency plan, or to decide that we're not going to have children, adopting, or something else.

FORTUN: What kind of explanation would be earth shattering? Would it help just to be told that you were, for sure, exposed?

PECK: Exposed to what? That's the crucial question. Answer that, then I can make my own conclusions. Maybe the headaches are genetic, even if I never had one before I went to the Gulf. I'm not looking for someone to blame; I'm just trying to get on with my life. Everyone wants a little revenge, every now and then. But I've come to the realization that it's more important to have a life than to spend the rest of my life trying to figure out who did this to me.

FORTUN: Do you think there's reason to continually demand that the government declassify, given that it's unclear how reliable any official release could be?

PECK: I don't want to say that I don't care anymore. It's a choice. I either have to make a major time commitment and pursue this thing right, or just accept whatever is and get on with my life. And I think I'm leaning toward the latter.

And, one thing is clear: I am a victim of Gulf War illness, even if my body is not the evidence. I've spent good time worrying about it, days at the hospital, nights arguing with my wife.

References

Cotton, Paul. 1994. "Veterans Seeking Answers to Syndrome Suspect They Were Goats in Gulf War." *Journal of the American Medical Association* 27, no. 20 (May 25): 1559–61.

Miller, Kenneth, Derek Hudson, and Jimmie Briggs. 1995. "The Tiny Victims of Desert Storm." *Life* (Nov.): 46–61.

DUES ABSCONDITUS:
WACO, CONSPIRACY (THEORY), MILLENNIALISM,
AND (THE END OF) THE TWENTIETH CENTURY

File 1: Millennialism, U.S., c. 1991 C.E.

This much is known: during the summer of 1981, a certain Vernon Howell first visited the Branch Davidian Seventh-Day Adventists, a sectarian community of perhaps some one hundred thirty congregants residing on a seventy-seven-acre compound known as New Mount Carmel, or simply as Mount Carmel, located just beyond the municipal limits of Waco, Texas.[1] Howell was born to an unwed fifteen-year-old mother in Houston on 17 August 1959. A sometime resident of Tyler, Texas, dyslexic, aspiring rock guitarist and songwriter, spiritual seeker, gifted improvisational preacher, Howell soon joined the Branch Davidians, and not long after found himself rather more than spiritually involved with their leader, sixty-seven-year-old Lois Roden.[2] He almost immediately fell out of favor with Lois's son and heir apparent, George. The acrimony between Howell and the younger Roden did not, however, reach its height for several years. In 1984 Howell broke off his relationship to Lois in order to marry fourteen-year-old Rachel Perry, daughter of a longtime congregant. In 1985 he traveled to Israel with Rachel, and while there claimed to have received a revelation of his distinctive spiritual mission.[3] Shortly after his return, George expelled Howell and forty of his supporters from Mount Carmel. In November 1986, Lois Roden died. In November 1987, Howell and Lois's son would finally come to blows. From a reliable source:

> George Roden dug up the body of Anna Hughes, a Davidian who had died at eighty-four and had been buried for twenty years on the Mount Carmel property. He put the casket in the [community's] chapel and challenged Koresh to a contest to see who could raise her from the dead. Koresh asked the McLennan County sheriff to arrest Roden for corpse violation but was told he would need to bring proof. Koresh and seven of his loyal followers tried to sneak onto the property to take a photo of the corpse. They were dressed in camouflage fatigues and heavily armed. A forty-five minute gun battle ensued, each side

blaming the other for firing first. Roden was wounded slightly in the hand. Koresh and his men were charged with attempted murder, and surely one of the strangest trials in Waco history was held in 1988. The jurors found the others not guilty but were split over the question of Koresh's guilt. The judge declared a mistrial. Six months later George Roden was charged with the murder of a fifty-six-year-old man in an unrelated incident. He was found not guilty by reason of insanity and was sentenced to an indeterminate stay in the state hospital in Vernon, Texas [from which, following an escape, he was indefinitely shifted]. In the meantime Koresh came up with the money to pay the back taxes on the Mount Carmel property, and his group returned triumphantly and began to rebuild.[4]

In 1990 Howell legally changed his first name to David, after the biblical king whose spiritual descendant he believed himself to be. He changed his surname to Koresh, the Hebrew form of the more familiar Greek "Cyrus," the Persian monarch whom the Old Testament prophet Isaiah designates "messiah" (or "anointed"; cf. the Greek χριστός, "christened"), and the ordained conqueror of an imperious and infidel "Babylon."

By 1991 David Koresh was (it would seem) in his own eyes and (rather more certainly) in the eyes of those who lived with him at Mount Carmel a "messiah," a "christ," a man divinely chosen and divinely touched. He was, more precisely, among Max Weber's "emissary prophets,"[5] the voice and instrument of "news," of a revealed truth. The boy Koresh (still Howell at the time, of course) had the example of the emissary Nazarene. But he had also been tutored in the more immediate, perhaps less exotic examples of William Miller and Ellen White, the latter the founding prophetess of the Seventh-Day Adventist Church. Like the majority of those who believed in him, the boy Koresh had belonged to the Church.[6] The man Koresh was no longer welcome in its mainstream.[7] He nevertheless continued to regard Miller and White as his own precursors. He continued to embrace many of White's practical and ritual prescriptions.[8] He continued with even greater constancy to embrace White's doctrine that revelation was historically emergent, and that until its completion, each prophet would of necessity be succeeded by yet another prophet, each "present truth" by yet another present truth.[9]

In its general outlines, the message that Koresh finally formulated was itself strikingly faithful to Miller's, but especially so to White's. Indeed, in its general outlines, it merely renovated the urgency of an eschatology a less determinate and—again to borrow from Weber—more "rationalized" expression of which informs the doxa of the majority of those sectarian churches of nineteenth-century origin whose ranks have swelled so dramatically since the Second World War.[10] Focused exegetically on the New Testament's Book of Revelation, it announced the imminence of a fateful battle, an Armageddon that would at once precede and pave the way for a Christly kingdom, due to last "a thousand years"—a millennium.[11] With Lois Roden and a great many of his exegetical contemporaries, Koresh was inclined to presume that Revelation's reference to Armageddon (16:16) was a quite literal reference to the plain enclosed since 1948 within the borders of the modern state of Israel.[12] By 1991, he would add a qualification. By 1991 Koresh was (it would seem) in his own eyes and (rather more certainly) in the eyes of those who lived with him at Mount Carmel the seventh and final angel (from the Greek ἄγγελος, "messenger") of the Book of Revelation, that emissary through whom the present truth would be made eternal (cf. 10:7). His flock and he were that assembly of testimonialists whom Revelation (6:9) destined to be slain "for the word of God." Their moment was the moment of the breaking open of the fifth of those seven vials in which the elixirs of both epistemic and historical plenitude are stored. Their enemy: the "beast" (Revelation 13:1) who presided at "Babylon" (17:5) and from Babylon ruled over the whole world (13:7). By 1991 Koresh may not yet have fixed the identity of the beast. The identity of the beast's political apparatus was, however, patent enough.[13] The final Babylon could only be the United States, and its instrument of global hegemony, the United Nations. Before 1991, Koresh seems to have envisioned that his flock and he would be among the first to fall at the literal Armageddon, defending the state of Israel against the onslaught of an international invasion. Not an advocate of aggression, but no advocate, either, of the uncompromising temporal pacifism of the Nazarene, he had accordingly begun to build a sizable arsenal. Not, however, until reflecting upon the locus and the agencies of the Gulf War does he seem determinately to have envisioned the possibility that the battle for which he was preparing, that battle which would culminate on the Israeli plain, could begin almost anywhere; that it could indeed begin at the Mount Carmel compound itself, that his arsenal could thus have its first deployment before it ever left home.

Koresh is reported not to have been unduly surprised, is even reported to have expected, to discover that in early 1992[14] the compound had been infiltrated by one Robert Rodriguez, an undercover agent of the U.S. Bureau of Alcohol, Tobacco, and Firearms (ATF) appointed to gather evidence of the violation of law—at least of that law governing the possession, the buying, and the selling of weapons.[15] Before Koresh had arrived, the Branch Davidians had lived peaceably enough on the Texas prairie, beneficiaries of the entrenched conservative tolerance that had attracted so many other Christian sectarians to the environs of Waco. If not widely admired for their commitments, they were often simply ignored. The strife that led to the deposition of George Roden may, however, have been pivotal. In any event, in response to rumors that began to circulate not long after Koresh settled in as leader, the local Bureau of Child Protective Services subjected the community to a somewhat

At the edge of the ruins of the Branch Davidian compound, crosses tally the dead. Photograph by William R. Dull.

perfunctory and ultimately inconsequential investigation.[16] By late February 1993 the Waco *Tribune-Herald* was set to publish a seven-part exposé of both leader and community tellingly entitled "The Sinful Messiah." [17] Could all the instruments, all the signs have pointed more definitively to special trials, special troubles? Sometime during the morning of 28 February 1993, shortly before the fact, Koresh in any event is reported not to have been unduly surprised to learn that a substantial and heavily armed brigade of ATF agents was set to move on the Mount Carmel compound in order to deliver a search warrant. Opinion is still divided over whether he was at all surprised by what transpired in the aftermath of the brigade's arrival: an exchange of gunfire, still of uncertain provenance; a standoff, unresolved for some fifty-one days, concluding—though we can hardly even yet speak of conclusion—with a catastrophic fire; the death of four ATF agents and what official tallies reckon at eighty Branch Davidians, David Koresh prominent among them.[18]

Excursus: Transcendental Reflections

The millennialist imagination, past or present, can hardly be reduced to a conspiratorial imagination; millennialist doctrine, past or present, can hardly be reduced to the theorization of conspiracy. Yet the machinating beast who looms so prominently and so fearsomely in Revelation's thirteenth chapter, a beast who has served as the typological template for myriad alleged Antichrists ever since, is merely the most vivid of many other indications that the affinities between millennarianism and the theorization of conspiracy are intimate and enduring. Millennialism may regularly offer a theodicy for which the most cynical theory of conspiracy fails to provide even a functional equivalent. Millennialism may promise redemption, at least to a few, while the theory of conspiracy promises none at all. Millennialism may proffer a philosophy of the historical process while the theory of conspiracy merely proffers piecemeal empirical speculation. But both tend even so to address strikingly similar existential concerns: the apparent arbitrariness of the distribution of good and ill fortune, and the apparent interminability of suffering.[19] Both also tend to address in particular the inherent tension of the relationship between the will to power and the will to justice. And both reveal a central and abiding preoccupation with the determination of the identity of an "elect," whether scapegoats, martyrs, saints, or all of these, whether sacred or secular, whether embodied in a collectivity or embodied in the extraordinary person of some single woman or man.

The existential ground that millennialism and the theorization of conspiracy tend to share leads to another, more basic ground. As doctrines and as engagements, both rest and both depend on an epistemological skepticism that finds its purest methodological instrument in what might be called a *sémiotique du soupçon,* a semiotics of (the) suspicion, of the inkling, or the trace. The author of the Book of Revelation posits a limit, at once historical and logical, at which such a semiotics would no longer have any methodological rationale whatever: "the days of the voice of the seventh angel, when he shall begin to sound, [and] the mystery of God should be finished" (10:7). At precisely that limit, David Koresh understood himself to stand. Beyond its threshold, all signifiers would be fully adequate to their references; a condition of absolute semiotic clarity and absolute semiotic transparency would hold sway. The evidential relationship would be delivered of all its semantic poverty and all its pragmatic ambiguity. Beyond the threshold, conspiracy might still be possible, even if deprived of virtually all its most serviceable tools. But "theory," whatever its object, would be nothing more than idle speculation. Or it would revert to its Aristotelian—which, in modern parlance, would have to be deemed either its "pretheoretical" or its "post-theoretical"—modality.[20] No longer sustained by phenomenal or factual indeterminacy, theory could be nothing more (nor anything less) than the synchronous contemplation of the real. It would demand no specialization, no research, no training. Like critique in Marx's communist society, theory would be radically popular. A semiotics of suspicion is a semiotics for a far less perfect world, less crystalline and less crisply visible, like so many reflections *in speculum aenigmate.* In such a world—in "our" world—signifiers are likely to distinguish their referents crudely at best, or even to have no referents. Both semantic and pragmatic obscurity are constant, and often incorrigible. Intentions—as "we" know—are often articulated vaguely even when they are not actively being disguised.[21]

A semiotics of suspicion is a semiotics, in short, for a world that cries out—just so long as it cries out—for interpretation. It is thus peculiarly well suited to the world of the Bible, especially to the Bible of Erich Auerbach's *Mimesis,* in which every pivotal historical moment is the *figura,* the figure, the always suggestive but always partial figuration, of yet another, later historical moment, and in which history itself, "with all its concrete force," thus "remains forever a figure, cloaked," and so forever inviting and forever in need of the final disclosure, the final demystification, of which the author of the Book of Revelation dreams.[22] Auerbach's habit of identifying the biblical view of the historical process with the "Judeo-Christian view" should, however, be resisted.[23] It is at the very least ethnologically uninformed, all the inspiration that the Bible has provided to millennialists and theorists of conspiracy alike—especially during the past two centuries—notwithstanding.[24] As Vassilis Lambropoulos has pointed out, it also constitutes the first principle of an anti-Hellenic celebration of Judeo-Christian tolerance and Judeo-Christian relativism against an allegedly Homeric and allegedly pagan attraction to "everything sceptic, static, autocratic, absolutist."[25] Lambropoulos might more forcefully have suggested that it further constitutes an equally prejudiced refusal to acknowledge the myriad semiotic obfuscations (and conspiracies!) on which the central events of both the *Iliad* and the *Odyssey* (among many other texts in the Greek corpus) turn. Or perhaps one might better, might more accurately, write less of prejudice than of self-deception. Auerbach, a fierce critic of Nazi tyranny, was compelled to cast himself and to cast his readerly enterprise as direct heir to a Judeo-Christian legacy of epistemological fallibilism, epistemological openness. Was he thus compelled to suppress all that his enterprise owed to the precedent of the godly point of view adopted and canonized by so oracular and so wry a poet-interpreter as Homer (whoever he, or they, might have been) himself?

Some two centuries ago, Friedrich Schiller declared ancient Greek poetry, and with it the ancient Greek sensibility, "naive"—semiotically untroubled, perhaps even semiotically complaisant.[26] Long before Auerbach, Schiller may thus be the first modern Western thinker to turn away from what might well have been an uneasy, somewhat unflattering, and somewhat too revealing encounter with the ancient hypostasis of the interpretive craft. Aristotle's epistemological self-confidence aside, the Greeks certainly knew of both the necessity and the dangers of interpretation. Their theology suggests indeed that they knew of both all too well. Hermes was among the first order of their gods, though not the equal of Zeus—lawgiver and the hand of justice. Hermes' special domain was that of the μεταφορά, "transference" or "haulage" but also "change," as of one phase to another, also "metaphor." Divine messenger, Hermes also presided conjointly over boundaries and over crossings and journeys. He was the master of commerce; the master, too, of λόγος, of communication, of speech and writing and eloquence. And who, after all, but the god whose distinctive virtues were those of making and securing connections should also be able to boast of that complementary virtue, that accessory power or talent called δεινότης, "cunning" or "guile," but also "marvelousness," "awesomeness"?

One must accordingly be struck by the symbolic overdetermination of that gesture through which a group of conspirators, whose identity was never firmly established, undertook one March night in 415 B.C.E. to cast a pall over the success of what the good citizens of the Athenian assembly had agreed to be a most timely invasion of Sicily. Throughout the Athenian city-state, Hermes stood in small stone effigies, "Herms," registering and attesting to the limits of lots and parcels of private property. He bore most often only what might be thought of as his barest essentials: the formal, smiling face of the benign host or patron; and an erect penis, the ubiquitous ancient icon at once of the power of continuity and of the power of transgression. The conspirators, who seem to have gone undetected in spite of the noise their chisels must have made, "mutilated" what Thucydides carefully specifies to be "the faces" of the Herms.[27] Other commentators have insisted that the mutilations were more thorough.[28] Partial or more complete, the widespread desecration amounted to a slap in the face of a democratically adjudicated policy, and so in the face of the Athenian democracy itself. But the scandal was not merely political. It was also moral, also religious, a matter of what ancient wisdom continued to regard as a cardinal sin. The conspirators had committed ὕβρις, "hubris," the "outrage," the "overweening arrogance" of having done insult to a presence to whom they should only have done honor. Even worse, in having sought to spoil through their own devices the divine auspices under which the Sicilian expedition could have been expected to set sail, in having thus taken the matter of the blessedness or cursedness of the expedition into their own hands, they had not merely dishonored Hermes; they had—the very quintessence of hubris—presumed to dethrone him, to put themselves in his place.

Whoever they were, the conspirators managed to inaugurate an enduring tradition. Their epigones appear again in the Renaissance. Some are Neoplatonist mystics; others, alchemists. They are united in their dedication to the Egyptian god Thoth, whom they presume to be a more original, more pure, and more mighty incarnation of the Greek Hermes and whom they accordingly call Hermes Trismegistus, Hermes "Thrice-Great." Pious, perhaps; but there is little question that these Hermeticists, as they called themselves, were hardly content merely to honor the divinity whose cunning gave him special entry into the realm of the secret, the mysterious, and the occult. There is little question that they also sought to acquire his secrets from him. And if such a man as David Koresh could regard himself as heir to the example of the prophets, the messiahs who had preceded him, to whose example are "we"—secular and modern semioticians of suspicion— proper heirs? Do we not—almost conspiratorially— strive to dissemble, by appeal to such secular pieties as those of "scientific rigor" and "methodological restraint," the actual ambitions that come almost to light especially when we refer to ourselves by that most precious of our occupational titles, "hermeneut"?

File 2: Revelations and Counterrevelations

But who was Vernon Howell; who was "David Koresh" really? The leader of hardly more than a hundred devotionalists camped together in the open Texas prairie: What could Koresh really have been planning to do, what could he really have been doing, to have garnered such exceptional governmental attention, to have provoked such an exceptional show of governmental force? Were these putative gunrunners really so dangerous that they could not have been trusted to accept a warrant from a single deputy's hands? Whatever their dangerousness, was the ATF really justified—legally or tactically—in undertaking so intimidating and confrontational a raid on the Branch Davidian compound? What was the real rationale for its strategy? Who were the real aggressors? And what really happened that fateful April morning in 1993? And why?

On the one hand: If a *hiatus irrationalis,* a certain incommensurability, separated the magnitude of the threat to peace or to order that the Branch Davidians posed from the magnitude of the forces of peace and order they faced, the national media were slow to perceive it. Initially, at least, most of the networks and wire services would accept—would often repeat verbatim—the diagnoses and accusations that the Waco *Tribune-Herald* had already begun to circulate. The 1 March edition of the *New York Times* was slightly more cautious. It reported an ATF raid on "the heavily armed compound of a religious cult" that had, only the day before, been the subject of a "long, investigative article . . . in a local newspaper." It noted that the article had "called attention to the weapons" of which the Branch Davidians were in possession. It noted that the article had also "discussed accusations by former members that Mr. Koresh sexually abused girls in the compound," but sought neither to confirm nor to deny them.[29] It had nevertheless managed to inscribe the terms—said and unsaid—of what would become shortly and would remain in the aftermath of the standoff a standard, an official portrait. Upon reflection, David Koresh could be seen as "a creature of his time and place, an archetypal anti-establishment figure of the American present and past."[30] But this hardly made him less a "thug and a terrorist,"[31] and it hardly made him any less larger than life. If

Relics of the fire. Photograph by William R. Dull.

anything, precisely the opposite. "Once in the cult, Davidians surrendered all the material means of independence, like money and belongings, while Koresh seemed to have unlimited funds." [32] The leader "indulged liberally in sex with the women of the cult, including young teenage girls—all of whom he said he could claim as wives and none of whom were permitted to have sexual relations with their husbands or anyone else." [33] "Behind the mind games and psychological sadism," moreover, "lay the threat of physical force. In addition to . . . paddlings, administered in a room called the spanking room, offenders could be forced down into a pit of raw sewage, then not allowed to bathe." [34] "Allegations surfaced that Koresh physically abused the children [of the compound] with frequent harsh beatings for infractions as minor as crying after a nap." [35] "Denied traditional family bonds and subjected to Koresh's warped teachings, the children became compliant playthings." [36] They had learned "to substitute the word love for fear." [37] The *Times* thus raised no questions when Attorney General Janet Reno pronounced in a news conference "that there was a particular urgency in the decision to move" upon Mount Carmel on 19 April. " 'We had information that babies were being beaten,' she said. 'I specifically asked, "You mean real babies?" "Yes, that he's slapping babies around." These are the concerns that we had.' " [38]

On the other hand: Only a day after her conference, Reno publicly acceded to FBI Director William Sessions's insistence that the "information" upon which she had premised her decision was in fact incorrect. Rumors, however, of David Koresh's transgressions had been circulating, in the United States and in several of the other countries of which members of the Mount Carmel community were native, well before either the ATF or the reporters of the Waco *Tribune-Herald* began seriously to attend to them. They were familiar to the local staff of the Texas Department of Child Protective Services, whose investigations nevertheless had failed to uncover any evidence of crime. Activist attorney Linda Thompson would identify Koresh's primary detractor as Marc Breault. In the controversial video that Thompson's American Justice Federation first offered to public scrutiny late in 1993, Breault is characterized as "a self-proclaimed 'prophet' from Honolulu, Hawaii," who joined the Branch Davidians in 1987 but left under pressure in 1989 after trying "to take over the leadership of the Mount Carmel Center from David Koresh." [39] It goes on to recount an ambitious enterprise of revenge. Among its claims: that Breault sought out various "international agencies" before which to accuse David Koresh of adultery, the abuse of children, and gunrunning; that he took pains to cultivate alliances with bitter kinspeople whose wives and daughters had abandoned them to join Koresh's flock. It reproduces the interview that an Australian television reporter conducted with Koresh in 1991. In the interview Koresh insists against his detractors that he has only a single wife. He proclaims that he does not commit adultery. He denies that he "beats children." [40]

The video then reviews the affidavit that ATF Special Agent Davy Aguilera filed with the Western Texas District Court on 26 February 1993 in order to procure a warrant to search the Branch Davidian compound. The narrator notes several peculiarities: that Aguilera makes note of purported polygamy and sexual abuse at the compound even though the ATF has no authority to investigate them; that Aguilera confuses the legal meanings of the terms *machine gun, destructive device, explosive,* and *explosive device;* that "bottom line, the raid on February 28, 1993, was launched because the ATF merely suspected that the Branch Davidians might have a machine gun that they failed to pay a $200 tax on." In Texas, at least, citizens have every legal right to own machine guns, so long as they pay the appropriate tax. [41]

On the one hand: In the early weeks of March 1993, the media regularly recorded the speculations and insinuations through which various spokespersons and agents of the ATF sought to assign responsibility for a raid that had come to be widely regarded as an embarrassing failure. The ATF strategists had sought to catch David Koresh and his community off guard, to surprise them. But the residents of Mount Carmel were expecting their visitors. Somehow, they had been forewarned. Initial scrutiny fell upon employees of the Waco *Tribune-Herald,* all the more so because "on-the-spot" representatives from both the local newspaper and a local television station had themselves already arrived at the Mount Carmel property by the time the raid commenced. ATF agent John Risenhoover thought their culpability likely enough that he filed a civil suit against the newspaper, seeking damages for the wounds he had suffered.[42] Other agents looked more toward their superiors, who were rumored to have decided to proceed with the raid in spite of having known that they had lost "the element of surprise."[43] By late April 1993, in the aftermath of the fire, treasury secretary Lloyd Bentsen had come to take such rumors so seriously that he was prepared to ask ATF Director Stephen Higgins to resign.[44] Amid all the confusion, all the finger pointing, and all the denial, however, one point seemed secure; the Branch Davidians had fired first. They had orchestrated an ambush.[45]

On the other hand: Thompson's video is constituted in part of "the first film footage of the initial raid as it was provided to all the network television feeds." The narrator suggests that the footage is "heavily edited," though not quite heavily enough "to remove the truth." She instructs the viewer to "watch closely" as eight ATF agents use ladders to climb to the roof of the compound. She draws attention to governmental helicopters that appear as three inky spots low on the horizon; to the sound of the automatic fire of ATF guns. Even having achieved the roof, the team of eight seems, for its part, to have met with no hostile response. Two of its members break open an upper-story window. They toss what appears to be "smoke grenades" into the room that they have breached. They follow the grenades into the room, accompanied by a third agent. A fourth agent appears briefly on the screen; then the tape jumps with a "badly edited cut." Its next image captures the same agent tossing yet another grenade into the breached room. The narrator wonders whether he can have had any intention other than that of injuring his own men. It makes no sense for him to be throwing anything at all into a room where the three ATF agents have just gone, unless he intends to injure his own men. She remarks that he also fires his automatic weapon into the room "twice, without looking." The video shifts to slow motion, and offers a reprise. The agent fires his weapon into the room. From inside, someone returns fire. The agent on the screen fires again. Another return of fire. On the roof, the agent falls. A bullet has struck his helmet but has not penetrated it. He manages an awkward retreat down the nearest available ladder. For the three agents who had entered the room, a different fate: all were killed.

Was it merely coincidental that all three ATF agents had happened to serve as Bill Clinton's bodyguards during the course of his campaign for president? Had they perhaps seen something that they should not have seen? Did they know something that they should not have known? Could the raid possibly have served at once as the cloak and the technology of their elimination?

On the one hand: By the fourth day after the shootout, the ATF had ceded control of all police operations to the FBI. Henceforth, the media would be restricted to a site some three miles from the Mount Carmel property. FBI agent Rob Ricks would offer them an official version of each subsequent day's events. Nearby Fort Hood would provide tanks and other material with which the compound was soon effectively surrounded.

On the other hand: The narrator of Thompson's video informs the viewer that "it is illegal to use military troops against United States citizens under the Posse Comitatus Act, 18 United States Code 13855," but adds a qualification. The National Guard and military materiel might in fact be deployed legally against citizens involved in the manufacture or sale of illicit drugs. The narrator dismisses the possibility that the Koreshite community might have had any such involvement. Yet what of the rumor that Mount Carmel hid a methamphetamine laboratory? Could the ATF have promulgated the rumor in order to secure then Governor Ann Richard's authorization of the use of tanks? And why, even long after it had become clear that the rumor was ill-founded, did the governor not retract the authorization she initially granted? Did she find the course of events wrested from her hands? Or was her inaction by her own design?

On the one hand: In consultation with a select group of behavioral scientists, the FBI is increasingly inclined to view David Koresh as matching the general profile of the mass murderer and to view his Mount Carmel followers as hostages. Seeking to break Koresh's will, or to provoke a mutiny, it launches a campaign of increasingly aggressive psychological warfare. Almost immediately it deprives the compound of the flow of public utilities. During the third week of March it resorts to an array of tactics that bemused reporters tend for a while to render almost carnivalesque. "Decibels, not Bullets, Bombard Texas Sect," read one headline in the 25 March edition of the *New York Times;* "It's Got a Beat and You Can Surrender to It" read another, on 28 March.[46] Both articles refer to the medley of Tibetan chants, screaming rabbits, and Nancy Sinatra's version of "These Boots Are Made for Walkin' " that blares at the compound twenty-four hours a day. On 18 April a frustrated agency finally persuades the attorney general to give approval to move ahead with a plan first proposed in detail some six days previously. On 19 April, at about 6:00 a.m., tanks would begin consequently to inject limited quantities of an irritant gas through holes that they had made in the compound's exterior walls. They continued their work, with little result, until midday, when a fire erupted on the compound's second floor. An FBI sharpshooter reportedly "saw at least one cult member apparently sprinkling liquid in a room moments before it erupted in flames." [47] The Mount Carmel Center was entirely destroyed within an hour. Nine of those who still resided in it on 19 April survived. Seventy-four of their fellow residents died.

On the other hand: The narrator of Thompson's video interprets the climax of the standoff rather differently. On the screen, the day is still 19 April, but the time is shortly before 6:00 a.m. The viewer looks upon the roof of an underground bunker, located several yards from the compound. A tank sits between the bunker and the compound, on top of a tunnel that connects the one to the other. For some two hours agents regularly enter and exit the tank, but at the first sign of their movements, the photographer filming them "conveniently cuts away." At about 6:10 a.m. the camera nevertheless reveals smoke drifting up from out of the bunker. None of the media bother to attend to its appearance. Nor do they attend to a tank that simultaneously moves against the compound itself, effecting the collapse of that end of the building at which a "trap door" might have allowed anyone taking refuge in the bunker to escape. Yet there is further footage to "prove that the Branch Davidians were murdered." The screen shows what appears to be a bright orange jet of fire twice spouting from another of the tanks that punctured the compound walls. Shortly after flames begin rolling out of a second-story window, it shows an agent riding atop yet another tank, apparently removing a "fireproof-type hood." It shows other agents, walking casually about the burning compound, apparently unconcerned about the risk of further assault. Over their heads helicopters circle, the passengers within them brandishing rifles. The narrator reminds the viewer that "in any ordinary crime scene, great pains are taken to preserve the evidence." On the screen, tanks busily push and press debris into the center of the fallen, smoldering compound, where it, too, might gradually disintegrate into ashes.

The evidential relation is notoriously difficult to formalize, and the relative weight of various modalities of evidence notoriously difficult to determine. The video, in any event, favors the visual. It thus remains silent about rumors of a connection between the explosion that damaged New York City's World Trade Center on 26 February 1993, and the initial ATF raid, which took place two days later. It remains silent about many other rumors as well. Much of what it professes to prove—whether it be the illegality of the use of military equipment and personnel or the actual sources of the final conflagration—remains, if not entirely dubious, still irresolutely disputable. But in the aftermath of the conflagration, the media—in company with both their scholarly and their lay publics—have gradually left David Koresh to rest in the pursuit of some of Thompson's own culprits: the president only very rarely; the "cultbusters" on occasion; the ATF and the FBI surely more frequently than either agency would care to have to bear.[48] Even those more moderate citizens who were at first apparently inclined to applaud the demise of David Koresh have thus increasingly come to discover that they might in fact have had something in common with him. Like him, they seem to have developed a distinct distrust of the system.

After the fire, assessors determine the precincts of the compound to be contaminated by lead. Security is imposed. Photograph by William R. Dull.

Excursus: Toward a Critique of Politicocybernetic Alienation

Theorists of conspiracy have no need of actual conspiracy, but semiotic indeterminacy alone is hardly enough to sustain them. Consider a heuristic analogue, a constellation of discourses and practices that continues even today to excite the imaginations of anthropological exoticists: witchcraft. As Jeanne Favret-Saada and many others have observed, believers in witchcraft, witch hunters, even unwitchers can do very well without witches.[49] Like millennialists, like theorists of conspiracy, they would be virtually bereft without the copious supply of indeterminate events—the "accidental" or the repeated misfortune, death, bad and good "luck"—over which their own semiotics of suspicion ranges so effectively.[50] The discourses and practices of witchcraft are, however, further in need of a metaphysics, nonetheless essential even when it remains inarticulate, or merely implicit. In its logically most simple expression, it might even be monological—an unqualified metaphysics of evil.[51] Most commonly it resolves into a dualism, a contest, whether equal or unequal, between good and evil. In any event, its abiding inspiration is an anxiety, at once metaphysical and moral, over the reach and touch of evil. As Kai Erikson and

Mary Douglas have both observed, witchcraft is thus well equipped to serve, and does frequent service, as a discourse of dangerous alterity, of the malign other.[52]

Witchcraft is also well equipped to serve—and in contemporary Africa apparently serves widely—as a moral critique of the distribution and the exercise of both economically and socially conditioned, both "material" and "ideal" power.[53] In this respect as well, then, millennialism, theories of conspiracy, and witchcraft have a common discursive and functional dimension. But two qualifications must be appended. First, if witchcraft is always "ready"—conceptually able—to contribute to the critique of the distribution and exercise of socioeconomic power, it does not always function critically in fact. Among E. E. Evans-Pritchard's Azande, for example, its applications are as often as not diagnostic, and its specific utility as a diagnostics of fault or blame is compromised by a physics that postulates witchcraft to be beyond the control of the individual's will.[54] The millennialist critique of power is, in contrast, not merely a typical but a fundamental aspect of millennialism itself. It is the discursive distillation of a "corrective" theodicy and an urgent soteriology alike. Deprive millennialism of what might be called its "politics of suspicion" and it becomes what Saint Augustine would have it be: an indefinite allegory of the world process. Deprive theories of conspiracy of their politics of suspicion and they become mere parlor games. Second, it is still possible to agree with those neo-Marxist ethnologists who insist that millennialist movements are "prepolitical" or "protopolitical"—but only at the expense of presuming the political domain to consist exclusively of acts and interests. The political is, however, also an experiential domain. Millennialism virtually never generates a "platform," a program of secular reform. Its characteristic program is rather a program of waiting.[55] But waiting can itself be a political strategy. It can very often be a response—in its way, a perfectly cogent response—to the experience of an abiding political fecklessness.

What millennialists experience as politically given, theorists of conspiracy may sometimes experience merely as a threat. They may sometimes accordingly embrace a secular activism directed toward controlling, more often toward annihilating, whom, or what, they fear. They may opt—as the apparently burgeoning leagues of American survivalists and militias attest—for strategic and often bellicose withdrawal. But just as often, they, too, opt for quietism, even for resignation, in the face of conditions they feel themselves unable to alter. It is tempting to construe the experiential reference point that millennialists and theorists of conspiracy share as one of oppression, even of subjection. Neither label would seem, however, precisely to capture the political experience of the Branch Davidian community, at least before the ATF began to take such special interest in their affairs. Neither label would seem precisely to capture the rather more distant political sensibility that informs Linda Thompson's

At the edge of the ruins of the Branch Davidian compound, a permanent memorial now stands. Photograph by William R. Dull.

video. Nor in fact is either label sociologically appropriate; neither all millennialists nor all theorists of conspiracy hail from subaltern strata. Millennialists are not unlikely to come from the legions of those petty venture capitalists who have never acquired their pot of gold; from the lesser, but notable, ranks of those nouveaux riches who do not believe that they really deserve the economic clout that they have acquired; from among the ranks of those supernumerary heirs who find themselves with fortunes they did nothing to earn; from among the ranks of those who, whatever their poverty or their privilege, find themselves constantly invited, constantly pressured to consider their experiences invalid, irrational, mad. Similarly, many of the most avid, and most activist, theorists of conspiracy can be found in the highest echelons of the politico-economic elite, and especially in those echelons whose privileges are (but then, aren't they always?) open to dispute, and in danger—real or imagined—of usurpation.

Curious bedfellows, perhaps: but an unlikely source offers a key to clarifying their intimacy. Durkheim had neither millennialists nor theorists of conspiracy specifically in mind when he formulated his definition of the "social fact." Seeking a "positive," an empirical ground for a social science, he ap-

pealed to what he evidently presumed to be a virtually universal human experience: that of a force imposing itself coercively and as constraint from without.[56] From the same experience, he would much later argue the original
postulation of the sacred to have its wellspring.[57] Pierre Bourdieu, among others, has suggested that the social, thus delimited, is virtually "empty." [58] At first
reading, Durkheim indeed seems to conflate a variety of modalities of coercion
that are experientially distinct: that of the conclusion validly derived from its
premises with that of moral duty; that of moral duty with that of such practically inescapable conventions as driving on one or the other side of the road;
that of convention with that of punishment; that of punishment willingly
suffered from that of punishment unwillingly suffered; and so on. There can,
however, be no doubt that some of Durkheim's conflations are intentional.[59]
Whether intentional or not, they bring to light a number of structural relationships that intuition may hesitate to entertain.

With the addition of only a single variable, Durkheim's experiential model
of the social fact yields an experiential model of paranoia. Intuition may incline
toward positing that what the sense or sensation of being subject to an external
coercive force lacks in order to be paranoid is a "reality check." But not only
is such an addition extraexperiential, it is also insufficient, even for as secure a
sociological realist as Durkheim, who would surely have to admit that even
paranoiacs occasionally have very real enemies. What the experience of the
social lacks in order to pass as paranoid is simply that additional sense, or
sensation, of "election"—positive or negative from one "case" to the next. If
positive, the paranoid sense of election often finds its symbology in the imagery
of the messenger or messiah in the symbology of a sometimes burdened but
distinctive blessedness that psychomedical discourse casts as the "delusion of
grandeur." If negative, the paranoid sense of election often seeks out those
symbologies of the scapegoat and sacrificial victim that psychomedical discourse takes as the stuff of a "persecution complex." Nor are the values mutually exclusive: the sense of election can be negative and positive at once.

The phenomenological proximity of social and paranoid experience does not
merely suggest that paranoia is itself a social, not a psychological, phenomenon. It further suggests that each of the two modalities of experience implicates
the other, as presence implicates absence, or better, as one pole of a continuous
scale implicates the opposite pole of the same scale. The difference between
the two seems, in other words, to be merely a matter of degree, not genuinely
of kind. Durkheim hints at their fundamental unity in noting that, at its most
"social," social experience goes unnoticed. Or at least it passes for something
else: having been internalized, having become an aspect of the habitus, external
coercion has the feel of personal inclination.[60] At such an extreme lie the practitioners of Bourdieusian theory, who reproduce the structural conditions that
have made them who and what they are without knowing or needing to know

what they are doing. The palpable externality and the palpable coerciveness of the social both increase, however, with even the slightest failure of the reproductive circuit, with even the slightest lessening of social investment. At the opposite extreme lies Weber's charismatic leader and his or her radically revisionary slogan: "It is written; but I say unto you."[61] In the company of the charismatic, standing nearer or farther away, are those like-minded souls who, for no doubt widely variable reasons, find themselves inclined to listen, perhaps to "convert," perhaps to realize their own election, negative or positive (or both) from one case to the next. At this extreme, the semiotics and the politics of suspicion are virtually constitutive of common sense. Here, paranoia has its structural correlate. Here, members of the ruling strata are likely to rub shoulders with the subaltern. Here, the theorist of conspiracy, the millennarian, and the messiah all meet.

Though Durkheim would probably have chosen a different label, the extremes at which paranoia thrives can well enough be deemed extremes of "alienation." But from what? Not from the social itself, for even such extremes stop well short of that boundary that divides the "outsider" from the true alien, the critic from the true enemy. They stop short, too, of the boundary that divides "deviance" from actual anomie. Nor do either theorists of conspiracy or millennialists stand beyond or leave behind the realm of the cultural. They are not preoccupied with meaninglessness, with the Absurd. They are rather preoccupied with mysteries. Both are aware of the sometimes terrible ironies of ignorance. But the aura of the uncanny that abides in even the most abstract of conspiratorial and millennialist revelations stems from an anxiety over more than mere ignorance. Even the theorist of conspiracy who does not think himself or herself a victim of conspiracy raises the specter of a double alienation: from the truth, but more immediately, from the regime of signification that, effecting an organization of the production and the distribution of the truth, also allows for the harboring of secrets. Even the rather rare millennialist who entertains no thoughts whatever of conspiracy still tells of an errancy, or a perversion, that has placed both truth and power beyond human managing. At its paranoid extremes, alienation is "politicocybernetic." Whatever the position of the subject who suffers it, such alienation would appear to have the sense of election, positive or negative, as its most common and most spontaneous fetish. Whatever its precise sources, which are surely multiple, its objective measure lies in the gap between the individual subject, the individual subjectivity, and that ideal-typical subjectivity perfectly tuned to use and to serve the steering mechanisms of the politicocybernetic regime in which it subsists.

Can it merely be accidental that the most intricate diagrammization to date of the components and processes of the politicocybernetic economy emerges not in religious studies or psychology, not in political science or information theory, but rather in Michel Foucault's analytics of those curious—and also very familiar—enterprises known in French as *les sciences humaines?*

File 4: The Beast Revisited

"You think there'll be a war."

"Perhaps." Profane's newspaper reading was in fact confined to glancing at the front page of the *New York Times.* If there was no banner headline on that paper then the world was in good enough shape. "The Middle East, cradle of civilization, may yet be its grave." (Thomas Pynchon)[62]

Official language, particularly the system of concepts by means of which the members of a given group provide themselves with a representation of their social relations, . . . sanctions and imposes what it states, tacitly laying down the dividing line between the thinkable and the unthinkable, thereby contributing to the maintenance of the symbolic order from which it draws its authority. Thus officialization is only one aspect of the objectifying process through which the group teaches itself and conceals from itself its own truth, inscribing in objectivity its representation of what it is and thus binding itself by this public declaration. (Pierre Bourdieu)[63]

The seals will either save you or destroy you. (David Koresh)[64]

Linda Thompson came to visit me again. We had met and compared notes on her previous visits. She was investigating Koresh's involvement with the C.I.A. She thought he was running a safe-house for them. She told me that there were two dozen large orange blobs in the back yard before the fire and I told her about the people who had heard a live voice over on C.N.N. in Bellmeade and the W.T.H. report of a pile of bodies inside a door and Debbie's account of her daughter Stardust pulling up a whole bunch of body markers in one place out back. A group of twenty people had run out the back door according to C.N.N.[;] it seemed to me that the other information confirmed it.

Accusation

Other confirmations of a link between Koresh and the government also tend to verify the C.I.A. safe house theory. The autopsies of 49 of the Branch Davidians showed lethal levels of cyanide in their blood. CS gas breaks down into hydrogen cyanide under high heat. According to the T.N.R.C.C. Cleanup Coordinator Don Fawn cyanide specific gas mask filters were found on the site as well as syringes of a type to penetrate clothing. In addition to indicating that the government set the fire, this also suggests they expected to be inside

the building during the fire and to need to treat persons for cyanide
exposure. . . .

Next Linda and I compared notes on the Feds. who were trying to
stop us. Ken Faucett was lying to both of us, and we both suspected
Gary Hunt. Ron Cole was spreading lies too. In fact we were surrounded by self-professed civil rights activists who were spreading
disinformation as quickly as possible. Linda traveled with a bodyguard and she had a gun in her shoulder holster too. Her bodyguard
was so big he could scarcely fit in my 8 by 8 house.

She left with hugs after two hours. I felt that we were kindred spirits
both seeking justice in an evil world. A year has past and I have made
repeated attempts to contact her again with no success. (Amo Paul
Bishop Roden, Branch Davidian)[65]

That the Encyclopedia Americana records American paranoids to be
generally better integrated than other psychotics is likely a symptom
of our police state. (Amo Paul Bishop Roden)[66]

I am not saying that the human sciences emerged from the prison. But,
if they have been able to be formed and to produce so many profound
changes in the episteme, it is because they have been conveyed by a
specific and new modality of power: a certain policy of the body, a
certain way of rendering the group of men docile and useful. This
policy required the definite involvement of relations of knowledge in
relations of power; it called for a technique of overlapping subjectifi-
cation and objectification; it brought with it new procedures of indi-
vidualization. The carceral network constituted one of the armatures
of this network of power-knowledge that has made the human sciences historically possible. (Michel Foucault)[67]

Someone asked about the plot to kill Hitler. The discussion moved
to plots in general. I found myself saying to the assembled heads, "All
plots tend to move deathward. This is the nature of plots. Political
plots, terrorist plots, lovers' plots, narrative plots, plots that are parts
of children's games. We edge nearer death every time we plot. It is
like a contract that all must sign, the plotters as well as those who are
the targets of the plot."

Is this true? Why did I say it? What does it mean? (Don DeLillo)[68]

It is because subjects do not, strictly speaking, know what they are
doing that what they do has more meaning than they know. (Pierre
Bourdieu)[69]

We must agree with Galbraith (and others) in acknowledging that the
liberty and sovereignty of the consumer are nothing more than a mys-
tification. The well-preserved mystique of satisfaction and individual
choice (primarily supported by economists), whereby a "free" civilization reaches its pinnacle, is the very ideology of the industrial sys-

tem. It justifies its arbitrariness and all sorts of social problems: filth, pollution, and deculturation—in fact the consumer is sovereign in a jungle of ugliness, where *the freedom of choice is imposed upon him*. The revised sequence (that is to say the *system* of consumption) thus ideologically supplements and connects with the *electoral system*. The drug store and the polling booth, the geometric spaces of individual freedom, are also the system's two mammary glands. (Jean Baudrillard)[70]

Technocratic organizations wrap themselves in secrecy and distrust public information and debate. They aggressively build their own power, impose more and more rigid social integration on their members, and manipulate the channels of production and consumption. They are centers of power that create new forms of inequality and privilege. On the global level, we speak of central and peripheral nations, a de facto distinction between the rulers and the subjects. Similarly, within a particular nation, there is a growing separation between the central and ruling elements within the great organizations and a new *plebs* which is subject to change beyond its control, to public campaigns and propaganda, and to the disorganization of its earlier social structures. (Alain Touraine)[71]

The structural force of system imperatives intervening in the forms of social integration can no longer hide behind the rationality differential between sacred and profane domains. The modern form of understanding is too transparent to provide a niche for this structural violence by means of inconspicuous restrictions on communication. Under these conditions it is to be expected that the competition between forms of system and social integration would become more visible than previously. In the end, systemic mechanisms suppress forms of social integration even in those areas where a consensus-dependent coordination of action cannot be replaced, that is, where the symbolic reproduction of the lifeworld is at stake. In these areas, the *mediatization* of the lifeworld assumes the form of a *colonization*. (Jürgen Habermas)[72]

Advances in substantial theory may have side effects on the theories that are supposed to control the research. Until the eighteenth century these problems were assigned to religion—the social system that specialized in tackling paradoxes. We have retained this possibility, but the normalization of paradoxes in modern art and modern science seems to indicate our desire to eventually get along without religion. Apparently our society offers the choice either to trust religion or to work off our own paradoxes without becoming aware that this is religion. (Niklas Luhmann)[73]

I believe that the future lies in religion. (Shoko Asahara)[74]

Excursus: From Millennialism to the Conspiracy of the System

The vast majority of societies, "simple" and "complex," are distinctly accommodating of their politicocybernetically alienated members. They may violently reject the most extreme of extremes. They may at least confine or psychopharmaceutically neutralize them. But with what one might deem a wily consistency, societies tend by and large to accord a tolerable, even a generous space of action and authority to those who would—by temperament, for example, or by situation—be disposed to become politicocybernetic malcontents. So the blind in Japan often find a place as mediums, if not millennialist messiahs.[75] So the psychically high-pitched around the world often find a place as healers, as shamans, as spiritual therapists or spiritual consultants, as oracles. So the "graceless" and the "haunted" often find positions as jesters, as artists, as university professors.

The functionalist might note that such "compromises" deceive and dilute a *vue à loin* that could easily turn subversive. The functionalist might note at the very least a preventative and a compensatory reintegration. Even short of its extremes, the politicocybernetically alienated consciousness is dangerous. It threatens to remind the regime in which it resides and against which it projects itself of what, even in the most politically and cybernetically "liberal" and "democratic" of climates, must remain outside, must remain unspeakable, must remain unthought. The ancient Greeks allegorically acknowledged the shortcomings of their own politicocybernetic regime in such figures as Tiresias, but especially in the figure of Cassandra, a seeress condemned to reveal truths that would always be remarked too late, or not at all. The canonists of the biblical testaments, old and new, sought at once to acknowledge and to transcend similar shortcomings in casting the ancient Hebraic prophets as witnesses to a more vast tableau, a more vast historical plan than ordinary men or women could discern. In both cases, Greek and Hebraic, these epistemic saints and martyrs stand at the rough edge of a rupture that separates the proximate from the ultimate order of things. Mortal counterparts of Hermes—this broker in symbols and signs, this "intellectual" divinity—they are messengers of the ultimate, of a supreme authority that always threatens to expose the pretensions and deceptions of lesser powers. The threat they pose is thus not of their own devising. They are mere instruments, their apparent arrogance only a side effect of their service and their submission to cosmos or God.

Both Greeks and Hebrews nevertheless knew the occasional temptation to kill even the most blameless of messengers. Perhaps the ATF and the FBI let temptation get the better of them at Waco. But then again, David Koresh was no ordinary, no run-of-the-mill messenger, either. Some of his sympathizers, especially religious scholars, have seen him as a man of his calling whose spiritual depth and spiritual sincerity an allegedly secular populace could not comprehend.[76] Others, rightist if not always militant, have touted him as a patriot[77] who chose to sacrifice himself in the name of a liberty that a corrupt and increasingly despotic government would have had him surrender. But Koresh seems to have aggravated both the press and the FBI less for his religiosity than for his insistence always upon talking about it, and less for his sovereign airs than for what could only be seen as his relentless whimsy. He simply did not behave as expected. He made promises that he failed to keep. He offered to negotiate only to revert to obstinacy. Mortally wounded at one moment, he was hale the next. He could be repentant and sorry. He could be consummately defiant. He spoke in parables. He spoke in sound bytes. When he appeared to be near defeat, he would return restored. The behavioral experts working for the FBI construed his "profile" as that of the mass murderer. But Koresh was so susceptible to the vilification of press and experts alike precisely because he refused to fit any profile neatly. This "sinful messiah," this "demon," this "madman" could not be characterologically normalized. He refused ethical resolution.

In this respect, at least, David Koresh was a follower of the letter of his favorite book. Like the *Iliad,* the Book of Revelation imposes a double ethical vision, a blurry ethical parallelism that defies ready clarification. On the one hand, it tells a tale of action and reaction, of choices made and abandoned, of the exercise and the thwarting of will. On the other hand, it tells a tale of pre-ordination, of a destiny always already inscribed or intoned in the divine logos. Tropological synthesis, tropological escape: Revelation cannot help but allow these, and has been vulnerable to both from Saint Augustine forward. Only with its ambiguities intact, however, can it simultaneously do service as a theodicy and as a secular apology. Only with its ambiguities intact can it simultaneously be a recounting of God's just distribution of merit and demerit, of earned reward and earned punishment, and of the fateful incapacity of both elect and condemned to do any more, or any less, or anything else but what they in fact do. Little comfort for the condemned: but only an ethically ambiguous Revelation can absolve the elect of their sins, the sin of pride perhaps paramount among them.

David Koresh remains sociologically and culturologically ambiguous. At first, even at second sight, he is countermodern, antimodern, even premodern. So, too, his favorite book. But here as elsewhere, historicism proves to be too simple, too simplistic. Many biblical scholars have urged a generic distinction between such strictly "prophetic" books as those of Isaiah or Jeremiah and the visionary, properly "apocalyptic" books of Daniel and Revelation. The former date largely from the period preceding the Babylonian exile, the latter from the politically more pessimistic period following it.[78] The former tend toward explicit exhortation and practical application, the latter toward an occult eschatology. The prophetic books appear to be the product of a socially

At Amo Paul Bishop Roden's offices, testaments on view. Photograph by William R. Dull.

more integrated spiritual practice. The apocalyptic books hint of dispersion
and isolation; the content of the Book of Revelation putatively came to the
apostle John during his lonely imprisonment on the island of Patmos. The terrain of the prophetic books can be wide, but their primary concern is always
with the Israelites. The terrain especially of the Book of Revelation is the terrain of all the known world. The deposition of a radically alienated sojourner
in the Roman empire, of a Hebraic Cassandra, Revelation oscillates world-
historically and world-systematically between the millions of the condemned
and the one hundred forty-four thousand troops of the Lord's chosen army
(7:4), between the vast presence of an imperialist "Babylon" and the intimate
particularities of the Christ and the Antichrist. Part epical, part tragic, part sublime, the book that David Koresh believed himself appointed at last to unlock
is at once totalizing and individualizing. It is a book of calculuses and codes,
the most haunting perhaps that "brand" or "mark"—666—that the Antichrist would impose upon all who hoped to participate in his world economy
(Rev. 13:18). It is infused with the panoptic and the disciplinary. Even those
Branch Davidians who were dubious of David Koresh from the outset and who
would reject his exegeses still share his regard for Revelation itself. For all of
them, it is a book for our new Rome, a book very much of our time.

"We" may presume that God is dead—or never lived. But for all this, we
cannot ignore His lingering shadows. Or perhaps we cannot do without them.
In any event, from the end of the 1960s forward, just as we have ostensibly

been disburdening our sociological and anthropological imaginations of such "millennialist" schemata as that of the Marxist dialectic, just as we have ostensibly been laying our worn and weathered "master narratives" and "grand theories" to rest, we seem unwittingly, almost compulsively, to have returned to the semiotics of suspicion, to the politics of suspicion, to the structural motifs and structural matrices of apocalyptic. We may thus have more in common with David Koresh—whoever he really was—than we presume. In this "late" era of ours (but late for what?), a certain double vision can often pass not for confusion but for the pinnacle of ethical wisdom. And perhaps it is. Apocalyptic totalism for its part is a practically inescapable principle of the representation—whether in our novels of paranoia or in our more analytical essays—of a "system" of myriad dimensions and myriad brands and marks whose tentacular "flows" now stretch to virtually every inhabited outpost of the globe. Whatever might be said of typological hermeneutics, does the Book of Revelation not also hold at least the prototypical epiphany of a system whose infrastructure is very like the one in which we have only recently begun to realize, or to believe, that we increasingly live? Is the beast's regulatory number not the original index of a "programmed society" that rests in and thrives upon the ever more intricate intersection of the political and the cybernetic, of power and knowledge? Is the beast himself not, in his way, the prototypical global technocrat, the prototypical world manager? This heteronomic creature of "seven heads and ten horns, and upon his horns ten crowns, and upon his heads the name of blasphemy" (Rev. 13:1), this monster destined to fall to the very instruments of his sovereignty (Rev. 13:10), this victim/executor and executor/victim, is he not, after all, what we increasingly encounter in our contemporary hall of mirrors? And who are *we,* who *are* we, to say?

Notes

1. Since the events of the winter and spring of 1993, both the Branch Davidians and Vernon Howell (or David Koresh) have been the subject of extensive attention and documentation, the latter of widely variable reliability. For a concise history of the Branch Davidian community, see B. Pitts, "The Davidian Tradition," in *From the Ashes: Making Sense of Waco,* ed. J. R. Lewis (Lanham, Md.: Rowman and Littlefield, 1994), 33–39. See also J. D. Tabor and E. V. Gallagher, *Why Waco? Cults and the Battle for Religious Freedom in America* (Berkeley: University of California Press, 1995), 33–43.

2. This rather delicate issue is a source of some controversy among Branch Davidians themselves. See, however, Tabor and Gallagher's judicious treatment in *Why Waco?* 41.

3. Howell claimed to have had a personal revelation during a visit to Israel early in 1985. He derived from it his self-conception as a latter-day Cyrus (Hebrew Koresh), appointed to free the "Israelites" from the oppressions of "Babylon." Cf. Tabor and Gallagher, *Why Waco?* 42.

4. Ibid., 43.

5. Weber's distinction between the emissary and the exemplary prophet is of particular pertinence here. Koresh did not present himself to his followers as an exemplar worthy of emulation. His role was strictly that of messenger. For the distinction, see M. Weber, "Religious Rejections of the World and Their Directions," in *From Max Weber: Essays in Sociology,* ed. trans. H. Gerth and C. Wright Mills (New York: Oxford University Press, 1946), 323–59.

6. As an adult, Koresh took his message primarily to Seventh-Day Adventist congregations, from which the great majority of his followers, whether from the U.S. or from abroad, actually came (*Why Waco?* 24–25). Amo Roden has indicated to me that the membership of the community before Koresh arrived was of a somewhat more diverse religious background.

7. Like the leaders who preceded him at Mount Carmel, Koresh had been formally removed from the rosters of the Seventh-Day Adventist Church (ibid., 44).

8. Or at least to require his followers to embrace them. On Ellen White, see ibid., 48–49; and R. E. Graham, *Ellen G. White: Co-Founder of the Seventh-day Adventist Church* (New York: Peter Lang, 1986).

9. White held that a prophetic remnant would gradually reveal the remaining divine mysteries to the elect in the Final Days. Each element of the remnant would thus have his or her "present truth" until suspended by the next revelation.

10. Paul Boyer reports that the Assemblies of God Church grew some 121 percent between 1965 to 1989, to 2.2 million members; that Jehovah's Witnesses have a current membership of some 860,000 U.S. adherents; and that the Seventh-Day Adventist Church, which has also experienced a virtual doubling of membership in the past thirty years, has a current U.S. membership of more than 700,000. See P. Boyer, "A Brief History of the End of Time," *New Republic,* 17 May 1993, 31. For a comprehensive overview of U.S. sectarianism, see T. Weber, *Living in the Shadow of the Second Coming: American Premillennialism, 1875–1925* (New York: Oxford University Press, 1979); and Boyer, *When Time Shall Be No More: Prophecy Belief in Modern American Culture* (Cambridge, Mass.: Harvard University Press, 1992).

11. For a formal synopsis of Seventh-Day Adventist tenets, see *Adventism in America,* ed. G. Land (Grand Rapids, Mich.: William B. Eerdmans, 1986), 231–50. Seventh-Day Adventist eschatology is technically a variety of "historicist premillennialism," concerning which see T. Weber, *Living in the Shadow,* 9–10.

12. On the location of Armageddon, literal and figurative, see Boyer, *When Time Shall Be No More,* 125–250.

13. On the belief that the United States and/or the United Nations are Babylon, see ibid., 246–64.

14. Tabor and Gallagher, *Why Waco?* 11. Agent Rodriguez was apparently unable to disguise his actual identity for any length of time. Koresh nevertheless permitted him to stay at Mount Carmel, and he was present the morning of 28 February. He had, however, departed from the compound before the raid, in part to inform his superiors that the residents expected their arrival. See M. Oliver Jr., "Killed by Semantics: Or Was It a Keystone Cop Kaleidoscope Kaper?" in *From the Ashes,* 72–73.

15. The types of violations over which the ATF has jurisdiction.

16. In his affidavit for a search warrant, Agent Aguilera lingers at some length on his conversations with Joyce Sparks, the social worker who visited the Mount Carmel

compound twice, first in February and again in April 1992. He reports Ms. Sparks's complaint that the tours she was provided seemed "staged" and that Koresh was minimally cooperative.

17. For a critique at once of the series and of its rapid proliferation in the national press, see Tabor and Gallagher, *Why Waco?* 117–19.

18. For the official tally, see R. Scruggs et al., *Report to the Deputy Attorney General on the Events at Waco, Texas, February 28 to April 19, 1993* (Washington, D.C.: U.S. Government Printing Office, 1993), 313–28. Unofficial tallies vary widely, as will become evident below. If not on the death toll, the government's report diverges in many other respects from such relatively rigorous journalistic accounts as that of D. Reavis. See Reavis's *The Ashes of Waco* (New York: Simon and Schuster, 1995).

19. For a detailed recent analysis of the *topoi* of apocalyptic rhetoric, see S. D. O'Leary, *Arguing the Apocalypse: A Theory of Millennial Rhetoric* (New York: Oxford University Press, 1994), chap. 23.

20. On the modern "functionalization" of theory, see H. Blumenberg, *The Legitimacy of the Modern Age,* trans. R. M. Wallace (Cambridge, Mass.: MIT Press, 1983), 200. These distinctions derive from Blumenberg's discussion of the semantic divergence between modern "theory" and Aristotle's θεωρία.

21. For an expansive historical survey of something very like a semiotics of suspicion, see M. Foucault, "Nietzsche, Freud, Marx," in *Aesthetics, Method, Epistemology,* vol. 2 of *Essential Works of Michel Foucault,* ed. J. D. Faubion (New York: New Press, 1998), 269–78.

22. See E. Auerbach, *Mimesis: The Representation of Reality in Western Literature,* trans. W. R. Trask (Princeton, N.J.: Princeton University, 1953), 58; cited in V. Lambropoulos, *The Rise of Eurocentrism: Anatomy of Interpretation* (Princeton, N.J.: Princeton University, 1993), 11.

23. Auerbach, *Mimesis,* 73; cf. Lambropoulos, *Rise of Eurocentrism,* 14.

24. There can be no question that millennialist movements outside the West have often been the inspiration, or the result, of "contact" with both Western missionaries and Western fortune hunters. But for one argument that the millennialist consciousness cannot always be supposed to derive from a Western predecessor, see K. Burridge, *Mambu: A Melanesian Millennium* (Princeton, N.J.: Princeton University, 1960), 25–44.

25. Lambropoulos, *Rise of Eurocentrism,* 14.

26. F. Schiller, *On the Aesthetic Education of Man, In a Series of Letters,* trans. R. Snell (New York: Frederick Ungar, 1965), originally published in 1794–95.

27. Thucydides, *History of the Peloponnesian War,* trans. C. F. Smith (Cambridge, Mass.: Harvard University Press), 6: xxvii, 1–2.

28. Among many others, Eva Keuls, who writes of the "castration" of the Herms and, departing even further from Thucydides, postulates that the league of vandals was in fact made of Athenian women (*The Reign of the Phallus: Sexual Politics in Ancient Athens* [Berkeley: University of California Press, 1993], 381–403).

29. *New York Times,* 1 Mar. 1993, A1, B9.

30. Boyer, "Brief History," 30.

31. J. M. Wall, "Eager for the End," *The Christian Century,* 5 May 1993, 476.

32. R. Lacayo, "In the Grip of a Psychopath," *Time,* 3 May 1993, 35.

33. H. Rainie, "The Final Days of David Koresh," *U.S. News and World Report,*

3 May 1993, 320; cf. G. Carroll et al., "Children of the Cult," *Newsweek,* 17 May 1993, 50; and S. Rimer, "Growing Up Under Koresh," *New York Times,* 4 May 1993, A1.

34. Lacayo, "In the Grip of a Psychopath," 35.

35. Ibid., 38.

36. S. S. Gregory, "Children of a Lesser God," *Time,* 17 May 1993, 54.

37. Ibid., 54, quoting psychiatrist Bruce Perry.

38. S. H. Verhovek, "Scores Die as Cult Compound is Set Afire after F.B.I. Sends in Tanks with Tear Gas," *New York Times,* 20 Apr. 1993, A20.

39. L. Thompson, *Waco: The Big Lie.*

40. For an appropriately skeptical discussion of these remarks, see Tabor and Gallagher, *Why Waco?* 67–68.

41. The Thompson video indeed cites the relevant state law (ibid., 100–101).

42. Verhovek, "Agent Injured by Cult Gunfire Blames Texas Newspaper in Lawsuit," *New York Times,* 18 Mar. 1993, A16. In the end, the informer turned out to be a mail carrier who encountered the troops of the ATF on his way to the Mount Carmel compound. The media, for its part, had apparently intercepted conversations among the ATF troops on short-wave radio.

43. See D. Terry, "Authorities Plan to Wait for End of Cult Standoff," *New York Times,* 4 Mar. 1993, L16, for report that undercover agent R. Rodriguez, who had left the compound a few hours before the raid took place, informed the ATF command that the Branch Davidians had received a telephone call warning them of the imminent raid.

44. S. Labaton, "Bentsen Signals Official's Ouster over Initial Raid on Cult in Texas," *New York Times,* 29 Apr. 1993, A1.

45. P. Applebome, "Negotiations with Texas Cult Cover Ever-Shifting Ground," *New York Times,* 11 Mar. 1993, A11.

46. Verhovek, "Decibels, Not Bullets, Bombard Texas Sect," *New York Times,* 25 Mar. 1993, A16; J. Pareles, "It's Got a Beat and You Can Surrender to It," *New York Times,* 28 Mar. 1993, IV2.

47. Verhovek, "Scores Die" (see n. 38).

48. Tabor and Gallagher note the largely negative review that Thompson's video received in the Waco press (*Why Waco?* 132). The press would begin to call for a "rational" investigation of the Waco fiasco almost immediately (M. Kelly, "After Waco's Inferno, an Inquisition that Insists on Rational Answers," *New York Times,* 25 Apr. 1993, IV3. Several of the more reflective journalists would also begin to assess the role that the media may have played in inciting hasty governmental action (J. Holley, "The Waco Watch," *Columbia Journalism Review* [May–June 1993], 50–53; J. Kamen, "A Matter of 'Live' and Death," *American Journalism Review* 5, no. 15 [June 1993]: 25–31). The standoff and fire have been the subject of two governmental investigative panels, the second in the aftermath of the Oklahoma City bombing. In contrast to earlier "fast-breaking" exposés, but in closer accord with the conclusions of the second panel, such monographs as those of Tabor and Gallagher or Reavis have tended to be pointedly critical of the FBI.

49. See J. Favret-Saada, *Deadly Words: Witchcraft in the Bocage,* trans. C. Cullen (Cambridge: Cambridge University Press, 1980), 133–36.

50. See E. E. Evans-Pritchard, *Witchcraft, Oracles, and Magic Among the Azande*

(Oxford: Oxford University Press, 1976), 18–32. Cf. Favret-Saada, *Deadly Words,* 110–36; T. Luhrmann, *Persuasions of the Witch's Craft: Ritual Magic in Contemporary England* (Cambridge, Mass.: Harvard University Press, 1989), 115–72.

51. To my knowledge, such an unremitting metaphysics of evil remains merely a theoretical (or "structural") possibility, though a possibility perhaps approached by certain putative expressions of "Satanism."

52. See K. Erikson, *Wayward Puritans: A Study in the Sociology of Deviance* (New York: Wiley, 1966), 3–29. See also M. Douglas, *Natural Symbols: Explorations in Cosmology,* 2nd ed. (New York: Random House, 1973), 136–42. Cf. J. Comaroff and J. L. Comaroff, introduction to *Modernity and Its Malcontents,* ed. Comaroff and Comaroff (Chicago: University of Chicago, 1994), xi–xxxvii.

53. Comaroff and Comaroff, *Modernity,* xxiii–xxviii.

54. See Evans-Pritchard's discussion of "witchcraft substance" (*Witchcraft,* 1–8).

55. Tabor and Gallagher rightly remark, but perhaps exaggerate, the action that the Koreshians expected to be required of them as elect in the unlocking of Revelation's seven seals (*Why Waco?* 53–54).

56. E. Durkheim, *The Rules of Sociological Method,* ed. G. E. G. Catlin, trans. S. A. Solovay and J. H. Mueller (Glencoe, Ill.: Free Press, 1938), 1–4.

57. Durkheim, *The Elementary Forms of the Religious Life,* trans. K. E. Fields (New York: Free Press, 1995), 192–216.

58. P. Bourdieu, *Outline of a Theory of Practice,* trans. R. Nice (Cambridge: Cambridge University Press, 1977), 23.

59. For example, the conflation of logical with social "necessity."

60. See Durkheim, *The Rules of Sociological Method,* 2.

61. M. Weber, "The Sociology of Charismatic Authority," in *From Max Weber,* 250.

62. T. Pynchon, *V.* (New York: Bantam, 1964), 362–63.

63. Bourdieu, *Outline,* 21–22.

64. From a letter dated 11 April 1993, included in appendix E in Scruggs et al., *Report to the Deputy Attorney General.*

65. A. P. B. Roden, *Cracking the Cover-up* (unpub.), 47–48. The sources of Ms. Roden's claims about CS gas are not clear. She may be confusing cyanide with carbon monoxide; high concentrations of the latter were indeed found in many of the bodies recovered from the fire. Though not a by-product of the heating of CS gas, carbon monoxide is a by-product of the metabolization of methylene chloride, a chemical with which CS powder was combined in the effusive canisters that Bradley tanks inserted through the punctured walls of the compound (see D. Reavis, "What Really Happened at Waco," *Texas Monthly* 23, no. 7 [July 1995]: 129). It should be noted, however, that Ms. Roden's charges have been repeated in *Rules of Engagement,* a documentary on the Waco catastrophe that gained widespread public attention after its debut in late 1996.

66. Roden, "The Politics of Murder: The Why of the Branch Davidian Massacre" (unpub.), 5.

67. Foucault, *Discipline and Punish: The Birth of the Prison,* trans. A. Sheridan (New York: Vintage, 1979), 305.

68. D. DeLillo, *White Noise* (New York: Penguin, 1985), 26.

69. Bourdieu, *Outline,* 79.

70. J. Baudrillard, "On Consumer Society," in *Rethinking the Subject: An Anthology of Contemporary European Social Thought,* ed. Faubion (Boulder, Colo.: Westview, 1994), 199.

71. A. Touraine, "Post-Industrial Classes," in ibid., 184.

72. J. Habermas, vol. 2 of *Lifeworld and System: A Critique of Functionalist Reason, The Theory of Communicative Action,* trans. T. McCarthy (Boston: Beacon Press, 1987), 196.

73. N. Luhmann, *Essays on Self-Reference* (New York: Columbia University Press, 1990), 16–17.

74. Quoted in Murray Sayle, "Letter from Tokyo: Nerve Gas and the Four Noble Truths," *The New Yorker* 1 Apr. 1996, 58. Shoko Asahara is the partially blind leader of Aum Shinrikyo, the millenarian organization that appears to be responsible for the recent gassing of the Tokyo subway system.

75. See M. Ivy, *Discourses of the Vanishing: Modernity, Phantasm, Japan* (Chicago: University of Chicago Press, 1995), 142.

76. Such is the position, for example, of Tabor and Gallagher in *Why Waco?*

77. See Ron Cole, "God Rocks," one of many unpublished but freely circulating manuscripts that have appeared since Koresh's death.

78. P. Hanson, *The Dawn of Apocalyptic* (Philadelphia: Fortress Press, 1975), 12; cf. T. Overholt, *Channels of Prophecy: The Social Dynamics of Prophetic Activity* (Minneapolis: Fortress Press, 1989), 150–51.

An American Theme Park: Working and Riding Out Paranoia in the Late Twentieth Century

Theme Park Street

To walk slowly down lively streets is a special pleasure. To be left behind by the rush of the others—this is a bath in the surf. But my dear fellow[s] . . . do not make it easy, however gracefully one might move out of their way. I always receive suspicious looks whenever I try to stroll as a flaneur between the shops. . . . I would like to linger with the first glance.

—Hessell 1994, 420–21

My life began and ended in a theme park.

It was the Halloween Festival and the greatest show of the year began. A giant Pumpkinhead dancer tromped around the stage while music roared through speakers. By the end of the show, most of the cardboard props and scenery had been trampled and knocked over by the Pumpkinhead. Patrons and workers rejoiced in harmonious laughter, and for just this brief moment of kitsch, both parties were in unanimous agreement. Cardboard truths.

This writing tracks two years' work in a major American theme park. Many historic and extant studies of amusement and theme parks have emphasized the symbolic linkages of parks and American culture through the foci of consumerism and consumption, most notably, nationalism, the family, and class, while others have stressed the contrast between the "outside" appearances of parks and the "real inside" of such places with worker apathy, management scandal, and public relations nightmares—a sort of evil underbelly of the theme park. This particular study identifies such approaches, yet it takes a different path.

I understand the American theme park as a lived environment of fear, yearning, distrust, circumscribed conspiracies, and unrealized threats and posturing. Fear, as it is understood in popular perceptions and representations of the object theme park,[1] is manifested as a symptom of life in contemporary American culture. Going to the theme park is seen as an avoidance of the nightmare landscapes of crime, poverty, the declining family, and street-driven paranoia. This is, after all, Disney's mode of existence: construct the society-that-isn't, yet hope it *could be*. What I seek to undertake is a representation of the latency of fear in the magical midways and spaces of pleasure parks. I argue that the majority of theoretical studies of theme park environments have rarely addressed the existential conditions of the worker and the patron as well as their mediated relationships.

Fear, latency, panic, suspicion, and conspiracy are here lumped together as a series of symptoms of both the contemporary United States and popular amusements. On the theme park street a moment is had: a patron and worker exchange glances, each wondering what the other is thinking; each assuming dark motives and desires in the other. Like much of the quotidian activities of the theme park, this moment is the product of a glance between persons. Later, a third person and patron comments to the first: "Even this place isn't safe anymore."

The theme park is a moderate sized place, some fifty acres, but rather small considering the standards of large parks today. It is located on the outskirts of a major United States city, in the shadow of some of the city's major sporting complexes. Originally built in 1961 and owned by an influential city politician, the park was sold to the CFC Entertainment Corporation in 1975. As of this writing, CFC owns five parks across the country. Since Disney's surges in the business, many independent parks have been gobbled up by other major corporations. Some argue that such mass-ownership benefits park patrons in offering them spectacular rides and attractions while creating a standardized product visible in its various manifestations at different locations throughout the country.

The theme park has undergone significant changes since its opening in 1961. Now running with some two thousand employees in a season, the park is constantly updating its operational and managerial procedures. Departments are continually being merged with other departments; park training programs are constantly modified and updated.

When I was very young I enjoyed visiting theme parks, though I was too small to ride the rides. In fact, I was terrified of them. Instead, I made the theme park my fantasy playground in which I was the secret agent on a mission to avert disaster. Perhaps the movie *Rollercoaster*[2] inspired some of this persona, and I distinctly remember looking at each patron as the potential enemy—each one could be the mad bomber or the ride saboteur as I would follow people relentlessly through the park. It was a great place upon which to build suspicion.

The pleasure of walking down the lively streets of the theme park is a reuniting with the carefree hours of childhood as John Kasson suggests of Coney Island visitors (1978), or as Michel de Certeau proposes of the experience "to be other and to move toward the other" (1988, 110). It is no longer possible to go to a public place like a theme park and expect to be "safe." Nor can one assume that the park's "Main Street," if it has one, will be any more idyllic than its best bathroom. The theme park adjusts in proportion to the world outside its confines: more thugs, bring in more cops or add some metal detectors at the front gate. Even patron attitudes have begun to change in regard to the pleasure gardens. If you wanted "fear," or at least its simulation, you would ride the "white-knuckle rides," scream, and laugh with your family and friends later. Today, even the rides will not do. The only fear you might have is of getting mugged in the parking lot or getting punched out by a ride attendant. So at least in one way the average patron of the theme park is compensated for the exorbitant amount he or she spends on a given visit.

Why all the hype about fear and loathing, and why write about it at all? My two years experience in the theme park would not, after all, suggest that the American theme park is the exemplary site of moral panic and conspiratorial actions. Compared to other sites in the ecology of fear, this story would not even come close, yet there is a tale here that shows its own eccentricities and also resonates with the other antecedents in the ecology of which the essays in this volume seek to describe. The way I employ this conflation of conspiracy, fear, trembling, and suspicion is through a series of conversations with myself, my former fellow workers in the industry, and other voices and metaphors of theme parks extinct and extant. In most instances, I feel my role as a surveyor and representative of the topic to be more akin to the roller coaster mule than the boutonniere-wearing rider.[3] Theme parks make me shudder.

In so writing of these experiences here, I do not expect to propose a complete explanation of the space I have delimited. Rather, I hope to take a few glimpses of a place which still personally gives me the willies for a variety of reasons. The theme park, something I would like variably to evoke, is its own space of trembling. I suggest the following preliminary observations on the work as a way of establishing some priorities in the essay which resonate with my personal experiences with theme parks.[4]

Panic is the psychological mode of the contemporary world (Kroker, Kroker, and Cook 1989). In the theme park panic is often as minor as a spilled drink or as serious as a ride that will not work. It is the lifeblood of the circular geography surrounding its weary patrons and workers.

Fear is realized as both a waiting and a wanting (see Massumi 1993). In the theme park the boundaries of kitsch fear and real fear have completely disintegrated. Themed fear is the uniformed worker slugging the patron, or the costume character making sexual advances at a child.

Conspiracy has become the theoretical expression of panic and fear in the defined moment in which an individual feels a loss of agency and/or explanatory social power. In the theme park, for the worker it is the little voice that tells one "something is up" (De Becker 1997); for the patron it is an acknowledgment of a capricious park with less than ideal workers.

Consumption is the Rosetta stone that drives the theme park. Forget about television advertising, Coca Cola is sponsoring the newest ride in the park! After Coney Island, it is the only excuse that gives the theme park its tangibility.

Trembling is the psychophysical response to the apparent decline of human will and the rise of chaotic world conditions. It is also the response of the nonliving world as it increasingly casts doubt on the validity of human rationality and subjectivity. The theme park trembles because it is tired of people having fun (Baudrillard 1990a).

Surveillance is what makes the theme park plausible; it is the emotive source that draws people together and pushes them apart. Surveillance "is not simply applied, it is also *experienced* by users, subjects, and audiences" (Marx 1996, 193).

Berm

It is like something in a corner of your life which just won't finally die. (Baudrillard 1996, 4)

One of these days this place is going to explode! (David, a rides supervisor)

The earliest amusement parks had no established boundaries between the park and the outside world, no real attempt to embellish the *inside*. Coney Island's Steeplechase Park was the first large park to have enclosed itself from the rest of the world. It soon became the passion of amusement park owners to school their patrons: it was as if rude fellows became "hushed, moderate and careful" as they entered the park (Kasson 1978, 15). In the contemporary theme park the berm has become a mere formality, something unnoticed and not generally reflected upon by the patron or the worker. No longer would the theme park owner wish to or believe that he could school the patron. What the berm functions as instead is an unconscious wall of opposition between persons—patrons, workers, management, the media.

The theme park, perhaps more than any other mass-produced and service-operated work environment, produces a landscape of immanent hostility, suspicion, and ill will. Yet strangely it functions day to day like an almost perfect, slightly rusted machine. From my first day of employment I had been trained to think, This is the best place you could work at because you'll meet people and begin to think of your fellow employees as family members. I used to give the sixteen- to twenty-year-olds in the classes I teach a similar, though modified pitch. For the typical high school person working at the urban park, life was sometimes a mess, sometimes carefree. A lot of them came to the park to get laid; some had been forced by their parents to get a job; many needed the work to support themselves and their low-income families; some actually wanted to work at the park because the idea of becoming a lead or a manager at the age of seventeen or eighteen seemed pretty good; others worked in the park because they thought the job would be an easy way to make a summer living, and a great way to meet other persons their age. I couldn't help but wonder, looking across the mostly lifeless tundra of their stares, what motivated them to come here? After teaching a few classes and after working at the park for a month or so, the question I would have asked would have been, Why do you want to work here for *these* people?

Do you think they trust you, respect you? Do you trust them? On one of my first working days at the park I was doing some paperwork and filing in the Operations office. On this particular day, employee paychecks were also being distributed. A disgruntled custodian walked in and became quite irate when he discovered that his paycheck was not ready. "This is the second fucking week without a check! This is bullshit!" The timid office workers did not know how to react to the individual and they kept their silence while he continued his tirade. He then proceeded to rip a top off of a table and throw it across the room, followed shortly by a round of miscellaneous binders, folders, and papers. Things got a bit tense in the office until the vice president of Operations came barreling down the hall.

"Calm down! Do you think you can act like this to one of our guests?"

"No! But I want my paycheck!"

"Well just think of how our guests depend on you. The people in Operations are also your guests so you need to treat them just the same."

Security then arrived and took the custodian outside. Later as he was being "termed out" (short for "terminated") in the Operations office, he pulled down his pants and with exposed buttocks exclaimed, "Tell me when you're finished fucking me up the ass!"

Everyone's always looking for someone to blame. Walking through the park on one of my first days I was given a guided tour by one of my supervisors. Eventually we met up with a group of two workers and a rides supervisor. The workers had a number of grievances and my supervisor motioned for all of us to go to the Haunted House. This attraction, located behind the Roarin' Twenties ride Street Joust, was a rundown funhouse used only during the park's Halloween Festival. As you entered you noticed the sheer cheapness of the place. Skeleton and cobwebs behind a piano. Demon hanging from ceiling. Haunted knight in shining armor. Past all of the props was the "gossip area," where we all sat and talked. I mostly listened as I did not know anyone there, nor really anything about the park and its operation. Two grounds-control workers were complaining about the lack of support they had been getting from other departments, mainly Food Service.

"No one helps us with the trash situation in the park, yet we go and help Food Service and empty their trash cans!"

My supervisor sympathized and later added some comments about other departments. "Food Service never does shit for us. And then they blame us for every last thing that goes wrong in the park!" A ride manager there added some other comments about the lack of cooperation and effort given by some of his fellow ride managers and leads. Everyone was down on everyone, but at least there were convenient places in which one could hide and discuss such matters: "conspire," etymologically, "breathing together."

What's the best way to get a promotion? Threaten someone with something you know. In one case a rides supervisor had rigged a conveyer on a pontoon boat ride while in the presence of another rides worker, and in turn a patron was injured. The second ride attendant gave management an ultimatum and threatened that he would report the company negligence to all of the local newspapers and television stations if he was not appointed a rides supervisor. He was given the position, and whenever promotions for rides supervisor occurred, many of the candidates failing promotion told the story as a way of recalling management practice and lessening personal disappointment. The practice of the threat seemed to carry more influence and greater effectiveness than trying to show one's abilities or negotiate one's position with management.

It was generally known that the park's vice president had little respect for the park's rides and ground-control supervisors. Many knew the story of the vice president once referring to rides supervisors as "pencil-necked geeks." The supervisors, perhaps more knowledgeable of park operations and power management than their bosses, responded when park situations led to frustration and impossibility. In one season three-fourths of the rides supervisors, after having been down-sized from twenty-two to four, threatened Operations with quitting if staffing did not improve in their ride areas. The supervisors, of course, did not quit, knowing that staffing was only partially controlled by Operations, as Human Resources, the department responsible with all aspects of initial employee matters including hiring, was commonly unable to hire "quality" workers to run the rides.

Playing off an other. We had all done it throughout the season. When you couldn't regenerate the self, you looked to an other—one who could make things seem almost real and ordinary again in a place which never lived up to its expectations. No one really remembered the words of Coney Island's bearded woman Lady Olga: "If the truth was known, we're all freaks together" (Kyriazi 1976, 75), when we went about and fashioned season after season out of a world of inanimate machines and stucco landscapes. Employees walk into the canteen one day and see eight insects walking proudly under the red hue of heat lamps. For a moment they are uncertain as to whether they identify with the roaches or the thirty-minute-old chicken strips under the light. Another fellow is terminated and returns to the park late one night to jump his former manager in the bushes near the park's historic 1895 carousel. Other managers and workers played department off of department, spreading a certain suspicion of the other. One wondered which was more parodic, departmental relations or a four-part choir singing in unison at the park's Christmas festival?

"What's Going On?" a rhetorical question posed by management and the name of the follow-up class given to all employees after a month of company service. I had to lead a few of these seminars, and I was caught in the unhappy position of speaking for management. This was the employee's time to vent his or her frustrations with the company, although management was absent. It was told that management would later hear these comments and the problems would be addressed systematically. Actually, they wouldn't be addressed or even seen; and even if they were, would it make any difference? The most important comments for management were generally shared from worker to worker in locker room and canteen. Every morning when you "got in costume" in the locker room you wondered who wrote "Fuck This Place!" on the locker. Who was that guy? What did he dream of at night? Would he in fifty years remember some repressed memory he had of the time in which he sat in an office getting terminated for punching a patron in the face? And perhaps the patron too recalled the time that she sat for seventy-five minutes with twenty others aboard the stationary Skyneedle brought to a stop by a faulty drive motor. All she could remember then was a fear of falling from a place that offered a different view of the same thing she had seen every season as a season ticketholder.

She went nuts once in the park—something you did not want to show the guests. Falling down on a crowded day due perhaps to a temporary bout of psychosis and heat exhaustion, she got transferred to the Operations office and became more bitter. She had worked for a season and a half to become a rides supervisor, and one bad day in the sun had gotten her this. She left the company shortly after having laid down for some ten minutes in the Operations office during rush hour. Other workers had ignored her and continued to do their office work. Just walk around her.

In the theme park the worker was a member of a nameless race whose hard, underpaid work was justified by his or her willingness to partake in the pleasure of work. It was often said that work in the theme park was not work: "How can you call it work when it's fun? After all, you get to ride all the rides after work!" From the first day of the season at the parkwide kickoff, slides of happy workers and managers accompanied the musical lyrics of "Right here, right now. There is no other place that I would rather be!" Even then, at that defining moment of the season, three employees were terminated for the use of foul language.

Throughout the season, from the top to the bottom of the company hierarchy, the characteristic mode of employee interaction was strain. Distrust and misunderstanding were only understandable given the open segregation and class marking of employees with colored name tags based on employee rank. Promotions themselves were for some the metaphors of the petite conspiracies they suggested. If one applied for a promotion, management would often simply not fill the position if they felt strongly against the available candidates. "Corrective interviews," or CI's, were disciplinary meetings between workers accused of a violation and their supervisors. They were perhaps one of the most contested arenas of employee interaction as they were more often than not conducted in a rushed manner with little regard for the rights of the accused. The employee was expendable. You could always hire more, and best of all, to avoid sticky legal situations with many trouble employees, many who were, for example, accused of sexual assault, you could place them in Receiving to handle boxes and paperwork. In the theme park's most famous case, an older man who had sexually harassed female workers and patrons over the steam engine's microphone, and later actually stalked some employees, was offered a position in Receiving. Though he eventually left the company, it was later reported that some employees suspected him of listening in on Operations radio frequencies from outside the park. He was an amateur radio operator.

I remember very vividly the words of the secretary to the vice president of Operations on my final day of employment at the park: "This place keeps you coming back. It leaves something in your blood." What made you come back was the berm, and only the berm.

Blocks

"Doesn't surprise me!" This being the response of a worker taking a ride examination in the training center as a police officer discovers a bullet on a patron in the same room. This was a strange visual montage as the place was simultaneously being used for employee training and patron body searches. It must be odd for the trainee, I thought, only later realizing that it was odd that the circumstance seemed to be nothing out of the ordinary for the worker taking the test.

Signal 3. Ride down due to major injury. Generalized panic among the crowd. Emergency procedures are set into motion as radio silence is maintained to assure communication between Medical Services, Security, management, and lower-level supervisors. The crowd mobilizes to view the developing spectacle, while miscellaneous personnel attempt to control its emotions. An ambulance is brought inside the property and the situation eventually subsides. The ride is closed indefinitely. Next, cause and suspicion. All the crowds, patrons, and workers have their own reasons that they attribute to theme park situations of panic.

The block system, present on every roller coaster in the park, is not terribly complex nor completely efficient. When you first begin work as a ride operator in the theme park you usually gain "certification" on a flat ride, but sometimes you are fortunate enough to start on a roller coaster. Even then your first job is as a ride attendant, meaning your only responsibilities would be checking safety restraints, measuring the height of children, and depressing a ride dispatch button in tandem with the certified ride operator—the person who actually operates the ride—though you might later become a "driver," one with greater responsibilities for the actual functioning of the machine.

Safety is a primary form of social control and creator of suspicion in the park. Management depends on it: each worker was required to pass a series of departmental and state-regulated safety examinations. Throughout one's tenure as a ride operator, management would monitor the level of operational safety at each work location. As a trainer I would stress this to new employees: "Management will periodically visit your work location to make certain that all crew members are following both operational and safety procedures. We want to emphasize that management is not out to get anyone. If a problem exists at your work location, we will fix it and inform you on how to do your job safely and correctly so that a potential accident or a near miss doesn't become a serious accident. And remember, even if you are safe, conscientious, and are doing things correctly, if something looks unsafe, it is unsafe. For our guests, *perception is reality*." It was inside knowledge that safety was to be stressed heavily in training, but in reality budgeting and personnel problems often dictated otherwise. Fear works at appearance.

"Being safe" meant that you were willing to "be watched." The numerous policies implemented and altered seasonally did little in terms of curbing the small to moderate number of park accidents; instead, they reinforced the eye and increased the chasm of suspicion between management and employees. Management was aware of the problems related to safety and its enforcement, yet in their view the block system had less to do with the movement of machines or the operations of employees. For them, safety stretched to the public.

The Mantis was at the top of the lift, halted by the lift-stop button. Each coaster operates with antirollbacks to assure that the train does not fall backwards down the lift. This day these safety features failed. Though unloaded, the train slammed backwards into the station and into a second parked train. One of the supervisors there knocked an Operations manager out of the way averting disaster as the train flew off the track and crushed the first car of the second train. Later, employees and managers speculated, "Can you imagine if those trains had been loaded?"

The accident at the Mantis was uncommon, yet minor accidents were common at this and other rides in the park. As an employee, one learned to accept things as they happened. Working in a theme park is akin to a readiness to recognize the disaster when it happens and to bathe in it as it happens, but did a disaster signify a breakdown in management efforts, poor teamwork skills, mechanical corrosion, patron negligence? Management had many statistical analyses on the percentages of each of these factors. As they expressed their thoughts in managerial meetings, they suggested that with competent worker skills and appropriate park leadership, most accidents could be avoided, save those attributed to patron negligence.

Before the Spinner, a troika, was located in its current theme land, the Roarin' Twenties, it was enclosed in a circular concrete building. Entirely in the dark it spun around until one day a small child jumped out of the lap restraints only to be thrown violently against the wall to her death. Other patrons and employees had been ground inside drive motors and crushed by miscellaneous roller coasters, and the question always came up in training classes, "Has anyone ever died here?" My response was always a denial of such stories.

Essentially, such dramatic incidents were primarily historic and rare. Management, though, did worry about accidents which had occurred at other parks. In 1995 a woman was thrown to her death on a Kansas City roller coaster. The following morning at Park Com, the twice-daily meeting of all department managers, the assembled anticipated attendance drops and weary patrons afraid to ride the park's coasters. The solution was for the park to distance itself from the accident by having its employees tell the public that the Kansas City park was not a member of the CFC conglomerate, and in addition mentioning that this park *is safe*.

"Don't ever let the guest think that you're not in control." The Mantis seemed to be always "going down." One incident left the train stuck at the top of the lift. After being unable to send the train through, Operations management decided to unload patrons on the lift. Operations hated the prospect of unloading any ride outside of the station as the task increased the likelihood of further accidents and potential legal liability. The Mantis situation forced the individual unloading of some twenty patrons down the lift stairs: each person had to be flanked in front and in back by an Operations supervisor. It was an almost sublime sight: the blue-and-white uniformed supervisors and motley patrons moving slowly down the stairs. Some patrons actually enjoyed the walk as it proved to be more interesting than the dull ride—a one-looper with few jerks and turns. The ultimate ride might be that which defeats the anticipation of the mundane: get up the lift and stop just before you plunge; then walk down slowly and go away. A conceptual roller coaster is a machine that requires each patron to never make it over the first drop.

Before the unloading could take place, Operations had decided to temporarily stop operation of the Skyway, the overhead gondola ride. It was suggested by some managers that it was bad publicity to have other patrons witness the unloading of a ride which had malfunctioned. Ironically, as the patrons of the Skyway were turned away, they found it attractive to walk to the nearby Mantis to watch the rescue operation from the ground. Would it not have been more ideal for management to have left the Skyway running, thus allowing all patrons to see the effectiveness of the rescue mission?

During the evacuation, to my chagrin, I was not charged with helping patrons on the lift. Instead, I was ordered to collect a tray full of drinks to pass out to the rescued patrons. Of course, the Coke machine was pumping slowly that day, so by the time I had returned to the Mantis the patrons had already departed. Later that week a worker reads a series of comments from Guest Relations: "Mantis—broke! Tsunami—broke! When we went to the Ball Lightning it had shut down. Then, the two girls working there told us, Okay, folks, it's time to turn your butts around and go home!"

It is rare to visit any theme park and expect that all rides will be operating. At the theme park it was an interesting activity to glance at the "downtime" sheet in the Operations control center. What's shut down today? And for how long? Patrons expected things to not work; one once telling me, "I haven't been here a day when something isn't broken!"

Generally, even with the fears of "rides crashing and burning," most patrons became apathetic about rides. This cynicism seemed to spread throughout the park: unhappy family visits a few bad rides, then attends a low-budget show with bad actors, then eats greasy food for forty dollars, then argues, then purchases kitsch items, then exits the park on the tram, then goes home. Having participated in various research and exit polls in the park, I found it rare to locate more than a small percentage of patrons who thoroughly enjoyed the theme park, and even the ones who gave you the answers you wanted to hear couldn't be trusted; they had a funny look about them.

Following most accidents there was a period of investigation in which Operations and Fire and Safety conducted interviews with any personnel potentially involved in or having witnessed the accident. These investigations were extremely secretive and most details of the accidents became the subjects of theme park urban myth and rumor.[5] In many cases, legal teams from the corporate office would arrive days after the incident to collect vital documentation. One such team once set up an entire ensemble of cameras near a roller coaster to verify and document its operation. A number of employees were asked to ride the coaster in plain clothes. Some, when riding and nearing a camera shouted like normal patrons, "This ride sucks!" Operations saw little humor in the outbursts and the "guestliness" of the riders, so they ordered the workers to ride the coaster around again, silently! After four cycles and numerous camera changes, the work was complete. The workers were then told that the purpose of the videotaping was for the production of a television commercial.

The purpose of a block system on a pleasure railway was to prevent any train from occupying a block already occupied by a second or third train. A setup is the name given to the situation described by its prevention.

The View from Above

There was a rumor which passed through the theme park concerning the park's highest ride and vertical point of reference, the Skyneedle. Hovering some two hundred and seventy feet above the ground, the ride was popular with families and persons who liked to relax and take the park slowly rather than partake in the major thrill rides. Rotating on its 360-degree axis, the Skyneedle offers the perfect view of a park in microscopic symmetry below. A story suggested that in the park's early years before corporate ownership, its boss had installed spy cameras atop the Skyneedle. It was also said that this boss could watch and zoom in on park locations from a command post of monitors located in his comfortable house near the front gate. Overhead invisibility.

"Scanning is the key to being a rides operator"—this is what we taught our employees at the theme park. If you were working a flat ride or a coaster, you had to be prepared for the stray child who might run into the ride area unexpectedly. Hit the ride stop button. You have to learn how to watch, and report. As surveillance got increasingly contagious, Operations installed a "hush hotline," which offered a reward for any employee who turned in another worker for committing larceny.

In a typical day of surveillance the morning began with a check of all locations. All the ride operators complete their inspection checks; all show personnel check their staging areas; all games, concessions, and retail locations prepare for opening. Grounds-control persons survey the park for trash while rides supervisors, seventeen- to twenty-two-year-olds responsible for governing the rides in their areas, communicate by phone and foot to speed up the opening of the rides. At the front gate security officers patrol the roped-off front mall area which is to be opened at 10:00 a.m. Occasionally an officer might ask a "suspicious character" to open his or her bag or purse;[6] once a child was accosted by an officer for carrying a knife which actually turned out to be a camera.

As the day unfolds, disaster management begins to click: We're running out of ice here at the Coke stand, or, Pull one of your crew members from the Skyneedle to the Lobster so we can get the RPG (rides per guest) up a bit. As things move along, it was a common sight to see an Operations manager or assistant manager atop the Demon Drop, a vertical drop ride which is also the second highest location in the park. From this point of view many attendants had been fired for having been observed committing a VOCP (violation of company policy) below. Even I remember looking up from time to time to see if I was the object of a gaze.

At midday there are two things one has to know as an Operations supervisor: how to watch your employees and how to keep an eye on the patrons. The problem then becomes, who is the assailant, and who is the greater assailant? Even the former CEO of CFC knew how to watch. Like a good chairman, he actually "worked" in the parks, once adorning a grounds-control costume at one of the other CFC parks. It is then said that while working with the other GC employees, one of the workers said, unaware of the CEO's prominent status, "Yeah, this job is great! Except for all of this guest interaction shit we have to do!" As I read of so many times on employee disciplinary sheets, he was later "taken care of"—another number in a series of employees who had passed through the theme park's front gates.

Like the theory of the panopticon, one might intuit the theme park as a site of universal policing, though the policing there is not that orderly. The theme park hums and spews out from its gears, each person a distortion of the other. Catch ten "perps" a day among the crowd; throw them out after scaring them with a pot-bellied rent-a-cop. Fire three employees a day for VOCP; hire six more the next.

As the day passes on the crowd became more menacing. Operations did not mind the circular layout of the park. Anyone who knows the histories of theme park geography understands the significance of shape and flow. Their thoughts were more practical: search and destroy. Security could only do so much alone. Essentially, park security served as both guide and symbolic enforcer, mainly with kids and "punks." On weekends, local police officers were brought in (with guns) to add a more deliberate presence. Especially on weekends, fights would often break out in one of the Q-houses (the lines in which patrons wait to board rides) or elsewhere in the park.

The most elite security force was invisible: known as "Internal" they were

composed of persons who had already worked in Security or had secretly transferred from another department. Once I saw a former ride operator at a meeting
for rehire employees. He mentioned that he was now in security, to which I
replied, somewhat loudly in the company of other miscellaneous employees,
"Good luck with your new job." Later in the day he pulled me aside and said,
"Hey, don't tell anyone I'm in Security or I'll get fired. I'm in Internal!" As
an Internal you had no identity in the park. You instead became the ultimate
flâneur, strolling from shop to shop in "plain clothes" or working invisibly in
a department for any number of dark reasons.

"We can't catch all of them, maybe 10 percent!" Internal would complain.
The idea of the theme park suggests a design of easy and open access—patrons
came to move freely and quickly—yet the open design (two to four unblocked
and unmonitored openings in a given retail shop) presented inescapable problems. The Security identification card and a radio was the Internal stock and
trade. When they apprehended a wrongdoer, he or she was taken to Item Recovery, where merchandise was "recovered" and the perpetrator was processed. Usually, the person was a juvenile, so he or she was yelled at by a
security officer and then released. Older offenders might be prosecuted, but
usually a warning never to return to the park was given. If ever again seen on
park property, he or she could be arrested on sight.

Many employees knew about Internal's activities as Item Recovery was
located directly adjacent to the employee training facility. Most, though, were
not aware of Internal's nuanced covert actions. Once a team of two Internals,
known so often by their array of AC/DC shirts and baggy shorts, walked by a
group of ride supervisors wearing costumes normally worn by front-gate auditors. One of the supervisors laughed and said, "I guess someone is dipping
their hands in the front-gate tills!" It turns out that one of the major areas of
employee larceny was ticket-till theft.

The park was plagued with all sorts of "criminal" employee activities. Due
to staffing problems, management hired temporary workers to work in some
areas of the park. This in turn led to increased theft and difficulties between
patrons and temporary employees. More frustrating to some were the "underground" activities occurring among employees throughout the park. Once a
roller coaster operator devised a scheme to have his lead operate his ride while
he stole the other's park I.D. With this piece of plastic he was able to pick up
the lead's check and attempted to cash it. Upon being caught, the employee
offered a bargain: he said he would provide names and details on an underground drug ring in the park. It was known that such economies existed, and
Internal tried in vain to eradicate them. Some employees actually joked about
the number of ex-cons working on rides and at other park attractions. One
individual was once carted away by the police after it was learned that he had
eight arrest warrants. He had been operating the Log Flume. As he was being

taken away he told a park trainer that he was trying to clean up his life. The trainer looked at another worker and made a motion with his finger near his head indicating that the flume operator had the problem of "nobody home."

One of the goals of the theme park employee training program was to assess the effectiveness of the training classes given to employees. The management team had practiced the strategy of "auditing" to judge what in their own words was "actually going on in the park." Our training crew was assigned to conduct both uniform and plain clothes audits. Although we were no Internal, our plain-clothes audits struck fear in the hearts of the typical ride operator. Due to employee turnover and the constant juggling of staff between work locations, many of our training staff went unnoticed during plainclothes audits. This of course was the point from the management perspective: keep the worker on his or her toes through surveillance. Audits were designed to assign a numerical point scale to various categories, including cleanliness, stage appearance, safety, enforcement of rider policies, and operator duties such as height check-ing. The reality was that staffing problems in the park required that the training team often had to staff the very rides they had just audited. Other times, even when there were a number of "samples" taken throughout the park, the audits actually assessed nothing, as staffing at a given ride could change multiple times in a given day. Management realized this but felt that the numerical scores and audit forms gave them a bargaining tool with Human Resources for staffing requisitions, as well as with the vice president of Operations, who might approve additions or changes to rides and/or ride operational procedures. It was also argued that the audits gave both the auditor and the employee an appreciation of the "guest's-eye view." Most of all, the audits gave Operations a sense of security in an environment which was anything but secure.

Toward the end of my stay in the park, management had given me the dubi-ous honor of updating the park audits for the end of the century. They had asked me to scrap paper audits so that I might concentrate on video portrayals of employee activities. The operations Assistant Manager had on occasion used video to "trap" employees outside of various park locations. Basically, he would place a cup or piece of trash somewhere and then, out of view, he would catch the employee offender "in the act." [7] I was charged with a similar opera-tion, yet I was told to get a picture of the park during an entire working day. In plain clothes I would traverse the park, looking, watching, and waiting. Other members of the Operations department, including my supervisor, would par-ticipate with me in the video audits. Are they checking that kid for height? Are they grouping riders correctly? Do they make an effort to pick up trash inside the trains? Do they smile at patrons? In the past, the paper audits had provided one picture of employee performance, yet management offered that they had no way to "prove" who had underperformed or committed a VOCP. The video would allow such precise assessment, and it turned out that the camera I was operating had a twenty-four-to-one digital zoom—great for picking up names on name tags.

As the season passed from good staffing to bad at "burnout time" (typically the middle of July), the video documents became more central to Operations philosophy. Originally, the undercover assignment was designed to judge only the work of Operations personnel (ride operators, grounds-control workers, and front-gate persons), but as the summer heat beat on, many in the Operations team grew upset with a perceived lack of cooperation between them and other departments. "Get anyone you can," one of my supervisors informed me. It was a tactical mission against everyone in the park. Even patrons learned to be photogenic as once my inadvertent shooting captured three youths firing M-80s in the park. Security loved it. "It's just like *Cops!*" one officer remarked to me as he hauled the offenders off to Security base.

As the video campaign spread throughout the park, I was assigned to edit the footage for viewing. This second stage of the operation was crucial as it mattered how the footage would be shown and received. Once, I remember shooting a grounds-control worker running over a "trash trap" previously placed on the ground. After he realized what he had done, he went back and picked it up, but for the final edit I cut the video just after he ran over the trash. It was a scene too good to happily resolve. The Operations team took the tape, watched it, and passed it along to other supervisors and managers throughout the park. I had become infamous and some workers would actually approach me to ask about particular (famous) scenes I had shot. Eventually, no one felt safe and at times I took on a "killer's mentality," stalking the fellow employee and waiting for things to happen. Other departments began to feel the wrath of Operations and they quickly involved Human Resources as a third party.[8] In one case a high-ranking manager from Food Service was seen failing to pick up trash. This case prompted Human Resources to call me in to discuss my video work. They suggested that I discontinue the airing of the videos until a clear written policy had been established by their office. Later I was told by Operations to ignore HR's requests and was instructed to keep producing the videos.

It became management's obsession to watch, and the employees learned throughout a season how to watch to themselves avoid being watched. I recall rides and grounds-control supervisors trying to bargain their way out of difficult and often illegal situations. "You have to watch my back, and I'll help you out," a supervisor once stated to me in reference to a project to which I was assigned. The project was demanded by the increasing filthiness of the park and the scarcity of grounds workers. Often the workers would sit all day in the canteen along with their supervisors, and everybody knew it. I shot more video. Meanwhile, greater numbers of employees learned how to post lookouts at various locations to watch for approaching auditors and managers. Management had given most of the grounds-control workers radios in an effort to open better communication and create quicker response times during park crises. The radios were handy as the workers used them to hide from auditors and to "scope out babes or hunks" in their work areas.

Perhaps the patron really had the best eyes. The strange man or the strange woman was there to personally check his or her child's safety restraint. The stranger watched the Food Service employee to ascertain that he had gotten the right portions. The visitor would watch other patrons and often argue with workers suggesting that her child was unfairly denied riding privileges while another child was allowed them. Other patrons made sure that Guest Relations knew of their experiences at the end of the day. Racist and sexist in their representations, these patrons shared their own theories of culture and amusement management. It was very obvious that many of the theme park's ten to twenty thousand patrons resented and distrusted both their fellow consumers and the employee producers they came in contact with on a given day.

For all of her or his eccentricities, the theme park worker can only sympathize with the patron. Once, in preparation for a plainclothes audit I wore a Motorhead shirt with the word *bastards* emblazoned on the bottom. Unfortunately, I had also been assigned to set up equipment in a room during a Park Com meeting. The theme park president noticed the shirt and instructed an Operations manager to notify me of my error in judgment: "He wanted me to tell you to get rid of the shirt. We know that you're doing audits, but we wouldn't even let one of our guests wear something like that!"

Hypothetico-Deductive Pleasure

> All situations are inspired by an object, a fragment, a present obsession, never by an idea. (Baudrillard 1996, 1)

Surveillance is where suspicion begins, yet measurement marks the ultimate end of the theme park. Everyone gets measured: the child who is suspected of being under fifty-four inches tall, the worker who is rumored to not be doing his job, and the front-gate auditor whose survey numbers haven't convinced the corporate office. The child under fifty-four inches is no different than the suspicious character-as-worker; both are overcome by a power exponentially greater than they. On a late summer day the Operations manager stated that rides per guest had gone up and the corporate office was pleased. The manager then announced that this was not due to increased worker productivity, rather the Hedge Maze—not technically a ride but a place for children to run through—and the new employee posted there with a counter were the causes for celebration.

Perhaps the greatest cheers were heard across the Operations hallways during the employment of OPCO, a prestigious survey and training team. OPCO was composed of various educators, Ph.D. academics (mostly engineers), and business owners from the Oklahoma City area. The team was reportedly consulted across the country, even by prestigious governmental agencies. The group served two important Operations functions: they addressed park leadership problems through a three-day training seminar known as Big Gun, and they reassessed the effectiveness of the course through three annual audits of the entire park.

For many of the rides and grounds workers, Big Gun was the culmination of much hard work and demonstrated leadership out in the park. Class attendees were hand picked by Operations management, and this alone led to much suspicion of park "suck-ups." The class was even more controversial, in the words of those not invited to attend, because it seemed to produce only temporary and superficial effects in the park.

The seminar began with a combination of miscellaneous park testimonials from supervisors and managers who had learned the gentle art of management. "Are you the kind of person others enjoy being around? The answer to that question will be deceptively important to you and to your life," the seminar leader began at seven in the morning. "By the end of these three days you will be leaders, but it ain't gonna be easy!" Ed, the seminar leader and manager of OPCO, was a Ph.D. engineer who was virtually deified in the park. Managers and employees loved this guy, who spoke from the heart and offered age-old wisdom to complex problems. As the class rolled along, Ed and his four to five henchmen lectured on outdated management theory: at times, one instructor actually discussed phrenology and leadership qualities. The lectures were interspersed with a variety of group activities, all designed to stress leader-follower relationships. From blanket games to blindfolded loading and unloading on actual park rides, each participant was supposedly learning how to lead and give directions.

Near the end of Big Gun, each participant was assigned to be an auditor. Like the OPCO team would do in several months, Ed and the others divided the seminar members into four groups and instructed the teams to produce a system of "quantifiable measures" to use in auditing each ride in the park. The teams went out and practiced their audits. Their fellow park workers who had not been invited to Big Gun got even angrier as they were being audited by their colleagues.

When OPCO returned to perform their audits, morale had already gone down in the park. Only during the first week following Big Gun could anyone say that employee-employee and employee-patron relations had significantly improved. The OPCO members made their rounds and frequently frustrated more employees than not. One told me angrily, "Those dorks come to my ride and check to see if there's any dirt in the bottom of my ride! And then they have the audacity to talk about those 'little blue circles' which, if they knew

anything, they would know are 'limit switches'! I can't believe those guys."
The OPCO comments and measurements were analyzed and interpreted by the
Operations staff and the vice president in order to "improve things in the park."
Again, nothing happened. OPCO was the continuation of a tradition which
Operations had intensified in the 1995 season. Returning from a New York trip
and some Broadway shows, the park's management and upper-level training
staff announced that the focus of park operations from that point onward would
be *measurement* and making all employee activities measurable.

A Later Destiny

> This is where the rest of life begins. But the rest is what is given to
> you as something extra, and there is a charm and a particular freedom
> about letting just anything come along, with the grace . . . of a later
> destiny. (Baudrillard 1990b, 3)

The artificial energy of human actions perpetuated by their self-made pleasure
wheels and odd mills gives way each night as all but a few lights in the park
go dim. At seven in the morning, just past sunrise, one can truly appreciate
the latent energy of the machines and landscapes of the theme park. Before the
mechanics arrived one morning I happily snapped seven to ten pictures of the
roaring fountains, the unattended trains, trams, and boats, and the commercial
effigy-mounds of cartooned animal toys—the glory of the nonhuman, in its

simple pleasures. Realizing its own insular agency, the theme park spins around on its planned circular orbit to see itself no longer as the sign of human pleasure enacted but the arbiter of human fate.[9]

It is no mistake or coincidence that for at least one year a fortune cookie verse sat taped to the Operations base radio bearing the slogan, "Enjoy what you have; hope for what you lack." The only thing we have to gain as the end of the millennium theme park patrons and ride operators is the acceptance of the destiny assigned by the silence of unattended trams and empty troikas. As many in the theme park had discovered, the reliance on the old forms of existential retribution and explanation had produced tragedies greater than those previously experienced. The only way to confront themed fear was through the realization that the source of the fear was *you* and only you. We made the theme parks; we are their sources; we realize their fears in our fears; we get off the ride feeling like we have to ralph.

Each day the greater apocalypse of the former. Each worker a symptom of the longing to build heroic monuments and amazing machines: from the Elephant Hotel of Coney Island to the prolific contemporary inverted-loop roller coaster. The destiny of the individuals with whom I worked was an eternal frustration with the world around them. When you terminated someone you were supposed to have a stiff lip as you walked the worker around to be processed out of the park. This was the environment of fear, yet really it was one of anesthesia.

Perhaps the image of the *flâneur* is only slightly appropriate in assessing the mutual fates of the theme park's victims. "If only the cause were known, then all tensions would be gone," an Operations worker once remarked to me. If things *were known,* what really happened? Someone got fired, followed by a potential death threat, followed by more blame and suspicion between individuals and departments. Later, perhaps, staffing falls low in one section of the park causing a reaction by patrons as they flood Guest Relations. You have to avoid fear, what I call fear, or what Operations managers knew as operational inefficiency or company disorder. Drinking with these persons on many occasions, I could not help but reflect on their souls and mine forming and having been formed in the complex situations we had all experienced.

At times banal and nihilistic, working and riding out one's paranoia in the theme park was neither fulfilling nor unique. All the uniqueness and the delight lay in the possibility unrealized: to take a bath in the surf's wake with the rest— patron, worker, machine—and to completely fall victim to the sheer potential of the theme park's hidden nature. The end of the millennium theme park worker begins to resemble more the *flâneur* as performance artist, the great maker of myth and mystery, than the analyst, great communicator, or public relations specialist. The patron, likewise, is attracted to the possibility of having to do nothing but wade in the surf.

"It's nothing like the stuff they tell you about in theme park guide books! This place has a much darker side to it." I vividly recall these words coming from a worker one night before I had agreed to work as the rest-room custodian at a park concert. The concerts at the park typically got out of control, and this night was no exception. The bathrooms began to overflow with drunks who pissed in any utilitarian device they could find. Defecating smells raised the consciousness of the place. The crowd began to take over and soon all purpose was lost. This came before the mob trampled its way out of the park.

A second memory here is only a prelude to a million more. This one was the case of "vomit boy," a name seemingly saying it all. One of the workers, the son of an influential electrician in the park, had some mental difficulties and was frequently reprimanded for making sexual remarks to many of the female workers. On the occasion of the monthly park party, when employees got to ride two to three rides and enjoy free food after the park had closed, a group of administrators from various departments was about to board the Perpetuator roller coaster. One entry-level worker saw the developing situation and quickly asked "vomit boy" to get in the front seat with the other administrators. True enough to form, a row of four bosses was covered with vomit as the coaster returned to the station. Their evening had been spoiled, but every knowledgeable theme park worker knows that vomit is a way of life in the theme park.

There is "no carnival without loss. No Luna Park without a slaughterhouse" (Hollier 1992, xxiii), and reading these words I cannot help but think of what

is ultimately left of the theme park, on what has been left out, on what remains, on what has come to pass there, and what is yet to come. The remnants of the theme park, the accidental moments and the unforeseen of what I would describe as a "Sacrificial Economy of a Theme Park," [10] have been purposefully or unintentionally deleted from the record of theme parks, academic and actual. Perhaps what is needed is one final, sacrificial commentary on this site of popular amusement—a realization of the theme park as a temporary autonomous zone (Bey 1991), a place of happening which forgets its own origins, its very purposes from the beginning. And like the great amusement parks of Coney Island, all of these memories ultimately go up in flames, and with those cinders stays the loathing, the fear, suspicion, and dread that reverberated for two seasons in the theme park, and, yet, "I would like to linger with the first glance. I would like to regain or rediscover my first glance" (Hessell 1994, 421) of the theme park in which I worked.

Notes

Thanks to Marian Rubchak of the Department of History at Valparaiso University for comments on this paper, as well as all the participants of the May 1997 Late Editions meetings at Rice University. All photographs are my own.

1. The "theme park" represents both the specific park discussed in this study as well as the "American theme park"—the extinct and extant histories, events, environments, persons, machines, and feelings associated with the author's experiences with theme parks.

2. *Rollercoaster* (1977), directed by James Goldstone.

3. The earliest roller coasters used mules in the back of the trains to bring the coaster back to the station after the patrons had departed (Mangels 1952, 86).

4. In responding to a few independent readers of this piece, I would offer that this writing does not attempt to follow the analytic lead of the previous literature on popular amusements and theme parks. Though governed by experiences from the "real world," its form follows the mode of an extended conversation, and its ethnographic component is based more on the mood I attempt to describe and evoke than on the embellishment of anthropological field sensibilities.

5. As Avital Ronell offers, "rumors are in the air; they fly" (1994, 95).

6. In 1994 a local television station reported on the apparently racist and sexist policy of front-gate scanning and searching of persons of color. Operations dismissed the claims of racism and sexism.

7. Picking up trash continues to be one of the main obsessions of theme park culture.

8. In fact, Human Resources served as the mediators and investigators of any employee situation which resulted in employee dismissal.

9. "But the comet is no longer looked upon as the sign, but the agent of destruction" (Mackay 1995, 258).

10. The idea of the park is to create theme lands based on underrepresented or excluded themes, objects, persons, and events in United States history. Such representa-

tions might include a ride on abortion politics, an end-of-the-century Los Angeles theme area, an Exxon Valdez ride, a serial-killer play area for children, a memorial to theme park victims, and a theme land dedicated to the memory of extinct theme parks, such as those of the Coney Island era. Ultimately, this sacrificial theme park would reflect excess in its midst.

References

Baudrillard, Jean. 1996. *Cool Memories II.* Durham, N.C.: Duke University Press.
————. 1990a. *Fatal Strategies.* New York: Semiotext(e).
————. 1990b. *Cool Memories.* London: Verso.
Bey. Hakim. 1991. *T.A.Z.: The Temporary Autonomous Zone, Ontological Anarchy, Poetic Terrorism.* Brooklyn, N.Y.: Autonomedia.
De Becker, Gavin. 1997. *The Gift of Fear: Survival Signs That Protect Us from Danger.* Boston: Little, Brown.
De Certeau, Michel. 1988. *The Practice of Everyday Life.* Berkeley: University of California Press.
Hessell, Franz. 1994. "The Suspicious Character." In *The Weimar Republic Sourcebook.* Ed. Anton Kaes, Martin Jay, and Edward Dimendberg. Berkeley: University of California Press.
Hollier, Denis. 1992. *Against Architecture: The Writings of Georges Bataille.* Cambridge, Mass.: MIT Press.
Kasson, John F. 1978. *Amusing the Million: Coney Island at the Turn of the Century.* New York: Hill and Wang.
Kroker, Arthur, Marilouise Kroker, and David Cook, eds. 1989. *Panic Encyclopedia: The Definitive Guide to the Postmodern Scene.* New York: St. Martin's Press.
Kyriazi, Gary. 1976. *The Great American Amusement Park: A Pictorial History.* Secaucus, N.J.: Citadel.
Mackay, Charles. 1995. *Extraordinary Popular Delusions and the Madness of Crowds.* Hertfordshire: Wordsworth.
Mangels, William F. 1952. *The Outdoor Amusement Industry: From Earliest Times to the Present.* New York: Vantage.
Marx, Gary T. 1996. "Electric Eye in the Sky: Some Reflections on the New Surveillance and Popular Culture." In *Computers, Surveillance, and Privacy.* Ed. David Lyon and Elia Zureik. Minneapolis: University of Minnesota Press.
Massumi, Brian. 1993. "Everywhere You Want to Be: Introduction to Fear." In *The Politics of Everyday Fear.* Ed. Brian Massumi. Minneapolis: University of Minnesota Press.
Ronell, Avital. 1994. *Finitude's Score: Essays for the End of the Millennium.* Lincoln: University of Nebraska Press.

Contributors

Andrea Aureli is a graduate student in anthropology at Rice University. He is currently doing his fieldwork on Italian social movements of the 1970s and their legacy.

Tatiana Bajuk is a graduate student in anthropology at Rice University, completing her dissertation on the period of post-Yugoslavian transition in Slovenia and the role of intellectual culture and professional economists.

Michael F. Brown teaches anthropology at Williams College. His books include *War of Shadows: The Struggle for Utopia in the Peruvian Amazon,* coauthored with Eduardo Fernández, and *The Channeling Zone: American Spirituality in an Anxious Age.*

James D. Faubion teaches anthropology at Rice University. He has written *Modern Greek Lessons* and is now at work on a critical ethnography of the events at Waco, Texas, and their aftermath.

Kim Fortun is a cultural anthropologist who teaches at Rensselaer Polytechnic Institute.

Michael Fortun is a historian of science and executive director of the Institute for Science and Interdisciplinary Studies (ISIS) at Hampshire College.

Bruce Grant teaches anthropology at Swarthmore College. His study of the proletarianization of a Siberian indigenous people, *In the Soviet House of Culture: A Century of Perestroikas,* received the 1996 Prize for First Book from the American Ethnological Society. He recently completed editing Lev Shternberg's *The Social Organization of the Gilyak* for the Presses of the American Museum of Natural History and the University of Washington.

Douglas R. Holmes teaches anthropology in Houston, Texas.

Jamer Hunt teaches on design and cultural theory at the University of the Arts in Philadelphia.

John Kadvany is a writer and consultant at Applied Decision Analysis, Inc., in Menlo Park, California. He has collaborated with János Radványi on various essays and articles, and they are now working on a book titled *Imre Lakatos and the Guises of Reason.*

Myanna Lahsen is a post-doctoral fellow at The National Center for Atmospheric Research (NCAR) in Boulder, Colorado. She is currently writing a book on the sociocultural and political dimensions of the production, mobilization, and contestation of the science underpinning environmental concern about human-induced climate change.

Scott A. Lukas completed his dissertation, *Signal 3: Ethnographic Experiences in the American Theme Park Industry,* in the Department of Anthropology at Rice University. It will be published as his first book. He has taught sociology and anthropology at Valparaiso University, in Indiana, since 1996.

George E. Marcus is professor and chair of the Department of Anthropology at Rice, and the founding editor of this series.

Luiz E. Soares is professor of anthropology and political theory at the Graduate Institute for Social Research of Rio de Janeiro (IUPERJ), and at the State University of Rio de Janeiro (UERJ). His most recent books are *O Experimento de Avelar,* a novel; *A Invenção do Sujeito Universal; Violencia e Politica no Rio de Janeiro;* and he is editor of *Cultural Pluralism, Identity, and Globalization.*

Kathleen Stewart teaches at the University of Texas, Austin. Her first book is *A Space on the Side of the Road: Cultural Poetics in an "Other" America.* She is currently working on a second book, called "The Private Life of Public Culture," and a third project on Las Vegas and the culture of risk and abjection in the United States.

Robin Wagner-Pacifici teaches in the Department of Sociology and Anthropology at Swarthmore College. She has published *The Moro Morality Play: Terrorism as Social Drama,* and *Discourse and Destruction: The City of Philadelphia versus Move.*

abuse: childhood, 137–38, 141–42; ritual cult, 142–43
accountability, 186. *See also* disclosure
Adorno, Theodor, 47, 54
Agency for International Development, U.S. (AID), 179, 182
Agent Orange, 372
Aguilera, Davy, 384, 400n16
Alcohol, Tobacco, and Firearms, U.S. Bureau of (ATF), 377–78, 382, 384–87, 389, 396
aleatory effect, 345
Alekseev, Iurii, 261
Ali, Quaddus, 321–22
alienation, politicocybernetic, 392, 396
aluminum, 248–49
American Coaster Enthusiasts (ACE), 297
American Institute of Certified Public Accountants, 188
American Justice Federation, video on Branch Davidians, 384–87
American Physical Society, 66
Americans, collaboration with Mafia to run Sicily, 281, 312
Andreotti, Giulio: and collaborators, 301–2; corruption trial of, 8, 293, 303–5, 311–14; and the Gladio conspiracy, 205; interview with Montanelli, 309–12, 315–16; the Judas kiss, 8, 218, 303–5; meeting with Pope John Paul II, 306; political power of, 307
antifascism, 214–15, 271, 322, 340n14
Anti-Nazi League (ANL), 322, 340n13
apocalyptic thought, and conspiratorial discourse, 153n1
Archimedes, 59

Arhar, France, 276
Aristotle, 44, 100–102, 380
Armageddon, 377
Arruda Camara, Diogenes de, 235
Artese, Erminia, 306
Asahara, Shoko, 395
Aspect, Alain, 78
Auerbach, Erich, 380

B-1 bomber, 164, 166
Banham, Reynard, 273
Barings Bank failure, 170, 177
Barnett, Tim, 117
baryga, 258
Bataille, Georges, 267
Baudo, Pipo, 307
Baudrillard, Jean, 395
Baumann, Gerd, 339n3
Beackon, Derek, 321, 331
Benjamin, Walter, 14, 218
Bennett, Charles, 34, 66, 75, 91
Bentsen, Lloyd, 385
Berezovskii, Boris, 242
Berlusconi, Silvio, 307, 313
Bernstein, Herbert: mock trial of, 71–72, 74, 79–81, 83–86, 88–90, 93–97, 99–106; and quantum theory, 78–79; and teleportation, 34, 65, 90–93; theoretical physicist, 27, 32, 71; and the willies, 33, 70
Bertani, Philip, 72
Bertoli, Gian Franco, 203
Bhopal disaster, 294–95, 368
Black Prince, the. *See* Borghese, Julio Valerio
blat, 258

Blunt, Anthony, 58
Bobbio, Norberto, 312
Boehmer-Christiansen, Sonja, 124
Boeing Corporation, 283
Boesky, Ivan, 191n7
Bohm, David, 55, 78
Bohr, Niels, 77, 81–82
Bolin, Bert, 119
Bologna bombing, 210
Boniface VIII, Pope, 314
Borden, James, 145
Borghese, Julio Valerio, 201–2, 208, 212, 215, 221n28
Borneman, John, 9n2, 10n
Borsellino, Paolo, 303
Bourdieu, Pierre, 9–10n4, 391, 393, 394
Bowden, Charles, 149
Bowman, James, 9n1
Boyer, Paul, 400n10
Boyle, James, 189
Bracy Williams and Company, 116
Branch Davidian compound: ATF raid on, 382–87; at New Mount Carmel, 296, 389; prelude to violence at, 375–78
Branch Davidian Seventh-Day Adventist Church, 296, 375
Braun, Bennett, 148
Brazil: Communist Party, 229, 235; conspiracy in, 194–95, 227–28; stories on the edge of conspiracy, 228–39; Trotskyite Communist Party, 235
Breault, Marc, 384
Brecht, Bertolt, 53
Brecht-Lukács debate, 53
Breeden, Richard, 176
Brezhnev, Leonid, 241
Britain: conspiracy in, 326–27, 330, 332–33, 337–38; environment for national socialism, 320–22; housing in, 321, 329, 334–37; immigration to, 323–27, 329–30, 339n9; interview with Richard Edmonds, 322–36; and multiculturalism, 327–28, 337–38; national socialism in, 293–94, 319–22, 326, 330–32, 338n1; unemployment, 325–26, 337. See also London, East End
British Nationality Act, 323–24
British National Party (BNP), 8, 319–22, 326, 330–32, 338n1
Briusov, Valerii, 259
Brizola, Leonel, 228, 237–38

Brooke, Warren, 129
Brooks, Jeffrey, 242
Brusca, Giovanni, 308, 314
Buford, Bill, 341n22
Burgess, Guy, 58–59
Burke, Don, 144
Bush, George, 351
Bush administration, and the Marshall Institute, 115, 117
Byng, John, 335–36

Cage, John, 345
Calabresi, Luigi, 203
Calabresi affair, 220n17
Cambridge University, 58
Canciani, Mario, 304–5
Canetti, Elias, 225–26
capitalism: and democracy, 159, 173; Russian, 195, 241–44, 257–58; Slovenian, 289
capitalist conspirators, 157, 243
Carabinieri, 202–3, 207
Carnap, Rudolph, 50
Carter, Elliot, 146
Casey, William, 190–191n3
Cavallo, Luigi, 204, 220n20
Central Intelligence Agency (CIA): and the Carabinieri, 207; collaboration with Bertoli, 203; and Italian intelligence, 221n31; and Koresh, 393; payment of Arruda, 235; and right-wing conspiracy in Italy, 198, 208
Certeau, Michel de, 407
CFC Entertainment Corporation, 406, 415, 418
channeling, 36, 81–82, 138, 145–53
Chechnya, 274
Chekhov, Vadim Vladimirovich, 252
childhood abuse, 137–38, 141–42
chlorofluorocarbons (CFCs), 111, 113
Christian Democratic Party (Italy): alliance with Communist Party, 209–10; and Andreotti, 303; appearance of, 309; central position in Italian politics, 204, 206–7, 217–18; depoliticization of political struggle, 215; and the Mafia, 272, 281, 304, 312
Christian Democratic Party, Slovenian (SKD), 286, 287
Churchill, Winston, 87, 324
Civilna Iniciativa, 269–70, 286
Civilna Inicijativa, 269–70
Clark, Kennedi, 344
climate change research, 34–35, 111–34

Clinton, Bill, 134n6, 385
Clinton administration, 133, 275
Cohen, Benjamin, 160
Colajanni, Napoleone, 307
Cole, Ron, 394
Commonwealth Immigration Act, 324
Communist Party: Brazilian, 229, 235; Italian, 206, 209, 216, 218; Slovenian, 270; Yugoslavian, 270
Conference of the Parties, 112, 118
conspiracy: and the aleatory effect, 345; Americans, Mafia, and Christian Democrats in Italy, 272, 281; ancient Greek, 380–82; attraction to theory, 21, 24–25, 27–29; in Brazil, 194–95, 227–28; in Britain, 326–27, 330, 332–33, 337–38; capitalist, 157, 243; dystopian, 36, 142–43, 153; and entanglement, 32; in general, 106–7, 225; Gladio, 205, 221n31; in Italy (*see* Italy); Jewish, 162; and language, 107, 126–27, 195; and millennialism, 378–79, 388–90, 392; and multiple personality disorder, 142–43, 153; Rosa dei venti, 203, 205; in Russia, 243–44, 266–67; and science, 67, 70–71, 78–79, 108n5; in Slovenia, 270–71, 280–83, 287–89; and social science, 225–26; and theme parks, 407–8; in Yugoslavia, 277–78. *See also* information; semiotics of suspicion
conspiracy theory: and alienation, 392, 396; anti-Communist, 197–98; as a tactic, 133–34; and channeling, 147–48; and climate change research, 111–14, 117–18, 125–33; coherence and capabilities of conspirators, 129–30; and constructive political discussion, 132–34; and evidence, 25–26; and Gulf War Illness, 295; and the Internet, 18; LaRouchies, 130; and markets, 37, 157–59; and military funding of science, 97–99; the New Deal, 160–61; overview, 13–19; and personal relationships, 119; and right-wing political groups, 128–34 (*see also* Italy, right-wing conspiracies); of science purists, 34; surrounding Stanley Sporkin, 190–191n3; trust and convergence of views, 117–18, 119; in the U.S., 1–2, 358–63, 370, 385–87, 393–94. *See also* paranoia; semiotics of suspicion
conspiratorial: discourse, and apocalyptic thought, 153n1; politics, of Italy, 193, 197–219, 222n50, 222n53

contagion, theory of, 25–26
contrarians: anti-environmental activities of, 113, 125; and right-wing political groups, 128–34
Coppi, Franco, 313
Corcoran, Thomas, 160
Cornford, John, 58
corporate responsibility, 191n4
Cosa Nostra. *See* Mafia, in Sicily
Council of Securities Regulators for the Americas (COSRA), 180–82
coversion, 44, 50, 55, 63
Craxi, Bettino, 272, 307
Crick, Francis, 58
critical rationalism, 39–40, 44
Cronenberg, David, 73
cryptography, 70, 86–88

Dalí, Salvador, 6, 7, 21–23, 29n3, 29n6
DDT, 113
deconstruction, 57
DeLillo, Don, 4–5, 8, 158–59, 394
De Lorenzo, Giovanni, 198, 202–3, 207–8, 216, 220n16
democracy: and capitalism, 159, 173; in Italy, 205–10, 215–18, 221n26; in Russia, 252–53
DEMOS coalition, in Slovenia, 278
Department of Defense, U.S.: and chemical sensors, 27; and Gulf War Illness, 295, 344, 361–62, 370; and scientific research, 33, 65, 72, 74, 80
Department of Energy, U.S., 133, 346
Department of Transportation, U.S., 125
deregulation, 172–73
Descartes, René, 47, 59
Desert Storm, Operation: in general, 343–46; "Peck's" experience in, 350–56
Desvernine, Raoul, 160–61
dialectical reasoning, 55
Di Maggio, Baldassare, 317n6
disclosure: in financial markets, 36–38, 159, 161–68, 170, 179, 184–87; of scientific knowledge, 82
discourse: conspiratorial and apocalyptic thought, 153n1; economic, and conspiracy in Slovenia, 196, 270–71, 277–78, 282–83; illicit, 319
dissociation, 143–44, 150
Djilas, Milovan, 270, 290n2
Dobb, Maurice, 58

Douglas, Mary, 389
Drnovšek, Janez, 278–79, 282–84, 289, 290n5
Durkheim, Emile, 189–90, 390–92
dystopian conspiracy, 36, 142–43, 153

Ebola virus, 81, 89
Eco, Umberto, 212
economics, history of, 55–57
Edmonds, Richard, 8, 294, 319, 321–38, 339n5, 341n19
Einstein, Albert, 70, 76–78
Einstein-Podolsky-Rosen particles (EPR), 76, 91, 92
Eisenstein, Sergei, 241
Elias, Norbert, 226
Ellsaesser, Hugh, 125–26, 130–32
Energy and Environment, U.S. House of Representatives Subcommittee on, 133
Energy Group, 138–39, 143–45, 152
Engels, Friedrich, 50, 55
entanglement, 32–34, 70, 76, 90–92, 108n4
environmental issues: conservative backlash against, 114–15, 125, 129. See also climate change research
Environmental Protection Agency, 125
environmental reporting requirements, 167
Erickson, Kai, 388
ethics of experimentation, 33, 100–103. See also science
Eulau, Heinz, 157
Euler's theorem, 41
Evans-Pritchard, E. E., 389
exclusionary welfarism, 319, 336–37
experimental ethics, 33. See also science

Falcone, Giovanni, 303
falsification, 40, 45–46
fascism: in Britain, 322 (see also British National Party); in Italy, 207, 210–14
Faucett, Ken, 394
Favret-Saada, Jeanne, 388
Fawn, Don, 393
fear, in theme parks, 407–8
Federal Aviation Administration, 148
Federal Bureau of Investigation (FBI), 386–87, 396–97
Fehér, Ferenc, 52
Fermi, Enrico, 83
Feyerabend, Paul, 31, 39, 43, 44–47, 50–53, 285

Filho, Luiz Gylvan Meira, 119
financial markets. See markets
Food and Drug Administration (FDA), 343, 346, 362
Foreign Corrupt Practices Act, 167
Forlani, Arnaldo, 203
Forman, Paul, 97–98, 108n5
Foucault, Michel, 226, 393, 394
four color theorem, 42
Frankfurter, Felix, 160–61
Frankfurt School, 226
Freisen, James, 149
Freud, Sigmund, 22, 28, 29n2, 43, 140, 152
Friedman, William, 87
Friesen, Robert, 142
Fronte Nazionale, 201

Galbraith, John Kenneth, 394
Galileo, 59
Gambetta, Diego, 304
game theory, 3
Garrincha, 236
Gautier, Théophile, 107
Geertz, Clifford, 228
Gelli, Licio, 205, 216
General Accounting Office, U.S., 343, 345
General Motors (GM), 169, 179
genetic counseling, for Gulf War vets, 363–67, 372
Genex, 276, 282, 285
George, Laurel, 108n7
German Enigma code, 87–88
Germany, absence of securities markets, 168
Giddens, Anthony, 139, 153
Ginzburg, Carlo, 220n17
Giotto di Bondone, 305
Gladio conspiracy, 205, 221n31
Global Climate Coalition (GCC), 118, 120, 121, 131–33
Global Positioning System (GPS), 100–101
global warming, 35, 111, 116, 129, 133
Gödel, Kurt, 42
Goethe, Johann Wolfgang von, 53
Goldenhar's syndrome, 364
Gollnisch, Bruno, 294, 333
Gorbachev, Mikhail, 241, 247
Gore, Al, 134n6
grabification (prikhvatizatsiia), in Russia, 242
Gramsci, Antonio, 339n5
Greene, Graham, 53

greenhouse gases, 111–12, 113, 118, 121, 129–30, 133
Greenpeace, 124–25, 128, 131–32
Gribbin, John, 78
Gronchi, Giovanni, 207
Gruber, David, 71
Guerri, Giordano Bruno, 300
Gulf War Illness, 294–95, 346, 356–57, 361, 369, 373
Gulf War. *See* Desert Storm, Operation
Gulf War Veterans Resource Page, 360

Haaken, Janice, 151–52
Habermas, Jürgen, 46, 55, 395
Hacking, Ian, 39, 46, 48, 98–99, 141
Hammer, Armand, 165
Hampshire College, 71
Hansen, Jim, 111
Hanson, Paul, 343, 345
Harsanyi, John, 58
Hasselman, K. L., 123
hauntology, 70, 72, 75
Healy, Robert, 187–88
Heath, Edward, 341n21
Hegel, Georg Wilhelm Friedrich, 41, 45–49, 52–55, 60–61
Hegelianism: in Lakatos, 31, 39–44, 49, 53, 57–58, 60; in Lukács, 49, 53; in Marx, 59–61; in Popper, 40; in Soros, 63
Hegelian Marxism: of Lakatos, 53, 54, 61; of Lukács, 54, 60–61
Heidegger, Martin, 285–86
Heine, Heinrich, 107
Heller, Agnes, 52
Heraclitus, 55
Hermes, 380–81, 396
Higgins, Stephen, 385
historicism: of Lakatos, 39–44, 46, 49; of Marx, 39; and Popper, 45–46
historiography of mathematics/science, of Lakatos, 40–43, 47–48
history: of economics, 55–57; and language for Lakatos, 45; of mathematics, 39–42, 48; of science, 40–42, 44–52
Hobbes, Thomas, 226
Hofstadter, Richard: the cold war and U.S. conspiratorial paranoia, 227; critique of extreme paranoia in politics, 1, 3, 7; non-recognition of reasonable paranoia, 2; over-assumption of coherence by conspiracy theorists, 129; the paranoid style, 132;

perceptions of marginalization, 131; the renegade, 277; tendencies of paranoid scholarship, 114, 123, 280
Holmes, Doug, 271
Holmes, Oliver Wendell, 261
Hooke, Robert, 47–48
Hooker Chemical, 164–66, 185
Houghton, John, 119
housing, in Britain, 321, 329, 334–37
Howell, Vernon. *See* Koresh, David
Hribar, Spomenka, 285, 291n10
Hribar, Tine, 285–86
Hughes, Anna, 375
Hume, David, 226
Hungarian uprising of 1956, 61–63
Hunt, Gary, 394
Hussein, Saddam, 295

immigration, to Britain, 323–27, 329–30, 339n9
indeterminacy, 77–79
India, government of, 295
information: as a public good, 36–37, 170; and the SEC, 36, 159, 161, 166–70, 187, 188–90. *See also* Securities and Exchange Commission, U.S. (SEC), disclosure; transparency of markets
Information Council for the Environment (ICE), 116, 134n5
inner self-helper (ISH), 149
insider trading, 175–76
Institute for Science and Interdisciplinary Studies (ISIS), 32–33, 65, 70, 102, 105
Institute for Securities Market Development, 181–82
intellectuals, as parasites, 285–86
International Business Machines (IBM), 66, 72, 75, 173
International Panel on Climate Change (IPCC) procedures, 3, 112–13, 115–16, 123, 134n3
International Panel on Climate Change (IPCC) report: ambiguity, 124; conclusions, 111–12; conspiracy against, 131–32; criticized, 112–14, 116–18, 125–28; defended, 119–21, 128; impact of fossil-fuel interests on, 116, 124–25; revisions analyzed, 121–23
Internet, and conspiracy theory, 18
Irish Republican Army (IRA), 321
Isle of Dogs, 320–21, 329, 333–34. *See also* London, East End
Italian Communist Party, 206, 209, 216, 218

Italian Social Movement (MSI), 203, 218
Italy: antifascism, 214–15; conspiracy in, 193, 199, 300; corruption trials, 303, 305, 307–8; democracy in, 205–10, 215–18, 221n26; fascism, 207, 210–14; fascism and right-wing conspiracies, 215–18; honesty of, 302; left-wing conspiracies, 198–99, 220–21n24; Mafia in, 218–19, 272, 281, 300–316; as Purgatory, 293, 301; right-wing conspiracies, 197–98, 201–6, 208, 272

Jameson, Fredric, 4
Janša, Janez, 286, 291n12
Jaruzelski, Wojciech, 230
Jastrow, Robert, 117
John Paul II, Pope, 306

Kádár, János, 62
Kadijević, Veljko Dušan, 279
Kadvany, John, 31
Kardelj, Edvard, 274, 290n3
Kasson, John, 407
Kaufmann, Walter, 53
Kavčič, Stane, 274
Kelly, Michael, 9n1
Kennedy, Joseph, 164
Khakopian, Rafael Pavlovich, 244–54, 266
Khrushchev, Nikita, 241
Kierkegaard, Søren, 60
kiss, of Andreotti and Riina, 8, 218, 303–5
Kissinger, Henry, 79
Knight, J. Z., 147–48, 150
Konrád, Georg, 61
Kontakt, 247–49
Koolhaas, Rem, 6, 21, 23–24, 27
Koresh, David: and the Book of Revelation, 9, 379, 396–99; and the Branch Davidians, 375–78; character and intentions, 382–84, 399n3, 400n5; and the CIA, 393
Kostabi, Mark, 29n3
Kučan, Milan, 270, 283–84, 290n7
Kuhn, Thomas, 31, 39, 43–45, 50, 52, 285
Kuwait, 124, 174

labor theory of value, 55, 57
Lacan, Jacques, 28, 29n6
Lady Olga, 411
Lakatos, Imre, 5, 7, 31, 39–63
Lambropoulos, Vassilis, 380
Landis, James, 160–62, 188, 190
language: and conspiracy, 107, 126–27, 195;

and history for Lakatos, 45; and problems of translation, 262. *See also* discourse, economic
LaRouche, Lyndon, 130, 133–34
Lasch, Christopher, 36
Latour, Bruno, 25–26
leadership: in the Brazilian Communist Party, 229; in Lakatos, 54; in theme parks, 423
Lederberg, Joshua, 74
Lega, 306–7
Lenin, Vladimir Ilich, 49, 229, 230, 241
Leninism, 54
Leone, Giovanni, 300
Lessing, Gotthold Ephraim, 53
Liberal Democratic Party of Slovenia (LDS), 286, 290
Liberty League, 160
Life, article on aftereffects of Desert Storm, 343–44, 358, 364–65
Lima, Salvatore, 303–5
Lipsitz, Imre. *See* Lakatos, Imre
litigation reform, 186
Ljubljanska Banka, 276, 279, 288, 289
logical positivism, 45, 59
Lohse, Theodor, 219n1
London, East End, 8, 293–94, 319–21, 329, 339n3, 339–340n11. *See also* Isle of Dogs
London School of Economics, 43, 58
Lotta Continua, 220n17
Love Canal, 164
Luciano, Lucky, 312
Luhmann, Niklas, 395
Lukács, Georg, 31, 41, 43, 47–49, 52–55, 60–63
Lukas, Scott, 9, 27
Lyotard, Jean Francois, 190

MacLean, Donald, 58–59
Mafia: American, 281, 312; in general, 284; in Italy, 218–19, 272, 281, 300–316; in Russia, 195, 243, 250–51, 254, 266; in Sicily, 303, 316, 317n8; in Slovenia, 271 *(see also Udbomafija);* in Yugoslavia, 275, 279
Major, John, 327
Malek, Matthew, 108n6
Malyschev, Ivan, 261–67
Manhattanism, theory of, 23–24
Mann, Michael, 36–38, 71, 159, 164–88, 190
Marcus, George, 31
Marine Corps, U.S., life in, 347–50
Marinho, Roberto, 228

Marino, Leonardo, 220n17

markets: absence of securities in Germany,
   168; benefits of, 168–70; competition for
   capital, 177–78; and conspiracy theory, 37,
   157–59; culture of compliance, 171–72;
   and deregulation, 172–74; and information,
   166–70, 178, 189–90; origins of SEC regulation, 160–64; transparent, 180–81

Marshall Institute, 114–15, 117

Marx, Karl: as economic theorist, 55–57; and
   Hegel, 49, 59–61; and Lakatos, 41; mole
   metaphor, 62; role of critique in communist
   society, 379; use of footnotes, 50; use of
   skeptical tropes, 52

Marxism: conflicts surrounding in 1980s, 31;
   dialectical reasoning and science, 55; and
   Lukács, 48, 60–61; and Popper, 43; Western, 49

Massa, Vincenzina, 313

mathematics, history and philosophy of, 39–
   42, 48, 59–60

Maurras, Charles, 320

McClure, John, 158

McMartin Preschool, 142, 154n5

Mencinger, Joze, 285, 291n11

Michelson-Morley experiment, 47–48

Microsoft Corporation, 169, 177

Milan, bombing in. *See* Piazza Fontana
   Massacre

Milken, Michael, 173

millennialism, and conspiracy, 378–79, 388–
   90, 392

Miller, William, 376

mole: metaphorical, 58–59, 62; philosophical,
   39, 63

Molnar, Imre. *See* Lakatos, Imre

Montanelli, Indro, interview with Andreotti,
   309–12, 315–16

Montreal Protocol, 111

Moon, Rev. Sun Yung, 125

Morgenthau, Henry, 157

Moro, Aldo, 204, 306, 308, 311, 313

Moroni, Primo, 221n26

Mosley, Oswald, 321, 328, 332, 340n14

MSI. *See* Italian Social Movement

multiculturalism: failure in Britain, 327–28,
   337–38; and multiple personality disorder,
   154n6

multiple personality disorder (MPD): and
   channeling, 147–50; and conspiracy, 36,
   142–43, 153; in general, 140–42, 153–

154n3; and multiculturalism, 154n6. *See
   also* self

Musgrave, Alan, 50

Mussolini, Benito, 206, 212, 214, 281, 314

Mutolo, Gaspare, 301–2

Nader, Ralph, 188–90

National Association of Securities Dealers
   (NASD), 170

National Center of Atmospheric Research, 35

National Cryptologic Museum, 86–88

National Front (Britain), 338n1, 340n14,
   341n19, 341n22

National Front (France), 333

National Science Foundation, 78–79, 84

National Security Agency (NSA), 33, 70, 73,
   86–88, 91–92

national socialism, 293–94, 319–22, 326,
   330–32, 338n1

Netscape, 169

New Age movement, 36, 147–49

New Deal conspiracy, 160–61

New Mount Carmel. *See* Branch Davidian
   compound

New Russians *(novye Russkie),* 241–43, 259,
   264–66

Newton, Isaac, 47

new world order, 327

New York Times, 382–83

Nierenberg, William, 117–18

North American Treaty Organization (NATO),
   203–5, 207

Notabartolo, Emanuele, 317n8

Occidental-Hooker case, 164–66, 185

Occidental Petroleum, 164–66, 185

O'Leary, Stephen, 153n1

Olivetti, Adriano, 272

P2 Masonic lodge, 304

Pacciardi, Randolofo, 204

Pace e libertà, 204, 220n20, 220n22

Palermo trial, 313–14

Palizzolo, Raffaele, 317n8

paper tigers, 172

paranoia: and anthropology, 10n; as a social
   phenomenon, 391–92; and conspiracy theory,
   5–6, 13–14; fusion, 9n1; as interpretive
   strategy, 21–24; and lack of a "reality
   check," 391; and reason, 225; reasonable *(see*
   reasonable paranoia); in theme parks, 425

paranoiac method: 29n2. *See also* Paranoid-
    Critical Method (PCM)
Paranoid-Critical Method (PCM), 21–24, 26,
    29
Park, Robert, 66–67
parks, theme: and conspiracy, 407–8; em-
    ployee interactions, 409–13; and fear, 407–
    8; and measurement, 422–24; overview,
    296–97, 405–8, 424–27; surveillance at,
    408, 417–22; suspicion and safety, 413–16
Parmenides, 55
Parrish, Michael, 163
Pasolini, Pier Paolo, 212, 217
Pasteur, Louis, 25–26
Peck, Gregory, 344
"Peck," interview with, 8, 295, 344–73
Pecorelli, Mino, 304, 311, 315
Pelé, 236
Pennino, Gioacchino, 313
Pentagon, the. *See* Department of Defense,
    U.S.
perestroika, 247, 260
Perry, Rachel, 375
Pesce, Ottorino, 200
Petöfi circle debates, 58
Petrovich, Paramon, 261
Philby, Kim, 58–59, 62
philosophy: of mathematics, 39, 41–42; of
    science, 39–52, 55–57
Piazza Fontana Massacre, 198–200, 203, 212,
    218
Pietro, Antonio di, 303
Pinelli, Giuseppe, 200–201
Podobnik, Marjan, 290, 290n4
Podolsky, Boris, 76–78
Pollack, Milton, 175
Pólya, George, 58
Ponzi (pyramid) schemes, 183–84
Popper, Karl, 31, 39–40, 43–53, 55–56, 58–
    63, 285
Powell, Enoch, 324, 330, 338, 341n21
Prestes, Luis Carlos, 230, 235
Prisoner's Dilemma, 3
privatization *(privatizatsiia),* in Russia, 242
psychotherapy: energy techniques, 137–39,
    143–45; growth of, 153n2; as mediation
    between individual and social world, 151–
    52; and religion, 139–40
Purgatory, 293, 300–301, 302
pyramid (Ponzi) schemes, 183–84
Pyrrhonism, 51–52

quantum physics, 33–34, 70, 77–79, 83–84, 89
quantum teleportation (QT), 33–34, 65–67,
    70, 72, 75–76, 84–85, 89–90
Quine, Willard Van Orman, 47, 50

racism, 332
Radványi, Janos, 31, 39–64
Raskin, Marcus, 74
Ravetz, Jerry, 52
Ravnikar, Edo, 196, 269–90
Rayburn, Sam, 160–61, 163
Reagan administration, and the Marshall Insti-
    tute, 115
reason, and paranoia, 225
reasonable paranoia: as a cold-war legacy,
    2–4, 9n2; and the crisis of representation,
    4–5; and the hierarchy of taste, 9–10n4
Reck, Michael, 72
Red Brigades, 210, 220–221n24, 306, 308–9,
    313
registry exam, for Gulf War vets, 367–70
Reich, Robert, 172
religion, and psychotherapy, 139–40
renegade, Hofstadter's conception of, 277–78
Reno, Janet, 383
representation, crisis of, 4–5
research program, Lakatos's theory of, 44–47,
    49, 51–52, 55–57
Revelation, Book of, 376–80, 397–99
Revelli, Marco, 214
Reynolds, Katherine, 138, 144–45
Ricardo, David, 55–57
Richards, Ann, 386
Ricks, Rob, 386
Rieff, Philip, 139
Rigelnik, Herman, 269–70
right-wing political groups, and conspiracy
    theory, 128–34
Riina, Salvatore (Toto), 218, 303–5, 317n6
Risenhoover, John, 385
ritual cult abuse, 142–43
Roberts, Andrew, 324
Rockwell International, 164
Roden, Amo Paul Bishop, 296, 394, 400n6
Roden, George, 375–76, 377
Roden, Lois, 375, 377
Rodriguez, Robert, 377, 400n14, 402n43
Rohrabacher, Dana, 115, 133
Roosevelt, Franklin, 160, 163–64, 188
Rosa dei venti (Weather vane) conspiracy,
    203, 205

Rosen, Nathan, 76–78
Rossanda, Rossana, 218
Rossetti, Siro, 205
Rushdie, Salman, 327, 338
Russia: capitalism in, 195, 241–44, 257–58; conspiracy in, 243–44, 266–67; criminality in, 252–58; democracy in, 252–53; grabification (privatization), 242; Mafia in, 195, 243, 250–51, 254, 266; New Russians, 241–43, 259, 264–66; personal stories of life in, 244–66
Russians: New *(novye Russkie),* 241–43, 259, 264–66; SEC training, 182–83

Safire, William, 157
Salomon Brothers, 167
Salvo, Ignazio, 303, 314
Sanderson, Anita, 137–38, 143–47, 151, 152
Sanford, Charles Jr., 189–90
Sanna, Marco, 200
Santa Fe International, 174–75
Santer, Benjamin, 113, 117–21, 124, 126–27, 129, 133
Saudi Arabia, opposition to IPCC meeting, 124–25
Scassia, Mario, 314
Scelba, Mario, 204
Schelling, Friedrich, 53
Schiller, Friedrich, 380
Schor, Nacomi, 29n2
Schrödinger, Erwin, 77
science: conflict over climate change research, 35; and conspiracy, 67, 70–71, 78–79, 108n5; and environmental controversy, 111–34; history of, 40–42, 44–52; and Marxian economics, 55–57; and military funding, 97–99, 102–3; mock trial of, 71–72, 74, 79–81, 83–86, 88–90, 93–97, 99–106; and the Paranoid-Critical Method, 25–27; philosophy of, 39–52, 55–57; and politics, 115–16, 118, 126; and social change, 35; and social responsibility, 71, 79–83, 86, 89–90, 93–97, 99–106. *See also* ethics of experimentation; quantum physics
Science and Environmental Policy Project (SEPP), 125
science purists, conspiracy theory of, 34
Scripps Institute of Oceanography, 117
Securities and Exchange Commission, U.S. (SEC): and corporate responsibility, 191n4; culture of compliance, 171–72; and disclosure, 36–38, 159, 161–68, 170, 179, 184–87; Office of International Affairs, 37, 174–79; origins, 160–64; technical assistance program, 179–84; value neutrality, 187–90, 191n7
Segni, Antonio, 207–8, 220n16
Seitz, Frederick, 112–14, 116–22, 125–27
self: fragmented, 139–40, 150–53; and psychotherapy, 139–53. *See also* multiple personality disorder (MPD)
self-management, 274–75
self-regulatory organization (SRO), 172
semiotics of suspicion, 379–80, 392, 399
Serbs: and the disintegration of Yugoslavia, 279; majority ownership in Yugoslavia, 276–77; takeover of Yugoslavia, 271–72
Servizio Informazioni Difesa (SID), 198
Sessions, William, 383
Seventh-Day Adventist Church, 376, 400n10
sexual abuse, childhood, 137, 141–42
shareholder activism, 174
Shchipok, Valerii, 254–61, 267
Shull, Clifford, 72
Sindona, Michele, 205
Singer, Fred, 125–31
skepticism, 51–52
Slivnik, Danilo, 290n7
Slovenia: economic discourse and conspiracy in, 270–71, 280–83, 287–89; economic system and political control, 270–71, 279–80, 283–85; ideological conflict within, 287–88; and intellectuals, 285–86; mafia in *(Ubomafija),* 271, 272; political identity, 273; politics of, 269–70, 286; transition to independence, 195–96
Slovenska Ljudska Stranka (Slovenian People's Party, SLS), 286–87, 290
Smith, Adam, 55–56, 266
Smith, Karen, 143, 145
Social Democratic Party of Slovenia (SDS), 286, 291n12
social science: as a personal commitment, 194; and conspiracy, 225–26
Sofri, Adriano, 220n17
Sogno, Edgardo, 203–5, 216, 220n20
Sommer, A. A., 191n4
Soros, George, 54, 63
Sound Science Initiative, 119
Sparks, Joyce, 400n16
spies, Cambridge, 58–59
Sporkin, Stanley, 164, 190–191n3

Sraffa, Piero, 56
Stalin, Josef, 58, 61–62, 241
Stalinism, 53–54, 61–63, 257
Star Wars, 115
Steeplechase Park (Coney Island), 409
Steinem, Gloria, 142
Stille, Alexander, 304
strategy of tension, 200, 205
suspicion, semiotics of, 379–80, 392, 399
Swiss banks, 168, 175–76
Szilard, Leo, 81–83

Tajikistan, 248–49, 251–52
Tajnikar, Maks, 283, 290n6, 291n9
Tam (Slovenia), 279–80, 283, 290n6
Tam Deutschland, 279
teleportation, 32, 72, 75, 90–91, 97
teleportation, quantum (QT), 33–34, 65–67,
   70, 72, 75–76, 89–91
Thatcher, Margaret, 320
theme parks: and conspiracy, 407–8; employee interactions, 409–13; and fear, 407–
   8; and measurement, 422–24; overview,
   296–97, 405–8, 424–27; surveillance at,
   408, 417–22; suspicion and safety, 413–16
theory: of particle finance, 188; of research
   programs, 44–47, 55–57
Thompson, Huston, 160–61
Thompson, Linda, 384, 389, 393, 394
Thucydides, 381
Tito, Josip Broz, 274
Togliatti, Palmiro, 206, 215
Touraine, Alain, 395
Tourmey, Chris, 130
toxic substances, exposure to, 343–46, 351–
   53
transparency of markets, 37, 180–81, 264
trial, mock, of science, 71–72, 74, 79–81,
   83–86, 88–90, 93–97, 99–106
Trieste Credit Bank (TCB), 283, 285
Turkle, Sherry, 139

Udbomafija, 269, 272, 282, 288
unemployment, in Britain, 325–26, 337
Union Carbide, 295
Union of Concerned Scientists, 119
United Nations: Framework Convention on
   Climate Change (FCCC), 112, 118; as an
   instrument of global hegemony, 377

United States (U.S.): Branch Davidian conflict, 375–78, 382–87; conspiracy theory
   in, 1–2, 358–63, 370, 385–87, 393–94;
   conspiratorial activity in Italy, 198, 272, 281
   (see also Central Intelligence Agency); as
   the final Babylon, 377; genetic counseling
   for Gulf War vets, 363–67, 372; Gulf War
   Illness, 294–95, 346, 356–57, 361; interview with "Peck," 295, 344–73; Operation
   Desert Storm, 343–46, 350–56; registry
   exam for Gulf War vets, 367–70

Valle Giulia, 200
Valpreda, Pietro, 201
Verdery, Katherine, 243
Vesco, Robert, 191n3
Veterans Administration, U.S. (VA), 361, 367,
   369, 370
Voltaire, 335

Waco, Texas, 375, 376, 377, 396
Waco Tribune-Herald, 382, 384
Wallis, John, 59
Wartofsky, Marx, 39
Weber, Max, 189–90, 376, 392, 400n5
Wells, H. G., 81
White, Ellen, 376, 400n9
White, Hayden, 4
Whitney, Richard, 162
Wigley, Thomas, 117, 122, 124
willies, the: creation of, 21, 27; cure for, 106–
   7; effect of, 65, 72; feeling of, 19, 29, 33,
   70, 88, 92, 407
Winter, Paul, 311
Wittgenstein, Ludwig, 52, 212
Woodell, John, 88
World Trade Center, explosion at, 387

Yardley, Herbert, 87
Yeltsin, Boris, 241
Yugoslavia: communism in, 273–74; conspiracy in, 277–78; disintegration of, 195–
   96, 278–79; economic system and political
   control, 270, 275–77; liberalism in, 274;
   Mafia in, 275, 279; takeover by the Serbs,
   271–72

Zeilinger, Anton, 32, 34, 72